DOING SCIENCE

AND

DOING GOOD

DOING SCIENCE
AND
DOING GOOD

A HISTORY OF THE BUREAU OF CHILD RESEARCH
AND THE
SCHIEFELBUSCH INSTITUTE FOR LIFE SPAN STUDIES
AT
THE UNIVERSITY OF KANSAS

Edited by
Richard L. Schiefelbusch, PhD
and
Stephen R. Schroeder, PhD

·P A U L ·H·
BROOKES
PUBLISHING CO®

Baltimore • London • Sydney

Paul H. Brookes Publishing Co.
Post Office Box 10624
Baltimore, Maryland 21285-0624

www.brookespublishing.com

Designed and Produced by Columbia Publishing Services, Columbia, Maryland.
Typeset by Circle Graphics, Columbia, Maryland.
Manufactured in the United States of America by Sheridan Books, Chelsea, Michigan.

Library of Congress Cataloging-in-Publication Data

Doing science and doing good : a history of the Bureau of Child Research and the
   Schiefelbusch Institute for Life Span Studies at the University of Kansas / edited by
   Richard L. Schiefelbusch & Stephen R. Schroeder.
      p.   cm.
   ISBN-13: 978-1-55766-912-4
   ISBN-10: 1-55766-912-0
   1. University of Kansas. Bureau of Child Research—History. 2. Schiefelbusch
Institute for Life Span Studies—History. 3. Child development—Research—
Kansas—History. 4. People with mental disabilities—Research—Kansas—History.
5. Life cycle, Human—Research—Kansas —History. 6. Gerontology—Research—
Kansas—History. I. Schiefelbusch, Richard L. II. Schroeder, Stephen R.
   [DNLM: 1. University of Kansas. Bureau of Child Research. 2. Schiefelbusch
Institute for Life Span Studies. 3. Academies and Institutes—history—Kansas.
4. Child Development—Kansas. 5. Mentally Disabled Persons—Kansas.
6. Developmental Disabilities—Kansas. 7. Geriatrics—history—Kansas.
8. Research—history—Kansas.   WS 24 U58 2006]
HQ767.85.D655 2006
305.231071'178165—dc22

                                                                    2006024078

British Library Cataloguing in Publication data are available from the British Library.

Contents

Contributors

Carmen Arreaga-Mayer, EdD
University of Kansas

James F. Budde, EdD
University of Kansas

Judith J. Carta, PhD
University of Kansas

Paul D. Cheney, PhD
University of Kansas

Pamela J. Cress, EdS
University of Kansas

David J. Ekerdt, PhD
University of Kansas

Stephen B. Fawcett, PhD
University of Kansas

Jacob U. Gordon, PhD
University of Kansas

Charles R. Greenwood, PhD
University of Kansas

R. Vance Hall, PhD
University of Kansas

Robert K. Hoyt, MS
University of Kansas

Debra M. Kamps, PhD
University of Kansas

David P. Lindeman, PhD
University of Kansas

Kathleen Olson, PhD
University of Kansas

R. Matthew Reese, PhD
University of Kansas

Mabel L. Rice, PhD
University of Kansas

Sara H. Sack, PhD
University of Kansas

Richard R. Saunders, PhD
University of Kansas

Richard L. Schiefelbusch, PhD
University of Kansas

Stephen R. Schroeder, PhD
University of Kansas

James A. Sherman, PhD
University of Kansas

Charles R. Spellman, EdD
University of Kansas

Joseph E. Spradlin, PhD
University of Kansas

H. Rutherford Turnbull III, LLM
University of Kansas

Cheryl A. Utley, PhD
University of Kansas

Dale Walker, PhD
University of Kansas

Steven F. Warren, PhD
University of Kansas

Preface

The life span of the Bureau of Child Research (BCR) has been 85 years — between 1921 and 2006. The BCR was the progeny of Florence Brown Sherbon and her colleagues. Dr. Sherbon came to Kansas in 1917 and became the driving force behind the creation of the state statute that authorized the BCR in 1921. Her work was a hallmark in efforts to improve the lives of the children of Kansas and their families. She died in early 1944.

The focus of Part I of this history is largely centered on the University of Kansas before the impact of the BCR (and the relationships formed with other state agencies) began to reach throughout the state and relates mostly to the work between 1956 and 1990. It includes the early programs and relationships developed under the leadership of Richard L. Schiefelbusch. Part II begins in 1990 with the appointment of a new director when the BCR became a new entity, the Schiefelbusch Institute for Life Span Studies.

After the BCR was created there was little money on which it could grow. Chancellor Franklin D. Murphy changed that in 1954 when he authorized $30,000 for the operation of the BCR. He took an inactive legislative statute passed in 1921 and used it to create an infrastructure for research with children. A committee was formed to recommend ways to establish a new program. Chancellor Murphy appointed the first full-fledged director of the BCR, Richard L. Schiefelbusch, in 1956. Schiefelbusch held the position for 35 years.

The two-part breakdown is essential to understanding each period. The two periods combine to delineate an important effort by many professionals to improve the lives of children and their families and friends throughout the state.

In 1990, with the appointment of a new director, Stephen R. Schroeder, the BCR became part of a new entity named the Schiefelbusch Institute for Life Span Studies. The BCR continues as a subdimension of that division. The statute that formed the BCR remains in effect. However, the program that has evolved since 1954 clearly fits better into a life span framework than within a child research concept. The future of this expanding research and development program holds great potential in these days of increased national concern about the education and nurturing of children.

The history of the Institute for Life Span Studies will require a third section and is beyond the scope of what is undertaken in this writing. As we look back to write this early history of the BCR, it becomes evident that the institute's programmatic record must, in due course, also be recorded and filed. This first step is limited to the formidable task of presenting the first 85 years of the history of the BCR.

Acknowledgments

This work was 14 years in the making. We want to thank all of our contributors for taking the time from their busy schedules to reflect a bit on the big picture of the Bureau of Child Research (BCR) and the Life Span Institute (LSI). It has been a labor of love, but nevertheless a labor.

To our readers, whom we suspect will be mostly former faculty, staff, and students, we also want to give thanks for making the BCR and the LSI what they are today. The Kansas State motto is, "To the stars through difficulties." You are our stars, but you may have difficulties agreeing with some of the opinions and recollections of our authors. They are Kansas individualists, and we have tampered with their writing very little. If you are feeling included or excluded or in disagreement with some rendering of history, we hope you will remember fondly what it was like when you were here leaving your mark on the institution. The editors apologize in advance for such mistakes. Attribute them not to ill will, but to old age.

Introduction: A Cluster of Miracles

RICHARD L. SCHIEFELBUSCH

M y task in this introduction is to describe a cluster of miracles, and explain how they happened. But, first let me explain that I have been reluctant to use the term *miracle* because I have not really believed that one, much less several, could happen within my range of experience. Perhaps my problem was that I did not appreciate the widely useful ways that the term *miracle* is used in our society—for instance, in the field of medicine (miracle drug), or in the field of social work (miracle worker) or in aeronautics (the miracle of flight). I submit that the fields of administration and science are also entitled to a few miracle designations, especially in the field of research administration. This possibility is rendered the more justifiable if we use the dictionary definition of miracle: "an extremely outstanding or unusual event, thing, or accomplishment." I suggest that we could simplify all of this by using the term *awesome experience*. We should be allowed to use either awesome or miracle, depending on the context.

The first miracle in the 85-year history of the Bureau of Child Research (BCR) began when Dr. Florence Brown Sherbon came to Kansas. She was able to persuade the Kansas legislature to pass a legislative statute forming a Bureau of Child Research in 1921! This remarkable piece of legislation was so prescient that it served admirably as a mission statement for eight decades. It is still an effective functional guide for many aspects of the Life Span Institute (LSI) after 85 years!

The second miracle occurred in 1958 when Joe Spradlin and Sy Rosenberg teamed up to design and to institute an effective research program at Parsons State Hospital and Training Center. Their research was highly effective, even though its outcome purposes were considered to be impossible! In 2006, we will celebrate the 50-year anniversary of the second beginning of the BCR and their awesome impact on the teaching of language to children with severe mental retardation. Their work has resulted in an evolution of cultural changes for children with mental retardation throughout our land. The Parsons miracle was also the springboard for a huge leap ahead in the development of the research program of the BCR. We soon had some portent of these wondrous outcomes when visitors began to appear at Parsons soon after the project began. They simply wanted to see for themselves.

Another miracle began in 1964 when Frances Horowitz, the newly appointed acting chairman of the largely underdeveloped Department of Human Development and Family Life (HDFL) came to me and said, "Dick, I understand that Don Baer is considering a move from the University of Washington and I suggest that we try to recruit him." At that time, Don Baer was only a name to me, but it was a magical name. I knew that he was the intellectual leader of the Rainier School group with headquarters at the University of Washington in Seattle. Frances had apparently gotten to know him through experiences at the national level in the field of human development. She was aware that the University of Texas, which had a reputation for paying much higher salaries than did the University of Kansas, had approached Don. Frances contacted Don and apparently got the specifics of the Texas offer. She then enlisted my efforts in creating an even better offer for attracting Don to the University of Kansas. The strategy was to discuss the possibility with the university provost, James Surface, and the dean of the College of Liberal Arts and Sciences, George Waggoner. Our top offer would ordinarily have been at least $5000 below the offer at Texas. I detailed the wondrous advantages in having Don on our faculty and concluded with a bold statement, "This is the best bargain that you ever will have made." (Please note that my verb form was in the future perfect tense.) As it turned out, I actually understated the deal; but, anyway, they offered and he accept.

Then the big miracle really began to take shape. George Waggoner was keen to upgrade his faculty, especially his young faculty. I needed excellent scientists, especially at the Juniper Gardens Children's Project. Don was keen to recruit to Kansas several of his young colleagues with whom he was working or had worked at the University of Washington. Fran Horowitz wanted able young faculty for her newly designed Department at Human Development and Family Life. Also, as it soon became apparent, the perspective, gifted young scientists were keen to get back together because, at the time, they were somewhat scattered about the country.

So we became a team: Don Baer identified the recruits, George Waggoner manufactured the faculty slots, George Waggoner and Fran Horowitz found half-time academic funding for the recruits and the BCR blessed us and found the other half-time funding for each eager young research professor. In this way, Todd Risley, Montrose Wolf, James Sherman, and Barbara Etzel came to the University of Kansas to be Don's colleagues; George Waggoner's talismans for academic excellence, which he was extolling at that time; and Frances Horowitz's new faculty in the HDFL, which soon catapulted into the top five of such departments in the country. Other members, who were attracted almost immediately as a result of this wondrous migration to Kansas, were Don Bushell, Betty Hart, Nancy Reynolds, and Vance Hall. Vance would soon become the director of the Juniper Gardens Children's Project. Montrose Wolf would become the key investigator in the remedial academic program at Juniper Gardens, and then the developer of the remarkable Achievement Place Project. Todd Risley quickly became a formulator of the preschool program at Juniper Gardens, including the parent co-op. Betty Hart soon completed her doctoral degree and became the head teacher in the language-oriented preschool at Juniper Gardens. She also became a superstar in language acquisition research over a period of 30 years. Barbara Etzel became a prominent scientist and a departmental and university leader for many years. Jim Sherman eventually became the head of the HDFL and director of the Program Project in Language and Communication of the Mentally Retarded.

Included among the projects that soon evolved from their research at Juniper Gardens were the Achievement Place Project, the Follow-Through Project, and the Parent Cooperative Preschool. Each of these projects validated procedures that have been replicated in a variety of other publications and settings. It is important to note that the time interval, from start-up to publication of these research activities was 3 to 5 years.

While his protégés were developing this tidal wave of outstanding achievements, what was Don Baer doing? The answer, of course, was lots of things, but the most apparent among them were tutoring, advising, supporting, and encouraging his protégés. He also volunteered to help in many of the projects that ensued during the Years of the Miracles. For instance, in one of the many advising sessions that he had with me about Juniper Gardens in 1964, he suggested that we try to recruit Vance Hall, who at that time was completing his doctoral work at the University of Washington. Vance responded positively to our invitation and joined the group of colleagues in 1965. He now deserves special commendation for creating a stable research center in this high-risk district, where even the instrumental equipment could not be insured.

Vance instigated a highly innovative career as a scientist, administrator, publisher, and professor. He did so for many years without the benefit of an academic tenure salary. He was one of the most effective day-to-day administrators whom I have ever known. The long-term high morale of his colleagues (from 1965 to 1989) of all designations speaks to this.

Now, my insistence that this entire scenario was a miracle is actually supported and described by one of their colleagues who became a prominent part of the program soon after they arrived and who became director when Vance retired. I'm referring to Charlie Greenwood, who headed a second research wave that included Judy Carta, Joe Delquadri, Debra Kamps, Dale Walker, Ed Christopherson, and Jane Atwater, among others. Now, 17 years later Charlie and his colleagues are well on their way to matching or exceeding the research of their predecessors.

Let me quote from Charlie Greenwood, after the Juniper Gardens (JG) program had received the CEC Research Award in 1995. Charlie stated,

> By conventional wisdom the Juniper Gardens Children's Project shouldn't exist, let alone be successful. Before Juniper Gardens, who would have thought that meaningful programs for research could be conducted in the homes, schools and neighborhoods of the economically distressed community like northeast Kansas City, Kansas, a place where every conceivable risk to children and

to personal success exists in abundance? Who would have thought that moms, dads and teachers at JG could learn and apply new strategies that showed measurable improvements in their children's performance? Who would have thought that families in this community would participate in longitudinal studies lasting ten years or more? Who would have thought that some University faculty would eagerly spend their careers in the neighborhood? Who would have thought that extensive new designs, assessments, and intervention practices would be created? The Juniper Gardens Children's Project has existed because of the leadership of the Northeast Community who sought a better future for their children. It exists because of the vision of the University of Kansas faculty who demonstrated that meaningful research could be organized in homes, schools and playgrounds. It flourished because the families and teachers participated. It continues now in its fourth decade because its children, research leaders, graduate students, post-doctoral associates and alumni sought to use and extend what has been learned. It continues because community agencies, organizations and individuals have found the work to be important. It continues because it has made a difference in the lives of a countless number of children and families.

Now let me go back to the beginning of the Washington odyssey, which I am now labeling as a miracle. Before we go further we should acknowledge that a major program of research in the field of mental retardation had already been developed at Parsons, Kansas, by Joe Spradlin and his colleagues, Seymour Rosenberg, Fred Girardeau, John Hollis, Ross Copeland, and others. They had developed a major program using applied behavior analysis (ABA) to improve social and other functional skills of children with mental retardation. This work had gained considerable prominence. In fact, Don Baer often mentioned that the existence of a research program in ABA at Kansas was a prominent feature of his desire to come to Kansas. He actually was the first to describe the program developed at Parsons State Hospital by Joe Spradlin and his colleagues as a miracle.

Incidentally, Fran Horowitz had also done awesome work in establishing a departmental environment that was conducive for the newcomers. She had talked with Don Baer and realized that he could be the catalyst for bringing his colleagues here. A few colleagues, including Fred Girardeau, and I had already done a number of relevant things, including the discussion of the Juniper Gardens Children's Project with members of the National Institute of Child Health and Human Development in Washington, D.C. They were keen to have the Juniper Gardens program become a part of their newly conceptualized Mental Retardation Research Center program at Kansas. They had already taken in-house measures to fund a supplement to our existing program project—Language and Communications of Mentally Retarded Children—which was located largely at Parsons. I had also considered the possibility, even at that stage, that there could be a mental retardation center in Kansas for long-term research.

George Waggoner had done considerable work to accommodate this special program of events to the College of Liberal Arts and Sciences. Even the provost had considered the possibility of expanding the work of the Bureau of Child Research and had anticipated that he would support the development of new events.

The miracle perhaps exists in the fact that so many were willing and keen to support this emergent development as a part of their program. Resources were generated that were indeed valuable to many different components of the university. There were no losers, just winners. The miracle evolved in what seemed to be an unlikely place because nothing like this evolving miracle had ever occurred at the University of Kansas.

As these endeavors were beginning, most of the new faculty, including Don Baer, Fran Horowitz, and Joe Spradlin, were housed in a temporary setting called Varsity House at Eleventh and Indiana Streets in Lawrence, where everyone aspired to have either a desk or a drawer in a desk. Other members of the BCR staff were crammed in three rooms in the basement of Bailey Hall. During this period (1964–1969), space was the most urgent topic on everyone's mind. Thus, space was one of the major issues in the next chapter of the expanding cluster of miracles. Perhaps, we should call this the Miracle of Space.

In the early 1960s the university space designers decided to replace old Haworth Hall with a new building. One of the authors of the application for federal funds was a young English professor by the name of Floyd Horowitz. He and the building committee found office space in this building for the space-challenged HDFL and the space-deprived

BCR, the former on the basement floor and the latter on the second floor, both in the east section of the building.

Needless to say, both the HDFL and BCR were glad to anticipate this space, but neither knew that the locations were going to become strategic in an unprecedented range of new spatial events. This miracle began to emerge when I chaired a site visit committee at the George Peabody College of Vanderbilt University at Nashville, Tennessee. There I observed a master administrator (Nick Hobbs) convince an experienced group of reviewers to approve a plan in which a small, existing group of colleagues and a larger, nonexisting group of "promised" positions were artfully combined into a major Center for Research and Training for the Mentally Retarded.

So, when I returned home I got together with my own small group of colleagues and tried to convince them that we should create such a center. This was early 1965. This quest took me the next day to the office of Provost James Surface, who immediately made an appointment for us with Chancellor Wescoe for the following morning, which happened to be a Sunday. The appointment began at 9 o'clock and at 11 o'clock the chancellor stood in front of the map of the university and said, "We will put the KU unit right here." He was, of course, pointing to the space immediately east of the in-construction Haworth Hall. Thus, the Haworth Wing was born. Having participated in this ritual of selection, the chancellor then called the Kansas University Medical Center (KUMC) and talked with three key friends there. Then he turned to me and said, "You will have to call Howard Bair and convince him." There was no way that I was going to say, "I have already done that."

Of course, Howard Bair, superintendent of Parson State Hospital and Training Center, said, "Yes," and, of course, Robert Anderson, chairman of the State Board of Social Welfare, also said, "Yes." So did the Board of Regents, the director of the Governor's Budget Office, Jim Bibb, and the National Institute of Child Health and Human Development— and, best of all, so did the Kansas Association for Retarded Citizens. Now then, we have discussed three miracles of program development and several miraculous people, but the biggest space miracle was yet to come.

After Frances Horowitz invited Don Baer to Kansas and the Washington miracle was already under way at Juniper Gardens, and after the strength of the new additions to the Kansas scene were apparent, and even after we had become well acquainted at Varsity House, we moved into our long-awaited space in the Stewart Wing of Haworth Hall. But, alas, our anticipation of copious space for gracious scientific and teaching activities was soon dispelled. Space issues were carefully planned; why then were we crowded from the very beginning of our occupancy? Simple. We did not anticipate that upper echelon space committees at KU would figure in the decisions about who was to move into the new building. Essentially, the new occupants were primarily from the Departments of Special Education, Speech and Hearing, Human Development, and the BCR. Those were, indeed, the logical and functional selections. However, they did not just move their research personnel. The new center became the location for both graduate and undergraduate teaching, for sack lunches and social hours, and for visitors and class demonstrations. In short, "the place to be" for all functions, both professional and casual. Of course, a space committee was formed and it soon became the most important committee in the building. Thousands of compromises and new agreements were struck. Personal pride and privileges were frequently modified. Then it became increasing clear that the main problem was our increasing productivity. Between the times when the architectural plans were completed and the time of occupancy, the research and training activities had multiplied. These trends continued.

For more than 21 years, the group held together. The Center, including Parsons and KUMC, became known as a national and international leader in research and training in mental retardation. Also, the academic departments and, of course, the BCR, the Mental Retardation Research Center (MRRC), and the University Affiliated Program (UAP) achieved their goals and moved into the top ratings in their respective fields of endeavor. Eventually, the opportunity for space expansion appeared in the form of the Dole Human Development Center. It is indeed a wonderful place to do research and to teach. Actually, it is a wonderful place to have one's office, as well as one's lab. But I do not regard that as the space miracle. The overcrowded individuals and groups who transcended their stresses and their crowdedness for 21 years created the Miracle of Space.

The foregoing discussion of miracles is primarily a preamble—now for the main purpose of this discussion! One need only to look at the record of compounding resource development to realize that the current

Life Span Institute is the miracle that compounds all the others. The late 1980s were transition years for the Bureau of Child Research. There were several unsuccessful searches for Dick Schiefelbusch's successor; Charles Greenwood was taking over the Juniper Gardens Children's Project upon Vance Hall's retirement; and the BCR continued to grow in breadth and depth. Francis Horowitz asked Dick to take over the administration of the KU Center for Aging, an important initiative that was having trouble getting off the ground. Thus the name change to the Schiefelbusch Institute for Life Span Studies was adopted in 1990 to reflect this broadened mandate of the BCR.

At the same time, funding for a new Dole Human Development Center became available. This was a new concept at KU, involving the joint housing of academic departments (i.e., Human Development and Family Life; Speech, Language, and Hearing Research; and Special Education), with closely collaborating research centers (i.e., the Bureau of Child Research, the Center for Aging, and the Institute for Research on Learning Disabilities), in order to promote research and development efforts among them. The dedication of the new Dole Human Development Center also served as the occasion for the launching of the Institute for Life Span Studies.

The awesome curve of the Life Span Institute resource growth is the work of two miracle administrators: Steve Schroeder (1990–2001) and Steve Warren (2001 to the present). The latter is a work in progress (an emergent miracle), and in chapter 28, Steve Warren reflects on the future of the Life Span Institute, which will doubtless generate many more miracles.

PART I

THE BUREAU OF CHILD RESEARCH 1921–1990

Edited by
RICHARD L. SCHIEFELBUSCH,
ROBERT K. HOYT, AND JOSEPH E. SPRADLIN

1

How Child Research Came to Kansas and Stayed

RICHARD L. SCHIEFELBUSCH

Child care instruction and child research emerged in Kansas between 1917 and 1924. Dr. Florence Brown Sherbon, who was both a nurse and a physician, came to Kansas during the summer of 1917 to serve temporarily as chief of child health on the Kansas Board of Health. She was a divorced mother with 9-year-old twin daughters.

Before coming to Kansas, she was one of the prime movers in the establishment of the Iowa Child Welfare Research Station and she had done field research in Wisconsin and Indiana for the U.S. Children's Bureau. Her work included a survey of maternal and infant care. In 1912 the first baby clinic was established in Iowa, and Sherbon was one of the doctors presiding over that clinic. She and her colleagues recognized the need for a better method for testing all babies.

In the fall of 1917, Sherbon became the director of physical education for women at the University of Kansas. While serving in that capacity, she organized and taught two courses on home nursing in the Department of Home Economics. In 1919 she left the university to accept the position of chief of the Division of Child Hygiene on the Kansas Board of Health.

In 1921 she returned to the University of Kansas to join the home economics staff as a permanent member. Her assignment was to develop two courses in child care, while continuing to teach home nursing. No textbooks were available for either area. This led Sherbon to undertake the task of writing one for each course. The following year, Sherbon induced the Kansas State Legislature to pass a bill creating the Bureau of Child Research (BCR).

The University of Kansas also authorized the development of the BCR in 1921. For a number of years, Sherbon combined BCR responsibilities with her classroom duties. Chancellor Lindley had appointed an administrative committee for the BCR in 1922, with F. J. Kelly, dean of the School of Education, as acting director and Sherbon as an acting assistant director. In 1923 Sherbon was appointed director of the administrative committee. One member of her committee was Dr. James Naismith, the acclaimed "Father of Basketball." Little developmental money was appropriated for the BCR beyond $1,000 (one third of her salary; $100 per month for her assistant, Emily Ferris; and $50 per month for a part-time secretary). Apparently no additional money was available.

Nevertheless, Sherbon began a study. This study is one of the few tangible descriptions to be found in the files regarding the research activities of the BCR during those years. Other research was planned with representatives from other colleges and institutions of the state, but there was no money to implement them.

Despite these difficulties, Sherbon founded and developed the Pre-School Clinic in Lawrence in 1925. The clinic worked with the various elementary schools in Lawrence. Children of preschool age were brought to her clinic for a thorough examination. A record of every child was kept on file and checked each year until the child reached kindergarten age.

Sherbon eventually established preschools in seven grade schools in Lawrence. She helped to develop the Children's Bureau of Health in Kansas City, Kansas. From 1924 to 1928, she served as a member of the advisory group of the Metropolitan Life Insurance Company. She wrote many articles, and for years she was on the editorial board of the *Medical Woman's Journal.* Her books, *The Child* (published by McGraw-Hill in 1934), and *The Family in Health and Illness* (McGraw-Hill, 1935), established her as a major national contributor in the field of child care. She was one of 11 women from Kansas listed in the 1932–1933 edition of *Who's Who in America.* In addition, she also was featured in *Who's Who in American Medicine* and *Leaders in Education.* Professor Viola Anderson writes of her:

Her professional life was not allowed to overwhelm the personal. She was devoted to her twin daughters and cared for her aged mother during her difficult years. Her home always had an air of easy hospitality. Everyone was welcome: the young intellectuals who liked to get her into serious discussions; the distressed; the inept; the dependent, whom she took under her wing; her friends and colleagues . . . calmly, and methodically, she went about the business of teaching, writing, furthering the causes in which she was interested . . .

Toward the end of 1943, she became seriously ill and on February 11, 1944, upon reaching her 75th birthday, she retired. On February 16, she died. She had worked at the University of Kansas for 27 years.

Her career story is truly distinctive. It is told here only briefly. There is much more that should be told, but perhaps most of it can never be told. What we know about her is interesting but limited. What we do know is that Sherbon brought the best of professional skills in child care and child research to Kansas in 1917. She was ahead of the times, but unfortunately she was unable to raise funds for many of the research projects she wanted to undertake.

Nevertheless, she developed demonstration activities for students and health care workers. She created a preschool program, although the chair of the Department of Home Economics did not wish to sponsor it. She published two books and a number of journal articles. More importantly, she succeeded in influencing the Kansas legislature in 1921 to pass a statute that created the Bureau of Child Research that ultimately fulfilled many of her aspirations.

Her legacy is that she started a program that is still growing at the beginning of a new century. She also became a legend: a pioneer woman who could seemingly prevail against all odds. Through her teaching, her writings, and her example, she created an enduring program for the children in Kansas that inspires us decades later. Her creed for the BCR, which appeared on the BCR letterhead, stated: ". . . organized for the scientific study of child life through cooperative efforts of all groups in the state which are equipped and willing to contribute to such study."

The Kansas legislative statute, however, was her crowning success. It was farsighted, aptly stated, and prophetic. It enabled a planning committee and new leadership 34 years later to pick up the tasks and the philosophy she advocated and to work with other universities, agencies, and settings in creating an interdisciplinary research program on behalf of the children of the state. She likely would have approved of the initiatives that emerged two decades later. With characteristic intelligence and optimism, she probably would have suggested a number of ways to make them even more collaborative and more productive. The account of Sherbon's work and the quality of her life would not be complete without an explanation of how she was awarded Kansas's Outstanding Pioneer Woman of the Year for 1993. It is a most remarkable story. Her daughters Elizabeth and Alice (who accompanied her to Kansas as 9-year-olds) graduated from the University of Kansas in 1930. During their undergraduate years they took extensive training in modern dance in the physical education program for women that Sherbon had started in 1917. Sherbon was resourceful in arranging for special instructors from Kansas City to work with her physical education students. She also arranged scholarships for her most able students to study at other studios and schools.

Elizabeth went on to become a national and international modern dance legend. She taught dance at the University of Kansas from 1961 to 1975. After retirement, she continued to live in Lawrence and subsequently became acquainted with Janet Hamburg, professor of dance and head of the university's dance program. Hamburg describes Elizabeth Sherbon as our "muse" and one of the first to be interested in world dance, dance therapy, and dance education for all ages.

Acting on her admiration for her older dance colleague, Hamburg prepared an application on behalf of Elizabeth's mother, Dr. Florence Sherbon. Hamburg then invited her friend, Professor Boyd of the English department, to work with her to collect archival information for the application document. His brief account suggests several aspects of what might be called the Florence Sherbon legacy. She was a remarkable mother, teacher, program developer, and, most of all, an inspiration for later generations of colleagues.

2

The Continuing History of the Bureau of Child Research: The Second Beginning

RICHARD L. SCHIEFELBUSCH AND ROBERT K. HOYT

In 1951, Ethan Allen, director of the Bureau of Government Research, sent Chancellor Franklin Murphy a letter recommending the reestablishment of the Bureau of Child Research (BCR). It was a knowledgeable and persuasive letter, written by the right person at the right time.

Murphy responded by appointing a committee chaired by Dr. Herbert Miller, chairman of the pediatrics department at the Kansas University Medical Center (KUMC). Because Murphy had been dean of the medical school prior to becoming chancellor of the university, he was knowledgeable about whom to appoint from key departments on both campuses. Murphy was interested in having a research institute to coordinate programs for children on both campuses.

The committee was a diverse group with several divergent interests and without a common base of agreement. Allen's recommendation to Murphy and to the committee was to begin by attaching the BCR to the Bureau of Government Research, as Phase 1, then to work to create a bureau of child research with "independent" status as soon as it had the resources to do so.

The committee engaged in a number of discussions but failed to forward recommendations to the chancellor. In June 1954, Murphy accepted Allen's suggestion to place the BCR under the administration of Allen in the Bureau of Government Research. Thus, the second active beginning of the BCR was undertaken 20 years after the first beginning had been diminished by the Depression.

At the time of the second beginning, the status of children in the state had been modified considerably. An important organization in 1954 was the Kansas Council for Children and Youth. It coordinated a support system for 51 children and youth agencies and service programs throughout the state. Also, there were a thriving Department of Social Work at the University of Kansas and KUMC, a Kansas Institute for Research in the Education of Exceptional Children, and a number of preschools across the state working in conjunction with public and private schools.

There was also a range of child care facilities, infant centers, and pediatric services for children. Chief among these programs was the Children's Rehabilitation Unit (CRU) at the KUMC. The BCR soon had close working relations with these active programs.

A close look at the 1921 statute reveals that the BCR provided an even better fit to the state's 1954 resources and programs than it did with the 1921 resources. Under Allen's leadership, activities were planned to extend the BCR into collaborations with state agency programs. William Tucker, executive director of the Kansas Council for Children and Youth, was already a staff member of the BCR. Unfortunately, space in Allen's governmental research center was minimal and didn't offer room for expansion. Also, the total yearly allocation for the BCR was only $30,000. These funds barely paid for two clerk typists and the salary of the assistant director, leaving virtually no funds for program development.

Finding a Director

In 1954, Richard Schiefelbusch, director of the Kansas University (KU) Speech and Hearing Clinic, who had a PhD in speech pathology, was offered a tenured position at the University of Illinois to direct the Cleft Palate Clinic in the University Hospital Complex in Chicago. The Cleft Palate Clinic was probably the leading orofacial clinic in the country, if not the world. The director's position was a prestige appointment with a 50% larger salary than Schiefelbusch had at the time.

While waiting for the tenure appointment to clear through the University of Illinois system, Schiefelbusch discussed his plans with Dean George Waggoner who then arranged an appointment with Chancellor Murphy. These two conspirators apparently made an agreement with each other in advance of the meeting. Schiefelbusch was asked to discuss the kind of children's program needed at the University of Kansas. Schiefelbusch, thinking he was leaving the University of Kansas, did not hesitate to articulate several issues. He also suggested that he could make a better statement if he had a few days to write a plan. He met with the chancellor and the dean again in 3 days with a six-page statement.

Murphy read it and promptly suggested that Schiefelbusch should stay at KU and direct the BCR. Schiefelbusch accepted the offer on two conditions: that there would be an appropriate salary adjustment and that funds would be provided to permit Schiefelbusch to visit three leading children's centers (Iowa, Minnesota, and Florida). Murphy agreed to both conditions.

The transition from the speech clinic to the BCR was a more difficult shift than Schiefelbusch had expected. One difficulty lay in the continuing responsibilities he had assumed before accepting the BCR commitment. He was still chairman of the intercampus committee that managed the Graduate Program in Speech and Hearing at the University of Kansas. That role extended until 1967.

He continued to teach courses in speech pathology and to direct student projects and serve on thesis committees. In addition, he was working with a committee in the Department of Speech and Drama (he was still head of the Speech and Hearing Division of that department) seeking to attain the status of a PhD-granting sector of the university. The strategy involved both the KU and the KUMC campuses. PhD-granting status was approved in 1959.

His most extensive prior commitment was to the Institute for Research in the Education of Exceptional Children (IREEC). The Institute was an advisory agency for special education in the state of Kansas and was under both the Division of Special Education and the Board of Regents. The purpose of the institute was "to encourage, coordinate, evaluate and guide toward meeting the major needs of exceptional children in Kansas, the research efforts of members of college and university faculties, of personnel of public and private agencies, and of other individuals qualified to contribute to organized knowledge in this important field." A second purpose of the Institute was "to serve as a single public center for coordination, direction, and evaluation of training programs for specialists, other than physicians or nurses, who will provide services for exceptional children."

A director and an executive committee managed the institute. The dean of the School of Education at the University of Kansas was designated the director and also served as chairman of the executive committee. The director of the BCR at the University of Kansas served as the executive secretary of the institute. Schiefelbusch's duties as the executive secretary began in 1955 and extended until 1964. Products of this work were described in a final report to the regents at that time.

The Metamorphosis Begins

At the beginning of Schiefelbusch's tenure as director of the BCR, a coordination committee made up of 12 representatives of existing relevant programs was formed. The committee met five times in 6 months and then voluntarily agreed to meet again when "we have something more to talk about."

Representatives of roughly the same departments and divisions (10 years later) began a series of meetings to create the Kansas Center for Mental Retardation and Human Development. Schiefelbusch was gratified when many of the members of the 1956 BCR Coordination Committee ultimately were provided much needed space, and they also received "program" funds to help them develop and upgrade their programs.

With no development money and little to coordinate, the committee soon exhausted all meaningful agenda items. A few things did result from those early meetings. It became apparent that the BCR should become a research development unit rather than the coordination department that Chancellor Murphy had envisioned. The chancellor's recommendation had been to make the BCR a research coordination division for the: 1) Pediatrics Clinic, 2) Children's Clinic in Psychology, 3) Speech and Hearing Clinic, 4) Department of Social Work, 5) Education Clinic, 6) Hearing and Speech Clinic at KUMC, 7) Cleft Palate Clinics at KUMC, 8) Cerebral Palsy Clinics at KUMC, 9) School of Law, 10) Preschool in Home Economics, 11) Government Research Center, and 12) Department of Clinical Psychology. Fortunately, that did not come to pass. Without its own funding base, the BCR would not have the influence or the authority to coordinate the research efforts of so many diverse departments and projects.

Before the meetings were discontinued, a plan and a proposal were submitted to the KU chancellor for a Kansas University Children's Center for Training and Research. The primary purpose of this proposal was to secure working space. In 1956 there was almost no space in which to undertake children's activities. Child development, child psychology, and children's services in several sectors or departments were housed in makeshift off-campus space. The lack of space was constricting the development of several teaching and service departments.

Schiefelbusch met with Dr. Clarke Wescoe (who had replaced Murphy as chancellor of KU) to show him a plan for a child research center. Wescoe was very helpful and encouraging, but he said, "Dick, if you are to build a children's center at KU, you will have to find all of the money." As Schiefelbusch left, he paused at the door and said to Chancellor Wescoe, "Remember that you did not say no."

Marking Time

In the meantime, three projects were undertaken by the BCR, in addition to coordination meetings. The earliest was to produce topical booklets and to operate information dissemination projects that were planned during the 1954–1955 year and continued after the move to Bailey Hall. The second was a small research project series funded from applications to the University Research Fund (e.g., Underachieving Children in the Schools). The third was the coordinating and facilitation of the Institute for Research in the Education of Exceptional Children.

As the federally supported research program expanded, the state activities for children and youth also flourished. Politics became apparent, as did the chronic struggle for funding. The Kansas Council for Children and Youth (KCCY) and the BRC collaborated in developing the 1960 Kansas report for the nationwide President's Report on Children. The report was collated, edited, and submitted from the BCR's office in Bailey Hall. Also, KCCY and the BCR continued to develop and disseminate information on topics requested by agencies in the state. The BCR was active, successful, and enthusiastic in the interactive relationship with KCCY. In this spirit of exuberance, several members sought an audience with the governor. His Honor George Docking responded by inviting the group for lunch at the governor's mansion. It was a wonderful luncheon. Everyone left thinking that all had gone well.

A few days later the director of KCCY received a letter from the governor explaining that he was very sorry but that in the discussion he had learned that the KCCY was a private agency and that it was already receiving state funds. He explained further that not only could he not recommend an increase in KCCY's state funding, but he also was obliged to recommend that the current funds be deleted. The governor never changed his mind. His legal background had led him to construe the KCCY position as not only "private" but as "vested." He felt that he was protecting taxpayers' interests.

After long discussion, the KCCY board decided to move its remaining resources and most of its agenda back to Topeka where it had been before it was invited to join the BCR several years earlier. A few state agencies provided continuing support and the KCCY survived several more years. It was eventually discontinued and two file boxes of condensed, carefully selected material were sent to the BCR director to be turned over to the KU Spencer Research Library. That material provides information about children in Kansas after 1942, when KCCY was founded.

Early Funding for Research

The movement into research funded by federal grants was labored and tentative. The first positive step was for Schiefelbusch to visit Parsons State Hospital and Training Center (PSHTC). This visit was suggested by Lee Meyerson, a psychologist at KU with whom Schiefelbusch had developed a prior professional acquaintance through a mutual interest in children who were deaf or cerebral palsied. Meyerson had lost his hearing when he was 11 years old. He had already visited Parsons and suggested that Schiefelbusch get acquainted with Superintendent Howard Bair and seek to do research there. Meyerson subsequently suggested that Schiefelbusch cultivate staff members of the National Institutes of Health. His advice was not to send a letter to them, but to go see them. Lee Meyerson left KU shortly after that and worked with Jack Michael at the University of Houston in forming one of the first operant laboratory programs for human learning. When he returned to KU for Erik Wright's (one of the original BCR committee members) memorial service more than 25 years later, Meyerson's first question to Schiefelbusch was, "How much money has the BCR brought to KU?"

There were few indicators that the BCR, as it was originally constituted, would become a major research agency. There were no strong research credentials in the BCR's staff and there was a limited tradition for research administration or research support at the University of Kansas at that time (1955). In fact, federally funded research was regarded as risky and was discouraged by the executive vice chancellor under whom the BCR was initially placed. This negative arrangement extended across the first 7 years of the BCR's development (1955–1962).

The National Institute of Mental Health (NIMH) funded the first successful BCR grant in 1957 with a fiscal start date of January 1, 1958. NIMH was then an institute of the National Institutes of Health (NIH) and, fortunately, had a program initiative for hospital improvement grants. The agency contact was Dr. Harold Hildreth of their grants management staff. Hal was helpful, knowledgeable, and experienced in working through offices in Washington, D.C., and in the regional office in Kansas City.

Hildreth was more than a project officer. He introduced Schiefelbusch to other staff members at NIMH and the National Institute of Neurological and Communication Disorders and Stroke (NINCDS) and, in subtle ways, served as a tutor in the process of making grant applications. The grant proposed to teach language and communication skills to children with mental retardation at PSHTC. It was conceived and written by Schiefelbusch with informal assistance of a few colleagues at KU and Topeka, none of whom were researchers in the fields of language or mental retardation.

It is safe to say that there were no experts at the University of Kansas in these fields, including Schiefelbusch. Also, it was apparent to the applicant, his colleagues, and the reviewers that there were no well-known experts in language and communication of persons with mental retardation anywhere. The application and the resulting project was an act of faith on the part of a group of optimists, some of whom did not even know each other.

Perhaps the most positive force in the research development effort was Howard V. Bair, MD, superintendent of PSHTC. He never seemed to doubt the success of the project at any stage of its development. The collaboration between Parsons and KU began with a handshake between Schiefelbusch and Bair in 1957 and has lasted more than 25 years. It was understood that Schiefelbusch was not to interfere with Bair's political moves in Topeka and Bair was not to interfere with Schiefelbusch's personnel selections. The agreement worked well even though neither honored his initial agreement literally. At the time of the grant submission in June 1957, the BCR group was remarkably naïve about grants and grant processing.

The first indication of real interest from the federal government came when two representatives from the regional office of NIMH in Kansas City appeared in Schiefelbusch's tiny office in the basement of Bailey Hall on the KU campus. They announced that the BCR's first research grant application had received a high score, but that they had been instructed to ask Schiefelbusch to assure them that he would really direct the grant.

Schiefelbusch intended to hire an expert to do that. Because his name seemed important to grant reviewers, that first meeting with federal officials launched a series of "principal investigator" arrangements. In the years that followed, Schiefelbusch put his name on dozens of grants that he helped to write in order to secure the funding, but research teams assembled to carry out the work conducted the research.

The initial grant was, however, the only one for which the complete staff had to be hired after the grant was submitted and approved. The four researchers hired were Ross Copeland, MA, from Purdue University in speech science who had experience with children who were mentally retarded at Muscatatuck State School in Indiana; Dorolyn Ezell, MS, from KU who had a teaching background; Joseph Spradlin, PhD pending, from George Peabody College with experience at Winfield State Hospital and Training Center as a staff psychologist; and Seymour Rosenberg, PhD, from Indiana University with experience as a U.S. Air Force scientist.

The absolute importance of the philosophy that Spradlin and Rosenberg shared and the ideas they worked out soon after they met at Parsons must be emphasized. Spradlin and Rosenberg shared the conviction that behavior was affected by environmental conditions and that communication was behavior. They also shared the conviction that understanding how behavior was affected by environmental conditions could best be facilitated by the use of highly controlled laboratory experiments. Their approach was influenced by two general trends in psychology—social assembly research and learning theory (especially operant theory). Moreover, they believed that the principles derived from research in these two areas could be applied to attack the daunting task of improving the lives of institutionalized children with mental retardation. These two approaches provided the core of the science in the beginning years of the BCR and during the developmental years of the Kansas Center.

Rosenberg was appointed field director of OM-111, also known as the Parsons Research Project. The strength of this team soon became apparent, especially the collaboration between Spradlin and Rosenberg. They proceeded to develop pilot studies using single-subject designs and operant technology. Rosenberg frequently referred to the basic research unit as a dyad. By this he meant that the interrelationship of two people (a child and an adult) might establish the basis for operant contingencies. Studies that began in September 1958 were presented as papers at the American Association on Mental Deficiency (AAMD) Convention in Cincinnati in May 1959. Five papers were read to a large audience, who responded with gratifying enthusiasm. A large portion of the crowd wanted to talk with the presenters at the conclusion of the program. The project had tapped into a strong need felt by the audience in attendance.

The bold description of methods and an operational frame of reference for changing behavior offered hope for future programs of instruction and training that had long been needed in institutionalized care settings. The Parsons Research Project had sent a small message that was about to be heard across the nation as a call to innovation and mental retardation research productivity. Members of the project staff were encouraged to develop working papers and journal articles, as well as additional conference panels, that detailed procedures and data confirming the assumptions of functional behavior changes in children who were considered "subtrainable."

Surveying the Scene

The first research grant to the BCR and PSHTC produced several significant studies in the language of children with mental retardation. The time was right to create a larger program. In retrospect, and with only a superficial knowledge of the early BCR program, it would be easy to interpret the events of the 1960s as a confident plan that Dick Schiefelbusch had designed and was putting in place. That was not the case. The road ahead was not clear, and Schiefelbusch was searching and tentative in his odyssey. He was still finding his way around Washington, D.C., and looking for agencies that might be receptive to all the possibilities for research that he was considering. That is made clear in a memo he wrote to his staff in 1960.

MEMORANDUM:

April 4, 1960

To: Members of the Bureau of Child Research

From: R. L. Schiefelbusch

Regarding: Visits with representatives of the Children's Bureau, The U.S. Office of Vocational Rehabilitation, and the Institutes of Health.

The content of this memo pertains to research primarily but attention is also directed to facilities and training.

Children's Bureau

The section on Maternal and Child Health seems to be the only one with money. They already have invested in the Children's Rehabilitation Unit. I doubt that they would wish to finance us too. Our best bet from the CB would involve a plan, which pertains to the Welfare Department in Topeka. If we can develop a plan for research acceptable to the State, they in turn can use it as a means for increasing their federal allotment. There is no money for studies of delinquency at the national level.

U.S. Office of Education

The trick there is to resonate with them on some area of research they wish to support, then to convince them that we can develop that study in good shape. They are extremely eager to back winning horses. Dr. Clark is especially keen on small group learning studies.

Office of Vocational Rehabilitation

They have a fair amount of money for research and some to help construct or add to facilities for service programs—not research. Their research style is for the most part applied in nature. In other words, they like to see the direct utility of the research they support. The do not support studies in delinquency. I see no way for us to use the Office at this time.

Institutes of Health

They have the money! They have a widely diversified program for research support both as to the areas supported and types of grants to be allotted. The project grant seems to offer the greatest flexibility but other grants are likewise flexible. They would support studies of delinquency. Dr. Gladwin in the Community Service Branch seems to be the best contact at this time. However, Dr. Jerry Carter, Chief Psychologist, in the Branch seems also to be a good contact. Ditto for Dr. Hal Hildreth. My best assumption is that if we have a project we would like to do in the future we should spell it out and ask one of these gentlemen (or some other if more appropriate) to reply or to drop in if possible when they are out our way. We should not send any more cold projects to them. I gather that a good grant request has three minimal assets: 1) It is timely and in agreement with their support designs, 2) it is significant and meets the tests of importance as they set them up, and 3) it is well designed and admirably communicated. We cannot adequately satisfy these requisites without interacting with them. If we do we are just lucky.

Grants for new research facilities can be had for up to 50% of the cost. They seem less eager for allotments for service buildings. OVR on the other hand is more interested in service stipulations. These, to the best of my knowledge, are the only federal grant funds we might apply to for new building space.

Training stipends for research personnel can be had if we have good support from academic departments and have good training facilities. They seem a trifle blasé about training projects so I imagine we'd have to be somewhat novel in our approach. I was impressed with the cordial reception I received during my visits to the various offices. There are a number of new people whom I will feel free to contact for advice. I assume this to be a part of an unfolding story which is, for us, still in Chapter 1.

A New Federal Ingredient

In a report submitted in October of 1962, 1 year after President John F. Kennedy established his Panel on Mental Retardation, the panel recommended that ". . . high priority should be given for developing research centers on mental retardation at strategically located universities. . . ."

The day following the release of that report, President Kennedy signed into law the legislation establishing the National Institute of Child Health and Human Development (NICHD). Three and one-half months later, during the first week of February 1963, the Department of Health, Education, and Welfare (DHEW) announced the formal administrative establishment of the NICHD, and the next day President Kennedy's message on mental retardation called for the implementation of the recommendations of the President's Panel on Mental Retardation.

Eight months later, on October 31, 1963, President Kennedy signed into law the Mental Retardation Facilities and Community Mental Health Centers Construction Act of 1963. That new law authorized "grants for construction of centers for research on mental retardation and related aspects of human development." The law authorized construction appropriations of $6 million for FY 1964, $8 million for FY 1965, and $6 million each for FY 1966 and 1967. Under the law, the institutions seeking construction grants had to document their competence in mental retardation research and provide reasonable assurances that "for not less than 20 years after completion of construction, the facility will be used for the research purposes for which it was constructed." In addition, applicants had to provide assurances " that sufficient funds will be available for meeting the non-federal share of the cost of constructing the facility," as well as "sufficient funds when the construction is completed, for effective use of the facility for the research purposes for which it was constructed."

The Match-up

Schiefelbusch and his team quickly began to build ties to federal agencies and started putting together a Kansas resource base that would be complementary to the views in Washington, but that would also be true to the needs of many long-neglected persons. The initial project was augmented by a second grant in 1961 with a 50% increase in funding. A research training grant for predoctoral trainees was added in 1962.

Another major development came in the form of a 7-year program project grant application that was funded in 1963. It was a $2 million grant with provisions for research on three campuses—Parsons, KU, and KUMC in Kansas City. This grant was the largest funded research project that the University of Kansas had received up to that time. It was reviewed and awarded by the National Institute of Mental Health, the agency that had awarded the original grant for the Parsons Research Project. However, the NICHD would be managing the grant. (See chapter 4 for a more complete discussion of that grant.) Visits were soon undertaken that led to discussions about the program project and about the Juniper Gardens Children's Project that began in 1964 (see chapter 6 for a discussion of this project).

This program project grant, by mutual consent, established the precedent for a number of other research, service, and training projects that soon were to be conducted jointly at these sites. Even more significantly, the program project served as an intercampus model for the Kansas Mental Retardation Research Center to be established in 1966.

Conception of the Kansas Center

In 1965 Schiefelbusch was chosen (as a federally paid consultant) to be the chairman of the site visit team to evaluate the application of Peabody College of Vanderbilt University for one of the mental retardation research centers provided for in the legislation by the Kennedy administration. Peabody had a strong and growing program for training behavioral psychologists. Some of the graduates, including Joseph E. Spradlin and Frederic L. Girardeau, had already come to Kansas and were planning and starting programs with as much, if not more, promise than the work at Peabody. But the Kansas program lacked a strong base with a specific commitment to mental retardation research from which it could grow and compete for federal mental retardation research funds.

After the Tennessee site visit, Schiefelbusch called his research associates together and explained the mental retardation centers legislation to them, what would be involved in a national center, and how together they could create a program to operate a national center. Many of his associates were not immediately taken by the idea. Most of them were young and had deep interests in their labs and did not relish the prospect of becoming involved in a large organization that might make them administrators rather than researchers. During a coffee break at a long meeting in Varsity House, Fred Girardeau asked Joseph Spradlin, "Is RLS really trying to talk us into applying for a mental retardation center grant?" "He already has," was Spradlin's reply.

Schiefelbusch never really put the center issue to a vote by his closest associates. He merely assumed that they would support him and respect his instincts and his perception of the benefits of having a center for mental retardation and related aspects of human development in Kansas. No one openly opposed the idea, though a few did express some reservations about the amount of time and nonresearch effort such a program would impose on those who were a part of it.

One research associate good-naturedly observed that, "Dick, it is not possible to get buildings of that size and money in that amount and to manage it to do all the things you envision. It is not realistic. You have to be out of your mind to be thinking of it, and we have to be out of our minds for going along with it." "Progress is only a new set of problems," was Schiefelbusch's philosophical reply.

Thus, 8 years after Schiefelbusch made his decision to stay in Kansas, he set out to convince Jim Surface, provost of the University of Kansas, that he could secure federal funds to construct buildings at KU, KUMC, and Parsons State Hospital (for a new center for research in mental retardation), if he could secure official university approval.

"Jim," Schiefelbusch said in a meeting with Surface, "I've been in Nashville where I was chairman of a site visit team for an application Peabody has made for one of the National Research Centers programs. What they're proposing is good, but we have more to offer than they do. If we want a program, including new buildings and research laboratories on all three campuses—here, Parsons and Kansas City—we should try for it. I'm convinced we could make it work."

"Dick, I want to get you while you're hot," Provost Surface replied. Surface called for an appointment for Schiefelbusch to talk with Dr. Wescoe. The chancellor was completely booked up except for Sunday morning. Surface and Schiefelbusch were in the chancellor's conference room at 9:30 a.m. the following Sunday.

"This better be good," the chancellor said with good humor, "this would have been the first Sunday morning I would have had free in 13 weeks."

By 11:00 a.m. the plan had been laid out. "Let's do it," the chancellor said. Wescoe called the provost of KUMC, Arden Miller, and received his approval. He called old friends at KUMC and advocated that they concur. Then he went to the building charts of each campus and marked where the buildings might be placed. In this way KUMC eventually increased its laboratory space by 40%, and KU would soon secure space that was easily twice as large as the original plan for a children's center.

The chancellor gave Schiefelbusch one more task: "Dick, it's up to you to explain this to Howard Bair and to help him get approval from the Board of Social Welfare."

That was not as formidable a task as the chancellor might have thought. Bair and Schiefelbusch had already formed a good working relationship. Both were veterans of World War II. Bair had been a battlefield surgeon during the war. A B-24 bomber on which Schiefelbusch was the navigator had been shot down while making a raid on German submarine pens. Both were private pilots, and both had deep concerns about the care of children with mental retardation.

Schiefelbusch went to PSHTC the next day and enlisted Bair's concurrence and support. Bair needed little persuasion. He was ready to move in almost any direction that would improve his institution and solidify his political influence. This was before the massive state agency, the Kansas Department of Social and Rehabilitation Services, had been created. A group called the Board of Social Welfare had control of the state's institutions.

The chairman of the Board of Social Welfare, Robert Anderson, had visited the state institutions. He was appalled by the conditions in the institutions, but had not been able to come up with a plan to improve them. Thus Anderson was already a potential ally in such a cause, but Howard Bair did not know that. Bair loved to play politics. Rather than going directly to Chairman Anderson, Bair began calling state legislators he knew to enlist their support in the new program and the buildings. Although most of the construction would be paid for with federal money, state matching funds would be required for the Parsons setting, and for that it would be necessary to have support in the legislature. By Monday noon, Bair had drummed up enough support among the state legislators to be assured of getting the needed matching money. He was ready to let Anderson in on the plan.

Before Bair got around to sharing what he and Schiefelbusch were planning, Anderson got wind of what was afoot and called Bair to Topeka to explain. Schiefelbusch went along. Howard Bair was a portly man with an infectious sense of humor and a skill in practical politics. But that day he may have wondered if perhaps the temptation to dabble in politics had led him to try an end run on the wrong man. Bob Anderson was an even larger man than Bair, and though he affected a country-lawyer demeanor, both Bair and Schiefelbusch knew him to be an astute and effective politician and an effective administrator who was less than pleased if circumvented.

In the boardroom, Anderson let Bair and Schiefelbusch wait for him for a while, and then he entered and greeted his waiting audience, not with hostility but with a certain cool attitude. He sat down, leaned forward, placed his elbows on the table, looked directly at Howard Bair as a country lawyer might when facing an opponent in the courtroom, and stated,

> Howard, all day yesterday I kept getting calls from state legislators telling me how we are going to have some new facility in Kansas. In case you have forgotten it, your job is to run Parsons State Hospital. My job is to be a politician. Now, I've heard that you are cookin' up some big plan with the federal government, the university, and the legislature. If you don't mind, since I'm supposed to be in charge of institutions and superintendents, I'd like to know exactly what is going on.

Schiefelbusch says it was the only time he recalls Howard Bair looking small, but Bair quickly recovered and he explained the amount of money involved and the buildings that were possible. Schiefelbusch explained the research programs for children that were planned and that this was a one-time chance to get several new buildings and support for progressive research programs—but they had to act quickly and either pass or play. Anderson immediately understood what such a center could mean to the state and to the institutions under the Board of Social Welfare and abandoned any resentment he may have had because Bair had chosen to build his own political support base before seeking permission.

Without Anderson's support the whole plan and the future Kansas program for persons with disabilities could have died in that room, but Anderson accepted it all and became an ally in getting support for an unprecedented program for children with disabilities. It was done with no contracts and no written documents, all in a gentleman's agreement. That day was not Anderson's only contribution. He remained a friend and supporter of mental retardation research programs as long as he was in state service.

Thus, myriad factors led to the further vitalization of the Bureau of Child Research and the creation of the entity known as the Kansas Center for Mental Retardation and Related Aspects of Human Development. Leaders were made or stepped forward at the right time. The university was open to fostering a program, not for the most intelligent citizens of the state but the most disabled. It was not lost on anyone that the move would bring federal money to the university. Young and well-trained behavioral scientists were about to begin their careers and were eager for opportunities. The state system had persons in power who were supportive of an effort to change the lives of persons with developmental disabilities. And the administration in power in the federal government was not only supportive, but was about to develop advocates and provide research funds devoted to helping persons with mental retardation. The ideas, aspirations, and professional and personal commitments of the right persons were present at the proper time to allow the creation of a new social experiment that would become a credit to Kansas and a resource for the nation.

All that was not apparent at this stage in the development of the Kansas Center. Support among Schiefelbusch's academic peers was not widespread. Schiefelbusch had in fact been advised by one university leader to abandon his idea of working with children with mental retardation.

"It's professional suicide, Dick. Get into something else."

Dr. Florence Brown Sherbon was appointed the first director of the Bureau of Child Research in 1921. She had pushed for the establishment of the Bureau, testifying in support of Senate Bill 310. She said, "I grow weary knowing about the yearly increase in appropriations for research on the care and feeding of livestock knowing that we appropriate nothing for research on the care and nurture of children."

Dr. Lloyd Lockwood and Dr. Richard Schiefelbusch at the Speech Clinic Annex at the KU Lawrence campus. Schiefelbusch came to KU in 1949 to start the University-based clinic while completing his dissertation from Northwestern University.

The Turner House pre-school, located at North Third and Stewart Streets in the urban core of Kansas City, Kansas, was the cradle of the Bureau's bold move to "cultural-familial" research, or the role of environmental factors in the risk of mental retardation and developmental delay beginning in 1965.

Nancy Reynolds (*far left*) and Betty Hart (*far right*) with children in one of the first preschools developed by the Bureau. Hart went on to co-direct a milestone study with Todd Risley in early language development in children.

From left: Richard Schiefelbusch, Ross Copeland, and Howard V. Bair shown in a *Parsons Sun* story from November 12, 1966, on the Bureau's impending three-campus Mental Retardation Research Center that was ultimately inaugurated on June 14, 1972.

Dr. Howard V. Bair was the progressive administrator of the Parsons State Hospital and Training Center in Parsons, Kansas, where the Bureau launched its first research effort. The collaboration between Parsons and KU began with a handshake between Schiefelbusch and Bair in 1957 and continues to this day.

The Mimosa Cottage Project, "A Demonstration Program for Intensive Training of Institutionalized Mentally Retarded Girls" at Parsons State Hospital and Training Center, was not actually a cottage, but a multilevel red brick institutional structure built in 1931. However, the remodeled floors in 1968 included an office, classroom, dormitories, a carpeted living room, music and recreation area, and kitchen.

What came to be known as the Mimosa Cottage Project resonated across the country. The Bureau developed an intensive training program at Parsons State Hospital and Training Center based on a token economy for young women with moderate to severe mental retardation to prepare them to live and, in some cases, work in the world.

When John F. Kennedy championed legislation that would target resources and talent to address the state of mental illness and mental retardation in 1963, Richard Schiefelbusch was on the forefront. He was tapped to prepare the first guidelines for the federal program of applied research. He was in Washington, D.C. in the fall of 1963 with Kennedy's Special Assistant on Mental Retardation, Dr. Stafford Warren.

The Kansas University Affiliated Facility (UAF) provided major service functions from its four community settings and facilities in Lawrence, Parsons, and Kansas City, Kansas, built under the auspices of the Division of Mental Retardation of the Federal Social and Rehabilitative Services. On June 14, 1972, two buildings were dedicated at Parsons facilities to support professional training for approximately 300 graduate students. The clinical facilities provided diagnostic and treatment facilities for over 1,000 children with developmental disabilities each year.
From left: KU Chancellor E. Laurence Chalmers, Richard Schiefelbusch, Kansas Rep. Clyde Hill, and Howard V. Bair, director of the Parsons State Hospital and Training Center.

Joseph Spradlin became known as the scientific conscience of the Bureau of Child Research. He was an investigator with the Bureau's very first research project and went on to be known for his work in stimulus control applied to the problems of people with mental retardation. He held several posts including director of research at Parsons.

As the faculty and staff of the highly successful Bureau of Child Research began to expand rapidly in the 1960s, their space did not. Most faculty members, including Don Baer, Fran Horowitz, and Joe Spradlin, were housed in a temporary setting called Varsity House at Eleventh and Indiana in Lawrence, where everyone aspired to have either a desk or a drawer in a desk.

At one time, films produced by the Bureau of Child Research Parsons Media Group were estimated (from records kept by the film rental service of the Division of Continuing Education) to have an annual audience of up to 75,000 persons. *Top row, left to right:* Joe Crabtree, David Hosman, Myron Salhberg, Dean Cole, Carl Williams, Rich Lindsey. *Bottom row, left to right:* Gary Campbell, Betty Thomas, Gary Burge, Larry Thompson, Stan Roit.

In 1965, Richard Schiefelbusch, with Frances Horowitz, chair of the Department of Human Development and Family Life at KU, pulled off a coup that recruited some of the hottest young behavior shapers in the country, Todd Risley (*A*), R. Vance Hall (*B*), Donald Baer (*C*), and Montrose Wolf (*D*), away from the University of Washington in one fell swoop. They became so influential they were lighthearted-edly dubbed "The Kansas Mafia" by *Behavior Today.*

From the beginning, the Juniper Gardens Children's Project was a joint community–university project. Uriel Owens was arguably the strongest behind-the-scenes community leader in Kansas City, Kansas. Universally liked and respected, he was politically astute and knew how to get things done without seeking the limelight. He acted as the project's grants manager and director of community relations. His efforts also led to securing money from the Kansas state legislature as core support for Juniper Gardens. *From left:* Todd Risley and Uriel Owens.

Joseph Spradlin and the work at Parsons were featured in the most influential column in the country—page one, column one of *The Wall Street Journal,* June 15, 1979.

3

Background: The Times

ROBERT K. HOYT AND JOSEPH E. SPRADLIN

The growth of the Bureau of Child Research and the development of the Kansas Center for Mental Retardation and Related Aspects of Human Development began with a joint project with Parsons State Hospital and Training Center. To better understand that development, a brief look at the conditions existing for people with mental retardation in the late 1950s is useful.

The Institutions

More has been written and filmed in and about institutions for humans with mental illness than is the case for humans with mental retardation. But the conditions in the two types of institutions were similar in many respects in the early part of the 20th century. An institution was an institution. A state institution in those times was never a particularly good place for anyone with a developmental difficulty to live.

Institutional interiors had a similar essence. The odor could be sensed at the entryways, sometimes even on the front steps, where a half-moldy, half-stale organic odor poured over an arriving visitor. That sensory blanket announced the complete hopelessness that descended on anyone curious enough to probe the dwellings of residents with mental retardation.

Some wards included males of 10 through 70 years, roughly comprising men and boys of similar potential. Day rooms were sometimes orderly and clean and the residents were well groomed as they sat on benches and rocked back and forth under the watchful eyes of police-like aides.

In other wards the residents swept floors, washed windows, played games, and came and went in shifts to work in the laundry or the dairy. They were often paid in the range of a dollar a month for their work, unless the work itself was considered payment. Work has value in confinement, even for someone who struggles to perform and repeat each laborious step of a simple task such as sweeping the oiled wooden floors, mopping up urine, or physically assisting residents with debilitating motor handicaps. Simple work provides wonderful variety compared to a day of rocking and flicking fingers inches from one's face.

The Keepers and the Kept

Older women were often the most successful managers of institutional wards. They were commonly postmenopausal, red-faced women who managed the residents with a blend of applied and well-understood discipline and practical experience. These earth mothers of the wards were characteristically positive. Their faces might be coarse and their hands hard. They could be chunky and solid. Most had developed or inherited smiles that radiated warmth and solid, agrarian or peasant beauty. They loved and cared about the humble persons in their care. They understood which residents were reliable and docile and which ones needed to be watched for treachery and violence.

These women could have been, and many times were, grandmothers who, when off-duty, prevailed in homey kitchens emanating odors of baking apple pies that graced huge Sunday dinners for large extended families. Many were widows. Most kept modest homes and worked weekdays to bring extra money into the neat farmhouses where they lived near the institution or in tidy apartments at the edges of more prosperous suburbs or city neighborhoods.

These women welcomed visitors to their wards and made it a point to introduce their best residents. Their wards were clean, comfortable, friendly, and housed men and boys who were fond of the women who were their surrogate mothers. Women who ran the wards developed kind but firm systems and the *boys* (many of them as old as the manager) were reluctant to bring disappointment into what was their home.

Many women had managed wards for 30 years or more. They were difficult to replace when they retired or burned out or became too old to get up and face another stress-filled day. Few of their wards followed plans to advance the residents toward independence, but their buildings were clean and humane places.

Next to one of the better buildings run by an older woman might be a stark and dirty contrast commonly run by men strong enough to handle more active residents. The odor of those places was pungent and had an unmistakable tinge of excrement not easily tolerated by outsiders. The management might have a benign practicality about it, but it was nonetheless cruel. The manager might rip strips of cloth to tie an old man's hands to the arms of his wheelchair. Few managers knew any other way to keep the old men from intermittently pitching forward from wheelchairs to slam their faces against the floors.

The oldest and most physically disabled were most often afraid of the manager. When the manager moved, the residents watched him. If the manager moved toward them, the residents tried to get out of the way.

Mobile residents were kept on floors separate from those in wheelchairs. Some had low-slung scooter carts with castors for wheels. Many men had open sores they picked at through the hours of the day. Blind residents often pressed their sightless eyeballs back in their head, possibly because the pressure against the retina created the only sensation of vision they had ever known. Windows were placed so high on the walls that the inhabitants could not look over the sills into the outside world.

Testing was common at admittance. The test scores of most of the men showed that they had little potential to do anything except spend their lives in a sometimes benign cage. Few ward attendants questioned the accuracy of a patient's test scores. The test scores proved what was assumed. Visitors who came to the worst wards were quickly convinced that the lack of potential was both apparent and real.

For a visitor to enter a ward for the most active residents, it was first necessary for an aide to unlock the door. When the door swung open, the uproar and odor intensified. The noise level in the room dropped suddenly from a raucous din to near silence and then picked up again as the visitors stepped inside and the inhabitants saw that the visitors were not threatening. The high windows were screened on the inside with heavy steel mesh strong enough to provide a convenient hitching rack to which several boys at a time could be tied with soft rope and cloth strips.

Those who were tied often urinated or defecated and trampled a smeared, brown half-circle around the floor at their feet. An aide with a mop and bucket might be cleaning up puddles and piles but no one took the boys to the toilet. Padlocks secured the toilet doors. Aides were busy making rounds, checking the bindings of the boys tied to the gratings, and breaking up fights. They did not refer to the boys by name. Communications were limited to grunts and shouts of, "Hey, you! Quit that! Asshole!" There were no toys in the room and no furniture except wooden benches.

The day rooms in such places were without toys. Except to go to meals and to bed, the boys spent their lives in the open area of the ward. A few times a day they were admitted to the toilets for a brief and chaotic toileting time.

Stepping out of such a place is like coming out of a dark tunnel of bad odors and loud noises into sudden springtime, from the muck of a manure mine into mountain valleys and dogwoods in bloom at the end of the lifeless cold of the winter. But the inmates knew little about the change of seasons except that sometimes they wore coats to go to meals if the institution was located in a northern latitude. They rarely got a breath of air that was not befouled, except when they were lined up and led to and from the dining hall. Those whose behavior or physical disabilities made them difficult to manage were not privileged to receive even that simple break. They were fed in the wards.

The women's buildings were not much different. In the best buildings, the women might be free to come and go under loose supervision. Nothing was allowed out of place. Dolls and dainty items were arranged in the middle of each bedspread. The feminine touches were window dressing, not parts of the environment of any practical use to those who inhabited the place. The girls and women were clean and well dressed. They sat quietly in chairs along the walls, saying little and doing nothing, except rocking with a rocking chair.

In some of the more organized wards, women were not always under the care of kindly building managers. Burly female aides watched the residents and corrected them, sometimes physically with a slap to the hand or a jerk on an arm, to make certain they did not fight or disturb the artificial neatness of the ward. The women in the cleanest wards appeared to be much better off than most male residents, better off insofar as neatness and cleanliness were concerned. But in the night, screams sometimes came from those seemingly perfect places when wet towels smacked the bare backs and backsides of anyone who had been out of line the previous day. Aides in such places were often quite skilled in applying wet towel discipline. The institution's superintendent might have been aware of such abuses, either directly or by grapevine, but he was often content to have a place that was neat, clean, and disciplined without inquiring too earnestly about how it was done.

Then there were the unmitigated hellholes that resembled closed cattle sheds more than places where humans might live. They were not air-conditioned in those times. The barred windows and doors were left open around the clock in the warmer months. The building might have a large cement verandah on the front. These were rare buildings with limited outside access for the residents. Those verandahs held assortments of men without limbs, men with sunken faces, men in dirty diapers, men crawling about on the cement, sitting in corners, and pushing themselves in wheelchairs and four-wheeled dollies. A few men had heavy protectors on their arms. Unfettered and unpadded, they would beat their arms against a radiator shield or windowsill until the bones were broken. Others wore helmets to protect them when they battered their heads against the concrete floor. There would be a tall wire mesh fence around the perimeter of the verandah. A cement ramp allowed misshapen and limbless men to roll or drag themselves in and out of the building as they saw fit. Aides hosed off the cement verandah from time to time.

Many residents showed little sign of annoyance or discomfort as they sat in urine and feces with their bodies exposed through clothing that long since would have been abandoned by a tramp. Nude and half-nude men of various ages sat against the walls or lay in fetal positions on the floor, sometimes toying with sturdy erections. The piles of feces that cropped up on the floor in aimless, scattered patterns were not all fresh. Some had congealed and hardened.

The worst of the women's wards were quite similar, except that messes on the floors and the associated odors were more intense because the menstrual flow from several women overlaid the moldy, subterranean essence of the interior. Young women sat naked and half-dressed on benches with their institutional dresses cast aside. Their genitalia were revealed without modesty and as mysterious and unblemished as on the most lovely of women. The organs of motherhood were seemingly molded into them as mocking jokes. Their reproductive systems were fully intact and capable, even eager, to receive insemination to set them full-speed into a reproduction cycle. Any newborn issued by them would enter the world to find a parent who knew little of herself and nothing about motherhood beyond the primal urgings that instigated procreation. The women in these holes spent their days sitting on benches or edging across the floor of the ward to find spots of moving sunshine that crept dimly across the floor from some dirty and distant window.

It had been a common practice in the 1930s to send ungainly, slow, or even ugly young women to institutions. Some had no home and no known relatives who wanted them. They never learned to hold down a job or care for themselves. Some came from mental hospitals and from jail where they had been confined for prostitution. Some came to the institutions because a judge believed it kinder to send them to a mental retardation institution than to a mental hospital. In the 1950s many of these women still remained.

Judges often had strange reasons for their decisions. Decrees often contained fanciful, colorful if vicious statements such as: "masturbation during teen-age made him dumb; mother scared by a black dog or bear; father was drunk when the child was conceived; child fell off the back porch; mother smoked cigars and drank beer during pregnancy."

The Saddest Place

Institutional hospital wards had no waiting area and no reception desk. A string of visitors was not a problem. The private lounges for physicians were behind unmarked doors. Nothing in the design made the hospital different from the other buildings. Visitors and staff walked into the building to be confronted by large open areas crowded with beds. The nurses' station was near the center of the room where the nurse on duty could keep an overseer's eye on the patients and aides. The patients were grouped according to age and requirements for nursing care. The hospital was populated with adults and children, many of whom had been bedridden for years. Most patients had human contact only when an aide or a patient-helper changed the bed clothing or brought liquid food. The most severely handicapped were fed with a tube that piped a watery gruel directly into the esophagus.

Nearly everyone in the hospital wards had to be fed and changed and turned. Bedsores as big as grapefruits were not uncommon and some patients soiled the beds nearly as fast as they could be changed. The nursery for the very young had nothing except the cribs to identify it as a nursery. There were no flowered wall coverings, no mobiles hanging from the ceilings, no pictures of smiling faces, and no drawings of lambs. The environment was so harsh it might have been constructed to punish the children for being what they were. Most children simply lay in their cribs. A few could stand and shake the sides of their cribs and make baby-like sounds. They received most of the attention from aides and nurses.

Some hospitals had a corner or a room for a collection of organisms kept from death for no apparent reason except that they had been born alive and had somehow survived the grossest deformities. These corners or rooms were teratological nightmares. Waste tubes and catheters were permanently attached. Some patients were hydrocephalic with emaciated bodies and heads like fragile, transparent watermelons with sad eyes in deep sockets and delicate blue veins beneath the translucent cranial skin. There might be a child with no face. There were eyes below a small forehead and above an opening that was a gaping, pulsating, organic cavern leading to the throat cavity. There was no way to know if a sentient mind existed there.

Such institutions were facing changes. The changes would require the cooperation of progressive institutional superintendents. Parents, institutional administrators, and scientists (who understood that there must be a better way to care for the nation's severely developmentally disabled citizens) would shape the changes through a combination of humanitarian concern and science. It would be a long and difficult task that never had a clean end.

The Changing Times

The Awakening

In the early and mid-1960s, dramatic changes were beginning to occur nationally. What follows is an attempt to characterize those changes.

National professional organizations for persons who worked with individuals with mental retardation had been sleepy, good-old-boy confederations for generations. Superintendents of various competencies were in almost complete control. Chaplains dispensed advice in platitudes. In some institutions there were fastidious hand wringers of various disciplines issuing confident diagnoses with deep feeling but no substance. There were stacks and reams of plans deigned to never be implemented. The professional organizations were doing little to make changes.

Those organizations were easily taken over by coalitions of young professionals from a dozen major universities. The best and the brightest of the young professionals understood that the associations were about to become bulwarks for scholars. They understood that the federal government, with a supportive president, was ready to launch massive research programs for persons with mental retardation. Federal money was beginning to flow to universities to support scholars to meet and talk and argue with each other about mental retardation. The organizations would become the channels of power for a movement to change the way persons with retardation were trained and treated. The movement was proceeding on the philosophy that the power that came with abundant federal money could accomplish anything. As one observer said many years later: "We believed we could put men on the moon. The new president was saying so. Curing mental retardation seemed a small task compared to going to the moon. All we needed was enough money."

The government sent representatives to professional association meetings to deliver dozens of papers—some of them were obscure and pedantic and some of them crystal clear. All were spreading the word about federal money. There were position papers, feasibility studies, white papers, statements of policy papers, the future of social responsibility papers, the role of the federal government papers, the charge to the American public papers, the functional role of the states in the new era papers, and dozens of other papers meant to reassure parents who kept up with such things and to convince the academic community and the professional organizations that something was about to happen.

Progressive professionals who came to the conventions and meetings often paid their own expenses and took personal leave because their superintendents or their universities were too cash-strapped or too niggardly to provide travel money and time off. The best organizations were ripe for real change and the scent of a power shift was in the air. Many young professionals who had been working in institutions were highly motivated for everything and anything to change. They saw a bleak future for themselves under existing conditions. They also realized that the behemoth institutions had developed immune systems to kill off any puny virus of change.

The best of the papers presented at the professional conventions changed the lives of many young professionals. Older institutional workers at first assumed that the new papers were bluff and bluster from federal bureaucrats who could not deliver anything but restatements of obvious homilies. But it quickly became clear to even the most oblivious sideliner that new agencies in Washington were offering almost certain success to colleges and universities that could assemble teams to create a credible research grant. The call was clear in a document written by a source close to the president:

> We, as a nation, have too long postponed an intensive search for solutions to the problems of the mentally retarded. That failure must be corrected. That failure is damaging to our national fiber. Approximately five million of our fellow citizens are retarded. The condition affects all members of their families and their friends. Over 700,000 of our young men were rejected by the draft in World War II because they were retarded. Every year we have 126,000 more retarded children born. Mental retardation disables ten times as many persons as diabetes does, twenty times as many as tuberculosis, twenty-five times as many as muscular dystrophy and 600 times as many as infantile paralysis. If we do not do something, by 1970 we shall have another million retarded citizens in our institutions. Over half will be children under nine years of age. Our objective should be to prevent retardation entirely. Failing that, we must provide our retarded citizens opportunities that are the birthright of every American child.

The Research Grants

Federally supported social research programs at universities grew rapidly in the decades following the middle of the century. Aspiring researchers in the social sciences learned how to organize research teams and write successful grant applications. Departments within universities began perpetuating their research programs by training students to become scientists with skills in grant writing and research administration.

In the process of approving most peer-reviewed grant applications, the federal agency's procedures normally called for a site visit by a team of experts who came to determine whether the work should be supported. For 2 or 3 days they visited laboratories, asked questions, and probed the knowledge of those who proposed to do the research. The team evaluated the scientific credibility of the proposal. Their final report included a recommendation to approve all or part of the money or to deny the application. A council of bureau chiefs and expert consultants then met in Washington to read and discuss the merits of the competing applications. The council gave scores to the most promising. Numerical ratings were assigned as a guide to the priority order in which the successful projects should be funded. The projects with the best scores were funded until the appropriated funds were exhausted. Many applications might be approved because they were deserving, but only applications with the best scores received money before the year's appropriation was expended.

The Opportunity

The federal government, prodded by a progressive administration, was enlisting brainpower in a rare example of inspired governmental leadership. There was plenty of idle talk in the convention bars and coffee shops and dinner conversations, but there was already enough published research to point out effective tools to create training programs that would produce results. Many young psychologists were coming under the influence of B. F. Skinner. These Skinnerians, or operant psychologists,[1] became aware that behavior could not only be measured and correlated with other measures, but could be changed by changing environmental conditions.

These operant psychologists were not interested in the study of the human mind. They were not particularly concerned about probing into the real or imagined recesses of consciousness. They stepped around all that to design objective experiments to manage the way humans behave. They sympathized with institutionalized children, but they did not delude themselves with mystical talk or false hopes. Such children were to be studied objectively. The need for food, water, and social attention, built in through millions of years of evolution, were the avenues they would tap. They would seek success there because they saw no evidence that sympathy, praying, anguishing, and labeling could make a person with retardation into a free citizen. They believed that persons with retardation could learn more than conventional wisdom implied. They were not deeply interested in physiology or neurology in the early days, but they understood that many forms of mental retardation could be avoided by preventing developmental errors. The more pressing problem was to improve behavior in institutionalized people. Most operant psychologists were not hindered by illusions about humanity and its place in the animal kingdom. The illusion that humans are the chosen species is not an easy concept to maintain when one understands that humans are not immune to pathogens and errors in the workings of chemistry and electricity that cause developmental problems in all animals, and that errors are more random than ordered.

The extant problem was immediate for the thousands of persons confined to institutions. Effective intervention must be brought from the lab to the ward with some haste, while the federal government was supportive and parents of children with retardation were gaining influence. Observing and measuring human behavior and finding ways to manage human behavior were the keys. Devotees of B. F. Skinner developed laboratories to examine principles that had proved effective with pigeons and rats.

This was a turning point. Operant psychologists were proposing that the principles used in animal experiments should be extended into experiments to teach persons with mental retardation to perform simple tasks. Given control over a subject's[2] reinforcements, they could define the responses they wanted and condition those responses by providing reinforcement for approximations of new responses. Operant conditioning was sometimes described in oversimplified terms as "grandma's law." Grandma says, "If you pull the weeds out of the garden, then I'll give you some cookies." Certain behaviors bring certain rewards when Grandma is in control. It was more complicated and refined than grandma's law, but grandma's law is close to the spirit of operant conditioning.

Early operant research was carried out with individual subjects in specially constructed experimental settings that provided more control.

Behavioral laboratories were often small cubicles with one-way mirrors in one wall and a flimsy entry door. Experimental rooms were insulated to prevent outside sounds from disturbing the subject, and to prevent the sounds of the subject's frustration from disturbing persons outside the experimental room. Responses from the subject were recorded on event recorders or cumulative recorders controlled by relays and wires and a primitive patch panel. The subject made a response and it was recorded on paper tape or cards or a tape recorder. Lights blinked and relays and switches clacked. Early behavioral event-recording equipment was primitive. Experiments with rats helped in the development of event-recording systems that could handle hundreds or thousands of responses. While more elegant experiments with rats were being conducted, operant psychologists were also conducting experiments with human subjects.

Some of the earliest studies of operant conditioning with people with retardation were primarily close replications of earlier studies with rats and pigeons. The experimental room for the subject might include a bar that could be pressed and tray into which a candy could be delivered. Delivery of the candy might be accompanied by the click of a relay, momentary dimming of the house light, and brief lighting of the tray. The subject would be a child with profound retardation. That child might not be toilet trained and might be unable to feed or dress himself or herself. Initially, the child would make no response to the candy. Perhaps the experimenter would initially smash the candy and place it on the child's tongue. After a couple of smashed candies perhaps the child would take the candy from the experimenter's hand, take it to his or her mouth, and eat it. Later the experimenter would teach the child to take the candy when it was delivered into the tray. When the child was adapted to the experimental room and the delivery of the candy accompanied by the click, house light dimming, and the lighted tray, the experimenter would leave the room and view the child from the control room. Now when the child's hand was near the bar, the experimenter would press a button and a candy would be delivered. If the child touched the bar, a candy would be delivered. Through these successive approximations, the child would soon be reliably pressing the bar. Now the child might be required to make an increasing number of bar presses for each piece of candy. Later, by careful application of reinforcement techniques, the child might be taught to press the bar only when a loud tone was present. Such demonstrations were primitive, but they were impressive to people who had never been able to teach the child such simple skills as self-feeding. Laboratory studies soon demonstrated that children who did not imitate could be taught to imitate by use of these reinforcement techniques. These initial laboratory successes led some operant psychologists to apply these principles to teaching such functional skills as self-toileting and self-feeding. Once again success often followed.

From the Laboratory to a Rehabilitative Culture

The successes that operant-oriented psychologists had in the laboratory and simple applications led some to believe that they could design and implement rehabilitative cultures for people who were juvenile delinquents, mentally ill, or mentally retarded.

The Cottage

What follows is not meant to portray any specific operant cottage but to describe how many cottages were set up and operated. This is a mixed narrative meant to give the flavor of the times rather than a precise description of any project or any institution. That said, however, the cottage described here closely resembles the first such attempt to design a rehabilitative culture for people with retardation, called Mimosa Cottage at Parsons State Hospital and Training Center.

Rather than being allowed to sit around watching television or otherwise wasting each day, selected adolescent girls lived together where they could be given chips, beads, coins, cards, or points throughout the day as rewards for performing positive behaviors. Each day, or several times a week, they exchanged tokens for privileges, snack food, music, and a variety of other tangible objects or activities referred to as reinforcers. Through a system of behavior modification the girls learned the skills of their nonretarded peers. The intent was for them to learn what they needed to know to move into houses or apartments that would provide sheltered living and where they could continue to be trained.

Changing the behavior patterns of children and adolescents with mental retardation with the intent to make them more like children who are not mentally retarded was a revolutionary approach. Most institutional workers, including the superintendents, considered persons of a certain level of intelligence to be "subtrainable" and thus, by implication, subhuman.

Operant practitioners quickly established systems to encourage persons with mental retardation to learn to do things thought to be impossible for them to learn. Girls (and boys) learned to care for themselves, to cook, and to do housework. They learned to fix their hair and wash and iron their clothes. This was accomplished by token reinforcement systems and by teaching children with severe handicaps to imitate modeled behavior.

Cottages were set up with same-sex groups as research subjects. The most effective projects were free of the institutional system. Cottages were often two-story brick buildings apart from the rest of the institution. The upstairs provided space for a dormitory for 8 to 10 girls. The downstairs of the old wards were turned into living rooms, kitchens, recreation areas, and a training area, with a room at the end for an office and conference area or space for research assistants.

They were called research cottages because the purpose was to do good sound research, collect data, and develop effective procedures that allowed semiskilled persons to teach children with mental retardation the tasks of daily living. When there was enough money, cottages were remodeled and reorganized. Systems were designed to teach children how to prepare food, use the toilet unassisted, wash themselves, and brush their teeth.

In some cottages there were provisions for birth control. The institution's head nurse, a woman of advanced years and conservative persuasions, sometimes resisted birth control measures. But she understood how awkward it would be if any of the girls should become pregnant while part of an experimental cottage. And the girls, after all, were to learn how to live outside the institution.

The girls were between 12 and 18 years old. None had self-injurious behaviors and none was profoundly handicapped or cosmetically marked by birth defects. The cottage and its inhabitants might be photographed for professional journals and mass-circulation publications. Cottage residents were selected who had promise for rehabilitation and life outside the institution and whose physical characteristics were most like children of similar ages outside the institution.

The girls lived under the constant supervision of young women who wore carpenter's aprons to hold large foreign coins. Foreign coins had value nowhere except in the cottage store, thus discouraging the tokens from being stolen or hoarded by more devious, if enterprising, girls. If a girl persisted in stealing tokens belonging to other girls, the aides marked each token given to the girl. Marked coins were the only ones accepted from that girl when she traded her tokens for things she wanted from the cottage store. That discouraged stealing and did not require the girl to be overtly punished.

The young women who dispensed the coins were called research assistants. They worked part-time in brief but intense shifts. They were often recruited from a local college, trained in data recording, and given a crash course in the delivery of tokens and social reinforcement. The work was a challenge and the young women were eager and idealistic and genuinely wanted to "help people."

"That's good, Mary," a research assistant would say, following a well-defined routine. "That's right. Look at me when you speak. Always look at the person you are speaking to."

Thus vocally reinforcing the girl for that small bit of good social behavior, the research assistant also gave the girl a token. The girl immediately took the token to a row of vertical metal tubes on one wall of the cottage. The tubes were slotted on one side so the contents could be seen. Above the tubes was a sign that said BANK. Each tube bore the name of one girl. The girl, to whom the research assistant had spoken, Mary, found her name and deposited the token in the slot at the top of the tube. The token fell down the tube and rested on the others Mary had earned. She looked around for anyone watching, and then she counted her tokens by the increments marked on the tube. Another research assistant passed by.

"I see you're counting your tokens, Mary. How many do you have?"

Mary counted again, hesitated, then looked at the numbers on the tube once more and turned back to the research assistant. "Five," she said, hesitantly.

"Excellent, Mary, excellent! Here's another token for your right answer. Now, how many does that make?"

"Six?" Mary said, not certain that six followed five.

"You're right! Six!" The research assistant gave Mary a friendly pat and moved on.

The cottage hummed with such activity. Research assistants and aides moved from girl to girl, instructing and prompting girls who were learning words. The aides modeled the behavior they wanted and then delivered reinforcement when the girls imitated the behavior. It was slow going. Girls were clumsily brushing their own hair and learning to tie shoestrings, bake cakes, clean bathrooms, sweep floors, and make beds.

Their inappropriate behaviors—cursing, fighting, crying, arguing, wetting themselves—were managed with as little interaction as possible. Inappropriate responses or behaviors were ignored where possible. A research assistant who praised the girl and gave her a token immediately rewarded proper responses. Some of the girls imitated the research assistants, even to the point of giving other girls their own earned tokens when their cottage mates demonstrated some new skill.

Research assistants carried stopwatches and clipboards and constantly observed girls as individuals and in groups and recorded data on the occurrence and rate of specific behaviors that the researchers were attempting to change. Those data provided substance to scientific articles and convention presentations.

The Site Visitor

When grant applications received a site visit, there was often at least one site visitor who was skeptical, critical, or self-righteous.

"So you pay the girls for doing what you want? They save the tokens and then on a certain day they buy candy and privileges for the coming week?"

"Yes, generally speaking, that's how it works," was the common answer.

"Some girls immediately exchange their tokens for food or drinks or games. Immediate gratification is important to them. Others save their tokens until they have enough to buy the privilege of playing records, watching television, going to the canteen, or buying a new comb or toothbrush, or going to town for shopping and dinner. For a certain number of tokens they get to play records, watch television, go to the canteen, and get a new comb or toothbrush. They earn and save for their privileges."

"Isn't what you're doing bribery?"

"Bribery is wrong. Most people agree on that. The girls are not promised payment for doing something wrong, they are promised payment for doing something in a way that we expect. We pay the girls to learn to do what we generally agree that they should learn to do. They don't learn it any less well or forget what they learn any sooner because we pay them."

"You don't expect strangers on the streets to give the girls tokens for behaving like everyone else, assuming they someday try to leave here and live outside."

"The most important thing we're proposing to study is how to get the girls into a natural reinforcement system that will maintain the behavior."

"We're not concerning ourselves with the social or psychological origins of the behavior just now. We're concerned with the observable behavior and what we can do to change it by modifying the environment. We'd find an appropriate behavior to encourage rather than waiting to punish her for an unwanted behavior."

"These girls have common behaviors that can be shaped and molded. It's that area we want to study. After the behavior is under control, we hope that the girls who don't communicate well can be taught basic communication skills."

The early operant psychologists were not particularly concerned about economics, but federal, state, and local officials were preoccupied with costs. In the 1960s the estimated cost of a lifetime of care for one individual was more than $100,000. With inflation, that cost threatened to rise beyond $1 million in a few decades.

Taxpayers might benefit through reduced taxes as thousands of persons learned to live outside and support themselves. The researchers never proposed that every institutionalized person would learn to become completely "normal," or that money to support persons with severe disabilities would cease to be needed. But they did believe that federal and state governments stood to gain by getting more taxpayers in the work force. Advocates were soon pointing out the likely economic benefits.

Contradictions and Confusions

Some superintendents were thrilled with the new possibilities; others were suspicious. Some secretly worried that their waiting lists might grow short and the money from the state legislatures might dry up if institutionalized children learned too much and left the institutions in large numbers. They were not necessarily evil men. Children with retardation[3] obviously needed to be sheltered.

Some superintendents were threatened because institutions might be forced to become training centers. They might be required to do what they pretend to do—train residents to live outside and hold down jobs. That threatened the way traditional institutions were operated. Most superintendents were lords of all they surveyed. Their fiefdoms held power. The needs of the children were not the primary consideration. That does not mean there were not compassionate and wise superintendents. And there also were many who understood how inadequate their institutions were. They would join and become strong allies to science as the struggle progressed.

One of the first superintendents in Kansas to allow behavioral research in his institution had been a World War II battlefield surgeon. Howard V. Bair, MD, superintendent of Parsons State Hospital, had operated in forward hospitals on the most severely wounded soldiers. He was a tough man who had seen and adapted to things most persons never see, but his toughness did not preclude a deep concern for children with retardation and a willingness to try something new. He was among the new superintendents who were willing to take risks to make changes. Many of them put their own careers on the line by opening their institutions to research teams.

The operant psychologists understood that the best strategy to overcome resistance was to clothe the idea of changing the character of the institutions in layer after layer of research. Research was commonly assumed to be honorable (until proven otherwise) when conducted under the aegis of a state university. The right circumstances needed to be nurtured to bring the necessary parts together. Meanwhile, life went on in the institutions.

Not all superintendents were forward looking. One reactionary superintendent was once explaining to the state director of institutions how his workers could take fresh tomatoes from the field, peel and cook and can the tomatoes on the grounds, and 3 days later have the residents eating canned tomatoes in the dining halls. He didn't need anyone to study the way he ran his institution.

"Why don't you just serve fresh tomatoes," the state director asked, "while they're in season? Aren't they more nutritious?"

"Sir, if we served 'em fresh we wouldn't need all these people working here to keep the canning operation running at full speed in tomato season."

The road ahead would be rough. Operant psychologists would be accused of harsh and nefarious tactics, from aversive control to food deprivation. Some accusations were true. Operant psychologists would generate controversies through experiments that created both humanitarian and scientific disagreements that could never be conclusively proved or disproved one way or the other.

The popular press and television critics sometimes vilified early operant psychologists. Academics who were seeking to make themselves known often opposed the inelegance of operant conditioning. Some observers, looking back on the changes that have resulted from these experiments, have been tempted to deify the operant psychologists. The truth may be that these early operant psychologists deserve both respect and criticism. Operant conditioners were commonly very arrogant during the 1950s and 1960s. Many were convinced that the human mind was of little consequence so far as behavior was concerned. To some, morality was a bothersome social construct and any attempt to intervene in human behavior from an intellectual or moral point of view was a display of ignorance.

Too many operant conditioners were not well trained. The practitioners were sometimes abysmally ignorant of 100 years of psychology, mathematics, and statistics. They tried to make up for that with zeal. They were nearly messianic in their belief that operant conditioning was a brave new technology that could solve any behavioral problem, including mental retardation. There were far too many practitioners who believed that the end justified the means. It can be debated whether or not a practitioner is justified in stopping life-threatening head banging with electric shock when the behavior occurs. That may or may not be justifiable. In other cases it is quite clear that errors were made. It is difficult to justify experimenting with human beings of any intelligence level merely to see if humans behave the same way as rats, pigeons, or monkeys subjected to pain, shock, or severe deprivation.

Normalization and the Deinstitutionalization Movement

In the late 1960s and early 1970s a new trend emerged. Fueled by the concept of normalization, a massive deinstitutionalization movement began. The basic concept of normalization is that people with retardation should live in normal environments that do not stigmatize them. Clearly, institutions are not normal environments. Hence, in spite of all of the training that might occur in an institution, the conditions are far from optimal for teaching a person how to live in noninstitutional environments. Moreover, few would deny that institutions were stigmatizing.

The normalization model and some significant court cases led to strong calls, not for improving or revolutionizing treatments in institutions, but for the closing of institutions and the development of community programs. Many institutions were closed. Many of the advocates of deinstitutionalization considered any attempt to improve the treatment of people within institutions as unwise if not immoral. In such a climate, most competent professionals refused to work in institutions under conditions of reduced funding and stigmatization and the care and treatment of people who remained in institutions deteriorated.

Sometimes persons who were discharged from institutions went to group homes or apartments that offered far more freedom and opportunities than the institutions that they had left. However, unfortunately many persons who were discharged went to modified nursing homes that were worse than the institutions. Even in community group homes, the house parents or staff were often poorly trained and the conditions were no better. For the advocates of normalization, even good group homes were stigmatizing and hence inadequate. Nothing short of living in a family or independent apartment context was satisfactory.

In the case of education, the movement quickly evolved to the full integration model. Separate classrooms for children with any level of retardation could not be justified. Advocates of full integration maintained that every child should be educated with his or her age peers.

This movement toward normalization, deinstitutionalization, and full integration was in many cases quite productive. When adults were placed in group homes or apartments with a well-trained behavioral support staff, they often lived happy and active lives. When children with moderate or mild retardation were placed in classes with well-trained highly motivated teachers and support staff, all children could benefit. In these cases, the teachers and support staff members often relied on the principles and procedures that had been developed in the early institutional operant research programs. In other cases, the results of the extreme positions recommended by advocates were not so positive. An adolescent with profound retardation with self-injurious behavior may gain little from being in a high school algebra class with his age peers. Likewise the algebraic skills of his normally developing peers are unlikely to be enhanced by his presence. Nevertheless, the deinstitutionalization movement and full inclusion have had a positive effect on the treatment of people with disabilities. Moreover, attempts to develop quality environments in which people with severe mental disabilities can lead satisfying lives have led to a better understanding of how to develop positive personal relationships between support personnel and clients with severe mental retardation. Recent research shows the power of such relations on modifying problem behavior.

Children and Parents

In theory, the new teaching techniques and the normalization movement should have been of benefit to both the children with retardation and their parents. Parents had started the movement to change institutions, but many parents were not eager to see their children leave institutions.

Not every parent was emotionally equipped to live with a child with a disability at home, or to have their child with a disability in the family and around people they knew. They did not necessarily want them home or even outside the institution. Other parents would become martyrs or use their children to further their personal aspirations. A few parents would find careers through a family member with retardation.

Many parents had tried everything possible to "fix" their children. Others viewed their offspring with retardation as a cross to bear. Others knew that the public would not be 100% behind the idea of changing children with retardation and they were timid about demanding things for what were perceived as flawed children for which they were responsible. A few parents believed that Divine Providence created children with retardation for reasons beyond human comprehension and that tinkering was bound to bring Divine consequences. Most parents merely wanted the best for their children—a life of relative freedom and a chance for them to work and manage their own lives.

Summary

In summary, the period from the mid-1950s to the mid-1970s was a period of extremely rapid change in the treatment of people with retardation. In the mid-1950s, the treatment of people with retardation was largely appalling institutional care. In the 1960s, the application of operant principles within institutions led to greatly improved conditions. Moreover, the application of these principles led to optimism concerning the ability of people with retardation to learn. Finally, the late 1960s and early 1970s were characterized by deinstitutionalization and normalization concepts. The 1970s also saw an intense movement to integrate people with retardation into normal daily life. While these changes have generally improved the living conditions for people with retardation, not every result has been positive. There remains much to be done.

Notes

1. Although the terms "Skinnerians" and "operant psychologists" were common in the1960s, most modern-day adherents to Skinner's psychology would prefer to be called behavior analysts.
2. The term "subject" is used in the current text because that was the term most used in the 1960s. Currently most published articles use the term "participant."
3. We use the "child with retardation" or "person with a disability" terminology rather than the more direct "retarded child" or "disabled person" terminology. Although that may be mere political correctness, we feel person-first language focuses on the fact that we are dealing with people similar to ourselves first and to the condition second. When we state the disability first, the focus is on difference rather than our common humanity.

4

The Communications Program Project and the Parsons Research Center

JOSEPH E. SPRADLIN

In the early 1950s, Kansas citizens, legislators, and administrators realized that there was something terribly wrong with state mental institutions. A committee was formed to evaluate these institutions and to make suggestions on how to reform them. Karl Menninger was an influential member of that committee. The conditions that the committee found were appalling. A change was needed and the legislature was willing to liberally fund such changes. As a result, the Kansas mental health programs went from being rated the worst in the United States to being rated the best. Kansas went from spending the least money per patient to spending the most per patient of any state in the United States.

Massive changes were brought about in all state hospitals. The worst of the abuses were eliminated and professional positions were upgraded to include PhD psychologists, psychiatrists, and a variety of adjunctive therapists. Menninger Foundation personnel were heavily involved in these changes. While there was a general movement to improve the treatment provided in all institutions, there was also a specific plan to establish a model treatment and educational program for children with retardation and mental illness. That plan called for converting Parsons State Hospital for Epileptics to Parsons State Training School. Initially the institution was designed for ambulatory children from ages 6 to 21 years with mild mental deficiency or mental illness. The plan was essentially to create a high-quality boarding school for children with disabilities. The residential school was to have a complete professional staff, including qualified teachers, psychologists, psychiatrists, and a variety of adjunctive therapists.

A young and dynamic physician with psychiatric training, Howard V. Bair, was hired as superintendent. He initiated a plan for transferring children from Winfield State Training School and other mental hospitals and correctional institutions to Parsons. The new institution was renamed the Parsons State Hospital and Training Center (PSHTC). An ambitious building program began. Many old multistoried red brick buildings were replaced with new modern one-level cottages with individual bedrooms and pleasant day areas. New buildings were constructed to house education programs and adjunctive therapy programs, including speech and hearing. A first-rate clinical psychologist, Henry Leland, was hired to build the psychology program. A quality speech pathologist, Lloyd Lockwood, was hired to coordinate adjunctive therapies. Numerous other therapists were hired. Additionally, resident psychiatrists from the Menninger Foundation were recruited. Menninger Foundation consultants in psychiatry, neurology, and neuropsychology periodically came to Parsons to provide consulting services. All elements were in place for a model program to educate and treat children and adolescents with mild mental retardation and mental disorders.

Most of the therapies depended primarily on understanding and communicating by speech. Treatments in psychiatry, psychology, and speech therapy depended heavily on spoken communication with the patient. Even play therapy, occupational therapy, and recreation necessitated an understanding of speech. The caregivers had been trained in a general culture that sought to manage behavior by verbal means.

Children transferred to Parsons included those with mild, moderate, severe, and profound retardation. Children with severe and profound retardation usually did not speak or understand speech. Speech often fails to influence behavior of children with moderate or mild retardation in the same way that speech influences children without mental disabilities. So, although there was a noble attempt to establish a model treatment program, the new personnel whose treatment approaches depended so heavily on verbal control of behavior were ill-equipped to manage, educate, and treat many of the children who made up the population at Parsons.

Because treatment and management were so heavily dependent on speech and the understanding of speech, the quality of the programs varied greatly. Wards for children with mild retardation (new, single-level cottages) were often clean and well managed. The clothes were the latest fashions. The environments of the education and therapy programs for such children often appeared quiet, with children engaged in activities. Wards for children with moderate mental disabilities appeared less orderly and clean, but still passed as humane places for children in therapy. However, the wards for children with severe and profound mental disabilities (the old multistoried buildings) presented a far different picture. Day rooms were often dirty with urine-soaked floors and an occasional pile or smear of feces. The children might be wet or soiled or with runny noses. The aide might be just outside the day room engaged in folding clothes or bent over a table listening to the radio.

One might assume that these aides were lazy or uncaring. However, from a behavior analytic point of view, the major problems arose from the consequences of their behavior, not from their internal motivation. They, like most members of society, depended heavily on spoken directives to influence the behavior of other persons. In the case of children, when spoken directives did not work, the aides might use punishing consequences. Neither technique is effective in teaching or managing people who do not understand speech. The aides' efforts had no functional effect on the children and hence their attempts to influence the behavior of the children were ineffective. Moreover, clean rooms would simply get dirty very quickly, so why try? The children from these wards rarely were seen in therapies.

While verbal directions are ineffective in developing behavior among such children, making positive consequences contingent on desired behavior is effective. Hence, when operant psychologists introduced experiments and training based on reinforcement principles, the results seemed almost miraculous.

In short, the climate was optimal for a success. The state was ready for change and had money to support change. Bair, who wanted a progressive treatment hospital for children, had a problem for which even Menninger could offer little help. Schiefelbusch had a way of getting money for funding a grant to improve Bair's program, and researchers influenced by animal learning experiments had an effective tool for teaching children who neither spoke nor understood speech.

The Change Begins

It is difficult to determine exactly where the history of a given endeavor begins. This is certainly true of the Program of Research in Communication Disorders of Mentally Retarded Children (hereafter referred to as the Communications Program Project) and the Parsons Research Center, but a reasonable place to begin is with Mental Health Project Grant OM-111: A Language Program for Mentally Retarded Children. R. L. Schiefelbusch, director of the Bureau of Child Research, was the principal investigator and project director, and Howard V. Bair, superintendent of PSHTC, was co-principal investigator. That grant was approved in November of 1957 and funded on January 1, 1958. The first year's funding was $56,695, and the total approved funds for its 3 years were $165,025. The money was to hire a field director, speech pathologist, clinical psychologist, and speech therapist, as well as research assistants, and to pay for equipment, supplies, and travel. For these funds the director and staff were "to develop an optimal language and communication program for a selected group of mentally retarded and mentally defective children in an institutional setting." The subgoals included:

1. The formulation of a set of experimental constructs relative to language and communication as features of social adequacy;
2. Diagnostic assessments, which include descriptions of the negative and maladaptive habits and patterns affecting language and communication;
3. The development of a battery of language and communication tests for purposes of assessing verbal characteristics of institutional children and for determining gains made in the training program;
4. The development of clinical techniques for improving the verbal behavior of mentally retarded children with particular attention to variations needed for training children who fall into the various diagnostic classifications; and
5. The development of a team program for improving the environmental milieu of the institutional child for purposes of stimulating verbal development.

The last named subgoal would be an attempt to develop creative and motivational experiences in the daily activities of children living at PSHTC.

The proposed research was basically a two-group treatment design. Available test file data, as well as new speech and language evaluations and neurological data, were to be used in selecting experimental and control groups. The experimental group was to be 65 children between the ages of 6 and 16 years and mental ages between 3 and 12. The control group was to meet the same criteria. The language and communication program of the experimental group was to be developed with the help of hospital staff and consultants from the Menninger Foundation and the University of Kansas. The neurological exams were to be conducted by neurologists from the Menninger Foundation. In addition to Schiefelbusch and Bair, there were nine other members of the advisory board from PSHTC, the University of Kansas, and the Menninger Foundation. There were also eight consultants from the Menninger Foundation and various departments of the University of Kansas.

Original Staff Members

When the grant was funded, four staff members were hired in a remarkably short time. By August 1, 1958 all of the staff members were on board. Seymour Rosenberg, a PhD social psychologist trained at Indiana University, was selected as field director. Rosenberg was a student of William Estes at Indiana and had done research on aircrews for the U.S. Air Force. Ross Copeland, a master's degree speech pathologist from Purdue University who had had experience as an assistant superintendent at the Muscatatuck State School (an institution for persons with mental retardation in Indiana), was hired to fill the speech pathologist position. Dorolyn Ezell, with an MS in special education from the University of Kansas who had had public school teaching experience, was hired to fill the speech therapist position. Joe Spradlin, a PhD candidate in clinical psychology from George Peabody College for Teachers who had worked as a clinical psychologist at Winfield State Hospital and Training Center, was hired on a 75% basis as the clinical psychologist. The remaining 25% of his time was to be devoted to completing his dissertation.

Rosenberg was a talented and experienced experimental social psychologist who insisted that he be located at Lawrence and that he travel to PSHTC 2 or 3 days per week. Although some of the staff members at Parsons objected to this arrangement, Rosenberg was hired. He was stationed at Lawrence and commuted to Parsons. Copeland, Ezell, and Spradlin lived and worked at Parsons. Prior to August 1, little actual research occurred; however, two neurologists from the Menninger Foundation did provide neurological examinations for over 200 children at PSHTC. Copeland did a masterful job of designing research and office space for the research team in the old hospital building. Bair assigned the hospital maintenance crew to make the changes that Copeland had designed. By August 1, rooms were ready for conducting research. After that date, there was a flurry of research activity at Parsons.

Rosenberg provided education and guidance concerning research and research design to the remaining members of the project and to hospital staff members. Although the research that he directed and supported was in line with the subgoals specified in the initial grant request, he largely disregarded the procedures and tactics suggested in the initial request.

Early in the project, two practices that proved very valuable in establishing a common research approach and for facilitating productivity were initiated. First, Rosenberg and Schiefelbusch initiated a series of informal research meetings. A combination of Schiefelbusch's wry humorous comments and Rosenberg's satiric wit made these meetings lively and filled with laughter. Although the formal topics of the meeting were research methodology and conceptualization, the topics ranged far and wide— often involving sex and flying. However, the topic did not matter, because Rosenberg was a masterful teacher who could weave research methodological and conceptual issues into any topic. The second practice was the initiation of a working paper series. Staff members were encouraged to prepare working papers on research or conceptual ideas at every stage from the first poorly formed notion to the final draft of convention presentations or manuscripts to be submitted for publication. The new research environment fostered a spirit of humor, camaraderie, adventure, and purpose.

Rosenberg and I hit it off immediately, beginning on my second visit to Parsons, before I had moved from Nashville to Parsons. At times, we roomed together in a building on the hospital grounds at Parsons. It was there that we discovered that we each had a copy of Skinner's *Verbal*

Behavior (Skinner, 1957). Moreover, we had similar views concerning the quality of the existing research on mental retardation and the directions in which research should move. We immediately became a strong team. Rosenberg was an expert in all aspects of research from conceptualization, to equipment construction, to design and statistical analysis. I was sufficiently well trained to see that Rosenberg's plans and desires were followed at Parsons. With Rosenberg's support, I had what was probably the most productive year of my career. I constructed the apparatus for conducting my dissertation, a study to evaluate the effects of various schedules of reinforcement on resistance to extinction. That study was completed and I defended my dissertation in June of 1959 (Spradlin, 1962). I also developed procedures for evaluating verbal behavior (The Parsons Language Sample) based on Skinner's book, *Verbal Behavior* (Spradlin, 1963).

Rosenberg and I also conducted a series of two-person interaction studies that first year (Rosenberg, Spradlin, & Mabel, 1961; Spradlin & Rosenberg, 1964). We developed a primitive operant laboratory for the study of the behavior of children with severe retardation under reinforcement conditions. I also functioned as Rosenberg's on-site supervisor for the research activities of Ezell and Copeland (Copeland, 1962). The research conducted between August 1958 and the spring of 1959 was presented at the meeting of the American Association on Mental Deficiency in May 1959.

By May of 1959, Rosenberg and Schiefelbusch had purchased an airplane and Rosenberg had received his private pilot's license. Bair was an experienced pilot who owned his own plane, so the research group flew to Milwaukee by private plane. Such adventures added zest to the activities of the research group.

During that first year, as well as during subsequent years, there were periods of tension between the hospital staff and the research staff. However, several informal factors helped keep tensions from becoming acrimonious. First, key members of the research and hospital staffs often socialized with each other after work. In fact, they formed a flying club and purchased a small airplane. Informal, after-work social events were often arranged by Al Spector, the hospital property control officer. Second, during the early years, research and hospital staff ate lunch together at a small staff dining room.

Two persons played major roles in keeping the tension between a somewhat arrogant research staff and members of the hospital staff from becoming disruptive. When tensions became too great, Schiefelbusch would meet with individuals and groups to resolve issues and to calm the emotions of the participants. The second person who played a major role in maintaining smooth relations between members of the hospital staff and the research staff was Al Spector. Anyone who casually noted Spector's activities during the working day would assume that he was lazy and inefficient. He went from office to office, relating the latest innocuous gossip, telling and listening to risqué jokes, and sitting with his feet on somebody else's desk. However, during those conversations, he might casually note that a member of another department was bothered because of some activity of the person with whom he was gossiping, or that someone in another department would be very appreciative if a piece of equipment was made available, or that Bair was concerned about some activity that was or was not taking place. In this role, Spector served as Bair's eyes and ears. Information was passed on so casually that the results were almost always constructive.

Visiting Consultants

Another aspect of that first year's activities that added spice was a series of visiting consultants. Two of the consultants, Ignacy Goldberg and Rudy Capobianco, were well known in special education. Ignacy was an immigrant from a Balkan country and was a strong advocate for education of all children, including those with severe retardation. In 1959 and 1960, this was not the dominant position. Most persons believed that education was only for those who might make a positive contribution to society.

Ignacy's presentations were interesting because of his accent and use of the English language. While making an important point, he sometimes substituted "There is no use laughing ourselves" for "There is no use kidding ourselves." Some members of the research team wondered if part of his misuse of English was intentional. It certainly was charming.

Capobianco had done research demonstrating the differences in the reading and arithmetic skills of children classified as retarded as a result of exogenous causes versus children with retardation resulting from endogenous causes (Capobianco & Funk, 1958).

A third consultant, Ogden Lindsley, turned out to be a delightfully stimulating character. Ogden ("Og") had conducted ground-breaking operant conditioning research with persons who were psychotic (Lindsley, 1956). Og was an evangelist for single-subject research, free operant methodology. He believed that rate of response was the only worth-while measure of behavior. He had a neatly trimmed beard and he resembled pictures of Christ or Don Quixote. He had come west from Boston to the American Psychological Association meeting in St. Louis and we had lured him to Parsons by paying his additional travel expenses to and from Parsons.

Schiefelbusch met Lindsley at the airport in Kansas City to take him to Parsons. Schiefelbusch apologized to Lindsley because he had a class to teach and they would be delayed in going to Parsons. Lindsley went with Schiefelbusch to the class and Schiefelbusch recalls that before the class period was half over Lindsley had completely taken over the class and Schiefelbusch had become a mere observer as Lindsley held forth before the students.

Lindsley stayed 2 days in Parsons. He talked to the hospital staff, the research staff, and anyone else who would listen to him. He succeeded in annoying the psychiatrist by observing that it was the aides in the cottages who prescribed medicine and that he, the psychiatrist, merely signed the forms. He correctly observed that the group design procedures that Rosenberg and I were using were not the best way to conduct research on behavior. Finally, he gave every group essentially the same message: single-subject research was the only way to conduct research, rate was the appropriate measure, and psychosis was the inability to change behavior as a function of changes in stimuli.

When I pointed to him that he had had the same message regardless of the group, hence showing an inability to change behavior with changes in stimuli, Lindsley leaned back, roared in laughter, and said, "You got it, you got it." Before taking Lindsley to his plane, members of the research team had dinner with him at Mickey Mantle's restaurant in Joplin, Missouri. At this dinner, Schiefelbusch and Og Lindsley began telling stories about their prison camp experiences in World War II. Og was in the crew of a B-24 when he was shot down; Dick was a navigator on a B-24 when he was shot down. The evening was most congenial with more than enough alcohol flowing. Toward the end of the evening Dick attempted to cash a check and was turned down. Og pulled himself to his full 6 feet 2 inches and said "Give me that check, I'll get it cashed." When Dick handed him the check, Og confidently went to the clerk, asked for her name, whipped out a full yard of credit cards, and told her who he was. He quickly intimidated the clerk into cashing the check.

Schiefelbusch, Copeland, and I had many years of interacting with Og. The behavior exhibited on that first visit was not atypical. Og was always stimulating, usually superbly insightful, once in a while illogical, and sometimes a bit crazy.

The New Research Team

In August I went back to Peabody College to participate in graduation exercises. When I returned, a friend told me that Seymour Rosenberg had accepted a position at Bell Telephone Laboratory and that I was now the field director of the Parsons Research Project. I was well equipped, both temperamentally and by training, as a researcher, but ill-equipped as an administrator. I was primarily interested in my own and other behavioral research, especially if it had a learning thrust. However, I had no experience in managing budgets, writing grants, or dealing with the interpersonal conflicts that inevitably occur among professionals in a new undertaking. However, I accepted the position of acting field director.

Soon after Rosenberg announced that he was leaving, Jerry Siegel was recruited to fill a research associate position on the project. Jerry was a well-trained research speech pathologist from the University of Iowa. He immediately began to plan studies to evaluate the articulation of persons in the institution and to evaluate the comparability of articulation scores obtained by different examiners (Siegel, 1962). He was also fascinated by the two-person social studies that had been initiated by Rosenberg.

Rosenberg and I had conducted a study in which a college student interviewed two participants from the institution. One participant had a high score on the Parsons Language Sample and one participant had a low score on the Parsons Language Sample. Rosenberg and I had hypothesized that the college student would ask more questions that could be answered by yes or no when assembled with low-scoring participants than when assembled with high-scoring participants. This hypothesis was based on the notion that participants with low scores would be more apt to answer a yes/no question than an open-ended question. Hence the student's yes/no question would result in more reinforcement for such questions than for open-ended questions and the student's yes/no questions would increase in rate. That did not happen and we filed the study away. When Siegel became interested in the effects of participant level on interviewer behavior, he replicated the earlier study but used such traditional speech measures as length of response, repetitions, type/token ratios, and mean length of responses. Using these measures, he demonstrated differences in the effects on the adult's verbal behavior. The adult's verbal behavior also was affected by the type of task he or she was told to perform (i.e., interviewing or instructing) (Siegel, 1963).

After Rosenberg left, the research team at Parsons consisted of Dorolyn Ezell, a former general educator trained as a special educator; Jerry Siegel, a rather rigid, Iowa-trained speech pathologist who originally hailed from Brooklyn; Ross Copeland, a perceptive and flamboyant Purdue-trained speech scientist; and Joe Spradlin, a displaced farm boy who had a passion for understanding human behavior.

Approximately once a week, Dick Schiefelbusch would come from Lawrence for a meeting. The meetings were informal and held in Ross Copeland's office, which had a T-shaped arrangement with a table that readily accommodated the five researchers. Ross sat at the head of the table, as if he were chairman of the board. When the topic of the meeting was general and somewhat forward looking, Dick was enthusiastic and would often make encouraging, big picture comments. At these times I would become impatient and show little interest. However, if the topic turned to specific research designs or research data, Dick would often yawn and perhaps leave to consult with Howard Bair. Siegel and I would immediately lean forward and begin discussing the data and asking questions concerning experimental control, statistical outcome, and the next step in the study. Copeland would fully understand the experiment, but he would be more interested in the discussion of equipment, which could be developed and patented. Dorolyn Ezell was not trained as a researcher. She often seemed lost in the discussions. However, toward the end of the day the group often retired to Ezell's apartment for drinks and relaxation. Dorolyn was comfortable there. She filled the glasses with cold Gluckstite ale and kept the glasses full until her guests finally left.

While Siegel and I were extremely careful and conservative researchers, Copeland was flamboyant and entrepreneurial. He would discuss how we might have the project lease an airplane, which the members of the project would own after the lease period had ended. Although having the project purchase an airplane for the members appealed to me, I was too fearful of the consequences to encourage such plans. For Siegel, such machinations were simply unethical. So there was always a bit of antagonism between Siegel and Copeland.

Dick Schiefelbusch's broad statements concerning the big picture and administrative developments at these research meetings led Siegel and me to a very mistaken perspective that Dick was vague and unorganized. In fact when we were preparing a new grant request and Dick proposed to come to Parsons and help us, we both expressed concern about Dick's approach and we doubted that he would really aid in preparation of the grant. However, when Dick arrived and began to review what we had done and make suggestions, we both realized very quickly that Dick was not the one who was inept.

Prior to the summer of 1960, Jerry Siegel noted that a good friend of his who was a very competent child psychologist, Frances Horowitz, would not be teaching at her small college during the summer. So during the summer, Frances was employed to come to Parsons and work with the group. Frances was trained in learning theory and research design and she resonated quite well with the staff. She immediately implemented a study of the effects of partial and continuous reinforcement and different types of events as reinforcers on vocal responses of children with retardation (Horowitz, 1963). Each child was instructed to find out which of three words (cat, dog, or bird) resulted in a positive consequence. The consequences were presented on 50% and 100% schedules. The consequences were trinkets, experimenter smiles, experimenter verbal feedback, verbal feedback and trinkets, and experimenter smiles and trinkets. The basic results were that only the children in the 100% reinforcement conditions learned the verbal response. During her summer at Parsons, there were vigorous discussions of experimental research.

The year 1961 marked major changes in the research project. Dorothy Ezell and Jerry Siegel left the project. John Hollis and Fred Girardeau were hired as replacements at Parsons. Frances Horowitz joined the Bureau of Child Research (BCR) at Lawrence, where she shrewdly began to remake the Department of Home Economics into a Department of Human Development and Family Life.

John Hollis was probably one of the most interesting and competent researchers ever at Parsons. John was the only son of a very rich Canadian family. Before joining the U.S. Air Force he had been a bush pilot. When he came to Parsons he was married, had a child by a former wife, and had none of the family's money. This constituted no problem to John. He left the family finances to his current wife, Jody, and focused exclusively on any research topic that happened to interest him at the time. That topic might be the sexual behavior of termites or the social behavior of children with profound retardation. He had extensive research experience as a research assistant in the Air Force with Mike Woolman and at the primate labs of the University of Wisconsin and at Yerkes with Bill Mason. He had numerous publications and a BS degree from the University of Wichita. While he did not have an advanced degree, he certainly had more extensive research experience and more research skills than any of his PhD colleagues. He also was an idiosyncratic, outspoken, and excitable colleague, who did not hesitate to express his disdain for activities he considered useless.

Hollis was hired to develop an experimental living unit for 18 young girls with severe to profound retardation. The 1962 Progress Report states that a committee had been established consisting of a psychiatrist, social worker, psychologist, director of education, and a nurse, Patricia Devine, from the hospital staff. The field director of the Parsons Research Project represented the Research Department. No one remembers much about that committee. It is possible that the committee met prior to the initiation of the project. If so, the committee had little effect on the decisions made.

An article by Hollis and Gorton (Hollis & Gorton, 1967) describing the cottage suggests that the education director did have some impact on the cottage. Nurse Devine undoubtedly had an impact on the project. She was listed as the director of nursing; however, functionally she was the operations officer of the institution. Assistant superintendent would have been a much more appropriate and less confusing title. She was a very tough and competent administrator with superb organizational skills.

Hollis and the key hospital staff members selected a ward (designated as 1S1) which was divided into a large day room, a sleeping room, and a bathroom. There was a small caregiver desk outside the rooms. The children would often be in the day room alone and caregivers would be at the small desk outside the ward with their heads bent over as they listened to the radio. Hollis redesigned the area so that what had been the large day room remained an open area. He proposed dividing the open area by four 12-foot by 12-foot plywood enclosures which where also divided into four 6-foot by 6-foot enclosures. The plywood enclosures were approximately 4 feet high. The aim was to provide separate areas where children could be worked with individually or observed individually by a researcher or caregiver. He also designed an experimental room with an observation booth (a glass-enclosed caregiver station), a playroom, and a sleeping area as well as an area for visitors. With the exception of the plywood enclosures, all of the modifications worked out well. The caregivers now had an aid station from which they could view the sleeping area, the playroom, and the open area with the enclosure. However, since the plywood structures obstructed the caregiver's view unless the caregiver was either in the enclosure with the child or looking directly into the 6-foot by 6-foot enclosure, such restriction of vision was impractical. Only one of the proposed enclosures was ever built. Although not everything worked out well on 1S1, Hollis' redesign resulted in improvements in the lives of both the children and the caregivers.

During the year that Hollis was redesigning the cottage, he also was designing and conducting a flurry of experiments on the social behavior of young girls with severe retardation (Hollis, 1965a, 1965b), the teaching of perceptual motor skills (Hollis, 1967a, 1967b), and communication (Hollis, 1966). Such rapid research development could never occur today because of the need to meet the requirements of the human rights committee at Parsons State Hospital and the University of Kansas. Hollis' research demonstrated that even children with profound retardation were not impervious to environmental influences.

Soon after Hollis came to Parsons, he enrolled in Pittsburg State University (PSU) to work on his master's degree. His advisor was Henry Leland who was the chief clinical psychologist at Parsons State Hospital and a Professor at PSU. John Hollis and Henry Leland formed a strange professor–student dyad. Both were intelligent, strong men who did not hesitate to express their opinions. Their styles of research and scholarship were not compatible. Leland was a brilliant insightful psychologist who made intuitive judgments based on either reading of cognitive literature or casual observations. Hollis was a hands-on researcher whose judgments were often influenced by his knowledge of nonhuman primate research. Nevertheless, Leland served as Hollis' advisor and Hollis successfully completed his master's degree at PSU. Hollis then began pursuing an EdD in the education department at the University of Kansas with Ogden Lindsley as his major professor. Hollis and Lindsley resonated well.

Lindsley had published a paper in which he clearly distinguished between procedures and functions in the analysis of behavior (Lindsley, 1964). Typical behavior analysis talks about discriminative stimulus (SD), response (R), contingency (C), and reinforcement (SR). Lindsley noted that the SD-R-C-SR terms were all defined together. For example, an event was not a discriminative stimulus unless it controlled a response. A movement was not a response unless it was controlled by an SD and the subsequent contingencies of reinforcement. An arrangement (specification of when a delivered event was dependent on a response) was not a contingency unless that arrangement produced a given effect on the movement. Finally, an event was not a reinforcer if its contingent presentation did not result in an increase in responding. Lindsley proposed four terms that paralleled the standard behavior analytic terms: antecedent event (AE), movement (M), arrangement (A), and subsequent event (SE). These terms were described procedures and made no assumption concerning their actual functions. This distinction is a very useful distinction for experimenters, because an experimenter may set up an experiment in which a given movement (M) in the presence of a specific environmental event (AE) may result in a specific environmental change (AE). However, that arrangement (A) may or may not result in an increase in the rate of movement in the presence of that event, in which case one would not use the standard terms SD, R, C, and SR. This conceptual system guided Hollis' research for many years. Hollis completed his EdD; his dissertation topic was the stereotypic behavior of children with profound retardation under reinforcement conditions. Only Lindsley would have considered Hollis' dissertation as relevant to education at that time.

Fred Girardeau was a PhD who came from the same psychology program in which I had participated at George Peabody College. Girardeau and I had been fellow students and friends at Peabody and we shared many of the same aspirations concerning research. When Girardeau graduated in 1960, I attempted to recruit him to Parsons, but Girardeau opted to spend a year working with Norman Ellis who had recently accepted a professorship at George Peabody College. Today, such blatant "good ole boy" procedures for hiring would never be allowed. Girardeau was a delightfully engaging 27-year-old researcher who had grown up on a farm in Claxton, Georgia. His father was a tobacco and peanut farmer and his mother was a schoolteacher. Girardeau and his brothers learned the give and take of negotiating in the farmer's market in Georgia. Although the family was relatively poor, all of the boys were educated and became professionals. Two of Girardeau's brothers became physicians and a third became a lawyer who orchestrated Jimmy Carter's campaign for governor of Georgia.

When Girardeau came to the Parsons Research Project, he immediately began to set up a laboratory and conduct research. He had conducted a number of discrimination studies at Peabody. His first study at Parsons was designed to determine whether adolescents with moderate mental retardation could learn a conditional discrimination in which gestures served as the conditional stimuli (Girardeau & Spradlin, 1964). Having been trained by Gordon Cantor, a good Hull–Spence-type psychologist, Girardeau also studied the role of verbal pretraining on subsequent learning of a simple discrimination (Dickerson & Girardeau, 1964). Later, he and Spradlin collaborated on a series of operant conditioning studies with persons with retardation (Spradlin, Girardeau, & Horn, 1965, 1966). They also collaborated on a series of studies on sharing and communication among persons with retardation (Spradlin, Girardeau, & Corte, 1969; Spradlin, Girardeau, & Horn, 1967).

Girardeau's most significant contributions to the Parsons setting was his establishment of Mimosa Cottage, a residential program based on positive reinforcement procedures (Girardeau & Spradlin, 1964). The Mimosa Cottage program was based on a similar program for patients with mental illness at Anna State Hospital in southern Illinois. The Anna State program, headed by Nate Azrin, was certainly the most productive operant research program in 1962. Among the activities at Anna was a token reinforcement program for mentally ill patients based on operant principles (Ayllon & Azrin, 1968). When during a visit to Anna State

Hospital, Girardeau saw the results of that project, he immediately decided to implement such a program at PSHTC.

Girardeau began working with Patricia Devine, director of the nursing department, and Dr. Jackie Baumiester, clinical director, to develop a program for about 20 adolescent girls with moderate retardation. Very soon the project was in operation and girls who had previously been doing nothing were now productively engaged. Girardeau was a master at designing programs to solve behavior problems based on positive reinforcement techniques. When a girl from the cottage clung excessively to Girardeau, he did not punish her. He simply gave her tokens if she walked beside him for short periods of time without clinging. Gradually he increased the time required for delivery of a token. And soon, the girl was walking beside Girardeau without clinging. When a girl stole tokens from other girls, he did not punish the girl, but he simply had the caregivers, mark each token that was given to the girl, and the girl was only allowed to spend marked tokens. Stealing other girls' tokens was thus eliminated. Although the program had few resources, it resulted in marked changes in staff and resident behavior.

In 1963, Girardeau went to the University of Kansas Medical Center (KUMC). At KUMC he established a productive behavioral laboratory and became a key member of a team, including Dick Schiefelbusch and Herb Miller (head of the Child Development Unit), that established the community program that became internationally known as the Juniper Gardens Children's Project. When Girardeau left the Mimosa program, it deteriorated for a couple of years until James Lent, a postdoctorate trainee, revived it and acquired a federal grant which resulted in an expansion and better organization of the program.

John deJung came to Parsons in 1960. John was an EdD in educational measurement from Syracuse University. During his late teenage years and early 20s, deJung had been a traveler. He did not finish his BA until he was 27 years old. Although he did not detail his life during those years, he would occasionally make comments that suggested that during those years he was a borderline delinquent. For example, as we traveled, he might comment that he had spent a night in jail in a particular town for vagrancy, or about his travel through the west with a friend in a stolen car. He credited an older sister with steering him back toward school and a more conventional life. However, his activities during his stay at Parsons indicated that he had not quite given up being a rebel or his desire for adventure.

John was somewhat of a mismatch with the staff at Parsons. His research interests were in person perception and his methodology depended on interviews and paper-and-pencil surveys. He was skilled in statistics and computer use. When he came to Parsons, he said that he required very little for his research, just some paper and pencils. However, while John's work did not require expensive equipment, it required large amounts of personnel time. Soon after his arrival, he had all of the clerical staff busily engaged in tabulating data and doing statistical operations.

In 1963 a new institute (National Institute of Child Health and Human Development) was established in the federal government with a major emphasis on funding research on mental retardation and related disabilities. This institute was funding program projects. When Schiefelbusch learned of this program, he immediately began planning a three-campus research program. There was a small cadre of researchers at each setting: Hollis, deJung, Copeland, and Spradlin were located at Parsons; Girardeau, Haring, and Winitz were at KUMC; Schiefelbusch, Horowitz, and Howard Rosenfeld were located in Lawrence. None of the researchers had strong publication records or was particularly distinguished in academics. The general weakness of his research staff did not deter Schiefelbusch. To expand his Lawrence research staff, he recruited Stanley Harms, an associate professor of speech, and James Neeley, an assistant professor of speech, to participate in the grant. Neither Harms nor Neeley became instrumental participants in the Communications Program Project.

Norris Haring soon left the KUMC and went to the University of Washington. His role merits discussion. First, as a graduate of the special education program of Syracuse University, and then the director of the education department at the Children's Rehabilitation Unit of KUMC, he added considerable strength to the grant request. Second, when he moved to the University of Washington, he established a strong education program based on the same behavior analysis principles that guided much of the significant research conducted in the BRC program. Haring established a strong behavior analytic program at Washington.

Harris Winitz, like Jerry Siegel, was an Iowa-trained research speech pathologist and an energetic researcher who studied the language development of young children. He was a prolific publisher and later developed programs for teaching second languages. Because of his learning bias and commitment to strong experimental designs, he resonated well with Girardeau, Horowitz, and Spradlin.

Howard Rosenfeld was a Michigan-trained social psychologist with an impressive academic background. He earned his Phi Beta Kappa key as an undergraduate at Stanford and was a Woodrow Wilson fellow. During his tenure with the Communications Program Project, he conducted research on social psychology but had little interest in the problems of retardation. He left the program project in a few years, but remained as a professor in the psychology department of the University of Kansas.

After the first Communications Program Project grant application was submitted, the dreaded site visit took place at Parsons. Two of the six members of the site visit were Charles Ferster, a devout Skinnerian, and T. Ernest Newland, a traditional cognitive educational psychologist. When the site team met at Parsons, they visited the laboratories. After visiting the laboratories, they took the members of the research team (individually) into a conference room and questioned them in a fashion that resembled an oral examination for a master's or PhD degree. Needless to say, the diversity of opinions of Ferster and Newland created problems for the participants. Schiefelbusch was grilled first, then each member of the research team was interviewed. Although Winitz, Girardeau, Horowitz, Hollis, deJung, and Spradlin participated, Harms, Haring, and Neeley did not. Perhaps they were interviewed in Lawrence or Kansas City, or perhaps they were not interviewed. In any case they were never an integral part of the Communications Program Project, which was funded in September of 1963. John deJung left Parsons in 1963 to take a position in the University of Oregon's education department.

Gary Evans joined the communications project soon after deJung left for the University of Oregon. Gary was a pragmatic and creative researcher, but he was also a professional gambler. As an undergraduate, he had attended the University of Kansas on a track scholarship, until an injury ended his track career. At that point, he transferred to

Pittsburg State University. While at Pittsburg State, he often traveled to Arkansas on weekends to play poker. These poker games financed his college education. After finishing his undergraduate degree, he enrolled at Oklahoma State University, where he completed a PhD in psychology. Gary was bright, charming, and a master of statistics and design. Although he published a number of articles (Evans, 1965; Evans & Banks, 1966), his greatest contributions were to research design. He had rare skills in developing simple and elegant designs to solve specific problems. Gary left the program project in 1968 to pursue full-time business endeavors.

Don McManis, who had come to Kansas as a postdoctorate trainee, was hired as a research associate in 1964. Don was a rigidly methodical PhD from the University of Oregon, where he had earned his Phi Beta Kappa key. He was a prolific publisher, publishing articles on the effects of praise and reproofs on motor skill performance (McManis, 1965) and serial learning performance (McManis, 1966, 1967). McManis designed and carried out each study in a rigidly systematic fashion. During the period that Don was at Parsons, he probably published more articles than any other researcher.

From the beginning, there was a strong but largely informal research training program at Parsons. Many early research assistants were psychology students from Pittsburg State University who worked part time in the research setting. When these students finished their degrees at Pittsburg, they were encouraged to pursue advanced degrees at other universities. Several went on to very successful research careers. By 1962, Schiefelbusch had obtained a training grant which supported both predoctorate and postdoctorate trainees. Initially, nearly all of those trainees conducted their research at Parsons. Among those trainees were James McLean and David Yoder, who both went on to make major contributions in the field of language and retardation and in 2002 received national awards from the American Speech-Language-Hearing Association. Moreover, McLean became a major contributor to the research, training, and demonstration programs of the BCR. The Research Center at Parsons has been a major setting for research training, and research training continues to be a major function at Parsons.

Three early trainees on the research training grant were Bill Locke, Don McManis, and James Lent. Locke, an Oklahoma State University

PhD student, finished his doctoral dissertation while at Parsons and stayed on as director of research training. Bill Locke had initially come to Parsons to finish his dissertation for his PhD. He conducted research on verbal conditioning with adolescents with mild retardation (Locke, 1966). Bill stayed on as a postdoctorate trainee and, after John deJung left, became director of the training program at Parsons. McManis came from the University of Oregon as a postdoctorate trainee after receiving his PhD from the University of Oregon. James Lent came as a post-doctorate trainee and stayed on to direct the Mimosa Cottage Project.

In addition to the Communications Program Project, the BRC also had a federally funded demonstration grant that funded many of the activities of the speech clinic at Parsons. Two of the early directors of the speech clinic were Ed Leach, a KU-trained speech pathologist, and Lyle Lloyd, an Iowa-trained audiologist. Lloyd was an energetic, productive clinician and researcher. While at Parsons, he developed operant procedures for evaluating hearing (Lloyd 1965, 1966; Lloyd, Spradlin, & Reid, 1968). After Lloyd left to go to Gallaudet College, McLean became director of the Speech and Hearing Clinic and conducted significant research on the use of operant procedures for articulation training (McLean, 1970).

When McLean left to become a professor at Peabody College, Robert Fulton, an audiologist, became director of the Speech and Hearing Clinic. Fulton collaborated with Spradlin in the further development of operant procedures for testing hearing (Fulton, 1974; Fulton & Spradlin, 1971, 1972, 1974a, 1974b, 1974c). Fulton was not only a careful researcher, but also a good communicator who developed two excellent films on the establishment of stimulus control and the evaluation of hearing. Although Lloyd and Fulton were interested in the development of operant procedures for testing hearing, they were also interested in the development of nonoperant techniques. They held conferences and produced two edited books on techniques for evaluating the hearing of people who were difficult to test (Fulton & Lloyd, 1969, 1975).

In addition to the programs of the BCR, E. Thayer Gaston, the father of music therapy, had a music therapy training program at Parsons. Gaston never anticipated a music therapy program based on operant principles, but that is what happened. Gaston hired Vance Cotter as director of the program at Parsons. Vance had completed all the requirements for his PhD in music therapy with the exception of his dissertation. He appeared to be destined to become a respectable music therapist following in the footsteps of E. Thayer Gaston. However, two events resulted in him becoming a behavior analyst. First, during the summer that Cotter arrived, Jack Michael had been hired to come to Parsons and work with the research team. Jack, always the proselyte for behavior analysis, held a series of lectures on behavior analysis. Vance sat and listened intensely to each lecture. Jack also conducted hands-on training concerning soldering, wiring relays and timers and the other skills that any good operant conditioner needed. Additionally, Howard V. Bair had obtained a hospital improvement grant and had hired, as the director, Sam Toombs, a student of Jack Michael while Jack was at Houston University. Cotter and Toombs developed a procedure for evaluating music preferences for nonverbal people (Cotter & Toombs, 1966). From that point on, all of Vance's music therapy trainees were well trained in the principles of behavior analysis.

As noted above, James Lent came to Parsons on a postdoctorate traineeship. He too fell under the influence of Sam Toombs and became a behavior analyst. After his training with Toombs, he became interested in Girardeau's Mimosa Cottage and developed a grant proposal to fund the further development of the project. Soon after the grant was funded, Lent hired Judith LeBlanc. Together they developed a token cottage system, which was an elaboration of that designed by Girardeau in 1964, that became a model for institutional programs and also for many group home programs (Lent & LeBlanc, 1970).

In addition to these university programs, Henry Leland had a grant from the American Association on Mental Deficiency to develop an adaptive behavior scale (Nihira, Foster, & Shelhaas, 1970). That project also drew very talented people. PSHTC was a very exciting environment in which to conduct research and research training during the 1960s.

A Boost from the University of Washington

In 1965, the Communications Program Project received a major infusion of talent when the psychology department of the University of Washington forced Sidney Bijou, Donald M. Baer, Montrose Wolf, and Todd Risley to leave. Frances Horowitz, Dick Schiefelbusch, and George Waggoner combined resources to hire Baer, Wolf, and Risley. Jim Sherman, Betty Hart, R. Vance Hall, Nancy Reynolds, and Barbara Etzel soon followed. The recruits from Washington combined with the behavior analysts already in the BCR to establish the BCR and Horowitiz's new Department of Human Development and Family Life as one of the foremost behavior analytic groups in the world.

The behavior analytic research at Parsons established that persons with severe retardation could be taught simple laboratory tasks using reinforcement principles (Spradlin et al., 1965, 1966; Spradlin & Girardeau, 1966). These principles were also applied to the evaluation of hearing (Lloyd et al., 1968), teaching simple self-help skills, and designing a reinforcement-based cottage for adolescent girls with mild and moderate retardation (Girardeau & Spradlin, 1964; Lent & LeBlanc, 1970). Parsons researchers had confined their research primarily to the laboratory and to audiometric studies. It remained for Baer, Wolf, and Risley to develop observation procedures and techniques to generate reliable research data in natural settings. Moreover, in 1968, they established the *Journal of Applied Behavior Analysis* and provided a seminal editorial which has since guided applied behavioral research (Baer, Wolf, & Risley, 1968).

While the immigration of the Washington group established a very strong behavior analytic research program in Kansas, it also resulted in tension. While Fulton, Girardeau, Hollis, Lent, Lloyd, and I, working at Parsons, made contributions to laboratory analysis and application, we never had the prominence that came to the Washington group under the leadership of Don Baer. The tension between members of the two groups deteriorated into conflict when Todd Risley and Mont Wolf became members of the Juniper Gardens Children's Project headed by Girardeau. Todd and Mont were extremely ambitious young men in a hurry. This ambition sometimes caused conflict.

Girardeau's response to these situations often involved harsh lectures. After the harsh lecture, Girardeau usually took care of the problems by negotiating solutions through the university bureaucracy. Unfortunately, Girardeau commonly got credit for the harsh lectures, but he rarely received credit for the problem solution.

While I was somewhat intimidated by Baer, Wolf, and Risley, my relation with Wolf and Risley was rather remote, so I was never involved in the conflict that Girardeau experienced. Now I digress to give some personal evaluations of Wolf, Risley, Baer, and Sherman. All four were extremely competent behavior analysts. Wolf was socially as smooth as glass. His students and colleagues never reported hearing a negative comment from Wolf. He was also extremely creative in applying behavior analytic principles to practical problems. Excellent examples of that can be seen in his early work with Risley in teaching an autistic child (Wolf & Risley, 1964), in his development of a behavior analytic classroom for underachieving adolescents (Wolf, Giles, & Hall, 1968), and in his development of Achievement Place (Phillips & Wolf, 1973). Wolf also introduced the concept of social validity (Wolf, 1978).

Risley, like Wolf, was extremely creative in applying behavior analytic principles. His accomplishments with his colleague Betty Hart matched those of Wolf. They include demonstrations of the relationships between saying and doing (Risley & Hart, 1968), language training in the natural environment (Hart & Risley, 1975, 1980), and the longitudinal developmental study of young children in natural settings (Hart & Risley, 1995). As he matured, his rough edges were rounded and he became a senior statesman in the field of behavior analysis and developmental disabilities.

Don Baer was initially the spiritual leader of the Washington group. He was one of the most articulate speakers I have had the privilege of hearing. When he spoke, one could simply transcribe his speech and it would be ready for publication. Baer was very comfortable in the give and take of academic debate that took place in national or local meetings. From his first months at the University of Kansas, he was an active participant in the Communications Program Project. He often wrote introductory statements for proposals. At site visits he was usually the last person to present, because we knew that he could answer any question that might be raised, or repair any damage that might have been done by previous presenters.

Baer had a way of disagreeing without being disagreeable. When he disagreed with a speaker, his introduction was frequently, "Let me play devil's advocate." Then, he would question the speaker's point with logic and knowledge. It was a rare privilege to attend a student's orals in which Don Baer and Mont Wolf participated. Both were masters of the Socratic method of teaching. Through a series of well-designed questions, they would lead the candidate to a presentation that was logical and insightful. I often left a student's oral examination with the feeling that I didn't know that the student was that bright and insightful. I later realized that neither the student nor I had been that insightful before the orals, but we both were afterwards.

Although Baer was comfortable in any academic setting, he was extremely uncomfortable and somewhat awkward in informal social settings. In spite of our long collaboration on two program projects, I had always been uneasy in Baer's presence, until after I retired and when I sat in on his research seminar. There I saw a side of Baer that most people never saw. During these meetings he was extremely concerned that he not exploit students, and that the children or adults who served as subjects in experiments were treated with dignity and respect. There I saw how extremely fair Baer was in his interactions with others. He told of going to a garage sale in which the unknowledgeable seller was selling a fine piece of camera equipment for a ridiculously low price. Baer refused to buy the equipment until he had given the seller what he considered a fair price. The opportunity to participate in Baer's research seminar was a rare privilege.

I had similar discomfort in interactions with Jim Sherman. Sherman was extremely logical and direct. If he thought a plan or idea was inadequate, he quietly informed the purveyor of his opinion. As a chairman of the Department of Human Development and Family Life, he was conservative and fair. Hence, while others, like myself, might be somewhat intimidated by Sherman, he had the complete trust of everyone who dealt with him. When Schiefelbusch gave up the principal investigator position on the communications grant, the researchers on that grant unanimously selected Sherman as the new principal investigator.

During the 1960s, there were no equivalent groups applying behavior analytic principles to problems of mental retardation. Baer, Wolf, and Risley immediately began their professional ascent. Baer attacked a critical problem for behavior analysis, namely the problem of producing generative behavior (Baer & Guess, 1971, 1973). Wolf and Risley immediately became involved in the activities at Juniper Gardens. Wolf established a remedial educational program for inner-city children based on operant methods (Wolf et al., 1968). Risley, Betty Hart, and Nancy

Reynolds established a preschool for inner-city children. Research in that preschool resulted in behavior analytic studies of truth telling (Risley & Hart, 1968) and incidental teaching (Hart & Risley, 1975).

Behavior analytic theory had been criticized for not being able to account for novel yet appropriate behavior such as occurs in imitating movements or vocalizations that the person had never imitated before. Chomsky (1959) had emphasized this point in his criticism of Skinner's book, *Verbal Behavior*. Baer, Peterson, and Sherman (1967) had begun to study imitation while still in Washington. However, Baer, Sherman, and their students and colleagues quickly established laboratories at the Kansas Neurological Institute to teach grammatical structures (Baer & Guess, 1971, 1973; Guess, 1969; Guess & Baer, 1973a, 1973b; Guess, Sailor, & Baer, 1974; Schumaker & Sherman, 1970; Sherman, 1971). While the results of this research seem so obvious that one may wonder why it was conducted, the trainability of such behavior was not always so obvious. In fact, in a late 1960s site visit, a noted psycholinguist (Fodor) confidently asserted that such training of grammatical structures could not be accomplished. Baer and colleagues had to remain quiet because Fodor was confidently informing them and the site team of the impossibility of what they had proposed and already accomplished. Fodor won out and that program project proposal was not funded.

Although I was poorly suited to being an administrator, between 1958 and 1968, my title had morphed from research assistant, to acting field director, to field director, to director of the Parsons Research Center, to associate director of the Bureau of Child Research. After Rosenberg left the BCR, I became more and more uncomfortable with my administrative roles and titles. In 1969, I resigned as associate director of the BCR and director of the Parsons Research Center and moved to Lawrence where I served as a research associate and courtesy professor in the Department of Human Development and Family Life.

When I resigned as director of the Parsons Research Center, William Bricker was recruited from George Peabody College as director. Bricker assumed responsibility for developing a new program project proposal. Bricker developed the grant and was to serve as principal investigator. However, in order to maintain continuity with the previous grant I was listed as co-principal investigator.

The proposal that Bricker developed had three major aims:

1. To execute an interrelated network of specific investigations intended to expand professional knowledge and skill in areas related directly and indirectly to language including phonology, morphology, semantics, syntax, and memory;
2. To develop and test a language training program to be synthesized from research outcomes of these programs recently completed. The competence of this training program would serve as a demonstration criterion of the sufficiency of the theory and process research generating it; and
3. To provide a relevant and exciting base for graduate and postdoctoral training through the active execution of this research.

The personnel of the program project at Parsons were to be: Bricker, who would study reinforcement control, imitation, and develop training aids; H. V. Bair; Lawrence Larson, a recent PhD from Peabody, who would study verbal input and output organization; James Lent, who would study direction following and question asking; Robert Fulton, who would study auditory assessment and discrimination; and James McLean, who would study linguistic rules. The personnel at Lawrence included: Spradlin, who would serve as co-principal investigator and study semantics; Schiefelbusch; Ross Copeland; Don Baer and James Sherman, who would study imitation and linguistic rules; Howard Rosenfeld and Kenneth Ruder, who would study nonverbal communication; and George Kellas, who would study associative learning. The researchers at KUMC were to be: Earl Butterfield, who would study memory retrieval; Fred Girardeau, who would study semantics and would supervise graduate training; and Leija McReynolds, who would study phonological development.

In March of 1969, after the grant was submitted, Bricker announced that he was returning to George Peabody and Lawrence Larson accepted a position in North Carolina. I became principal investigator and Don Baer and Earl Butterfield became co-principal investigators. One can see both in the aims and the labeling of the areas of research that the request had incorporated the terminology and research methods of linguistic and cognitive thought. Moreover, Bricker had organized the research of the proposal and presented a diagram of the research that gave the illusion of an integrated whole. In a sense, the researchers selected for the grant and the rationale expanded the conceptual base of the program project to include linguistic and cognitive perspectives. That pattern has been maintained. Although Bricker was only with the BCR for 1 year, he was a major contributor to the Communications Program Project research program.

After Larson left, funds were available to hire a new research associate. In 1970 Sebastian Striefel joined the program at Parsons. Striefel had been a predoctorate research trainee at Parsons during Bill Locke's tenure as research training director at Parsons. During that period he had been accepted into the PhD program of Frances Horowitz's new Department of Human Development and Family Life and had completed two readings courses with Don Baer and me. In August 1968, Striefel moved to Lawrence to complete his work on his PhD, which he announced that he would complete in May of 1969.

The faculty of the department considered such a statement as foolish, since he would need to take three courses, write six comprehensive answers, do a review paper, meet a research skills requirement, write a comprehensive review paper, pass his comprehensive orals, collect the data for a dissertation, write it up, and pass his final orals. Striefel completed his work for his PhD in August of 1969, becoming the first PhD of the new Department of Human Development and Family Life. The completion of so much work in such a short time seems almost impossible. Striefel was highly motivated. He had been in the ROTC during his undergraduate work at South Dakota State University. He had the choice of finishing his PhD and entering the army as a captain in the psychology department at Fort Riley, or he could not finish the PhD and enter the army as second lieutenant in the field artillery and go to Viet Nam. Striefel served a year in the army at Fort Riley and then was hired as a research associate at Parsons. At Parsons, Striefel was extremely productive both as a researcher and as a mentor for graduate students. He published research on imitation (Striefel & Eberl, 1974) and instruction following (Striefel, Wetherby, & Karlan, 1976, 1978). This work served as a basis for later research by Ruder and others.

From 1970 until about 1978, the Communications Program Project had three main themes: behavior analysis, linguistics, and information processing. In 1971, the participants in the program project were Donald Baer, Earl Butterfield, Joseph Spradlin, Robert Fulton, Fred Girardeau, George Kellas, James Lent, Leija McReynolds, Ken Ruder, Howard Rosenfeld, James Sherman, and Sebastian Striefel.

A brief glance at the noncompeting proposal submitted in 1971 suggests that behavior analytic and psycholinguistic concepts were well integrated. Fulton proposed to study discrimination among phonemes. McReynolds was studying distinctive features as a source of generalization in articulation therapy (McReynolds & Bennett, 1972; McReynolds & Elbert, 1981; McReynolds, Engmann, & Dimmitt, 1974). Girardeau was studying stimulus control over relative terms such as over and under. Spradlin proposed to study the development of stimulus classes without physical defining features. Baer and Sherman were studying the development of grammatical structure. Lent was to study instruction following and Rosenfeld was studying the role of paralinguistic behavior in communication. Nearly all of the research based on combined behavior analysis and psycholinguistic concepts involved training and probes for generalization. Studies by Butterfield and Kellas (based on information-processing concepts) were less well integrated.

In retrospect, it is not surprising that behavior analysis and linguistics became integrated. The subject matter for both linguistics and behavior analysis involves behavior. Linguists are interested in the structure of behavior, whereas behavior analysts are interested in the functions of behavior. In many ways these two approaches provided for a productive marriage. Information-processing concepts were never really integrated with the rest of the research. Information-processing researchers were making models of what was going on between the environmental inputs and the response outputs. So their interests were far less in the behavior than in hypothetical cognitive processes. While behavior analysis and linguistics provided guides for immediate training and remediation, the fruits of information processing often were quite remote.

The following discussion provides some of my personal recollections of the participants. I have already discussed Baer, Sherman, Striefel, and Girardeau. Other members of the group who were present in 1971 were equally interesting and talented. Robert Fulton was a bantam rooster, who, when he was recruited to Parsons, told me that his research cost a lot because he used expensive equipment. His statements about costs were exaggerated. He did buy equipment, but he used it productively. Moreover, he did not use large amounts of personnel time, so his research turned out to be a bargain. Although he did not have the sophistication of Ross Copeland, he had many of the same tastes. He considered himself a clotheshorse, and at one time was a joint owner of a small clothing store in Parsons. He owned a sports car and a motorcycle. With his friend, Bob Hoyt, he might take off on his motorcycle and ride halfway across the United States. He enjoyed playful one-upsmanship. I recall an occasion in which I was writing a chapter for a book that Fulton was editing. I had submitted a section to Bob for his reaction. He came to my office and immediately began raving about the quality of what I had written. After a minute or so of his highly complimentary review, he said, " I really like the material, especially the material that you plagiarized directly from me." Bob and I had written many articles together, so sometimes it was a little difficult to determine who had plagiarized from whom. In any case, Bob meant it as a joke and no offense was taken.

Earl Butterfield, like Girardeau and Spradlin, was a George Peabody graduate. After graduating form Peabody, Earl had done post-doctorate study with Ed Zigler at Yale University. Butterfield was extremely bright and effective. His primary research interests were in information-processing differences between people with and without retardation (Butterfield & Belmont, 1971a, 1971b, 1972; Butterfield, Peltzman, & Dickerson, 1971; Butterfield, Wambold, & Belmont, 1973). However, he also wrote articles on more general issues in the field of retardation (Butterfield, 1961; Butterfield & Dickerson, 1976). Unlike Baer, who seemed comfortable and relaxed during formal presentations, Butterfield's hands trembled noticeably during formal presentations. Despite very visible signs of anxiety, Butterfield's presentation style was confident, clear, and a model of logical thinking. Although his research and conceptualizations were a bit discordant with the other aspects of the Communications Program Project, he was always a major asset. He left the University of Kansas in the late 1980s to take a position in the psychology department at the University of Washington.

Leija McReynolds, a Stanford graduate in speech pathology, was a careful, productive researcher whose research was programmatic, conceptually sound, and meticulously conducted. She was an excellent teacher and many of her students became prominent researchers in the field of speech and language. She was quite reserved and presented both the value and limitations of her research. Although such honesty is a major asset in developing a high-quality research program, and in training graduate students, it can be—and was for Leija—a major defect in the salesmanship game of competition for grant funds. Hence, Leija's research was never as highly regarded by granting agencies as it was by scientists in the field of speech and hearing.

George Kellas was a graduate of the University of Alabama. He was a careful nonflamboyant colleague of Butterfield. His work was primarily directed toward isolating differences in normal and retarded children in memory. This work was couched in terms of storage and retrieval mechanisms. In the early 1980s, Kellas discontinued his participation in the Communications Program Project and, until his retirement at KU, was a full-time professor in the psychology department.

Kenneth (Ken) Ruder was a graduate of the University of Florida, with a strong interest in psycholinguistics. Ken was a creative and productive researcher who inspired his graduate students. He conducted research on fluency (Ruder & Jensen, 1972), speech perception, the relation of language reception to production (Ruder, Hermann, & Jensen, 1977), and articulation therapy (Ruder & Bunce, 1981). He could be extremely charming and was usually quite reasonable about major issues. However, he could be resolute when he believed in his cause. The department had granted Ken tenure and advanced him to associate professor. Ken had been trying for an appointment as a full professor. When the professorship was not granted, Ken abruptly resigned, even though he had no immediate alternative plans for employment. Fortunately for Ken, he was hired as chairman of the speech department at Southern Illinois University at roughly twice his University of Kansas salary. At Southern Illinois University, and at later positions, Ken became a strong advocate for programs for individual children with disabilities.

This role fit Ken perfectly, because he enjoyed a good fight under any circumstances, and especially for a moral cause.

Jim Lent was a postdoctorate trainee at Kansas. He had obtained his EdD in special education from Syracuse University. Jim, like Vance Cotter, was influenced by Sam Toombs and had come to believe in the utility of operant procedures in the management and education of people with retardation. Jim was not a researcher, but a practitioner, and was quite goal directed. Moreover, he was not only steadfast in his adherence to a goal, but he was also equally steadfast in his methods for achieving the goal. For the most part, his firmness served him well in his management of Mimosa Cottage.

At the end of the Mimosa grant period, Jim obtained an Office of Education grant for a project to develop mediated operational research (Project MORE). He moved the project to Peabody College (taking Project MORE and staff with him), where he became a full professor and remained until he retired. Project MORE developed training materials and techniques to train children with retardation in daily living and hygiene skills.

In 1974, three new researchers joined the program project. They were John Belmont, Lois Dixon, and Ann Rogers-Warren. In the 1974 program project renewal grant proposal, Butterfield, Belmont, and Kellas proposed to study executive function among normally developing children, persons with mental retardation, and normal adults. They maintained that their studies had shown that most of the cognitive functions of people with retardation were intact, but they failed to organize and use these functions in ways that would solve cognitive problems. According to Butterfield, Belmont, and Kellas, executive function selects, sequences, evaluates, reorders, or abandons mechanisms in view of information-processing goals. They were active in conducting and publishing research (Belmont & Butterfield, 1976). However, this research had little impact on the treatment and education of persons with retardation.

John Belmont received his PhD from the University of Alabama, where he was a student of Norman Ellis. Like Butterfield, he had done postdoctorate study with Ed Zigler at Yale University. John was a researcher who placed great value on making judgments based on accepted scientific findings. There is a story that John broke his arm, and while being treated by the orthopedist, John questioned him regarding whether the procedures that he was using were based on scientific studies reported in refereed medical journals. The story may or may not be true. However, it illustrates how heavily science guided John's actions.

Dixon and Rogers-Warren were graduates of the Department of Human Development and Family Life. Ann was a student of Don Baer's and Lois was a student of mine. Ann was a bright articulate ambitious woman. She could be quite charming or extremely direct in her evaluation of others' behavior. She was a vocal feminist who once told me, after I had told a joke that had both sexist and prudish themes, "I don't like sexist jokes." I later gave her a copy of John Stuart Mill's book, *On the Subjugation of Women*. I told her that when I bought it, I thought it was a "how to" book. She could give as well as she got. Initially, Ann worked with Baer on saying and doing (Rogers-Warren & Baer, 1976). Later she collaborated with Steve Warren to conduct a series of studies to determine how language forms that were trained in one-to-one settings generalized to naturalistic settings (Warren & Rogers-Warren, 1983). They also developed the Mand model procedure for encouraging children to use language in natural settings (Rogers-Warren & Warren, 1980). They accepted positions at Vanderbilt University in 1978. Later, Steve Warren returned to the University of Kansas to become director of the Life Span Institute.

Lois Dixon was a shy, critical researcher with extremely high standards. Her work was geared primarily toward studying stimulus control. Working initially with Fred Girardeau and Barbara Etzel of the Department of Human Development and Family Life, Dixon developed techniques for teaching children with severe retardation to understand such spatial terms such as *above* and *below* (Dixon, 1972). Later she demonstrated that some children with severe retardation did not match pictures of objects with the actual three-dimensional objects, and she developed procedures for teaching such symbolic matching. However, her most frequently cited research was on "exclusion." The procedure involved reinforcing a participant for selecting one of two stimuli in response to a sample stimulus. After the participant had learned this response, the experimenter then introduced a new sample. Most participants select the previously incorrect choice. That is, they respond away from the previously correct stimulus and toward the stimulus indicated by the new sample stimulus (Dixon, 1977; Dixon & Dixon, 1978). Although her work was carefully conducted and was often cited by researchers in the field of behavior analysis, it was not always viewed favorably by grant reviewers in the 1980s. She left the field of behavioral research and took a position as chief psychologist at the Kansas Neurological Institute in Topeka.

Mike Dixon joined the Communications Program Project in 1973 as a graduate research assistant and continued on after he received his PhD as a research associate until 1980. In addition to his work with Lois Dixon on stimulus control, he worked with me on the development of stimulus classes (Dixon & Spradlin, 1976; Spradlin & Dixon, 1976).

During the 1970s, Melissa Bowerman, a PhD graduate of Harvard University who had studied with Roger Brown, participated in the program project. Although she conducted no research herself, she provided a conceptual analysis of the development of semantic and syntactic behavior in young children (Bowerman, 1974, 1976). Her conceptualizations had considerable influence on the research conducted on the project, especially that of Ken Ruder.

When I left Lawrence to return to Parsons as the director of the University Affiliated Programs in July of 1978, I resigned as principal investigator (PI) on the Communications Program Project and Don Baer took over as PI. My reasons for not continuing as PI on the grant were twofold. First, I simply did not want to take on the onerous task of putting together a new program project, and second, I felt that the grant would have a higher probability of success with Don as the PI. Don was an extremely well-respected scientist who wrote and spoke exquisitely.

In 1983, Dick Schiefelbusch exercised his uncanny leadership and assembled a new team, which included projects by Jim and Lee McLean, Don Baer, Jim Sherman and Jan Sheldon, Frances Horowitz and Kenneth Roberts, Joe Spradlin and Richard Saunders, and Betty Hart. After a brief hiatus in funding, the communication grant under Dick's leadership was refunded. Between the time when the grant was approved and when it was funded, Kenneth Roberts was replaced by Marion O'Brien in the Horowitz project. The next few years were extremely productive. Jim and Lee McLean analyzed the communication behavior of children and adults with minimal speech in terms of the topographics of communication behavior and pragmatics. They were able to classify severely limited individuals as those who communicated their needs via physical contact, through gestures, and by speech (McLean, McLean, Brady, & Etter, 1991). They also made a clear distinction between symbolic and nonsymbolic communication.

Saunders and I conducted research on the development of stimulus classes that shared no defining physical properties (Saunders, Saunders, Kirby, & Spradlin, 1988; Saunders, Wachter, & Spradlin, 1988; Spradlin & Saunders, 1984, 1986). Saunders was bright and creative and had endless energy and the skills to handle almost any task assigned to him. Kate Saunders came to Parsons as a postdoctoral trainee after graduating from the University of Florida. She immediately began to conduct research with myself and Dick Saunders (no relation) on stimulus equivalence (Spradlin, Saunders, & Rosenberg, 1992). Later Kate conducted work on the development of stimulus control among people with severe retardation (Saunders & Spradlin, 1989, 1990; Saunders, Williams, & Spradlin, 1995).

Neither Don Baer nor Jim Sherman was enamored with the research on stimulus equivalence. There were many spirited discussions at research meetings concerning whether research on stimulus equivalence was an important area or a mere fad. Don and Jim maintained that that research field would be dead in 5 years. Don Baer and his colleague Ken Silverman conducted research that demonstrated that college students did not show equivalence dependent on the instructions and choices given. However, Baer collaborated with Silverman on a study demonstrating that if one trainer (Trainer A) taught a participant to respond to a set of questions with one set of synonyms, and a second trainer (Trainer B) taught the participant to respond to the same questions with a second set of synonyms, and then a new trainer (Trainer C) taught the participant to respond to some of the questions with the same answers as required by Trainer A, the participant would respond to the remaining questions as had been required by Trainer A (Silverman, Anderson, & Dison, 1986). In other words, Trainer A and Trainer B had become members of the same stimulus class.

Sherman and Jan Sheldon conducted research on social skills training with adults with retardation. This research focused on critical social skills such as proper responses to criticism and how to respond to directions and how to ask for clarification when a direction is not understood. Because Sherman was always interested in utility or social validity, the trained behavior was evaluated not only in the training setting but also in the person's daily life at the cottage. During Sherman's observations, it become apparent that different teachers could give the same instructions and provide the same consequences for compliance or noncompliance and the participants would respond quite differently. With one teacher, the person might willingly comply, while with another teacher, the same request might result in a tantrum. Casual observation suggested that a teacher–client pair in which instructions were readily followed had a good relationship or liked one another. Now, the question became, "How does one measure a good relationship." After trying several measures, Sherman settled on proximity and found that those pairs who were judged to have a good relationship spent more time in close proximity than pairs not so judged. Although Sherman was interested in measurement of good teacher–client relationships, he was most interested in how to establish such a relationship. He first started with the view that perhaps if a teacher simply provided a high density of reinforcers to the client, a good relationship would be established. However, this procedure was soon shown to be ineffective in establishing good relationships. Clients would smile and be happy as long as reinforcers were being delivered, but when the teacher gave an instruction, it was often greeted by tantrum behavior. Sherman then introduced a procedure in which the teacher started by giving almost noncontingent reinforcers; however, the teacher would soon begin to require some simple, appropriate, high-probability response from the client. Gradually the requirements were increased until the teacher could give instructions for even low-probability behaviors and the client would respond appropriately. Then the client and teacher might be seen in close proximity with one another and be said to have a good relationship.

Hart conducted a longitudinal parent–child interaction study comparing young children from culturally deprived families to children from professional families. This ground-breaking work clearly demonstrated that the amount and type of language used by caregivers dramatically influenced the type and amount of language used by children as they develop. Moreover, the research strongly indicates that social class is not the determinant of differences in the development of language, but rather that the determinant is the amount and quality of language used by the parent when interacting with the children (Hart & Risley, 1995, 1999). Hart's research was conducted with Todd Risley. Risley and Hart were an excellent team. Hart, because of her long work with young children, had great observation skills, sensitivity to the variables affecting children's behavior, and the ability to interact with parents. Moreover, she exhibited a phenomenal tenacity. Risley was able to organize and conceptualize the data, which Betty had so meticulously collected.

O'Brien and Horowitz studied the relationship between early stimulus categorization and later language development. The O'Brien and Horowitz research did not result in publications, but they were later joined by John Colombo who continued and refined the infant procedures and developed a very productive research program (Colombo & Horowitz, 1985, 1986; Colombo, Mitchell, & Horowitz, 1988; Colombo & O'Brien, 1986).

I have been a participant and an observer of the research of the Communications Program Project for about 40 years. Many times when the program project was subject to its 5-year reviews, I felt that little had been accomplished in the previous 5 years. However, looking back on the 40 years of research, I have developed a new perspective and a feeling of pride. Research conducted on the program project has led to marked changes in the way in which people with retardation are viewed. When the project was first initiated, few people believed that children with retardation could be taught. Speech pathologists were told not to attempt speech therapy with children with retardation. Now almost no knowledgeable person has that view. Early operant studies clearly demonstrated that children with retardation were teachable. In those early years, there were no procedures for evaluating the vision and hearing of people with severe or profound retardation. Now procedures for such evaluations exist. The program project provided new information concerning categorization by infants. The work of Baer, Risley, and Sherman demonstrated procedures for teaching generalized imitation and grammatical rules. The program project led the design of therapeutic environments for people with retardation as well as children who were classified as delinquent. The project has made contributions in the past and its contributions will extend well into the future.

I have outlined the work of many of the researchers of the program project and I have noted some of the accomplishments, but that is only a small part of the story. The success of the endeavor depended on the efforts of many people who did not publish the research. I have not included the work that was done by Dick Schiefelbusch in mediating between the researchers, members of the National Institute of Child Health and Human Development staff, and the committees. That story is best told by Dick. Nor have I included the stories of the graduate students who made major contributions while serving as research assistants on the program project. Many of these graduate assistants went on to have very illustrious careers after they left the program project. I have focused primarily on the researchers who have their names on research articles published in refereed journals. That list of names is far too short. There were other researchers who made significant contributions. There were always support personnel who were sometimes more important to the overall success of the program project than the researchers. There were electronic and computer technicians, without whose expertise the research could never have been completed, including Riley Worthy, Greg Diaz, and Janet Marquis. Ruth Staten and Pat White turned my illegible incoherent, handwritten scribbling into readable requests, reports, and publications. Wilma Hull kept careful records of all expenditures, hence keeping us from overspending budgets. Bob Hoyt edited and revised almost all Communications Program Project requests and reports from 1970. Ed Zamarripa managed budgets and purchases so that they met university, state, and federal guidelines. Paul Diedrich made sure that all the numbers of a request were accurate and the necessary details were included. That work was often done when the principal investigator presented the request or report at the last possible minute before the deadline. So at this point, I want to say thanks for your contributions and thanks for the memories.

References

Ayllon, T., & Azrin, N. (1968). The token economy, A motivational system for therapy and rehabilitation. New York: Appleton-Century-Croft.

Baer, D. M., & Guess, D. (1971). Receptive training of adjectival inflections in mental retardates. *Journal of Applied Behavior Analysis, 4,* 129–139.

Baer, D. M., & Guess, D. (1973). Teaching productive noun suffixes to severely retarded children. *American Journal of Mental Deficiency, 77,* 498–505.

Baer, D. M., Peterson, R. F., & Sherman, J. A. (1967). The development of imitation by reinforcing behavioral similarity to a model. *Journal of the Experimental Analysis of Behavior, 10,* 405–416.

Baer, D. M., Wolf, M. M., & Risley, T. R. (1968). Some current dimensions of applied behavior analysis. *Journal of Applied Behavior Analysis, 1,* 91–97.

Belmont, J. M., & Butterfield, E. C. (1976). The instructional approach to developmental cognitive research. In R. Karl & J. Hagden (Eds.), *Perspectives in the development of memory and cognition* (pp. 101–112). Hillsdale, NJ: Erbaum.

Bowerman, M. (1976). Semantic factors in the acquisition of rules for word use and sentence construction. In D. Morehead & A. Morehead (Eds.), *Directions in normal and deficient child language* (pp. 99–179). Baltimore, MD: University Park Press.

Bowerman, M. F. (1974). Development of concepts underlying language. In R. L. Schiefelbusch & L. L. Lloyd (Eds.), *Language perspectives: Acquisition, retardation, and intervention* (pp. 191–209). Baltimore, MD: University Park Press.

Butterfield, E. C. (1961). A provocative case of over-achievement by a mongoloid. *American Journal of Mental Deficiency, 66,* 444–448.

Butterfield, E. C., & Belmont, J. M. (1971a). Relations of acquisition and retrieval strategies as short-term memory process. *Journal of Experimental Psychology, 89,* 319–328.

Butterfield, E. C., & Belmont, J. M. (1971b). Effects of recall requirement on acquisition strategy. *Journal of Experimental Psychology, 90,* 347–348.

Butterfield, E. C., & Belmont, J. M. (1972). The role of verbal processes in short-term memory. In R. L. Schiefelbusch (Ed.), *Language research with the mentally retarded* (pp. 231–248). Baltimore, MD: University Park Press.

Butterfield, E. C., & Dickerson, D. J. (1976). Cognitive theory and mental development. *International Review of Research in Mental Retardation, 8,* 106–137.

Butterfield, E. C., Peltzman, D. J., & Dickerson, D. J. (1971). The effects of practice upon rehearsal in short-term memory. *Psychonomic Science, 23,* 275–276.

Butterfield, E. C., Wambold, C., & Belmont, J. M. (1973). On the theory and practice of improving short-term memory. *American Journal of Mental Deficiency, 77,* 654–669.

Capobianco, R., & Funk, R. A. (1958). A comparative study of the intellectual, neurological, and perceptual processes as related to reading achievement of exogenous and endogenous retarded children. Syracuse, NY: Syracuse Research Institute.

Chomsky, N. (1959). A review of B. F. Skinner's *Verbal Behavior. Language, 35,* 26–58.

Colombo, J. O., & Horowitz, F. D. (1985). Aparametric study of the infant control procedure. *Infant Behavior and Development, 8,* 117–121.

Colombo, J. O., & Horowitz, F. D. (1986). Infant attentional responses to frequency modulated sweeps. *Child Development, 57,* 287–291.

Colombo, J. O., Mitchell, D. W., & Horowitz, F. D. (1988). Infant visual behavior in the paired-comparison paradigm: Test-retest and attention performance relations. *Child Development, 59,* 1198–1210.

Colombo, J. O., & O'Brien, M. (1986). Stimulus salience and relational processing. *Infant Behavior and Development, 9,* 377–380.

Copeland, R. (1962). Therapy considerations for the institutionalized mentally retarded. *Training School Bulletin, 59,* 53–58.

Cotter, V., & Toombs, S. (1966). A procedure to determine music preference in mental retardates. *Journal of Music Therapy, 3,* 57–64.

Dickerson, D. J., & Girardeau, F. L. (1964). Verbal pretraining and discrimination learning by retardates. *American Journal of Mental Deficiency, 68,* 476–484.

Dixon, L. (1972). Training an in-front spatial discrimination using a programmed stimulus series. Lawrence: University of Kansas.

Dixon, L. S. (1977). The nature of control by spoken words over visual stimulus selection. *Journal of the Experimental Analysis of Behavior, 29,* 433–442.

Dixon, M. H., & Dixon, L. S. (1978). The nature of standard control in children's matching-to-sample. *Journal of the Experimental Analysis of Behavior, 30,* 205–212.

Dixon, M. H., & Spradlin, J. E. (1976). Establishing stimulus equivalence among retarded adolescents. *Journal of Experimental Child Psychology, 21,* 144–164.

Evans, G. W. (1965). Opportunity to communicate and probability of cooperation among mentally retarded children. *American Journal of Mental Deficiency, 70,* 276–281.

Evans, G. W., & Banks, M. (1966). Paired-associate verbal learning by preschool children: Prompting vs. confirmation. *Psychological Reports, 18,* 838.

Fulton, R. T. (Ed.). (1974). *Auditory stimulus-response control.* Baltimore, MD: University Park Press.

Fulton, R. T., & Lloyd, L. L. (1969). *Audiometry for the retarded: With implications for the difficult to test.* Baltimore, MD: Williams & Wilkins.

Fulton, R. T., & Lloyd, L. L. (1975). *Auditory assessment of the difficult-to-test.* Baltimore, MD: Williams & Wilkins.

Fulton, R. T., & Spradlin, J. E. (1971). Operant audiometry with severely retarded children. *Audiology, 10,* 203–211.

Fulton, R. T., & Spradlin, J. E. (1972). SISI procedures with the severely retarded. *Journal of Speech and Hearing Research, 15,* 217–224.

Fulton, R. T., & Spradlin, J. E. (1974a). Basic stimulus-response control training procedures. In R. T. Fulton (Ed.), *Auditory stimulus-response control* (pp. 13–27). Baltimore, MD: University Park Press.

Fulton, R. T., & Spradlin, J. E. (1974b). Puretone threshold measurement. In R. T. Fulton (Ed.), *Auditory stimulus-response control* (pp. 34–52). Baltimore, MD: University Park Press.

Fulton, R. T., & J. E. Spradlin (1974c). The short increment sensitivity index (SISI). In R. T. Fulton (Ed.), *Auditory stimulus-response control* (pp. 53–64). Baltimore, MD: University Park Press.

Girardeau, F. L., & Spradlin, J. E. (1964). Token rewards in a cottage program. *Mental Retardation, 2,* 345–352.

Guess, D. (1969). A functional analysis of receptive language and productive speech: Acquisition of the plural morphene. *Journal of Applied Behavior Analysis, 2,* 55–64.

Guess, D., & Baer, D. M. (1973a). An analysis of individual differences in generalization between receptive and productive language in retarded children. *Journal of Applied Behavior Analysis, 6,* 311–329.

Guess, D., & Baer, D. M. (1973b). Teaching productive nonsuffixes to severely retarded children. *American Journal of Mental Deficiency, 77,* 498–505.

Guess, D., Sailor, W., & Baer, D. M. (1974). To teach language to retarded children. In R. L. Schiefelbusch & L. L. Lloyd (Eds.), *Language perspectives: Acquisition, retardation, and intervention* (pp. 529–564). Baltimore, MD: University Park Press.

Hart, B., & Risley, T. (1980). In vivo language intervention: Unanticipated general effects. *Journal of Applied Behavior Analysis, 12,* 407–432.

Hart, B., & Risley, T. (1995). *Meaningful differences in the everyday experience of young American children.* Baltimore, MD: Paul H. Brookes Publishing Co.

Hart, B., & Risley, T. R. (1975). Incidental teaching of language in a preschool. *Journal of Applied Behavior Analysis, 8,* 411–420.

Hart, B., & Risley, T. R. (1999). *The social world of children learning to talk.* Baltimore, MD: Paul H. Brookes Publishing Co.

Hollis, J. H. (1965a). Effects of social and nonsocial stimuli on the behavior of profoundly retarded children: Part I. *American Journal of Mental Deficiency, 69,* 755–769.

Hollis, J. H. (1965b). The effects of social and nonsocial stimuli on the behavior of profoundly retarded children: Part II. *American Journal of Mental Deficiency, 69,* 772–789.

Hollis, J. H. (1966). Communication within dyads of severely retarded children. *American Journal of Mental Deficiency, 70,* 729–744.

Hollis, J. H. (1967a). Development of perceptual motor skills in a profoundly retarded child: Part I. Prosthesis. *American Journal of Mental Deficiency, 71,* 941–952.

Hollis, J. H. (1967b). Development of perceptual motor skills in a profoundly retarded child: Part II. Consequence change and transfer. *American Journal of Mental Deficiency, 71,* 953–963.

Hollis, J. H., & Gorton, C. (1967). Training severely and profoundly developmentally retarded children. *Mental Retardation, 5,* 20–24.

Horowitz, F. D. (1963). Partial and continuous reinforcement of vocal responses using candy, vocal, and smiling reinforcers among retardates: Part I. *Journal of Speech and Hearing Disorders, Monograph Supplement No. 10,* 55–69.

Lent, J. R., & LeBlanc, J. (1970). Designing a rehabilitative culture for moderately retarded adolescent girls. In R. E. Ulrich, T. T. Stachnik, & J. Mabry (Eds.), *The control of human behavior* (pp. 121–135). Glenview, IL: Scott Foresman.

Lindsley, O. R. (1956). Operant conditioning methods applied to research in chronic schizophrenics. *Psychiatric Research Reports, 5,* 118–139.

Lindsley, O. R. (1964). Direct measurement and prosthesis of retarded children. *Journal of Education, 147,* 62–81.

Lloyd, L. L. (1965). Use of the slide show audiometry technique with mentally retarded children. *Exceptional Children, 32,* 93–98.

Lloyd, L. L. (1966). Behavioral audiometry viewed as an operant procedure. *Journal of Speech and Hearing Disorders, 31,* 128–136.

Lloyd, L. L., Spradlin, J. E., & Reid, M. J. (1968). An operant audiometric procedure for difficult-to-test patients. *Journal of Speech and Hearing Disorders, 33,* 236–245.

Locke, B. J. (1966). Stimulus exposure rate in verbal conditioning. *Psychological Reports, 19,* 343–346.

McLean, J. E. (1970). Extending stimulus control of phoneme articulation by operant techniques. In F. L. Girardeau & J. E. Spradlin (Eds.), *A functional analysis approach to speech and language* (vol. 14, pp. 24–47). Washington, DC: American Speech and Hearing Association.

McLean, J. E., McLean, L. K. S., Brady, N. C., & Etter, R. (1991). Communication profiles of two types of gesture using nonverbal persons with severe to profound mental retardation. *Journal of Speech and Hearing Research, 34,* 294–308.

McManis, D. L. (1965). Pursuit rotor performance of normal and retarded children in four verbal incentive conditions. *Child Development, 36,* 667–683.

McManis, D. L. (1966). The von Restorff effect in serial learning by normal and retarded subjects. *American Journal of Mental Deficiency, 70,* 569–575.

McManis, D. L. (1967). Intra-list differentiation and isolation effect in serial learning: A test of the S-R competition hypothesis. *Journal of Verbal Learning and Verbal Behavior, 6,* 714–720.

McReynolds, L., Engmann, D., & Dimmitt, K. (1974). Markedness theory and articulation errors. *Journal of Speech and Hearing Disorders, 39,* 93–103.

McReynolds, L. V., & Bennett, S. (1972). Distinctive feature generalization in articulation training. *Journal of Speech and Hearing Disorders, 37,* 462–470.

McReynolds, L. V., & Elbert, M. F. (1981). Generalization of correct articulation in clusters. *Applied Psycholinguistics, 2,* 119–132.

Nihira, K., Foster, R., & Shelhaas, M. (1970). *AAMD Adaptive Behavior Scales.* Washington, DC: American Association on Mental Deficiency.

Phillips, E. L., & Wolf, M. M. (1973). Achievement place: Development of the elected manager system. *Journal of Applied Behavior Analysis, 6,* 541–561.

Risley, T. R., & Hart, B. (1968). Developing correspondence between the nonverbal and verbal behavior of preschool children. *Journal of Applied Behavior Analysis, 1,* 267–281.

Rogers-Warren, A., & Baer, D. M. (1976). Correspondence between saying and doing: Teaching children to share and praise. *Journal of Applied Behavior Analysis, 9,* 335–354.

Rogers-Warren, A., & Warren, S. F. (1980). Mands for verbalization: Facilitating the display of newly trained language in children. *Behavior Modification, 4,* 361–382.

Rosenberg, S., Spradlin, J. E., & Mabel, S. (1961). Interaction among retarded children as a function of their relative language skills. *Journal of Abnormal and Social Psychology, 63,* 402–410.

Ruder, K., Hermann, P., & Jensen, P. (1977). Effects of verbal imitation and comprehension training on verbal production. *Journal of Psychology and Research, 6,* 59–71.

Ruder, K., & Jensen, P. (1972). Fluent and hesitation pauses as a function of syntactic complexity. *Journal of Speech and Hearing Research, 15,* 49–60.

Ruder, K. F., & Bunce, B. H. (1981). Articulation therapy using distinctive feature analysis to structure the training program: Two case studies. *Journal of Speech and Hearing Disorders, 65,* 59–65.

Saunders, K. J., & Spradlin, J. E. (1989). Conditional discrimination in mentally retarded adults: The effect of training the component simple discriminations. *Journal of the Experimental Analysis of Behavior, 52,* 1–12.

Saunders, K. J., & Spradlin, J. E. (1990). Conditional discrimination in mentally retarded adults: The development of generalized skills. *Journal of the Experimental Analysis of Behavior, 54,* 239–250.

Saunders, K. J., Williams, D. C., & Spradlin, J. E. (1995). Conditional discrimination by adults with mental retardation: Establishing relations between physically identical stimuli. *American Journal on Mental Retardation, 99,* 558–563.

Saunders, R. R., Saunders, K. J., Kirby, K. C., & Spradlin, J. E. (1988). The merger and development of equivalence classes by unreinforced conditional selection of comparison stimuli. *Journal of the Experimental Analysis of Behavior, 50,* 145–162.

Saunders, R. R., Wachter, J., & Spradlin, J. E. (1988). Establishing auditory stimulus control over an eight-member equivalence class via conditional discrimination procedures. *Journal of the Experimental Analysis of Behavior, 49,* 95–115.

Schumaker, J., & Sherman, J. A. (1970). Training generative verb usage by imitation and reinforcement procedures. *Journal of Applied Behavior Analysis, 3,* 273–287.

Sherman, J. A. (1971). Imitation and language development. In H. W. Reese & L. P. Lipsitt (Eds.), *Advances in child development and behavior* (vol. 6, pp. 239–272). New York: Academic Press.

Siegel, G. M. (1962). Experienced and inexperienced articulation examiners. *Journal of Speech and Hearing Disorders, 27,* 28–35.

Siegel, G. M. (1963). Language behavior of adults and children in interpersonal assemblies. In R. L. Schiefelbusch (Ed.), *Language studies of mentally retarded children* (pp. 32–53). Danville, IL: American Speech and Hearing Association.

Silverman, K., Anderson, S. R., & Dison, D. M. (1986). Establishing and generalizing audience control of new language repertoires. *Analysis and Intervention in Developmental Disabilities, 6,* 21–40.

Skinner, B. F. (1957). *Verbal behavior.* New York: Appleton-Century-Crofts.

Spradlin, J. E. (1962). Effects of reinforcement schedules on extinction in severely retarded children. *American Journal of Mental Deficiency, 66,* 634–640.

Spradlin, J. E. (1963). Language and communication of mental defectives. In N. R. Ellis (Ed.), *Handbook of mental deficiency* (pp. 512–555). New York: McGraw-Hill.

Spradlin, J. E., & Dixon, M. H. (1976). Establishing conditional discriminations without direct training: Stimulus classes and labels. *American Journal of Mental Deficiency, 80,* 555–561.

Spradlin, J. E., & Girardeau, F. L. (1966). The behavior of severely and profoundly retarded persons. *International Review of Research In Mental Retardation,* 257–298.

Spradlin, J. E., Girardeau, F. L., & Corte, E. (1969). Social and communication behavior of retarded adolescents in a two-person situation: Part II. *American Journal of Mental Deficiency, 73,* 572–577.

Spradlin, J. E., Girardeau, F. L., & Horn, G. L. (1965). Fixed ratio and fixed interval behavior of severely and profoundly retarded subjects. *Journal of Experimental Child Psychology, 2,* 340–353.

Spradlin, J. E., Girardeau, F. L., & Horn, G. L. (1966). Stimulus properties of reinforcement during extinction of a free operant response. *Journal of Experimental Child Psychology, 4,* 369–379.

Spradlin, J. E., Girardeau, F. L., & Horn, G. L. (1967). Social and communication behavior of retarded adolescents in a two-person situation: Part I. *American Journal of Mental Deficiency, 72,* 473–481.

Spradlin, J. E., & Rosenberg, S. (1964). Complexity of adult verbal behavior in a dyadic situation with retarded children. *Journal of Abnormal and Social Psychology,* 64, 694–698.

Spradlin, J. E., Saunders, K. J., & Rosenberg, S. (1992). The stability of equivalence classes. In S. C. Hayes & L. J. Hayes (Eds.), *Understanding verbal relations* (pp. 29–42). Reno, NV: Context Press.

Spradlin, J. E., & Saunders, R. R. (1984). Behaving appropriately in new situations, A stimulus class analysis. *American Journal of Mental Deficiency, 88,* 574–579.

Spradlin, J. E., & Saunders, R. R. (1986). The development of stimulus classes using match-to-sample procedures: Sample classification versus comparison classification. *Analysis and Intervention in Developmental Disabilities, 6,* 41–58.

Striefel, S., & Eberl, D. (1974). Imitation of live and videotaped models. *Education and Training of the Mentally Retarded, 9,* 83–88.

Striefel, S., Wetherby, B., & Karlan, G. R. (1976). Establishing generative verb-noun instruction-following skills in retarded children. *Journal of Experimental Child Psychology, 22,* 247–260.

Striefel, S., Wetherby, B., & Karlan, G. R. (1978). Developing generalized instruction-following behavior in severely retarded people. In C. E. Meyers (Ed.), *Quality of life in severely and profoundly mentally retarded people: Research foundations for improvement* (pp. 267–326). Washington, DC: American Association on Mental Deficiency.

Warren, S. F., & Rogers-Warren, A. K. (1983). A longitudinal analysis of language generalization among adolescents with severely handicapping conditions. *Journal of the Association for Persons with Severe Handicaps, 4,* 18–31.

Wolf, M., & Risley, T. (1964). Application of operant conditioning procedures to the behavior problems of an autistic child. *Behavior Research and Therapy, 1,* 305–312.

Wolf, M. M. (1978). Social validity: The case for subjective measurement, or how applied behavior analysis is finding its heart. *Journal of Applied Behavior Analysis, 11,* 315–329.

Wolf, M. M., Giles, D. K., & Hall, V. (1968). Experiments with token reinforcement in a remedial classroom. *Behavior Research and Therapy, 6,* 51–64.

5

The Emergence of the Kansas Center

RICHARD L. SCHIEFELBUSCH

The organization referred to as the Kansas Center (the Kansas Center for Mental Retardation and Related Aspects of Human Development) was always difficult to precisely define or diagram. It began as a single effort that quickly became a confederation of research projects growing and spreading from the original Parsons Research Project. The Mental Retardation Research Center (MRRC) soon became the primary component of the Kansas Center. The MRRC led to funding for a large research center and buildings to house it. The Kansas University Affiliated Facility (UAF) was the clinical partner to the MRRC. It also came with buildings.

As the Kansas Center grew, it acquired more and more projects. It expanded significantly for many years. As it matured, and the emphasis shifted from the institutions to community programs, dozens of new projects were spun off. Those projects experienced varying degrees of success in establishing valid areas of research and service and in maintaining their funding as semi-independent components of the Kansas Center.

The Planning

The original Kansas Center and the growth of the Bureau of Child Research (BCR) was possible because of many agreements reached among the scientists and staff members of the BCR, with officials of

Kansas University (KU), with the KU Medical Center (KUMC) administration, with the Board of Social Welfare, and with the federal link to the National Institute of Child Health and Human Development (NICHD) and several other major federal departments. The accumulating projects led to a vastly increased workload within the BCR administration.

A grant had to be written that would enfold numerous agreements across three campuses, one that would be approved by officials of both the university and the state systems. Furthermore, the BCR's small group of inexperienced planners had to learn quickly how to work and think with architects, medical laboratory scientists, politicians, fiscal planners, and various official committees to create a plan for a center with no real precedent.

There were no experts at what needed doing. No one knew if such a center could be built, or if it were built, that it would be productive. KUMC had already prepared a preliminary center grant application and had been advised by staff members at NICHD to team up with the Lawrence campus. KUMC soon formed an expert group of scientists and administrators to work with the BCR. Together they created work groups that visited each campus and established collaborative projects. The Children's Rehabilitation Unit (CRU) at KUMC became an interdisciplinary program model for both university campuses. CRU was a well-regarded program that served children who were to be included in the new center.

Herbert Miller, chairman of the Department of Pediatrics, agreed to talk and to plan with several of the medical investigators. He turned those discussions into content for the application. Russ Mills, associate vice chancellor of KUMC, became an adviser on many controversial issues and intercampus policy. At Parsons, Howard Bair was especially supportive in planning new facilities. Bair also had aspirations of his own, such as a chalet to be used for visitors and a centralized media center to be used for training and public information. Joe Spradlin and other members of the Parsons research staff became prime advocates for new research and new research space, even while they managed to hide space that was already temporarily available. Because the number of hospital residents was dwindling at that time, unoccupied space was especially abundant. The space was often aged and dispersed. The center undertaking was justified in having new space because planning was well underway for new research in a new program project that would radically change Parsons State Hospital and Training Center (PSHTC).

One of the early investigators at Parsons was Frances Degen Horowitz, who subsequently became chairperson of the newly constituted Department of Human Development and Family Life at KU. In 1964, she approached Dick Schiefelbusch with a daring plan to recruit Donald M. Baer.

Don was seeking to move from the University of Washington. He had been working at Rainier State School, where he and several of his students and professional colleagues had also developed a program of applied behavioral applications. Frances' interest led to the recruitment of Don Baer and to the subsequent recruitment of Montrose Wolf, Barbara Etzel, Betty Hart, Todd Risley, Jim Sherman, and Vance Hall. Each of these investigators was given an appointment that allowed for at least half-time research. Thus, a new major academic department came into being, and the number and quality of the members of the research cadre for the MRRC application increased significantly.

Applied behavior analysis was especially useful in the creation of the MRRC because at that time there were few proven research strategies available for attacking the national problem of mental retardation. The congressional appropriations that enabled the newly formed NICHD to develop procedures for creating 12 centers throughout the United States was indeed a bold move. In like spirit, the various scientific groups that competed for construction and center support grants also were bold and confident. The Kansas Center application was especially "innovative" because it included construction and program plans for three sites (a state hospital, a university, and a teaching hospital).

The application for the MRRC included an administrative and technical plan that had been evolving for about 10 years. This extensive proactive experience included management, accounting, clerical, media capabilities, data processing equipment, and personnel and research training. The new center was for the most part simply an extension of ongoing activities and assumed responsibilities involved in the BCR's mandate. Also, the BCR was prepared to provide in-kind contributions in applications for the center. These resources were detailed in the center grant application and subsequently in each application and at each site visit review.

The BCR's staff members at Lawrence began looking forward to having more spacious accommodations for their work. Most of the candidates for new space were crowded in an off-campus makeshift facility called Varsity House. It had at one time been the meal site for varsity athletes. The building had been converted into temporary office and laboratory space with funds that had been granted for the recently funded Communications Program Project. Most of the research staff at Varsity House had been recruited the year before and were already part of this intercampus development.

Varsity House was actually the launch cite for the anticipated Center Unit in Lawrence. At the same time, Varsity House also housed the emerging Department of Human Development and Family Life. Many Varsity House residents were spearheading the new community site in Kansas City that soon was to be the Juniper Gardens Children's Project under the direction of R. Vance Hall. (See chapter 6 for a discussion of this project.)

In the meantime, the central office personnel of the BCR still were jammed into three small rooms in the basement of Bailey Hall, striving valiantly to relate functionally to the entire plan. To facilitate the efforts in such a growing enterprise, Ross Copeland moved to Lawrence from Parsons to become associate director of the BCR. Ross organized the office to handle the numerous new transactions and to handle the overwhelming job of monitoring the architectural activities that ensued. Ross proved to be more than a troubleshooter and a man of many talents. He was primarily responsible for designing the central office of the BCR for the new center. He had also designed both old space and new space at Parsons. He made a lasting contribution in building the BCR's international program and also its media program as a colleague of Robert Hoyt.

Fred Girardeau agreed to move his research operation from Parsons to KUMC and to set up a research lab in the basement of the Children's Rehabilitation Unit. He also assumed responsibility for directing the early activities of the Juniper Gardens Children's Project program. He soon became the director of research training for the BCR when Vance Hall became coordinator then director at Juniper Gardens.

Other individuals agreed to serve important new functions on behalf of the center. Don Baer agreed to be the director of the KU unit of the new Kansas Center for Research in Mental Retardation and Human Development. Herb Miller agreed to direct the KUMC unit and Joe Spradlin agreed to direct the unit at Parsons. The plan called for Dick Schiefelbusch to be the coordinator of the new center. This title was upgraded to director by a request from the staff of NICHD as soon as the center grant application was approved.

It would be difficult to list all of the responsibilities of the Kansas Center's director. His role as BCR director expanded and intensified when the Kansas Center was formed. Along with a stream of "red-eye" trips to Washington, hundreds of trips to visit outlying state agencies markedly increased the interactions with bureaucrats and politicians in Topeka and with researchers in Kansas City and Parsons. Soon after the application was completed, the site visit was scheduled. A practice site visit was held to prepare for the real site visit. Chuck Strother, director of the Mental Retardation Center at the University of Washington in Seattle, was invited to visit and critique the plans. Several sessions were held in which key participants explained their research plans to each other in great detail and to a visiting scientist. These sessions tested the validity of center plans and the team's ability to explain them.

After the first day of discussion, there was a dinner at the Kansas Union Building on the KU campus at which key administrators were invited to express their views "in rehearsal." After dinner, Chancellor Wescoe invited everyone to the chancellor's mansion for further coffee talk. During the evening, Bob Anderson, chairman of the Board of Social Welfare, leaned toward the chancellor and said, "Do you want the Governor to be at the site visit?" After it was explained that his honor's visit might seem to be a bit excessive, Anderson said, "Okay, but if you do, he'll be there." Later, Strother observed, "It seems to me that you have the State well under control."

The site visit went well. All of the facilities were subsequently approved as presented; even Howard Bair's vaunted Media Center was accepted. It would be placed in what would become the new PSHTC UAF. The site visit was an encouraging experience in which the presenters learned as much about the center as the visitors did. The team soon learned, unofficially, that the plan would be funded. After a wait of several days, official word came down from Washington. The Kansas Center was in business.

The Real Thing

The preparation was strenuous, but the application process for the Kansas Center turned out to be the easy part of the experience. After the grant application was formally approved for funding, the work began for real. Building contracts had to be let for bids and contractors selected in accordance with state regulations. NICHD requested applications for center development grants that were designed to facilitate administrative and technological resources and to provide the substance for a true center. But the most strenuous activities were related to the construction and furnishing of the buildings. We did not anticipate cost overruns or funding moratoriums. We did not expect that we would be required to approach the legislature on two occasions to increase our matching funds beyond those we had assembled in our initial agreements. However, on the positive side, one could say that if these exigencies had not emerged, we would never have learned how supportive our colleagues in Topeka really were.

When the research transactions were at their full state of uncertainty, we decided to develop a three-campus clinical center. For this effort, we were required to work under a different agency in Washington, the Division of Hospital and Medical Facilities, Public Health Service. This center program was officially labeled the University Affiliated Facility. The name was later changed to the University Affiliated Program (UAP). Altogether there were 12 MRRC research centers and more than 30 UAP clinical centers constructed throughout the United States. Kansas was the only site that was initially granted funds for the construction of buildings for both research and clinical activities, each with three locations: Lawrence, Parsons, and Kansas City. The clinical center proved to be somewhat easier to construct, perhaps because these building units were placed at the same locations as the research center buildings. We even secured a third building unit for Parsons that was labeled the Community Support Unit. It was actually constructed as a wing of the UAF unit and served as a new hospital facility for the institution.

The placement of the clinical center with the research center units proved to be a fortunate strategy. However, this plan was not always acclaimed. Scientists tended to doubt that other scientists would want to work in a service environment. Clinicians doubted that their colleagues would benefit from working next to scientists. Our views of this arrangement were, of course, that each would benefit individually and would likely contribute to better science and better service.

The primary purposes of the center, as considered initially, were to research critical problems associated with mental retardation, to train a new generation of scientists for this field, to provide the leadership in developing improved services for persons with developmental disabilities, and to train the critical personnel who would be needed to maintain and to further advance these services. At the time, we were greatly impressed with the amounts of our overall construction awards, which were significant for those times.

The grants included $5,049,521 in federal funds and $2,621,000 in state and private funds, in addition to the two construction grants. Federal grant funds were awarded for renovation of two BCR facilities. In 1963, $36,500 was awarded to renovate Varsity House on the KU campus, and in 1965, $14,700 was awarded for renovation of the Juniper Gardens research facilities in Kansas City, Kansas. Thus, the amount of federal funds awarded for construction and renovation totaled $5,100,721 and the amount of state and private gifts totaled $2,621,000, for a total dollar figure of $7,721,721.

The total package of building space, more than 200,000 square feet, could not be built today for this amount of money. But 30 years ago it seemed to us that we had completed an awesome project. And so we had. The center, in addition to the newly constructed space, had, or soon utilized, substantial space in the Juniper Gardens area of Kansas City, Kansas; the Kansas Neurological Institute in Topeka, Kansas; the Children's Rehabilitation Unit at KUMC; and in Haworth Hall, adjacent to the center's space at KU in Lawrence. The latter provided space for the administrative offices of the BCR and office and staff space for the Department of Human Development and Family Life. These personnel moved to that location from Varsity House, located at 1046 Indiana Street.

At KU the John T. Stewart Children's Center (the name given to the Kansas Center space in Lawrence) housed most of the Lawrence setting of both the MRRC and the UAP. It was almost immediately overcrowded. Despite the fact that all of the space in the new construction was committed to center activities, we were soon required to find space for faculty members from three academic departments that were initially deemed to be relevant to the center's mission. The Council of Deans together with the University Space Committee had reached that decision in concert with the administrative and research committees of the center. There is no doubt that these decisions greatly increased the research, the training, and the service resources of the combined center, but it is also true that the building facilities at KU were immediately over-crowded. Thus, for the next 21 years the most active and possibly the most important committee in the John T. Stewart Children's Center (or, as it was generally known, the Children's Wing of Haworth Hall) was the Space Committee.

The most chronic issue before the committee was how to make opti-mum use of space in the Lawrence MRRC unit. The committee fre-quently had to work through several levels of university authority, as well as several layers of competing needs. Despite frequent inconve-niences and disappointed space applicants, the growing number of MRRC participants created the most active and possibly the most pro-ductive research group at the KU campus. The other units in the center had problems too, but their difficulties were mostly related to nonspace issues. For instance, the KUMC had difficulty accepting a unified plan for data collection and analysis within their unit and with the center as a whole. The Parsons group wanted autonomy in designing their com-puter systems. These problems simply reflected the difficulties in devel-oping an efficient centerwide data system. For this reason, it was sometimes difficult to convince site visitors that we had an efficient interactive system for managing our center's technical resources.

The Challenge and the Foundation

In the 1960s, the accepted and overwhelming scientific opinion was that persons with mental retardation could not learn. The self-fulfilling prophecy that they could not learn was based on the idea that these persons had insurmountable, inherent, inabilities. "What you see, is what you get, and you may as well not waste your time," summarized such thinking.

The young behavioral scientists in Kansas, and at selected sites across the country, were establishing research projects that flew in the face of such fatalism. They were committed to scientific principles; they believed it was possible for persons with retardation to learn functional, daily living skills; and they were not slaves to academic stuffiness and professional truisms.

The operational philosophy quickly established in Kansas was to study problems important in making improvements in the lives of humans with personal or environmentally induced disabilities. However, when the BCR's first major research project began at PSHTC, there were few data to demonstrate that the behavior of persons with severe retardation was influenced by the environment in which they lived.

Careful observation in laboratory conditions soon determined that the behavior of these persons was not capricious. It became apparent that persons with mental retardation would repeat acts that resulted in pleasant consequences, and that new skills could be taught through the careful management of behavioral consequences. The extensions of contingent reinforcement (or operant conditioning) applications by BCR researchers had profound implications in the study of persons with severe mental retardation and in the deinstitutionalization movement that was to follow.

Almost all of the visible and vocal leaders of the deinstitutionalization movement came from places other than laboratories. They represented parents' groups, legislators, religious and human rights groups, legal action groups, and various advocacy groups. Their preoccupation was with the human rights features of the movement. The realism of scientists in the nascent Kansas Center focused on the feasibility of teaching self-help skills, functional (if limited) language skills, and adaptive responses to persons in circumstances encountered in daily living. Without scientists such as those at Parsons, and at in a few other places in the nation, the movers and shakers of the deinstitutionalization movement would have never become movers and shakers.

Research projects in Kansas, and elsewhere, soon demonstrated that children in institutions could learn substantial new skills. The early behavioral work influenced a whole generation of young scientists by setting an example of research uniformly impeccable and oriented toward learning processes that led to practical application in teaching children with and without disabilities. The investigations dealt with concerns that are commonly labeled "cognitive," to which were applied the behavior analytic framework of stimulus control. Although much of the early work took place in institutions, the behavioral researchers were early, unsung deinstitutionalizationists.

The Kansas Mental Retardation Research Center

Through the years the work in the MRRC reflected the research progress that was being made in changing developments in public policy and increasing demands for self- sufficiency and independence for persons with developmental disabilities. Small biomedical projects were supported and an emphasis was placed on disseminating both research data and functional training techniques.

The large center that is commonly referred to as the Kansas Center had several different names and various guiding thematic areas during its evolution. The center within the center, the Mental Retardation Research Center, changed through the years. This large grant was funded in 5-year periods and it was necessary to reapply every 5 years in competition with other universities. The names and the thematic areas reflected a changing and adapting program that kept pace with government funding programs and the perceived needs of persons with developmental disabilities. In the first core implementation grant that began in 1966, the five thematic areas included:

1. Biochemical and genetic correlates of retardation;
2. Other biological correlates of retardation;
3. Educational correlates of retardation;
4. Interpersonal correlates of retardation; and
5. Environmental correlates of retardation.

As the early behavioral work matured and was more widely applied, the changing nature of the search for definitive answers to the problems of mental retardation began to take on a somewhat different character. In 1971, after 5 years of operation, the thematic areas of the MRRC were revised to include more biomedical work in addition to the behavioral studies. The application stated that "The Kansas Center for Mental Retardation and Human Development is prepared to undertake research that bears upon a broad range of critical problems," and the renewal application listed eight thematic areas:

1. Physical Processes of Reproduction;
2. Fetal and Neonatal Development;
3. Biochemical and Metabolic Factors;
4. Neurophysiology;
5. Sensory and Perceptual Development;
6. Language and Verbal Behavior;
7. Depriving Environments; and
8. Learning Disorders and Special Education.

As the MRRC matured further, thematic areas in the next 5-year reapplication reflected the changing emphases brought about by research advances, the nature of the mental retardation problems that resisted solution, and the changing character of public expectations for persons with disabilities. Language and Verbal Behavior and Fetal and Neonatal Development endured, reflecting a continuation of the original language work and the importance of early childhood as a viable research challenge.

Other themes were modified somewhat, again to reflect research progress and the perceived priorities of the Kansas Center and the skills of its investigators. The next reapplication specified research listed under nine themes:

1. Language and Verbal Behavior;
2. Learning Disorders and Problem Behaviors;
3. Neurobiological Mechanisms;
4. Early Childhood Intervention;
5. Special Classrooms;
6. Teachers and Parent Training;
7. Reproductive Physiology and Neuroendocrinology;
8. Fetal and Neonatal Development; and
9. Dissemination of Intervention Programs.

In the 1981 reapplication, the continuing evolution of the MRRC and the ability to adapt to changing needs and technological progress were becoming subtler, with only slight modifications in the thematic areas, with a clear explanation of why the changes were necessary.

During the past few years there has been a steady tendency, not only to follow the original stated goals and subgoals, but also to continue to refine those statements into finite thematic areas of investigation. This has resulted in a progression, which examines the problem of mental retardation from conception to the optimum development of life skills in persons handicapped by retardation.

The rationale and disseminated data stemming from research in several thematic areas included:

1. Language and Communication Acquisition and Intervention;
2. Social, Conceptual, and Cognitive Development;
3. Neurobiological Mechanisms;
4. Infant and Preschool Programs;
5. Assessment and Intervention Techniques;
6. Teacher and Parent Training;
7. Reproductive Physiology and Neuroendocrinology;
8. Fetal and Neonatal Development; and
9. Dissemination of Intervention Programs.

The thematic areas in the 1986 reapplication reflected a combination of the most viable biomedical and behavioral themes, themes that had been shaken down and revised to reflect a program that allowed "research areas to bind together on a common theme and approach the solutions from a multidisciplinary front. Information from this type of approach cannot help but produce the most informative results possible in a research center." The themes continued to combine the talents of many different investigators proposing increasingly complex biomedical studies, while the behavioral research strategies extended into cognitive, social, and educational domains. These included:

1. Cognitive Development;
2. Family Center, Ethics;
3. Language and Communication;
4. Neurobiology of Mental Retardation;
5. Social and Environmental Management and Intervention; and
6. Experimental Training/Professional Training.

The 1991 reapplication reflected the reality that the MRRC is still a developing organism. The MRRC had passed through several evolutionary stages that allowed it to survive and flourish and to continue to find a viable mission. Beginning in a quite primitive state, the MRRC examined fundamental principles of behavior and applied those principles to modify specific behaviors in persons with severe disabilities. Those principles were generalized into community and home environments. Later, projects and programs designed specifically to develop and support home-like and community environments for persons with developmental disabilities took over where the research left off.

In a parallel development, the biomedical puzzles of developmental disabilities were studied and continue to be studied. Those studies are important, and many of them merged into studies called "biobehavioral." Where the behavioral projects were dominant in the beginning, it was anticipated that the biomedical projects became full partners in a combined approach to the solving of common problems. Thus, 1991 thematic areas were:

1. Language, Communication and Cognition;
2. Strategies for Prevention;
3. Prenatal and Postnatal Risk Factors;
4. Cellular and Molecular Studies of Information Processing; and
5. Cell Biology and Molecular Genetics of Pregnancy.

The thematic areas changed to accommodate the progress of science, the makeup of the MRRC, and the professional and public demands and expectations of the nation. Some researchers perhaps foresaw that possibility with the MRRC programs. But no one could have predicted the exact nature or the course of the science that proceeded from the MRRC and other concerted research efforts or how much specific information we would have amassed by this time. As an example, the mapping of the human genome is not only possible, it is well underway. Genetic links have been established for numerous human disabilities, including Down syndrome, cystic fibrosis, and Huntington's chorea. Other links emerge as the work continues. Biomedical research perhaps holds the most promise for preventing developmental disability in the coming generations. And as a full partner to biomedical research, behavioral and biobehavioral research holds the most promise for positively affecting the lives of persons whose lives are presently affected by developmental disability.

Thus the Kansas Mental Retardation Research Center is arguably at the time of its greatest promise, with research plans that will influence the prevention of developmental disabilities in children yet to be born, and behavioral research that will continue to affect the way persons of all ages with disabilities live.

The Kansas University Affiliated Facility

The partner of the MRRC in the Kansas Center is the UAF. It has been at various times referred to as the Kansas University Affiliated Facility (KUAF) and the Kansas University Affiliated Program (KUAP). Those names reflected the preoccupations of the various government agencies that supported the University Affiliated Facilities across the nation. While there were originally only 12 MRRC research centers, there were up to 30 UAF programs at different times and states. NICHD was a primary source of support for the MRRC. The UAF programs were funded by numerous agencies; some of them where new but many of them were the same agencies with name changes.

The UAF programs were to take the tools, techniques, programs, and procedures developed in research programs and apply the findings in clinical settings. That was often the case, but not always. The UAF programs are subject to a great deal more political and interdisciplinary tinkering than were the MRRC programs.

At Kansas the UAF grant application was designed with three settings with three constructed facilities. Each of the UAF units is arranged to have convenient interaction with the MRRC units constructed prior to the UAFs. Kansas, in effect, got three new buildings and three new programs for both the MRRC and the UAP.

The three-setting Kansas UAF application was virtually assured of approval from the beginning. However, we did not take the submission casually. We organized planning committees and studied agency committee minutes and recommendations, and we also secured verbal approval from state agencies and university administrative offices.

Chancellor Wescoe suggested that we should create a name for the combined MRRC and UAF centers. Thus came the name: The Kansas Center for Mental Retardation and Human Development.

The KUMC setting already had a constructed facility that reflected the general mission of the University Affiliated legislation. The Children's Rehabilitation Unit (CRU) was created in 1958 and already had several years of collaborative programming that included pediatrics, orthopedics, obstetrics and gynecology, special education, deaf education, speech pathology and audiology, psychology, and physical therapy. Many of the children served in the CRU had developmental and multiple disabilities, and for them and their families, CRU provided an urgent service.

Nevertheless, the prospect of a UAF was promising because the CRU service system had become overcrowded. There was a waiting list of applicants with developmental disabilities. CRU provided an impetus for all the settings, especially because CRU had a major grant for exemplary program activities, both service and training, and would likely be able to expand that funding by means of a UAF.

Other existing programs at Lawrence and Parsons were favorable for the development of the UAF. KU had major aspirations for the expansion of their special education program, but had no other prospects for space expansion. Other groups urgently needing space were Human Development and Family Life; Speech, Language and Hearing; and the Bureau of Child Research. The BCR, of course, was active on all three campuses in planning and development of interdisciplinary training.

At Parsons the situation was vastly different. PSHTC actually had space that it was not using. This was due largely to the downsizing of the resident population and also to Bair's successful campaign in recruiting funds to build facilities for existing needs (e.g., food services, recreation, music therapy, and additional cottages). But, the need for facilities equipped for better services and resources was very strong (i.e., for audiovisual and clinical laboratories, community-based programs, and improved staff training).

Another important feature of the UAF planning was the relationship with state agencies that were charged with improving statewide services. These agencies generally regarded the university departments and divisions as ivory tower operations that had little relevance to the difficult aspects of service for persons with developmental disabilities in the state. The UAF application plan required a set of strategies for relating to state realities. In the application we tried to break the exemplary service and the training designs down to practical dimensions that could be endorsed by state agency planners, as well as by the federal review team and university departments.

The BCR was a valuable resource for each construction, for program planning and development, and for administrative organization. The BCR staff had already logged time in intercampus planning, designing, and organizing. So, they played approximately the same role in preparing the UAF application that they did for the MRRC application. Schiefelbusch played the same coordinative for each application in turn. As a case in point, BCR worked with the executive officers of each campus in adjusting indirect cost rates, in coming to interactive agreements, in making management decisions, and in planning for the new space.

Staff members in the federal agencies also became part of the planning and implementation processes on each campus for each program. Because members of the BCR had experienced numerous encounters with federal agency personnel prior to the beginnings of the Center's activities, it was natural to exchange information and opinions throughout the entire complex effort. Here again, the enterprise of the UAF was not a start-up experience, but rather a continuation of relationships, routines, and mutual support strategies. In some instances the Washington staff members unhesitatingly made suggestions for strengthening the plans for the UAF applications.

Some surprise disappointments and successes were apparent during the development years. The policy differences between the State Office of the Secretary for Social and Rehabilitative Services (SRS), which had replaced the Board of Social Welfare, and the several instrumental offices of the UAP were especially abrupt. The conflict resulted because of the state bureaucracy's need to preserve institutions that were at odds with disabilities advocates who had joined the UAP and wanted to immediately bring about deinstitutionalization and alternate systems of service delivery. In a generic sense, the conflict related to almost any alteration that might change existing structures of state services. These apparent impasses seemed to be fueled by several dissonant contributors, including the secretary, Dr. Robert Harder, who was very powerful and at times inflexible, and the associate director of BCR and UAF director, Ross Copeland. Copeland had always been at odds with institutional systems.

The first penetration of this mounting problem came when the legislative assistant to the chancellor called Schiefelbusch and instructed him to go to Topeka and "make peace" with Harder. An appointment was made and at the beginning of this 2-hour conference, Schiefelbusch was told by Harder that the only reason he had agreed to the conference was that he did not want it said that he would not talk about the differences.

The two "colleagues" covered many topics germane to each other's role, including who was the most sincere about helping the people of Kansas and about whose roots were the deeper in the Kansas culture. In short, they broke through to each other and were able to form critical issues of agreement. The final step was an offer (or challenge) that was extended by Harder for the UAP to demonstrate a sustained contribution to as many as three crucial problems that the secretary was concerned about in serving the children of Kansas.

These "problems" were: 1) newborn birth-impaired babies and their mothers, 2) program designs for vocational and other rehabilitation and training for youth with severe retardation, and 3) training of regional SRS personnel. Each area led to concrete proposals for funding support and the assigning of UAP staff to work with SRS personnel at regional and local community locations.

At this point we encountered dissonance with assigned staff members of the SRS state system. This led to still more accommodations. In retrospect, an interactive university–state system was created and has continued to this day. We were indeed fortunate that the officials of that time at both ends were wise enough to rise to that challenge. These officials included the secretary of SRS, the director of Institution Management, the superintendent of PSHTC, the chancellor, the executive vice chancellor for the Medical Center, and selectively, members of the Board of Regents, the Board of Social Welfare, and legislative staff members. It may have been also a validation of the aphorism that "crisis is the time of opportunity."

About 15 years later a second crisis presented itself. This one was critical to the federal funding at Winfield State Hospital and Training Center. An evaluation of the Winfield program by the federal evaluation team had turned up a number of deficiencies. These deficiencies, if unchanged, would terminate a large amount of federal service funds for the hospital. The deficiencies were detailed, and a brief interval of time was allowed for compliance. Joe Spradlin and about 25 colleagues from Parsons, both caregivers and scientists, volunteered to go to Winfield for an intensive effort to bring the care program there up to compliance.

The results of this effort were: 1) compliance was achieved, 2) state funds were set aside for a follow-up monitoring period of 3 or more years, 3) the legislative charter of the BCR was changed to include the possible "management of State institutions," and 4) major federal funding was created for management assistance to institutions in Kansas and beyond Kansas.

The initial success of the Mimosa Cottage Project in teaching socially effective skills resulted in the placement of 40 teenage children with severe retardation in community settings. This, of course, was what the project was designed to do. However, it soon became apparent that communities were not accepting the idea and were not preparing to provide the essential training of staff to manage or to oversee the routines in the community settings.

The crisis that resulted from the deinstitutionalization movement was felt all across the country in both the mentally retarded (MR) and the emotionally disturbed (ED) service settings. Often the problem was not limited to specific sites because the institution residents were simply turned out to no designated community setting. The problem that was presented by this change in service arrangements created a need for new resources and new training services. The UAP's responded to this need by combining efforts with both agencies and settings. They also were soon to combine in creating surveillance and evaluation resources and in-training service personnel.

It was apparent that Kansas research personnel and service personnel were resources that the agencies, settings, and families needed. But that would require a vast, new, urgent focus on environmental design for appropriate living alternatives to institutions. This urgency continues and has long since been extended to aging populations and to other service groups.

This changing emphasis of care and support has forced the UAPs to assume responsibilities that include costs, education and training, management, and information collection and evaluation. The UAPs have led the campus to move from their "ivory towers" to a condition of shared responsibilities within statewide community designs for group-oriented environments. Beyond the UAP role in designing new service strategies and resources is the formulation of policy and political action. In a very general perspective that is where we are now. The paradigms and the technologies for management and planning have become, and are likely to continue to become, more effective and more sophisticated. Designs have been formulated and validated for making environments and ecologies more practical, attractive, and cost-effective. Furthermore, UAP personnel have become involved in developing policy and legislative language for the future.

That is not to imply that all, or even most, of the problems associated with the care and treatment of persons with developmental disabilities have been solved. Far from it, but when one looks back at where we were, significant progress has been made and hundreds of thousands of lives have been changed for the better. The Kansas Center is arguably at the time of its greatest promise, with research plans that will influence the prevention of developmental disabilities in children yet to be born, and will continue to affect the way persons with disabilities of all ages live and work.

Technology and the Kansas Center

Nearly everyone associated with the BCR and the Kansas Center has had reason at one time or another to give deference to "technology." In some cases, this involved ways to use electronics to help persons with severe disabilities in their daily living. Telecommunications and other forms of communications were used. But one of the most important technological advancements was the computer.

Looking back from 1990 it would have been easy to say that computer technology and the BCR came to their maturity together. That may or may not be true. Who knows what computers will become? It is true that much of modern, computer-based technology developed during the 69 years of the BCR. When BCR researchers first set up their laboratories, the only efficient electronic assistants were relay racks and patch panels. Each data collection system for each experiment had to be programmed by wiring a panel that directed the responses through relays into a data recording system. Complicated compilations and analyses of data were done by tabletop calculators that were effective but were time consuming and prone to operator error.

At the end of the period covered by this history, every scientist in the BCR (except those who never troubled themselves to become computer literate) had access to personal computers with sophisticated software that could do in a few minutes what would have taken days or weeks when some of them began their careers.

Gregorio Diaz was the first director of what later became known as the BCR Computer Applications Unit. He came as a student from Latin America and he left in 1984 to work as the Latin American representative for Microsoft.

Personal computers had entered the market by the time Diaz left and they were beginning to be widely used. Diaz noted in his final report before he left that 30 microcomputers had been installed in the BCR during the past year (1984), but there was no efficient way to share data among them.

The university also had a Honeywell mainframe computer that was available to BCR scientists. The university's statistical software at that time was too limited to meet the needs of everyone in the BCR. The capability to use computers to communicate and transfer data from Parsons to Lawrence or Kansas City was very limited. The BCR had a PDP 11/34 in Lawrence and one in Kansas City, but they could each support no more than three users simultaneously.

Diaz and his staff had also done considerable planning to acquire a VAX super minicomputer. The VAX was fast for its time and had software to support scientific and administrative needs. It was also among the early machines that had networking capabilities.

Davida Sears became director of the Computer Applications Unit following Diaz. Diaz was retained as a consultant until his duties at Microsoft precluded his further assistance.

The VAX required a sizeable capital investment. The money was put together from a number of sources, most from line items in grants for data processing and analysis. The VAX also required personnel to program and maintain it. Thus a commitment was made to a central computer system in the BCR. From the beginning, that central system was in competition in many ways with the burgeoning personal computer (PC) technology. PC technology was changing so rapidly it was difficult to keep up. That was a problem, but PC technology also offered great flexibility and adaptability and software that had been tested.

It was a challenge for the Computer Applications Unit to keep a handle on both a central computer system and a growing number of

PCs. Communications and media technology were also coming together to form telecommunications capabilities, graphics production, text processing, and other functions vital to the operation of a research organization.

When the Dole Center was planned and constructed, numerous committees investigated, planned, proposed, promised, and otherwise looked at the technology needs of the new building. People talked about "fibering" it, meaning that fiber optic cable should be put in the building while it was under construction. Other committees talked about being "telecommunications intensive," which was never really defined, but it probably meant that it should be possible for people in the new building to communicate with each other by closed-circuit television. In the case of the BCR, there was also a need for teleconferencing with Kansas City and Parsons.

Although much of the deliberation turned out to be only committee fodder, one extremely positive development was the establishment of a research and design and statistical capability within the Computer Applications Unit. That allowed researchers to come to Lawrence to get consultation on designing the experiments that they intended to conduct and on how to collect and analyze the anticipated data. By this time PCs had become so powerful that an organization like the BCR had no real need for a centralized computer system.

Perhaps the remarkable thing about technology and the BCR is that the BCR was often ahead of other parts of the university in the development and use of technology, in film making, video production, data processing, computer networking, and communications. While we were really ahead, we always seemed to be struggling to catch up, and that is most likely destined to be the nature of technology in any viable, growing, and progressive organization.

Looking ahead from 1990, it would have been safe to predict that planning, debating, anguishing, and pontificating about technology and how to support it would endure. What we could not have predicted is the effect that unforeseen advances such as the Internet would have on organizations such as the BCR. Whatever is in store for the future, it is quite plain now that technology will change more things, make more things possible, and require the ability to use tools undreamed of in 1921, in 1954, or in 1975.

6

The Juniper Gardens Children's Project

R. VANCE HALL, RICHARD L. SCHIEFELBUSCH,
CHARLES R. GREENWOOD, AND ROBERT K. HOYT

The Juniper Gardens Children's Project was first named the Northeast Children's Project because of its location in the northeast area of Kansas City, Kansas, and because it was sponsored in part by the Northeast Neighborhood Action Group (NAG). The population of the northeast area was, and is today, primarily African American (99.5%) with a preponderance of the working force employed as laborers. The median yearly income is the lowest of any area of the city and has always been below government poverty levels.

The Northeast Children's Project name was changed after the first 2 years because people confused it with the better-known northeast area of Kansas City, Missouri, and because, as it began to receive national recognition, outsiders often assumed that it was located somewhere in New England. Because its offices and some of its first programs were located in or near the Juniper Gardens Housing Project, the new name chosen was the Juniper Gardens Children's Project which locally was usually shortened to Juniper Gardens.

The name Juniper Gardens was derived from the juniper bushes that grew on the banks of the Kansas and Missouri rivers. Prior to the Civil War, a number of African Americans settled along the banks of the two rivers on the Kansas side. The area included the historic town of Quindaro just to the north, which had been a terminus of the Underground Railway in Civil War times. Former slaves who managed to cross over the Missouri into Kansas were free. Because of the profusion of junipers, the settlement on the riverbank became know as "Juniper Town," or to be more accurate in the vernacular of that time, "Junicky Town." After the Civil War, many other African Americans from Arkansas and further south migrated north. Many went farther north, but some settled in Kansas City, congregating on the hillside among the juniper bushes where they constructed ramshackle shelters while they were finding jobs and getting settled and building better homes.

Kansas City, Kansas grew into a major industrial site, boasting more that 300 manufacturing firms that attracted large numbers of low-salaried and unskilled workers. Meat packing became a leading industry, which along with structural steel, flour milling grain storage, frozen food, fiberglass, furniture, and soup manufacturing were labor-intensive places of employment. Jobs came and went, with the supply of labor nearly always exceeding the demand. Because of the low incomes and the uncertainties in the labor market, and the general debilitating effects of discrimination, much of the community housing was chronically unsafe and unsanitary. Deprivation in the form of substandard clothing, food, and shelter has always taken a toll on the children living there.

The Parsons State Hospital Influence

The Juniper Gardens Children's Project was the scientific child of another research program located primarily at the Parsons State Hospital and Training Center (PSHTC), 148 miles to the south in Parsons, Kansas. In October 1963, the National Institute of Child Health and Human Development (NICHD) funded a 7-year program project entitled Program of Research in Communication Disorders of Mentally Retarded Children. The program was based in part on the grounds of PSHTC and was one of many research, service, and training projects conducted jointly by the Bureau of Child Research (BCR) and the PSHTC. Under the leadership of Joe Spradlin, researchers at Parsons embarked on the long-term project, developing procedures for teaching children with retardation the communication skills they needed to get along in society.

It quickly became evident that the problems that children with retardation faced were not all located within institutional walls, and that the work needed to be broadened to include what was then called "cultural-familial" research, or the role of environmental factors in the risk of retardation and developmental delay. Scientists easily identified Juniper Gardens as an ideal setting for conducting research and service into the effects of "depriving" environmental factors, but the idea of integrating a university research program into a community of mostly poor, increasingly militant, and suspicious residents presented no small challenge.

Entry into the Community

Using a supplement to the program project as a temporary bridge, several university and medical center professionals began a cautious move into the then-political hotbed of the Juniper Gardens community. It fell to Richard Schiefelbusch and Fred Girardeau to go into the community and begin the process of winning support and finding research space. Frederic L. Girardeau was a young psychologist trained at Peabody College of Nashville, Tennessee, who came to the BCR to study mental retardation as a profession. After winning his spurs in basic research at Parsons, he became research training director for the BCR and moved to Kansas City, Kansas to begin work in new laboratories in the university's medical center. Girardeau immediately became interested in reducing the possible impact of poverty on young children.

Girardeau and Schiefelbusch spent several frustrating weeks merely finding a likely place to begin. In the process of this search, they became acquainted with a number of supportive colleagues in the community. Several public meetings were held to announce their intentions to the community, but their first break did not come until Father Harris Collingwood of St. Paul's Episcopal Church (and several other local pastors and local civic leaders) took an interest in the two academics who were proposing to establish a research laboratory within the community to study the effects of urban poverty on children.

Father Collingwood and Schiefelbusch persuaded the Episcopal Diocese to invest $95,000 in a building, with provision that the BCR would rent a large part of the building for laboratory and experimental classroom space. The Soroptomist Club and the Junior League of Kansas City raised over $5,000 to help equip the classrooms and laboratories. However, because this space was not sufficient to house a central office, the headquarters for the project was located in a rented basement under a local liquor store owned by C. L. Davis. The space was remodeled and modernized mostly by parents who volunteered their time and labor, working at nights and on weekends as well as during the day.

About 300 home visits were made in 1964 and 1965 to find children for experimental classes and to locate mothers who were willing to participate in preschool classes. One hundred and fifty-eight mothers of preschool children were interviewed to assess their opinions and to find out what they thought was most needed in the way of education for their children. Thus, the precedent was established to involve the community and its citizens rather than working from the top down from an agenda designed entirely by the scientists.

Girardeau, and later R. Vance Hall, who arrived at the project in 1965 from the University of Washington, regularly attended meetings of the NAG, one of several neighborhood action groups formed in Kansas City, Kansas as a part of the Office of Economic Opportunity's War on Poverty. The purpose of these groups was to give the people of the affected communities a voice in setting goals and carrying out action designed to help solve the problems of poverty in America's cities.

Girardeau and Hall worked closely with such community leaders as Uriel and Chester Owens, John Burris, Kermit Kitchen, Virginia Kirkwood, Sethard Beverly, Vernon Burleson, and Elmer Jackson. Although a number of persons were initially suspicious of the university representatives, Girardeau and Hall were able to answer the questions of community members who feared that their children would be used as "guinea pigs." Once convinced that the project would have as its goals not simply the description of problems existing in the community, but improved health, learning, and educational opportunities for the community's children, and that persons from the community would be hired and trained to work in the project, NAG and its leaders became strong supporters.

In subsequent years, the strong liaison between the community and the Juniper Gardens Children's Project was maintained. This was accomplished through a community advisory board and the continuous efforts of the project staff to keep community representatives informed about project programs and activities. The liaison also continues because project offices are located within the inner-city areas served. Perhaps most importantly, the project made good on its promise to employ members of the community. These persons benefited directly from employment in the project, and over the years they interpreted the program to their friends and neighbors.

Mary Wilkins helped overcome community suspicion and resistance as the project social worker. She grew up in the northeast area of Kansas City, Kansas. She was well known and well respected by everyone in the community. Mary had struggled to raise her family and, though middle-aged, went back to school and received her master's degree in social work just as the project was beginning to solicit children for participation in the preschool and after-school remedial programs.

Although capable, the white social worker originally hired to visit parents of potential candidates for Juniper Gardens Children's Project programs was having little success. When Mrs. Wilkins was hired, the picture changed immediately. Her standing in the community and her ability to communicate with its residents enlisted community support that had begun to seem impossible to gain.

Another major player was Uriel Owens. Owens was arguably the strongest behind-the-scenes community leader in Kansas City, Kansas. Universally liked and respected, he was politically astute and knew how to get things done without seeking the limelight. He became the chief administrative assistant of the project. Owens acted as the project's grants manager and director of community relations. He excelled in interacting with other members of the community and in keeping the project staff abreast of community issues and views. His input helped ensure that research and training were directed toward the best interests of the community. His efforts also led to securing money from the state legislature as core support for Juniper Gardens.

In 1965, having laid much of the groundwork for the community research program, Girardeau stepped aside from his responsibilities at Juniper Gardens. Schiefelbusch appointed R. Vance Hall to serve as coordinator of the Juniper Gardens Children's Project. Hall served in that capacity for 24 years. Although Girardeau continued in an advisory capacity, the responsibility for moving the project forward fell to Hall and the three other recruits to the BCR, Todd R. Risley, Betty Hart, and Montrose M. Wolf, all from the University of Washington. All three were at the early stages of their careers and were to become prominent behavioral psychologists.

The First Grant in Its Own Right

In 1965, the BCR received a supplementary grant from the NICHD to carry out a community-based program of research to help teachers, parents, and others motivate children to improve their social and academic skills. The Episcopal Diocese of Kansas established a community development center called Turner House and, as promised, built the building that was to house the experimental preschool. The preschool developed effective approaches for teaching language and other preacademic skills to young children. Other project facilities were eventually located in the basement of a local business, in the community center building of the Juniper Gardens housing project, and in the basement of a nearby church.

The Juniper Gardens Children's Project was funded in its own right in October 1967, following 3 years of supplemental support from the NICHD. The 3-year supplement and the subsequent series of five, competitively won, 5-year program project support periods, enabled the project staff to maintain a relatively stable level of core support complemented by a small state budget after 1985. These core funds have supported the research setting, which in turn, enabled investigations to acquire additional research and training funding from the U.S. Department of Education and other federal sources, resulting in a stream of significant investigations.

The Juniper Gardens staff also obtained support from various other agencies to carry out research, training, and service programs in the local schools and in the community. Supporting agencies include the Office of Economic Opportunity, Head Start, the Bureau for the Education of the Handicapped, the National Institute of Mental Health, and the State of Kansas. The Juniper Gardens Children's Project rapidly became a national model for community-based projects. In 1982, the project was described as one of several projects "that work" by the President's Committee on Mental Retardation.

In addition, key support has come from the city government of Kansas City; the Kansas City, Kansas Public Schools; the Economic Opportunity Foundation; the National Association for the Advancement of Colored People; the Neighborhood Action Group; and various church and civic groups. Small research and training programs have also received support and implementation through agencies such as the Shawnee Mission; Kansas Public Schools: Kansas City, Missouri Public Schools; and the Kansas Community College.

The Early Mission of Juniper Gardens

The original mission of the Juniper Gardens Project, as seen by the idealistic young researchers in charge of its programs, was to use applied behavior analysis to overcome the behavioral and learning deficits of poverty-area children "in order to break the poverty cycle." They knew that systematic behaviors in special preschools, institutions, and behavioral laboratories had been successful. They proposed that similar techniques be used in a poverty-area community. It was their goal to teach parents better behavior management techniques, to set up preschool programs that would result in rapid acquisition of language, to develop powerful classroom remediation procedures to overcome education deficits and reduce school dropouts and delinquency, and to increase good family health practices.

The Parent Cooperative Preschool

Todd Risley and Betty Hart soon started a parent cooperative preschool operation. Mothers from the community brought their children to the community center building in the Juniper Gardens housing project each day to learn basic skills and to prepare them for similar work in the public schools. The mothers themselves learned how to teach their own children and how to encourage children to learn new words and how to write numbers and letters. The curriculum was a sequence of 150 daily lessons developed by the project staff. Lessons included training in colors, numbers, matching, rhyming, size, and recall. The mothers were observed by the staff and taught to use praise and encouragement to motivate their children to learn rather than nagging and threatening them when they made errors or misbehaved.

The program later came under the direction of Donald Bushell of the Department of Human Development at the University of Kansas and his colleagues, including Gene Ramp. It provided the prototype program for Bushell's long-running behavior analysis follow-through model, which produced academic gains for low-income school children in public schools across the nation.

Preschool Research Programs

Risley and Hart also started an experimental preschool in the basement of Pleasant Green Baptist Church and later in Turner House, the building constructed by the Episcopal Dioceses of Kansas. The experimental preschool at Turner House focused on language development in young children. The program was to be a prime language research program involving mothers and children in their homes in a sophisticated analysis of the spoken language interaction histories of young children and their family members. The data collected formed the Juniper Gardens home-language database, one of the largest and most comprehensive of its kind anywhere in the country.

A strand of the research and training programs at the Juniper Gardens Project over the years dealt with preschool-aged children. Initially headed by Betty Hart and Todd Risley, numerous programs were developed for improving learning opportunities for children in Head Start and day-care centers that could be carried out by paraprofessionals. Hart and Risley with their staff, many of whom were recruited from the Juniper Gardens neighborhood, investigated the development of language in inner-city poverty-area children. They pioneered a number of procedures, including "incidental teaching" for increasing language usage and teaching verbal skills to youngsters.

In addition to the continuing work of Betty Hart, in later years, Judith Carta, Charles Greenwood, Jane Atwater, and Ilene Schwartz developed ecobehavioral assessment strategies for evaluating preschool programs. These strategies are employed to examine interactions among classroom environmental variables, teacher variables, and student behaviors to determine the specific aspects of early intervention programs that differentially affect students' later development. They also examine the effects of preschool-based interventions on later successes in kindergarten and first grade.

The After-School Remedial Program

Working in the basement of the Pleasant Green Baptist Church, Montrose Wolf established an after-school remedial program. Through cooperation with the local school system, Wolf was able to assemble a group of fifth-grade children who were underachievers. Students in this experimental group had been getting "D" grades before coming to the after-school remedial program. The children came to the remedial class for 3 hours each day and during the school year the class average rose to "C." The early research demonstrated that inner-city students could be motivated to improve their grades and school achievement using procedures that structured the environment to reward them for academic efforts and achievement. Wolf also established a token reinforcement classroom for high school dropouts. These projects provided the basis for the well-known Achievement Place programs and the teaching family model for motivating predelinquent youth in foster home settings. In this model, teaching parents used systematic reinforcement procedures to teach social and academic skills needed for young men and women to become successful citizens. The project was later refined and implemented in over 100 different locations in the United States.

Public Schools Research

Vance Hall began working directly in the community public schools teaching teachers how to use reinforcement principles in the classroom instruction. It was there that he developed and evaluated the responsive teaching model. Hall had been a public school principal in Washington state before obtaining his PhD. He was familiar with the problems that principals faced and he saw the development and extension of operant conditioning techniques as a possible solution to many of the discipline and motivation problems plaguing students and teachers. With modifications by Jasper Harris and Herb Rieth, the responsive teaching model was packaged to help teachers and other school staff learn to use systematic consequences and objectively observe and measure behavior. The responsive teaching model was widely replicated across the country.

A second continuing strand of research and training since the earliest years focused on working with principals, teachers, parents, and paraprofessionals within the public schools. This strand initiated by Vance Hall, and later headed by Charles R. Greenwood and Joseph Delquadri, included their colleagues, Carmen Arreaga-Mayer, Jane Atwater, Judith Carta, Marleen Elliott, Debra Kamps, Barbara Terry, Ilene Schwartz, and Dale Walker. In the early years at Juniper Gardens, the school research focused on helping teachers and principals use systematic consequences to decrease disruptive behavior and increase attending in the classroom. Some of these studies showed that teachers could decrease classroom disruptions if they systematically attended to appropriate rather than inappropriate behavior of pupils.

With refinements provided by Marilyn Clark Hall, the responsive teaching model became the responsive parenting model in which over 3,000 parents were trained locally and nationwide to observe and measure their children's behavior and to use systematic consequences natural to the home in order to teach children skills in a nonpunitive way.

Home visitor programs designed initially to train parents as paraprofessionals sought to teach parents simple aspects of behavior analysis. Parents learned to observe child behavior, employ differential attention to strengthen or weaken specific behaviors, and employ home-based tutoring procedures. However, because the home visitors found themselves often helping parents solve everyday problems (e.g., a housing problem), in addition to assisting parents with their child's behavior problems, this program eventually grew into the group-based Program for Women's Survival Skills developed by Linda Thurston and her colleagues. Women were trained in skills designed to make them more employable and to assist them in budgeting and child management. It also served to end the isolation of many women in the community. This program was used by area businesses to increase the productivity of employees and it continues in a number of states, most notably in Kansas, Missouri, Iowa, and Texas. The program has been used in centers for battered women and in community service agencies, alternative schools, and the public welfare system. In Texas, the program is part of their welfare reform package.

Health Interventions

A fourth strand of research concerned child and family health. During the early years, the Juniper Gardens project sponsored a well-child health clinic headed by Alice Marsh of the Kansas University Medical Center (KUMC) and coordinated by social worker Mary Wilkins. Marsh and Wilkins developed flexible scheduling and other innovations to increase the well-child clinic use by poverty-area mothers. Juniper Gardens Children's Project investigators, including Edward Christopherson and Michael Rapoff, developed procedures to improve the prenatal care for the teenage mothers whose babies are at increased risk for handicapping conditions. Their procedures also focused on increasing medical compliance in children (including diabetics) whose health was endangered if they failed to follow instructions in medication and dieting. They also sought to decrease the incidence of dangerous behaviors in the home and accidents, which are the number one cause of death and injury in young children, especially those from poverty areas.

The Continuing Mission of Juniper Gardens

The success of the Juniper Gardens Children's Project has been based on a continually changing model or series of models. The program has never become static or bureaucratic. The early investigators demonstrated that behavior analysis procedures could improve language, preacademic, and academic skills and could result in improved health status and academic achievement. They demonstrated that poverty-area parents could learn better methods for teaching their own children and could become more effective managers of behavior. Nevertheless, the Juniper Gardens staff in those early years came to realize that the mission they had set out to accomplish was much more complex and would take much longer than they anticipated. That is why the mission of Juniper Gardens in 1990 remained largely the same as it was when the project began.

The project has developed systems and procedures for increasing children's use of language, for helping teachers and parents to better manage behavior, for improving compliance with medical treatment, and for implementing systems to improve social behavior. The staff is also engaged in finding ways to ensure that the intervention programs have an ongoing and lasting influence on the lives of the community's parents and children.

Although Wolf and his colleagues demonstrated how to remediate delinquent behaviors over the short term, they also discovered that remediating them over a lifetime is much more difficult. It is necessary to explore alternative programs that will follow youths at risk on into adulthood and provide the support network they need in their jobs, marriages, and in rearing of their own children after they are no longer members of a group home. We have learned that achieving these outcomes will require changes not only in family members but also within institutional systems as well.

Work in public school classrooms demonstrated that even though we could teach teachers better ways to manage classroom behaviors, the results did not necessarily maintain and did not always result in improved academic achievement or schoolwide adoption. Therefore, it has been necessary to develop better strategies, better methods of analysis, better teaching procedures, and more powerful means of intervening.

Thus, the mission of Juniper Gardens remains very much the same as it was when the project began. The staff now realizes that it takes much more than simple systematic reinforcement systems to bring about the changes necessary to affect the life outcomes of children born in poverty. Although necessary, reinforcement procedures alone are not sufficient solutions. It takes long-term, ongoing systems if important change is to occur. The beauty of Juniper Gardens and some of its off-shoots is that such long-term development and implementation have been possible. It has taken the unique cooperation of members of the community, the project staff, the support of the University of Kansas, and various federal funding agencies, all of whom have seen the necessity of continuing to help children from a hard-core poverty area.

The Juniper Gardens Children's Project has carried out research studies to demonstrate that behavioral and learning deficits could be overcome in individual children and in entire preschool and public school classrooms. The analysis of problems and the approach to intervention now reflect sophistication based on this prior experience. Through longitudinal studies of individuals and groups, we are demonstrating that these procedures can be carried out on a larger and grander scale. We developed systems for training and monitoring large numbers of teachers so that effective practices can be implemented on a schoolwide or a districtwide basis. New projects have emerged from year to year. New community laboratory sites have been found and incorporated into the project. The project has become the center of professional careers of young investigators who continue to explore and implement better developmental outcomes for children and families.

In 1988, Vance Hall submitted a history of his 23 years of work as director of the Juniper Gardens Children's Project. This submission was prepared in conjunction with his retirement from the University of Kansas and the Juniper Gardens Children's Project. His carefully prepared information included sections on preschool programs, parent training programs, and public school programs. In addition, he included sections on the impact of Juniper Gardens Children's Project research, publications, and presentations at professional meetings, training services for children, incidental training of Juniper Gardens employees, and training at professional levels. He explained that the staff productivity was augmented by neighborhood friends, by colleagues in the schools, by the University of Kansas, by the State of Kansas, and by several funding agencies. The collaborative information was truly impressive. Also the accompanying summary of the impact of the Juniper Gardens Children's Project speaks for itself.

Impact of Juniper Gardens Children's Project

Estimates of children affected 1965–1986
    Directly through intervention: 7,463
    Indirectly through training of teachers, parents, paraprofessionals: 361
Trainers of paraprofessionals: 92
Parents trained: 5,841
Professionals trained
    Teachers: 1,223
    Master's degrees: 91
    PhD degrees: 86
    Postdoctoral trainees: 22
    Other students: 17
Persons from community who worked at Juniper Gardens, improved
    skills, and went on to better paying jobs: 161
Number of publications in professional journals, chapters in books,
    and training manuals: 354

At virtually the same time, Charles Greenwood, who was due to replace Hall as director of the Juniper Gardens Chilren's Project, prepared a manuscript detailing "the longitudinal affects of classwide peer tutoring." He shared the authorship of the work with Joseph Delquadri and Vance Hall. Along with this summative report was a letter addressed to Dr. David L. Lusk, superintendent of Kansas City and Kansas Public Schools:

April 29, 1988
Dr. David L. Lusk
Superintendent, Kansas City Kansas, District #500
625 Minnesota, Kansas City, Kansas 66101

Re: Summative Progress Report on the Juniper Gardens *Classwide Peer Tutoring Longitudinal Study* Implemented in the District During the Period 1983–1987.

Dear Dr. Lusk:

Please find enclosed a summative report on this Project for you and your staff. I have also sent copies of the report to the Principals whose building faculties participated. We are intending to submit this report for publication to either the *Journal of Educational Psychology* or the *Elementary Education Journal*.

In brief, we found that after four years, the Chapter 1 experimental group students whose teachers implemented our Classwide Peer Tutoring Program in Grades 1 through 4 approached the 50th percentile National Norm on the Metropolitan Achievement Test Battery with Subtests in Reading, Mathematics, and Language. In comparison, the Chapter 1 control group performed significantly below this level in the 30th percentile range. Achievement effects of this magnitude appear to be quite large compared to other studies of effective teaching practices in the literature that we reviewed. The report further describes the levels of tutoring implementation achieved by experimental group teachers, changes in classroom process variables we observed, such as tutoring effects on student's academic engagement, and time devoted to academic and nonacademic subject matter. We are very pleased with the results and I expect that we will produce two additional reports from this study for publication.

Two years ago, I made a presentation to the Board on the results at that time. I would like now to request an opportunity before the end of the school year to provide the Board with a summary of the overall results, if possible.

I am also pleased to tell you that our recent application for funds to conduct a follow-up study of the students in this study (now in Grade 5) has been funded by the National Institute of Child Health and Human Development (NICHD). Two years ago I was asked by Board members about a follow-up study and at that time I told them we intended to submit a proposal for such a study. This new project will allow us to conduct follow-up assessments of these students during their middle school years. Thus, I'm certain the Board will be pleased to hear that it has been supported. I will shortly forward this new proposal to you and your staff so that we may begin discussions that may eventually lead to beginning this work during the 1988/89 school year.

Thank you for your continued interest and support.

Sincerely,

Charles R. Greenwood, PhD
Research Director

Cc: Dr. Don Moritz, Dr. William Beckley, Dr. Walter Davies, Dr. James Jarrett, Dr. Lowell Alexander, Dr. Joe Delquadri, Dr. R. Vance Hall, Dr. Richard Schiefelbusch

This information provides an obvious prediction of continuing productivity for the Juniper Gardens Children's Project. Further historical accounts will reveal how fully this prediction has been fulfilled.

In addition to the peer tutoring work in the schools, Charles Greenwood soon began to plan and develop other community laboratories for experimental studies. For instance, he is creating new models for promoting urban children's mental health: accessible, effective, and sustainable school-based mental health services. These and other projects are described and discussed in part II, which details the continuing history of the Institute for Life Span Studies from 1990 to 2006.

7

Projects of the Kansas Mental Retardation Research Center

RICHARD L. SCHIEFELBUSCH

This chapter examines the growth of the Mental Retardation Research Center (MRRC) up to 1990. The MRRC and the Kansas University Affiliated Facility (UAF) (see chapter 8) are presented in the same time frame. Upon completion of the UAF building, the program was ready to begin and the UAF became the Kansas University Affiliated Program (UAP). At the end of chapters 7 and 8, we consider a special group of projects that maintained their growth and have since become centers within the Institute for Life Span Studies (LSI). Those projects form a portion of the continuing LSI substance. In part II, Stephen Schroeder discusses these activities as they developed (1990–2006) under his leadership.

Background

The MRRC has from its beginning been a broadly based, multidisciplinary program of research and research training for students and staff conducting research in developmental disabilities. Likewise, the UAP has fostered supporting projects devoted to designing and implementing better services.

Not all these projects fit into a specific time frame. Projects often overlapped into both the MRRC and the UAP. Many projects that were part of the MRRC were not directly funded by the MRRC center grants. Many were quickly completed. Some continued for years, going through several cycles of reapplication and refunding. Others continue today, and there are many that continue under different names or themes. They adapted to changing problems and different funding priorities.

The research program (MRRC) and the clinical program (UAP) emerged as investigators in the Kansas setting accepted dual roles as scientists and technologists. The programs drew on improved scientific knowledge to provide data and technical assistance in areas where such support was nonexistent, incomplete, or inadequate. The Kansas program incorporated the skills and knowledge of behavioral scientists, speech clinicians, audiologists, special educators, linguists, psychologists, biologists, and other specialists and generalists in a systematized, cooperative, and functional manner. There were few places in the United States where such a diverse concentration of disciplines attempted to integrate methodologies in basic sciences, education, and training. With a continuing and expanding emphasis on biological and psychobiological research, the MRRC developed an increasingly progressive and comprehensive approach to solving or ameliorating developmental problems.

That investment in Kansas led the way to systematic, procedural attacks on a number of developmental problems. The professional staff developed systems that incorporated many different disciplines and experimental approaches. Their sustained investments resulted in a significant number of valuable products for persons who worked to improve the lives of persons with developmental disabilities. Along the road there were dozens of exemplary programs that contributed to the training of children and adults, with and without disabilities. Such programs often served as models for other centers and projects outside Kansas.

To establish a center capable of producing effective products, MRRC administrators developed approaches to problems common to the various units within the MRRC, while also encouraging each setting to strengthen those features unique to it. This included constructing novel laboratory equipment and instrumentation for the control of experimental variables. Such equipment was often a requirement of a number of investigators at each setting. Researchers also developed procedures that generalized to the natural environments of the settings. Partners in the research efforts were the clinical and community programs in which the results of research could be tested and applied.

Behavior Analysis

The staff of the MRRC excluded no approach and no reasonable technique in working with children. Any method or precept that seemed effective was tried and used in the environment of the Kansas setting. The most productive and most functional general tool was the analysis of behavior or positive reinforcement. Many behavioral scientists in the Kansas setting developed sophisticated reinforcement systems to produce measurable and desirable changes in the deficient or defective behaviors of children who were disadvantaged and developmentally disabled. New developments in basic behavioral research were translated into programs of applied research to clearly demonstrate improved learning, educational achievement, and appropriate behavior in disadvantaged and institutionalized children. The technology employed was essentially one of action for progress. Rather than define what the problems were, put them in categories, and write articles about what was wrong with the child, the researchers and clinicians in the MRRC concentrated on what was wrong with the child's environment and what could be done to reshape it into a plan to stimulate and contribute to the child's learning process. These tools and techniques were then placed in the hands of workers who learned to apply the precise principles to change deficient behaviors.

In 1965, when the MRRC planning began, the behavioral analysis paradigm had been adapted to a range of research activity, much of which was "applied," hence the term *applied behavior analysis* (ABA). The more familiar term at that time was *experimental analysis of behavior*. The two terms were intended to characterize the activities in the same general manner that *basic* and *applied* were used by psychologists to designate laboratory science as contrasted with clinical procedures. ABA research was often placed somewhere outside the field of basic science. It is no wonder then that some observers were skeptical that the emerging work would achieve the distinction of *important* research. In response to this, Don Baer, Montrose Wolf, and Todd Risley, who had recently joined the Kansas group at the University of Kansas (KU) and at Juniper Gardens, founded the *Journal of Applied Behavior Analysis* in

1968. For the first several years, they took turns editing it. A rich and varied literature soon emerged. Shortly thereafter, *Psychology Today* published a substantial report declaring that Kansas was the world's leader in Applied Behavior Analysis. This, of course, was only one major event in a continuing debate among behavioral and cognitive scientists for many years. The central question of the debate was, "Is ABA productive research?" This question in some form or context confronted the Bureau of Child Research (BCR) group at site visits, grant reviews, discussion panels at national organization meetings, and academic seminars across the country.

Throughout this period of controversy, which extends, in limited ways, up to the present, it has been essential to maintain that behavior analysis is a scientific system. In the beginning, when the work at Parsons was considered to be suspect (by many of our professional colleagues) it was essential to demonstrate how explicit and rigorous the behavior analytic system really was.

Another major controversy emerged between behavioral and cognitive psychologists over the merits of explicit data that had not been organized within cognitive theory. This controversy was also active in discussions with linguists about our language data. It was most often a battle between the followers of Chomsky (linguist) and Skinner (behaviorist). It is safe to say that neither group won the debate, but the discussions were good for both sides.

At this point it should be acknowledged that the early Kansas Center group had three significant credibility problems: 1) behaviorism, 2) language intervention, and 3) mental retardation. In the initial grant application, submitted in 1957, there was a bold statement of intent to teach language and communication to children with mental retardation living in an institution. Furthermore, the intent was to alter the environment and the programs of the institution to further this objective. It soon became clear that behavioral analysis was the method of choice. In retrospect it is clear that our initial plan placed our research products outside the academic and research worlds of cognitive psychology and linguistics. The very lively controversies that followed were difficult for all concerned. These challenges were extended to research planning, site visits, journal and book editing, and grant reviews. The methods of choice were *applied behavior analysis* and *language inter-*

vention with children who are mentally retarded. The issues that pertain to each of these terms appeared frequently in accounts of our methods and products.

Of course, we were really studying the social (interpersonal) behavior of children who had limited repertoires for responding to adult scientists or clinicians. More specifically, we were studying the changes that specific reinforcers had on behavior. Better yet, we were seeking to determine whether specific reinforcers could be used to change the behaviors of children. The latter could be regarded as the true beginning of our work at Parsons. (Robert Hoyt and Joe Spradlin have presented an excellent description of our early and continuing behavioral analytic work in chapter 3.)

The best remembered of the early projects at Parsons was the Mimosa Cottage Project. It attracted attention from various groups interested in the deinstitutionalization of both children and adults with mental retardation. Montrose Wolf and his colleagues at Juniper Gardens also used ABA to design a foster environment for delinquent and predelinquent children known as Achievement Place. A brief description of the Mimosa Cottage Project follows. A description of Achievement Place is provided in the section on Juniper Gardens.

The Parsons Research Center

The Parsons Research Center quickly became a creative, interactive system of shared activity in which aides, nurses, and other care staff members joined with the research staff in pilot studies on selected problems, such as self-care, recreation, and other daily activities. Such activities served several purposes for the children, the staff, and the scientists. For instance, Joe Spradlin was an active participant in designing an eating program and a bathing program for children with severe developmental delays. Also, a Journal Club was formed to encourage any and all participants to prepare "working papers" for discussion and possible publication. Many of these papers are still available in the archives at the Parson's State Hospital and Training Center (PSHTC). In the following pages, several of the larger and more significant research projects are presented. A sizable number of the young staff members at the PSHTC attained advanced academic degrees under the tutelage of Parsons researchers.

While they were attending to the early stages of their academic work, they were also a part of the research of the Parsons setting. These activities provided valuable background for the subsequent project on research training (see section on research training).

Mimosa Cottage

The Mimosa Cottage Project at PSHTC was a pioneering effort of Fred Girardeau's to design a homelike atmosphere based on a token reinforcement system. Mimosa Cottage became a nationally known demonstration project where severely retarded, institutionalized girls learned independent living skills. As an example of the cooperation between KU and PSHTC, Mimosa Cottage was begun as a combined research endeavor. It became a national model for a token reinforcement system to train adolescent, severely retarded girls in personal skills, social skills, educational skills, and occupational skills. The girls learned how to care for themselves, how to get along socially in the outside world, how to read and write, and how to make change and to do their own shopping. They were specifically trained for employment so they could contribute to their own support once they left the institution.

The system supported the academic and social development of the girls and allowed many of them to progress to the point at which they were able to live and work outside the institution. The Mimosa Cottage Project became a model for similar training environments in other institutions in other states (Lent, LeBlanc, & Spradlin, 1970).

MESH

Model Education for the Severely Handicapped (MESH) began as a project for developing total programming to provide children with severe disabilities with adequate educational programs within the public schools of Parsons, Kansas. The project served a student population of children from the PSHTC and from the community, all diagnosed as having severe or profound disabilities. The activities included a comprehensive language and communications program and a number of practical educational and vocational programs. It was probably the first zero reject program in the state.

A particularly important aspect of this project was the development of a mechanical reading program and an expectancy concept known as "Tinker toys to TV sets." Beginning with the mechanical reading program, the student was taught to "read" figures and drawings in a task sequence, such that he or she learned to prepare foods, or complete complex vocational tasks, by "reading" the picture sequence in flip-books. Initially, the student was taught by match-to-sample techniques to recognize objects in front of him or her.

Next, the child learned "mechanical reading" for assembling such objects (i.e., Tinker toy parts). This training advanced to other skills, such as assembling nine-part bicycle brakes and electronic units such as signal generators and circuit boards. Trainees eventually learned to assemble complete items, including television sets and whole bicycles. The project staff demonstrated that the individual diagnosed as severely disabled was limited foremost by what we "expect" he or she can do. His or her potential is always considerably more. The mechanical reading program provided the person with severe disabilities with a significant new structure to reach that potential. Because the stimulus came from the task books, rather than verbal instructions from the trainer, the student could recall the procedure independent of assistance by merely taking the procedure book from the shelf.

Another project that evolved from MESH was the development and marketing of the Parsons Visual Acuity Test, the first commercially available tool for testing students who were unable to perform on standard visual screening tests. Other accomplishments were methods for teaching health fitness and the use of assistive technology. This last project established a comprehensive activity system that has become the largest in the LSI. All of these and others were established by Charles Spellman and his colleagues, whose work is explained further in part II, chapter 26.

Audiology and Language Research

Researchers at Parsons soon developed techniques for testing the hearing responses of children who were nonverbal and unresponsive to spoken instructions. All these fields or project areas included graduate training programs. Students worked side by side with professional researchers in conducting research projects and in preparing findings for publication.

Early researchers developed precise audiometric evaluation procedures that produced exact hearing assessments for persons unable to respond in traditional audiometric evaluations. Robert Fulton, Joseph Spradlin, and Lyle Lloyd developed precise audiometric evaluation procedures for hearing assessments for persons who were unable to respond in traditional audiometric evaluations. For the first time it was possible to evaluate the hearing of persons with severe retardation and to fit them with hearing aids designed to compensate for their particular hearing deficiencies. Precise hearing evaluations and resulting hearing devices meant that persons with disabilities no longer needed to have their other problems compounded by deficient hearing.

Audiometric programs developed at PSHTC were some of the most advanced in the country. Many children who are retarded also have associated disabilities that interfere with their learning and communication processes. This is especially true of hearing problems. Because many children with retardation do not respond to verbal or vocal stimuli, it is very difficult to assess their hearing capabilities. Operant techniques were used to condition children to respond to auditory cues by pressing a button upon receiving a signal through a headset or bone-conduction device.

A hearing disability impairs intellectual growth and development and may cause a hearing-impaired child with nearly normal intelligence to be committed to an institution for mental retardation. A deaf child who may be capable of learning may be committed to an institution because of severe behavior problems associated with an inability to respond to spoken directions. Once committed to an institution and denied adequate stimuli for normal growth and development, many in fact do become functionally retarded.

For children who are retarded, advances in the science of audiology have made it possible to provide better training and evaluation. It was possible through the use of basic operant procedures to teach even children with severe retardation to make auditory discriminations. That opened a whole new training area for such children and allowed their participation in programs previously considered too complex for them. Once a subject was systematically trained to respond, by being brought under stimulus-response control, a variety of tests could be administered. Such a training program can be a basic key to training in other forms of communication (Fulton & Lloyd, 1975).

Language Training and Demonstration

Extensive demonstration programs for language training have been an enduring part of the regular program of the MRRC and the BCR. These programs include research in the basic communications process and extend through the whole range of language and communications problems to include the clinical application of newly developed language programs inside and outside clinical environments. The strength of the Parsons Research Center was traditionally communication projects in speech, language, auditory training and assessment, and environmental influence on communications. The systematic integration of the components into one coordinated program for clinical management of children with severe communication disabilities was accomplished through the Clinical Center for Communications Research. The project provided children diagnosed as severely and profoundly mentally retarded with intensive training in auditory processing, language reception, speech production, and expressive language. The project gave total day care coordinated with other formal communications training. Data were gathered in both formal training environments and day-care programs for the study and quantification of the interactions between these components. These data were used to generate an integrated, data-based program of clinical management, as well as to suggest new areas of additional research directly applicable to clinical processes. (The work was initiated by Ross Copeland and later expanded and modified by James McLean and several colleagues.)

Research Mediation

A full-blown, U.S. Office of Education-funded, research mediation project to develop and disseminate improved instructional technology for children with disabilities began on the grounds of PSHTC. Project MORE (mediated operational research for education) developed instructional programs to overcome specific behavioral deficits among children with disabilities. The instructional programs were empirically validated; organized through the application of systems technology; implemented by optimal, multimedia materials; and disseminated in a way to assure immediate application in educational environments by virtue of their systematic nature and their multimedia format. The mediation project was developed and managed by Barbara McLean and James Lent.

In addition to Project MORE, researchers in the Parsons Research Center contributed to tangible products relevant to deinstitutionalization by changing patterns in community services and education strategies. One program resulted in a nonspeech symbol system, which allowed children with retardation to communicate without spoken speech and language.

Psychobiological Investigations of Auditory Processes

Extended efforts in psychobiological investigations of auditory processes provided a greatly increased potential for correlating behavioral performances in auditory processing with anatomical differences in brain structure. The first study established the hearing differences among mammals and then correlated the results to various morphological parameters reflecting the selective pressures operating in the evolution of the various hearing abilities. This research thrust, coupled with a second study in ablation-behavioral analyses of specific auditory abilities and their relationship to various areas of auditory cortex, generated definitive data regarding the relationships between brain structure and certain specific auditory processes. A third study included initial work comparing intensive behavioral data on the performances of children with severe retardation on certain auditory processing tasks to the brain tomograms obtained on these children by CT scans. The pilot data provided atypical tomograms on two of six children with severely deficient auditory processing performances.

Nonspeech Communication

This project began at PSHTC and later moved to the Kansas Neurological Institute (KNI). It was developed to study ways of using nonspeech responses to teach communication. The project investigated the utility of nonspeech (visually displayed) responses for teaching communications skills. The project utilized the carefully designed and explicitly defined training programs in a nonspeech language initiation program (non-SLIP). The programs were effective with many low-level, retarded children with whom other management tactics had failed.

The specific aims of this project included: 1) determining the function of the nonspeech response mode in clinical management of children with severe communications disabilities; 2) determining the most effective and efficient tactics for bringing about transfer of linguistic rules from a nonspeech to a spoken symbol system; 3) determining the effect of an internal shaping procedure on memory; 4) determining the reliability and validity of a statistical procedure for establishing criterion levels; and 5) comparing the effects of different types of stimuli on training.

The several programs in the non-SLIP system consisted of step-by-step procedures for teaching children linguistic rules without requiring that they also emit spoken responses. The children used geometric forms of various shapes as words and morphemes. They learned to select appropriate forms and to arrange them in a response tray as if writing sentences. The data indicated that these programs and this approach were successful with many children with severe and profound retardation. This finding was particularly significant because children from such populations have traditionally been considered poor candidates for language training.

Non-SLIP required no speech from a child with disabilities. Instead, the child learned to say "tree" by picking up the geometric form for "tree" and placing it on a tray in front of him or her. From such beginnings, the training radiated to noun–verb–noun structures and more complex sentences, while still requiring only the simpler motor skill of placing the forms on the sentence tray. Thus the pattern of communication was greatly simplified. This made communication, and therefore learning, more accessible to the disabled and nonverbal person. A training film was produced to demonstrate this work, and a kit was produced commercially for a broader application. Joseph Carrier developed the non-SLIP system.

The results of this work contributed significantly to the effectiveness of the nonspeech programs already in existence and also had implications for work with other types of communication disabilities and for teaching in general. It was estimated that there were approximately 130,000 children in this country who could benefit from an effective and easy-to-use nonspeech communications training program. This program of research was featured on the front page of the *New York Times* and the *New York Times Magazine*.

Communication and Language Behavior

A study area called "Applications of Sociolinguistic Constructs to Communication and Language Behavior Among Severely Mentally Retarded Populations" provided new knowledge about the human organism and made definitive analyses of the effects of retarding conditions on these organisms. The behavioral performances of persons classified as severely retarded are of great concern to professionals in human development and mental retardation. One need only have a cursory experience with persons labeled severely mentally retarded to appreciate that there is great heterogeneity in the behaviors of individuals within that group, and that such heterogeneity is poorly represented in the programs and the treatment environments provided for them.

Similarly, it takes only minimal experience with persons with severe mental retardation to recognize that there are extreme variations in the qualitative nature of these persons' interactions with other humans. Attention to, and commerce with, other human occupants of the environment is an extremely important variable in the prognosis and treatment of individuals with severe retardation.

It was the contention of a group of investigators at Parsons that the levels of important social commerce between persons with severe retardation and other human occupants of their environment could be well defined and measured by the application of several taxonomies for analyzing language forms and communicative acts identified in developmental sociolinguistic research. For example, taxonomies concerned with definition of the functions of human communicative acts would be highly useful in this context. Similarly, the dimensions that classify levels of intent-to-communicate to other humans are also highly productive in the analysis of interactive performances by persons with severe retardation.

Such information was used in determining the social treatment targets and contexts to be applied to various individuals and groups of persons with severe retardation. Such data were also useful in analyzing and evaluating the relative responsiveness of treatment and living environments.

Deinstitutionalization

The focus of the programs of the MRRC was to integrate disadvantaged and developmentally disabled children into natural environments that had frequently rejected them. This concept has sometimes been referred to as deinstitutionalization. Children with retardation and delinquent children had for years been prime candidates for institutions. Traditional institutions of reform or custodial care have too often contributed more to the perpetuation of the problems than to their solutions. Thus the MRRC scientists aimed for the ultimate development of a technology for re-educating children with developmental disabilities in homes and schools and communities rather than in institutions. Not only was the public saved the additional tax burden caused by residential care, but also the children who would have been institutionalized had an opportunity to live fuller and more productive lives in more natural settings.

This research and demonstration program was derived from its thoughtful and productive study and utilization of parents and community organizations and resources and produced gains for children and their parents and for the community. As the effectiveness of the programs developed in Kansas become better known, and as more citizens became aware of the applications of the technology, programs were extended into social and commercial operations much as they had been utilized in the more controlled situations of education and training. Again, it was most significant that the behavioral techniques developed in the Kansas setting came to be used by ordinary people for public benefit.

Almost all of the visible and vocal leaders of the deinstitutionalization movement came from places other than laboratories. They represented parents' groups, legislators, religious and human rights groups, legal action groups, and various advocacy groups. Their preoccupation was with the human rights features of the movement. The realism of scientists in the nascent Kansas Center focused on the feasibility of teaching self-help skills, functional language skills, and adaptive responses to persons in circumstances encountered in daily living. It soon became apparent that children in institutions could learn substantial new skills.

Thus, the early Kansas scientists and their colleagues across the nation provided the vehicle on which the deinstitutionalization movement rode into the headlines to change the way thousands of Americans with disabilities were living at that time.

The University of Kansas Campus

The MRRC literally brought research in developmental disabilities to the KU campus. Fortunately, the MRRC was preceded by the Parsons Research Project that provided funds to renovate a building on the outskirts of the campus for a sizable number of research personnel who occupied the building shortly before the MRRC was funded. These personnel subsequently filled key roles in the Department of Human Development, the Juniper Gardens Children's Project, and the MRRC, although they did not know about the last involvement when they came to Kansas from the University of Washington. So, much of the strength of the MRRC at KU was recruited prior to 1969 when the John T. Stewart Children's Center (the Children's Wing of Haworth Hall) was completed. By this time research projects were well established in Juniper Gardens and the Department of Human Development.

The Department of Special Education and the Department of Speech and Hearing were also provided space in the Children's Wing. It was the first reasonably adequate space that either department had ever had. Thus, three departments that were soon to play important roles in the new center were provided reasonably adequate space in functional relationship to each other. Also, fortunately, each was situated in functional relationship to the office suite of the Bureau of Child Research. So, for the first time there was a nucleus for a combined center!

The following sections discuss several projects and programs that evolved. Much of the productivity evolved in interactive designs that are difficult to describe, so there is no sequential format in the reporting here; instead, the productive units are presented as a cluster. Some of these programs are discussed in more detail in other chapters.

International Program

In 1970 the chancellor of the University of Kansas signed an agreement for an international program between KU and the Inter-American

Children's Institute. The agreement laid the foundation for an extensive cooperative program between KU, its Bureau of Child Research, and the Inter-American Children's Institute. The program included working exchange visits by MRRC staff members to teach in various Latin American countries. Similarly, professionals from Latin America traveled to the United States to share their knowledge and to participate in ongoing programs in the MRRC. Films were produced in Spanish for Latin American consumption, and professionals in Latin America made Spanish translations of the work of Kansas' researchers for use there.

Graduate students in academic departments and in the center at KU arranged with student colleagues in two universities in Mexico to exchange visits and to present their research products (usually behavioral data) from areas of common interest. These events took place for several years in the late 1960s and early 1970s. The spirit of these events is still maintained by Joe Spradlin, who is regularly invited to give a workshop at a university in Brasilia, the capital of Brazil. Currently, Mabel Rice maintains a research program with colleagues at the University of Perth in Western Australia. Beyond these international activities it is apparent that web sites and the Internet opened many opportunities for research exchanges and possible collaborations with other countries.

The BCR has also worked through The Partners of the Americas, an independent organization, to assist our partner (Paraguay) in developing preschool and day care centers. It has also contributed books, educational methods, and materials. The most extensive efforts, however, resulted in a revision of their nationwide plan for special education. Conchita Augelli and Dick Schiefelbusch worked with representatives of several agencies of the Paraguayan government in this endeavor. This work was completed by 1981.

More recently, Judy LeBlanc worked with her colleague, Liliana Mayo, in developing Centro Ann Sullivan del Peru (also known as CASP) in Lima, Peru. Today CASP is an international award-winning demonstration, training, and investigation model center where over 300 people of different abilities and their families are educated annually. Eight programs in different parts of the world actively follow the educational model of CASP. These endeavors were greatly aided by Stephen Schroeder and members of his family who organized a fiscal and an administrative support system for long-term development.

Juniper Gardens Children's Project

The Juniper Gardens Children's Project (JGCP) indirectly sprang from the early work in applied behavior analysis at PSHTC. The linkage was provided by Fred Girardeau who had moved to the KU Medical Center (KUMC) shortly after the program project (Language and Communication of the Mentally Retarded) was announced. His work, and the work of Norris Haring, Herbert Miller, and Dick Schiefelbusch, in 1963 established a presence in the Northeast District of Kansas City, Kansas. Their work, and the surprising interest and assistance of staff personnel at the National Institute of Child Health and Human Development in Washington, D.C., led to a supplement to the program project in 1964, forming a continuing link between Parsons and the emerging Juniper Gardens research team. The result of this liaison was the formation of behavioral research systems similar to those that had already been developed at Parsons. Researchers in the Juniper Gardens community worked in the schools and helped parents become more effective in home instruction and in managing problem behaviors. That work soon became prominent with children and families living in conditions of poverty, developmental disability, and educational delays. The JGCP gained a national reputation and is still active in the same area of northeast Kansas City, Kansas. The project includes language training programs for preschool children, training programs for parents, assistance to local public school teachers in the management of problem behaviors, and participation in community organizations to improve the condition of an economically deprived neighborhood in an urban metropolitan area.

The JGCP is a nationally known setting for research in economic deprivation. The early work was portrayed in a film "Spearhead at Juniper Gardens." Although the surface character of the project has undergone significant changes during the past few years, the focus of the project still remains as research into the developmental factors for children from depriving environments. The concentration is still on procedures and strategies for preventing and remediating learning and social deficits.

The responsive teaching (RT) model, which evolved from research in that setting, came to be applied in one form or another in the schools in nearly every state in the nation. The RT model was a scientific behavior management system applied in home, school, and other settings to remediate the problem behaviors of children with and without disabilities.

The Juniper Gardens staff has continued the development of the RT model for training parents and teachers to increase appropriate social and academic behavior of children. Research has indicated that children with developmental disabilities can be more effectively taught if teachers and parents reward them with their attention and with privileges when they behave appropriately. Parent training has been an important focus of JGCP programs.

Achievement Place

An offshoot of the early behavioral research from the Juniper Gardens Children's Project led to Achievement Place and the development of a "teaching-parent" system that placed couples trained in behavior management in a home-based living arrangement. Predelinquent boys (and later girls) lived in the Achievement Place homes under a point system based on school performance and home behavior that helped them gain control of their own problems. The system was subsequently implemented in homes all over the United States, and became the primary model for group-home systems in Boys Town in Omaha, Nebraska. The original home model was generalized to various environments to include girls as well as boys. The home featured applied behavior analysis in the treatment of adolescents with demonstrated problem behaviors that put them in danger of being incarcerated.

The approach to the treatment of juvenile behavior problems was to establish programs in community-based settings rather than in large institutions such as reformatories and mental hospitals. The community-based programs created environments to establish the behavior necessary to bring troubled youths back into contact with the normal community resources that would develop academic, social, and vocational skills. Also, these programs strengthened the natural family to the point that it was often able to reassume the family's goals and responsibilities.

The Achievement Place model, developed largely with National Institute of Mental Health funding, was more effective than more traditional approaches. It could be maintained at a lower cost than most institutions, based on a per-client cost. From a base of 17 Achievement Place type homes in Kansas, similar homes were established in other states. The most prominent of these is at Boys Town in Omaha, Nebraska (Wolf, Phillips, & Fixsen, 1972).

Language Intervention Research

Perhaps the most dominant impression conveyed by a person with severe limitations is that person's inappropriate language and sparseness of productive speech. This results in a mismatch between the limited responses of the retarded speaker and the more complex behavior of other speakers. Thus language research was our first major research effort. Language is one of the most significant requisite skills to the placement of a person with developmental disabilities in the mainstream of our social system. Language research was accomplished in many far-ranging areas. The specific details of the research are voluminous. The fruits of this research had a significant impact on the traditional methods and procedures of language training.

Through research into ontogenetic speech response systems, semantic and syntactic features of early language, relationships between receptive and expressive language, the utility of special language systems, the generative nature of language, and the rationale for language intervention in natural and controlled environments, researchers at the MRRC designed intervention systems that changed the lives of thousands of persons with retardation who would otherwise have lived their lives apart from mainstream society. The products of this work are available in films, monographs, books, and numerous articles.

Research Training

Research training was a prominent feature of the MRRC program from the early years. The first research training grant was awarded to the BCR as a part of the original Parsons Research Project. The emphasis was always on individualized programs. Each trainee had a research mentor to work closely with him or her, usually in activities related to the mentor's ongoing research. As soon as the trainee was ready, he or she was encouraged and supported in developing new research. Senior investigators formed the base for the program by providing day-by-day assistance and by recruiting well-qualified and interested trainees. Graduates of the Kansas training programs went on to develop new programs for persons with retardation and disabilities in several outlying states. Peer tutoring and parent training programs developed in Kansas were applied in urban ghettos, on Native American reservations, and in rural depressed areas to help deprived or disadvantaged citizens help themselves.

Fred Girardeau, who served as research training director from 1966 to 1976, described the training process as follows:

The Kansas training program is based largely on our experience that a close tutorial relationship of a trainee with a senior investigator is an effective procedure for training researchers. The trainees are selected for their interest in a problem area currently being investigated by a senior person and are required to become involved in this research immediately upon acceptance into the program. As rapidly as possible the trainee moves toward independence in the design, execution and write-up of experiments. Throughout the program, though, the emphasis is on day-by-day behavior involved in conducting research. In many cases, trainees in the Kansas program have had several publications by the time they complete the program. In addition to the day-by-day research activities required of trainees, they participate in research seminars and workshops, both locally and nationally.

In summary, the training program included five general areas:

1. Knowledge and experience in relevant research methodologies;
2. Day-by-day conduct of research, beginning immediately with the awarding of the traineeship;
3. Academic scholarship in the trainee's professional area;
4. Integration of research projects into larger, more systemic bodies of knowledge; and

5. Appreciation of the relevance of research to current clinical problems and the need for more research-based information about mental retardation and other developmental disabilities.

Earl Butterfield assumed the directorship after Fred died in 1976.

Experimental Preschools

The Experimental Preschool Project for Handicapped Children was a collection of several projects to extend the outreach activities of the university into community and institutional programs of service delivery. This project served children between 3 and 6 years of age. It included an interdisciplinary educational clinic program. The program was based on an integrated classroom model in which normal children of about the same developmental level as the children with retardation were also enrolled in the class. The normal children served as models for the children with disabilities and training activities were organized to capitalize upon the modeling and imitation potentials of this arrangement. The interdisciplinary service model brought together a number of related disciplines to work cooperatively in the evaluation and the clinical testing, program planning, and therapy services provided to each child.

Model Education Program

This project established a model education program for severely handicapped, orthopedically impaired children that was extended to KNI from PSHTC. The project established a model class for the target population, in conjunction with a program for deinstitutionalization at KNI. The program was a joint effort of the University of Kansas Bureau of Child Research and the Kansas State Department of Special Education, in cooperation with KNI and the Topeka, Kansas School District 501.

The project included the following components: a model service delivery system; a deinstitutionalization class at KNI for experimental applications of new assessment tools and curricula for preparation for movement into the community class; a deinstitutionalization model including early infant stimulation and intervention; a rural, sparsely populated area educational service model; a parent support and assistance model; a comprehensive package for dissemination; and a series of educational products for teachers and personnel working with the target population. The project provided, over a 3-year period, a system of comprehensive diagnostic program planning and educational delivery for orthopedically impaired children with severe disabilities who resided in institutions. The program enabled movement of these children into community-based schools with adequate support systems to maintain them in their communities.

Animal Research on Neurobiological Mechanisms

Animal research on neurological mechanisms led to experimental animal models for children who are hyperactive during their neonatal to adolescent stages and who show various degrees of recovery from that hyperactivity during adolescence. Several causes for such hyperactivity were isolated in young rats and investigations identified the anatomical basis for differences in hyperactivity and the ability of the developing central nervous system to recover normal functions after a period of hyperactivity.

Other investigations clarified the process of chemical communication between specialized regions and the individual neurons. This chemical communication is essential in normal development, maturation, maintenance, and regeneration of the nervous system. Unraveling this biochemical mystery contributed to intervention in the developmental process to prevent retardation.

An additional goal of this research is to develop sensitive techniques for the detection of subtle neurological changes that are important in the manifestation of learning disabilities and to identify target sites for potential pharmacological intervention.

The University of Kansas Medical Center

Biological Research

Prominent among the biological areas studied were reproductive physiology, metabolism, and neurophysiology. Of equal importance were areas generally regarded as behavioral, educational, interpersonal, and

environmental. Most problems in learning disabilities, sensory impairments and perceptual disorganization, language impairments and communication disorders, seizures, neonatal disorders, and so forth lend
themselves to a combined biobehavioral approach.

Research on Fetal Development

Realizing that the ultimate solution to the problem of mental retardation lies in prevention, research on fetal development at the KUMC setting of the MRRC focused on various prenatal and postnatal problems.
Important work identified parents with a potential risk of bearing a
retarded child and developed tests for screening them for possible progesterone deficiency, as well as an evaluation of ovarian progesterone
production.

Other work concerned the control of seizures. The safe and successful management of seizures was imperative for the optimal intellectual and emotional development of children with disabilities, as well as
to prevent further central nervous system deterioration from repeated
seizures. This research resulted in a study that provides a practicing
physician with a quantitative basis from which an optimal schedule of
drug administration may be derived. This provided better control of
seizures as well as a minimization of adverse effects from drugs.

Basic Cognitive Functioning

Classification and representational strategies are the most basic of
human concepts. Certain objects are related because of common functions, common physical properties, or any number of other factors. Similarly, persons with retardation were offered experiences designed to
show how various experienced objects or events were represented by
spoken or written language forms or by pictures or modeled replicas.

In all of this training experience, both the content of the training
and the exemplars of this content were often ineffective because they
were developed on the basis of normal adult perceptions of both the
content and the exemplary arrangements that best display this content.
It does not take much experience in teaching language, for example, to
find that most arrangements selected to display hard/soft comparisons,

kitty/puppy contrasts, or exemplars of *in, on,* and *under* are often ineffective. Relationships that seem so clear to an adult (or even a normal child) are often not so clear when presented for acquisition in a teaching relationship with persons with retardation.

Again, the treatment of the relative performances of persons with retardation in classification and representation strategies and skills was at this time relatively gross, except for the laboratory research done with persons with mild retardation. Educational and training practices reflected very little empirically based accommodation to possible variations in classification strategies or in abilities to represent objects or events at levels more abstract than the real objects or events. Most attempts at educational accommodation to such important differences were relatively simplistic approaches, such as repetitive presentations, increased gesture and/or paraphrasing, and slowed-down speech rates. These strategies can be likened to the common tendency to talk louder to the hearing aid wearer—well-meaning, but essentially useless in combating the problems.

Language and Cognitive Development

Research on language and cognitive development with early childhood populations concerned different programming strategies on the behavior of developmentally delayed children with behavior problems. One procedure, which involves returning to an easier, higher probability event contingent upon an error, produced fewer intervals of crying in a child than during a baseline which involved a return to a different but equal probability event.

Observations were made concerning the effects of carbon monoxide exposure (hypoxia). Periods of hypoxia in excess of 60 minutes produce behavioral alterations and neurochemical deficits (dopamine, norepinephrine, and 5-hydroxytryptamine), which persist over long periods.

When neonatal rats (4–5 days old) were exposed to carbon monoxide to the point of severe respiratory difficulty, the animals developed locomotor hyperactivity, which lasted past the weaning period. The hyperactivity disappeared with maturity (4–5 months of age). Golgi staining and Nissl staining allowed neuronal morphology to be examined during growth and maturity of the central nervous system. Three morphometric measurements were made: the size of the neuronal nuclei, dendritic branching patterns, and dendritic spine counts. Considerable recovery from damage occurs in neuronal morphology during the period of behavioral recovery. Neurons in the caudate nucleus of the brain were selected for study.

Comparable studies used X-irradiation on gestational day 15 during the period of development of the telencephalon. Locomotor action of the young rats was normal until maturity, then they developed hyperactivity. Neuronal morphology in these rats was compared with that of carbon monoxide-induced anoxic rats.

A 2-deoxyglucose brain functional mapping procedure provided a powerful new "window" for new insights about which brain regions are involved in brain function, both normal and pathological. Brain regional changes in rats and monkeys consequent to 1) acetylcholine esterase poisons (pesticides), 2) injury-induced seizures, 3) the anesthetic ketamine, 4) brain tumors, and 5) amphetamine have been identified.

Genetics

Biopsies were taken from a number of patients with tuberous sclerosis, neurofibromatosis, and a family with hereditary hemorrhagic telangiectasia. Human genetics studies concerned the production of collagen utilizing [^{14}C]proline and its incorporation into procollagen by skin fibroblasts from such patients.

Considerable research was directed to the elimination of particular memory deficits (through training) in children with developmental disabilities. This work helped develop more effective educational techniques for children with disabilities. The problem was to determine whether it is possible to train trans-situational cognitive functions which effect general improvements in young and retarded children's cognitive performances.

One major undertaking was an attempt to chart the development of receptive and productive processes that occur during the first year of life and which allow later use of speech and language. The hypothesis was that systematic developmental changes normally occur during the first year of life and that, lacking those normal developments, effective language use does not emerge later. These investigations established that by 43 hours of life, infants can discriminate the stop consonants /b/ and /p/, and that there is correlational evidence that experience with the voiced consonant /p/ promotes this discrimination capacity.

Neurobiological Mechanisms

Neurobiological mechanisms in the microtubule-associated proteins strengthen the axial forces between the subunits of tubulin in the microtubule. The sensitivity of microtubules to antimicrotubule agents is increased in the absence of microtubule-associated proteins. The amount and the composition of the microtubule-associated proteins play an important role in the response of microtubules to pharmacological agents and these "associated proteins" may regulate the polymerization–depolymerization of tubulin.

Antimicrotubule agents arrested fast axoplasmic transport concomitant with the disappearance of axonal microtubules. This supports the concept that the functional integrity of the microtubules is essential for axoplasmic transport. Further, vincristine-induced neuropathy may be a consequence of fast axoplasmic transport disruption.

The synaptic membrane fraction obtained following asmotic rupture of the nerve endings isolated from rat brain is enriched in glutamate-binding activity with the characteristics of the excitatory amino acid receptors. This high-affinity glutamate-binding activity is associated with a small molecular weight glycoprotein that interacts strongly with the lectin concanavalin A.

The purified glutamate-binding protein (GBP) has a selectivity in that it binds L-glutamic acid most strongly, L-aspartic acid less strongly, and kainic acid not at all. This protein from synaptic membranes in association with membrane phospholipids could be the glutamate receptor. This GBP is not the carrier for glutamate uptake because these two systems have a number of different properties.

Children with thantophoric dwarfism, achondroplasia, homozygous achondroplasia, diastrophic dwarfism, Kniest syndrome, asphyxiating thoracic dwarfism, osteoporosis (two different types), vitamin D-resistant rickets, and osteopoikilosis were studied. In diastrophic dwarfism, there appears to be an abnormal distribution of collagen within the cartilage matrix, suggesting a defect in collagen synthesis or fibrogenesis. In Kniest syndrome there is a degeneration of cartilage matrix, leaving a delicate network of proteoglycan and reduced amounts of collagen throughout most of the matrix. Two forms of autosomal recessive osteopetrosis were distinguished histologically: 1) classical severe neonatal form, characterized by an excessive hypertrophic growth plate cartilage and an overabundance of osteoclasts within newly made bone, and 2) a mild form, with a relatively normal growth plate and a normal number of osteoclasts in bone.

Reproductive Physiology

Preovulatory and postovulatory "overripeness ovopathy" was postulated to underlie a broad range of developmental anomalies in studies of reproductive physiology. Although the evidence for untoward consequences of ovulation defects in the human subject was imperfect, the concept was not without support and is so crucial to mental retardation that a better understanding is imperative. How the antral follicle responds to "ovulatory delay" and how its characteristics change as it approaches the atretic phase were systematically studied. A single injection of anti-LH serum not only interrupts pregnancy in the hamster, but also results in the superovulation of 30 eggs. A model for inducing follicular atresia in a synchronized population of large antral follicles was tested and found to be a promising approach for learning the biochemical changes in follicles undergoing atresia.

Ovarian steroid-induced behavior was mediated by selective protein synthesis in discrete brain areas. This hypothesis received support from experiments that revealed a significant change in ovarian steroid-induced behavior following protein synthesis inhibition in the preoptic area and the ventromedial hypothalamus.

Special Centers

Several centers that were established during the transition years of the Bureau of Child Research and the Life Span Institute are briefly described below. Stephen Schroeder and others expand on these in part II.

The Research and Training Center on Independent Living

The Research and Training Center on Independent Living (RTCIL), founded by and directed for 21 years by James F. Budde, was formed in 1980 to develop systematic approaches to enable individuals with physical and/or intellectual disabilities of all ages to live independently, control their lives, and shape their futures. The RTCIL has increasingly focused on the needs of people with disabilities in developing countries, as well as in minority and rural communities in this country.

Work Group on Health Promotion and Community Development

The mission of the Work Group is to promote community health and development through collaborative research, teaching, and public service. Formed in 1976 and still directed by Stephen B. Fawcett, its current work is in three domains: community/public health, child/youth health and development, and community development. The Work Group has assisted with state and community initiatives in many critical areas, including substance abuse, adolescent pregnancy, youth development, rural health, health promotion, child well-being, systems change, and neighborhood development in urban communities.

Juniper Gardens Children's Project

The Juniper Gardens Children's Project is the subject of chapter 6.

Beach Center on Disability

The Beach Center, founded in 1988 and still directed by H. Rutherford Turnbull III and Ann P. Turnbull, has a steadfast commitment to making a difference in the quality of life for persons with disabilities and their families. It is committed to listening to the priorities of families and service providers, incorporating those priorities into the center's research agenda and carrying out research in a participatory way. Primary areas of Beach Center research include access to the general curriculum, disability policy, family–professional partnerships, family quality of life, positive behavior support, and self-determination. The

Beach Center is affiliated with the School of Education's Department of Special Education. It was named for Ross and Marianna Beach in 1988 in honor of their significant roles in advocating for families affected by disabilities in Kansas and throughout the world, especially in South America.

Child Language Doctoral Program

The Child Language Doctoral Program was established in 1983 as the first specialized degree program in the emerging field of child language acquisition and intervention. The program focuses on the interdisciplinary academic preparation and research training of child language specialists. The internationally recognized faculty brings diverse approaches to the study of how children communicate and speak. The program offers students a wide choice of research tools, facilities, and field sites, including the Child Language Acquisition Studies Lab, which has the largest known archive of transcribed spontaneous samples from specific language-impaired children. Research sites and practica are provided by the Life Span Institute, the Language Acquisition Preschool, and the clinical and research facilities of the Speech-Language-Hearing Clinic.

Planning for the program emerged during the 1980–1981 academic year when a number of faculty colleagues and several students met and considered the advantages of an interdisciplinary graduate curriculum. The pre- and postdoctoral students were extremely active in providing advice to faculty members about possible graduate programs. These students included Etti Dromi, now at the University of Tel Aviv; Amy Finch-Williams, now at the University of Wyoming; Mike Casby, now at Michigan State University; Mary Ann Romski, now at the Language Research Center, Georgia State University, and Emory University; and Ken Roberts, now at Kent State University. Also, research associates Ken Ruder and Ann Rogers-Warren were active leaders in the planning sessions. Most active from the faculty at that time were Frances Ingemann, linguistics; Sue Kemper, psychology; Mary Moran, education; Mabel Rice, speech-language-hearing; and John Wright, human development and family life. In addition, the proponents of the Child Language Program were advised and encouraged in substantial ways by Frances Horowitz, vice chancellor for research, graduate studies, and public service. An interesting feature in the chronology of events is that the team was notified that they had been awarded three new federal predoctoral training grants in the same week that the University Board of Regents approved the new program.

Merrill Advanced Studies Center

The Merrill Advanced Studies Center, directed by Mabel L. Rice, was founded in 1990 with an endowment from Virginia Urban Merrill and Fred Merrill. It is a catalyst for scholarship on disabilities and policies that shape university research. Merrill conferences and publications establish new directions and build collaborative projects in both science and policy. World-class experts often meet as a group for the first time at Merrill conferences and go on to develop national projects that answer key questions in science. The center publishes books on topics relevant to developmental disabilities and makes policy papers available online and in print. The Merrill web site at *Merrill.ku.edu* has fact sheets and discussions on science and policy for the general public.

References

Fulton, R. T., & Lloyd, L. L. (Eds.). (1975). *Auditory assessment of the difficult-to-test* (pp. 145–178). Baltimore, MD: Williams & Wilkins.

Lent, J. R., LeBlanc, J., & Spradlin, J. E. (1970). Designing a rehabilitative culture for moderately retarded adolescent girls. In R. E. Ulrich, T. T. Stachnik, & J. Mabry (Eds.), *The control of human behavior* (pp. 121–135). Glenview, IL: Scott Foresman.

Wolf, M. M., Phillips, E. K., & Fixsen, D. L. (1972). The teaching family: A new model for the treatment of deviant child behavior in the community. In S. W. Bijou & E. L. Ribes (Eds.), *First symposium on behavior modification in Mexico* (pp. 51–62). New York: Academic Press.

8

Projects of the Kansas University Affiliated Facility

RICHARD L. SCHIEFELBUSCH

The service program of the Bureau of Child Research was extensive and widespread in Kansas. The Kansas University Affiliated Facility (UAF) provided major service functions from its four community settings and facilities in Lawrence; Parsons; Kansas City, Kansas; and Topeka. A primary assumption of the program was that service, research, and training personnel would work together to create improvements in service delivery. It was further assumed that these services should focus on community settings and involve community resources and community personnel. Training was designed for in-service workers, paraprofessionals, supervisors, specialists, parents, and so forth. Likewise, research also helped improve education, social skills, living environments, vocational and work skills, recreational activities, and community adjustment for children with developmental disabilities.

The service programs of each setting were mutually related. However, there were areas in which each setting had special interests. The training programs also offered different student experiences and opportunities at each setting.

The UAF facilities were built under the auspices of the Division of Mental Retardation of the Federal Social and Rehabilitative Services. The facilities were built to support professional training for approximately 300 graduate students pursuing degrees in areas of child development, clinical neurology, education, hearing and speech, music therapy, nursing, pediatrics, psychiatry, psychology, recreation, social work, vocational rehabilitation, and occupational therapy. The clinical facilities also provided diagnostic and treatment resources for over 1,000 children with developmental disabilities each year. The construction program of the UAF was begun in 1969 and the facilities were dedicated on June 14, 1972.

The building at the Kansas University Medical Center (KUMC) housed a clinical training unit that included facilities for students and professionals. Children entering the facility came from the surrounding metropolitan area, from outlying areas of Kansas, and from the Children's Rehabilitation Unit (CRU). The building at KUMC included an interdisciplinary diagnostic area to evaluate the condition of each entering child. There were laboratory units for cytogenetics, electrodiagnosis, orthopedic surgery, metabolic studies, pediatrics, neurology, physical medicine, psychiatry, social work, nursing, and education. The KUMC unit was named after Dr. Herbert Miller who also continued as its director.

The UAF unit at Parsons State Hospital and Training Center (PSHTC), like the unit at KUMC, provided complete diagnostic facilities for incoming children with mental retardation as well as training for students who were entering the profession as clinicians or researchers. The diagnostic and treatment unit was devoted largely to training activities involving the diagnosis and disposition of cases, in-service and professional training, and intensive treatment and training. In addition, there were psychological and educational diagnostic laboratories for nursing education, and a large studio for audiovisual activities related to research and clinical training, as well as the development of audiovisual products.

The Lawrence UAF facility was in a children's unit on the top two floors of the east wing of Haworth Hall, the bio–life sciences building. The children's clinical unit (John T. Stewart Children's Center) included a day training program for young children with retardation and their parents from the Lawrence area, a nursery and play area, individual training and counseling rooms, an observation area, and an area for a mental retardation psychology clinic. In addition, there was a language clinic and an area used by the Bureau of Child Research (BCR) for special projects related to mental retardation.

(For a complete description and analysis of these resources, see two articles in *Tracks,* published by The Kansas Association for Retarded Children in January and May, 1973: "A New Center for Children" and " Kansas University Affiliated Facility." Each article was directed to parents as an explanation of possible involvement of UAF professionals and trainees in the evaluation and training of children with mental retardation.)

Each of the center's units had features that differed from the others. For this reason a special feature of each of the settings should be considered briefly. The unit at KU included a research institute and three academic departments that were starved for space so each of them pressed vigorously for office space as well as for research and training space. It was often difficult to determine what were center and what were departmental preserves. In addition, all of them were growing rapidly and, of course, did urgently need more space. In some respects the situation was awkward from the beginning and became steadily worse as we continued.

The center's unit at KUMC also had a built-in problem. The federal support agency was well aware that the CRU and the new UAF unit had overlapping purposes and functions. Although the two programs really were complementary, the funding agencies were inclined to cut the project funds back during periods of funding shortages or during frequent periods of shifting priorities.

PSHTC was primarily an institution for children and youth with mental retardation. As such, some reviewers doubted that it was or could be a combined center for research, training, and service. *Teaching* activities were especially suspect in the minds of our federal evaluators.

Interestingly, each unit took its built-in problem and turned it into a positive agenda. For instance, the Stewart Children's Center reached out to various locations off campus to develop their preschools, follow-through teaching unit, co-op center, and/or technical assistance unit and thus achieved a better ecological arrangement than they might have designed on campus. The daily conversations of the participants frequently included the location names: Varsity House, Roof House, Turner House, Kansas Neurological Institute (KNI), and so forth. The ecology of these settings was enhanced by student participants, parents, volunteers, and observers.

The KUMC situation was even more complicated. Their funding agency in Washington simply deleted program funding in 1982, shortly after they had approved continuing funding for a 5-year major grant ($850,000 per year). After going through the usual effort to convince the agency that the program was urgent and highly qualified, we decided to send a five-person delegation to Washington to talk with the agency representatives. The meeting was arranged through Senator Dole's office.

Our delegation was headed by the chancellor of the university. At the meeting with the assistant commissioner of the U.S. Department of Health and Human Services and the head of the funding agency, we explained that we were not there to question the agency's decision, but rather to explain the nature of our unexpected problem, to wit: we had made commitments to families all over Kansas for assistance for their children. "We have no fall-back position. Even our legislature is not in session. Could the agency please fund us for one more year so that we can make appropriate adjustments?"

The agency agreed to our request and we subsequently were able to get $225,000 yearly from the Kansas legislature, $100,000 yearly from the KU Medical Foundation, *and* $535,000 yearly from the reapplication of the original application. Thus, we not only recaptured our funding but we established a better funding package for the long haul!

Howard Bair and the Parsons Unit may have fared equally well with their problem. They requested funds to construct and to operate a media center in order to facilitate the development of instructional materials for instructional purposes at Parsons and also to disseminate them to a wide range of consumers throughout the state. The plan was to display the products of their application research and to strengthen the unit's productive interaction with the other two units and to assist with other dissemination plans.

The participants of the UAF generally regarded the differences among their units as positive features of the overall program. The productive record among the units may suggest that they were right. In any event, a closer look at the various projects at each setting produces a positive effect. They indeed provided resources that had been needed for a long time by service providers and their clients.

The Training Program

The clinical training centers were places where retarded children and their parents came for systematic and specialized help, where professionals of all kinds devoted part of their professional time to research and training with children, and where graduate students received the professional training they needed to carry their work forward. These facilities were sources of professional help for the communities. Trained clinicians and researchers based at the UAFs went into the communities, homes, shops, clinics, and businesses to work with children with developmental disabilities and persons associated with them. Children who returned to their communities from institutions found the UAF and the Kansas Center a resource to which they could turn if their developmental disabilities led to problems that they could not solve alone or with the help of the family.

International Program

UAF influence was largest in Kansas, but not restricted to Kansas. In 1970 the KU chancellor signed an agreement between KU and the Inter-American Children's Institute. This laid the foundation for an extensive cooperative program. Ross Copeland, head of the International Program and an associate director of the BCR, was appointed by President Richard Nixon to represent the United States on the Director's Council of the Inter-American Children's Institute. The International Unit of the UAF in Lawrence was instrumental in developing an ongoing exchange program involving Latin America, Europe, Australia, New Zealand, and the Far East. The exchange program varied from short visits to in-residence visits of 9 months to a year. Primary exchange visitors came from Latin America, but extended visits were made by persons from other countries. The purpose was to train foreign scientists and practitioners to use the models and programs available in the United States for persons with disabilities. Formal agreements between KU and Mexico, and between KU and the International Children's Institute (an arm of the Organization of American States) allowed for the exchange of research information and visiting scientists. (See chapter 7 for further information about the international program.)

The Lawrence Setting

The Lawrence UAF was initially a community outreach program, which extended the tools developed in research laboratories into applications by parents and teachers who were seeking alternatives to institutional care. The Lawrence UAF developed and demonstrated exemplary new programs and procedures for care and training for the children, their families, community service workers, and educators. The Lawrence UAF was a community resource where parents brought their children for special educational and behavioral training programs and where the parents themselves received training in the care and management of children with developmental disabilities. It was a resource base for professionals who extended the service, care, and research strengths of the UAF into community outreach programs in various parts of the state. The Lawrence UAF, on the central campus of the University of Kansas, provided facilities for graduate training in special education, occupational therapy, psychology, speech and hearing, and human development. The service delivery system provided direct service and served as a vehicle for practical training for university students preparing for careers in the developmental disabilities field.

Academic credit was arranged through cooperating university departments. The various research and training programs provided environments for graduate and undergraduate students to actively participate and earn college credit. Data collection, observation, charting, graphing, and experimental design were important aspects of the training program. The availability of ongoing programs encouraged student participation in these areas as enhancements to their classroom work. Training for parents, paraprofessionals, professionals, and other caregivers furthered the program goal of helping develop and disseminate exemplary services to persons with developmental disabilities while meeting outside manpower needs.

Management Training Program

A management training program was initiated to train administrators to manage community programs for persons with developmental disabilities. The need for trained personnel was substantial, particularly with the movement toward deinstitutionalization. The movement away from the institutions required a concomitant increase in community resources to meet the needs of the persons with disabilities. The continuing expansion of community programs required a trained administrative staff to maintain quality programming, monitor legislation, and assure compliance with multiple regulations. The management training program was an attempt to provide such a trained staff.

This program, sponsored by the Federal Region VII Developmental Disabilities Office, was a response to the severe shortage of master's level managerial-level personnel in the developmental disabilities field. The project was designed so current directors or staff of community agencies could further their training without leaving their jobs. In cooperation with several academic departments and the Division of Continuing Education at KU, they prepared the curriculum for this course of study. Following its approval as an official degree course by the university administration and the Board of Regents, the role of the Lawrence UAF became one of coordinating, facilitating, and monitoring progress of students who participated in the course.

A training program for administrators of child care centers helped train these administrators in providing a service for children and their families by establishing a stimulating care center for young children 2.5 to 5 years of age whose parents were at work or at school. It also provided a training experience for students to work as administrators of child development centers. This training included classroom management of program activities and behavior, parent involvement, supervision of personnel, food service procedures, and elementary financial procedures. While it was not possible to provide training in all areas useful to an administrator, the training gave exposure to a number of necessary areas of expertise. A component of research was included in the training. A student was expected to carry out teaching duties and simultaneously develop a system for collecting necessary data in a baseline/intervention type of research that increased observation and programming skills and gave a base for noting progress and planning for children. The program served about 608 graduate and undergraduate students per year.

The project was initially directed by James Budde, who was located at Lawrence and supported by a number of his young colleagues. In due course, it became the title of the technical assistance program developed by Chuck Spellman and his colleagues at Parsons. It is now a statewide program that uses state-of-the-art technology to meet widely ranging needs of children with developmental disabilities.

Technical Assistance Program

The technical assistance program provided training to State Developmental Disabilities Council members and community agency administrators, managers, and staff on techniques, strategies, and directions for developing programs for persons with developmental disabilities. The deinstitu-tionalization movement created a need for more and better community services. The establishment, funding, staffing, and programming of such services were major undertakings. The technical assistance staff provided training to new and existing agencies.

The program was created to develop the least restrictive environments for the developmentally disabled population. Technical assistance staff were involved from the beginning in "gearing up" assessments to meet accredi-tation standards, and in the application of systems technology and other sophisticated management techniques to community programs. The staff consisted of specialists who: 1) worked directly with organizations of devel-opmentally disabled citizens; 2) consulted with vocational and residential facilities for adults; 3) consulted with preschool and child care facilities; 4) prepared and conducted training workshops on relevant topics for agency staff; and 5) developed manuals, slide presentations, and other media productions used in training and planning.

Music Therapy

A music therapy program housed in the UAF at Lawrence provided a clinical practicum for more than 200 music therapy students per year. Practicum training was necessary because music therapy was a major program for children with mental disabilities. Students worked with clients who were mentally retarded, learning disabled, emotionally dis-turbed, orthopedically handicapped, deaf or blind, or senile.

The music therapy program in Lawrence was directed by George Dierkson. A concurrent program at Parsons was directed by Vance Cot-ter. A highly functional music therapy building was constructed at PSHTC to facilitate both research and training in music therapy procedures.

Speech and Hearing

The speech and hearing program exposed students in speech and audi-ology to all ages of clients with all types of communication dysfunctions. Practicum training on assessment techniques and therapy was provided for the many students in the program. Diagnostic evaluations and reme-diation techniques as they relate to persons with developmental disabilities were stressed to improve the quality of service once the students become practitioners. The "hands-on" experience was one of the most valuable parts of student training. Margaret Byrne and James Lingwall were, in turn, directors of the program. In recent years, Jane Wegner has added further quality and diversity to the Speech-Language-Hearing Clinic. Kim Wilcox, former dean of the College of Liberal Arts and Sciences and head of the Department of Speech-Language-Hearing: Science and Disorders maintains that the Bureau of Child Research put the term *language* into the departmental and the disciplinary designation.

The language project preschool served as a practicum site for undergraduate and graduate students working with language-delayed and language-deficient children. The program provided excellent opportunities for students to observe treatment, to participate in the treatment procedures, to participate in a preschool curriculum, to work with children, to work with professionals, and to design and implement their own research.

The preschool program, designated the Language Acquisition Preschool (LAP), provided a research setting for improving teaching generalized language skills to children with language deficiencies and for remediating problems related to early childhood education of children with disabilities. This program served children between the ages of 2.5 and 5 years. Most were diagnosed as language deficient or language delayed. Betty Bunce is the director of this program.

The speech and hearing program provided diagnostic evaluations and remediation programs for persons with communication disorders. Speech therapy and audiological assessment were available, along with parent training to assist with in-home therapy to maintain and extend treatment gains. Speech-language-hearing skills were of prime importance because the ability to communicate and understand others is a basic requirement in our society. Consequently, these services fulfilled both a personal and community need.

The Kansas UAF Speech Pathology Project engaged in training, service, technical assistance, research and development, and coordination of training and service with the department. The program was begun to train speech pathologists and audiologists with an emphasis in working with people with developmental disibilities, working with an interdisciplinary staff, and providing speech services to people with developmental disibilities in the Lawrence and Kansas City communities. Since the department was a two-campus undergraduate and graduate program, KU and KUMC, the activities on both campuses were coordinated.

The training program consisted of several categories. First, undergraduate and graduate students in speech pathology received clinical practicum training with clients with developmental disabilities. Academic credit was obtained through the speech-language-hearing department. Interdisciplinary training, in the form of lectures, audio- and videotapes, and observation, was conducted with staff members of the UAF special education experimental classrooms in Haworth Hall and with the CRU in Kansas City. Parent training was conducted with the parents of children from these classrooms to enable them to understand and work with their children at home.

The service program consisted of providing diagnostic, program planning, direct therapy and coordination of clients' programs with the classroom teacher. The students in training did much of the diagnostic work and direct therapy. From 800 to 850 hours of direct service were provided each year. On request from community service agencies, diagnostic evaluations, individual program planning, in-service training of staff, follow-up, and guidance in choosing appropriate training materials were provided. Research and development centers were kept up to date on new evaluation tools, and training and evaluation procedures for adults were developed. The entire UAF Speech Pathology Project was coordinated with the Department of Speech-Language-Hearing: Science and Disorders.

An associated project in Topeka at the KNI involved a unique program to teach communication skills to children who lacked functional speech. The children were taught a "symbol" language consisting of various shapes. These symbols have meaning and the children were taught to manipulate these symbols into meaningful groupings that enable the children to communicate. This program served as a foundation for later speech therapy and training. It was an early version of what is now known as augmented instruction or language augmentation.

Occupational Therapy

The occupational therapy program offered clinical services to children with developmental disabilities ranging in age from birth to 18 years in the area of fine, gross, and perceptual motor development. Proper motor development is essential in normal development. When motor skills do not develop, the child is at risk and should have therapy programs to assist motor development and to improve skills.

The occupational therapy clinic likewise provided a practicum site for students to work with children who were developmentally disabled. It also exposed students not intending to enter this area to the problems of persons with developmental disabilities so they could recognize the need for proper treatment. Service providers came into contact with persons with disabilities during the course of their professional careers whether or not they were working in clinics for persons with disabilities. Community programs for all levels generally find persons in need of special programming. Recognizing that this approach increased the services available to children with developmental disabilities, the occupational therapy clinic provided hands-on experience and at-home care techniques.

The services available in the fully equipped occupational therapy clinic in Lawrence included thorough evaluation of motor skills, reflexes and self-help skills, direct therapy, home programs, and parent training (to keep treatment going) to follow up the clinical programs. Three academic courses available through the occupational therapy department, and the UAF gave students without prior knowledge or experience a chance to work with children in a clinical environment. Consulting services were provided to the southeast section of the state of Kansas in collaboration with the Parsons UAF.

Mildred Copeland was the founder of this program. She received valuable assistance at the beginning from Bill Hopkins, the initial director of the KU UAF.

Experimental Education

A unique special education experimental class that included both normal and exceptional children allowed students to work with children with disabilities in a school atmosphere. The mixture of normal and disabled was a model not commonly used in public schools. Students learned techniques to enable them to implement similar programs in their professional careers. The project included a preschool serving children 2.5 to 5 years of age, and a primary school class serving children 5 to 8 years of age. Based on an integrated model, the program also included approximately half nondisabled children enrolled in both preschool and primary classrooms to serve as models for the children with disabilities. Approximately 35 children were enrolled in the classes each year. Major progress was made in designing a classroom environment in which children with disabilities could learn from normal children (as well as from the teacher), while the normal children could continue to learn as efficiently as they would in classes comprised completely of normal children. This program, called "Super School" and directed by Bill Hopkins, had a major impact as school districts moved to provide educational services to children with severe disabilities who were previously excluded from participation in public school classes.

Early Evaluation

The PEED (Program for Early Evaluation of Development) project was twofold. The first goal was to train staff of agencies holding major purchase contracts with the State Department of Social and Rehabilitation Services (SRS) to work more effectively with developmentally delayed infants and preschool children (ages birth to 6 years) or those suspected of having developmental problems. This part of the program was developed by Jennifer Ashton Lilo for the SRS. It began as a program to assess low birth weight and birth defect babies.

The second goal was to train SRS staff to enable them to determine appropriate referrals, arrange for acquisition of helpful services, and acquire skills in monitoring the progress of children at various stages of early childhood development. The training methods were flexible. Design and delivery were tailored to fit each agency's needs. General areas available for training included: normal development, developmental assessment, classroom management and curriculum behavior management, teaching and observation techniques, infant stimulation, and other related topics. This part of the program was developed by the UAF at KU under the leadership of Jim Budde.

Parent Training

Various parent programs provided services to children. After proper training in certain treatment techniques, the parents become extensions of the treatment program. Moreover, the parents have the most contact with the child; consequently, home-based treatment procedures exponentially increase the amount of treatment that the child receives. Improvements in the child were more likely to occur with continual and consistent treatment procedures than in weekly scheduled therapy sessions. Parent training programs were initiated in Lawrence based on the results of research with children with disabilities. One important factor in maintaining treatment gains in service programs was to continue the treatment program in natural settings, such as the home. In order to provide a continuity of treatment, parents were trained to provide an environment at home so the child responded to appropriate stimuli. The parents were taught to elicit appropriate behavior and to reinforce this behavior. The inappropriate behavior was not reinforced.

Consequently, after training, parents implement reading, math, speech, and other school programs in the home. The increased opportunities for learning enhanced the skills of the child. The parent training activities were developed by Ann Rogers-Warren and Lynn Embry in Lawrence and Vance Hall and Marilyn Hall at Juniper Gardens.

Predelinquent Youths

A major program in cooperation with the Department of Human Development was the Achievement Place Research Project. It became increasingly apparent during the early years of the BCR and the Kansas Center that there was a great need for alternative, community-based treatment programs that could supplement or replace institutional programs for delinquent and predelinquent youths. In 1967 work began on developing and evaluating a Teaching-Family model program at Achievement Place, a community-based, community-directed, family-style group-home treatment program for six to eight adjudicated adolescents. The Achievement Place program was administered by two teaching-parents (a married couple) who were specially trained to operate the program and to teach the youths more appropriate behavior. The treatment program was designed to provide maximum motivation and instruction to the youths when they first enter the program. As the youths developed skills and self-control, the structured elements of the program were reduced and replaced by more natural feedback conditions. The youths all came from the local community and the teaching-parents worked with the youths' parents and teachers to solve the youths' problems at home and at school and to prepare the youths to return to their natural homes. The preliminary results of the program indicated that while the youths were in the program, they had substantially fewer offenses than youths from comparison homes. One measure of the success of the program is that the Achievement Place model was duplicated in 98 communities in Kansas and other states. The teaching-parent training program prepared group-home treatment personnel. Married couples (at least one had a BA in the social sciences) participated in a 1-year, practicum-based, professional training sequence to prepare them to implement the teaching-family model of community-based, family-style, group-home treatment for predelinquent and delinquent youths. The need for more group homes was continually growing. A program model that assured proper treatment of the residents was essential. This program (based on several years of research) provided the trained personnel to administer these group homes. This program, under the direction and leadership of Montrose Wolf and his colleagues, was developed in a number of other settings and has been continued extensively about the United States and at Boys Town in Nebraska.

The Parsons Setting

PSHTC was equipped and staffed to handle about 650 children with mental retardation. The UAF program located on the grounds of the PSHTC served children with disabilities in residence and provided community outreach services to communities in the southeast quarter of Kansas. PSHTC had made a programmed effort to get away from the concept of custodial care. It extended the professional services of the facility into community programs designed to alleviate the problems of persons with developmental disabilities in the community environment. Parsons had a history of developing university and college affiliations which replaced the custodial approach with a developmental approach. It was a progressive research and demonstration center and a training facility for professional and paraprofessional workers aspiring to careers in developmental disabilities. More than 300 trainees received training in various programs at Parsons. In line with the emerging UAF programs,

Parsons became a community resource center with growing capabilities to help develop local programs to support family and community care for persons with developmental disabilities.

The Parsons program in research and clinical programs provided an excellent site for practicum training for students, professionals, and paraprofessionals working with children with mental retardation. The purpose was to increase the effectiveness of persons providing services and resource development, and to increase the number of persons who could provide effective services in remediating developmental disabilities. The Parsons program provided opportunities for observation and participation in various therapy programs, training programs, and research studies in an institutional setting.

The UAF at Parsons coordinated a network of training resources. University students from a number of colleges and universities spent internship periods with the various departments (e.g., psychology, social work, music therapy, speech therapy, audiology, education, nursing, etc.). Seminars covered various aspects of treatment for developmental disabilities. Training lectures by visiting consultants were open to staff and community personnel. Finally, interdisciplinary projects and presentations provided information, fostered cooperation, and demonstrated innovative treatment techniques Directors of the UAF at Parsons have included Sid DeBriere, Joe Spradlin, and Lee McLean.

Child Development Services

The Child Development Services (CDS) of the UAF at Parsons, under the direction of Lee McLean, provided a major direct service program. The CDS provided comprehensive medical, psychological, social work, speech and language, and hearing evaluations to children and young adults suspected of having one or more developmentally disabling conditions. These services included comprehensive evaluations involving all professional disciplines, partial evaluations involving selected staff, emergency evaluations involving selected staff, or screening evaluations involving most or all professional staff. The diagnostic and evaluation services determined program needs for the child and follow-up treatment was provided at the CDS or in community programs. These services included ongoing medical treatment, behavior management, special training programs, referral, counseling, and program consultation services. In addition, the staff worked with parents to train parents to provide therapy in the home. The use of parents to continue treatment in the homes was a valid procedure with demonstrated effectiveness. The child progressed much more rapidly when treatment was continued at home rather than at scheduled, hourly sessions in the clinic.

Early Intervention

An infant and early childhood intervention program was initiated as a volunteer effort of local professionals and the Parsons staff under the guidance of Lee McLean. The county health departments, SRS, and Parsons UAF staffs joined to provide early identification and intervention to at-risk children in southeast Kansas. Utilizing back-up support from the KUMC, KU, and the UAF at all settings, and others, the program developed an effective model for serving the area. The model provided a continuing community resource to recognize, refer, evaluate, and help treat children with developmental disabilities. The services were provided by cooperating agencies in the area. For the very young, this early intervention made a major difference in the child's development.

Visual Acuity

The Visual Acuity Project (Research and Development of Subjective Visual Acuity Assessment Procedures for Severely Handicapped Persons) developed and validated alternative methods for visual acuity assessment. The work enabled persons whose vision cannot be assessed by conventional methods to receive accurate and subjectively validated assessment and correction. The project office was located in a building adjacent to the Parsons MRRC and UAF buildings on the grounds of the PSHTC. The research program offered a service component as part of its validation procedures.

Nearly half of all the people in the United States over age 3 wear eyeglasses. Conventional visual acuity assessment procedures rely on verbal responses by the subject to indicate to the ophthalmologist or optometrist how well the stimuli are perceived by the subject. However, for children under age 3 and for other children and even adults with communication disabilities, these procedures are insufficient. Very young children and persons with severe retardation frequently cannot respond verbally to the questions posed by the tester. Consequently, these patients often have visual acuity problems that go undetected. Because vision is so important in so many activities, especially learning, early assessment and correction could (in a number of cases) prevent the compounding of disabilities that may occur because of a lack of adequate vision. Thus, the subjects tested in this program were fitted with corrective lens. This program enabled the testing and visual correction of severely disabled and other difficult-to-test children. It also provided a procedure for the testing of very young children who were normal in every other respect. Visual correction for very young children can increase learning and strengthen the child's vision. This program served residents of the PSHTC, clients of the UAF at Parsons outpatient clinic, and other community members with severe disabilities.

The Visual Acuity Project experimented with various modifications of training of attending and participation behaviors and developed and validated improved techniques for assessing visual acuity. The impact of new adequate techniques for each individual whose vision needs correction, but for whom conventional testing was inadequate, was significant. Nearly half of the persons with severe disabilities and who were given visual acuity assessments were found to be in need of correction of visual acuity problems.

The Visual Acuity Project grew out of the MESH project directed by Chuck Spellman. It is also described in chapter 7.

PRIDE

A project, Programming Regionalized Intervention for Difficult to Educate (PRIDE), provided in-service training and direct service for teachers and to students with severe, profound, and multiple disabilities who were enrolled in public school programs in southeast Kansas. Delivery of services was a cooperative effort among the Southeast Kansas Regional Educational Service Center (SKRESC), the SEK Special Education Cooperative, the Parsons Special Purpose School, the ANW Special Education Cooperative, and the Bureau of Child Research.

Severely multiply handicapped (SMH) students from multiple special education cooperatives received services from a regional resource team approach funded by this project. Resource team members acted as consultants to classroom personnel and were closely involved in the planning and implementation of educational programs for this population. All SMH students between the ages of 6 and 21 who resided in the nine-county area, as well as 16 SMH students who were residents of PSHTC, were included in the project. Demonstration sites were located at: Lone Star School, Pittsburg, Kansas; SKRESC Special Purpose School, Parsons, Kansas; and ANW Special Education Cooperative.

The long-term goals of this project, in conjunction with other agencies and organizations in the state were: 1) to establish a model public school demonstration project for all SMH children living in rural, sparsely populated regions; 2) to provide technical support to rural schools, state departments, and universities in need of assistance in developing educational programs for SMH students in rural areas; 3) to disseminate significant aspects of the procedures that were assembled, developed, and evaluated and which could be implemented in other rural areas.

The short-term objectives were: 1) to identify, evaluate, and serve all SMH school-aged children residing in two rural special education cooperatives in southeast Kansas and one classroom at PSHTC; 2) to implement, evaluate, and modify the curriculum developed by Project MESH with students from the county region in southeast Kansas; 3) to develop sites to be used for training new personnel to implement effective education procedures with SMH students; 4) to develop sites that allow research on the applied problems relating to the education of SMH students; and 5) to provide dissemination opportunities for communicating various aspects of educating SMH students. PRIDE also was an outgrowth of MESH under the leadership of Chuck Spellman.

Adult Service Provider In-Service (ASPIN)

Project ASPIN developed and delivered in-service training to staff members of agencies, which contract under Title XX guidelines with the Kansas Department of Social and Rehabilitation Services to provide residential and vocational services to adult developmentally disabled clients. In-service training was also provided to SRS staff members concerned with locating and monitoring residential and vocational services for adult developmentally disabled clients. The in-service training content and methods were designed to improve the skills of personnel in training adult clients for normalized daily living and vocational accomplishments. Project personnel developed training workshops and practicum plans and then implemented on-site training sessions with personnel of contracting agencies and SRS.

With the assistance of Title XX funds and program guidelines, a number of communities in Kansas developed normalized vocational training and community residential services for adults with mental retardation and other developmental disabilities. Personnel working in these community programs had relatively little sustained access to research and program development advances which would directly benefit their efforts to help their adult clients acquire and utilize additional work skills and daily living skills. Project ASPIN was a model for making fully accessible and applicable the information developed in centers of research and program innovation to the personnel who were striving to deliver services to adult clients across the state. Project ASPIN also emerged from MESH.

Project LEARN

Project LEARN, which was developed at KNI in Topeka under the leadership of Wayne Sailor, established a model education service delivery program for children with severe disabilities, with orthopedic impairment as a primary disabling condition. The project established a model class for the target population in School District 501, Topeka, Kansas, in conjunction with a program for deinstitutionalization at Kansas Neurological Institute. The combined model provided, over a 3-year period, a system of comprehensive, diagnostic, program planning and educational delivery for orthopedically impaired, severely disabled children residing in institutions. The system enabled movement of these children into community-based schools with adequate support systems to maintain them in their communities as part of a comprehensive, coordinated state and local plan for special education. The project included: 1) a model service delivery system class in School District 501; 2) a deinstitutionalization class at KNI for experimental applications of new assessment tools and curricula, and preparation for movement into the community class; 3) a preinstitutionalization model including early (infant) stimulation and intervention; 4) a rural, sparsely populated area educational service model; 5) a parent support and assistance model; 6) a comprehensive package for dissemination; and 7) a series of educational products for teachers and personnel working with the target population.

Infant and Early Childhood Intervention Program

The earlier a child is recognized to have a developmentally disabling condition, is evaluated, and is provided with a therapeutic educational program designed to meet the "whole" child's individual needs, the more effective and lasting is the alleviation and/or correction of the child's problems. Thus, the county health departments, SRS, and the Kansas UAF joined together voluntarily in southeast Kansas to provide training in the evaluative and intervention procedures appropriate for these children. This program was developed under the leadership of Lee McLean and was based on four assumptions:

1. The earlier the identification and intervention, the better.
2. The parents are the primary programmers of their children and must be the central focus of any effective intervention program.
3. The transdisciplinary model of team utilization is the most viable in working with this population.
4. The transdisciplinary teams should be composed of professionals located in each county working together on behalf on the children and families in their communities.

The composition of the individual county transdisciplinary teams included physicians, nurses, social workers, speech pathologists, psychologists, physical therapists, human developmentalists, special education teachers, learning disability teachers, nutritionists, foster parents, and concerned parents from the local county health department, SRS, county mental health departments, hospitals, Head Start programs, preschool programs, public and private schools, Kansas UAF, and other local agencies. These groups received further professional support from allied professionals at the University of Kansas, the University of Kansas Medical Center, Children's Rehabilitation Unit at Kansas University Medical Center, the Kansas UAF, Wichita State University, Kansas Crippled Children Commission, and others.

The goals of these concerned groups were as follows:

1. To provide a continuing community resource to recognize, refer, evaluate, and help treat children with developmental disabilities;
2. To help provide a comprehensive developmental management program for infants and their parents through various service models;
3. To offer service to the parents of these children that will enable them to understand their child's disability; to overcome barriers or threats to their child's early development of cognition, gross fine and perceptual motor skills, communication skills, and social behavior; and to participate with programs as their child's trainer and teacher in an effort to help achieve the child's highest potential; and
4. To provide interagency "child advocacy" by planning and providing for the continuity of appropriate services for each child through adulthood.

The Kansas City Setting

The Kansas City UAF was on the campus of the KUMC. This facility provided extensive diagnostic services, but it also featured interactions with the urban community and emphasized the development of health care delivery services which provided new approaches and new solutions to the problems associated with health care and education of citizens with retardation. The Kansas City UAF featured service delivery programs and supplements and complements the existing capacities of the Birth Defects Center, which was, itself, a service-oriented program. The UAF was also operated in close association with the existing CRU at KUMC. The UAF served many of the same types of children served by the rehabilitation unit, but the UAF included a much heavier training commitment. All types of developmental disabilities, including mental retardation and related problems in human development, were included in the patient population. This program emerged under the leadership of Herbert Miller and John Spaulding.

Children's Rehabilitation Unit

The Children's Rehabilitation Unit and the KUMC's UAF provided a whole range of services. The population included children with multiple disabilities, qualitative and quantitative problems in growth and development, mental retardation, cerebral palsy, hearing and visual impairments, learning disabilities, emotionally disturbances, autism, and birth defects, as well as battered children. A range of services was offered including diagnosis and evaluation, therapy, corrective medical procedures, complete assessments, and special classes and training. The ages served ranged from birth to 21 years.

The UAF greatly expanded the resources of the CRU and enabled the program to better support its research, training, and service activities. John Spaulding became the director of the UAF in 1969 and led an interdisciplinary effort on behalf of this program.

Mid-Central Legal Center for the Developmentally Disabled

As part of the UAF in Kansas City, a legal advocacy regional resource center for persons with developmental disabilities was established to provide information and training regarding advocacy and legal matters. The program served state councils on developmental disabilities, protection and advocacy councils, citizen and parent groups, and persons with developmental disabilities themselves. As part of this program, project staff developed a manual on the rights of persons with developmental disabilities. Intended as a resource, it explains the legal rights and other matters such as education, right to treatment, guardianship, sterilizations, commitment, estates and trusts, and so forth.

This center provided in-house training to CRU/UAF trainees on legal rights of persons with developmental disabilities, child abuse, and special education mandates. It also provided direct legal assistance to clients and patients in other programs at CRU, who may incidentally have need of legal assistance. But the bulk of activity of the legal center was directed at the community.

Legal center staff were involved in the planning committee for the Kansas protection and advocacy system, a product of which was the incorporation of the Kansas Advocacy and Protective Services, Inc. (KAP). The legal center director was chairman of the legal committee, which advised KAP's Board of Directors. Similar consultation services were provided to TALL, Inc., a United Cerebral Palsy project providing job training and community employment for persons with severe physical disabilities.

Legal center staff have also conducted numerous workshops and participated in conferences throughout Kansas, on topics which included child abuse and the juvenile court, guardianship, special education laws, legal rights, and sterilization. The number of participants in one of these presentations totaled 550 persons. More far-reaching in its impact, however, were the two manuals produced by the legal center. One was a comprehensive publication on the legal rights of persons with developmental disabilities in Kansas, which encompassed 15 areas of the law. The other was a layman's guide to Kansas guardianship laws. Both these publications served as an invaluable resource to Kansas attorneys, community professionals, and persons with developmental disabilities. This program was directed by Barbara Blee and Jan Sheldon.

Resource Access Project

Another resource program was the Resource Access Project (RAP) to assist Head Start services to children with disabilities. A major goal was to promote collaboration between Head Start and other agencies serving young children with disabilities, especially local and state education agencies.

The Region VII RAP was funded by the Administration on Children, Youth, and Families (Federal Contract HEW-105-76-1150, KUMC Grant #8522) to assist Head Start services to children with disabilities in Iowa, Kansas, Missouri, and Nebraska. The RAP offered or arranged direct training and technical assistance to 67 Head Start agencies for the design and implementation of individual programs for children and for the development of agency policies and procedures. Also maintained was a comprehensive clearinghouse of curricula, training packages, kits, diagnostic tools, and audiovisual materials, all concerned with preschool children with disabilities and their families.

Although the RAP served 1,600 children in Region VII Head Start agencies, services were also offered to other preschool service agencies. RAP staff members sat on coordinating committees for preschool services at regional and state levels and on national task force committees with other staff from the RAP national network. The immediate and projected benefits of coordination of agencies included an increased public awareness of the need for early intervention and legal access to educational programs for young children with disabilities, as well as increasing individual agencies' competence in serving this population.

Social Skills Training

An outgrowth of research with adjudicated youths was a social skills training program for youths on probation. The project staff worked with probation officers in Johnson County, Kansas, who worked with adjudicated youth. Probation officers were trained in treatment, assessment, and evaluation techniques. Those officers worked with 18 to 20 youths each year in an effort to train these youths in appropriate social skills. This skill training lessened the chances of the youths coming into contact with the court again.

Social Skills Training for Youths on Probation was a major and longstanding research training program supervised out of Kansas City, but with programs and trainees at all settings. This program was interdisciplinary in scope, cutting across traditional academic disciplines. The training program was based primarily on the premise that close working relationships among trainees and senior investigators were an essential component for training researchers. The trainees were selected for their interest in an area under investigation by a senior scientist and were required to become involved in this research upon acceptance into the program. As rapidly as possible, the trainee moved toward independent design, execution, and research reporting. The emphasis was on the day-to-day behavior required to conduct quality research. The program offered postdoctoral stipends and predoctoral traineeships with concurrent enrollment in a doctoral program.

Concerned Care

Another research effort with service aspects involved Concerned Care, a program patterned after the Achievement Place model and developed by Montrose Wolf and his colleagues. The program served adults with developmental disabilities in all ranges of severity and consisted of six group homes and three apartments. The environmental aspects of group homes were important in determining the best ecological makeup to assure or enhance opportunities to learn and grow. While working with adults who needed further training, the staff also worked with teaching parents in specific skill training programs and in the development of behavioral checklists for evaluations.

Concerned Care was a nonprofit corporation that operated residential programs for adults with mental retardation in the Clay and Platte County areas of metropolitan Kansas City, Missouri. The purpose of the Concerned Care program was to integrate citizens with retardation into the mainstream of community life. In this developmental process, Concerned Care had the following objectives:

- Residents were taught (to the extent they were capable) to take normal risks in the community.
- Nothing was done for residents that they were capable of doing or learning for themselves.
- Residents were taught the necessary skills to live independently or semi-independently in the community.
- Residents were allowed to live in the least restrictive environment that they were capable of managing.

Concerned Care operated six group homes housing from four to eight persons. Additionally, a supervised apartment program accommodated 16 residents. The 60 residents ranged in age from 17 to 57 and had IQ levels ranging from 18 to 80. Approximately one third of the residents previously lived in state institutions. The others previously lived with family members or were housed by the local county.

Concerned Care group homes were located in residential neighborhoods and were similar in size and appearance to other homes in the community. In each residence, a couple (teaching-counselors) conducted a continual learning program as an integral part of home life. The training included all areas of personal growth and was directed toward the individual becoming as self-sufficient as possible in the community setting. The following were examples of the subject matter covered with each resident on both a one-to-one and small-group basis: self-care skills including grooming, personal hygiene, and health; money management skills ranging from counting and making change to making and following a budget; food skills involving making a grocery list, grocery buying, menu planning, meal preparation, and cleanup following a meal; the complete spectrum of appropriate social behaviors; sex education; academic endeavors mainly in the areas of reading and mathematics for practical living; laundry skills; and care and maintenance of a home.

Each home, under the supervision of the staff, was operated in a democratic manner. Self-government principles, adapted from the Achievement Place model, were implemented. "Family meetings" were held from once a day to once a week in the respective homes. In the "family meetings," residents discussed and made decisions regarding problems in the home, purchases for the home, and individual and group activities. In this context, each resident was given the opportunity to have input regarding the circumstances of day-to-day living.

Finally, as Concerned Care residents become more productive and self-sufficient, many graduated into the supervised apartment living program and into jobs in competitive employment. The apartment living program was structured to foster growth and development that could eventually lead to complete and total independent living in the community.

Juniper Gardens Children's Project

The Kansas City area program, including Juniper Gardens, offered many services to developmentally disabled, economically deprived, delinquent and predelinquent, hearing-impaired, language-delayed, and other children with disabilities and their parents. The Juniper Gardens program was located initially in a public housing area of Kansas City, Kansas. This research program investigated the effects of environmental conditions on the development of children. By applying behavioral techniques and principles of learning, quality developmental interactions were made available to children in day care and school settings. New strategies and intervention procedures were developed to overcome the behavioral deficits of economically disadvantaged children in the area. The research and service aspects were interdependent.

The Juniper Gardens Preschool Special Children's Project was designed to train paraprofessional personnel as early intervention strategists in group day care, home day care and other preschool settings that served the needs of behaviorally disturbed and developmentally disabled preschool children and their parents. The training sequence involved modules in behavior management, positive approaches to solving behavior problems, assessing children's behavior, positive teaching strategies, and parent training/community liaison. The program served minority residents of northeast Kansas City, Kansas but there were no geographic or other restrictions. Fifteen students were trained each year. They worked with 300 to 400 children. In addition, the project was a practicum site for graduate student research and training experience.

"Training and Maintaining Paraprofessionals as Early Intervention Strategists and Day Care Home Consultants for Handicapped Pre-School Children" was a grant funded by the Bureau of Education for the Handicapped and located at the Juniper Gardens Children's Project. The purpose of this project, the Juniper Gardens Preschool Special Children's Project, was to train, at the paraprofessional level, personnel working in group day care, home day care, and other preschool settings to serve the needs of behaviorally disturbed and developmentally disabled preschool children and their parents. Trainees received up to 20 hours of undergraduate credit from either the University of Kansas or from Kansas City Kansas Community Junior College for the complete 11-month training. Trainees held a high school diploma or GED and must have been working (or be able to arrange) simultaneously with their training a compatible paid or voluntary work experience to serve as their practicum sites. Primary preference in admission was given to minority residents of the northeast area Kansas City, Kansas, but there were no absolute restrictions. Final development and dissemination of the complete training package was planned. Program evaluation included data on changes in trainees' knowledge and skills and also child behavior change data.

The Responsive Parenting Project, directed by Vance Hall, trained parents to use applied behavior analysis principles and procedures. The effects of techniques used for children with behavior deficits were well documented, but there was little information about how parents of "normal" children can use applied behavior analysis principles and

procedures. The program was significant because mental health workers, school authorities, and parents expressed concern because their children were having difficulty and there was a shortage of trained manpower
to help those who had developed patterns of maladaptive social and
learning behavior. The children were generally considered "normal"
but the behavior problems could become severe. Consequently, this program trained parents to work with their children to increase appropriate
behaviors in the home and school.

Day Care

One area of investigation sought to facilitate child development through
an urban community center. As a part of this research, day care centers
were established to investigate specific objectives. An infant day care center provided full day care to 20 children aged 4 weeks to 12 months.
Based on an open environment design, the children received early stimulation and the parents were able to work. The early stimulation was
important in normal child development.

The toddler and preschool day care center had a similar design but
served toddlers (1 and 2 years) and preschoolers (3 to 5 years). A fall
program was utilized and marked increases in early preacademic performance were noted.

Recreation

As children grow older, they no longer need direct care but instead need
guidance in establishing the skills necessary for successful and appropriate adult behavior. Research in school settings enabled Juniper Gardens
staff to take the treatment gains made in the younger children and maintain and extend these gains in the public schools. The technology was
made available to inner-city schools that incorporated it as part of the
regular teaching functions. Academic performance of high-risk children
showed gains and the teachers perceived themselves as better perform-
ers. Consequently, the service aspects of the research model enhanced
the lives of the inner-city children. The model carried over into the
homes, and staff worked with the parents who were able to maintain
gains by working with their children at home.

Home Intervention

Also at Juniper Gardens, a home intervention program was designed to investigate the effectiveness of a home-based, family-centered treatment program for children referred for behavior problems. The program demonstrated the effectiveness of intervention strategies into community settings and natural homes for implementation by parents. The behavior improved and the parents reported improved home life.

The Juniper Gardens staff worked with the Economic Opportunity Foundation to improve programs for the Juniper Gardens community. The Foundation improved the economic base of the community by providing skill training, referrals, and day care. This program was developed and maintained by Vance and Marilyn Hall.

Language Training

The Turner House preschool project in Juniper Gardens, developed and maintained by Betty Hart and Todd Risley, helped improve the productive language of neighborhood children. Inner-city children frequently have early language problems. The Turner House program served 16 4-year-old children and provided intensive language training in addition to preschool activities.

Family Reading Program

An in-home parent tutoring designed at Juniper Gardens to improve the reading skills of children in northeast Wyandotte County developed as an outgrowth of a doctoral dissertation study. The program was a volunteer service program sponsored by local PTAs and involved staff of the Juniper Gardens area. Parents were trained at monthly reading workshops held in local schools to help their children choose appropriate reading materials, to use the public library, to use several different tutoring procedures when they read with their children at home for 10 minutes a day, and to model, prompt, and motivate additional teaching of their children. Over 40 parents, with a combined total of 95 children, were trained. This work evolved naturally from the public school work of Vance Hall and his colleagues.

Paraprofessional Training

A program for training and maintaining paraprofessionals as early intervention strategists and day care home consultants for preschool children with disabilities was created in Juniper Gardens. The training program filled a need and the service aspect had far-reaching implications for the community. The 10 to 15 students trained each year affect an estimated 300 to 400 children. In addition, the economic impact in the community was enhanced with paraprofessional employability.

Paraprofessional training at Juniper Gardens apparently had its beginning in the Parent Cooperative Preschool in the early stages of the Head Start Preschool Program. Parents who brought their children to the setting were invited to participate in the classroom activities, under the guidance of Betty Hart, Todd Risley, and Don Bushell. Fifty-one parents subsequently qualified as teacher aides and were employed in community preschool programs as they evolved.

Many other paraprofessionals have also received training at Juniper Gardens. One level of training has been the training of research and clerical staff. Whenever possible, the research and clerical staffs of the various Juniper Gardens projects have been recruited from within the inner-city community. As a result, many who began as Job Corps, Youth Corps, or CETA workers or who were formerly on welfare have become skilled as research assistants, teacher aides, day care staff, and clerical workers. A high proportion of those who have worked in the project have found better paying jobs in the community. A number have gone on to community college to earn associate degrees, nursing degrees, or baccalaureate degrees at the University of Kansas. One doctoral student was initially employed as a research assistant with no intention of continuing her education. At least 160 persons from the community received on-the-job training by 1987 and went on to other employment. Ross Copeland was a key member of the paraprofessional training during the first 10 years of the program.

Mental Health

A training program for community paraprofessional mental health workers also had an important service function. The 120 persons who were trained to monitor and facilitate the socialization and educational process of inner-city children who were experiencing social or learning problems affected some 1,800 children. The program helped children stay in school and avoid encounters with police and other authorities. This program was under the primary auspices of Ed Christopherson and Mike Rapoff, who extended it to KUMC for extended use.

Parent Training

An in-home educational program for parents of young children with disabilities provided a service component to the Wyandotte County area. Parent training to stimulate cognitive and social development in their children and training in behavior management and skill-building techniques helped parents work with their children at home. A Kansas State Personnel Summary for Preschool Handicapped Children estimated that 8,750 children (ages 0–5) were in need of service. The use of parents for early intervention reduced the service gap and helped the children develop.

This program was developed by Vance and Marilyn Hall. The work has been widely disseminated and utilized.

The Development and Validation of Survival Skills for Low-Income Minority Women

This project concentrated on developing, evaluating, and disseminating a model program designed to build the capacity of human service agencies to serve low-income minority women. The project provided a tool for agencies to help women learn basic competencies that were prerequisites to successful participation in job training and educational programs. The training involved the teaching of survival skills, which included many of the behaviors necessary to take control of elements of the individual's environment, to increase self-concept, and to decrease the sense of isolation and powerlessness felt by low-income, minority women. The program was developed by Linda Thurston and has been active for more than 20 years.

Lakemary Center for Exceptional Children

Lakemary Center for Exceptional Children, in Paola, Kansas, was a school and residential facility serving children with mental retardation from ages 3 to 21. About 100 children comingled in the school program, and benefited equally from a full panoply of supporting services provided by a 100-person professional and paraprofessional staff. Lakemary was primarily a teaching, training, and treatment facility. It provided a demonstration facility for the UAF in the development and implementation of individualized program plans (IPPs). In addition, it was a research facility wherein investigations were conducted into effective and efficient organization, administration, and management of its teaching, training, and treatment services, as well as more general research studies of an applied nature. Lakemary offered consultative services and served as a demonstration model for facilities of its kind. It was funded through public as well as private sources.

One of Lakemary's demonstration project founders, John Throne, subsequently developed a second program in Asuncion, Paraguay, where it was referred to as Alegria. (Find information about the activities there in the files of the Partners of the Americas and the Inter-American Children's Institute.) The program lasted several years and became a prominent feature of the ongoing early childhood services in Asuncion. It was also replicated in outlying communities of Paraguay.

An Epilogue to Chapters 7 and 8

The content of chapters 7 and 8 is intended to show the interrelationships of research, training, and service. Each has been used to strengthen both the MRRC and the UAP. Our efforts have been presented in at least three ways:

1. *Research application.* If the data show research procedures to be effective, colleagues in applied settings can use the information to strengthen their service activities, both clinical and educational. The service efforts, in turn, can be observed and considered by researchers as procedural information for additional research. Likewise, if both scientists and their application colleagues have first-hand exposure to

each other's procedures and resulting data, the chances are that valid and reliable new events will emerge in their collaborative efforts.

2. *Training.* Research training was enhanced by pre- and postdoctoral training grants, by organizing the training to fit into ongoing research projects, programs, and settings. (See Fred Girardeau's discussion of research training in chapter 7.) Training was also provided for parents, children, paraprofessionals, teachers, observers, and many others. The ecology in which the training was provided was also evaluated in the Juniper Gardens Children's Project as a part of the training. In some instances, the training procedures, as well as the trainees and the trainers, were available to other settings to be used in other programs. It may be apparent that training has a compounding effect, both for the training setting and the affiliated setting.

3. *Service.* Sometimes called *exemplary* service, this can also attract attention and, thus, draw interaction from colleagues with research and/or training interests. If so, this interaction may also facilitate the productive strength of the service program, as well as the research institute and the participating academic departments. A colleague of mine in the bio–life sciences referred to the above interactions as an ecology for research.

While preparing this material (for chapters 7 and 8), I recalled an experience I had in the mid-1970s at the National Institute of Mental Health (NIMH). I was a member of an ad hoc committee that was formed to study a problem that the agency had in conjunction with their efforts to develop a functional library to process a vast amount of information from final reports of funded research grants. They had stacked these reports for three decades on shelves in two rooms that they labeled as "the Library." It seemed that no one had ever collated this information. Consequently, when a staff member was commissioned to write a report for public information, the author did not consult their own treasure trove! The ad hoc committee spent several days talking with staff members before writing a report. During the discussion time we found out that the research that produced the uncollated material covered most of the serious conflictive emotional and social problems of our society. The aggregate of the direct and indirect cost of these projects was more than $1 billion. Our report included a procedural plan that was called RIDU (research information, dissemination, and utilization). But actually, our thinking was that if a reporting-back feature were added, the agency could set better priorities for future funding. In that event, the system would be called RIDUR. The agency elected to use the shorter version. Incidentally, they still use RIDU at NIMH. The purpose of my commenting on this long-ago experience is simply to point out that the description I gave about our MRRC–UAP combination, is a RIDUR system and that it is a system that does not cost anything to arrange. In fact it saves money. Admittedly, RIDU was designed for a national agency and the Kansas program was arranged for the Mental Retardation and Human Development Center. Nevertheless, they both are designed to put the process together—the process being from research to service and instruction and back again. In other words, it is a circuit of events that can have a compounding effect.

9

The Transition Years

RICHARD L. SCHIEFELBUSCH

he 1980s proved to be strenuous years of unanticipated complexity. The 1960s and the 1970s had been years of expansion
and development. But, from the beginning, the 1980s seemed
destined to be a period of transition, planning, and recommitment.
Indirectly, the period of transition was induced by the vice chancellor for research and graduate studies. Dr. Horowitz obviously wished
to use my upcoming administrative retirement, due to take place
in 1983, at age 65, to do an in-house review of the entire Bureau of
Child Research (BCR) program. So, at the beginning of the decade, a
planning committee was formed with Joe Spradlin and Ann Kaiser
as co-chairs.

At roughly the same time, the BCR and its university leaders became
aware that the Reagan administration was planning to reduce the funding base of the Health, Education, and Welfare department by cutting
back on the congressional appropriations and by sending a substantial
portion of federal research funds to the states as block grants. The still
remaining funds would be used to finance a smaller portion of research
applications, estimated in some agencies to be about 7% of *approved*
applications.

Also, in 1982, the associate vice chancellor for research informed
the director of the BCR that the University of Kansas viewed the BCR
as a successful program but not as a high priority program. This
apparent view was emphasized further when the BCR's associate

director's position was transferred that year to the Institute for Public Policy and Business Research. This is the position that had been occupied by Ross Copeland, whose contributions to media development, building construction projects, fiscal management, and international activities had been huge! Unfortunately, Ross had died in 1980.

Also, by 1983, the BCR's annual budget had eroded by nearly $1 million from its previous high. At that time, the intercampus staff of the BCR set about the task of repairing the damage. In 1 year, the number of funded grants was increased from 18 to 28. In 3 years, the total budget had increased by 30% above the previous high. Among the fiscal events were three pre- and postdoctoral training grants that accompanied a new Doctoral Program in Child Language and a reestablished Program Project for Language and Communication of the Mentally Retarded. This increase continued on throughout the decade and into the transition to the Life Span Institute that occurred in 1990. Perhaps the most important feature of these increases is that they took place across the entire face of the BCR—Parsons, Kansas University Medical Center, Juniper Gardens, Topeka (Kansas Neurological Institute), and the University of Kansas.

Officials in Washington have since informed us that the shortage of federal funds that was anticipated at the beginning of the 1980s did happen but that there was also a drop-off of submitted applications brought on by the apparent lack of confidence of former applicants. But, it was also true that the depletion percentage of federal funds was reduced by Senator Robert Dole and some of his colleagues in the Senate who worked in congressional committees to reduce the block grant transfer to about 15%, and thus to prevent the major crisis that was anticipated by many participating scientists.

But the 15% depletion produced continuing stresses on the Kansas scene. However, they were manageable stresses. The upcoming years also were filled with still other uncertainties. For instance, the plans for new technologies were still tentative and incomplete. The Computer Application Unit was overdue for a technological revolution. The following letter that we sent to the acting vice chancellor in 1984 explains our survival plans.

To: Ed Meyen

Dear Ed:

Greg Diaz prepared the attached status report of the Computer Applications Unit before he departed Sunday, September 30. As you know he is assuming new responsibilities with Microsoft Corporation in Bellevue, Washington. We are continuing in the development of the network described in this report. Greg is keen to maintain his relationship with us. The feeling is mutual.

The plan described here began last February–March shortly after a site visit on the Program Project (Communication Research With the Mentally Retarded). This is a multisetting plan (actually six different sites), which calls for a networking design. The experience cued us to believe that we were due to experience an even more state-of-the-art problem in the upcoming Mental Retardation Center site visit. Consequently, we analyzed the functions that the Center must account for during the next grant period ending in 1991. The plan is geared to these functions. Incidentally, the plan would keep us well ahead of the expectations of NICHD review committees and would facilitate a round of new research developments. These realities come at a very good time.

Sincerely,

Dick Schiefelbusch

Of course, Davida Sears soon replaced Greg Diaz as director of the Computer Application Unit. Other changes in the central office included Paul Diedrich as associate director for program development and Ed Zamarripa as associate director for fiscal management. At the end of the decade of transition, the administrative office was in excellent working order.

It is important now to return to the Task Force Report of 1982 in order to give appropriate credit to its participants. Without doubt, it is the most comprehensive planning document prepared during the entire history of the BCR. It was especially valuable in detailing the management and leadership that had existed and the changes that were needed for the future. The document describes the attributes that a new leader should have as well as the research management structure that should be developed for the future.

The recommendations did not detail failures as such, but instead provided challenges for the BCR to match changes in technology and in basic and applied sciences for the future. The only questionable content in the entire self-study document, in my opinion, was a section reporting future strategies for developing needed research funding. Apparently, the formidable number of University of Kansas administrators and scientists who were interviewed in the Future Planning Study felt that the BCR could not possibly continue the growth of its research program if it continued to depend primarily on federal grant applications. This view was conveyed to all who read and discussed the document. The doubts and concerns that were expressed by university and relevant state planners were, of course, the logical and natural expressions of concerned leaders.

Nevertheless, the transition years demonstrated that the BCR had adequate leadership and an adequate administrative system for "confronting the future" during that time of adversity. But after all of the events and strategies are presented to explain the success story of the 1980s, the BCR's last director is impelled to explain that as the concerns and doubts of university leaders mounted, key staff members in key roles, in the BCR had already learned to provide additional effort and support wherever and whenever needed, to meet the changing demands of the transitional situations. They were accustomed to challenging circumstances. During the 1980s they were indeed challenged to confront some especially difficult circumstances. The results speak for themselves. The resources of the Bureau of Child Research and much of the Institute are their legacy—and a remarkable legacy it is.

It includes the development of the Dole Human Development Center (the Dole Building). This is the facility that the BCR group and their functional colleagues had needed desperately for more than a decade. This group had decided collectively to stay the course until new space could be arranged. In many respects the Dole Building was the outstanding achievement of the transition years.

In addition, the existing leadership of the BCR developed or added improved technology and new programs that were eventually to become centers in their own right. The programs were: The Child Language Doctoral Program; The Merrill Advanced Studies Center; The Gerontology Center, which was soon to develop its own doctoral program; The Research and Training Center on Independent Living; and The Beach Center on Disability. Two additional centers could also be listed with these programs. They are: The Center for Research on Learning, which was initially (1978) the Institute for Research on Learning Disabilities, co-directed by Ed Meyen and me; and The Work Group on Health Promotion and Community Development, begun in 1976 by Steve Fawcett. Both of the latter two were begun prior to the transition years but evolved substantially during that time. These centers, in aggregate, make up a substantial portion of all the long-term research and training centers managed by the Life Span Institute in 2004.

In addition to increases in the project and the program grant funding during the transition years, there were also major changes in the scope of the program. The "life span" designs of the institute called for the addition of the Gerontology Center to the Life Span Institute (LSI). For this purpose, the vice chancellor for research appointed me as acting director of gerontology. My most difficult task in this new role was to move the center from its location in Strong Hall to the newly built Dole Building so that it could be combined with the other components of the LSI. All of the space in the new building had already been consigned to other occupants. I examined the space plans of the Dole Building and the adjacent Haworth Wing where the Dole Building occupants would be vacating. Unfortunately there was to be no space available in either building! Shortly thereafter, I happened to be visiting with Jim Budde, director of the Research and Training Center on Independent Living, about the space problem. Without hesitation, Jim proposed that the Gerontology Center be invited to share his administrative space and that otherwise they both would garner as much project space as possible in relevant areas of the building. In this manner the Gerontology Center joined the other components of the LSI. When these space moves were eventually completed I found myself serving as acting director of both the Gerontology Center and the LSI. Fortunately, Steve Schroeder soon became the director of LSI and Rhonda Montgomery became the director of the Gerontology Center.

The transition years, of course, include Schroeder's entry into the Kansas scene. His even-handed research and administrative tactics were immediately regarded with favor by the long-standing research and other staff members of the BCR and the newly accrued members of the LSI, including the Gerontology Center. His force, intelligence, and experience impacted the growth of the LSI immediately. The overall yearly budget of his institute grew from about $6 million to about $16 million over the next 10 years. He was also instrumental in balancing the research portfolio more evenly between biological and behavioral research activities. He expanded the impact and the image of the LSI to a national and international group of colleagues. In short, Schroeder effected a positive, effective transition from the BCR to the LSI with finesse and good results.

10

Communications and Media in the Bureau of Child Research

ROBERT K. HOYT

O n a spring morning in 1970, I was miles off the western Panama shoreline in a helicopter under the command of the dictator of Panama, General Omar Torrijos. The Pacific Ocean below was changing from the color of brown coastal silt to emerald green. I could see what seemed to be dozens of huge manta rays swimming just below the surface. We were on the way to the island of Coiba, a Panamanian prison colony and farm community, and to Coibita, the general's private island hideaway separate from Coiba.

We were on a film-making venture. The sister of the dictator had arranged for us to spend several days in Panama, filming at a children's institute that she directed. After a week of filming, we were headed for a tropical island for a weekend with the dictator. Before we took off for Coiba, the Guardia Nacional soldiers loaded several cases of Johnnie Walker Red scotch on board. El Jefe knew how to socialize as well as how to command.

The trip was a creation of Ross Copeland, associate director of the Bureau of Child Research (BCR). He had an affinity for power and politics and moving in fast circles in a manner that brought notice. As on all BCR film projects, Copeland was the producer. I was the writer. Others from the University of Kansas also on the way to Coiba were Bob Gardner, cameraman, director, and film editor; and Frances Horowitz, chair of the University of Kansas Department of Human Development and Family

Life. Frances had addressed a student gathering at Berta d'Arosamena's Children's Institute during the past week.

The general was a physically powerful, intense, handsome, and proud man. He spoke English, but not to Americans; he spoke to Americans through an interpreter. He wore the green uniform and campaign hat of his Guardia Nacional. There were about 40 guests flying to Coiba (not all of them Americans, and mostly women) on two airplanes.

There was indeed a beach party that night. We sat around a table in the beach house and talked politics with the general, drank scotch, talked more politics, drank scotch, walked on the beach, drank scotch, and listened to music. As I said, not all the guests spoke the same language, or, perhaps more accurately, not all spoke the same Spanish. There were several different regional and national Spanish dialects at work through the evening. Gardner had an almost perfect sense of imitation of voice inflections. That evening Gardner stood by the bar in the beach house and carried on a long and animated conversation with a Spanish-speaking doctor who was having marital problems. The doctor never realized that Gardner could not speak real Spanish; he assumed Gardner was from a region with a dialect that the doctor did not quite understand.

We slept through what was left of the night anywhere we could find a spot to stretch out on the screened veranda of the beach house. Sentries from the Guardia Nacional walked the beach all night. Next morning we got up whenever we felt like it or when the foot traffic near us got heavy enough to make us stir. Copeland was still sleeping somewhere when Gardner and I went swimming for a bath in the surf and a vain search for a hangover cure. There was no breakfast. Instead the general sent some of his men out fishing. They came back with barracuda, which they cooked with vegetables in a huge iron pot over a fire on the beach. It was delectable.

Copeland, with the cooperation of Richard Schiefelbusch, had brought Gardner and me to the University of Kansas a few years earlier to help build a communications program for the Bureau of Child Research. Although the Panama shoot was not a routine film project, it was typical of the manner in which Copeland preferred to work and move. Even my own hiring had been an unusual move by university standards.

Before returning to Lawrence from Washington, D.C., 3 years earlier, I had been working as an intelligence officer. The place where I worked was located in an extremely depressed area of the city. A high fence topped with razor wire surrounded a building that had no windows. There were guards on the fenced entrance, and guards on the front door, where the first badge bearing a picture had to be shown. Another guard waited inside at a station behind bulletproof glass. Each person entering had to ask for an admittance badge by number. The guard found the badge and compared the picture on the badge with the person asking for it before handing it over. The person entering then passed through an opening in a steel door capable of stopping a tank round. Upon finding his or her way to the right floor, the employee entered a work area through a door that was essentially a locked vault. My new Kansas environment was quite a change!

Barbara McLean and I had become almost immediate friends after we met at a writer's workshop when we were both in graduate school at the University of Kansas (KU) before either of us went to Washington. She was completing her master's degree in English. I was completing my master's degree in journalism. After we had both taken jobs in Washington, Barbara and I had lunch one day in northern Virginia and she told me about the new research center job in Lawrence. The position was an information specialist on what was called a core implementation grant recently awarded to the University of Kansas. Copeland and Schiefelbusch had built the position into the core implementation grant. They were also planning the construction of a 7,000-square-foot media center at Parsons State Hospital and Training Center (PSHTC), complete with a sound stage and a film vault. Part of the plan included closed-circuit television on the grounds.

The job was somewhat uncertain, diverse, and complex and would have required her to relocate. Barbara was working for an educational materials producer in Washington at that time. She elected not to accept the position for a number of reasons. Her husband, Jim, was working for the Department of Education. Jim was later to become director of the Speech and Hearing Clinic at PSHTC. She also returned to Kansas not much later.

My wife, who by now was not surprised by anything I might suggest we attempt, encouraged me to interview in Kansas. We had met in Nashville while I was a paratrooper stationed at Fort Campbell, Kentucky. After the Korean War and before Washington, we had spent

7 years running a 1,600-acre cattle and wheat operation in western Kansas, until I decided to go back to school. She thought Kansas might be a better place than Washington, D.C., to raise our two small daughters.

I took the job when Copeland and Schiefelbusch called me (after I returned to Washington) and raised the salary figure they had offered by an additional $1,000 a year. They had already offered me more than I was making in Washington.

After I went to work in Lawrence, I waited in my office in Varsity House (at Tenth and Indiana Streets) for about a week for Copeland or Schiefelbusch to tell me what I should be doing. It finally dawned on me that they weren't going to tell me what to do. They instead pointed out several opportunities and then let me pursue what I thought to be most promising. That turned out to be routine communications products, and more.

Copeland had a deep, well-developed resonant voice. He had been a college radio announcer and was interested in film narrations. He was one of those rare individuals who can deal with delayed auditory feedback. Some people joked that Copeland was not real, that he had actually been built in Max Steer's speech and audiology laboratory at Purdue University where Copeland went to college. Copeland could listen to spoken words through earphones and then, without discontinuity, deliver the lines orally. He was looking for a speaking role as well as an executive role in making films.

Gardner had worked for a time on the Route 66 show, one of the classics of early black and white television. He knew film making from film stock to release print. He was a skillful cameraman and a brilliant film editor.

A few years later, our film crew was strengthened by the addition of David Lutz. He came to the university after working at a local commercial film company. He was a dedicated and fastidious sound man. Two words we never heard from Lutz were, "good enough." If the sound was not perfect, he would not accept it, and he would stop the filming of a scene anywhere the sound faltered. Lutz also had the reflexes of a cat. He and Gardner and I were once driving down a highway on the way to make a film in Nebraska when the hood on Gardner's pickup came open, flew up, and blocked the windshield. I was sitting in the middle. Gardner was momentarily stunned by suddenly being unable to see the road. Lutz immediately reached across me, took the steering wheel in his left hand, and guided the pickup off the road and to a stop by watching the white line out of his window.

Before coming to Lawrence, Gardner had been working in Parsons where Howard Bair, superintendent, had established a film project under a federal vocational rehabilitation grant. Bair was a believer in media. He had arranged that first media grant through his contacts in Topeka. It was a vocational education grant to produce a series of vocational training films to be used to train vocational counselors who worked with persons with mental retardation.

Working with the Parsons media group, we made half a dozen films about counseling persons with mental retardation. Although not a writer himself, Gardner (who worked in Parsons during the series of counseling films) taught me how to write technical film scripts by making suggestions and critiquing rough scripts and explaining to me what was possible and what was not possible, and what it would cost for special effects. The film project was only one of the things that the media department at Parsons was responsible for doing. Much of the work those days was routine photography and the production of teaching and presentation materials.

Gardner later left Parsons and moved to Lawrence, mostly because he wanted to make films, and because Copeland and I were there and we were more interested in film production than in other media formats. Our first film made from the Lawrence base was *Spearhead at Juniper Gardens*. Copeland, R. Vance Hall, and Schiefelbusch had agreed that it might be time to publicize what was happening in that model project in Kansas City, Kansas. We had nothing in the way of equipment except an old, wind-up Bolex 16-millimeter camera. While I worked out a script, Gardner managed to borrow sufficient equipment from Parsons and from the radio-television-film department of the university to begin production.

Copeland found a room in a nearby renovated house owned by the Endowment Association. Gardner set up his editing studio, again with loaned, borrowed, and used equipment. Gardner was well known in Lawrence. He had done favors for lots of people around the university and had located most of the local people who could help him and whom he could help. He called in enough favors to get an old reel-to-reel editing system and a light table with a film viewer set up. We found projectors somewhere. Gardner settled into Hodder House, which was a special education instructional materials center at the time. It was on Louisiana Street, not far from Varsity House. With almost no camera equipment and no editing equipment in Lawrence, and very little in Parsons, we began looking for gear. Copeland found a mother lode of excess federal film equipment in New Mexico and Arizona. The gear had been part of secret government projects at Los Alamos and Fort Huachuca. Because we were getting federal research grants, we were eligible to get surplus federal equipment. I flew to the Southwest and picked up several cameras; among them were 16-millimeter and 35-millimeter Mitchells, the Cadillacs of the industry at the time.

R. Vance Hall, a recent PhD from the University of Washington, had come to Kansas to join what *Psychology Today* later named the Kansas Behavior Modification Mafia. Vance had taken the job as director of the Juniper Gardens Children's Project (JGCP). Vance's approach to living and to research was down-to-earth and practical. Although he was fond of being called "doctor," he had little patience with academic or scientific pretense. He immediately saw that a good teaching motion picture would be a valuable tool as he worked to spread the influence of behavior modification and the work for Juniper Gardens.

The project was designed to help low-income parents learn to manage the behavior of their children, and to help teachers in the local public schools use operant techniques in their classrooms. Todd Risley, Montrose Wolf, and Donald Baer, all of whom were to become prominent behavioral scientists, were cooperating in JGCP research and demonstration projects. The projects were set up in the local community center, in the basements of churches, and in classrooms in cooperating public schools. Vance Hall's office was in the basement of a liquor store.

These were the days of Lyndon Johnson's War on Poverty and there was federal money to be had for successful projects. To be successful, a project had to be known. *Spearhead at Juniper Gardens* was about the work in JGCP and the science on which the work was based. The film was made for teachers, principals, and anti-poverty project directors, to demonstrate that behavior modification techniques were effective in controlling classroom behavior and motivating students from inner-city areas.

   Bob Gardner was the chief ingredient in what became the production of a string of nationally accepted education and training films, most of them having to do with operant conditioning. Although he did attend Brooks photography school in California, Gardner had learned most of his craft from observation and practice. He was brilliant at improvising. He was hard working, humorous, and accommodating.

   During the production of *Spearhead,* I rewrote and rewrote the script and carried camera gear. Gardner filmed and edited. Copeland acted as executive producer and narrated. He was also chief screening critic. He loved to preside over the screening of the check print of a new film where he could turn the lights out, watch reactions of others in the audience, and then hold forth on the merits and flaws of what we had viewed. Schiefelbusch sometimes worried that we would take too many liberties with the respectability of science, but he never interfered or micromanaged us. That is not to say that he didn't express some concern over a few things that we did. We started grinding them out. By the time 16-millimeter films became too expensive for us to produce, and the focus of the research had shifted away from easy-to-film behavioral projects, we had made over 50 films that were in national distribution among research centers, schools, institutions, and training facilities. Many were very good films. A few were self-serving propaganda. All were the best we knew how to make them in the circumstances under which we operated.

   Spearhead at Juniper Gardens was long (40 minutes), black and white (which contributed to the austere atmosphere of the housing project), preachy (academics talking to academics but hoping that teachers would also listen), and timely. The idealistic survivors of Lyndon Johnson's War on Poverty were hungry for anything that would look like success in the struggle against chronic poverty. The audience included teachers, administrators of federal projects meant to help low-income families, colleges and universities eager to get into the federal grant game, and social service workers in state and local departments and agencies looking for tools.

   Unlike most of our later film projects, *Spearhead* had no accompanying printed materials. It was used by too many different persons in too many different ways. We never got a grip on what was needed in the way of accompanying instructional materials. The film merely demonstrated how behavior management could produce measurable academic changes in children. That seemed to be sufficient. But as it turned out, the film was only a stepping-stone to extensive training programs that were developed later to provide a path through the long list of not-so-successful attempts to deal with the problems of poverty and substandard education. Vance Hall developed an extensive training program called Responsive Teaching. It trained teachers to use reinforcers (rewards) in their classroom teaching. Vance's successor, Charles Greenwood, and his associates developed what was called Peer Tutoring. That program used the brightest children in the classroom to help children who were having problems keeping up.

Barbara McLean had returned to Kansas from Washington to join her husband Jim. She found a job in the KU Division of Continuing Education. She was a pert and petite intellectual whose conversation was sometimes difficult to follow. She had an enduring interest in literature and writers and she was an excellent editor, writer, and teacher.

Our approaches to media were quite different, but over the years Barbara and I worked on several projects together, talked about many more, and held many long, nocturnal, scotch-fueled conversations about writing and writers and how one day we were going to score big in the literary world. We had those conversations intermittently from time to time over the years, nearly until she died in a nursing home after a brain cancer operation.

Barbara was also a friend of both Ross Copeland and Richard Schiefelbusch. They all three appreciated the value of quiet public relations and good training materials. Schiefelbusch was also a dedicated educator and scholar. After graduating from college, Schiefelbusch went into the Army Air Corps and was shot down in World War II while navigating a B-24 back from a bombing raid against German submarine pens. He spent what was left of the war in a German prison camp. He was trained as a debater. He learned to be a survivor, motivator, and negotiator in prison.

After the war he picked up university politics when the department in which he was studying for his doctorate fell apart, mostly because of faculty squabbling. Early in his career he understood university politics. He was cosmopolitan. He could talk to anyone about almost anything. He has to this day a skill for being tenacious but kind. During my years of observing him at work, I learned that he would suffer the mistakes and outright misbehaviors of people who worked for him beyond all reasonable expectation, but when it was necessary he would take appropriate measures to correct a problem situation.

On my first visit to interview for the KU job, I quickly learned that the key players in the center at the beginning were Ross Copeland, Joseph Spradlin, Fred Girardeau, and Vance Hall. Spradlin was field director for the Bureau of Child Research at PSHTC. Girardeau held a similar position at the KU Medical Center (KUMC). There were many other good scientists in the organization in those early days, and more were joining as the organization grew. Some came and made careers. Others came briefly or for a few years and then moved on. Ed Zamarripa was hired a few months after I joined the BCR, just as we were moving into the new research center building. Zamarripa served a long under-study with Copeland and eventually became manager of the budget of the organization.

To get back to the media story, my introduction to mental retarda-tion took place at Parsons State Hospital and Training Center. Joe Spradlin had set up a demonstration project to show that adolescent girls with severe retardation could live together in a training cottage where they would learn to behave in a fashion that would allow them to be integrated into the community. When I went there to interview for the job, Joe was handing the Mimosa Cottage Project off to Jim Lent and some of Lent's colleagues. It was in that transition when I visited PSHTC for the first time. I visited that demonstration project, then another cottage where Lent had prepared a little surprise for me. He opened the door to a room full of Down syndrome girls and sent me in like Daniel into the lion's den. A few weeks before, I had been looking down at satellite photography of intercontinental ballistic missile sites in the Soviet Union. Now I was looking down into the faces of what seemed to be dozens of young Down syndrome girls all looking up at me, crowd-ing around, holding their hands out as if they expected to be picked up, while chanting their best versions of "Daddy! Daddy! Daddy!"

During my employment interview, I had learned that some researchers supported the idea of having a staff member to produce man-uscripts, films, newsletters, and other communications from the research that would be conducted. Others were not so positive. Ogden Lindsley told me flatly "the only scientific communication that is worth a damn is one written on the back of a used envelope and passed to a colleague."

Fred Girardeau at the Children's Rehabilitation Unit in Kansas City was generally suspicious of journalists and newspapers. A reporter who distorted Fred's research in an oversimplified newspaper feature soured Fred's view of journalists. There was no point in my pursuing media projects with Fred. He was amiable and friendly and a good researcher, but he saw scant benefit in trying to translate his work to the public, especially if he had to be processed through a journalist.

Schiefelbusch had a well-earned reputation for being fair, brilliant, highly motivated, and ambitious. It took a few months for me to fully grasp that Schiefelbusch and Copeland had hired me and set me free from a Washington bureaucracy to help them build a diverse communications program to get the new research center up and going. That was to be done through a combination of scientific reporting and public relations. It became obvious that Dick was not going to tell me how to do that. He would explain his views, hint at what he thought was needed, support my efforts (within reason), and expect something to happen, the sooner the better. He expected everyone who worked at the BCR to circulate through all its components rather that sitting in the KU office.

Schiefelbusch referred to Joe Spradlin as the "conscience of the Bureau." Spradlin was always a consummate scientist—a behaviorist through and through. He remains a thoroughly principled man who was willing to be convinced in those early days that media exposure had benefits for the organization, but he saw little there to help his own science. Joe understood the need for public relations and science reporting, and he advised and participated in many media projects, but rarely included his own work. Joe was much like Schiefelbusch in that he understood a range of disciplines and interdisciplinary problems. Before I arrived, Joe was already on the way to becoming the chief mentor, field leader, and scientist in the Parsons Research Center and for the Bureau of Child Research.

Ross Copeland was a flamboyant, intellectual, clotheshorse, a gourmet cook, an aficionado of the arts, an influence merchant, and a hell of a party-thrower. His, and Millie's, annual opening-game soirée was one of the major university social events. After the opening game, each year their house received a string of the university's best, coming and going in celebration of the start of another academic year and another football season. Copeland was also an accomplished speaker, debater, and film narrator. He was all the things I was not, which may have been why we could work so well together.

The chief thing we had in common was a love of the English language and its use. Ross was a purist and I was a pragmatist. I once complained because he had not read a narration as I had written it. He replied, "Bob, you must remember. I don't always listen to me when I'm talking." The next time he complained about some grammatical or usage error I had made, I said, "Ross, you must remember. I don't always read what I write."

Along with the newsletters, press releases, and other routine communications that go along with most organizations, I almost immediately began helping Schiefelbusch get scientific and technical books ready for publication. Schiefelbusch had an abiding skill for communicating coherently with professionals from many disciplines. He was an expert in the field of language and in persons with retardation. The federal government supported one project after another that he organized to bring language scientists from all over the nation together in language conferences. They presented papers that we turned into book chapters and published as texts and technical reference manuals.

We were also making teaching films and project demonstration films in addition to the behavior management projects that were in use throughout the emerging center. Scientists were learning how to apply operant conditioning to children who had been institutionalized with mental retardation, or who were having trouble in school and whose language development was at risk. The goal was to change the behavior of institutionalized children (and other children with aberrant behaviors) so they could live outside the institutions. It was working.

Because behavior management, operant conditioning, or behavior modification (which are essentially the same to laypersons) is so visual, it was natural that we should make 16-millimeter films to demonstrate to the rest of the world what was happening in Kansas. While we were finishing the vocational training films, we were also in production on a film we called *Operation Behavior Modification*. It was about Mimosa Cottage at PSHTC, where adolescent girls with severe retardation were being trained to live outside the institution. It was made with equipment that the Parsons media department had acquired through the federal vocational rehabilitation grant. It was as widely accepted as *Spearhead at Juniper Gardens* had been.

A spin-off of the Juniper Gardens Children's Project was H & H Enterprises, Inc. Vance Hall was a great promoter of behavior modification. He and I went to a local, commercial film company and proposed that, if they would make a series of training films showing the use of behavior modification techniques in schools and homes, Vance would write a series of instruction manuals to go along with them. The corporation was not interested. They saw it as a gamble and were not eager to invest in anything having to do with children with disabilities. Vance put up some money and we formed a company to do it ourselves in our spare time. We made only two films, but we did produce a series of manuals that Vance wrote (sitting at my dining room table for a few days), which sold over 250,000 copies. H & H Enterprises, Inc. flourished for a few years. We published a range of special education materials, most of them for parents and teachers. In the mid-1980s, when companies all over the country started swallowing each other, the owner of Pro-Ed in Austin, Texas, made us an offer we chose not to refuse. H & H Enterprises, Inc. was loaded on a truck or two and carted off to Texas. We were happy to see it go, in many ways. It was taking nearly all our spare time. We were operating on borrowed money, and we occasionally heard the sound of gnashing and grinding of teeth coming from the higher echelons of the university over something H & H was or was not doing. Some administrators who imagined themselves to be highly principled scholars were profoundly disturbed that a company nearly under the skirts of academia was producing and selling educational materials for kids who didn't have a prayer for getting into college. In a few years, the university would be encouraging people to market the results of university projects.

When the Mental Retardation Research Center (MRRC) building was completed as a two-floor wing attached to new Haworth Hall on the south slope of the University of Kansas campus, Gardner had moved out of Hodder House. The Lawrence component of the film operation was concentrated in one room filled with editing tables, rewind reels, cameras, projectors, film bins, and recording equipment. When Schiefelbusch and his team won a grant for what was called a University Affiliated Facility, two more floors were built on top of the research center. Copeland made certain that a room above the media operation was dedicated to expanded media space. He then had a spiral staircase built to provide access between the two media rooms. It was the envy of the other occupants. It was pure Copeland.

Juniper Gardens gave Lawrence filmmaking a jump-start, but PSHTC was the parent of the BCR media empire. It was an exciting time. Many talented students and temporary employees took part in the media program. Many moved on to new jobs. A couple of cameramen (Chuck Bemis and Mike Herzmark), whom Gardner had trained, went to the West Coast to work for a national television network. One of Joe Spradlin's research assistants joined the media operation (after he had devised a system to produce research photos for Spradlin in a tenth of the time required by the media department). Norman Baxley went on to form his own film production company that specialized in research and medical films.

One cameraman from Parsons went off to film a miracle. As a deep and fundamentalist believer, Mac Owen's life ambition was to get a miracle happening on tape. He was a good cameraman, but he had trouble at times. Mac had spent days waiting to film a scene in a cottage for boys with severe retardation. He was trying to film some very aggressive behavior so we could use it in a training piece to demonstrate how such behavior could be managed with operant techniques. One day Mac sat down to tie a shoestring and several boys got in a fight. They were engaging in the specific behavior that we wanted filmed. The boys screamed and shouted and turned over a bench. Mac leaped up to turn on the camera, stumbled over his loose shoestring, and fell flat on the floor. By the time he got up and found the camera, the boys had stopped fighting and were all staring at him to see why he was sprawled on the floor. We didn't let him quickly forget that. He was embarrassed for weeks. We never heard if Mac filmed his miracle after he left PSHTC.

A man named Don Reedy was director of the Parsons media operation when I arrived. He was followed by Wade Ramsey, Larry Thompson, Jim Bird, and Gary Burge.

Larry Thompson was one of the most flamboyant in a series of directors of the media department of PSHTC. He had also learned his skills from Bob Gardner. Thompson was a careful and dedicated film producer who eventually left to pursue television and telecommunications interests in Kansas City. Before he left, he was negotiating production contracts with other state agencies. He and his crew produced some outstanding public relations media products that brought money into the organization. That was the exception. Most of the film projects returned little in terms of monetary gain, though the public relations, training, and demonstration benefits were major. Thompson, one of the early members of the PSHTC media department, was an advocate for spectacular openings for films. We were among the first to use the stock NASA film footage of a booster separating and falling back to earth from one of the early launches in a film opening. I have since seen that sequence on television in other productions hundreds of times.

Thompson had the idea that we should get some aerial shots of Big Brutus, a mammoth, electric-powered dragline that was working strip mines east of Parsons. We were not sure how we might use the footage, but Big Brutus was about to be retired and made into a museum. We decided to get some film against the possibility that we could use it in the future. The film may still be around on a shelf or in a vault at Parsons. It was spectacular, but during the course of filming Big Brutus, Larry got airsick when his equilibrium was disturbed from peering through the eyepiece. He opened a window to stick his head out and threw up all over the inside of the airplane that Joe Spradlin was flying around and around Big Brutus while Larry ran the camera.

The last director before I left was Joe Crabtree, a mild-mannered, calm director whom everyone liked and who made some marginal scripts I had written into good productions. By that time, 16-millimeter film was becoming too expensive for us and we were struggling to enter the television world.

Crabtree was a dedicated and hard-working director. He was conscientious and devoted to television. He struggled valiantly to build a better television capability at PSHTC, despite being in almost continual pain from postpolio syndrome, which had required him to have a steel rod inserted along his spine. It was also a time when the Parsons media department was being pulled in different directions by different needs and interests among the research, clinical, and hospital staff. There was a chronic shortage of production money. Crabtree was also caught in the beginning of the transition to computers. It was almost impossible at the time to find technicians who had creative talents along with computer skills. Some of the existing staff did not want to change how things were done. New recruits sometimes wanted to change the way everything was done.

Media services had many supporters and many advocates over the years. There were those who could not wait to get their next film finished. Nancy Peterson, a very bright and attractive PhD, made several films, one of which she narrated about a classroom that integrated children with disabilities into regular classes. It was a hit.

We occasionally had an investigator who was reluctant to relinquish control of filming a project. One investigator insisted that we must not set up a situation or edit the film to demonstrate the behavior he wanted to capture on film. It had to happen naturally and in a certain sequence. He spent the whole production budget of several thousand dollars on the raw film we expended with the camera running on the subject, waiting for the behavior to happen "naturally."

Bob Fulton, researcher and audiologist, produced some of the best technical films to come from the organization. He was fastidious in testing the hearing of several persons with disabilities. He designed a stimulus and response measurement technology that precisely defined the auditory limitations of children who could not communicate through speech or gestures. We filmed those techniques for a film called *Hearing Assessment for the Young and Difficult to Test*. It was the third in a series of technical films on audiology.

Bob and I were also close friends and fellow motorcyclists. We rode from the Grand Canyon to the Smoky Mountains, from Atlanta to the Black Hills. We rode through some of the most beautiful land in the country and swaggered into some of the toughest bars in Texas. We spent many starry nights by campfires and far too many days in freezing rains or baking sun. He died too soon of a heart attack and prostate cancer.

William Diedrich in the hearing and speech department at KUMC produced several quality films and slide shows, complete with instructional materials that enabled other speech clinicians to benefit from his research and clinical experience and expertise. His *Counting and Charting Target Phonemes From Conversation* was accompanied by a user's guide for the film and a reference text for students.

Jim McLean and Lee McLean were perhaps the most consistent supporters of the media department at PSHTC. Nearly every grant they won included support for film or other mediation for teachers, speech therapists, and parents. Unlike many of the top researchers in the organization, they realized that it was not practical to maintain a large media organization on the crumbs from federal grants. They also understood that they could get the products they needed by putting production money in their grant budgets and then depending on a few skilled technicians to produce what they needed.

I do not mean that we never had any large media projects. We did, but they were projects within themselves and did not support general BCR productions. Barbara McLean, not long after she proposed me for the job at the BRC, had taken a job working for the Department of Continuing Education at the university. After several years there, she was offered a media position at PSHTC running a project directed by Jim Lent. The project produced educational materials for persons with severe disabilities. Barbara was not one to do things half-heartedly. She named the project MORE (Mediated Operational Research in Education). In a few months she had hired a staff, including graphic artists, writers, editors, and printers. She bought a printing press, after a protracted struggle with the university printing service and the state printer about why PSHTC needed its own press. The press was so large that it would not pass through the doors of the building that was to house it. Large double windows were removed so the delivery crew could hoist it through the opening with a crane to get it inside. In a few months Barbara had a media operation set up. It had a huge capacity. She could produce full-color, fully illustrated, bound publications. There was only one problem. She was set up to flood the world with training materials based on scientific projects at Parsons, but the input stream to her media operation was a trickle. Barbara and the whole project finally moved to Peabody College at Vanderbilt University in Nashville, where the project produced a series of effective materials before she died. The project also held workshops for teachers, paraprofessionals, and parents in the United States and Canada. The workshops were discussions of the philosophy of the operation, design, and dissemination of systematic instructional packages for teaching daily living skills to children with severe disabilities.

In 1978, the entire media services department at PSHTC was transferred from the control of PSHTC to the BCR. That added six staff members to the BCR; brought several thousands of dollars worth of film, television, and photographic equipment to the BCR; and added approximately $100,000 a year to the BCR budget in funds that were annually appropriated to support media production—or at least it should have. Somewhere in the shuffle, the $100,000 disappeared at the state level, was diverted into someone else's budget at the university level, or was appropriated from a media line item at the BCR administrative level. The media department was left with no annual state budget for production costs.

Meanwhile, on the KU campus, it was a time of major campus unrest. The student union was partly destroyed by a fire said to have originated in the ballroom. A rumor was that some imitation revolutionary had tied a 5-gallon can of gasoline to the ceiling by a rope, punched a hole in it, set it swinging, and tossed a match.

There were protests and riots. A bomb was placed near the Computer Center. It produced some minor damage and left a crack in the wall that was visible for years. Drugs were everywhere. The Kansas attorney general, Vern Miller, was making regular trips to the KU campus. He would hide in the trunk of an unmarked car and have his driver take him and a photographer to a place where students were smoking pot. Miller would then leap out of the trunk and make an arrest.

We once hired a group of rock musicians to record a music track on a film we were making. The film was called *Wheels*. The film demonstrated a project at Kansas Neurological Institute that modified and fit wheelchairs to conform to the different physical needs of persons with different physical disabilities. We needed contemporary music to go with the title. We had no sound booth of our own, so we used a soundproof room in the speech and hearing clinic next door to the media center in Lawrence to make recordings. The room was wired to an adjoining control room. When the recording session was over, the door to the soundproof room was opened and the rather scruffy looking group poured out of the soundproof room followed by a thick cloud of marijuana smoke. It was a career-threatening moment for us, but the air conditioning system was working well that day and it cleared out the smoke before any truly responsible authority arrived. We never hired that group again.

Bob Gardner found all kinds of talented people to help with the films: artists to do graphics, musicians to record music, and bit-part players. Some of the filming was done off-campus. It was hard work with long hours, and the crew sometimes felt the need for relaxation. We had two or three station wagons at that time, which were randomly assigned to whomever needed transportation. One day Dick Schiefelbusch came out of his office to get in a car to go to Kansas City or Parsons and found that the floorboard in the back of the car (that had been returned late the previous night) was all but covered with debris that had no place in a state vehicle. He could easily have fired the whole lot of us, or at least me, because I was responsible for that motley crew. I always suspected that some fun-loving student had planted the trash. Dick patiently decreed that the film crew would henceforth not use any state car except the oldest one belonging to the BCR. He made it clear that, in the future, woe be unto the person who had checked out any car, new or old, and left it cluttered with beer cans or any similar debris.

There were some unexpected moments in those days. We were once taping an adolescent boy in Jim McLean's speech and hearing clinic in Parsons. He was supposedly nonverbal and the speech therapist was working hard to get the boy to utter one intelligible word. We were pouring light into the cramped room, standing around, and watching the therapist take the boy time after time through a series of exercises, stimuli that were meant to elicit a response. After about an hour the temperature rose to an uncomfortable level. We made take after take, with the director yelling "Cut!" each time the boy refused to utter a sound.

Finally, after a particularly long and drawn out series of stimulus presentations, the boy looked at the speech therapist and said, "Cut! It's too damned hot in here!"

When the self-advocacy movement came along, the BCR hired a talented man with cerebral palsy, Randy Kitch. Kitch was very interested in media and took part in some of our later productions. He had one dependable leg and foot; the rest of his body was unreliable. He spoke by typing out words with his big toe on a child's spelling machine. It was called a "Speak and Spell," manufactured by Texas Instruments. When a key was hit, the machine spoke the sound of the letter. Kitch was quite proficient at making his wants known with the machine. He was also a strong advocate for the right for persons with disabilities to live their own lives as independently as possible. He was not known for hiding his disability or for any reluctance to try to do what everyone else did, including steering a moving car with one foot while the driver behind the steering wheel worked the brakes and the throttle.

As awkward as it was for persons who had never seen anyone with cerebral palsy eat in public, Kitch had no reluctance to take his rightful place in a public restaurant. Persons in those days were not accustomed to seeing persons with either physical or mental disabilities eating out. Kitch could walk after a fashion and he got up and down stairs by scooting on his backside. When he ate, we put a sheet on the floor and Randy sat in the middle of the sheet. The waitress, sometimes with tears and great distress, placed Randy's meal in front on him and he fed himself by holding a spoon between the first two toes of his functioning foot. We took turns cutting up Randy's food (and taking him to the bathroom). He was not a neat eater. The sheet around him was normally littered with pieces of food that missed his mouth. He loved for someone to say, loudly, after the meal, "Is it time to get the chicken to clean up around you, Kitch?"

The deinstitutionalization movement was very divisive. People seemed to line up on either side and take truculent positions. It was not always the old versus the new. It was a matter of believing that all persons, no matter how disabled, could live independently. On the other side were those who believed that the more realistic approach was to free as many persons as possible from the institutions, but to always have institutional services for persons with the most severe disabilities.

Bob Gardner, who had normally been apolitical, took a strong stand with those who wanted to close the institutions, toss the superintendents out in the street, and find a way to help even bedridden persons live on their own. It came to a head when Gardner and I found ourselves on opposite sides when we were trying to finish a film on self-advocacy. Gardner had sided with the radicals. I agreed with much of what they said, but I could not see my way clear to join those who were accusing the university and the state hospital of conspiring to obstruct the best interests of persons with disabilities. Gardner left and went to California with his wife-to-be to search for new filmmaking opportunities. I missed him sorely. Copeland died nearly at the same time at age 50. He had turned from media promoter to promoter of an international program, but he remained a supporter and participant in film and video until the last few years of his life.

Gardner and I were estranged for years, but my colleagues had the grace to invite him to my retirement party. Bob and Nancy flew back from California and we mended our fences.

In some ways, media was always a hanger-on in the Bureau of Child Research. The BCR had only a small state budget amid an ever-growing portfolio of federal research grants. The grants generated what are called indirect cost funds. That is an amount the federal government agrees to pay the university as compensation for the janitorial, utilities, upkeep, and other associated costs incurred by the federal grants awarded to the institution. That money, while disbursed through the state system, is not beholden to the state budgeting or the tinkering of state bureaucrats. My salary came out of state funds and indirect cost funds, most of the time. It was supplemented by other funds from time to time, according to who was doing the money managing and deal cutting.

The point is that most of the professionals in the research center were compelled to be successful in getting grants in order to support their projects and themselves, but I was spared that. I held a privileged position. I was free to devote my time to producing products, when there was money, while many of my associates were ever under the gun to get the next grant. On the other hand, it was easy to starve the media program because it ended up with no line-item production budget of its own. The PSHTC media operation was more stable in the early days because it, for a time, had a line-item production budget in the hospital budget that was not so subject to the good graces of the grants budget managers. The media projects generated some income, but that income was insignificant. How much good will, public relations, and reputation building were produced by the media products can be debated, but the Kansas Center was among the best known and most respected of all the 14 federally funded mental retardation research centers and the 30-some University Affiliated Facilities.

There were mixed opinions about the value and status of media. To this day some will say it was critical to the reputation of the Kansas Center. There were other researchers in the center who disdainfully regarded motion pictures as mass-appeal frivolity that would corrupt science. They scoffed at me for putting script-writing credits and magazine and newspaper feature stories on my vita. Yet they saw nothing amiss in making an entry on their own professional record for having spoken at some professional convention to an audience of half a dozen persons with hangovers and sleep deprivation.

Toward the end of my career at KU, the name of the Bureau of Child Research was changed to the Schiefelbusch Institute for Life Span Studies to honor Dick Schiefelbusch, who was retiring by then. It was in some ways a fortuitous time for him to retire. The center had become a huge tent under which anyone with a federal grant for human or social research was welcome.

An organization chart is the most basic of media products. I drew many organization charts in the 28 years I worked for and with Dick Schiefelbusch. But somewhat like modern physicists who are still seeking the grand theory that will explain how strong nuclear forces, weak nuclear forces, electromagnetism, and gravity may fit together and not contradict each other, I never ceased trying to fit everything under what Dick always referred to as the Kansas Center. I once, half-seriously, suggested to Dick that our organization charts should be drawn on latex so we could stretch them to suit the needs of the moment.

In the beginning there was the Bureau of Child Research. Then came the Mental Retardation Research Center. To that was added the Kansas University Affiliated Facility. For a time that seemed to be the Kansas Center. But hundreds of other projects came and went. Some were BCR programs; others were not. But they could be combined into the Kansas Center in different ways depending on the report we were preparing or the grant we were submitting. Finally, there was the Schiefelbusch Institute for Life Span Studies. It seemed to replace the Kansas Center and the BCR, but it did not. It was merely a means to shift the budget of the BCR under different control and open up the operation to include gerontology and other interests. Outsiders and even insiders, continued to refer to the Kansas Center or the Kansas operation or the Kansas program, or more often, Schiefelbusch's Center. I retired still scratching my head and wondering how to create the great organization chart that explained it all.

Steve Schroeder moved from Ohio State to replace Schiefelbusch— a most difficult undertaking. Schiefelbusch was probably as near to being irreplaceable as any person on campus. But even he faced major challenges during his last few years. All the little centers and big projects were clamoring for their own space and more money. The most important research was being done in the biomedical field. Schroeder was an asset to what remained of the Bureau of Child Research because he could, much like Schiefelbusch, work across medical disciplines to change the direction toward biomedical projects.

Political correctness swept across the campus and it became difficult to make a product that would not get someone's underwear in a knot. When Copeland's influence waned and he died, several successful and unsuccessful runs were made against the scant resources of the media program. As an example, a sound man on the staff at Parsons, Rich Lindsey, died suddenly. Before he could be replaced, his position disappeared from the table of organization only to pop up as a clerical slot in the office of the vice chancellor for research. The university was threatened with a lawsuit because of a magazine story I wrote about a classroom that integrated children with and without disabilities. One child without disabilities was shown in a picture without a caption to note that the child was not one of the children with disabilities. The parents were sorely irritated. I had become so accustomed to not viewing persons according to disabilities that I neglected to consider there were other views in the world.

Efforts to modernize the media operation by increasing its technological base and training staff to combine media and computer technology to move into the digital era failed. Too many of its staff members were too old to change and too rigid to see the future. Too many new research administrators wanted their own media staff where they could exercise more control rather than a central production unit that had different production standards. They were right, of course, in a way. More troubling was that media projects were out of favor with administrators who controlled the budgets. The new computer and video technology had not yet settled into something that could be predicted more than a few months ahead. Administrators were reluctant to venture into areas about which they knew little and where the value of technology remained to be proved. The files of the BCR are sprinkled with study after study and reports from committee upon committee that studied, pondered, argued, recommended, and planned for grant communications programs, but not much happened. Up-to-date communications technology always seemed out of reach, too expensive, too uncertain, and too difficult to define and implement.

But we left a record with what we had. At one time, films produced by the BCR were estimated (from records kept by the film rental service of the Division of Continuing Education) to have an annual audience of up to 75,000 persons.

In the early 1980s, over half of all the professional literature on teaching language to persons with mental retardation had been written by scientists associated with the BCR and the Kansas Center. When Richard Schiefelbusch was awarded the title of Distinguished University Professor, the university provided funds to hire a research assistant for a limited time. Marilyn Fischer, a graduate of the Department of Human Development, was selected to fill that role. She became a skilled editorial assistant, fact checker, proofreader, manuscript coordinator, and general publishing assistant and member of the small media staff in Lawrence. Her care, attention, and professional dedication were major contributions to the production of the series of language books edited by Schiefelbusch. She later earned her master's degree and went on to teach in the public schools in Baldwin.

It was estimated that at one time 300,000 copies of books produced by BCR scientists were in use in classrooms and institutional training facilities. Several books were translated into Spanish, Dutch, Portuguese, and Polish. Research citations published by BCR and Kansas Center researchers filled two fair-sized volumes.

Perhaps the most significant aspect of the Kansas program (including the media program) is that no matter how circuitous the route it took, Kansas played a major part in finding the ways and the means for thousands of children to live their lives in the relative freedom of community programs, rather than being locked up to scream and rock out their lives in human warehouses. The BCR media program had a part in that accomplishment.

By the way, we did other things with the general in 1970, in addition to drinking scotch. We visited the penal colony and watched him hold court for prisoners who came before him one at a time, asking for leniency, commutation, or pardon all without benefit of a lawyer. We did not film that.

We watched prisoners (who had been sent to what was essentially a Panamanian Devil's Island) stage a cockfight for the general. We rode to the interior of Coiba in the backs of Guardia Nacional vehicles covered with olive drab canvas. The general stopped along the road and asked if anyone was thirsty—we were. The general nodded to one of the Guardia Nacional soldiers and he turned his machine gun up into a palm tree and coconuts rained down. The soldier took a machete and topped the coconuts and gave them to us. The coconuts were green and the water inside tasted if it had just come from a warm spring.

In the interior of Coiba, the farm workers and supervisors of a sugar cane plantation gathered under a large shaded pavilion to hear the general. The general asked the head of the farming operation how long it would take before he could raise more than one crop a year. The man said it would take several years. The general snorted, "I may be dead by then." He was killed in a helicopter crash a few years later.

PART II

THE SCHIEFELBUSCH INSTITUTE FOR LIFE SPAN STUDIES, 1990–2006

Edited by
STEPHEN R. SCHROEDER

11

The Roots of the Schiefelbusch Institute for Life Span Studies

STEPHEN R. SCHROEDER

The Schiefelbusch Institute for Life Span Studies (commonly referred to as the Life Span Institute, LSI) was created because of the growing national realization that all Americans, disabled or not, are living longer and their developmental problems at any age affect families and communities as well as individuals. The LSI came about through the partnership of two visionaries, Richard Schiefelbusch, the director of the Bureau of Child Research, and Frances Degen Horowitz, a highly regarded researcher in child development and gifted administrator with a knack for research and development. As the first chairperson of the Department of Human Development and Family Life and later the vice chancellor of research, graduate studies and public service, Frances promoted an entrepreneurial spirit at the University of Kansas which has had a lasting impact at the university as well on the field of life span development.

The roots of the LSI go back to the beginnings of the Bureau of Child Research (BCR) and they are chronicled in detail in part I, which covers the period from 1921 up to 1990. Part II covers the period of 1990–2006. Chapter 9, The Transition Years, recounts the foment and changes that were presaged by Dick Schiefelbusch's retirement after 35 years as director of the BCR. The university had difficulty replacing him. Indeed there were four separate nationwide searches before they finally found Stephen Schroeder to replace Dick at the age of 72.

These uncertainties as to future leadership, as well as budget cuts in federal funding for research and training on human development and disabilities during the Reagan administration in the 1980s, left the BCR in a state of high alert as to its future. Fortunately, with the aid of Senator Bob Dole, some cutbacks were reduced and funds were found for a new building, the Dole Human Development Center. Dedicated in 1990, it allowed the housing of three strong related academic departments (Human Development and Family Life; Speech Education; and Speech-Language-Hearing: Science and Disorders) as well as two research centers (the Institute for Research on Learning Disabilities and the Bureau of Child Research, which became the Institute for Life Span Studies after the Gerontology Center was merged into it).

These five units at the time accounted for more than 25% of all federal grant funding to the University of Kansas (KU). They all fostered a highly entrepreneurial interdisciplinary spirit, which is now widely accepted in universities, but was then rather unique. In fact, there was only one other similar unit at KU, that is, the Higuchi Biosciences Centers (HBC) attached to the School of Pharmacy. The LSI and HBC have since been close partners in research and development (R&D) efforts, HBC being the main neurobiological sciences research resource and LSI being the main behavioral and biobehavioral research resource for KU and the state. They provided a "functional action system" (in Dick's words), which, along with their many collaborative ties to the KU Medical Center (KUMC) in Kansas City, laid the platform for tremendous growth in research and development at KU. The LSI is now a model for R&D at the University of Kansas and other universities across the United States.

The LSI facilitates life span research, service projects, and training programs conducted by investigators who study human developmental problems. The LSI provides opportunities for more than 150 scientists of diverse disciplines (and a broad range of 35 professional specialties) to unite in the study of the human developmental cycle from birth through aging, preimplantation to death, and bench lab to field studies.

The central office of the LSI moved in 1990 to the new Robert Dole Human Development Building on the University of Kansas campus in Lawrence. Components of the LSI are in Lawrence at the university; at the Juniper Gardens Children's Project in northeast Kansas City, Kansas;

at the KUMC in Kansas City; and at the Parsons Research Center and Kansas University Affiliated Program (now renamed KU Center on Developmental Disabilities) in Parsons, Kansas.

Mission

The mission of the LSI is to enhance the quality of life for the citizens of Kansas (and the world) by supporting excellence in research, training, technical assistance, and services in studies of human development across the life span. The LSI's mission consists of four interrelated functions:

1. To discover (through research) knowledge to improve the quality of life in all phases of the human life span;
2. To provide technical assistance, consultation, and direct services on problems that interfere with a life of dignity and the social and economic contributions that persons with disabilities can make to themselves and others;
3. To provide practicing professionals and students (in formal academic preparation programs) with intensive experiences in conducting research and providing services in an interdisciplinary learning environment; and
4. To shape the direction of national policy and research by attracting nationally and internationally recognized experts to the university for advanced studies on issues related to life span development.

Professional Profile of the LSI

The LSI has affiliated centers and projects in more than 35 departments and divisions on the Lawrence campus and the KUMC campus. The LSI has off-campus research, training, and service sites in Kansas City, Parsons, and other urban and rural areas of the state, as well as in other collaborative universities in the United States.

An array of resources help the LSI accomplish its mission. The most important resources are people committed to collaborative, interdisciplinary research, service, and training under several broad thematic areas, which change according to investigators' research interests and availability of federal grant funds:

1. Cellular and Molecular Biology of Early Development
2. Neurobiology
3. Risk, Intervention, and Prevention
4. Language, Communication Disorders, and Cognition
5. Aging
6. Behavioral Analysis
7. Family Support Systems
8. Independent Living
9. Cultural Diversity

Program Development

The process of developing LSI research programs (including planning, analysis, evaluation, and monitoring) follows an integrated approach that considers all the implications of policy, research strengths, resources available, traditional areas of investigation, relevance to the mission of the LSI, and relevance to national funding patterns in sponsored research. Developing new programs and maintaining old programs must address all these issues to match the strengths of the organization with the practical aspects of maintaining a diverse funding base, including local, state, federal, and foundation support.

The principles of operation of the LSI remain the same as those of its namesake, Dr. Richard L. Schiefelbusch, written in 1986 in an important paper entitled, "Research Administration." The operational philosophy is based on support rather than control, encouragement rather than structured demands, and positive rather than negative consequences. This is a functional rather than a structural administrative model with several enduring tenets:

1. To give the greatest administrative effort to securing favorable outcomes for the projects of professionals who collaborate in LSI programs;
2. To maintain an administration that is informed, committed, and persistent in pursuit of consensus goals and objectives;

3. To balance administrative functions with the philosophical pursuit of excellence, change, efficiency, and good will; and
4. To provide an administration that is supportive, nutritive, and attentive to productive collaborations and the development of professional colleagues.

These ideas seem self-evident in principle, but they are difficult in practice because they sometimes mean that an investigator's personal priorities may also have to accommodate those of the larger group, especially when large research programs and center grants are concerned. In order to succeed at the larger research enterprises, the research group may need to close ranks and share resources for the common good. Fortunately, all major federal funding agencies recognize this fact, and they have built these contingencies into their grant application and management policies. The more successful investigators come to learn these contingencies and use them. This circumstance puts R&D action systems like the LSI in a facilitative and information-giving role rather than the role of policemen most of the time. This is mostly an advantage. The downside, of course, is that the LSI is very subject to funding whims and regulations. Because it is leveraged so highly (6:1 ratio of federal to state dollars), it has to go where the funding is available.

Transition to the General Motors Model at LSI

How did we implement the Schiefelbusch principles of research administration at LSI? The LSI helps investigators negotiate the sometimes troubled waters of grantsmanship by providing program supports in all of the core resources necessary to be successful at the grantsmanship enterprise. The larger grant programs help and nurture the smaller ones. Junior investigators are developed through an apprenticeship model attaching them to more senior colleagues who are successful grantees. Preapplication reviews and guidance are given if requested. Expertise on all of the technical aspects of grant application are provided, so that grant applicants can learn their craft.

How did we operationalize this plan? When Steve Schroeder arrived at LSI in 1990, it became apparent to him that all the basic ingredients for a large expansion of LSI were already there in the Bureau of Child

Research. All they needed were a little organization, focus, and encouragement through total quality management (TQM) principles. The occupation of the new Dole Human Development Center and the dedication of the Schiefelbusch Institute for Life Span Studies were the public occasions for launching the effort.

The General Motors model for R&D was to promote the development of a broad collection of centers within the LSI. It fit the funding pattern for federal granting agencies, and it encouraged the development of more autonomous programmatic research groups, with individual grants clustered around the larger center grants and program projects. Programmatic grants fostered the group cohesion and incentives to collaborate on interdisciplinary projects where the goal was for the whole to be greater than the sum of its parts and where larger research questions could be attacked that no individual investigator could accomplish by himself or herself. Each center or program would be more autonomous and develop a sense of ownership of its program, generating ever more individual projects that over time could develop themselves into new research programs. These programs would then serve as the core resource for training grants, demonstration grants, and dissemination grants. Program grants always had a multiplicative effect. Even if the program grant application was unsuccessful, the collaborative effort could be resubmitted as a cluster of individual grants (IRPGs). So they were a win-win strategy that LSI investigators pursued very successfully. Over a 12-year period, the LSI expanded from 8 to 16 centers and program projects.

Decentralization and Total Quality Management

A key feature of the TQM approach was consensual decision making. All major programmatic decisions were vetted with the LSI central office staff, the LSI center directors, and funded individual investigators at regular program support committee meetings. These meetings occurred weekly in the early 1990s until everyone was "on the same page." Eventually they tapered off to semiannual meetings. The guideline was: "Meetings cost money. Meet only if you have to."

A second key feature of TQM was decentralization of authority down to the lowest unit level possible. The final say was always left up to the principal investigator of the grant unless there were issues of ethics, compliance with regulations, or privacy involved beyond the group, in which case the LSI central administration had to step in. Two manuals, the *Pattern of Administration* and *Manual for Surviving at the LSI,* were distributed to each investigator at LSI. They made explicit the guidelines and procedures for decision making, budget allocation, space allocation, promotion and tenure, merit raises, sharing joint authorship, dealing with fraud or academic misconduct, affirmative action, compliance with university regulations, and so forth.

A third key feature was decentralization of the LSI budget. Budgets were negotiated with each center director on an annual basis and allocated for the year based on the center's performance, just as the LSI had to negotiate with the university for its budget. This gave the centers an opportunity to do multiyear planning in defining their programmatic direction, recruitment of new investigators, and rebudgeting more efficiently to meet their individual needs. They could opt to use one half of the overhead returned to the LSI by the university to cover administrative and financial costs peculiar to their environment (e.g., rental of space).

A fourth key feature of TQM was annual performance self-review. Since the university required an annual performance review of all academic and research faculty, we developed a self-review questionnaire with the help of the Program Support Committee. Needless to say, these meetings raised many questions about such a system and about how individuals from diverse backgrounds, disciplines, and interests could be compared fairly. Eventually, it was agreed that each person should be compared with himself or herself based on each person's performance expectations. Center directors did individual evaluations on members of their center and passed them on with recommendations to the central office, and these recommendations were used as the basis for annual merit raises. This system worked very well because our director of finance and administration, Ed Zamarripa, had just completed his dissertation on a survey of over 350 comparable research centers in the United States. We simply adopted his top 25 ranked criteria for productivity of a research center which we referred to as "Z Scores." The Zamarripa Criteria are now adopted widely in the United States and in two foreign countries.

Annual Goal Setting

LSI centers were encouraged to set annual goals for themselves. This was usually easy because they had to do this for their federal grant reports anyway. Individuals set their goals through their performance self-evaluations. The LSI set its annual goals through Program Support Committee meetings and negotiations with the vice chancellor for research, graduate studies and public service. We also adopted the long-range goals of increasing our grant holdings by 10% per year, because this was the minimum rate deemed necessary to keep pace with our competitors across the United States who often had many more core resources than KU had. It would also allow LSI to double in size every 10 years and stay ahead of its competitors in the university. LSI had to compete for university funds just as all other units did. Their major selling point was leveraging federal grant dollars for dollars invested in them by the state. This tactic always kept the LSI in a favorable negotiating position with the University in budget allocations, a position that it still occupies today.

Core Resources at the Central Office of the LSI

The central office of the LSI was blessed with a group of gifted specialists in grants development finance and administration over the years. They have been the glue that has held the organization together, helped investigators realize their dreams, and, when necessary, kept them out of jail by enforcing federal, state, and university regulations. These cores are described briefly below.

Project Development

Activities in the LSI provide an umbrella for a broad array of innovations that foster an expanding research program based on quality and substance. The LSI director's staff includes project development personnel to assist in preparing, processing, and submitting applications for sponsored research. The procedure is kept as simple as possible to make this service convenient for investigators. Generally, any investigator who wishes to be a part of the LSI meets with the LSI director. Considerations of relevance to the mission of the LSI, the quality of the research proposed, the accountability for the project, space for conducting the research, and the soundness of the conceptualization are addressed by the director and the proposed investigator. If the director and the investigator agree that the project should become a part of the LSI, and under what conditions, an application is prepared and processed through the LSI. The associate director for project development works with the investigator to prepare budgets, to satisfy state and federal guidelines that apply to the application, to respond to University submission requirements, and to prepare an application document in the proper format and with the appropriate content for the agency to which it will be submitted.

Administration

The LSI director's staff includes 24 persons with different specialties who provide services that lend cohesion to the LSI. Under the supervision of the associate director for finance and administration, staff accountants and bookkeepers are responsible for accounting reporting on the receipt and disbursement of state and federal grant funds. The associate director for finance and administration ensures that all state and federal guidelines are followed, that funds are disbursed according to regulations, and that the resources of the LSI are up to date and are used effectively and efficiently.

A word-processing pool provides manuscript preparation services for grant applications, progress reports, book and journal articles, correspondence, university reports, and numerous other formal and informal documents for internal consumption, university consumption, and for conveying information to federal funding agencies and publishers. An administrative officer and various assistants handle telephone traffic, mail, and university communications, greet visitors, and respond to public inquiries about the work of the LSI. These services are key to coordinating and sifting information among all of the many research sites of LSI grantees in the state and the United States. There is always one final portal of entry where inquirers can get their questions answered.

Computer Applications

Each major setting and satellite setting of the LSI includes an array of microcomputers. The Computer Applications Unit (CAU) maintains a staff of programmer/analysts, network support staff, electronics technicians, and clerical help. This staff provides services for all settings and supports over 300 microcomputers dispersed in Lawrence, Parsons, and Kansas City. The microcomputers supported by the CAU communicate with the KU central computers through one of the KU networks by direct connections or through modems.

Communications

The LSI maintains a staff of professional video production personnel to support research and clinical training activities. The LSI has available within the organization, or has access to, the technical and artistic talent and equipment necessary to produce professional videotape programs and printed publications. Media services facilities are located in the Kansas University Center for Disabilities building in Parsons and in the Dole Human Development Center in Lawrence. The videotape production facility is at Parsons and comprises a sound studio, production staff, and equipment. The media and communications program provides quality production in almost all existing media formats for scientific and public information dissemination.

Research Design and Analysis

Established in 1994, the Research Design and Analysis (RDA) Unit advises LSI scientists on research design, measurement, and selection of appropriate statistical techniques, as well as data management. It also coordinates a consortium of faculty statistical consultants who provide their expertise to LSI associates at every stage of the research process from grant writing through implementation and final report preparation. The RDA Unit also provides opportunities for updating quantitative skills through workshops, seminars, and brown-bag sessions.

Major Centers and Programs of the LSI

The LSI is made up of programs and projects that fluctuate in number from year to year as new grants are awarded and old projects are completed. The following descriptions are thus not the sum and substance of the work of the LSI. Rather, these major programs are the entities under which most of the other grants are grouped because of commonality of purpose, common research interests, or the relevance of the projects to a priority area of investigation. Each is described in a subsequent chapter in this book.

Kansas Mental Retardation and Developmental Disabilities Research Center

When the national Mental Retardation Research Centers program was put into effect in the 1960s by the National Institute of Child Health and Human Development (NICHD), it was recognized that no single discipline could unravel the complex problems surrounding the causes, prevention, and treatment of mental retardation. That was very much in line with the research already underway in Kansas. The operation philosophy established in the Kansas setting in the 1950s was to study problems important in making improvements in the lives of humans with personal or environmental disabilities. The first federally funded project (located on the grounds of Parsons State Hospital and Training Center) was to study language intervention with children with severe mental retardation. Researchers at Parsons put together a behavioral technology that included recording of behavioral events that emphasized reinforcement theory. That work led to a program project grant and (in 1966) to an implementation core grant. At the same time, pediatrics, obstetrics, gynecology, and biomedical programs expanded at KUMC to form basic and clinical research projects in fetal, neonatal, and early developmental problems in children.

For four decades the work has expanded. Associated with the intervention mission is a continuing effort to improve state and national service delivery systems so persons with disabilities can continue to move away from living in large, segregated institutions toward inclusive living environments that more closely resemble family life. The mission of the Kansas Mental Retardation and Developmental Disabilities Research Center (MRDDRC) is to foster research on mental retardation and developmental disabilities. The research includes both behavioral, biobehavioral, and biomedical investigations. A primary goal of the Kansas MRDDRC is to be a catalyst for overcoming barriers in establishing interdisciplinary research on problems of mental retardation and developmental disabilities. The MRDDRC provides resources and access to the synergism required to develop new proposals and new programs. Facilitation of multidisciplinary and interdisciplinary research and research training is a hallmark of the MRDDRC. A strength in this approach to the study of mental retardation and human development is that most MRDDRC research initiatives involve more than one discipline and more than one campus. Different academic orientations bring different questions to similar areas of study—questions that help investigators unite under common themes to produce a participatory commitment on a multidisciplinary front.

Four themes reflect the MRDDRC mission:

1. Language, Communication Disorders, and Cognition in Mental Retardation
2. Risk, Intervention, and Prevention in Mental Retardation
3. Neurobiology of Mental Retardation
4. Cellular and Molecular Biology of Early Development

Kansas University Center for Excellence on Developmental Disabilities

Interdepartmental and interdisciplinary cooperation influences the composition of the Kansas University Center for Excellence on Developmental Disabilities (formerly referred to as the Kansas University Affiliated Program, KUAP). The three-setting (Lawrence, Kansas City, and Parsons) KUAP began in 1969. The Division of Mental Retardation of the federal Social and Rehabilitation Services granted funds to construct facilities for interdisciplinary training for approximately 300 graduate students pursuing degrees in child development, clinical neurology, education, hearing and speech, music therapy, nursing, pediatrics, psychiatry, psychology, recreation, social work, vocational rehabilitation, and occupational therapy. The Kansas City site of the KUAP was also charged with providing diagnostic and treatment facilities for children with developmental disabilities. In the year 2000, due to a name change in the federal Developmental Disabilities Act, its funding source, the name was changed to Kansas University Center for Excellence on Developmental Disabilities (KUCDD).

Community outreach, clinical evaluations, diagnoses, program models, and teaching materials are among the services extended to the citizens of Kansas. The KUCDD develops alternatives to institutional care for persons with developmental disabilities. The KUCDD helps families of persons with disabilities define their needs and find resources and plan and evaluate services on a cost–performance basis. The KUCDD also provides in-service training to service providers. KUCDD applied research activities in Lawrence, Parsons, and Kansas City include model programs to serve children with disabilities and their families. Educational and behavioral training programs assist in developing individual talents that support more rewarding lifestyles.

The KUCDD supports training to university students at undergraduate, graduate, and postgraduate levels. In-service training is provided for persons already working in habilitation programs for children and adults with disabilities. The KUCDD promotes the development of community services and training for parents and others concerned with the needs of persons with developmental disabilities in home and community settings, and with the full inclusion of children with disabilities in their own public schools.

The University of Kansas at Parsons

KU's first extensive and collaborative program to conduct research and provide research-based service programs for persons with disabilities began in the mid-1950s when KU and Parsons State Hospital and Training Center (PSHTC) were awarded a federal research grant to study language intervention for children with severe mental retardation. For nearly 50 years, KU has maintained research and training programs on the campus of PSHTC, including a component of the Kansas MRRC and a component of the KUAP. These stable and productive components of the LSI have produced nationally recognized Parsons Research Center behavioral research and training information for professionals in both institutional and community-based provider programs. Further, the university program at Parsons houses the media service department that provides communications and support services to the LSI.

Today, research and training staff are focusing their efforts on many timely issues including: studies of reading; effects of reinforcement variables on self-injurious and destructive behaviors; effects of drugs on aberrant behaviors, adaptive behaviors, and cognitive skills; movement-related brain potentials in individuals with Down syndrome; relational and symbolic learning; stimulus control and stimulus classes; treatment of sexual deviancy; and smoking cessation. This site also provides extensive service, training, and technical assistance to the state of Kansas, as well as the outreach into other states, in areas of assistive technology, early childhood and child care, respite services, services for persons with dual diagnosis of mental retardation and mental illness, causes and treatments for disruptive behavior in school-aged children, and training for community-based provider organizations and agencies.

The Robert Dole Human Development Center

In Lawrence, the various units in the Dole Center have discrete space, but share clinical and educational areas for children, and laboratories dedicated to interdisciplinary research. The Dole Center is designed to set a standard for accessibility for all persons, and to position the University of Kansas as a national leader on the frontiers of research on human disabilities in persons of all ages. The Dole Center contains several preschools for children with and without disabilities. Those preschools provide settings for extensive research in early childhood development. The Dole Center and the adjoining John T. Stewart Children's Center include the Beach Center on Disability, the Center for Multicultural Leadership, the Research and Training Center for Independent Living, MRDDRC research and office space, space for the KUCDD, and components of speech-language-hearing research. The graduate program for the study of child language in children with disabilities is also part of the Dole Center and the LSI.

Research in the Dole Center is concerned with developing biomedical and behavioral strategies to prevent disabilities; procedures for early diagnosis and intervention to remediate disabilities; preschool programs to prepare children with disabilities and children without disabilities for the public schools; educational techniques and curricular materials for children with disabilities; tools to measure and define the individual needs of children and adults in the educational, nutritional, medical, social, and employment aspects of their lives; and a range of service and training programs for families with members with disabilities. Ongoing research in the Dole Center also includes basic research on infant behavior and development, studies on how children learn, and various projects on learning disabilities and normal development across the life span.

University of Kansas Medical Center

The Ralph L. Smith Research Center at KUMC operates in two buildings on the KUMC campus. These buildings are part of the MRDDRC and KUCDD components of the LSI. The two adjacent buildings were constructed in 1972 and dedicated to research on mental retardation and developmental disabilities. One features laboratories and animal care facilities designed and equipped to support biological research. This building is a six-story structure occupied by MRDDRC investigators, with some space shared in common use. The second of the dedicated buildings is a three-story structure designed and equipped to support behavioral and speech and hearing research.

These buildings contain modern, attractive research space and provide an environment highly conducive to interaction among the scientists they house. Over 20 MRDDRC scientists have laboratory space in these buildings. Multiuser facilities include walk-in coolers and freezers, an histology and tissue-processing laboratory, tissue culture laboratories, animal care unit, conference rooms, and computer facilities. Major equipment resources cover a large range of high-cost units such as radioactivity counters, high/ultra-speed centrifuges, microtomes, ultratomes, and microcomputers.

The KUCDD was constructed as a three-setting complex and the largest of the three is the KUMC facility. The building was designed to house a mental retardation/developmental disabilities clinical training unit, including seminar facilities for students and professionals. The program functions under the name of the Developmental Disabilities Center (DDC). Children served in the facility come from the surrounding metropolitan area, the outlying areas of Kansas, and the nearby region. The program constituents include representatives from 11 disciplines, as well as close working relationships with other departments such as pediatric neurology and genetics, orthopedics, special education, nursing, and physical medicine. Interdisciplinary clinics with a strong training component make up the majority of the clinical programs. Additional resources of the DDC include a Maternal and Child Health LEND grant (interdisciplinary training), an Early Head Start research program, and a close working relationship with the state Title V Program, Services for Children with Special Health Care Needs.

Gerontology Center

The University of Kansas Gerontology Center's mission is to: 1) promote and conduct applied research on issues of aging; 2) develop and administer a multidisciplinary program of education for students, practitioners, and researchers in the field of aging; and 3) assist in the development and evaluation of programs and policies addressing the needs of elders. While the center is interested in all areas of aging, it has a special interest in the social and behavioral sciences. A particular focus is on public policies and studies of long-term health care and housing alternatives, communication and aging, service utilization, and aging among minority populations.

The center also coordinates an interdisciplinary graduate concentration in gerontology for students enrolled in any master's or doctoral program at the university. The concentration prepares students to apply their specialized knowledge of the social, psychological, demographic, and biomedical aspects of aging. In addition, KU has created a multidisciplinary graduate program that offers both master's and doctoral degrees in gerontology. Program faculty are drawn from several departments and professional programs on the Lawrence campus, along with the Center of Aging and several academic departments at the KUMC. The first group of doctoral students was recruited to begin the program in the fall of 1998. Center staff members also work with a wide variety of public and private agencies in developing programs for older persons and their families. Staff also assist agencies and organizations with evaluations of programs and public policies.

Juniper Gardens Children's Project

Juniper Gardens Children's Program (JGCP) began in 1964 when citizens from the northeast Kansas City, Kansas community joined with faculty from the University of Kansas to address child development concerns in a low-income community. The goal was to develop effective procedures to improve the developmental experiences and academic and social achievements of children. The project has grown over the years from a small, community-based research project housed in the basement of a liquor store to an environment that includes multiple community sites, projects, and investigators. Together, the community and the university have designed programs to intervene and improve the caregiving and education received by children on a local, state, and national level. The specific projects addressed by JGCP's investigators change over the years. However, most of the projects fall in one of the following major areas: educational research, early childhood research, parent and family support projects, technology research, and student and postdoctoral training. In 1996 JGCP was given the Research Award of the International Council for Exceptional Children in recognition of its outstanding research.

Merrill Advanced Studies Center

Closely aligned with providing program support within the LSI is a center to help guide the national conscience in matters relating to the needs of persons with disabilities. The Merrill Advanced Studies Center provides leadership in policy development and helps set new directions for research in a variety of human life span issues. Virginia and Fred Merrill established an endowment at the University of Kansas to create the Merrill Advanced Studies Center. The Merrill Center is an exemplary program for scholarly exchanges, including professional conferences, symposia, and book conferences. Future plans include producing and disseminating scholarly information and applied intervention products. The Merrill Center disseminates information in support of scholarly investigations and develops systems to help apply research discoveries to human developmental problems. Future support facilities envisioned for the Merrill Center include a forum for national conferences on topics related to life span development. The intent is to isolate areas that have not been thoroughly studied and to locate the best professional minds in those areas and bring them together to address specific topics.

Communication of People with Mental Retardation

This is the longest-running NICHD-funded program project in the LSI. It began at Parsons over 30 years ago and led to the reputation of Kansas as one of the premier language research settings in the nation. The current project uses developing research methodology to clarify the developmental history of several crucial communication abilities:

1. Categorization;
2. Progression from natural gestures to symbolization and from non-verbal concept to language;
3. Verbal mediation of problems; and
4. Generalization and transfer, in ways that provide more effective facilitation of communication competence.

The projects provide an interface between nonlinguistic knowledge and language, and two broad aspects of language–vocabulary and verbally mediated problem solving. An important strategy is to highlight the individually different ways that children, who are developmentally "different," function within the experimental conditions of the six studies and how, collectively, the studies may provide important information about acquisition performance and retention. The studies are designed to provide information about rule knowledge and interpersonal experiences in acquiring and in applying this knowledge.

Child Language Program

KU has the first academic program in the nation devoted exclusively to the study of language development in children. The multidisciplinary graduate program offers both master's and doctoral degrees in child language. The Child Language Doctoral Program is a multidisciplinary program spanning linguistics, psychology, human development, and speech pathology. It trains five predoctoral and four postdoctoral students in child language in three research areas: cognitive and linguistic bases of language acquisition, social and environmental bases, and the identification and remediation of atypical patterns of language acquisition. The program emphasizes the mastery of research methodologies for enhancing the "teachability" of language within this framework. Trainees are expected to be experts in a variety of research methodologies for studying language acquisition processes, and knowledgeable of seminal theoretical and applied issues in language acquisition, intervention, and remediation.

Rehabilitation Research and Training Center on Families of Children with Disabilities (Beach Center on Disability)

Funded as a rehabilitation research and training center, the Beach Center connects its research, training, and dissemination activities to family empowerment. Each research project supports and strengthens families' motivation, resources, and skills. Current Beach Center research projects focus on parent-to-parent mutual support, positive behavior support, fathers, friendships, empowerment, transition planning, assistive technology, family-centered service delivery, early childhood programs, family support policy, and other areas. A hallmark of Beach Center research is the active collaboration of the intended beneficiaries of the research in conducting, disseminating, and utilizing research. The Beach Center also offers the only doctoral program in the United States that focuses on family studies and disability.

Research and Training Center for Independent Living

The Research and Training Center for Independent Living (RTCIL) was formed in 1980 to develop systematic approaches to enable individuals with disabilities of all ages to live independently and work in their home communities. The RTCIL is based on a philosophy of consumer control where individuals with disabilities take responsibility for their lives and lessen the burden of care for their families and financial cost to taxpayers. It is a center where disabled citizens themselves study and help resolve their own problems. A needs-based intervention model supports the development of intervention products and the development of research and training programs, fosters technical assistance to other independent living organizations, and disseminates RTCIL products nationwide. The primary objective of RTCIL interventions is to help individuals with disabilities (particularly those from underserved and culturally diverse populations) develop skills, knowledge, and motivation to control their lives and shape their futures.

The Center for Multicultural Leadership

This center was established at KU in 1986 and became part of the LSI in 1991 to address a growing crisis in Black leadership in Kansas and the nation. It is a resource center for the development of Black leadership in the region and a forum for addressing issues that affect African Americans. In 1995 the center altered its focus to a multicultural approach and it now sponsors leadership training symposia and research into multicultural economic and social issues. By promoting the advancement of culturally diverse people in both the public and private sectors and preparing culturally diverse youths for leadership positions, the center encourages pride and excellence in the improvement of race relations.

International Program

In May of 1970, a *convenio* (agreement) was signed by representatives of KU and the Inter-American Children's Institute of the Organization of American States. The agreement laid the legal groundwork for an international program of research, service, and professional exchange visits among cooperating nations of Latin America. The international program has fostered exchange study visits for dozens of professionals from Latin America, Japan, Australia, New Zealand, Canada, Europe, and other countries developing programs for persons with disabilities. Graduate and undergraduate students spend part of their professional careers studying in the Kansas program, and senior scientists from Kansas participate in exchange programs to share professional skills with researchers and clinicians in other countries. The International Program has firm ties with the Ann Sullivan Center in Lima, Peru, and with the Alegria School in Asuncion, Paraguay where LSI staff conduct joint, ongoing research in a Latin American school for children with autism and other severe disabilities.

Work Group on Health Promotion and Community Development

The mission of the KU Work Group is to enhance community health and development through collaborative research, teaching, and service.

Staff assist community partnerships and grant-makers in building capacities to address issues that matter to local communities. We have worked with community initiatives in a variety of areas, including: substance abuse, adolescent pregnancy, youth development, rural health, health promotion, and neighborhood development in urban communities. Research and evaluation includes studying factors that affect community initiatives for health and development and conducting field experiments and case studies with collaborating partnerships. Teaching consists of graduate training in behavioral science, community development, and public health, and undergraduate practica in community leadership and development. Technical assistance, consultation, and distance learning are enhanced by an Internet site, the "Community Tool Box" *http://ctb.ku.edu/*, that connects people's ideas, and resources for promoting community health and development. The Work Group is also one of three approved dissemination sites for the World Health Organization in the United States.

Summary

The success of the Life Span Institute in the 1990s was the result of a fortuitous confluence of people and historical setting events (e.g., the U.S. economic boom, the favorable democratic administration that promoted the doubling of the federal budget for research in health and education, and the unique culture of research centers at KU that exists in only a few public universities). These are discussed in chapter 12. Dick Schiefelbusch was finally able to retire. Frances Horowitz became the president of the Graduate School of the City University of New York, her hometown, in 1991. When Steve Schroeder retired in 2001, it was possible to recruit a premier new director, Steven Warren, from Vanderbilt University. Steve had been educated at KU from undergraduate degree through doctoral dissertation, so he knew the culture at KU and he was really just coming back home. His coming to the LSI has taken it to a new level of excellence and there is no end in sight.

12

Important Historical Events Setting the Stage for the Life Span Institute

STEPHEN R. SCHROEDER

D eveloping and maintaining a university research center is much like betting at the racetrack. The evaluation processes are always a gamble, based on the horses you have, their readiness for the race, the track conditions, the weather, and good old-fashioned luck. Interestingly, the analysis of these setting factors is called "handicapping the race."

The analogy is remarkably similar to the federal grantsmanship game in which grant awards are extremely competitive, with few winners who take the money and those who place win little or nothing. At the Life Span Institute (LSI) over 85% of its budget comes from federal grant awards to its investigators, so handicapping a race for a grant is very important, and early detection of grant trends is crucial. Much of the success of the Bureau of Child Research and its successor, the LSI, was the result of good handicapping, that is, seeing the opportunities at which we might succeed, based on our strengths. The 1990s were optimal years in several ways for development and expansion of the LSI.

The Economy of the 1990s

The dot.com boom of the 1990s and the fiscal policies of the Clinton administration provided economic growth in the United States that also made available federal and state funds for research grants. It permitted the smaller as well as the larger research universities to prosper. This was especially important to public universities like the University of Kansas (KU), whose primary mission was teaching undergraduates and whose secondary mission was research or graduate research training. During the early 1990s, the United States Congress set as a national goal the doubling of the National Institutes of Health (NIH) budget within 5 years to $35 billion. The era of big science had arrived. At the NIH and the Office of Education, research branches relevant to LSI's mission began to fund larger centers and program projects more frequently. Because the LSI already had a critical mass of funded projects under way, it was very successful in competing for these larger grants, which, of course, also helped investigators to win their smaller individual grants. More linkages with other universities became possible through multicenter collaborative grants. Some NIH institutes (e.g., National Institute of Child Health and Human Development) even began partnering with private foundations (e.g., Down Syndrome Congress) to leverage private funding to enhance their federal funding. As a result, more grants per review cycle were funded. As goes the economy, so goes grant funding, usually lagging a year or two behind. So projecting economic trends was very important to the LSI's success in the 1990s.

Changes in Research Administration at KU

When Frances Horowitz left the University of Kansas in 1991, many of the LSI staff were concerned that we had lost a great advocate for our research priorities and the university had lost one is its best entrepreneurs. However, before she left, she succeeded in having Howard Mossberg, dean of the School of Pharmacy, appointed as interim vice chancellor to replace her. Dean Mossberg was also a gifted administrator who had developed the School of Pharmacy into one of the top three in the United States. He had a great ability to spot talent and he had a very entrepreneurial spirit. The Higuchi Biosciences Centers were developed under his aegis.

Howard also established a Research Development Fund, a new tool to fund larger scale pilot projects ($30,000–$100,000), with a view to making them competitive for federal grant funding. LSI was very successful in competing for these in-house grants. Besides, assisting investigators, these grants also helped to identify gifted faculty whose grant-writing skills could be shaped to make them more competitive grant writers in the future. This program was very successful in increasing federal grant funding at KU over the years.

A second important development in university administration was the recruitment of a new chancellor in 1995, Robert Hemenway. A native of Nebraska, and former chancellor at the University of Kentucky, Hemenway had a good understanding of research and development (R&D) operations in a public university. He also was very good at public relations and selling his ideas to the faculty and staff. He was a great fit for the culture at KU. Coming into a mild budget crisis induced by overspending by the state legislature, he needed to cut the KU budget by 3%. He took the opportunity to collect much more from the KU budget, reducing the faculty and staff roster by 500 positions, thereby increasing his discretionary budget.

Another tool that the new chancellor used to "get the fat out" of KU's budget was to appoint a universitywide committee to restructure and reengineer the University of Kansas, headed by Steve Schroeder and Deb Teeter, a gifted KU administrator. This committee met weekly for the next year, conducting focus groups with representatives of every sector of the university, to make recommendations to the chancellor for structural and policy changes that would streamline administration at KU.

Many recommendations were made by the Restructuring and Reengineering Committee, some of which the chancellor adopted, but others which were not. Three especially impacted the research sector at KU:

1. Going to the model of a research foundation, which allowed research investigators to bypass some of the gothic state rules of contracting, purchasing, and disposing of equipment which were irrelevant to the research enterprise. The research budget could then be used to grow the research operation at KU, and, in fact, it doubled over the next 6 years.
2. Moving from a vice chancellor model to a more hierarchical and accountable provost model, which streamlined the budgeting and decision-making process.
3. Striving for a paperless system of accounting and information technology, which speeded up and allowed more redundant information flow, while reducing needless duplication of effort. While this latter process was never fully achieved, it did improve significantly. Ability

to respond rapidly to federal program announcements and accounting crises is essential in the grantsmanship game.

The Ascendance of Designated Research Centers at KU

The idea of designated research centers at KU was a brainchild of the new vice chancellor of research and public service. The Graduate School had been made a separate entity as a result of reorganization. Robert Barnhill, another KU graduate, was recruited from Arizona State University in 1997. A mathematician by profession, he put his skills to good use, clarifying and "incentivizing" the role between the research centers and schools and the College of Liberal Arts and Sciences in the R&D enterprise at KU. There had been a good deal of discord between the research centers and the academic units at KU. The academic units felt that they provided most of the manpower for research at KU while not reaping the benefits (i.e., academic credit and overhead return from grants). They wanted all research centers to report to the deans instead of to the vice chancellor for research. The research centers steadfastly maintained their desire to remain interdisciplinary units pursuing the research talent wherever it was and not confining themselves to a particular school. Because almost all researchers also taught classes and supervised students, the trade-off was deemed fair.

The Research Foundation resolved this problem by encouraging individual research centers to negotiate a split of their indirect cost return with the deans instead of the department heads, and they gave duplicate academic credit to each department, and each of the other academic units, as well as to the research centers according to the level of involvement of each investigator. These were complicated formulae, but, once the rules were worked out, they worked well after a debugging period. This was a significant administrative contribution that encouraged collaboration rather than competition among the research centers and the academic units.

The Research Foundation also decided that they would emphasize their six largest and most productive research centers, rather than all 44 research centers, as designated research centers. The remaining centers were grouped according to their core functions and were allowed to grow according to criteria more suited to their needs. The LSI is the largest of the six designated research centers at KU, which puts it in a favorable position to compete for state core funds at annual budget negotiations. This fact has also been a strong selling point to federal granting agencies at site visits and in grant applications. It is an excellent resource and environment for R&D, something highly prized by granting agencies.

Continuity in Leadership at LSI

The above three points have had a very salutary effect on the continuity of leadership at LSI. All investigators know that they must do research and win grants to survive, but they also have an excellent resource system to help them in time of need. They have access to bridging funds if their grant portfolio weakens or falters for a period of time. They have the possibility of opportunistic recruitments, spousal accommodations, and so forth. if an important figure in their specialty wants to move to KU. The net result is a very high retention rate of research talent and little staff turnover due to financial exigencies at LSI. This is a very strong recruiting point in the highly competitive research grants marketplace. As Dick Schiefelbusch says, a good research center really runs on trust.

Transition to the New Director of the LSI in 2001

As Steve Schroeder approached retirement age in the late 1990s, he was resolved to accomplish the transition to the new director smoothly and seamlessly, so as to maintain continuity in leadership of the LSI and not risk a lapse in major grant funding that occurred at the transition to a new director in the late 1980s. Fortunately, the Research Foundation had made a practice of allowing overlap of the tenures of the outgoing and incoming directors of their designated centers. This allowed time to transfer all appropriate grants and the administrative reins of the LSI to the new director. This was a key factor in smoothing the transition.

In the case of LSI, it was especially complicated because the LSI director was also the director of two federally funded center grants plus an NIH program project. Because of university affirmative action policies, this transition had to be done in phases, that is, a separate search for the directorship of the Mental Retardation Research Center (MRRC), then the LSI directorship. This was costly and inefficient, but required by the rules. It also affected the candidate pool. The potential candidates had to be tolerant to subject themselves to such redundant and gratuitous screening. Therefore, informal contacts of potential candidates began 6 years in advance of the deadline for Steve Schroeder's retirement, in order to find a suitable candidate pool.

Fortunately, a KU native son, Steven Warren, was recruited from Vanderbilt University and he accepted the job, first as director of the MRRC in 2000 and then as LSI director in 2001. Steve was another great fit for KU, because he had all of his college degrees from KU and had been an understudy to Dick Schiefelbusch and Joe Spradlin as a student. So he knew and valued the unique research culture of the Bureau of Child Research and the LSI, and he was a very quick study. Steve Warren has taken the LSI to a new level of excellence, both scientifically and administratively. The LSI has continued to grow under his leadership.

13

The Kansas Mental Retardation Research Center

STEPHEN R. SCHROEDER, RICHARD L. SCHIEFELBUSCH,
AND PAUL D. CHENEY

The Kansas Mental Retardation and Developmental Disabilities Research Center (MRDDRC) has been one of the main driving engines of the whole research enterprise at the Life Span Institute (LSI) from its very beginning. It provided core resources which helped to spin off many other large projects and programs over the years. Mental retardation research is still a central focus of the LSI today.

Early History (1963–1990)

The Kansas Mental Retardation Research Center (MRRC) had its beginnings at several different settings and in several different ways. Perhaps there was no exact time that it first came into being. If forced to say that it began at a specific time, one must declare that it began when the center grant application was approved by the federal review process and when we were further informed that we were funded (fall of 1966). However, there were other key dates, such as, when the enabling Kennedy legislation was passed (1963); when the "machinery" was established for center grant applications; when we at the University of Kansas (KU) arrived at a multisetting decision to prepare and submit an application; and, earlier on, when we in the Bureau of Child Research received a 7-year, three-campus (KU, KU Medical Center [KUMC], and Parsons) program project on the Language of the Mentally Retarded (1963). Of course, there were other milestones and collaborations that determined our eligibility for applying. Then, too, interactive projects and committees had appeared on the scene as far back as 1953. The earlier events enabled potential participants to form working relationships and to gain confidence in collaborations. However, until the federal center program funds were legislated, there simply was no mechanism for establishing and supporting a MRRC-type program.

The Kansas Center, it should be understood, was made possible by the creation of a "franchise in mental retardation." The reality of this franchise could be described as a prior investment in the creation of research resources, professional group experiences, development of leadership and scientific personnel, and so forth. It should be remembered that the "Kennedy legislation" emerged quickly, seemingly without warning, and did not allow for enough time for a large number of potential centers to "establish" themselves. The franchise, essentially, must have been there already. For this reason, we should first introduce the beginnings of the Kansas Center as a series of project and program events that produced the franchise realities that we built into our application.

Early Beginnings at the Parsons Site

The first significant event was OM-111, a grant funded by the National Institute of Mental Health in 1958. It was a hospital improvement grant designed to develop a program for teaching language and communication to children with severe retardation at Parsons State Hospital and Training Center (PSHTC). Actually, although it did make progress in that area of work, it even more significantly created a research presence in PSHTC that initiated a number of professional objectives, such as recruitment, training, daily care improvements, and hospital–university collaborations. But, most significantly, it brought Seymour Rosenberg, Joe Spradlin, and Ross Copeland to Parsons in 1958 and Jerry Siegel in 1959. Before leaving for Bell Telephone Laboratories in 1959, Rosenberg was instrumental in designing the original studies. Copeland played an important role in the development of Parson's projects and other projects, especially media projects, for 23 years. Spradlin became the central figure in research development up to the present time (40 years).

The OM-111 project was expanded and refunded in 1961 and was subsequently replaced by a program project in 1963. Prior to that, a research training grant was generated by the hospital–university consortium in 1962. The program project provided a direct link to the MRRC because it established laboratories at the university and the KUMC to complement the research at Parsons. Also, a supplement to the program project enabled a group at the Lawrence and KC areas to establish the Juniper Gardens Children's Project in 1964. Two additional research training grants were also established in 1964. The Juniper Gardens Children's Project was expanded with a program project grant in 1967.

The MRRC was submitted as a center grant in 1966 and approved in the fall of that year. This approval was soon followed by a center support grant and other funded projects to support research and related activities on each of the campuses.

Applications Research at the Lawrence Site

It would not have been possible to develop the interactive and collaborated program of research leading up to the three-campus MRRC without the applied behavior analysis projects that were designed and implemented during the period from 1958 to 1965. The beginnings of this explicit, functional system were laid out initially by Joe Spradlin and Seymour Rosenberg during the first year of the original Parsons Research Project in 1958. They needed a single-subject research design with which to undertake the difficult task of demonstrating that children with severe retardation could learn socially useful skills such as responding (communicating), eating, toileting, play activities, and so forth. It was soon apparent that individually charted events could be used to demonstrate that the Parsons children could learn (be taught) socially useful behavior and that the primary objective of the new research project should be to design and to refine intervention studies that could make a difference in the daily lives of the children.

The procedures, once devised, could be extended functionally for use by graduate students, aides, teachers, nurses, and other hospital staff members. Furthermore, the studies could be replicated, revised, expanded, or situationally adjusted to fit into daily routines or caregiver plans. These tactics became the focus of informal seminars in which principal investigators, such as Joe Spradlin, Ross Copeland, Fred Girardeau, John deYoung, John Hollis, and their students and assistants could look closely at each other's data and research paraphernalia. One of the early investigators at Parsons was Frances Horowitz, who subsequently was appointed acting director of the newly constituted Department of Human Development and Family Life at KU. In 1964, she approached Dick Schiefelbusch with a daring plan to recruit Don Baer. Don was apparently seeking to move from his post at the University of Washington. He had been working at Rainier State School, where he and several of his students and professional colleagues had also developed a program of applied behavioral applications. Frances' instigation led to the recruitment of Don Baer and to the subsequent recruitment of Montrose Wolf, Barbara Etzel, Betty Hart, Todd Risley, Jim Sherman, and Vance Hall. Each of these investigators was given an appointment that allowed for at least half-time research. Thus, a new major academic department came into being, and the number and quality of the research cadres for the MRRC application were expanded and improved significantly.

The applications research (applied behavior analysis) was especially useful in the creation of the MRRC, because at that time there were few proven research strategies available for attacking the national problem of mental retardation. The congressional appropriations that enabled the newly formed National Institute of Child Health and Human Development (NICHD) to develop procedures for creating 12 centers throughout the United States were indeed a bold move. In like spirit, the various scientific groups that competed for these constructions and center support grants also were boldly imbued. The Kansas Center application was especially "innovative" because it included construction and program plans for three sites (a state hospital, a university, and a teaching hospital).

The Bureau of Child Research

The application for the MRRC included an administrative and technical plan that had been evolving for about 10 years. This extensive experience included management, accounting, clerical, media products, data processing, and personnel and research training. The new center was for the most part simply an extension of ongoing activities and assumed responsibilities involved in the Bureau of Child Research's (BCR) mandate. Also, the BCR was prepared to provide in-kind contributions in applications for the projected center. These resources were detailed in the center grant application and subsequently in each application and at each site visit review.

Resources and Developers

Beyond the BCR, other resource groups should be considered. The director, Dick Schiefelbusch, had had extensive interactions with virtually all aspects of the MRRC enterprise for the previous 10 years and some crucial aspects for approximately 20 years. In the period from 1948 to 1970, he had participated in developing special projects for the State Department of Special Education, the Department of Social Welfare, and the Department of Health. From 1951 to 1958, he had participated in developing team clinics at KUMC. He had also served on review teams in Washington from 1957 to 1980 and had consulted with an advisory team in Washington regarding the Kennedy legislation. He had also chaired state committees formed during the 1940s, 1950s, and 1960s to determine how Kansas should respond to the obvious need for research and training on behalf of persons with developmental disabilities. This background subsequently helped in the selection of resources in the preparation of the center grant application and the subsequent development of the center.

The effectiveness of the director was greatly augmented by other leaders in the settings and, of course, by researchers in the laboratories. A brief scan of these effectors brings out only a few of the contributors who were active in developing the centers and in making the center effective in the years that followed.

- *Clark Wescoe* had been vice chancellor of the KUMC and dean of the Medical School prior to his assumption of the chancellorship. When presented with the possibility of a Kansas Center for Mental Retardation, he selected the location for the construction of the KU unit and also called his colleagues at KUMC and secured their cooperation for the center's application agenda.
- *Herbert Miller,* a major national figure in pediatrics, volunteered to organize his colleagues and to write a research plan for the KUMC unit. Dr. Miller and his wife also had developed a day center and preschool for children with retardation prior to development of the MRRC plan.

- *Howard Bair,* superintendent of Parsons State Hospital and Training Center, was an extremely effective advocate for the center in the Department of Social Welfare and the Department of Institution Management. He also created cooperative strategies within the hospital and the state.
- *Donald Baer,* although relatively new to the Kansas scene, recruited the cooperation of his colleagues to the prospective center and helped to write the research protocol for the Lawrence unit. He also agreed to serve as the research director for the KU unit for the first few years of its existence.
- *Russell Mills,* executive associate vice chancellor of the KUMC, was a good microbiologist who also had a good feel for organization, for science, and for crisis management. Richard Schiefelbusch spent many hours in Dr. Mills' office and ran many possibilities by him before taking them to planning committees.
- *Robert Anderson,* chairman of the State Board of Social Welfare and a formidable political leader, endorsed the center plan and helped to arrange for state matching funds to create construction at Parsons.
- *Clyde Hill,* chairman, House Ways and Means Committee, helped to engineer emergency funding on crucial stages of center construction.
- *Ross H. Copeland,* research associate, had instrumental competencies in designing construction facilities, and in working with architects, technical teams, and other planning groups. He helped to write scores of change orders.
- *Joe Spradlin,* research associate, helped most of all to design and implement an enlarged protocol of research for the MRRC and helped to nudge all of us toward technological and scientific competencies.

These few examples emphasize that effective collaborators were available and that without them, the center would not have been possible. Following are a few more enabling colleagues—a few among many.

- *R. Vance Hall,* director, Juniper Gardens Children's Project, came to the project at a crucial time and brought vision, diplomacy, courage, and unity.
- *Uriel Owens,* director of the OEO Foundation of Kansas City, Kansas, provided an incredible link with the community.

- *Fred Girardeau,* research associate, volunteered to develop a three-campus research training program.
- *Bob Hoyt,* associate director for communications and the center media expert, brought the center to the attention of the world.
- *Edward Zamarripa,* director for finance and administration, created an efficient plan and was responsible for the fiscal details of the center. Federal, state, and university audits never questioned the center's fiscal transactions.
- *Greg Diaz,* director of the Computer Application Unit, guided the center through an awesome transition toward computer literacy.
- *Frances Horowitz,* chair, Department of Human Development and Family Life, gave an incredible lift to academic support.
- *Montrose Wolf,* research associate, provided immediate credibility for the research program at Juniper Gardens.
- *Melissa Bowerman,* professor of linguistics, was the tutor and acknowledged scientist in residence for language research.
- *William Argersinger,* vice chancellor for research administration at KU, served on the administrative committee of the MRRC and was instrumental in creating a viable design for managing an officially accepted center.
- *Paul Diedrich,* developed the best grant application skills among all the centers of the MRRC network.

Initial Strengths and Weaknesses

It was customary for review committees in the 1960s and 1970s to list strengths and weaknesses in evaluating program grants and center grants. Perhaps it is appropriate to list these polar issues now in summarizing the background of the MRRC.

Strengths

The strengths of the center included the following:

1. Support of state agencies and state organizations;
2. Support of university, medical center, and Parsons administrative offices (also tacit support and encouragement from federal agencies and other key personnel in Washington, D.C.);

3. An existing record of successful research development and research management;
4. A cohesive (small) cadre of able young scientists and technical personnel;
5. A validating reputation for ongoing quality research application activities;
6. A unifying collaborative management and leadership system;
7. Resources and experiences in research training in the areas covered by the center; and
8. Unusual enthusiasm among members of the instrumental planning cadre.

Weaknesses

The weaknesses included the following:

1. The center activities were scattered over three dispersed settings and two other active sites (Actually this was both a strength and a weakness. Today, with modern telecommunications, it is no longer an issue).
2. The history of research activities was relatively short and required a "leap of faith," because the center contract required long-term projective (20 years) operations. Although it was brief, it was also robust.
3. The research protocols were initially skewed in favor of behavioral strategies, leaving a relatively smaller emphasis on biological and neurophysiological issues (this was also a plus as well as a minus).
4. The bold investigations into application research were hardly *mainstream* scientific programs. A number of basic science members of review committees privately expressed their doubts that scientists could be recruited to Parsons and to Juniper Gardens. At least initially, this was the greatest risk factor of all.

Center Development

When the MRRCs were conceived, the huge national undertaking was hampered by the lack of research resources and strategies. Furthermore, NICHD, which was selected to administer the program, was a relatively new institute, and most of its personnel were inexperienced. Nevertheless, their efforts on behalf of the centers were effective. They set up an open system of communication with center settings so that information flowed in both directions.

The most effective funding, in addition to center support grants, was the program project grant. This multi-investigator research strategy allowed for several investigators to work together on related projects clustered within a larger theme. Usually the program project was in one or more of the MRRC's primary center objectives. These larger research programs were ideal for young investigators who needed experiences with older or more experienced investigators. Training grants were also valuable in recruiting good-quality young investigators as pre- or post-doctoral trainees. The center support grants were valuable also in providing for equipment, support, personnel, travel, and technical resources of various kinds. Program projects grants were 5-year awards and for this reason were stable support vehicles.

The impact of the MRRC for these reasons was to accelerate the quality of work and thus the career progress of a number of investigators. In short, the MRRC proved to be a magnet for both senior and junior investigators who wanted to enhance their roles as scientists.

It soon became apparent also that the MRRC was a desirable resource base for academic departments on both the KU and the KUMC campuses. The resulting interaction seemed to be advantageous for both academic departments and center personnel. Likewise, the research unit at Parsons thrived and in turn helped to enhance the hospital. The three campuses also created interactive strategies and, in aggregate, were more substantial than any single setting could have tolerated.

Development of the Ralph L. Smith Center on the Kansas City Site

The Kansas City site of the Kansas MRRC had its origin with funding of the MRRC grant from the NICHD. This grant, headed by Dick Schiefelbusch, provided funds to "kick start" what has become widely accepted as the university's "crown jewel" of interdisciplinary cross-campus research. With a combination of federal funds from the NICHD center grant and a generous gift from the Ralph L. Smith Foundation, construction of the R. L. Smith MRRC began in 1967 on two buildings that have housed the research programs of the Kansas City Center since their completion and dedication on June 14, 1972. Speakers at the dedication included Lawrence Chalmers, chancellor of the University of Kansas at that time, and Gerald LaVeck, then director of the NICHD, who both expressed pride and optimism that the new center would apply cutting-edge research tools to understanding and treating the many different forms of mental retardation and developmental disabilities. And so the R. L. Smith MRRC was born and has continued to the present day as a vibrant interdisciplinary environment where the convergence of biological and behavioral approaches on problems related to mental retardation and developmental disabilities has flourished.

From the beginning, the Kansas City Center had an emphasis on both human behavioral research and more basic biomedical research using animal models. The two wings of the R. L. Smith MRRC, comprising 50,000 square feet of space, reflected this emphasis, with one wing devoted to human research and another wing devoted largely to basic research into mechanisms of mental retardation and developmental disabilities. The individuals chosen to lead the R. L. Smith MRRC also reflected this dual emphasis with Fred Samson moving from his position as chair of physiology and cell biology on the Lawrence campus to become the first director of the center, and a behavioral scientist, Earl Butterfield, serving as co-director. Soon after the center opened, Butterfield accepted a position at the University of Washington in Seattle and left the center. Samson continued on as director until his retirement in January of 1989.

The leadership team of Dick Schiefelbusch on the Lawrence campus and Fred Samson at the medical center, along with many others, led the Kansas MRRC through a number of successful renewals of the NICHD-funded center grant. Throughout those years, site visits by NICHD review panels were held in the first-floor conference room of the R. L. Smith MRRC. Every competitive renewal site visit held in this room was successful, leading to the widely held belief that the room might have supernatural qualities favoring the inhabitants of the building. The last site visit in this room was in 1996 and it again was successful. The 2001 site visit moved to a much larger room in the new School of Nursing building on the KUMC campus. It was also a highly successful site visit. Given the competition for these center grants and the scrutiny they received during review, the track record of the Kansas MRRC with its multiple sites is truly remarkable.

Over its history, the R. L. Smith MRRC has been fortunate in having three very capable individuals as director. As mentioned above, the first director was Fred Samson. Fred was a neuroscientist considered by many to be the "father" of neuroscience at the University of Kansas. His work focused on neurochemical aspects of neuronal function, specifically the role of microtubules (the pipelines of axons), and the role of reactive oxygen species in neuronal injury associated with various perturbations of the brain, such as seizures. After serving as its director for more than 16 years, Fred Samson retired in 1989 but remained at the center as an emeritus professor. Fred was a scientist at heart and continued a very active schedule until his death in 2004. Paul Cheney was selected as the second director of the R. L. Smith MRRC. Paul is a systems neuroscientist with research interests in the brain control of movement and the neurological disease associated with AIDS (neuro-AIDS).

Over its entire history, research at the R. L. Smith MRRC has had two major areas of focus that have been complementary to the overall Kansas MRRC. One major area of emphasis has been, and continues to be, a focus on molecular and cellular aspects of normal and abnormal early development. Various researchers have addressed questions concerned with all the early stages of development, including follicular development, fertilization, implantation in the uterus, and early development of the embryo. This group was established in the early days of the center by Gilbert Greenwald and Donald Johnson, who were two of the original occupants of the new R. L. Smith MRRC space. Gil Greenwald later became chair of the physiology department and was in a position to build further strength in the area of early development and reproductive biology. This occurred through his recruitments in the 1970s that established a world class, internationally renowned group in this field of research. The strength of this group continues to the current day and this group remains a very important contingent of the R. L. Smith Center and overall Kansas MRRC. One of the true success stories of the MRRC, in fact, has been the growth of this highly cohesive and eminent research group working on aspects of early development. The MRRC had an important role in fostering the development of this group over its entire history. A landmark accomplishment for this group was the funding in 1996 of its own NICHD center grant on reproductive biology under the leadership of Paul Terranova, a former postdoctoral fellow of Gil Greenwald. Paul Terranova has emphasized on many occasions that the new center grew out of the highly supportive and interdisciplinary environment provided by the MRRC.

The second major, long-standing area of research emphasis in the R. L. Smith Center that continues to the present day is concerned with the neurobiology of mental retardation and developmental disabilities. Neuroscience is a large and diverse field and that is reflected in the composition of the members of this research group within the center. Work from members of this group have addressed questions related to development of the nervous system, neuroplasticity, mechanisms of neurodegenerative disease, ischemic brain injury, and brain motor function. Unlike the group working on early development, which is located primarily on the KUMC campus, the neuroscience group has a substantial representation on both the KUMC and Lawrence campuses. Neuroscience continues to be a vibrant and growing component of the Kansas MRRC.

It did not require much time to demonstrate that the Kansas MRRC was one of the most successful centers among the 12 MRRCs that had been established nationally. It should also be explained that the three units of the Kansas University Affiliated Program (KUAP), which were created in 1967 to be congruent with the MRRC units, were also thriving. The MRRC research, including the program projects, drew from and contributed to the units of the UAP. Research was frequently extended into the UAP's exemplary service and training units and, of course, the application research methods were equally productive in the units of both centers.

Transition to New MRRC Administration

Dick Schiefelbusch had been the only director of the MRRC as well as of the Bureau of Child Research from the beginning. From the point of view of the funding agency, this was a strength and a weakness. On the strength side, it was an indication of the university's strong support for the MRRC, but it also added to the complexity of its administrative organization vis-à-vis the Bureau of Child Research, which was difficult to explain to site visitors. Thus, when Dick was approaching retirement, it was difficult to find an internal candidate to replace him as MRRC director. Eli Michaelis, the director of the Higuchi BioSciences Centers, was an eminent neuroscientist and administrator at KU; but the MRRC was not renewed under his direction because of the issue of "complexity" of the organization and of the appearance that the KU MRRC was moving away from its traditional strength (i.e., behavioral research in MR).

Steve Schroeder had just taken the job of director of the BCR and it was decided to go back to the original administrative structure of the MRRC, but to delineate it more clearly. So Steve also became director of the MRRC in 1990. Paul Cheney, the newly appointed director of the Ralph L. Smith Center at the KUMC, became the MRRC co-director. Paul was an eminent neurophysiologist in the Department of Molecular and Integrative Physiology, a major department at KUMC and the academic home of many MRRC scientists. Paul was also a superb administrator who was highly respected by the KUMC administration. He was a perfect fit for the MRRC, and this team proved to be very successful over the next decade.

The MRRC revised proposal in 1990 successfully addressed the criticisms of the site visit team and of the Mental Retardation Review Committee. The two main general criticisms were that the Kansas Center had a complex, multilayer administrative structure and that it proposed a transition in emphasis away from the center's historical strength in behavioral research. These two criticisms were addressed as described in the specific steps discussed below.

1. *Simplification of the Organization.* The major governing body became the Internal Scientific Advisory Committee, which consisted of the MRRC director, the MRRC co-director, the administration core director, the coordinators of the four main MRRC sites, the thematic leaders, and the directors of the scientific core units.
2. *Elimination of the Multilayered Reporting System.* The layers in the administration core were greatly reduced by making Steve Schroeder, who was the director of the BCR and the Schiefelbusch Institute for Life Span Studies (LSI), also the director of the MRRC. Each theme, each core function, and each major research logistic site had representation on the Internal Scientific Advisory Committee. Each core

unit was directed by a faculty member who was a research scientist in the MRRC. The division of labor between the MRRC, the BCR, and the LSI was clarified.

3. *Identification of Scientific Leadership in All Thematic Areas.* We revised the titles of the thematic areas and added the theme of behavior analysis, which had always been an overarching theme of the Kansas MRRC. The themes acknowledged the many contributions to basic as well as applied research in all areas of the MRRC. We considered the research scientists on the Internal Scientific Advisory Committee as both the present and future scientific leaders in the MRRC. They ranged from the junior to the senior investigator level.

4. *Review and Revision of the Criteria for Access to MRRC Core Units to Require Evidence of Recent Productivity.* Those criteria were: 1) recent history of grantsmanship, peer-reviewed publications, and relevance to the NICHD mission; 2) current published research in the KU MRRC thematic areas; 3) project's functional relationship to thematic areas; and 4) evidence of integration into the MRRC structure.

5. *Integration of Behavioral and Biomedical Components.* See Table 1, which summarizes most of the main MRRC thematic areas and sub-themes within areas. Note that considerable integration of bio-behavioral themes existed within columns (e.g., animal and human neuropharmacological models of aberrant behavior) and across rows (e.g., behavioral and biological risk factors at the behavioral, cellular, and molecular levels in columns 4, 5, and 6).

6. *Clarification of Core Access.* In determining whether any project, behavioral or biomedical, had access to core unit services, the rules for access to core unit services were made more explicit, and were monitored by the core unit directors as well as the Internal Scientific Advisory Committee. New investigators and new program development were identified by any of the MRRC advisory groups, were invited to present at MRRC monthly seminars, and were reviewed for inclusion at the time of the annual MRRC retreat.

7. *National Advisory Committee.* This committee consisted of six nationally recognized experts, one for each of the proposed thematic areas. The committee members were invited to review program progress of the MRRC, as well as to suggest new areas of leading-edge research that the MRRC should develop.

Table 1. *Mental Retardation Research Center Central Organizing Theme: Integration at the Behavioral, Organ System, Cellular, and Molecular Levels*

Behavior Analysis	Language, Communication	Intervention and Treatment in MR	Risk Factors in Development	Neurobiology of Mental Retardation	Cellular and Molecular Biology of Early Development
	Disorders and cognition in MR				
Stimulus classes	Behavioral and cognitive processes	Environment & behavioral systems	Behavioral risk factors	Neurodevelopment and neuroplasticity	Fertilization and embryonic development
Generalization	Competence limitations	Mitigating effects of depriving environments	Television effect	Experience and brain maturation	Blastocyst formation
			State organization		Blastocyst implantation
Imitation		Transition hazards	Newborn risk status	Disc renewal in retinal visual cells	Cadmium
					Embryogenesis
	Developmental disorders	Educational and emotional intervention			Maintenance of fetal integrity
	Processing in aging	Biological and behavioral systems	Biological risk factors	Neural control of limb movement	Hormonal regulation of pregnancy interruption
	Biological processes	Scaling facial impairments due to cleft palate		Neonatal sympathetic neuroplasticity	

(continued)

Table 1. *Mental Retardation Research Center Central Organizing Theme: Integration at the Behavioral, Organ System, Cellular, and Molecular Levels (Continued)*

Behavior Analysis	Language, Communication	Intervention and Treatment in MR	Risk Factors in Development	Neurobiology of Mental Retardation	Cellular and Molecular Biology of Early Development
Ecobehavior analysis	Otoacoustic emissions	Implantable glucose sensors	Alcohol and brain model membranes	Mechanisms of brain damage	Environmental toxins and pregnancy establishment
	Thalamocortical auditory organization	New flow injection techniques for immunoassays	Neurotoxicity of X-irradiation	Neurocytotoxins	Hypothalamic control of prolactin
Social skills			Kinin regulation of BBB permeability	Glutamate NMDA receptor	Immune system in pregnancy
Chronic aberrant behavior			Hormonal deficiency and maturation	Sublethal cyanide	Immunoregulation of pregnancy
Health and human behavior				Free radicals	Decidual cell/placental interactions
Clinical behavioral pharmacology				Behavioral neuropharmacology	Gene expression of human trophoblast cells
Pharmacology pharmacotherapy				Hypersensitivity to pressor effects of NPY	
				Animal models of aberrant behavior	

BBB, blood–brain barrier; NMDA, *N*-methyl-D-aspartate; NPY, neuropeptide Y.

Integration of Research Themes of the Kansas MRRC and Participation in Functional Groups

Table 1 summarizes the main themes and subthemes of the MRRC. The central organizing theme for the Kansas MRRC became the *Integration of Mental Retardation Research at the Behavioral, Organ System, Cellular, and Molecular Level*. Each thematic area, except the Cellular and Molecular Biology of Early Development, had substantial behavioral and biological components. The thematic areas primarily described the composition, activities, and achievements of the functional working research groups. They were devices for organizing the main thrust of the MRRC. Faculty functional groups were the true subunits within and across thematic areas. They functioned as tightly organized groups of investigators who met frequently, shared findings with each other, critiqued each other's work, and solicited advice, consultations, and access to core unit services. Functional groupings changed from time to time depending on research outcomes, funding, and scientists' interests, but the overall thematic areas of the Kansas MRRC remained remarkably consistent.

The challenge for the KU MRRC was to bring behavioral and biological research efforts to bear on one another, in order to answer integrative questions (e.g., to bring the study of the social effects of poverty into synchrony with the biological effects of the interacting biobehavioral milieu). The frequently found specific effects observed in behavioral science needed to be supported by a broadly based biological basic science in a consistent fashion. Such activities created a scientific environment where breakthroughs and paradigm shifts could occur.

The Kansas MRRC is still developing these themes today. The MRRC has passed through several evolutionary stages that have allowed it to survive and flourish and to continue to find a viable mission. In the beginning, the MRRC examined fundamental principles of behavior and applied those principles to modify specific behaviors in persons with severe disabilities. Those principles were generalized into community and home environments. Later, projects and programs designed specifically to develop and support homelike and community environments for persons with developmental disabilities took over where the research left off. In a parallel development, the biomedical puzzles of developmental disabilities were studied, and continue to be studied. Those studies have continued to be important, and many of them are merging with behavioral studies until today we find the term *biobehavioral* widely applied to many contemporary studies. Where the behavioral projects were dominant in the beginning, biomedical projects have become more prominent. In many cases the behavioral and the biomedical projects have become full partners in a combined approach to solving a common problem. Thus, in the 1995 MRRC renewal, the resulting thematic areas became:

THEME 1: Language, Communication Disorders, and Cognition in Mental Retardation

THEME 2: Risk, Prevention, and Early Intervention in Mental Retardation

THEME 3: Neurobiology of Mental Retardation

THEME 4: Cellular and Molecular Biology of Early Development

In the 1995 MRRC renewal, we also upgraded resources and facilities to MRDDRC investigators reconstituting scientific and technical cores. In response to the critique in 1991, we invited outside consultants to review three of our cores. Their visits and recommendations were very helpful. One major result was to split the computer, statistics, and electronics core into a *research design and analysis core* and a *technology enhancement core*. The communications core was discontinued and folded into the technology enhancement core, in order to position the MRDDRC to take advantage of new developments in electronic communications technology. The other three cores (i.e., administrative core, tissue culture and monoclonal antibody core, and histology and image analysis core) remained essentially unchanged.

In addition to the usually provided core services, special emphasis was placed on training investigators in the core services they needed to update and improve their research skills. Information on research design and analysis and communications technology was increasing so rapidly that investigators needed help in keeping up with them. Modern instructional technology was used to ensure the success of this training.

Developing research, training, and dissemination programs relevant to critical problems of people with mental retardation and developmental disabilities (MRDD) has always been important to the Kansas

MRDDRC. It had its beginnings in programs that showed the capacity for learning and independence of people with MRDD that served as the research basis for the deinstitutionalization movement. These findings were generalized to programs for juvenile delinquency, school interventions in poverty areas of Kansas City, and communication programs for the most difficult to assess and train. The MRDDRC renewal proposal took a life span perspective, incorporating relevant research programs in early pregnancy as well as in aging. The life span perspective continued and developed during the next 5 years. The Kansas MRDDRC conducted research in 19 of 21 NICHD priority areas for MRDD research.

A special effort was made to foster interdisciplinary collaboration both within the Kansas MRDDRC and across other MRDDRCs in the United States. Within the MRDDRC, a high proportion of the research was collaborative and interdisciplinary. Collaboration was promoted by three organizational tools: 1) at the time of recruitment scientists who wished to work on the central organizing theme were given preference; 2) scientists were recruited into one or more of the thematic groups so as to enhance that theme; and 3) scientists were encouraged to form new functional groups to address a new area of interest within the MRDDRC. Such groupings might lead to program project applications or center grant applications. For instance, the language communication disorders and cognition theme group applied for a center on specific language impairments, a program project on communication and aging, and a successful renewal of the program project on communication in mental retardation; the early development theme group applied for and won a Reproduction Center grant; the brain damage subgroup submitted a program project on central nervous system effects of reactive oxygen species; and the risk, prevention, and intervention group applied for and received a program project of severe aberrant behavior and mental retardation. Although not always successful, application for a large program grant was an excellent way of fostering interdisciplinary collaboration. It almost always has led to successful spin-off individual grants on the same topic or on a closely related topic.

Much of the success of the MRRC can be attributed to the close, synergistic working relationship between Paul Cheney and the two directors of the LSI during this period: Steve Schroeder in 1990 and later Steve Warren in 2001. After a year as interim chair of the Department of

Molecular and Integrative Physiology, Paul accepted the permanent chair position in September of 2002 and resigned as director of the R. L. Smith MRRC after nearly 14 years of service. Another highly capable internal candidate, Peter Smith, then accepted the directorship of the center and continues to serve in this role. Peter is a neuroscientist with an interest in molecular and cellular mechanisms of neuroplasticity. The Smith Center continues to thrive under his leadership and a strong, mutually supportive working relationship with the director of the LSI, Steve Warren, continues to be a cornerstone of this success.

Since 2000 the Kansas MRRC has maintained nearly the same administrative structure that was developed in 1990. Steve Warren, the director of the LSI, is also director of the MRRC. The cores, however, received another review and change. The tissue culture and monoclonal antibodies core was dropped and a new biobehavioral measurement and technology core was added. The Kansas MRRC is currently at the time of its greatest promise, with the ability to perform truly outstanding bio-behavioral research affecting important problems of people with mental retardation and impacting U.S. society.

Finally, another exciting new development deserves mention. We are about to enter a new chapter in the history of the R. L. Smith MRRC. After 33 years of operating out of the original dedicated buildings, the MRRC on the KUMC campus will move to new space in a 210,000-square-foot biomedical research building. Two floors of this building will be devoted to the two areas of strength of the MRRC: neuroscience and early development/reproductive biology. This building will allow for growth and will bring together cutting-edge technologies, some of which are cores within the MRRC. This is an exciting development that will help ensure the continued success of the MRRC well into the 21st century.

14

The Kansas University Center on Developmental Disabilities (Formerly the Kansas University Affiliated Program)

STEPHEN R. SCHROEDER, RICHARD L. SCHIEFELBUSCH, R. MATTHEW REESE, DAVID P. LINDEMAN, KATHLEEN OLSON, AND RICHARD R. SAUNDERS

The Kansas University Center on Developmental Disabilities (KUCDD) has evolved over the years, starting in 1969 as a federally funded program by the Maternal and Child Health Branch of the U.S. Department of Health and Human Services called University Affiliated Facilities (UAFs). Later, additional federal core funds came from the Administration on Developmental Disabilities authorized by the Developmental Disabilities Act of 1975. UAFs originally were funded to train professionals in mental retardation and developmental disabilities (MRDD), because there were few formal mechanisms to provide such training at that time. Later, the mandate was expanded greatly. UAFs changed their name to University Affiliated Programs (UAPs), and finally to their current name as result of the name change in the Developmental Disabilities Act of 2000. Each name reflects a different emphasis as the developmental disabilities movement grew in the United States in the late 20th century.

The Kansas program was in on the ground floor from the beginning. As the Kansas Mental Retardation Research Center (MRRC) was the major research engine of the Bureau of Child Research (BCR) and the Life Span Institute, so was the Kansas UAF (then UAP, then UCDD) its major companion core grant program for training, service, research, and outreach on developmental disabilities to the Kansas community from which many other similar grant-funded programs have spun off.

In this chapter, Dick Schiefelbusch gives a brief history of the formative years of the Kansas UAP (KUAP) (1969–1990) in the marvelous retrospective piece that follows. A fuller treatment of the early years of the KUAP is in chapter 8. A subsequent section of the present chapter chronicles the recent evolution of the KUCDD from 1990 to 2002.

The Origins of the UAP (1969–1990)

Sarge Shriver informed Richard Schiefelbusch at a Kennedy Awards dinner in 1969 that the strategy behind the University Affiliated Facility program begun in 1963 was really quite simple. He said, "We wanted a number of professionally strong settings to commit their talent to programs for the mentally retarded." He assumed that the best way to secure their support was to promise them a building. In other words, busy, productive settings already were crowded with existing clinical/teaching activities. Many of these settings, however, had little, if any, activities involving persons with mental retardation. If promised new construction of their own design, they were more likely to apply for a UAF. (The designation of UAP came later after the construction grants were already transacted. So, construction did indeed beget programs.)

At Kansas the UAF grant application, submitted in 1972, was designed with three settings and thus with three constructed facilities. Each of the UAF units was arranged to have convenient interaction with the approved, but not yet constructed, MRRC units. The MRRC units were approved for construction a year prior to the UAFs. Kansas, in effect, got three new buildings and three new programs for both the MRRC and the UAP.

The three-setting UAF applications were virtually a "sure thing" from the beginning. However, we did not take the submission casually. We organized planning committees and studied statewide agency committee minutes and recommendations, and we also secured verbal approval from state agencies and university chief officers. Chancellor Wescoe suggested that we create a name for the combined centers: The Kansas Center for Mental Retardation and Human Development.

Existing Resources

The Kansas University Medical Center (KUMC) setting already had a constructed facility, the Children's Rehabilitation Unit (CRU). In fact, CRU was created in 1958 and already had several years of collaborative programming that included pediatrics, orthopedics, obstetrics and gynecology, special education, deaf education, speech pathology and audiology, psychology, and physical therapy. Many of the children who were served in the CRU had multiple disabilities; and for them and their families, CRU provided an urgent service. Nevertheless, the prospect of a UAF was indeed exciting because the CRU services had become overcrowded, and there was a waiting list of applicants, especially those with developmental disabilities. Needless to say, CRU provided an impetus for all the settings, especially since CRU had a major grant for exemplary program activities, both service and training, and would likely be able to expand that funding by means of a UAF.

Other existing conditions at Lawrence and Parsons were favorable for the development of the UAF. For instance, KU had major aspirations for the expansion of their special education program, but had no other prospects for space expansion. Other groups urgently needing space were Human Development and Family Life, Speech, Language, and Hearing; and the Bureau of Child Research. The BCR, of course, was active on all three campuses in planning and development of interdisciplinary training.

At Parsons the situation was vastly different. The Parsons State Hospital and Training Center (PSHTC) actually had space that it was not using. This was largely because of the downsizing of the resident population and also because of Howard Bair's successful campaign in recruiting funds to build facilities for existing needs (e.g., food services, recreation, music therapy, and additional cottages). But, the need for facilities equipped for *better* services and resources was very strong (i.e., for audiovisual and clinical laboratories, for community-based programs, and for improved staff training).

Another important feature of the UAF planning was the relationship with state agencies that wished to improve statewide services. These agencies had generally regarded the university departments and divisions as having ivory-tower operations that had little relevance to the difficult aspects of service for persons with developmental disabilities in the state. The application plan required a set of strategies for relating to state issues. In the application, we tried to break the exemplary service and the training designs down to practical dimensions that could be endorsed by state agency planners, as well as by the federal review team and the respective university departments and dimensions.

These brief comments indicate that the UAF planners were willing to undertake research, training, and service-oriented projects far beyond the tentative activities of their past. This, of course, was what the UAF policy developers in Washington had hoped for in their UAF legislation.

Common UAP and MRRC Resources

The BCR was a valuable resource for each construction, for program planning and development, and for administrative organization. The BCR staff had already logged time in intercampus planning, designing, and organizing. So, they played approximately the same role in preparing the UAF application that they did for the MRRC application. Richard Schiefelbusch played the same coordinative role for each application in turn. As a case in point, the BCR worked with the executive officers of each campus in adjusting indirect cost rates, in coming to interactive agreements, in making management decisions, and in planning the new space.

Interestingly, the staff members in the federal agencies also became part of the planning and implementation processes on each campus for each program. Because members of the BCR had had numerous encounters with federal agency personnel prior to the beginnings of the center's activities, it was natural to exchange information and opinions throughout the entire complex effort. Here again, the enterprise of the UAF was not a start-up experience, but rather a continuation of relationships, routines, and mutual support strategies. In some instances the Washington staff members unhesitatingly made suggestions for strengthening the plans for the UAF applications. One of the suggestions was for the director of the BCR to be also the director of the three-campus UAF. In the original plan, the BCR director was to be the intercampus *coordinator.* The Washington staff made a strong pitch for a *director* designation instead. The chief officers of each campus were persuaded to agree to this strengthening of the role of the "coordinator."

Some surprise disappointments and successes were apparent during the developmental years. The policy differences between the state Office of the Secretary for Social and Rehabilitative Services and the several instrumental offices of the UAP were especially abrupt. These policy differences seemed to focus on plans and activities that related to deinstitutionalization and to other possible structural changes in service delivery.

In a generic sense, it related to almost any alteration that might change existing structures of state services. These apparent impasses seemed to be fueled by several dissonant contributors, for instance, the secretary was very powerful and at times inflexible. The associate director of the BCR (at that time, Ross Copeland), was also a contributor to the impasses.

The first penetration of this mounting problem came when the legislative assistant to the chancellor called Schiefelbusch and instructed him to go to Topeka and "make peace" with Dr. Robert C. Harder. An appointment was made and at the beginning of this 2-hour conference, Schiefelbusch was told by Harder that the only reason he had agreed to the conference was that he did not want it said that he would not talk about the differences.

The two "colleagues" covered many topics germane to each other's role, including who was the most sincere about helping the people of Kansas and about whose roots were the deeper in the Kansas culture. In short, they broke through to each other and were able to form critical issues of agreement. The final step was an offer and/or challenge extended by the director of UAP to make a sustained contribution to as many as three crucial problems that the secretary was concerned about in serving the children of Kansas.

Three "problems" were indeed selected: 1) newborn birth-impaired babies and their mothers, 2) program designs for vocational rehabilitation and training for severely retarded youth, and 3) training of regional Department of Social and Rehabilitation Services (SRS) personnel. Each area led to concrete proposals for funding support and the assigning of UAP staff to work with SRS personnel at regional and local community locations.

At this point we encountered dissonance with assigned staff members of the SRS state system. This led to still more accommodations. In retrospect, an interactive university–state system was created and has continued to this day. We were indeed fortunate that the officials of that time at both ends were wise enough to rise to that challenge. These officials included the secretary of SRS; the director of institution management; the superintendent of PSHTC; the chancellor, executive vice chancellor, and vice chancellor for research graduate studies and public service at KU; the vice chancellor for the medical center; and selectively, members of the Board of Regents, the Board of Social Welfare, and legislative staff members. It may have been also a validation of the aphorism that "crisis is the time of opportunity."

About 15 years later, a second crisis presented itself. This one was critical to the federal funding at Winfield State Hospital and Training Center. The evaluation of the Winfield program by the federal evaluation team had turned up a number of deficiencies. These deficiencies, if unchanged, would terminate a large amount of federal service funds for the hospital. The deficiencies were detailed; and a brief interval of time was allowed for compliance. Joe Spradlin and about 25 colleagues from Parsons, both care workers and scientists, volunteered to go to Winfield for an intensive effort to bring the care program there up to compliance.

The result of this effort was: 1) compliance was achieved, 2) state funds were set aside for a follow-up monitoring period of 3 or more years, 3) the legislative charter of the BCR was changed to include the possible "management of state institutions," and 4) major federal funding was created for management assistance to institutions in Kansas and beyond Kansas. This Active Treatment Training Program continues today with Dick and Muriel Saunders.

Another challenge to the KUAP came when Ronald Reagan became president in 1980. David Stockman, his budget director, decided that he was going to reduce "Big Government." He took a knife to many federally funded social programs, including the Maternal and Child Health (MCH) core funding for UAPs. The Children's Rehabilitation Unit was one of the six programs targeted for drastic reduction in funding. Dick Schiefelbusch and the new KU chancellor, Gene Budig, went to visit Senator Bob Dole, to get help with this crisis. Senator Dole was a life-long advocate for people with disabilities in Congress. Together they got MCH to postpone defunding for a year while they went to the Kansas legislature to get replacement funds. The net result was that the Kansas legislature appropriated state funds for the UAP into the budget of the KUMC. This was a tremendous vote of confidence for the UAP, and it emerged even stronger in subsequent years because of this additional state core funding to add to its reduced federal core funds.

Success and Failure

The initial success of the Mimosa Cottage Project in teaching socially effective skills resulted in the placement of 40 teenage children with severe retardation in community settings. This, of course, was what the project was designed to do. However, it soon became apparent that communities were not prepared to provide the essential training for the care staff to manage or to oversee the routines in the community settings.

The crisis that resulted from the deinstitutionalization movement was felt all across the country in both mentally retarded (MR) and emotionally disturbed (ED) service settings. Often the problem was not limited to specific sites because the institution residents were simply turned out to no designated community setting. The problem that was presented by this change in service arrangements created a need for new resources and new training services. The UAPs responded to this need by combining efforts with both agencies and settings. They also were soon to combine in creating surveillance and evaluations resources and in training service personnel.

It has been all too apparent at Kansas that both the application research personnel and the exemplary service personnel were resources that the agencies, settings, and families needed. Also, it required a vast new, urgent focus on environmental design for appropriate living contexts. This urgency continues and has long since been extended to aging populations and to other service groups.

This changing emphasis of care and support has forced the UAPs to assume a prominent set of responsibilities that include cost factors, educational and training factors, management designs, and information collection and evaluation factors. The UAPs have moved from their ivory tower to a condition of shared responsibilities within statewide community designs for group-oriented environments. Beyond the UAP role in designing new service strategies and resources is the formulation of policy and political action. The paradigms and the technologies for management and planning have become, and are likely to continue to become, more sophisticated. Designs have been formulated and validated for making environments and ecologies more practical, attractive and cost-effective. Furthermore, the UAP personnel have become involved in evolving the policy and the legislative language for the future.

Recent History of KUAP (1990–2002)

Historical Forces Shaping New Roles for the KUAP

In many respects the disability movement came of age in the 1980s, and the KUAP was right in the thick of it. Special education rose to prominence in this decade, and many special educators at KU were key players. The KU special education department became the top one in the United States. The Department of Human Development and Family Life was one on the tops of its kind. The Department of Speech-Language-Hearing: Science and Disorders was a younger, up-and-coming department. These departments were a great resource for attracting excellent trainees in MRDD to the KUAP. Thus the KUAP had great preservice and in-service training opportunities for students. Many KUAP trainees are now leaders in the field of disabilities as a result of this partnership between KUAP and these three academic departments.

In the 1990s, with the advent of good academic educational programs in disabilities in the United States, the acute needs for the UAPs changed, and they began to expand into other fields. The MCH-funded programs, with their well-established training in the biomedical disciplines, stressed leadership education in neurodevelopmental disorders (LEND), especially in pediatrics and related disciplines. The DD Act core-funded programs, on the other hand, stressed training, technical assistance, and outreach training for all people with disabilities across the life span. This naturally led them into networking with community resources, consumer empowerment and advocacy, inclusion into all aspects of society, social policy development, and disability legislation.

Shortly after Steve Schroeder came to KU in 1990 to direct the Bureau of Child Research, the KUAP received a negative site visit from the Administration on Developmental Disabilities, notifying it that it was out of compliance with the DD Act, one of its core-funding agencies. As a result, we had an outside peer review by consultants who recommended that Steve take over the KUAP, so that its relationship to higher levels of KU administration was clearer. So Steve also took over administration of the KUAP along with the MRRC and the BCR, as had his predecessor, Dick Schiefelbusch.

We also reorganized the KUAP slightly, clarifying our role with other important nationally recognized research and demonstration centers within the Life Span Institute, such as the Beach Center on Disability, Assistive Technology for Kansans Program, the Center for Community and Neighborhood Policy, and the Research and Training Center on Independent Living, whose director, Jim Budde, became the associate director of the KUAP. These moves solidified our position in the social policy and consumer empowerment and advocacy fields.

In addition to in-house activities, KUAP also partnered more closely with our two sister state agencies who were also being funded by the DD Act (i.e., the DD Planning Council and Protection and Advocacy Services). Together we formed the DD Network for the state of Kansas. We monitored every bill related to disability in the state legislature, helped legislators draft bills, provided expert testimony before the legislature, got out the vote, helped bring lawsuits when necessary to protect and advocate for individuals with disabilities, and effected closure of state institutions that needed it. This was and still is a very effective coalition for change in the state. Each year we would meet at a retreat, set a legislative agenda, and then push for it.

All KUAP components were responsible for all four mandates (i.e., training, service, outreach, and research). They had to juggle the four plates simultaneously. At the KUAP, our slogan was that you had to be good at all four mandates, but great at one of them. KUAP's great training programs on both the Lawrence campus (i.e., mainly preservice academic degree programs) and the Medical School campus (i.e., the LEND program with interdisciplinary preservice and in-service training programs) were then complemented with great outreach training and technical assistance at the Parsons UAP, which extended over the entire state of Kansas as well as to many universities across the United States. The KUMC site became known as the interdisciplinary diagnostic training, research, and service center of the KUAP; the Lawrence campus became known as the academic degree training and social policy research center; the Parsons campus was the outreach connection and demonstration site for the state of Kansas.

The next sections briefly review the important historical developments of each KUAP site from 1990 to 2002.

The Lawrence Site

In the early 1990s, much effort was made to retool the Lawrence site, to bring it into harmony with current thinking on DD advocacy and to capitalize on its strengths. While the degree programs in the departments of Special Education; Human Development and Family Life; and Speech-

Language-Hearing: Science and Disorders were flourishing and in no need of change, other KUAP affiliated programs did need some adjustment.

Early intervention programs across the United States had moved from center-based programs to community-operated programs with strong ties to home training. The KUAP Early Intervention Program moved to support these programs with consultancies rather than with competing center-based programs at the university. Some of the people left this program, but Millie Copeland, a very experienced occupational therapist, stayed on and provided valuable consultant services to these programs until she moved to Texas in 1994.

A second initiative at the Lawrence site was disability policy. KUAP had two very strong nationally prominent National Institute of Disability and Rehabilitation Research–funded affiliated research and training centers (i.e., the Beach Center on Disability and the Research and Training Center on Independent Living) which did research on consumer empowerment of people with physical disabilities. These two centers were very instrumental in shaping the national legislative agenda and the research agenda for their respective constituencies for the next decade. Their history is covered more fully in chapters 19 and 20. Many of their outstanding students are now national leaders in the field. For instance, just one contribution they both made was involvement of consumers with disabilities in setting the research agenda. Participatory research was controversial at the time, but now it is commonplace in federally funded research programs.

With the help of Ann and Rud Turnbull and the Beach Center, the Lawrence KUAP site was able to hire Wayne Sailor, a nationally known educator in school reform policy. Wayne also was a participant in the University of Oregon-based R&T Center on Positive Behavioral Support (PBS), which he brought with him to KUAP. Wayne expanded the KUAP social policy groups, convening legislative work groups, testifying to the state legislature on disability issues, and promoting PBS in Kansas, not only in disability programs, but also in regular schools to curb school violence. In 2000 Wayne left the UAP to devote himself full-time to these efforts at the Beach Center.

In 1995 Wayne recruited Martin Gerry, former assistant secretary of the U.S. Department of Health and Human Services (HSS) for disability planning in the first Bush administration. Martin directed a Center for

Community and Neighborhood Policy for KUAP. He was very interested in welfare reform and empowerment of people in poverty and he worked with several other university and community coalitions to try to consolidate poor peoples' federal funding programs, so that they could earn a living wage. This was especially helpful for people with disabilities who are usually underemployed or unemployed. When federal welfare reform legislation came into existence in 1997, Martin ran an Administration on Developmental Disabilities–funded National Technical Assistance Center for Welfare Reform. This center was very important in pointing out the effects of welfare reform legislation on people with disabilities and in preventing the erosion of their federal funding by mobilizing advocacy groups in many states across the United States. Martin left the KUAP in 2000 to become the associate commissioner of the Social Security Administration in the current Bush administration.

When Steve Schroeder was preparing for retirement in 2001, once again the KUAP and the Beach Center co-recruited a nationally known researcher, Michael Wehmeyer, to be associate director of the Beach Center and overall director of the KUAP, which had by now changed its name to the Kansas University Center for Excellence on Developmental Disabilities. This was done to keep it in compliance with the name change in the reauthorization of the DD Act in 2000. Mike took over in May of 2002 and has done an outstanding job since then.

The Kansas City Site

In 1990, the Kansas site of the KUAP was the Children's Rehabilitation Unit as described in the early history section. Joe Hallowell, the director, was a senior savvy MCH developmental pediatrician with a master's degree in maternal and child heath, who had come to us from the State Division of Maternal and Child Health. He was very knowledgeable about state Title V programs, and he had public health interests that were good training for UAP LEND trainees. Joe decided to leave CRU to join the Developmental Disability Program at the Centers for Disease Control and Prevention (CDC) in Atlanta. He often returned to CRU and was very helpful in guiding our relationships with CDC. Joe was one of the people who were instrumental during the 1990s in raising the level of consciousness of CDC on disability issues to its current level.

Donna Daily replaced Joe Hallowell as director of CRU. She was a perfect fit—a KU-trained developmental pediatrician with a MA in human development from the Department of Human Development and Family Life (HDFL) and a native of Dodge City, who knew Kansas issues in children's health and disability very well. She came to us from the neonatology program at Children's Mercy Hospital with research interests in the neonatal intensive care unit (NICU) and long-term follow-up of very-low-birth-weight infants, which was ideal for the job. During her tenure, Donna did many things for the LEND program. She got foundation funding and renovated the building and made it much more patient friendly. She changed the CRU's name to the Child Development Unit (CDU). She increased the patient flow by admitting more patients to CDU and by starting more clinics within CDU and by holding regional clinics around Kansas City. One of the people she hired in 1993 was the current training director, Matt Reese. Matt was also an HDFL-trained psychologist with extensive training in disabilities as well as in local community resources for people with disabilities. He has turned the CDU LEND training program into one of the model UAP training programs in the United States.

Donna gave the CDU focus and energy through a retreat process where the staff set annual goals and responsibilities. Some of the programs started during her tenure were: Early Evaluation of Autism, Aberrant Behavior Assessment and Intervention, School Re-evaluation Following Traumatic Head Injury, Adoption and Respite Care Project, Transition from NICU to Home Project, Foster & Adoptive Caregivers Education and Support, Child Passenger Safety Program, Jayhawk Medical Passport, Functional Analysis of Children's Behaviors, and Telemedicine Clinics across Kansas.

When Donna was first hired, CRU had just won a large federal research grant from Comprehensive Child Development Programs at HHS, Project EAGLE (Early Action Guidance Leading to Empowerment). The author, Jean Ann Summers, and the principal investigator, Joe Hallowell, had both just left the KUAP, leaving this grant in limbo. Donna was instrumental in hiring a gifted administrator, Martha Staker, who reorganized and shaped this grant into a major model program in the Kansas/Missouri region. This program later grew into the Early Head Start Program for the Kansas City region and continues today as such. This plus other grant programs that Donna started made the CDU the second largest externally funded center at the KUMC, behind the MRRC, the Ralph L. Smith Center next door.

Position in the KUMC organization was very important to both the existence of the CDU and the Smith Center, because the KUMC administration always had difficulty recognizing disability as a high priority, especially interdisciplinary training of health professionals in neurodevelopmental disabilities. CDU was commonly judged based on its clinic patient numbers rather than on its interdisciplinary trainee numbers. This has been a problem for all LEND programs across the United States from their beginning, and KUMC was no different. Most training, research, and service at medical centers is not interdisciplinary, unfortunately. Nevertheless, LEND faculty must all have regular academic appointments in their home departments in each of the 11 required disciplines, as well as strong ties to state Title V MCH programs, in order to qualify for federal core funding from MCH. Donna fought this battle well by positioning the CDU well within the KUMC, but eventually, she burned out. She left the CDU in 1999 to take a job overseas because of her difficulty in getting the dean to recognize the proper role of the CDU at the KUMC.

An opportunity arose to recruit Travis Thompson, a distinguished MRDD director of the Kennedy Center at Vanderbilt University. Travis began in 2000 with high expectations. The CDU was reorganized as the Institute for Child Development to develop a greater research capacity. The CDU itself was renamed the Developmental Disability Center (DDC) under the Institute for Child Development. Chet Johnson, a KU-trained developmental pediatrician and LEND director at West Virginia University, was recruited to head the DDC, and a new era began for the Kansas City site of the KUAP.

Unfortunately, the dot.com bust and the depressed Kansas economy conspired to undercut plans. At the same time, the dean of the Medical School who sponsored Travis left for the University of Minnesota to become dean of the Medical School there. The subsequent dean was faced with budget rescissions, and disability was not one of her priorities. The CDU took a large cut in their state core funding budget. Several staff had to be let go, and Travis took a job in 2003 directing a state program for autism connected to the University of Minnesota. The Institute for Child Development was disbanded and Chet Johnson remained to direct the remaining DDC UAP component. He was an excellent administrator and the program recovered the hit. Chet currently is also acting chair of the Department of Pediatrics and the DDC continues to thrive under his leadership. Fortunately, the DDC has developed their telemedicine capacity further, to compensate for the inability to travel to remote areas of the state to deliver training and services.

The Parsons Site

Just prior to 1990, Lee McLean assumed the position as director of the Parsons UAP. She accepted this role when the previous director, Joe Spradlin, moved to the leadership role of the MRRC at Parsons. Under her leadership a number of significant service, training, and model demonstration projects were initiated. In 1992, following the retirement of Joe, a restructuring of the program at Parsons occurred and Lee became the director for both the UAP and MRRC programs. It was at this time that David Lindeman accepted an administrative role as associate director for the UAP. In 1996, when Lee was recruited by the University of Connecticut to direct the UAP there, Dave Lindeman moved into the director's position.

The 1990's through 2002 was a time of tremendous growth for the Parsons site of the Kansas University Center on Developmental Disabilities. While a number of federal and state legislative initiatives fueled the activities of this center, growth focused on the overall mission of the KUCDD and built on the specific strengths of the personnel, the rural setting, and work that had preceded this time period. This continuity led to an emphasis on training and technical assistance, development and provision of exemplary services to persons with disabilities, and dissemination of information to local, state, regional, and national audiences.

Exemplary Service Programs

Children with Special Health Care Needs Clinic

The special health care needs clinic has been a long-standing service program of the Parsons KUCDD for southeast Kansas. Initiated prior to 1990 through funding from the Kansas Department of Health and Environment and the Maternal and Child Health Bureau, this program has supported the early identification of children at risk for or with disabling conditions or chronic disease. This early diagnostic and treatment program has provided services in the area of orthopedics, developmental pediatrics, pediatric cardiology, nutrition, and orthotics and prosthetics. In collaboration with the University of Kansas Medical Center and physicians from Wichita and the surrounding area, these services have provided needed care and services in this rural area of the state.

Most recently the program has expanded from on-site clinics to include diagnostic services from the University of Kansas Center for Telemedicine and Telehealth. These services utilize distance technology through interactive TV for services that otherwise might not be unavailable. Included are diagnostic services for young children with autism and challenging behavior.

Respite Care Services

In 1991, through a grant from the U.S. Department of Health and Human Services, Administration for Children, Youth and Families, a model demonstration project was initiated to provide respite care service to adoptive and foster families with children with special needs. This project focused on the provision and promotion of respite care services in two areas of the state, rural southeast Kansas and metropolitan Kansas City. The focus of this project was to improve the capacity of adoptive/ foster families to access respite care through the development of respite resources and training of providers, compilation of a directory for services, and linking of families and relevant agencies. An additional significant outcome for this project was the development of a consensus statement regarding respite services for the state. This statement was developed in conjunction with multiple agencies and organizations, such as Families Together, Governor's Office Liaison on Developmental Disabilities, Kansas Department of Health and Environment, Kansas Social and Rehabilitation Services, Kansas State Board of Education, Kansas Advocacy and Protective Services, and a number or other state and local organizations.

Over the past 20 years, this program has continued to flourish in southeast Kansas. Area mental health and disability organizations along with the University of Kansas program have worked together and incorporated a nonprofit corporation to continue respite services for southeast Kansas. In collaboration with the nonprofit corporation, the KUCDD has expanded this program to provide respite services to a number of other groups of individuals. These include all children with disabilities and adults with respite needs, including those with disabilities, aging, and Alzheimer's disease.

Coordinated Resource and Support Services

Individuals with a dual diagnosis of mental retardation and mental illness are often faced with unique problems. Because of their developmental disabilities they may not "fit in" to mental health programs or these programs may not have the capacity to respond to their needs. Further, because of mental health, psychiatric, and behavioral problems that can develop into crisis, developmental disability centers are faced with the ongoing problem of serving these consumers in emergency situations. As a result, beginning in 1993, five mental health centers and two community developmental disability organizations, along with the KUCDD, developed the Coordinated Resource and Support Services (CRSS) program. This program is designed to provide crisis intervention for persons with a dual diagnosis and prevent the need for hospitalization or institutionalization. CRSS is guided by a collaborative board of professionals from both the mental health and developmental disability communities and has been recognized as a model for the state.

Child Care Resource and Referral

The identification of and access to quality child care is of critical concern to any family. When other factors are considered, such as living in a rural area, financial constraints (working poor), or having a child with a disability, the selection of child care quickly becomes more complex. In response to these issues and the desire of the state of Kansas for the development of a child care resource and referral (R&R) system, the KUCDD at Parsons began an R&R with funding from the Kansas Department of Social and Rehabilitative Services. Beginning these services in one county, the program has now expanded to eight counties in southeast Kansas.

Although the basis of the program is linking families with child care providers, the program also offers significant training opportunities for providers and focuses on extended technical assistance for improving the quality of registered and licensed home and center providers.

Assistive Technology for Kansans

The Rehabilitation Act of 1988 provided support for the development of a statewide assistive technology network to link services and supports and to identify barriers in accessing technology. The UAP at Parsons, later known as the Kansas University Center on Developmental Disabilities, received funding from the United States Department of Education for the Assistive Technology for Kansans program (ATK) in 1993. The ATK program has been in operation for 13 years and while activities have changed over time, much of the structure that consumers set in motion is still in place today. Chuck Spellman and Sara Sack direct the efforts and work with the Advisory Council to select project staff, subcontractors, and develop strategies to address identified barriers. There is a detailed description of the ATK program in chapter 26.

Training for Community Service Providers

As the KUCDD has grown at Parsons, there has been a major change in the best practices for supporting persons with intellectual and other disabilities. Services moved from large congregate settings to small or individualized community living situations. The Developmental Disabilities Assistance and Bill of Rights Act and subsequent amendments solidified the vision of integration, productivity, and independence. Sheltered work and segregated educational settings were replaced with community employment and school options. Persons with disabilities and their families began to assume and to demand more control over their services.

The roles and responsibilities of direct support professionals (DSPs) employed in community settings changed to meet these needs. Training for DSPs in Kansas has been a focus of several KUCDD community training grants. In addition to being more autonomous workers, skills were needed to address the needs of individuals with significant behavioral, physical, and medical challenges.

A training initiative project from the Administration on Developmental Disabilities (1991–1993) developed a 56-hour values-based curriculum, "An Introduction to Developmental Disabilities" (AIDD). AIDD included modules on Values and Visions, Assessment and Planning, Communication (based on training developed by another team of Parson's investigators (McLean, Sack, McLean, O'Connor, and Simmons), Teaching Skills, Positive Behavior Change, and Health. The train-the-trainer format allowed consistent local delivery of information across service providers.

AIDD linked community service providers with local college resources and helped some staff progress toward formal degrees. Thirteen of the 17 Kansas community colleges as well as Washburn University provided college credit for training and in some cases AIDD was incorporated into formal degree programs. When the federal funding cycle was completed, Kansas Social and Rehabilitation Services continued to support the training of trainers. Funding continued through 1997 with revisions occurring annually. The training was required for DSPs as part of community service provider contracts. Several organizations continue to teach AIDD a decade later. The Kansas curriculum served as a model for several other states.

A subsequent federal initiative, Consumer-Centered Education for People Providing Support to Individuals with Disabilities (1994–1998), supplemented the AIDD training and focused on building training capacity within the state. Supplemental resources were introduced, distance education was promoted, and individualized learning approaches were supported. Community trainers became a cohesive group for exchanging resources. This group has continued as an InterHab training committee.

Concurrently (1997–1999) a train-the-trainer approach was used to develop a supported employment curriculum, "Competency-Based Training for Supported Employment Specialists." Training was provided to 70 community developmental disability organizations and affiliates, community mental health centers, independent living centers, and public school districts through 6-day workshops. The curriculum has received national and international attention resulting in purchase requests from several U.S. states and Northern Ireland.

Dual diagnosis continued to be an unmet training need faced by community service providers. Curricula were developed to provide an understanding of various psychiatric disorders experienced by people with developmental disabilities and to develop working relationships between mental health providers and community service providers. Beginning in 1998, a series of five training modules (including videotapes) was produced. These included: *Dual Diagnosis: Mood Disorders and Developmental Disabilities; Dual Diagnosis: Schizophrenia or Other Psychotic Disorders and Developmental Disabilities; Dual Diagnosis: Anxiety Disorders and Developmental Disabilities I; Dual Diagnosis: Anxiety Disorders and Developmental Disabilities II;* and *Dual Diagnosis: Autism and Coexisting Disorders.* A train-the-trainer format was used. National distribution occurred through the project and through national publishers.

The Corporation for National and Community Service (CNCS) oversees AmeriCorps, Learn and Serve America, and National Senior Service Corps. Through CNCS, citizens have various opportunities to improve their communities through service in the areas of the environment, education, public safety, homeland security, and other critical areas. A national service project in 2002–2003 encouraged Kansans with disabilities to participate successfully in national service. A small project with the Self Advocate Coalition of Kansas in 2003 developed training to explain state of Kansas waiver programs for home- and community-based services.

Recruitment and retention of DSPs pose a major challenge for persons with disabilities. Turnover is associated with poorer community outcomes for persons served, including poorer health and lower levels of community inclusion. Kansans Mobilizing for Change, originally a grant from the Kansas Council on Developmental Disabilities (2002–2004), funded a project addressing the complex needs of community service providers. The College of Direct Support, an on-line training for DSPs, began to replace the face-to-face training. It allowed more timely and individualized training. KUCDD customized this training for Kansas. An apprenticeship program, approved by the Kansas Apprenticeship Council, was designed and implemented to enable DSPs to obtain a professional credential. Assistance was provided to start a Kansas Chapter of the National Alliance of Direct Support Professionals (NADSP). A videotape was developed to provide applicants with a realistic job preview of the profession. Job applicants could use this to make an informed decision about the position before going through an expensive orientation process.

A set of marketing tools and techniques was used to attract and recruit quality and motivated staff into direct support roles. Training for frontline supervisors addressed how to recruit, train, reward, mentor, and support DSPs. This initiative was successful in reducing turnover by 15%. The project continues to have community support after formal funding ended.

Early Childhood Programs

Beginning in the early 1980s, Lee McLean initiated a service program for young children with disabilities with a model demonstration grant from the U.S. Department of Education, Handicapped Children's Early Education Program (HCEEP). This program was designed to develop a model service program for rural communities. This demonstration was followed by two additional HCEEP projects; one to evaluate and validate the model and the second to provide outreach training for replication of the model. This short history is noteworthy because these projects quickly led to a number of subsequent early childhood model demonstration, outreach, and in-service training projects under the Early Education Program for Children with Disabilities (EEPCD) program of the U.S. Department of Education and the Kansas State Departments of Education and Health and Environment throughout the 1990s to the present.

Preschool Services and Training

Following the model demonstration work of Lee McLean, Vikki Howard was awarded an EEPCD project designed to meet the spirit of PL 94-142 and to develop integrated learning and preschool opportunities for preschool-age children with disabilities. This project focused on the challenges of sparsely populated rural areas and inclusion of young children with disabilities in typical preschool settings. In its second year, Dave Lindeman assumed this project. The Rural Alternatives for Preschool Integrated Delivery of Services (RAPIDS, 1989–1991) demonstrated that integrated or inclusive services for children with disabilities could be successfully implemented in rural areas. This preschool program was successfully transitioned from a university-based model demonstration project to the local special education agency prior to the full implementation of preschools services under PL 99-457 and continues to the present time utilizing components of the model developed.

Following the RAPIDS demonstration project, two outreach training programs provided dissemination of the information learned. Under the direction of McLean and Lindeman, the Comprehensive Model of Appropriate Preschool Practices and Services (CAPPS, 1992–1995) and the Supporting Teams Providing Appropriate Preschool Practices in Rural States (STAIRS, 1995–1998) projects provided training regarding inclusionary practices, instructional strategies, and administrative structures for preschool programs. Each of these projects provided outreach training promoting the replication of the model in six states.

Building on these experiences, Lindeman received funding for the development of training and training materials for inclusion of children with severe disabilities into Head Start programs. The Head Start Integration, Training, and Support Systems for Children with Severe Disabilities (1992–1995) project funded by the Department of Health and Human Services (HHS) worked with area and state Head Start Programs in the development of these materials. Two videotapes from this project were selected by the Head Start Bureau to be distributed to all Head Start grantees across the United States.

The Kansas Inservice Training System (KITS, 1991–1994) under the direction of Juliann Woods and David Lindeman, initiated an in-service training program in collaboration with the Kansas State Department of Education (KSDE). This model project integrated four training components of in-service training, focused technical assistance, collaboration and linkages, and information management and resources to provide training across the state to preschool program professionals serving children with disabilities and their families. Initially funded by the U.S. Department of Education, KITS received additional support from the KSDE to expand its services in 1993. Soon after that (1998), the Kansas State Department of Health and Environment, the lead agency for Part C: Infant and Toddler Services, joined with KSDE in support of KITS. This program currently remains the central training program for Part B: Preschool Services and Part C: Infant and Toddler Services for the state of Kansas.

Early Intervention Services and Training

Prior to the passage of PL 99-457, which began services for infants and toddlers with disabilities and their families, the Parsons KUCDD received funding for the development of a model for service programs in rural areas implementing Part H (now Part C: Early Intervention Services). This EEPCD project from the U.S. Department of Education, The Southeast Kansas Birth to Three Program (1990–1993) under direction of McLean, Lindeman, and Woods, developed a model with five components. These components were referral and identification, screening and monitoring, family services, intervention and service delivery, and regional coordination. This program demonstrated and validated a number of specific program approaches for the delivery of quality services. This program was one of the first programs to utilize novel strategies for public awareness and child find, transdisciplinary and routine-based intervention, and utilization of local coordination councils. Two videotapes developed by the project, *Family-Guided Activity-Based Intervention for Infants and Toddlers* and *A Family's Guide to the Individualized Family Service Plan,* have been disseminated on a national level. Additionally, because this project was conducted in collaboration with a local education agency, the program has expanded and currently provides services to 11 counties covering 7,000 square miles in southeast Kansas.

Subsequent to this model demonstration project, Woods and Lindeman provided direction for two U.S. Department of Education outreach training projects related to early intervention programs for infants/toddlers and their families. Family-Guided Approaches to Collaborative Early-Intervention Training and Services (FACETS I, 1993–1996 and FACETS II, 1997–2000) each provided training to 18 programs in six states. The training modules in FACETS I were based on the Birth to Three model demonstration components. These modules were further refined for FACETS II and focused more on family-guided routine-based intervention and interdisciplinary team planning and intervention. Woods, although currently at Florida State University, has continued to build on this work, focusing on the related service providers and routine-based intervention.

Active Treatment Training Project

On an otherwise unremarkable day in early May 1985, and with no hint in the air of what would follow, Gary Daniels, then superintendent of PSHTC, prepared for a conference call with Gerald Hannah, director of

Mental Health and Retardation Services (MH&RS), a branch of the Kansas SRS. At Hannah's request, Daniels had invited a number of individuals from the UAP, the Special Purpose School, and the Parsons Research Center—all located on the grounds. As it turned out, Hannah's purpose was to seek assistance with a serious emerging problem: Winfield State Hospital and Training Center (WSHTC) was being threatened with decertification from the Medicaid program. Indeed, millions of federal dollars were at risk and the potential loss was imminent: about 10 days. Participants at the conference call learned that WSHTC had recently been surveyed by a federal survey team from the Health Care Financing Administration (HCFA) as part of the nascent "Look Behind" program. HCFA was initiating a series of surveys in which federal teams would survey for compliance with Medicaid regulations (42 CFR 442) to determine whether state survey teams had applied the regulations accurately. WSHTC was among the first facilities in the country to experience a Look Behind. These surveys first examined the services provided to determine whether the residents of the facility were afforded basic protections from sources of harm (e.g., abuse, neglect, poor supervision) and, if so, were the residents provided with "active treatment," a fairly aggressive program of individualized services to meet their various needs. In late April, the federal team concluded that protection from harm was not in place. If not corrected promptly, Medicaid funding would be terminated.

Before proceeding with this story, it is important for the reader to know that what occurred in April at WSHTC repeated itself in the months and years that followed at numerous facilities across the country. That is, WSHTC was not the only facility found out of compliance and the state survey team for Kansas was not the only team whose survey conclusions would be challenged. Although highly adversarial at the time, the Look Behind program is best viewed as HFCA's version of an in-service training program. That is, what were deemed to be acceptable, if not laudable, conditions in facilities for persons with mental retardation were changing rapidly in America. Thus, HCFA was under pressure to change what was acceptable where Medicaid funds were concerned, and the Look Behind program was a relatively speedy mechanism for clarifying just how much had to change. But those of us involved in these events in 1985 remember all too clearly that consensus even among federal surveyors regarding the specifics of protection from harm and active treatment had not been achieved. It was not until 1988, when the Interpretive Guidelines for 42 CFR 442 were rewritten, that reliable objectivity replaced well-intentioned, but often inconsistent guidance.

Gary Daniels and Joe Spradlin, then director of the UAP, formed a team of 21 individuals who shortly traveled to Winfield to see the conditions themselves and to offer ideas and assistance in responding to the emergency. Following a plan advanced by Dick Saunders, each team member assumed the role of temporary qualified mental retardation professional (QMRP) for one of the residential units at WSHTC. Working with the WSHTC staff, the QMRPs began an aggressive program of training of direct service staff to increase client engagement in functional activities, reduce self-injurious behavior and client-to-client assault, and eliminate the environmental antecedents of injurious behavior. Following 10 long days, the federal team concluded that the immediate sources of harm had been addressed, but active treatment was not yet in place. The facility was given 90 days to leap this next hurdle.

Ultimately, Dick Saunders and his wife Muriel, a teacher in the Special Purpose School, were asked to remain at WSHTC and guide the active treatment building process. Concurrently, Hannah appointed Dennis Tucker as the SRS active treatment administrator and liaison to the effort in Winfield. The Saunders worked with Tucker to draft an initial position description upon which the state could build a new civil service position: QMRP. The Saunders also quickly drafted a QMRP handbook from which Muriel would later train the newly recruited and employed QMRPs. Dick, serving as acting program director, focused on developing a quality assurance tool involving frequent direct observations of groups of clients and staff with subsequent graphic feedback to the QMRPs on the rate of development of active treatment outcomes in their units. The outcomes measured were indexed to the specific expectations of the QMRPs, as enumerated in their job descriptions. Perhaps the most important aspect of the new job descriptions was that it positioned each QMRP as the direct supervisor of the direct service staff who attended to the needs of the clients in the QMRP's caseload. Thus, active treatment expectations and outcomes were, for the first time in Kansas institutions, linked directly by supervision and accountability. To create consistency in the training and supervision of the direct service staff, the Saunders developed and implemented the Scenario System. In this system, a daily activity schedule was developed for every grouping of clients (8–12) that covered every waking minute. For every activity, the QMRP working with other unit professionals (e.g., speech pathologists, psychologists) wrote a script, called a Scenario, for every activity. The Scenarios revealed the precise expectations of the direct service staff throughout the day. Those expectations were directly linked to the QMRP's job descriptions and to the outcomes measured by the quality assurance observations.

During the 90-day effort at WSHTC, Tucker and Spradlin formed a program management team consisting of themselves and the program directors of the four Kansas institutions for persons with mental retardation. With funding from the Kansas Planning Council on Developmental Disabilities, the management team initiated a "train-the-trainer" project to build active treatment in the institutions and also in the private intermediate care facilities in Kansas that provided services under Medicaid.

There were a number of significant outcomes from the activities of the summer of 1985. WSHTC passed its active treatment survey in late August. The program management project was highly successful in exporting methods of building and maintaining active treatment, thus protecting Medicaid funding for many individuals with mental retardation. The indices of active treatment in the WSHTC quality assurance survey instrument were adopted throughout the Midwest by Medicaid-funded facilities. Ultimately, those indices became part of HCFA's 1988 revision of their Interpretive Guidelines for active treatment under 42 CFR 442. Also in 1988, the Saunders teamed with James Rast to update their QMRP handbook. The result, the *Handbook for Scenario-Based Active Treatment*, has been disseminated by the UAP at Parsons since then.

This project was so successful that Hannah created a long-term funding mechanism for its continuation. The Active Treatment Training Project, as it became known, is still funded. Guided by Dave Lindeman (current director of the UCD in Parsons), the project has addressed a wide variety of focused issues related to delivery of quality support and services to persons with developmental disabilities. The project has brought numerous national experts to the state to provide training in a variety of treatment, education, and system management issues. The program has also supported staff of public and private agencies in accessing training that otherwise would not have been available. Over the past 18 years, this program has been central to capacity building for the state, its programs, and community partners.

Summary

From the above it can be seen that the KUCDD/KUAP has been a major training, service, and technical assistance resource in disabilities for the state of Kansas and the nation. On average, its federal grant budget has been $13 million plus, covering approximately 80 different projects annually. These projects have made a great service impact in the state, and they continue to do so. For instance, in 2000–2001, KUCDD faculty trained 34 graduate-level students and 1,611 undergraduate KU students; gave 567 workshop presentations to audiences of 28,726 professionals and families in the community across the state; published 146 publications, videos, public service announcements, and so forth; and saw 1,257 new clients in their DD clinics.

15

The Gerontology Center

DAVID J. EKERDT

erontology, as the study of aging, is far from being a modern fascination. Observations about life change and longevity have been
recorded across all of history. Classical and biblical literature
abounds with descriptions of long life spans as well as explanations for such
good fortune. But it was not until longevity was "democratized" in the 20th
century that gerontology and geriatrics (the health care of older people)
were formally organized as scientific and professional specialty fields.

Gerontology's appearance in higher education, typically as an interdisciplinary endeavor, accelerated across the 1960s and 1970s, propelled by
three developments: rising scholarly interests among faculty; increased
student demand for instruction in age-related topics; and the availability
of federal research and training funds from the new National Institute on
Aging (NIA), created in 1975, and the Administration on Aging (AoA).
The latter agency administered the Older Americans Act of 1965, which
directed discretionary funds to higher education for the purpose of building knowledge, developing model programs, and training personnel for
service in the field of aging (Achenbaum, 1995). This federal support had
a catalytic effect on the development of interdisciplinary gerontology centers on United States campuses, including the University of Kansas (KU),
where a Gerontology Center was initiated in 1977.

Nearing its 30th anniversary, the KU Gerontology Center hews to
a constant set of objectives. The purpose of the Gerontology Center is
to design, sponsor, and maintain programs of research, education, and

service that address changes in structure, behavior, and function over the course of life. The Gerontology Center promotes aging-related activities within established departments; develops and sustains externally funded programs of research and training; encourages interdisciplinary collaboration among university faculty and staff interested in the study of aging; and assists professionals in the state of Kansas in meeting the needs of its aging citizens.

Reading three decades of documents pertinent to gerontology at KU, one often encounters a demographic rationale for promoting age-related research and training specifically in Kansas. Kansas is one of a tier of midwestern states with a proportion of persons aged 65 and over that is higher than the national average. That was true in 1977 and it remains true today. Between 1977 and 2002, the population of the state increased by 16%, but the population of older Kansans increased by 22%. In 38 of the state's 105 counties, one in five persons is aged 65 or older (Center on Aging, 2002). Although these demographic arguments support the significance of gerontology as a field of study and potential application, they are but a partial rationale. Even absent such numbers, inquiry into aging in all its dimensions is worthwhile because the passage from birth to death is a common feature of all life and fundamental to human culture. How and why aging proceeds are enduring questions with more contemporary relevance than ever.

The following organizational history focuses on the Gerontology Center. However, as will also be noted, age-related research, education, and training was proceeding across and within many sectors of the university.

Early Years

The center came into existence in September 1977, partly at the suggestion of the KU chancellor and partly to meet the interests of faculty in such disciplines as psychology, sociology, social welfare, and American studies. Supported by a state appropriation to the university budget specifically for that purpose, this center was established as a freestanding unit reporting to the vice chancellor for research, graduate studies, and public service. Walter (Hob) Crockett (professor of psychology and of speech, communication, and human relations) was named the first director and, until 1990, served longest in that position. Ron Harper and Brenda Crawley also had terms as director. Consistent with the national pattern, early organizational support came from center and training grants of the federal Administration on Aging.

In the first years of the Gerontology Center, few faculty members were prepared to engage in research and teaching on problems of aging. Consequently, the center instituted two programs to encourage such interest: 1) grants of aid to help faculty members attend courses and workshops that would bring them up to date on aging-related developments in their disciplines, and 2) small research grants, awarded on a competitive basis, to provide seed money for faculty research into gerontological topics. Beyond this, graduate and undergraduate stipends were provided to stimulate student interest in the study of aging. In addition, funds were committed to help develop interdepartmental training programs.

As a research organization, the center had funded projects on such topics as attitudes toward aging, geriatric psycholinguistics, long-term care and its financing, and the needs of Native American elders. A bimonthly national newsletter for professionals assisting family caregivers, Parent Care, was produced out of the center. Launched by an AoA grant and later sustained by subscriptions, it reported research summaries, model programs, policy, and resources. There was collaboration with Kansas State University in the training of service providers. Another initiative provided gerontological training for faculty of American Indian colleges and other technical assistance to those institutions. From 1985 to 1990, the center hosted the Midwest Council for Social Research on Aging (MCSRA), an interuniversity training program of the National Institute on Aging. This consortium of midwestern universities coordinated training in social gerontology for pre- and postdoctoral fellows. MCSRA eventually placed more than 100 alumni in teaching and administrative positions around the United States. Regionally, the Gerontology Center provided service or technical assistance to such entities as the Kansas Department on Aging, offices on aging in Douglas and Johnson Counties, and the Topeka Veterans Administration. Throughout this period, the center had informal ties to KU's Bureau of Child Research, the KU Medical Center's Long-Term Care Gerontology Center, and its successor, the Center on Aging.

Beginning in the mid-1980s, the Gerontology Center coordinated a 15- to 18-hour Graduate Concentration in Gerontology on the Lawrence campus for graduate students enrolled in any master's or doctoral-level program at the university. The course of study included a proseminar, core gerontology courses, electives, and practicum or field placement. The concentration was designed to prepare students to apply their specialized knowledge of the social, psychological, demographic, and biomedical aspects of aging to their own professional disciplines.

The story of the Gerontology Center next pivoted upon its affiliation with the Institute for Life Span Studies (LSI). The LSI, inaugurated in 1990, arose out of the realization that many of the important problems related to human development required a life-span perspective. The Gerontology Center joined other programs of the large, well-funded Bureau of Child Research (with its special focus on developmental disabilities and language) to complete the LSI. At this point in time, Richard L. Schiefelbusch was acting director of gerontology, and the staff had two doctoral-level research associates, along with Susan Kemper of the Department of Psychology who served as curriculum coordinator. An outside search for a new director of the Gerontology Center brought Rhonda Montgomery to KU in 1992. This began a period of growth that has continued to the present.

Expansion

The Gerontology Center has experienced remarkable growth since 1990 in the capability of its professional staff, the scope of activities, and the amount of research support. Great credit is due to Rhonda Montgomery who directed the center from 1992 through 2002. Within the supportive environment of LSI, the program was able to build a strong faculty that eventually consisted of six research scientists whose appointments were shared with academic departments. The center gained its own space for operations within the Dole Building. A doctoral program in gerontology, one of only several in the nation, was launched in 1997.

Research Activities

Across this period, the Gerontology Center summarized its research foci under four themes that reflected a primary emphasis on social and behavioral research. The major awards that supported these projects are listed in Table 1.

1. *Long-term health care and housing alternatives.* Projects include:
   • Nursing home programs and units that provide special care to persons with Alzheimer's disease; effects of environmental design features on staff and residents of special care units;

Table 1. *Major Awards to the Gerontology Center Beginning with Projects Active in 1990*

Year	Agency	PI/Project Dir.	Title
1987–1990	NIA	Peterson, Warren	Inter-University Training—Adult Development and Aging
1987–1991	NIA	Kemper, Susan	Geriatric Psycholinguistics
1988–1990	AARP	Schiefelbusch, Richard	Applied Research on Native American Aging
1990	HCFA	Montgomery, Rhonda	Secondary Analysis of Effects of Intervention on Family Caregivers
1990	AoA	John, Robert	Faculty Development in Gerontology
1991	UMKC	Osterkamp, Lynn	Dissemination of Training Materials
1991	AoA	John, Robert	Faculty and Program Development
1991–1997	NIA	Hummert, Mary Lee	Stereotypes of the Elderly and Communication
1992	AoA	John, Robert	Paraprofessional Home Care Workers
1993	AoA	John, Robert	American Indian Elder Campaign
1993–1996	NIA	Montgomery, Rhonda	Cultural Impact on Caregiving Outcomes
1993	Kansas SRS	Montgomery, Rhonda	Long-Term Care Services Workplan
1993–1994	NIA	John, Robert	Navajo Nation Long-Term Care Study
1993–1995	NIA	Montgomery, Rhonda	Special Care Units: Impact on AD Residents, Family, Staff
1993–1994	NIMH	Montgomery, Rhonda	Targeting Respite to Promote MH of Alzheimer's Families
1994	HRSA/PSA	Montgomery, Rhonda	Alzheimer Demonstration Project—Data Preparation and Monitoring
1994	KU-RDF	Kemper, Susan	Community and Aging
1994	Kansas Aging	Montgomery, Rhonda	Developing Survey Instruments for Health Care Suites
1994	Kansas SRS	Montgomery, Rhonda	In-Depth Investigation of the Income-Eligible Home Care Program and the Home- and Community-Based Services Nursing Facility Waiver Program
1994	NIA	Mathews, R. Mark	Healthcare Suites: SBIR Phase I
1994	NIA/Kentucky	Kemper, Susan	Independent and Dependent Life in the Elderly

(continued)

Table 1. *Major Awards to the Gerontology Center Beginning with Projects Active in 1990 (Continued)*

Year	Agency	PI/Project Dir.	Title
1994	Kansas SRS	Montgomery, Rhonda	Medical Consultation Services Contract
1994–2003	NIA	Kemper, Susan	Speech Accommodation by and to Older Adults
1994–2004	NIA	Kemper, Susan	Training Communication of Elderly
1995	State of Michigan	Montgomery, Rhonda	Study of Caregiver Satisfaction for the Alzheimer's Demonstration Grants to States Program
1995	Benjamin Rose	Montgomery, Rhonda	Cultural Expectations for Caregiving
1995	HHS	Montgomery, Rhonda	Data Collection: National Evaluation on Alzheimer Demonstration Grant
1995–1996	NIA	Mathews, R. Mark	Homecare Suites: A Homecare Alternative for Elders—SBIR Phase II
1995	Alz. Assoc.	Mathews, R. Mark	Legal and Policy Analysis of Assisted Living Facilities
1996–1997	HHS/HRSA	Montgomery, Rhonda	Continuation of the Alzheimer's Demonstration Data Collection
1996–1997	Ohio Aging	Montgomery, Rhonda	Cultural Expectations for Caregiving
1996–1998	HHS/HRSA	Montgomery, Rhonda	Integrating Support Service of Alzheimer Families into Managed Care Systems
1997	HRSA	Montgomery, Rhonda	HRSA Cultural Expectations for Caregiving (Alzheimer Demonstration)
1997	HRSA	Montgomery, Rhonda	HRSA Managed Care Initiative
1997–2001	NIA/Kentucky	Kemper, Susan	Independent and Dependent Life in the Elderly
1997–1999	Alz. Assoc.	Montgomery, Rhonda	Targeting Support Services for Markers in Caregiving Careers
1998–2004	NIH	Kemper, Susan	Speech Accommodations by and to Older Adults

1998	HHS/HRSA	Montgomery, Rhonda	Cultural Expectations for Caregiving
1998–2002	NIA	Ekerdt, David	Changing Decisions and Plans for Retirement
1998	Ohio Aging	Montgomery, Rhonda	Demonstration Grants to States with Respect to Alzheimer's Disease
1998	Kansas Aging	Mathews, R. Mark	Douglas County Senior Center Needs Assessment
1998–2000	Alz. Assoc.	Mathews, R. Mark & Altus, Deborah	Evaluation of an Active Treatment Program for Dementia Care
1998	NIA	Harwood, Jake	Intergenerational Communication Schemas
1998	Care Trak	Mathews, R. Mark	Where Did Grandma Go? Locating Wanderers
1999	HHS/HRSA	Montgomery, Rhonda	Development of Strategies to Replicate HRSA Projects
1999–2003	HHS/HRSA	Montgomery, Rhonda	Evaluation of Alzheimer Demonstration Grant to States Program and Managed Care Initiative
1999–2005	NIA	Hummert, Mary Lee	Social Cognition, Communication and Age Stereotyping
2000	Care Trak	Mathews, R. Mark	Locating Wanderers: Evaluation of Care Trak Mobile Locator
1999–2001	Resthaven	Mathews, R. Mark	The Environment and Its Effects on Resident Care
2001–2005	Lapeer	Mathews, R. Mark	Evaluation of the Engagement Model
2001–2002	HHS/HRSA	Montgomery, Rhonda	Alzheimer's Service System Analysis
2001–2004	NIA	Ekerdt, David	Strategies for Household Disbandment
2002–2006	NIA	Kemper, Susan	Tracking Older Adults' Eye Movements While Reading with Distraction
2002–2007	Iosco	Mathews, R. Mark	Iosco County Medical Care Facility—Alzheimer Special Care Unit Research
2005–2010	NIA	Kemper, Susan	Dual Task Costs of Language Production by Young and Older Adults

- Modular apartment units as an alternative to long-term care;
- A legal and policy analysis of statutes that regulate assisted living facilities;
- New technologies for controlling wandering;
- Evaluation of a treatment program for dementia patients that promotes engagement and independent functioning; and
- Elders' disposition of possessions when moving to smaller quarters.

2. *Communication and aging.* The Gerontology Center has had an internationally recognized program of research in geriatric psycholinguistics. Projects include:
   - Studies that investigate age-related changes to adults' production and comprehension of language, the impact of such changes on activities such as reading and listening comprehension, and strategies to minimize communication deficits;
   - Language and speech accommodation among persons with dementia and among minority elders;
   - The nature of stereotypes of the elderly;
   - How stereotypes affect communication styles with older adults; how stereotypes affect decision making for health and family issues;
   - Early life predictors of later cognitive and physical function in the Nuns Study; and
   - Use of eye-tracking technology to study age differences in reading styles.

3. *Service utilization.* Projects include:
   - Respite care use by family members who care for impaired elders;
   - A national study of volunteer home-repair programs;
   - Evaluation of a large, multistate service demonstration program for Alzheimer's families; studies of service utilization and client satisfaction;
   - Use of managed care systems to link caregivers with appropriate, timely services;
   - Evaluation of a multisite family education program for caregiver families;
   - Accessibility issues in consumer cooperatives;
   - Training for caregivers to reduce the incidence of incontinence; and
   - Sequential decision making for retirement among American workers.

4. *Aging among minority populations.* Projects include:
   - Training home-care workers to serve American Indian elders;
   - Long-term care of Navajo elders;
   - Cultural differences in the use of nursing homes; and
   - Ethnic differences in elders' evaluation of their quality of life.

Education and Training

As far back as 1982, Gerontology Center faculty had discussed the formation of a program to offer a doctoral degree in gerontology. In 1997, the University of Kansas became one of only several universities in the United States to do so. This freestanding program within the College of Liberal Arts and Sciences is governed by affiliated faculty drawn from various academic units including the Departments of Sociology, Psychology, Human Development, Communications Studies, Occupational Therapy Education, and Health Sport and Exercise Sciences. It is administered through the Gerontology Center. The program in gerontology is interdisciplinary in structure and is designed to provide a relatively broad, but advanced educational experience. It provides a common focus for all students, yet allows each student to select a course of study most appropriate for his or her career objectives. The university conferred the first PhD in gerontology in 2001, with two more to date.

In 2002, efforts were initiated to convert the interdisciplinary Graduate Concentration in Gerontology into a certificate program in order to place it on a common footing with other interdisciplinary certificate programs at KU. The certificate was approved in 2004.

Between 1992 and 2004, the Gerontology Center hosted a NIA-funded Research Training Program in Communication and Aging, directed by Susan Kemper. The program supported four predoctoral and two postdoctoral students training in gerontology, psycholinguistics, communication studies, and speech pathology. Trainees pursued a program of coursework, research participation, workshops, and tutorials under the supervision of faculty members from a variety of academic departments. The Gerontology Center has had a monthly faculty colloquium series since 1999, and has also co-sponsored occasional conferences and visiting lecturers with other departments and schools of the university.

Service to Profession and Community

Faculty members have had prominent roles in their respective disciplines. Three have recently served on standing study sections to review grant applications at the National Institutes of Health. Two major research journals have been edited out of the center, *Research on Aging* and *The Journal of Gerontology: Social Sciences*. Faculty also raise the national profile of the KU gerontology program by their service on several editorial boards and as officers of service organizations and scientific societies. Center members have collaborated on projects with Kansas state government and with Douglas County.

Additional Milestones

1993: R. Mark Mathews accepts a joint appointment in gerontology and in human development and family life. KU's Balfour Jeffrey Award for Excellence in Research in Humanities and Social Sciences is awarded to Susan Kemper.

1995: For the first time, the Gerontology Center attracts more than $1 million in external funding.

1996: Virgil Adams accepts a joint appointment in gerontology and psychology. The center proposes a new PhD program in gerontology.

1997: Kansas Board of Regents approves the doctoral program in gerontology. David Ekerdt accepts a joint appointment in gerontology and sociology.

1998: Susan Kemper accepts a 50% appointment in gerontology. First student enrolls in the doctoral program.

1999: Gerontology administrative offices move to the third floor of the Dole Building.

2000: KU's W. T. Kemper Fellowship for Teaching Excellence is awarded to Mary Lee Hummert. KU's Irvin Youngberg Award for Applied Sciences Research is awarded to Rhonda Montgomery. Susan Kemper is appointed Roy A. Roberts Distinguished University Professor of Psychology and Gerontology.

2002: KU's W. T. Kemper Fellowship for Teaching Excellence is awarded to Virgil Adams.

2004: The Gerontology Doctoral Program successfully completes its first program review.

2005: David Ekerdt is appointed director of the Gerontology Center and the gerontology doctoral program.

Other Programs in Aging at the University of Kansas

The portrait of gerontology at KU is not complete without the acknowledgment of other centers and programs that enrich the university.

The Landon Center on Aging at KU Medical Center

The Center on Aging is a state-funded interdisciplinary center that conducts, sponsors, and supports the development of educational, clinical, and research programs related to aging. Most center activities are carried out in partnership with other academic units of the KU Medical center (KUMC) campus, including the Schools of Allied Health, Medicine, and Nursing, and with affiliated institutions, such as area geriatric care centers, VA Medical Centers in Leavenworth and Kansas City, the Wichita branch of the School of Medicine, the University of Kansas in Lawrence, state agencies, and service organizations.

The center was established by Kansas legislative action in 1986 as one of the KUMC Centers for Interdisciplinary Concentration. Designed as an umbrella program, it built on existing campus strengths in aging, including an AoA-funded Long-Term Care Gerontology Center and faculty initiatives in geriatric education. Original objectives were: to participate in the development and sponsorship of model programs of clinical service which may serve as opportunities for clinical education and research; to help direct individual educational and research efforts toward issues of age and aging; and to serve as a clearinghouse for intramural aging activities and serve continuing educational needs in the state and region.

The research program grew considerably during the 1990s. The Center on Aging was instrumental in obtaining a multiyear grant from the NIA to create an Alzheimer's Disease Center on campus. A second large center grant from the NIA established the Kansas Claude D. Pepper Older Americans Independence Center with a focus on stroke rehabilitation research. To accommodate this expansion, faculty and staff took up residence in a new state-of-the-art facility in 2001, the Theo and Alfred M. Landon Center on Aging.

The Landon Center on Aging is presently led by Randolph J. Nudo. The strongest area of investigation is research on stroke, including pre-clinical animal studies, clinical trials, and rehabilitation. Another laboratory focuses on cognitive aging. The center has special collaborative interests with the Departments of Neurology, Physical Therapy, and Occupational Therapy Education. Other ongoing studies at the center focus on health policy research, caregiving, and psychosocial concerns at the end of life. The center has ties to researchers in aging in the School of Nursing.

Although the center does not supervise or administer clinical programs of geriatric care, it has a strong interest in quality clinical sites and educational programs, and so supports faculty time in the Departments of Medicine and Family Medicine to facilitate undergraduate and postdoctoral training. The center hosts a NIH-sponsored institutional training grant to prepare postdoctoral fellows for research careers in rehabilitation sciences. The Landon building also houses the federally funded Central Plains Geriatric Education Center, which provides online educational modules and curriculum resources for geriatric educators. The center has a long-standing interest in rural health needs and rural practice with elders. Finally, the center sponsors a recurring program of continuing education conferences, research seminars, visiting professors, seminars in medical ethics, and a community outreach series.

The Office of Aging and Long Term Care

The Office of Aging and Long Term Care in the School of Social Welfare was created in 2000 to improve social service practice and policy for older adults, with a special focus on experience in Kansas. Directed by Rosemary Chapin, the office also develops faculty and student expertise in gerontology and trains future faculty in gerontological social work. With support from foundation, state, and federal funds, the overall goal is to find ways to support older adults' independence and facilitate their ability to age in place. The office's projects have studied the future supply and demand for aging services, the forms and appropriateness of various types of supportive housing, the advisability of community versus institutional provision of long-term care, and the need for mental health services among older Kansans.

Elder Law Program

Since 1995, the University of Kansas School of Law has been a leader in offering both coursework and a clinical experience for law students wanting exposure to the practice of elder law. In recent years, the school has further expanded course offerings, created a certificate program for those law students wanting to pursue a focused study of elder law, and developed an LLM program in elder law, a postjuris doctorate program concentrated on the study and practice of this specialty. Initiated in spring 2005, KU's LLM program is one of the first in the United States. Students in these programs become knowledgeable and proficient in the law that affects elder citizens as well as the unique issues relevant to client counseling and professionalism when dealing with the older population. They receive law school credit for designated nonlaw school courses in the gerontology curriculum. Interns in the Elder Law Clinic draft wills and powers of attorney for clients, and represent clients in guardianship or conservatorship proceedings, public benefits matters, consumer protection, and abuse and neglect issues.

Osher Lifelong Learning Institute

The newest chapter of the gerontology story at KU is the Osher Lifelong Learning Institute, launched in 2004. Oriented to learners 50 and older, the institute provides noncredit classes taught by KU faculty and community instructors during fall, spring, and summer sessions. The curriculum encompasses culture, history, science, religion, literature, the arts, politics, and the environment. The institute is administered by KU Continuing Education and supported in part by funds from the Bernard Osher Foundation of San Francisco. The Osher Foundation has funded the development of 50 lifelong learning institutes in the United States. KU's institute is the first in the Midwest. Courses are held in Kansas City, Topeka, and Lawrence in collaboration with other community and educational organizations.

In addition to these units, the vitality of campus interest in aging is also shown by research programs within departments. There have been long-established research efforts in the neurobiology of aging and mechanisms of age-related neurodegeneration led by Elias and Mary Lou

Michaelis in the Department of Pharmacology and Toxicology. Michael Crawford of the Department of Anthropology maintains a longitudinal study tracking the environmental and genetic components of biological aging in Mennonite populations in Kansas and Nebraska. A promising cluster of scientists in the School of Engineering and the Department of Health, Sport, and Exercise Science is investigating the biomechanics and kinetics of aging, mobility, and exercise.

Conclusion

The Gerontology Center does not conduct all of the research and educational activities in aging at the University of Kansas, but it has always aimed to be a nexus of these efforts. Operating from the supportive environment and infrastructure of the LSI, the center bridges the research and academic sectors of the university and bridges its campuses. The center has recently started to maintain a list of KU faculty members from Lawrence and Kansas City who have research or educational interests in gerontology. This universitywide faculty now numbers over 60 individuals from 11 schools of the university and over 30 departments, programs, and centers.

Looking ahead, there are three developments that will compel further opportunities for the study of aging, basic and applied, in the years ahead. The first is population aging. Although population aging, as noted earlier, is not an exclusive rationale for gerontology, the growing number of older adults in America and worldwide will challenge the sustainability of welfare-state arrangements that were the context for aging in the later 20th century. Oncoming cohorts of elders will also present new markets for the economy, and new possibilities for participation in civic and community life. Second, today's elders are facing demands to cope with an increasingly rationalized and bureaucratized world. The simplest practical tasks and transactions can be confusing. Successful encounters between the individual and social structures require new knowledge and skills (literacy about health, finances, legal matters, and technology) in order to negotiate complex systems. Research that sharpens the everyday competencies of older adults can make immediate contributions to practice.

Third, the conceptual frameworks of gerontology are converging with those used in the study of growth and development. Where science once balkanized life into young, middle-aged, and old, scholars now invoke principles that address change in structure, function, and behavior at all stages of life. Explanatory frameworks in biology, psychology, and the social aspects of aging now embrace the entire life span and biographical life course. This is all the more reason why the Gerontology Center's location with the Schiefelbusch Institute for Life Span Studies some dozen years ago is proving to have been a fortuitous event.

References

Achenbaum, W. A. (1995). *Crossing frontiers: Gerontology emerges as a science.* New York: Cambridge University Press.

Center on Aging. (2002). *Kansas ElderCount.* New York: Milbank Memorial Fund.

16

The Juniper Gardens Children's Project

CHARLES R. GREENWOOD

with contributions by
CARMEN ARREAGA-MAYER, JUDITH J. CARTA, DEBRA M. KAMPS,
CHERYL A. UTLEY, AND DALE WALKER

I n the decades between the founding and establishment of the Juniper Gardens Children's Project (JGCP), 1964–1989, the JGCP had embarked on a path of productivity, relevance, and success. Under the leadership of Dick Schiefelbusch and R. Vance Hall of the University of Kansas (KU), and Uriel and Chester Owens, Noah and Virginia Kirkwood, and other strong and like-minded community leaders in Northeast Kansas City, the work had flourished for 25 years (see chapter 6). Over the period 1990–2001, significant new events continued to shape the program and its impact on the community and the field of knowledge. The first section in this chapter mentions some of the most salient of these events. The second section reviews the major research programs of the second generation of KU faculty and students to work at the JGCP and findings that emerged. The chapter concludes with a brief statement of current activities and events that are reshaping the JGCP's future.

Shaping Events

Transition in funding occurred as the sixth 5-year National Institute of Child Health and Human Development (NICHD) program project grant was not funded in the period when repeated efforts failed in 1988–1990. In this period defined by the Reagan administration, NICHD became increasingly disinterested in supporting behavioral research compared with the past. At the same time, the leadership and investigators of the founding period were increasingly in transition. Collectively, it seemed that these changes undermined the success of this effort. This mix of work and careers being completed with transitions in senior to junior investigators reasonably explains this change. Thereafter, the younger investigators found project funding was increasingly forthcoming from the Office of Special Education Programs, U.S. Department of Education (OSEP USDE), as this funder was concerned with children with disabilities served in public schools, general education classrooms, and access to the general education curriculum.

Transitions in leadership occurred with the retirement of R. Vance Hall and Dick Schiefelbusch. Subsequently in 1990, Charles R. Greenwood was appointed director of JGCP, and Stephen Schroeder was appointed director of the Life Span Institute (LSI) and the Kansas Mental Retardation and Development Disabilities Research Center. JGCP continued its roles as a research center within these units and Greenwood reported to Schroeder. Transitions in the first generation of JGCP's career scientists occurred. Ed Christophersen, who had developed a highly successful program in behavioral pediatric research, went into private practice at Children's Mercy Hospital. Todd Risley returned to his native Alaska and worked with the university's and state's programs. Betty Hart retired, but continued her work on young children's language learning at LSI headquarters on the Lawrence campus. Other retirements occurred, including Joseph Delquadri who returned with this family to his native Idaho. Others pursued new opportunities; foremost was Linda Thurston, who after leaving JGCP and a stint running a restaurant in Chase County, Kansas accepted an appointment at Kansas State, where, at this writing, she is assistant dean of education.

Reports of the major research findings of the prior decade were published in increasing numbers and benefited the current efforts immensely. Findings of Hart and Risley's ground-breaking 10-year longitudinal study of young children learning to talk, titled *Meaningful Differences in the Everyday Experience of Young American Children* (Hart & Risley, 1995, 1999), were published, and relatively overnight the work became a beacon message for both the Clinton and Bush administrations regarding advances in knowledge of brain development and the role of early experience and language learning in early literacy and school readiness. Christophersen published a range of popular "how-to" books of effective parenting strategies and a major synthesis of evidence-based strategies in behavioral pediatrics (Christophersen & Mortweet, 2001). Vance Hall revised and expanded his highly successful line of how-to books on applied behavioral intervention. Greenwood, Delquadri, and Hall's randomized trial of the educational benefits of classwide peer tutoring (CWPT) was published in the *Journal of Education Psychology* (Greenwood, Delquadri, & Hall, 1989), followed by follow-up reports on the long-term benefits of CWPT use in elementary school on later middle and high school outcomes (Greenwood & Delquadri, 1995; Greenwood, Terry, Utley, Montagna, & Walker, 1993).

Linda Thurston's development and validation of the Survival Skills for Urban Women program (Thurston, Dasta, & Greenwood, 1984) thereafter launched a life of its own as it was replicated widely in more than 40 states' programs and three countries, spawning similar programs designed for men and for youth. In many states, her programs were adopted as evidence-based, best practices as part of welfare reform. To meet this need, she founded Survival Skills Education and Development, Inc., a not-for-profit independent team of developers, trainers, and program staff (*http://www.ssed.org*). Like Hart and Risley's *Meaningful Differences* research, this program also received the attention of the Clinton administration, where it was presented as a program that works at one of Vice President Gore's Welfare to Work Program initiatives, as well as the United Nations Conference on Women held in Beijing.

For the first time, several syntheses of JGCP work were published. The history of the JGCP was published in a special issue of *Education and Treatment of Children* (Vol. 12, No. 4, pp. 1–428, 1989). In addition to its founding history (Hall, Schiefelbusch, Hoyt, & Greenwood, 1989), the then-current research programs of the JGCP were described (Carta & Greenwood, 1989; Greenwood, Carta, Hart, Thurston, & Hall, 1989; Kamps et al., 1989), as was JGCP's role in doctoral research training (Walker, Hall, & Greenwood, 1989). An important synthesis of the work at JGCP was published in the *American Psychologist* in the special issue commemorating the life's work of B. F. Skinner (Greenwood et al., 1992). Its message was a description of how Skinner's principles of behavior had been and were continuing to be extended from the laboratory to the Northeast community of Kansas City, Kansas. Three years later, a report on the doctoral and postdoctoral training at the JGCP was published in *Teacher Education and Special Education* (Greenwood & Walker, 1995). In 1996, the JGCP received the research award of the Council for Exceptional Children, for its 30-year record of work developing and testing interventions of importance to children with special needs. To the current date, this award has been the only one made to an organization, rather than an individual scientist. A paper summarizing the work that was the basis for receipt of this award was published in *Exceptional Children* (Greenwood, 1999). Important career awards also followed. For example, Division 25 of the American Psychological Associate awarded R. Vance Hall in 1989, and Charles Greenwood and Joseph Delquadri in 2001, the Fred S. Keller Award, recognizing their significant contributions to the field of education, all based on work conducted at the JGCP over the years.

Instead of existing in the basements of liquor stores or local churches, preschools, or community centers, JGCP programs and staff in September of 1996 were consolidated into a single facility designed for its use at 650 Minnesota Avenue, Kansas City, Kansas. Moving from two overcrowded offices located at 18th and Washington Boulevard, with new support from a KU Research Development Fund award for facilities, the entire staff of 60-plus individuals (scientists, support staff, and students) was consolidated on the second floor of this two-story office building.

Also for the first time, the entire staff had access to e-mail, the Internet, and the university's evolving wide area network through a central file server with direct links to the LSI and the KU library system, thanks to funds donated by JGCP graduate alumni and the UMB Bank. Location to key community partners and organizations here was significantly improved because we were now 5 minutes to any point in the Northeast community, and across the street or down the block on Minnesota Avenue, including the school district central office, Wyandotte Country Special Education Cooperative, Project EAGLE, and others who became collaborators in those years.

Several other initiatives marked Greenwood's leadership during this period. The first initiative involved several annual retreats during which JGCP investigators, support staff, and students engaged in facilitated strategic planning process. Previously, strategic planning at JGCP had only occurred in the context of "the next major grant writing project."

The second of these strategic planning meetings occurred in a facility owned by the newly operating Ewing M. Kaufman Foundation. During these events, the strengths, weaknesses, opportunities, and threats facing the organization at this time were envisioned, and planned initiatives were designed to strengthen vision, mission, and work of the JGCP over the next 5 to 10 years.

A second initiative was the institution of a formal governance structure that involved direct participation of all investigators and key support staff. Governance by the scientists was modeled on one existing at the time at the Oregon Research Institute in Eugene, Oregon. An "Executive Committee of Scientists" was established that included all principal investigators (PIs) and representative support staff for central office, computer, and program implementation staff. The JGCP Executive Committee met monthly, foremost to consider issues of budget/funding, but also collective issues of policy, governance, technology, science, safety in the community, and as needed, timely issues impacting the project. Supporting this committee's work were subcommittees who met regularly or as needed to address issues of personnel, grant development, space, computer, safety, and social events.

A third initiative was activation of a community advisory board charged with meeting three times per year with roles and subcommittees related to 1) themes of work at JGCP, 2) neighborhood and public relations, and 3) fund raising. This work benefited from the leadership of Noah Kirkwood, an original supporter of the project, who served as president of the Community Board during this period. One major change recommended by the Community Board and adopted by the Executive Committee was a reframing of the JGCP's mission to reflect the fact that its programs, research, and impact now routinely extended beyond just the residents of the Northeast Community, to the county, the bi-state area (Kansas and Missouri), and the nation. This was expressed in the new mission language:

Original Mission: To conduct research designed to improve Northeast Kansas City, KS area children's developmental and educational experiences and thus, their academic and social achievements.

Revised Mission: To conduct research designed to improve the quality of life for children and families in Greater Kansas City by identifying problems (e.g., educational, economic, social, environmental), providing solutions, evaluating their effectiveness, and informing others of their success.

The cumulative impact of the Postdoctoral Leadership Training Grant first funded in 1983 (Greenwood, PI) on the entire JGCP program itself became increasing clear during this period. Like the Research Development Fund and subsequent KU programs that followed through the new Kansas University Center for Research, which made investments to stimulate new research development programs, investigators, equipment, and infrastructure, the postdoctoral leadership program at JGCP funded by the OSEP USDE served a similar function—stimulating new research programs and building research capacity.

While the postdoctoral program had clear benefits on the individual careers of completing fellows (53 to date in March 2005) who received 1- or 2-year stipends to work at JGCP, the impact on JGCP itself was unplanned and unforeseen. That impact was the success that individual postdoctoral associates experienced in obtaining grant funding for their projects, and the fact that many decided to stay on at JGCP to develop these projects. Their new careers now represent long-running programs of research.

This was particularly true for Carmen Arreaga-Mayer, Judith J. Carta, Cheryl Utley, and Dale Walker, four postdoctoral associates who had obtained project funding resulting from applications made during their postdoctoral programs, who eventually earned KU promotions to associate and senior scientists because of their records of achieving new grants, growth in staff and doctoral research assistants, and impact on the field and local participants. This also proved true for Debra Kamps, who obtained initial project funding through her doctoral work at JGCP, another career path for scientists at JGCP. Interestingly, compared with other units at this university, direct investments to recruit and employ new, promising investigators to broaden and strengthen the work at the JGCP never occurred. Of all JGCP PIs during this period, only Greenwood in 1978 had been actively recruited to a position at JGCP from outside of the university because at the time new funds were available from the JGCP program project. Funds for outside recruitments at JGCP were few and far between, which helped evolve a mentality of developing and growing the program from within the organization—its graduate students and post-doctoral associates.

Research Programs and Findings

Alongside Greenwood and Delquadri's active research programs, the research of the younger investigators previously mentioned blossomed during this period. Largely due to the efforts of these younger investigators, the annual externally funded grant budget of the JGCP went from $1,095,148 in 1990, to more than doubling to $2,509,217 in 2001.

Several strengths lay behind the success of this group of PIs. Their first strength was their inherited knowledge and dedication to the mission of the JGCP. Their second was their shared grounding in the conduct of empirical research with strong implications for practice and social validity. Third, the unique disciplinary knowledge and diverse backgrounds of each one collectively formed a multidisciplinary group within general and special education and behavior analysis and developmental psychology. Fourth, they shared a number of frameworks and methods so that collaboration on projects was often the norm, rather than the exception. For example, Arreaga-Mayer's training was in learning disabilities and she was Spanish/English bilingual. Carta's training was in early childhood special education. Utley's training was in mental retardation and multicultural education. Kamps' training was in special education with an emphasis on emotional/behavioral disorders and autism and applied behavior analysis. Walker's training was in human development and early language development.

Collectively, they created programs of research and training focusing on infants and toddlers (e.g., parenting, child care, Early Head Start, etc.), preschool (e.g., Head Start), and K–8 schools. As in the past, JGCP investigators often worked across discipline areas either alone or in collaboration with each other. Carta, Walker, and Greenwood have worked across programs for children from birth to kindergarten; Arreaga-Mayer, Kamps, Utley, and Greenwood have worked across programs for children in kindergarten through middle school. Running through this work are key methodologies and practices shared in common, such as sensitive and

Table 1. *Human Impact: Juniper Gardens Children's Project in FYI 2001 (Count based on 14 funded projects, small and large)*

Region	Number in Program
Kansas City, KS (including Kansas City, KS schools)	
Children	432
Families	167
Students	1,278
Total	1,878
Regional (Kansas City Bi-State Metro Area)	
Children	3,152
Families	1,274
Students	2,445
Total	6,871
National	
Children	2,060
Families	0
Students	0
Total	2,060
Grand Total	10,809

valid observational measures of child, parent, and the environment; experimental studies of socially valid interventions that fit the needs of culturally and linguistic diverse populations; and empirically rigorous studies of risk and resilience in children and families living in vulnerable and dangerous communities. Collectively, the impact of this work on children, family, and students estimated for the peak year of 2001 in this period included 1,878 in Kansas City, Kansas, 6,871 for the Kansas City and Missouri/Kansas bi-state region, and 2,060 nationally (see Table 1). Additionally, we provided professional development to over 300 child care providers, preschool, and K–12 teachers in the local area. We mentor and support 16 master's and PhD students and postdoctoral associates from KU each year.

Carmen Arreaga-Mayer

Arreaga-Mayer's work sought to incorporate elements of ecobehavioral observation measurement in classroom-based research on bilingual special education. Her first PI project was funded in 1990 with collabora-

Table 2. *Cumulative List of Arreaga-Mayer PI Projects*

H023C00052DID, USDE, Development and Validation of an Evaluation Instrument to Measure Instructional Effectiveness of Bi-Lingual Special Education Programs (1990–1993)

H023C40064DID, USDE, Promoting Literacy Through Ecobehavioral Assessment and ClassWide Peer Tutoring for Racial/Ethnic Limited English Proficient Minority Students with Disabilities (1994–1997)

tions with Carta and Greenwood who had previously developed such measures of classrooms and preschools (Table 2). Her work led to a number of important findings including the observation that spoken language rarely occurred in bilingual instruction when it should occur very frequently (Arreaga-Mayer, 1996, 1998a, 1998b; Arreaga-Mayer, Carta, & Tapia, 1992, 1994, 1995; Arreaga-Mayer & Greenwood, 1986; Arreaga-Mayer & Perdomo-Rivera, 1996; Arreaga-Mayer, Terry, & Greenwood, 1998).

Judith J. Carta

As a consequence of her postdoctoral experience at JGCP, Carta's submitted grant application was funded in 1984, entitled, "The Development and Validation of an Evaluation Instrument to Measure Instructional Effectiveness of Early Childhood Handicapped Programs." As was the case with Arreaga-Mayer, this project sought to create an ecobehavioral observation measurement for use in intervention research in preschool early childhood special education (Carta & Greenwood, 1985; Carta, Greenwood, & Robinson, 1987). Since then, her program of research has focused on a range of early childhood issues that include 1) measurement and outcomes and indicators for children birth through kindergarten (Luze et al., 2001; McConnell et al., 1996; McEvoy et al., 2001; Priest et al., 2001; Walker, Greenwood, Hart, & Carta, 1994); 2) evidence-based practice (Carta, 1995, 1999, 1999–2002; Carta, Atwater, & Peterson, 2001; Carta, Atwater, & Schwartz, 1990, 1991; Carta, Estes, Schiefelbusch, & Terry, 2000; Carta & Greenwood, 1997); and 3) risk and resiliency in child development (Carta & Greenwood, 1988; Carta et al., 1994a, 1994b) (Table 3). Carta is currently the editor of the journal, *Topics in Early Childhood Special Education.*

Table 3. *Cumulative List of Carta PI Projects*

G008400654DID, USDE, The Development and Validation of an Evaluation Instrument to Measure Instructional Effectiveness of Early Childhood Handicapped Programs (1984–1987)

G008630226DID, USDE, Increasing Teaching/Learning Efficiency in the Mainstreaming of LD Students: Discovery and Validation of Effective Naturalistic Instructional Procedures (1986–1989)

H024J80003EEPCDE, USDE, The Validation of a Classroom Survival Skills Intervention Package: Measuring Short- and Long-Term Effects on Young Children with Handicaps (1988–1991)

H024U80001EEPCDE, USDE, Component Project in the Kansas Early Childhood Research Institute (1988–1993) (Carta/Greenwood)

H024V00008EPPCDE, USDE, A Programmatic Approach for Comparing the Effectiveness of Early Childhood Language Program Features (1990–1994)

H024D10009EEPCD, USDE Skills for Promoting Integration in Preschool, Kindergarten, and First Grade Classrooms: An Outreach Training Model (1991–1994)

H023B00043DID, USDE, Promoting Transfer of Academic Skills in Mainstreaming Through Recruitment of Contingent Praise Training in Elementary Students with Behavioral Disabilities (1990–1991)

H024R10004USDE, Early Childhood Research Institute on Substance Abuse (1991–1996)

H023B40037USDE, Milieu Language Teaching and Children Prenatally Exposed to Drugs (1994–1995)

H024DH0053EEPCD, USDE, Project SLIDE: An Outreach Training Model (1995–1998)

7421 HRY, DHHS (Subcontract/NewHouse), Promoting Early Resilience to Reduce Substance Use (1995–1998)

H023C50111DID, USDE, Longitudinal Study of Risk and Protective Factors Affecting the Development of Children Prenatally Exposed to Illicit Drugs and Alcohol (1995–2000)

90-YF-0005, HHS-Admin Children, Youth, Families, Local Research Partnerships for Early Head Start Programs (1996–2001)

8300-96-10, Mathematica Policy Research, Inc., Early Head Start Research and Evaluation (1996–2000), Carta

H024S60010, USDE (Subcontract/University of Minnesota), Early Childhood Research Institute on Program Performance Measures (1996–2001)

90YD0055, HHS-Admin Children, Youth, Families, The Effects of Acculturation, Demographics and Child–Caregiver Interactions on Children's Early Language Development in Bilingual Environments (1998–2000)

H324D990048, USDE, Improving the Delivery of Early Intervention to Children with Disabilities From High Poverty Backgrounds (1999–2002)

Robert Wood Johnson Project-Kansas Site, Assessing Neglect in Teen Moms (2000–2003)

90YF0032, HHS, Early Head Start Research Partnership (2001–2005)

UND45746, NIH Predicting and Preventing Neglect in Teen Mothers (2001–2005)

Debra M. Kamps

Following from her work with both Rich Simpson, a specialist in autism and behavior disorders in the Department of Special Education, and Joseph Delquadri at the JGCP, Kamps' first grant was funded in 1987–1990 by the USDE, entitled "An Ecobehavioral Approach to the Validation of Effective Education and Treatment Programs for Autistic and Developmentally Disabled Students." Since then, her work has focused on the development of evidence-based practices for use with children with autism and behavior disorders primarily in schools settings. This work has ranged from a focus on 1) arranging access for general education experiences for children with disabilities (Kamps, Dugan, Potucek, & Collins, 1999; Kamps, Gonzalez-Lopez, Potucek, Kravits, Kemmerer, & Garrison-Harrell, 1998; Kamps, Barbetta, & Leonard, 1994; Kamps, Potucek, Dugan, et al., 2002); 2) teaching and learning of social skills (Kamps et al., 1992; Kamps, Tankersley, & Ellis, 2000; Morrison, Kamps, Garcia, & Parker, 2001; Tankersley, Kamps, Mancina, & Weidinger, 1996); 3) prevention and early intervention for students with emotional and behavioral risks (Greene, Kamps, Wyble, & Ellis, 1999; Kamps, Ellis, Mancina, Wyble, Greene, & Harvey, 1995; Kamps, Kravits, Rauch, & Kamps, 2000; Kamps, Kravits, Stolze, & Swaggart, 1999); and 4) the relationship between behavior and academic problems in early schooling success (Kamps & Greenwood, in press; Kamps, Wills, Greenwood, et al., 2003) (Table 4). Kamps is past associate editor for *Education and Treatment of Children* and currently on the editorial review board for *Focus on Autism and Developmental Disabilities, Journal of Emotional and Behavioral Disorders, Journal of Autism and Developmental Disorders,* and *Journal of Positive Behavior Interventions.*

Cheryl A. Utley

Utley's first grant was funded in 1992 following her postdoctoral experience at JGCP. Her work has maintained a nice balance between in-service teacher training and professional development, and research on instructional intervention practices (Greenwood, Arreaga-Mayer, Utley, Gavin, & Terry, 2001; Greenwood, Terry, et al., 1993; Kamps, Greenwood, Abbott, Utley, & Arreaga-Mayer, 2001; Mortweet et al., 1999; Reddy et al., 1999;

Table 4. *Cumulative List of Kamps PI Projects*

G008730080DID, USDE, An Ecobehavioral Approach to the Validation of Effective Education and Treatment Programs for Autistic and Developmentally Disabled Students (1987–1990)

H237E20034DID, USDE, An Ecobehavioral Approach for Assessment and Prevention of Behavior Disorders for Young Children and Their Families (1992–1995)

H023C00024DID, USDE, Academic and Social Interventions to Promote Mainstreaming and Integration for Students with Autism in Public Schools (1990–1993)

H023C30055DID, USDE, A Longitudinal Study of Generalization and Maintenance in Integration Settings for Students with Autism (1993–1998)

H237F50019DID, USDE, Proactive Home-School Programming for the Prevention of Serious Emotional Disturbance in Children with Behavior Problems (1995–1999)

H234D990051, USDE, Use of Multiple Gating and Prescriptive Assessment Procedures to Improve Early Childhood Services and Accurate Identification of Young Children with Disabilities (1999–2002)

H324D990052, USDE, Multi-Content ClassWide Peer Tutoring and Self-Management Interventions: Research Improving Teaching Practice and Literacy Outcomes for Middle School Students with Disabilities in Urban Poverty and Suburban Schools (1999–2002)

H324X010011, USDE, Center for Early Intervention in Reading and Behavior to Improve the Performance of Young Children (2001–2006)

Sideridis et al., 1997, 1998; Utley, 1999; Utley, Mortweet, & Greenwood, 1997). Her work has focused on evidence-based practice in the context of urban schools and multicultural education and special education (Table 5). Utley is currently editor of *Multiple Voices,* the journal of CEC's Division of Culturally and Linguistically Diverse Learners.

Dale Walker

Following her graduate training at JGCP and postdoctoral experience, Walker's first grant was funded in 1993, entitled, "Observational Assessment Instrument for Parent–Child Interactions Related to Language Development." Since then, her work has focused on early language interventions and evidence-based practice in child care and other birth-to-3 programs (e.g., Early Head Start, IDEA Part C) and the assessment of infant and toddler outcomes (Luze et al., 2001; Priest et al., 2001). A major publication was her follow-up study of the school performance of

Table 5. *Cumulative List of Utley PI Projects*

H029K20029DPP, USDE, Trainers of Trainers In-Service Program for Minority and
Non-Minority Regular and Special Education Teachers Who Educate Multicultural
Students with Disabilities (1992–1997)
H023C20145DID, USDE, Ecobehavioral Assessment, ClassWide Peer Tutoring and
Racial/Ethnic Minority Students with EMR: Validation of Academic Engaged Time,
IEP's, and Achievement (1992–1995)
H029J60006, USDE (Sub-contract/University of Virginia), Subcontract with the
University of Virginia—Research in Urban Communities (1998)
H324D980041, USDE, The Sustainability of ClassWide Peer Tutoring: An Effective
Instructional Intervention for Students with Disabilities in Inclusive and Special
Education Classroom Settings (1999–2002)

the children participating in Hart and Risley's *Meaningful Differences.*
That study demonstrated that children with the least vocabulary development to age 3 years also had lower performance in elementary school
(Walker, Greenwood, Hart, & Carta, 1994). This work contributes to the
current understanding of school readiness and early literacy prior to
kindergarten. Her subsequent work in this period focused on the relative
effectiveness of language intervention and assessment practices in child
care programs (Walker, 1999; Walker, Greenwood, Hart, & Carta, 1994;
Walker, Greenwood, & Terry, 1994; Walker & Linebarger, 2002; Walker
et al., 2001) (Table 6).

Charles R. Greenwood

The work of Charles Greenwood continued developing practical and sensitive measures of student performance and instruction interventions. In
one line of work, he and colleagues developed computer software to make

Table 6. *Cumulative List of Walker PI Projects*

H023A30099DID, USDE, Observational Assessment Instrument for Parent–Child
Interactions Related to Language Development (1993–1995)
H324D980066, USDE, Beacons of Excellence in the Promotion of Language
Development of Infants and Young Children and supplement (1999–2003)
Child Care and Language Learning, Cornyn Foundation (2001–2004)

their ecobehavioral observational measures easier to conduct in research and practice (Greenwood, Carta, Kamps, & Delquadri, 1993, 1994; Greenwood & Hou, 1995). During this period, the use of computer technology tools involving expert systems and multimedia, combined with CWPT, were demonstrated and tested (Greenwood, Carta, et al., 1993; Greenwood, Delquadri, & Bulgren, 1993; Greenwood, Finney, et al., 1993; Greenwood & Reith, 1994). In the mean time, reports on the longitudinal follow-along of CWPT programs as well as other CWPT work was published (Greenwood, 1991a, 1991b, 1994, 1996a, 1996b; Greenwood & Delquadri, 1995; Greenwood, Delquadri, et al., 1993; Greenwood, Finney, et al., 1993; Greenwood, Maheady, & Carta, 1991; Greenwood, Terry, Arreaga-Mayer, & Finney, 1992; Greenwood, Terry, Delquadri, Elliott, & Arreaga-Mayer, 1995; Utley et al., 1997). Additional reports on advances in ecobehavioral observation were also published (Greenwood, Carta, Arreaga-Mayer, & Rager, 1991; Greenwood, Carta, & Atwater, 1991; Greenwood, Carta, Kamps, & Arreaga-Mayer, 1990; Greenwood, Carta, Kamps, & Delquadri, 1994) (Table 7).

Current Activities Shaping the Future and Final Remarks

This brief history of the JGCP between 1990 and 2001 is incomplete because many other doctoral-level program coordinators and support staff made significant contributions. We apologize for not mentioning them all, but space does not permit. For example, the senior of these is Barbara Terry, a master trainer, leader, and co-director (Terry & Arreaga-Mayer, 2002). The younger of these were additional postdoctoral examples, such as Debra Linebarger, who received grant funding and completed research (Linebarger, 2001; Linebarger, Kosanic, Greenwood, & Doku, 2003) but went on to a faculty position at the University of Pennsylvania. Support staff members such as Betty Smith, Alva Beasley, and Mary Todd received 20-, 25-, and 30-year service pins, respectively, as employees of the university.

The next addition to this history will be written in another decade or so, no doubt under new leadership. The current program is continuing the kind of progress previously described. Because the NIH has again become interested in behaviorally focused research and early literacy and preschool school readiness, new topics such as abuse and neglect and

Table 7. *Cumulative List of Greenwood PI Projects*

G008730085DID, USDE, Expert Systems Approaches to Consultant-Mediated Intervention: Efficacy Studies of the Delivery of ClassWide Peer Tutoring to Students with Learning Disabilities (1987–1990)

H180B00005DID, USDE, Integrated, Computerized Systems for Ecobehavioral Classroom Observation: Laptop Assessment Tools for LEA Personnel (1990–1993)

H029D00085DPP, USDE, Post-Doctoral Program in Research Concerning Effective Practices for Minority Group Students With Handicaps at the Juniper Gardens Children's Project (1990–1995)

H023A40040DID, USDE, Improving Future LEA Observational Assessment Practices Through Instrument Dissemination and Technical Support to Preservice Training Programs (1994–1995)

KU#6090 Kauffman Fund for Greater Kansas City, Parent-Home Tutoring Center and Mentoring Concept (1995)

H029K50068DPP, USDE, Promoting Literacy Through Multimedia Training Approaches for the ClassWide Peer Tutoring Program: Developing, Evaluating, and Disseminating an Interactive Learning Management System (1995–1998)

H023G50012DID, USDE, Development and Validation of a Partnership-Consultation-Collaboration-Professional Development Model to Bridge the Gap Between Research and Practice (1995–1999)

H180G60002, USDE, Promoting Literacy Through Materials, Media, & Technology Improvements in the ClassWide Peer Tutoring Program: Research on the Effects of a Computerized Learning Management System (1996–1999)

H029D60040, USDE, Post-Doctoral Leadership Training Program in Research Concerning Effective Instructional Practices for Culturally Diverse Students with Disabilities (1996–2000)

H023G50012-Project Supplement, USDE, The Development and Validation of a Partnership-Consultation-Collaboration-Professional Development Model to Bridge the Gap Between Research and Practice (1999–2000)

H327A000038, USDE/OSEP, ClassWide Peer Tutoring-Learning Management System (CWPT-LMS) Technology Supporting Literacy, Accountability and Access to General Education Curriculum (2000–2003)

H325D000034, USDE/OSEP, Post-Doctoral Leadership Training Program in Intervention Research for Culturally/Linguistically Diverse Students with Disabilities (2000–2004)

child maltreatment are being funded in increasing numbers. With the reauthorization of the Individuals with Disabilities Education Improvement Act in 2005, the special education research mission of OSEP was transferred to the new Institute for Education Sciences (IES) in the USDE. With this change, the new history will describe how we were challenged to continue existing and new lines of work that will be increasingly under new management, but also the themes of the work will likely change. As always, JGCP programs of research change to fit new realities in national and local need and policy.

In closing, an initiative of high importance to the future of the JGCP and in which JGCP is a central player is the development of the Children's Campus of Wyandotte County (CCWC), Inc. Based on the past 4 years of work examining feasibility, planning, location, architecture, funding, and governance, the CCWC at this writing is in its capital campaign phase of development with a goal of breaking ground in the fall of 2006.

This development of the CCWC, like the JGCP, has been very much a grass roots collaboration of directors and frontline staff in Northeast Kansas City from over 50 organizations (private and public), volunteers, and community residents (on-line at *http://www.childrenscampus ofwyco.org*). The collaboration scaled up to include monthly meetings 4 years ago; meetings continue today (now held in the Juniper Gardens Housing Projects' Community Center) (Nicely, 2004). Work groups made up of these collaborators have contributed to the outcomes, designs, plans, and services to be delivered on campus. Just one of these collaborations has led to the development of a central intake and referral process used by the CCWC partners to better serve and account for services provided to children and families. The current status of the CCWC is as a 501(c)3 (not-for-profit) organization responsible for governance, design and build, and tenants. Tenants (the partnering agencies), through both a tenant association and as tier-1 on-site service providers, will provide children and family services and support program operating costs.

Research linked to the use of evidence-based practices pervades the CCWC's themes of early childhood education, family support, health, and the arts. The Juniper Gardens Children's Project is the lead research partner, responsible for research planning and the conduct of studies with relevance to the mission of the CCWC. The JGCP will be responsible for orchestrating collaborations with partners, research methodology, recruitment, and reporting/disseminating results. A major process through which collaboration occurs at the grass roots level is at the monthly meeting of partners where the last hour of each meeting is devoted to work groups, of which research is one. In these meetings, research needs and ideas are discussed and findings are reported, but to partners. Additional reports will be published on the CCWC web site and in the professional peer-reviewed literature.

It is anticipated that the CCWC will be the future location of the JGCP. Also anticipated are many more important opportunities of the type previously described, including the opportunity of serving greater numbers of area children who are at risk and currently not receiving services as well as teaching and service related to effective practice in the education and treatment of children and families.

Acknowledgments

We thank the Northeast Community of Kansas City, Kansas for its continued participation and support. Also deserving thanks are the Office of Special Education Programs, U.S. Department of Education, whose programs funded the majority of work completed during this time; and the University of Kansas for its continued support for this program and its mission of research, service, and teaching.

References

Arreaga-Mayer, C. (1996). An ecological approach to effective service delivery for economically deprived ethnically diverse families. In I. T. Mink, M. L. de Leon-Siantz, & P. Berman (Eds.), *Ethnically diverse families with developmentally disabled or mentally retarded members: Theory, research and service delivery*. Washington, DC: American Association on Mental Retardation.

Arreaga-Mayer, C. (1998a). Increasing active student responding and improving academic performance through class-wide peer tutoring. *Intervention in School and Clinic, 34*(2), 89–94.

Arreaga-Mayer, C. (1998b). Language sensitive peer-mediated instruction for culturally and linguistically diverse learners the intermediate elementary grades. In R. M. Gersten & R. T. Jimenez (Eds.), *Promoting learning for culturally and linguistically diverse students* (pp. 73–90). Belmont, CA: Wadsworth.

Arreaga-Mayer, C., Carta, J. J., & Tapia, Y. (1992). *ESCRIBE: Ecobehavioral system for the contextual recording of interactional bilingual environments*. Kansas City, KS: Juniper Gardens Children's Project, University of Kansas.

Arreaga-Mayer, C., Carta, J. J., & Tapia, Y. (1994). Ecobehavioral assessment of bilingual special education settings: The opportunity to respond revisited. In R. Gardner, D. Sainato, J. Cooper, T. Heron, W. Heward, J. Eskleman, & T. Grossi (Eds.), *Behavior analysis in education: Focus on measurably superior instruction* (pp. 225–240): Brooks/Cole.

Arreaga-Mayer, C., Carta, J. J., & Tapia, Y. (1995). Ecobehavioral assessment: A new methodology for evaluating instruction for exceptional culturally and linguistically diverse students. In S. B. Garcia (Ed.), *Shaping the future: Defining effective services for exceptional culturally and linguistically diverse learners* (*Monograph 1*). Washington, DC: CEC-DDEL.

Arreaga-Mayer, C., & Greenwood, C. R. (1986). Environmental variables affecting the school achievement of culturally and linguistically different learners: An instructional perspective. *Journal of the National Association for Bilingual Education, 10,* 113–135.

Arreaga-Mayer, C., & Perdomo-Rivera, C. (1996). Ecobehavioral analysis of instruction for at-risk language minority students. *Elementary Education Journal, 96*(3), 245–258.

Arreaga-Mayer, C., Terry, B., & Greenwood, C. R. (1998). Classwide peer tutoring. In K. Topping & S. Ehly (Eds.), *Peer-mediated instruction* (pp. 105–119). Mahwah, NY: Erlbaum.

Carta, J. J. (1995). *Project SLIDE: Skills for learning independence in developmentally appropriate environments.* Kansas City, KS: Outreach Grant funded by Office of Special Education Programs (CFDA No. 84.024D), U.S. Department of Education.

Carta, J. J. (1999, December). *Implications of general outcome measurement for young children.* Paper presented at the 15th Annual Meeting of the Division for Early Childhood, Council for Exceptional Children, Washington, DC.

Carta, J. J. (1999–2002). Improving the delivery of early intervention to children with disabilities from high poverty backgrounds. OSEP, USDE Project H324D990048. Kansas City, KS: Juniper Gardens Children's Project, University of Kansas.

Carta, J. J., Atwater, J. B., & Peterson, C. (2001). *Examining children with special needs and their families in the Early Head Start national evaluation.* Paper presented at the International Division of Early Childhood Conference on Children with Special Needs, Boston, MA.

Carta, J. J., Atwater, J. B., & Schwartz, I. (1990). *Early classroom survival skills: A training approach* (Final Report). Lawrence, KS: Kansas Early Childhood Research Institute, University of Kansas.

Carta, J. J., Atwater, J. B., & Schwartz, I. S. (1991, June). *Early classroom survival skills: A training approach.* Paper presented at the New Directions in Child and Family Research: Shaping Head Start in the 90s, Arlington, VA.

Carta, J. J., Estes, J. S., Schiefelbusch, R. L., & Terry, B. J. (2000). *Skills for learning independence developmentally appropriate environments: Project SLIDE* (4th ed.). Longmont, CO: Sopris West.

Carta, J. J., & Greenwood, C. R. (1985). Ecobehavioral assessment: A methodology for examining the evaluation of early intervention programs. *Topics in Early Childhood Special Education, 5,* 88–104.

Carta, J. J., & Greenwood, C. R. (1988). Reducing academic risks in inner-city classrooms. *Youth Policy, 10,* 6–18.

Carta, J. J., & Greenwood, C. R. (1989). Concluding remarks. *Education and Treatment of Children, 12,* 425–428.

Carta, J. J., & Greenwood, C. R. (1997). Barriers to the implementation of effective educational practices for young children with disabilities. In J. W. Lloyd, E. J. Kame'enui, & D. Chard (Eds.), *Issues in the education of students with disabilities* (pp. 261–274). Mahwah, NJ: Erlbaum.

Carta, J. J., Greenwood, C. R., & Robinson, S. (1987). Application of an eco-behavioral approach to the evaluation of early intervention programs. In R. Prinz (Ed.), *Advances in the behavioral assessment of children and families* (Vol. 3, pp. 123–155). Greenwich, CT: JAI.

Carta, J. J., Sideridis, G., Rinkel, P., Guimaraes, S., Greenwood, C., Baggett, K., et al. (1994a). Behavioral outcomes of infants and young children prenatally exposed to illicit drugs: A review and analysis of the experimental literature. *Topics in Early Childhood Special Education, 14,* 184–216.

Carta, J. J., Sideridis, G., Rinkel, P., Guimaraes, S., Greenwood, C. R., Baggett, K., et al. (1994b). Behavioral characteristics of drug-exposed infants and young children: A review and analysis of the experimental literature. *Topics in Early Childhood Special Education, 13,* 243–254.

Christophersen, E. R., & Mortweet, S. L. (2001). *Treatments that work with children: Empirically supported strategies for managing childhood problems.* New York, NY: APA Books.

Greenwood, C. R. (1991a). Longitudinal analysis of time engagement and academic achievement in at-risk and non-risk students. *Exceptional Children, 57,* 521–535.

Greenwood, C. R. (1991b). Classwide peer tutoring: Longitudinal effects on the reading language and mathematics achievement of at-risk students. *Reading Writing and Learning Disabilities International, 7,* 105–124.

Greenwood, C. R. (1994, February). ClassWide Peer Tutoring and inclusion. In D. Fuchs (Chair), *Data-based approaches to inclusionary education: Strategies for the policymakers?* Paper presented at the Pacific Coast Research Conference, La Jolla, CA.

Greenwood, C. R. (1996a). Research on the practices and behavior of effective teachers at the Juniper Gardens Children's Project: Implications for the education of diverse learners. In D. Speece & B. K. Keogh (Eds.), *Research on classroom ecologies: Implications for inclusion of children with learning disabilities* (pp. 39–67). Hillsdale, NJ: Erlbaum.

Greenwood, C. R. (1996b). The case for performance-based models of instruction. *School Psychology Quarterly, 11*(4), 283–296.

Greenwood, C. R. (1999). Reflections on a research career: Perspective on 35 years of research at the Juniper Gardens Children's Project. *Exceptional Children, 66*(1), 7–21.

Greenwood, C. R., Arreaga-Mayer, C., Utley, C. A., Gavin, K., & Terry, B. J. (2001). ClassWide Peer Tutoring Learning Management System: Applications with elementary-level English language learners. *Remedial and Special Education, 22*(1), 34–47.

Greenwood, C. R., Carta, J. J., Arreaga-Mayer, C., & Rager, A. (1991). The behavior analyst consulting model: Identifying and validating naturally effective instructional models. *Journal of Behavioral Education, 1,* 165–191.

Greenwood, C. R., Carta, J. J., & Atwater, J. J. (1991). Ecobehavioral analysis in the classroom: Review and implications. *Journal of Behavioral Education, 1,* 59–77.

Greenwood, C. R., Carta, J. J., Hart, B., Kamps, D., Terry, B., Arreaga-Mayer, C., et al. (1992). Out of the laboratory and into the community: 26 years of applied behavior analysis at the Juniper Gardens Children's Project. *American Psychologist, 47,* 1464–1474.

Greenwood, C. R., Carta, J. J., Hart, B., Thurston, L., & Hall, R. V. (1989). A behavioral approach to research on psychosocial retardation. *Education and Treatment of Children, 12,* 330–346.

Greenwood, C. R., Carta, J. J., Kamps, D., & Arreaga-Mayer, C. (1990). Ecobehavioral analysis of classroom instruction. In S. R. Schroeder (Ed.), *Ecobehavioral analysis and developmental disabilities: The twenty-first century* (pp. 33–63). New York: Springer-Verlag.

Greenwood, C. R., Carta, J. J., Kamps, D., & Delquadri, J. (1993). *Ecobehavioral assessment systems software (EBASS): Practitioner's Manual.* Kansas City, KS: Juniper Gardens Children's Project, University of Kansas.

Greenwood, C. R., Carta, J. J., Kamps, D., & Delquadri, J. (1994). *Integrated, computerized systems for ecobehavioral classroom observation: Laptop assessment tools for LEA personnel* (Final Report: Project H180B00005). Kansas City, KS: Juniper Gardens Children's Project, University of Kansas.

Greenwood, C. R., Carta, J. J., Kamps, D., Terry, B., & Delquadri, J. (1994). Development and validation of standard classroom observation systems for school practitioners: Ecobehavioral assessment systems software EBASS. *Exceptional Children, 61,* 197–210.

Greenwood, C. R., & Delquadri, J. (1995). ClassWide Peer Tutoring and the prevention of school failure. *Preventing School Failure, 39*(4), 21–25.

Greenwood, C. R., Delquadri, J., & Bulgren, J. (1993). Current challenges to behavioral technology in the reform of schooling: Large-scale high-quality implementation and sustained use of effective educational practices. *Education and Treatment of Children, 16,* 401–440.

Greenwood, C. R., Delquadri, J., & Hall, R. V. (1989). Longitudinal effects of classwide peer tutoring. *Journal of Educational Psychology, 81,* 371–383.

Greenwood, C. R., Finney, R., Terry, B., Arreaga-Mayer C., Carta, J. J., Delquadri, J., et al. (1993). Monitoring improving and maintaining quality implementation of the classwide peer tutoring program using behavioral and computer technology. *Education and Treatment of Children, 16,* 19–47.

Greenwood, C. R., & Hou, L. S. (1995). *Ecobehavioral Assessment Systems Software (EBASS), Version 3.0: Technical manual.* Kansas City, KS: The Juniper Gardens Children's Project, University of Kansas.

Greenwood, C. R., Maheady, L., & Carta, J. J. (1991). Peer tutoring programs in the regular education classroom. In G. Stoner, M. R. Shinn, & H. M. Walker (Eds.), *Interventions for achievement and behavior problems* (1st ed., pp. 179–200). Washington, DC: National Association of School Psychologists.

Greenwood, C. R., & Reith, H. (1994). Current dimensions of technology assessment in special education. *Exceptional Children, 61,* 105–113.

Greenwood, C. R., Terry, B., Arreaga-Mayer, C., & Finney, R. (1992). The classwide peer tutoring program: Implementation factors moderating students' achievement. *Journal of Applied Behavior Analysis, 25,* 101–116.

Greenwood, C. R., Terry, B., Delquadri, J., Elliott, M., & Arreaga-Mayer, C. (1995). *ClassWide Peer Tutoring (CWPT): Effective teaching and research review.* Kansas City, KS: Juniper Gardens Children's Project, University of Kansas.

Greenwood, C. R., Terry, B., Utley, C. A., Montagna, D., & Walker, D. (1993). Achievement placement and services: Middle school benefits of ClassWide Peer Tutoring used at the elementary school. *School Psychology Review, 22*(3), 497–516.

Greenwood, C. R., & Walker, D. (1995). Post-doctoral fellowship at the Juniper Gardens Children's Project: Developing research leadership in special education. *Teacher Education and Special Education, 18*(3), 205–217.

Hall, R. V., Schiefelbusch, R. L., Hoyt, R. K., & Greenwood, C. R. (1989). History mission and organization of the Juniper Gardens Children's Project. *Education and Treatment of Children, 12,* 301–329.

Hart, B., & Risley, T. R. (1995). *Meaningful differences in the everyday experience of young American children.* Baltimore: Paul H. Brookes Publishing Co.

Hart, B., & Risley, T. R. (1999). *The social world of children learning to talk.* Baltimore, MD: Paul H. Brookes Publishing Co.

Kamps, D., Carta, J., Delquadri, J., Arreaga-Mayer, C., Terry, B., & Greenwood, C. R. (1989). School-based research and intervention. *Education and Treatment of Children, 12,* 359–390.

Kamps, D., Greenwood, C. R., Abbott, M., Utley, C. A., & Arreaga-Mayer, C. (2001). *Center for early intervention in reading and behavior to improve the performance of young children* (Grant No. H32X0100011, OSEP, USDE). Kansas City, KS: Juniper Gardens Children's Project, University of Kansas.

Linebarger, D., Kosanic, A. Z., Greenwood, C. R., & Doku, N. S. (2003). Effects of viewing the television program "Between the Lions" on the emergent literacy skills of young children. *Journal of Educational Psychology, 96*(2), 297–308.

Linebarger, D. L. (2001). Learning to read using television: The effects of captions and narration. *Journal of Educational Psychology, 93,* 288–298.

Luze, G. J., Linebarger, D. L., Greenwood, C. R., Carta, J. J., Walker, D., Leitschuh, C., et al. (2001). Developing a general outcome measure of growth in expressive communication of infants and toddlers. *School Psychology Review, 30*(3), 383–406.

McConnell, S. R., McEvoy, M. A., Carta, J. J., Greenwood, C. R., Kaminski, R., Good, R. I., et al. (1996). *Early childhood research institute on program performance measures: A growth and development approach.* Minneapolis, MN: University of Minnesota, Proposal funded by the Early Education Programs for Children with Disabilities, Office of Special Education and Rehabilitation Services, U.S. Office of Education.

McEvoy, M. A., Priest, J. S., Kaminski, R., Carta, J. J., Greenwood, C. R., McConnell, S. R., et al. (2001). General growth outcomes: Wait! There's more! *Journal of Early Intervention, 24*(3), 191–192.

Mortweet, S. L., Utley, C. A., Walker, D., Dawson, H. L., Delquadri, J. C., Reddy, S. S., et al. (1999). Classwide peer tutoring: Teaching students with mild mental retardation in inclusive classrooms. *Exceptional Children, 65*(4), 425–536.

Nicely, S. (2004). Children's Campus of Wyandotte County: A fertile learning field for children, parents, teachers, service providers, and researchers. Kansas City, KS: Children's Campus of Wyandotte County, Inc.

Priest, J. S., McConnell, S. R., Walker, D., Carta, J. J., Kaminski, R. A., McEvoy, M. A., et al. (2001). General growth outcomes for children: Developing a foundation for continuous progress measurement. *Journal of Early Intervention, 24*(3), 163–180.

Reddy, S. S., Utley, C. A., Delquadri, J. C., Mortweet, S. L., Greenwood, C. R., & Bowman, V. (1999). Peer tutoring for health and safety. *Teaching Exceptional Children, 31*(3), 44–52.

Sideridis, G. D., Utley, C. A., Greenwood, C. R., Dawson, H., Delquadri, J., & Palmer, P. (1998). An intervention strategy to enhance spelling performance and social interaction and to decrease inappropriate behaviors of students with mild disabilities and typical peers in an inclusive instructional setting. *Research in Education: An Interdisciplinary International Journal, 59*, 109–124.

Sideridis, G. D., Utley, C. A., Greenwood, C. R., Delquadri, J. C., Dawson, H., Palmer, P., et al. (1997). ClassWide Peer Tutoring: Effects on the spelling performance of students with mild disabilities and their typical peers in an integrated instructional setting. *Journal of Behavioral Education, 7*(4), 435–462.

Terry, B., & Arreaga-Mayer, C. (2002). Think, Get Ready, Respond! Class-wide responsive teaching to improve basic academic skills. Longmont, CO: Sopris West.

Thurston, L. D., Dasta, K., & Greenwood, C. R. (1984). A program of survival skills workshops for urban women. *Journal of Community Psychology, 12*, 192–196.

Utley, C. A. (1999). Peer-mediated instruction and interventions (Part 1). *Remedial and Special Education, 22*(1), 1–34.

Utley, C. A., Mortweet, S. L., & Greenwood, C. R. (1997). Peer-mediated instruction and interventions. *Focus on Exceptional Children, 29*(5), 1–23.

Walker, D. (1999, December). How individual growth and development indicators are used to direct intervention with infants and toddlers within a decision-making model. In D. Walker (Chair), *Measuring Growth and Development of Infants and Toddlers for the 21st Century.* Symposium conducted at the Conference for the Division of Early Childhood, Washington, DC.

Walker, D., Greenwood, C. R., Hart, B., & Carta, J. J. (1994). Improving the prediction of early school academic outcomes using socioeconomic status and early language production. *Child Development, 65*, 606–621.

Walker, D., Greenwood, C. R., & Terry, B. (1994). Management of classroom disruptive behavior and academic performance problems. In L. W. Craighead, W. E. Craighead, A. E. Kazdin, & M. J. Mahoney (Eds.), *Cognitive and behavioral interventions: An empirical approach to mental health problems* (pp. 215–234). Boston: Allyn and Bacon.

Walker, D., Hall, R. V., & Greenwood, C. R. (1989). Impact as a community, graduate, and post-graduate training site. *Education and Treatment of Children, 12*(4), 405–425.

Walker, D., & Linebarger, D. L. (2002, March). *Beacons of excellence in the promotion of communication: Project of national significance: Identifying elements of quality services within inclusive early childhood settings and the impact on child outcomes.* Paper presented at the Conference on Research Innovations in Early Intervention, San Diego, CA.

Walker, D., Linebarger, D. L., Bigelow, K. M., Harjusola-Webb, S., Small, C. J., Rogrigues, D., et al. (2001, April). *Language interactions related to quality of infant childcare.* Paper presented at the Biennial Meeting for the Society for Research in Child Development, Minneapolis, MN.

17

The Communication of People with Mental Retardation Program Project

RICHARD R. SAUNDERS, JOSEPH E. SPRADLIN, AND JAMES A. SHERMAN

The Communications Program Project was the first and longest running major program grant of the Bureau of Child Research. Funded in the 1960s, it has been one of its most generative research enterprises, from which many other research projects have spun off and many researchers have been trained, to the point where the University of Kansas has become an internationally recognized center for speech and language research. A detailed history is presented in chapter 4.

Early History

The first program project of the Bureau of Child Research to study the communication of people with mental retardation was funded in 1964. From the beginning, the researchers participating in this effort assumed that the speech and communication of children and adults with mental retardation could be improved by the systematic application of behavioral principles. Congruent with that assumption, some of the earliest experiments were directed toward changing specific aspects of speech. In the light of the enormous progress that has occurred during the years since 1964 concerning the development of speech and communication, the aims of many of the earliest studies may seem trivial. When the studies were conducted, however, they were significant and were attempts to demonstrate that, for example, the rate of vocalizations of children

351

with mental retardation could be modified through the systematic application of consequences (Horowitz, 1963) or that these children's vocal behavior was affected by the persons with whom they interacted.

In the late 1950s and early 1960s, many prominent researchers did not believe that the speech and language development of children with mental retardation could be enhanced or modified in any meaningful way via environmental means. Chomsky (1959), for example, had published his criticisms of Skinner's book (Skinner, 1957) and had proposed his theory that generative grammar was innate. Statements by Chomsky and other psycholinguists about the innateness of language led project researchers to initiate a series of studies that demonstrated that many of the aspects of grammar, whether thought to be innate or not, could still be taught through the systematic application of sound behavior principles (Baer & Guess, 1973; Guess & Baer, 1973; Guess, Sailor, Rutherford, & Baer, 1968; Schumaker & Sherman, 1970).

Although these early studies were aimed at demonstrating that generative aspects of spoken language could be taught, there was also a recognition of the substantial importance of receptive language. Because hearing is typically critical to such understanding and because there were not good ways of evaluating the hearing of children with severe mental retardation, project researchers at that time conducted a series of studies aimed at perfecting procedures for evaluating the hearing of such children. This research led to a set of procedures that could be used to evaluate such children with audiometric procedures previously applicable only to persons who understood and followed verbal directions (Fulton & Spradlin, 1971, 1972, 1974a, 1974b; Lloyd, Spradlin, & Reid, 1968). Project researchers also began a systematic study of the development of generative receptive language. Once again they demonstrated that generative receptive language could be developed with many children, to at least a limited extent, by the systematic application of behavioral principles (Baer & Guess, 1971; Striefel & Wetherby, 1973; Striefel, Wetherby, & Karlan, 1976). These early successes in demonstrating that some children with severe mental retardation could be taught many aspects of generative language led to subsequent attempts to develop a comprehensive program for language and communication training for children with severe and profound mental retardation (Guess, Sailor, & Baer, 1978).

In spite of the fact that specific aspects of productive and receptive language could be taught to children with severe and profound mental retardation, many problems were apparent. First, not all such children seemed to profit from such training and, second, even those children who demonstrated considerable language competency within teaching situations often failed to exhibit their newly acquired skills in their daily environments. The inability to teach some children to use speech led researchers (e.g., Carrier, 1974) to develop a symbol system for children who did not learn via the speech mode. The failure of children who had been taught specific language skills to use these skills in their daily environments also led project researchers to begin to look carefully at those environments. Observation of the children in their daily environments (at that time these were typically institutional environments) led to the conclusion that they frequently did not have sufficient opportunities to use their newly developed skills. These observations led to a number of developments. One development was that investigators began to observe carefully the interaction of persons with mental retardation and their caregivers in their natural (i.e., noninstitutional) environments (Hart & Risley, 1980). The results of these efforts to observe children and their caregivers led to another project by Hart and Risley. In this research, Hart and Risley examined the communicative interactions of young children in their home environments who were just beginning to develop language. This research resulted in the publication of a seminal monograph by Hart and Risley (1995), as well as to the current research of Hart within the present program project that examines the development of language by children with Down syndrome in comparison with that of typically developing children.

The observation that the systematic teaching of language failed to generalize led Stokes and Baer (1977) to develop a model of the procedures used to facilitate generalization. They proposed this in a classic article that has served as a basis for both the experimental clinical analysis of generalization problems and tactics for nearly three decades.

In the mid-1970s, project researchers began to develop procedures to be used in the children's natural environments to aid them to acquire and use new skills (Hart & Risley, 1975; Schumaker & Sherman, 1978). Hart and Risley (1975) developed an incidental teaching technique that encouraged children to request objects in their play environments. Halle and his colleagues (Halle, Baer, & Spradlin, 1981; Halle, Marshall, & Spradlin, 1979) demonstrated that if one introduced a delay between the time that a child made a nonspeech request and then prompted speaking by presenting a spoken model, the person would often begin requesting with speech after a few such occasions. Others have now replicated these "incidental teaching" and "delayed prompt" techniques to the point that the use of such procedures is standard practice in the fields of early intervention, special education, and speech-language pathology.

Among the early contributions of the program project are two initiatives that took on a life of their own. These were the Mimosa Cottage Project and the Juniper Gardens Children's Project. The Mimosa Cottage Project was the first major initiative to demonstrate that the systematic application of behavioral principles could make major changes in the lives of persons with mental retardation (Girardeau & Spradlin, 1964; Lent, LeBlanc, & Spradlin, 1970). That project demonstrated that many people who had previously been largely kept in custodial care could be productive and led to the deinstitutionalization of some of the women in Mimosa Cottage. Although the project was carried out in a house on the grounds of a large residential institution, it demonstrated the possibility of supporting such persons in noninstitutional environments and thus was an important step in the deinstitutionalization movement. The second initiative, the Juniper Gardens Children's Project, was an early model for improving the quality of education and life for urban children who were economically deprived (Wolf, Giles, & Hall, 1968). This unique "community-based" research program is going strong four decades later. Moreover, from that project sprung the Achievement Place model for treating adolescents who were "predelinquent" (Phillips, 1968). Many of the procedures developed on that project were adapted in the development of community programs for persons with mental retardation (Harchik, Sherman, Sheldon, & Strouse, 1992). These are but a few of the examples of the ground-breaking research associated with the early years of the Communications Program Project.

Recent History

Development in general can be seen as a seemingly cohesive sequence of changes. Some, but not all, of the later changes cannot take place until certain earlier changes have become stable and efficient; the earlier changes are prerequisites for the later ones. Of those prerequisites, some are necessary for only a few subsequent changes; others, by contrast, are necessary for many subsequent changes. The latter are referred to here as "cusps." The recent history of this program project has focused on various cusps that underlie basic communication and language development.

Cusps are attainments with two characteristics: 1) Once mastered, they open the way to the sudden and widespread development of many other important attainments; and 2) if not mastered, those important subsequent attainments will not be achieved. A familiar example is reading skill. Once achieved and made fluent, a huge world of knowledge and skills is available to the reader for quick, efficient access. Absent reading skill, that same knowledge would be acquired only slowly and inefficiently, if at all.

During the several recent funding periods for the program project (1985–1999), specific projects have studied communication-related skills and processes with participants with mild to profound retardation. The initial work by R. Saunders and colleagues was devoted to the cusp of classification, with research aimed at unraveling how dissimilar objects or other stimuli become members of important classes (Spradlin & Saunders, 1984). Classification is a building block skill that enables a broad array of knowledge attainment. Early on, they found that young adults with mild mental retardation did not develop stimulus classes when certain approaches to training were employed, but did with other approaches. The prerequisites to classes are usually taught by establishing conditional discriminations with sets of stimuli in common across the discriminations. Spradlin and Saunders (1986) found that whenever the in-common stimuli were the set of discriminative stimuli used in all the conditional discriminations, class formation occurred. When the in-common stimuli were a set of conditional stimuli, the reverse was true. Saunders, Wachter, and Spradlin (1988) replicated these results. In a follow-up, Saunders, Saunders, Kirby, and Spradlin (1988) found that with discriminative stimuli in common, classes were formed even when the conditional discriminations were "taught" without feedback, provided the subjects had a prior history of class formation. Thus, discrimination learning and class formation were found to generalize across problems. Research also showed that classes could be merged with conditional discrimination training without feedback (Saunders, Saunders, et al., 1988; Williams, Saunders, Saunders, & Spradlin, 1995).

Paralleling the work on establishing classes and assessing their stability, K. Saunders and Spradlin (1989, 1990, 1993) and Oppenheimer, Saunders, and Spradlin (1993) investigated methods for facilitating discrimination learning—the key prerequisite to stimulus class formation. This research highlighted the central role of simple discrimination acquisition as an important component of conditional discrimination learning. Concurrently, R. Saunders and Green (1992) mapped how training with conditional discrimination procedures could lead not only to arbitrary matching, but also arbitrary oddity (referred to as sample/S) control (see Carrigan & Sidman, 1992). Further, Saunders and Green (1999) determined that methods for establishing conditional discriminations could have an impact on whether certain simple discriminations important to stimulus classification would arise. Thus, care in arranging the conditional discriminations and interpreting test results emerged as a particularly important issue—that is, without appropriate safeguards subjects, could develop classes other than those intended by the experimenter or not develop classes at all.

Recently, Kate Saunders has been studying the development of reading and spelling with young children and adults with mild and moderate mental retardation. Saunders and colleagues have demonstrated that, through systematic programming that involves constructing words and nonsense syllables, both young typically developing children and adults with moderate and mild mental retardation can be taught word attack skills (Mueller, Olmi, & Saunders, 2000; Saunders, O'Donnell, Vaidya, & Williams, 2003). These word attack skills allow the person to read and spell words that involve new combinations of previously learned components. Word attack skills are a critical cusp for basic reading development.

Although the previous work by R. Saunders and colleagues on discrimination and classification and by K. Saunders on reading and spelling involved important cusps in communication, we have chosen to focus the proposed research on earlier ones. This shift in focus fits a 40-year progression of the research to extend the scope of communication studies to persons with even more severe impairments.

Recently, inspired by preliminary work of M. Saunders aimed at developing procedures for determining whether participants with the most severe physical and mental disabilities could learn to control aspects of their environment (M. Saunders et al., 2001) and R. Saunders' research on the role of contingency discrimination in interventions for aberrant behavior (Saunders, McEntee, & Saunders, accepted pending revision; Saunders & Saunders, 2000), the Saunders have studied aspects of cause-and-effect learning in people with profound multiple impairments. These individuals are adults with profound inability to tell those around them anything, including whether or not they have any awareness of the conditions around them. Typically they had not even responded to differential contingencies because there was no reliable response for an observer to detect. In this work, the participants were provided adaptive switches for control of events hypothesized to be reinforcing or enjoyable, such as music and vibration (e.g., Saunders, Smagner, & Saunders, 2003). This research has allowed for the development of procedures for demonstrating that many of these individuals are responsive to aspects of their environment provided that the appropriate contingencies are in effect.

Adaptive switches are constructed by housing a small electromechanical switch in a user interface designed to make closure of the switch relatively effortless. Commercially manufactured adaptive switches include pressure-sensitive disks, joysticks, mercury-filled tubes, and motion detectors. Switches can be used to control both alternating current (AC) and direct current (DC) sources. Adaptive switch programs usually are adopted and employed when efforts to establish more typical communication and environmental-control repertoires have failed. The individuals enrolled in switch programs often have severe motor skill deficits, with limitations in range of motion, grasp and release, coordination, and strength. Indeed, a common challenge to establishing a switch program is to identify a single physical movement that appears to be volitional and that also occurs with sufficient force and distance to displace a switch interface.

The Saunders' project team, including staff of Fircrest School and faculty and students of the University of Washington Department of Speech and Hearing Sciences, first found that response duration measures were more reliable indicators of contingency discrimination than rate measures (Saunders, Timler, Cullinan, Pilkey, Questad, & Saunders, 2003). With duration measures, a surprisingly large proportion (given the extant literature) of the participants showed evidence of cause-and-effect learning. The team also have found that adaptive switch use was more consistent when ambient stimuli (i.e., potential visual and auditory distractions) in the learning environment are minimized (Murphy, Saunders, Saunders, & Olswang, in press), that switch use was not greatly affected by changes in behavioral state (Mellstrom, Saunders, Saunders, & Olswang, in press), and that evidence of cause-and-effect learning was sometimes more robust when the individual controls social attention rather than mechanical sources of stimulation (Struve, Saunders, Saunders, & Olswang, in preparation). Most recently, these investigators demonstrated a novel method by which their participants could choose between two concurrently available sources of stimulation (Saunders et al., 2005).

Overall, the switch research has demonstrated that individuals with the most profound impairments and no conventional means of communication can be enabled to control their environment, including making choices about what to experience. In short, we have greatly enlarged our understanding of the potential capabilities of these individuals' cause-and-effect learning, a significant developmental cusp. This work is important because individuals with profound impairments are at risk of having switch supports discontinued, or never provided in the first place, because their motor responses are perceived to be involuntary and nonfunctional. These recent achievements also reflect passage by the investigators through their own cusp: Finding that these individuals could discriminate contingencies led the investigators to develop and arrange tests for preferences; finding preferences led the investigators to develop and test choice making; and the establishment of choice behavior leads them to hypothesize that a history of choosing is a fundamental prerequisite for establishing signaling a request for assistance. Two of the projects in the current application propose empirical tests of the investigators' hypothesis.

One goal of the previous research of Brady and McLean was to investigate whether certain behaviors of individuals who did not speak, use sign language, or use other alternative forms of symbolic communication could be described as communicative. They borrowed descriptive criteria of communication used by colleagues studying prespeech communication in typically developing infants (e.g., Bates, Benigni, Bretherton, Camaioni, & Volterra, 1979; Bruner, 1975; Carpenter, Mastergeorge, & Coggins, 1983), as well as behavioral criteria for nonspoken examples of "verbal behavior" (e.g., Savage-Rumbaugh, 1984; Skinner, 1957). Using these criteria, Brady and McLean described various forms and reliably identified functions of communication in adults with severe to profound mental retardation (McLean & Snyder-McLean, 1987; McLean, McLean, Brady, & Etter, 1991), thereby broadening our understanding of the cusp that is the transition from gestural communication to symbolic communication. McLean and colleagues described some gestural communication as "perlocutionary," or behavior lacking in communicative intent yet often assigned communicative intent by an observer. The Saunders' projects both extend work on perlocutionary communicative intent and explore certain switch use as reflecting perlocutionary, or perhaps illocutionary, communicative intent.

The work of Brady and McLean followed the pragmatics revolution in language. The outcome of this revolution was to consider how one's communication affected communication partners. What was the function of a communication act within a conversational framework? In applying this framework to studies of communication, Brady and McLean not only described the specific gestures and vocalizations used to communicate, but also the apparent functions of these communicative gestures and vocalizations. For example, an individual might point to an object on a shelf in order to comment on some distinctive feature of the object or to request access to that object. Brady and McLean developed observational criteria for reliably differentiating between these different communicative functions (McLean et al., 1991).

An additional accomplishment was the construction of communication protocols designed to observe different communication forms and functions in individuals with severe disabilities. Opportunities for participants to request, protest, and comment were all embedded within these protocols. The communication protocols have been adapted for portability (McLean, Brady, McLean, & Behrens, 1999) and to provide specific communicative opportunities such as repairs (Brady, McLean, McLean, & Johnston, 1995). These protocols added additional information from that obtained by surveying familiar caregivers (McLean, Brady,

& McLean, 1996). In the most recent Communications Program Project, protocols were designed to create opportunities for children to initiate and repair specific types of communication breakdowns. Similar protocols were used with adults (Brady et al., 1995) and have enabled researchers to analyze children's productions under equivalent conditions. That is, we are able to compare how children at different stages of preverbal communication development repair when given a set number of opportunities to repair. The protocols developed to date have been ideal for promoting gestural and vocal communication. However, they were not designed to maximize the likelihood of using augmentative and alternative communication (AAC). The proposed research calls for protocols that are adapted and individualized to promote use of AAC by children learning to use AAC.

Communication repair is a critical cusp; without its development, the child whose communication initiations are unclear or misunderstood will not be successful in achieving their communicative goals. Current work by Brady and colleagues is focused on delineating the parameters that facilitate a child's successful repair of communication breakdowns in interactions with mothers and experimenters. Relative communication levels and receptive language scores matter when it comes to repairs, even within the rather narrow range of prelinguistic communication. Brady and colleagues have found that children who communicate by pointing or with a few words repair commenting communication acts significantly more often than do children who communicate with more basic gestures, such as giving and leading by the hand. Results indicate that children who have crossed the cusp of distal gesture communication respond more often to overt indications of breakdown, such as a request for clarification, than they do to nonacknowledgments or changes in topic. This observation indicates that repair attempts by these children are not merely persistent behaviors. The children are showing a differential response to conversational rules that guide interactions. Results from these studies indicate that children become more successful as their repertoires of communication forms increase. This has direct bearing on the current proposal, wherein Brady will utilize her system for reliably quantifying successful communication to study growth in successful communication as children expand their expressive communication repertoire as they learn to communicate with AAC.

Sherman's previous research on the project has been focused on the development of more appropriate social and communicative interchanges between people with mental retardation and others. Two intertwined approaches have been explored: 1) the direct teaching of social and communicative skills to people with mental retardation; and 2) investigations of living and work environments that may foster more appropriate social and communicative interactions between people with mental retardation and their teachers.

The research on the direct teaching of social skills focused on those skills that were likely to be directly useful to people with mental retardation in both their employment and their everyday lives—skills such as following instructions, dealing with negative feedback, and resolving conflicts. Sherman and Sheldon examined the component behaviors of this cusp that were critical to the successful performance of these skills (Quinn, Sherman, Sheldon, Quinn, & Harchik, 1992; Sherman, Sheldon, Harchik, Edwards, & Quinn, 1992) and the generalization and maintenance of these skills in the everyday lives of the people with mental retardation (Sherman & Sheldon, 1992). The results of the studies of social skills taught to people with mental retardation, as well as studies of social skills taught to children with autism (Harchik, Harchik, Luce, & Sherman, 1990) and adolescents with behavior problems (Serna, Schumaker, Sherman, & Sheldon, 1991; Serna, Sherman, & Sheldon, 1996), clearly showed that the participants could be taught the social skills to a high level of performance, and that the skills generalized to real-life situations that required the use of the skills. Producing high levels of generalization, however, sometimes necessitated special generalization-enhancing procedures. Maintenance of the social skills often necessitated modifications of the real-life environments, such as providing more consistent feedback about the appropriate use of the skills as well as occasional, but more consistent, positive consequences for appropriate use of the social skills. In short, it seemed clear that the teaching methodology was sufficient to teach social skills and produce generalization of these skills to real-life settings. The maintenance of these skills, however, was not always assured unless the real-life environment was modified to be more responsive to the appropriate use of the skills.

The importance of the responsiveness of real-life environments in maintaining social skills is probably obvious, but the failure of many real-life environments to maintain newly taught appropriate behavior may not be. In any case, the research on maintenance of newly taught social skills reemphasized the need to investigate real-life environments of people with mental retardation that encouraged and supported the use of social-communicative skills. Some of that research was concerned with developing environments that promoted appropriate behavior in general (Anderson, Sherman, Sheldon, & McAdam, 1997; Bannerman, Sheldon, Sherman, & Harchik, 1990; Harchik, Sherman, & Sheldon, 1992; Harchik, Sherman, Sheldon, & Bannerman, 1993; Harchik, Sherman, Sheldon, & Strouse, 1992), under the assumption that appropriate social-communicative skills were most likely to be maintained in environments where people were engaged in desirable activities. Sherman's proposed project with the Saunders would continue research on the importance of engagement in establishing a context for communication.

Baer and Grote's research over the past several years has shown that self-instruction can enhance intellectual competence at problem solving, but also that self-instruction, like instruction, must be complied with to be effective. Their work with normally developing children and with adult participants with developmental delays has taught that a number among them require not only thorough, complete, and perfect mastery of the obvious task-analytic prerequisite skills; they also require explicit training to comply with what they tell themselves to do, as they task-analyze the problem at hand. Some participants made the appropriate self-instruction, even generalizing it correctly across various problems of the same or similar classes, yet did not obey it. They did not do what they had just said they should do, and accordingly they continued to fail at these problems. Currently, this research continues this year with an evaluation of that additional component: compliance with self-instruction.

Hart's research on the program project has been a longitudinal study of the developing language of children with Down syndrome reared at home, focusing on the cusp that is the transition from prelinguistic to linguistic communication. She has collected observational data each month in the homes of children with Down syndrome between the times when the children were 12 to 60 months old. For some children with Down syndrome, these language data have been collected for several years longer as well. Hart's research directly addresses the frequently noted need (e.g., Miller, 1987) for longitudinal data on the language development of children with mental retardation. The data Hart has collected show both the variability and the slower rates of language development characteristic of children with Down syndrome (Cicchetti & Beeghly, 1990) and provide a basis for examining the developmental trajectories of the language of these children in greater depth. The observation of unstructured interactions between parents and children during their everyday activities also has contributed to the understanding of the environmental supports provided in the homes of children with Down syndrome, and how the children's gains (or lack of gains) influence, and are influenced by, changes in the amount and complexity of environmental supports over time.

An important feature of Hart's longitudinal research with children with Down syndrome is that the research was designed to be methodologically identical to longitudinal observations of typically developing children conducted earlier, thus enabling the direct comparison of the slower language development of children with Down syndrome to the more rapid development of typically developing children (Hart, 1996). Additionally, because the data reveal aspects of language behavior, times, and contexts where language difficulties arise and the trajectories of language development diverge between children with Down syndrome and typically developing children, the results provide a basis for developing and refining attempts at remediation. Finally, Hart has continued to collect follow-up language samples of some children with Down syndrome beyond the age of 5 years old. Her data will contribute to a better understanding of the increasing deficit in language skills seen among children with Down syndrome as they get older and enter school (Miller, 1987). Thus, the totality of data collected by Hart from both children with Down syndrome and typically developing children will provide a basis for designing interventions to prevent language deficits of children with Down syndrome.

Current Research

Current research on the Communications Program Project is aimed at expanding our knowledge about and our ability to affect developmental cusps related to the development of communication. Generally, this application focuses on communicative development in individuals with severe or profound mental retardation or those at risk of such significant disability. Although the program project has moved gradually in this direction over several funding cycles, the shift was also influenced by the passing of Don Baer, whose recent work investigated self-instruction in typically developing children and adults with mild mental retardation. His associate, Irene Grote, has returned to Europe to pursue her career. Kathryn Saunders, whose current research on reading acquisition is also with adults with mild mental retardation, has chosen to pursue research independently. Hart is now completing some final analyses for portions of her next book. She will continue as a contributor to the program project as a member of our Internal Scientific Review Board, rather than as an investigator.

Researchers for the current program project include Richard and Muriel Saunders, James Sherman, Nancy Brady, Kathy Thiemann, and Steve Warren, from the University of Kansas, and Lesley Olswang, Gay Lloyd Pinder, and Patricia Dowden, from the University of Washington and the Kent Therapy Center. The cusps proposed for study in this application usually arise early in development. They are those involved in the ability to gain another's attention for the possible purposes of requesting assistance, interaction, or continuation of an interaction. Although these cusps ordinarily are encountered early in normal development, our proposed populations reflect a wide range of ages and have, or may develop, severe disabilities. Our purpose is to study these cusps across infants with severe motor disabilities, young children with severe language delays, and adults with profound multiple impairments and with few functional, adaptive skills. Two of the projects will study whether ACC devices can be functional in enabling mastery of cusps. Three will employ automated devices in various ways to gain and maintain the participants' attention or engagement as a step in establishing contexts for a communicative response.

Clearly, our interest is in human communication. Our concern is its delayed or precluded development. Our hypothesis is that communication problems are best studied at several key points in its potential development. Our intent is to apply approaches to intervention at those points that are both innovative and promising, but also informed by recent data. Thus, our overarching purpose is to improve our understanding of communicative development with novel demonstrations of problem remediation in people with or at risk of severe or profound mental retardation.

References

Anderson, M. D., Sherman, J. A., Sheldon, J. B., & McAdam, D. (1997). Picture activity schedules and engagement of adults with mental retardation in a group home. *Research in Developmental Disabilities, 18,* 231–250.

Baer, D. M., & Guess, D. (1971). Receptive training of adjectival inflections in mental retardates. *Journal of Applied Behavior Analysis, 4,* 129–139.

Baer, D. M., & Guess, D. (1973). Teaching productive noun suffixes to severely retarded children. *American Journal of Mental Deficiency, 77,* 498–505.

Bannerman, D. J., Sheldon, J. B., Sherman, J. A., & Harchik, A. E. (1990). Balancing the right to habilitation with the right to personal liberties: The rights of people with developmental disabilities to eat too many doughnuts and take a nap. *Journal of Applied Behavior Analysis, 23,* 79–89.

Bates, E. Benigni, L., Bretherton, I., Camainoi, L., & Volterra, V. (1979). *The emergence of symbols: Cognition and communication in infancy.* New York: Academic Press.

Brady, N. C., McLean, J. E., McLean, L. K., & Johnston, S. (1995). Initiation and repair of intentional communication acts by adults with severe to profound cognitive disabilities. *Journal of Speech and Hearing Research, 38,* 1334–1348.

Bruner, J. S. (1975). The ontogenesis of speech acts. *Journal of Child Language, 2,* 1–19.

Carpenter, R. L., Mastergeorge, A. M., & Coggins, T. E. (1983). The acquisition of communicative intentions in infants eight to fifteen months of age. *Language and Speech, 26,* 101–116.

Carrier, J. (1974). Application of functional analysis and a non-speech response mode to teaching language, *American Speech and Hearing Monograph No. 18,* Washington, DC.

Carrigan, P. F., & Sidman, M. (1992). Conditional discrimination and equivalence relations: A theoretical analysis of control by negative stimuli. *Journal of the Experimental Analysis of Behavior, 58,* 183–204.

Chomsky, N. (1959). A review of B. F. Skinner's verbal behavior. *Language, 35,* 26–58.

Cicchetti, D., & Beeghly, M. (1990). An organizational approach to the study of Down syndrome: Contributions to an integrative theory of development. In D. Cicchetti & M. Beeghly (Eds.), *Children with Down syndrome: A developmental perspective* (pp. 29–62). New York: Cambridge University Press.

Fulton, R. T., & Spradlin, J. E. (1971). Operant audiometry with severely retarded children. *Audiology, 10,* 203–211.

Fulton, R. T., & Spradlin, J. E. (1972). SISI procedures with the severely retarded. *Journal of Speech and Hearing Research, 15,* 217–224.

Fulton, R. T., & Spradlin, J. E. (1974a). Puretone threshold measurement. In R. T. Fulton (Ed.), *Auditory stimulus-response control* (pp. 37–52). Baltimore, MD: University Park Press.

Fulton, R. T., & Spradlin, J. E. (1974b). The short increment sensitivity index (SISI). In R. T. Fulton (Ed.), *Auditory stimulus-response control* (pp. 53–64). Baltimore, MD: University Park Press.

Girardeau, F. L., & Spradlin, J. E. (1964). Token rewards in a cottage program. *Mental Retardation, 2,* 345–352.

Guess, D., & Baer, D. M. (1973). Teaching productive noun suffixes to severely retarded children. *American Journal of Mental Deficiency, 77,* 498–505.

Guess, D., Sailor, W., & Baer, D. M. (1978). Children with limited language. In R. L. Schiefelbusch (Ed.), *Language intervention strategies* (pp. 101–143). Baltimore, MD: University Park Press.

Guess, D., Sailor, W., Rutherford, G., & Baer, D. M. (1968). An experimental analysis of linguistic development: The productive use of the plural morpheme. *Journal of Applied Behavior Analysis, 1,* 297–306.

Halle, J. W., Baer, D. M., & Spradlin, J. E. (1981). Teachers' generalized use of delay as a stimulus control procedure to increase language use in handicapped children. *Journal of Applied Behavior Analysis, 14,* 398–409.

Halle, J. W., Marshall, A., & Spradlin, J. (1979). Time delay: A technique to increase language use and facilitate generalization in retarded children. *Journal of Applied Behavior Analysis, 12,* 431–439.

Harchik, A. E., Harchik, A. J., Luce, S. C., & Sherman, J. A. (1990). Teaching autistic and severely handicapped children to recruit praise: Acquisition and generalization. *Research in Developmental Disabilities, 11,* 77–95.

Harchik, A. E., Sherman, J. A., & Sheldon, J. B. (1992). The use of self-management procedures by people with developmental disabilities: A brief review. *Research in Developmental Disabilities, 13,* 211–227.

Harchik, A. E., Sherman, J. A., Sheldon, J. B., & Bannerman, D. J. (1993). Choice and control: New opportunities for people with disabilities. *Annals of Clinical Psychiatry, 5,* 151–163.

Harchik, A. E., Sherman, J. A., Sheldon, J. B., & Strouse, M. C. (1992). Ongoing consultation as a method of improving performance of staff members in a group home. *Journal of Applied Behavior Analysis, 25,* 599–610.

Hart, B. (1996). The initial growth of expressive vocabulary among children with Down syndrome. *Journal of Early Intervention, 20,* 211–221.

Hart, B., & Risley, T. R. (1975). Incidental teaching of language in the preschool. *Journal of Applied Behavior Analysis, 8,* 411–420.

Hart, B., & Risley, T. R. (1980). In vivo language intervention: Unanticipated generalization effects. *Journal of Applied Behavior Analysis, 13,* 407–432.

Hart, B., & Risley, T. (1995). *Meaningful differences in the everyday experience of young American children.* Baltimore, MD: Paul H. Brookes Publishing Co.

Horowitz, F. D. (1963). Partial and continuous reinforcement of vocal responses using candy, vocal, and smiling reinforcers among retardates: Part 1. *Journal of Speech and Hearing Disorders: Monograph Supplement No. 10,* 55–69.

Lent, J. R., LeBlanc, J., & Spradlin, J. E. (1970). Designing a rehabilitative culture for moderately retarded adolescent girls. In R. E. Ulrich, T. Stachnik, & J. Mabry

(Eds.), *The control of human behavior* (Vol. II, pp. 121–135). Glenview, IL: Scott Foresman.

Lloyd, L. L., Spradlin, J. E., & Reid, M. J. (1968). An operant audiometric procedure for difficult-to-test patients. *Journal of Speech and Hearing Disorders, 33,* 236–245.

McLean, J., & Snyder-McLean, L. (1987). Form and function of communicative behaviour among persons with severe developmental disabilities. *Australia and New Zealand Journal of Developmental Disabilities, 13*(2), 83–98.

McLean, J. E., McLean, L. K. S., Brady, N. C., & Etter, R. (1991). Communication profiles of two types of gesture using nonverbal persons with severe to profound mental retardation. *Journal of Speech and Hearing Research, 34,* 294–308.

McLean, L., Brady, N., McLean, J., & Behrens, G. A. (1999). Communication forms and functions of children and adults with severe mental retardation in community and institutional settings. *Journal of Speech and Hearing Research, 42,* 231–241.

McLean, L. K., Brady, N. C., & McLean, J. E. (1996). Reported communication abilities of individuals with severe mental retardation. *American Journal on Mental Retardation, 100,* 580–591.

Mellstrom, B. P., Saunders, M. D., Saunders, R. R., & Olswang, L. B. (in press). Interaction of biobehavioral state and microswitch use in individuals with profound multiple impairments. *Journal of Developmental and Physical Disabilities.*

Miller, J. F. (1987). Language and communication characteristics of children with Down syndrome. In S. M. Pueschel, C. Tingey, J. E. Rynders, A. C. Crocker, & D. M. Crutcher (Eds.), *New perspectives on Down syndrome* (pp. 233–262). Baltimore, MD: Paul H. Brookes Publishing Co.

Mueller, M. M., Olmi, D. J., & Saunders, K. J. (2000). Recombinative generalization of within-syllable units in prereading children. *Journal of Applied Behavior Analysis, 33,* 515–531.

Murphy, K. M., Saunders, M. D., Saunders, R. R., & Olswang, L. B. (in press). Effects of ambient stimuli on measures of behavioral state and microswitch use in adults with profound multiple impairments. *Research in Developmental Disabilities.*

Oppenheimer, M., Saunders, R. R., & Spradlin, J. E. (1993). Investigating the generality of the delayed-prompt. *Research in Developmental Disabilities, 14,* 425–444.

Phillips, E. L. (1968). Achievement place: Token reinforcement procedures in a home-style rehabilitation setting for "pre-delinquent" boys. *Journal of Applied Behavior Analysis, 1,* 213–223.

Quinn, J. M., Sherman, J. A., Sheldon, J. B., Quinn, L. M., & Harchik, A. E. (1992). Social validation of component behaviors of following instructions, accepting criticism, and negotiating. *Journal of Applied Behavior Analysis, 25,* 401–413.

Saunders, K. J., O'Donnell, J., Vaidya, M., & Williams, D. C. (2003). Recombinative generalization of within-syllable units in nonreading adults with mental retardation. *Journal of Applied Behavior Analysis, 36,* 95–99.

Saunders, K. J., & Spradlin, J. E. (1989). Conditional discrimination in mentally retarded adults: The effect of training the component simple discriminations. *Journal of the Experimental Analysis of Behavior, 52,* 1–12.

Saunders, K. J., & Spradlin, J. E. (1990). Conditional discrimination in mentally retarded adults: The development of generalized skills. *Journal of the Experimental Analysis of Behavior, 54,* 239–250.

Saunders, K. J., & Spradlin, J. E. (1993). Conditional discrimination in mentally retarded subjects: Programming acquisition and learning set. *Journal of the Experimental Analysis of Behavior, 60,* 571–585.

Saunders, M. D., Questad, K. A., Kedziorski, T. L., Boase, B. C., Patterson, E. A., & Cullinen, T. B. (2001). Unprompted mechanical switch use in individuals with severe multiple disabilities: An evaluation of the effects of body position. *Journal of Developmental and Physical Disabilities, 13,* 27–39.

Saunders, M. D., Saunders, R. R., Mulugeta, A., Henderson, K., Kedziorski, T., Hekker, R., et al. (2005). A method for testing learning and preferences in people with minimal motor movement. *Research in Developmental Disabilities, 26,* 255–266.

Saunders, M. D., Smagner, J. P., & Saunders R. R. (2003). Improving methodological and technological analyses of adaptive switch use of individuals with profound multiple impairments. *Behavioral Interventions, 18,* 227–243.

Saunders, M. D., Timler, G., Cullinen, T. B., Pilkey, S., Questad, K. A., & Saunders, R. R. (2003). Evidence of contingency awareness in people with profound multiple impairments: Response duration versus response rate indicators. *Research in Developmental Disabilities, 24,* 231–245.

Saunders, R. R., & Green, G. (1992). The nonequivalence of behavioral and mathematical equivalence. *Journal of the Experimental Analysis of Behavior, 57,* 227–241.

Saunders, R. R., & Green, G. (1999). A discrimination analysis of training-structure effects on stimulus equivalence outcomes. *Journal of the Experimental Analysis of Behavior, 72,* 117–137.

Saunders, R. R., McEntee, J. E., & Saunders, M. D. (accepted pending revision). Effects of reinforcement schedules and a behavioral prosthesis on behavioral allocation in adults with severe or profound mental retardation.

Saunders, R. R., Saunders, K. J., Kirby, K. C., & Spradlin, J. E. (1988). The merger and development of equivalence classes by unreinforced conditional selection of comparison stimuli. *Journal of the Experimental Analysis of Behavior, 50,* 145–162.

Saunders, R. R., & Saunders, M. D. (2000). An analysis of contingency learning in the treatment of aberrant behavior. *Journal of Developmental Disabilities, 7,* 54–83.

Saunders, R. R., Wachter, J., & Spradlin, J. E. (1988). Establishing auditory stimulus control over an eight-member equivalence class via conditional discrimination procedures. *Journal of the Experimental Analysis of Behavior, 49,* 95–115.

Savage-Rumbaugh, E. S. (1984). Verbal behavior at a procedural level in the chimpanzee. *Journal of the Experimental Analysis of Behavior, 41,* 223–250.

Schumaker, J., & Sherman, J. A. (1970). Training generative verb usage by imitation and reinforcement procedures. *Journal of Applied Behavior Analysis, 3,* 273–287.

Schumaker, J. B., & Sherman, J. A. (1978). Parent as intervention agent. In R. L. Schiefelbusch (Ed.), *Language intervention strategies* (pp. 237–315). Baltimore, MD: University Park Press.

Serna, L., Schumaker, J. B., Sherman, J. A., & Sheldon, J. B. (1991). In-home generalization of social interactions in families of adolescents with behavior problems. *Journal of Applied Behavior Analysis, 24,* 733–746.

Serna, L. A., Sherman, J. A., & Sheldon, J. B. (1996). Empirically based behavioural treatment programs for families with adolescents who are at risk for failure. In C. R. Hollin & K. Howells (Eds.), *Clinical approaches to working with young offenders* (pp. 165–180). New York: Wiley.

Sherman, J. A., & Sheldon, J. B. (1992, May). *Social skills of people with mental retardation: Teaching, generalization, and social validation.* Invited presentation at the Association for Behavior Analysis, San Francisco, CA.

Sherman, J. A., Sheldon, J. B., Harchik, A. E., Edwards, K., & Quinn, J. M. (1992). Social evaluation of behaviors comprising three social skills and a comparison of the performance of people with and without mental retardation. *American Journal on Mental Retardation, 96,* 419–431.

Skinner, B. F. (1957). *Verbal behavior.* New York: Appleton-Century-Crofts.

Spradlin, J. E., & Saunders, R. R. (1984). Behaving appropriately in new situations: A stimulus class analysis. *American Journal of Mental Deficiency, 88,* 574–579.

Spradlin, J. E., & Saunders, R. R. (1986). The development of stimulus classes using match-to-sample procedures: Sample classification versus comparison classification. *Analysis and Intervention in Developmental Disabilities, 6,* 41–58.

Stokes, T. F., & Baer, D. M. (1977). An implicit technology of generalization. *Journal of Applied Behavior Analysis, 10,* 349–367.

Striefel, S., & Wetherby, B. (1973). Instruction-following behavior of a retarded child and its controlling stimuli. *Journal of Applied Behavior Analysis, 6,* 663–670.

Striefel, S., Wetherby, B., & Karlan, G. R. (1976). Establishing generative verb-noun instruction-following skills in retarded children. *Journal of Experimental Child Psychology, 22,* 247–260.

Struve, B., Saunders, M. D., Saunders, R. R., & Olswang, L. (in preparation). Preferences between social attention and automated stimulation in adults with profound multiple impairments.

Williams, D. C., Saunders, K. J., Saunders, R. R., & Spradlin, J. E. (1995). Unreinforced conditional selection from three-choice conditional discrimination training. *The Psychological Record, 45,* 613–627.

Wolf, M. M., Giles, D. K., & Hall, R. V. (1968). Experiments with token reinforcement in a remedial classroom. *Behavior Research and Therapy, 6,* 51–64.

From left: Stephen R. Schroeder, director 1990–2001; Richard L. Schiefelbusch, director 1956–1990; Steven F. Warren, 2001–present

FAMILY FIRST

New KU research center will tap strengths of families with disabled members

NEW DIRECTION: Rud and Ann Turnbull and Jean Ann Summers will lead the Beach Center as it focuses rehabilitation on families.

Rud and Ann Turnbull and Jean Ann Summers won a grant in 1988 to focus on policies and practices for families who have members with disabilities.

During their tenures at KU, Lee and James McLean were nationally recognized contributors to their fields and to the research program of the Bureau of Child Research.

The Robert J. Dole Human Development Center, which would house the newly designated Schiefelbusch Institute for Life Span Studies, was dedicated on August 25, 1990. *From left:* Richard Schiefelbusch, KU Chancellor Gene Budig, and Senator Robert Dole.

Meaningful Differences

in the Everyday Experience of
Young American Children

◆◆◆◆

Betty Hart & Todd R. Risley

Foreword by Lois Bloom

Meaningful Differences in the Everyday Experience of Young American Children, by Betty Hart and Todd Risley, one of the most groundbreaking studies in the history of the Institute, has been cited by other scientists over 400 times as well as journalists and policy makers, and has greatly expanded the understanding and appreciation of the environmental contribution to language development and literacy.

Kim Osbourne of Benedict, Kansas, is one of the more than 11,000 Kansans who get help from the Assistive Technology for Kansans project each year. Starting in 1992, Sara Sack and Chuck Spellman, among other Institute researchers, began to research and implement a statewide system to give people with disabilities access to life-changing assistive technology that has become a national model.

KU Chancellor Robert Hemenway paid homage to Life Span affiliate Directora Liliana Mayo on his visit to Lima, Peru, in June of 2002. Mayo, a KU graduate and KU Distinguished Service Citation award winner, started the internationally acclaimed school for children with cognitive disabilities and their families in her parent's garage in 1979. Today, Centro Ann Sullivan del Perú serves more than 350 people through 21 different clinical, professional, and parent programs.

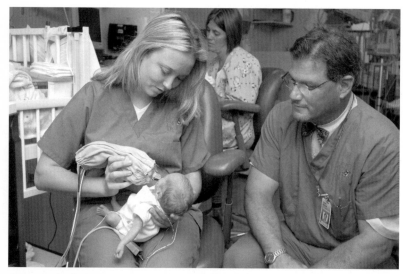

Steven Barlow's development of the Actifier is one of the Institute's most significant current projects. The motorized pacifier connected to a computer is an intervention procedure based on basic science findings to correct sucking deficiencies. The Actifier is currently in a clinical trial being conducted at KUMC and a Topeka hospital to test the cognitive impact of this intervention during infancy in high-risk preterm infants.

Susan Slothower, director of behavioral services at Creative Community Living in Winfield, Kansas, has benefited from the Institute's current intensive training program for practicing human services professionals in positive behavior support, directed by Rachel Freeman.

While 3-year-old Gael Martinez plays with his mother, Cynthia Zambrano, Early Head Start home visitor Jesse Schulz records his Early Communication Indicators, ranging from gestures to multiple words—in as little as 6 minutes. She, like others on the front lines of child care in Early Head Start sites in Kansas and Missouri, can input these data at a web site, developed by Charles Greenwood and associates, and instantly see a child's progress and how he compares to his peers and developmental norms.

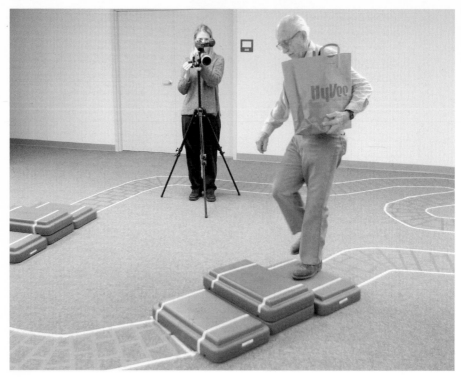

Life Span Institute researcher Susan Kemper explored the other end of the life span in her "Two Things at Once" study on the subtle cognitive deficits of people who were thought to have had excellent recovery from strokes.

Psychologist R. Matthew Reese is part of a "dream team" of specialists who transport their Kansas City Medical Center developmental disabilities diagnostic clinic to underserved parts of Kansas several times each year.

Isaiah Shannon, like several hundreds of his counterparts in Kansas schools, benefited from a Life Span Institute program called School-wide Positive Behavior Support, directed by Amy McCart and Wayne Sailor, that has reduced office referrals for behavior problems—dramatically in some schools.

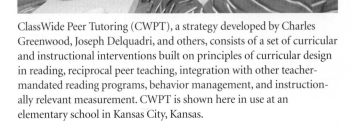

ClassWide Peer Tutoring (CWPT), a strategy developed by Charles Greenwood, Joseph Delquadri, and others, consists of a set of curricular and instructional interventions built on principles of curricular design in reading, reciprocal peer teaching, integration with other teacher-mandated reading programs, behavior management, and instructionally relevant measurement. CWPT is shown here in use at an elementary school in Kansas City, Kansas.

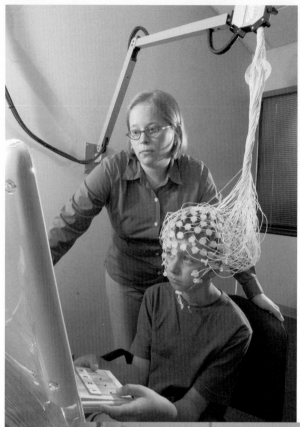

The Biobehavioral Neurosciences in Communication Disorders Center, directed by Mabel Rice, is the Institute's most recent affiliated center. Here, Stacy Betz, a child language doctoral student in 2003, documents the pattern of electrical charges of a child's brain when he hears a spoken sentence with the EEG/ERP.

Steven Fowler's Force Plate Actometer has been awarded a patent and a National Institutes of Health Small Business Innovation Research grant. The device can precisely discern and characterize subtle movement in laboratory rats and mice to test the effects of drug and gene therapy.

18

The Severe Aberrant Behavior and Mental Retardation Program Project

JOSEPH E. SPRADLIN AND STEPHEN R. SCHROEDER

This Severe Aberrant Behavior and Mental Retardation Program Project was funded by the National Institute of Child Health and Human Development (NICHD) and grew out of the long history of Bureau of Child Research investigations on chronic aberrant behaviors (CAB) and their modification among people with mental retardation who lived at the Parsons State Hospital and Training Center (PSHTC). Members of the Kansas University Affiliated Program (UAP) and the Mental Retardation Research Center (MRRC) at Parsons were often called upon to help out with the most difficult cases there and around the state and the country. The work soon became one of their foci of research interest, from both a behavior analytic and a psychopharmacological perspective.

The work of John Hollis in laboratory studies showing the effects of chlorpromazine on stereotyped rocking and complex covariations with other operant behaviors was published in *Science* in 1972 and was one of the first human behavioral pharmacological studies on this topic in the literature. Although Sprague had published a review of over 100 other studies of the effects of drugs on the aberrant behaviors of people with mental retardation, Hollis' study was one of the first to show the interactions between drugs and behavioral interventions.

Hollis and Meyers (1982) published an American Association on Mental Retardation monograph on life-threatening behavior in which several chapters showed the antecedents and consequences that affect generalization and maintenance of treatments for self-injurious behavior (SIB). Extensive functional analyses were used to delineate the environmental interactions which affected the occurrence of SIB. These were early seminal contributions which were developed by many investigators in the subsequent research literature on the treatment of aberrant behavior and people with mental retardation.

In the late 1980s there was a loud outcry against the use of behavior modification procedures which used aversive consequences to intervene with CAB. A reemphasis on the use of manipulation of antecedent conditions to control the occurrence of CAB emerged, and we tried to analyze why people with mental retardation were doing such counterintuitive behaviors as SIB.

At a Consensus Development Conference convened at NICHD in 1989, it became clear that: 1) there was little consensus on the proper treatment of aberrant behaviors of people with mental retardation, and 2) the database of empirical evidence undergirding an approach based on manipulation of antecedents was very small. At the suggestion of David Gray, then a program specialist at NICHD, Joe Spradlin assembled a team of researchers at the University of Kansas (KU) to help develop this research database.

The First Program Project

The first NICHD program project on CAB funded at KU, entitled "Severe Aberrant Behavior and Mental Retardation," was a straightforward application of pharmacological and behavior analytic procedures to the investigation of antecedent factors related to the development and maintenance of stereotyped, self-injurious, and aggressive behavior, and to the remediation of such behaviors among persons with mental retardation. The program project had three general aims:

1. To develop animal models for altered behavioral repertoires and to determine whether these altered repertoires increase the risk of stereotyped, self-injurious, or aggressive behaviors;
2. To analyze the effects of neuroleptic and antiseizure medications on the aberrant and adaptive behaviors of persons with mental retardation and on animals with restricted repertoires; and

3. To analyze the effects of various environmental events and routines on the aberrant and adaptive behaviors of people mental retardation in a broad range of ecobehavioral contexts.

Researchers at the University of Kansas, PSHTC, and Kansas Neurological Institute (KNI) were an ideal group to do such work. They had a long and distinctive history of applying behavior analysis to the investigation of basic behavioral processes and to the solution of important behavior problems of persons with retardation and developmental disabilities. Some of the accomplishments of these investigators are described briefly in the following paragraphs.

Laboratory Studies of Basic Processes

Researchers at the University of Kansas and the Parsons Research Center had maintained a program of research directed toward the study of basic behavioral processes of persons with mental retardation for over 30 years. These researchers were among the first to demonstrate that basic reinforcement procedures could be used to increase simple response rates of persons with retardation (Spradlin, 1962; Spradlin, Girardeau, & Corte, 1965), that new complex responses could be shaped (Hollis, 1967), and that reinforcers had discriminative properties (Spradlin, Fixsen, & Girardeau, 1969; Spradlin, Girardeau, & Horn, 1966). More recently, they had directed their efforts toward studying the development of functional stimulus classes and their control of the emergence of untrained but appropriate behavior in new situations (Dixon & Spradlin, 1976; Saunders, Saunders, Kirby, & Spradlin, 1988; Saunders, Wachter, & Spradlin, 1988; Spradlin, Cotter, & Baxley, 1973; Spradlin & Dixon, 1976; Spradlin & Saunders, 1986; Wetherby, Karlan, & Spradlin, 1983)— an extremely important process in adaptive behavior.

Adaptation of Laboratory Procedures to Evaluate Sensory Processes and Preferences of Persons with Severe Retardation

Researchers at the Parsons Research Center had adapted basic stimulus-control procedures to obtain precise evaluation of the hearing and vision of previously untestable children (Cress et al., 1981; Fulton & Spradlin,

1971, 1972; Lloyd, Spradlin, & Reid, 1968; Spradlin, Lloyd, Horn, & Reid, 1968; Spradlin, Locke, & Fulton, 1969), and to evaluate the music preferences of children with very severe retardation (Cotter & Spradlin, 1971; Cotter & Toombs, 1966).

Research on Basic Learning Processes

Researchers in the three settings of this program project had demonstrated the value of behavior analysis processes in establishing generalized imitation (Baer, Peterson, & Sherman, 1967), rudimentary generalized language skills (Dixon, Spradlin, Girardeau, & Etzel, 1974; Guess & Baer, 1973; Guess, Sailor, Rutherford, & Baer, 1968; McLean, 1970; Striefel, Bryan, & Aikins, 1974; Striefel & Wetherby, 1973; Striefel, Wetherby, & Karlan, 1976), mathematical skills, and socially useful language (Guess, Sailor, & Baer, 1978).

Application of Specific Behavior Analytic Procedures to Change Specific Behaviors in Natural Settings

Researchers from these same settings had shown how to reduce problem eating behaviors (Barton, Guess, Garcia, & Baer, 1970) and how to increase socially appropriate verbal requesting in dining, snack, and classroom settings (Halle, Marshall, & Spradlin, 1979).

Application of Behavior Analytic Techniques to Ensure That Taught Behavior Generalized

Baer, Wolf, and Risley (1968), in their seminal article on behavior analyses, delineated three types of generalization that were critical to successful treatment. Later Stokes and Baer (1977) categorized many of the procedures for ensuring that generalization occurred. Researchers in the three settings have designed procedures to study and ensure appropriate generalization across responses (Guess & Baer, 1973; Guess et al., 1978; Risley & Hart, 1968; Rogers-Warren & Baer, 1976) and across settings (Halle et al., 1979; Stremel-Campbell & Campbell, 1982).

Application of Behavior Analytic Principles to the Design of Living Environments

Throughout the history of behavior analyses in Kansas, researchers had designed environments in which persons with mental retardation or other disabilities could lead happy, productive, and harmonious lives. Early studies at Parsons to design reinforcement-based cottage environments were described by Girardeau and Spradlin (1964) and Lent, LeBlanc, and Spradlin (1970). Researchers at Lawrence and Juniper Gardens had developed and analyzed classroom and home environments for young delinquent boys (Bailey, Wolf, & Phillips, 1970; Braukmann et al., 1975; Braukmann, Kirigin Ramp, & Wolf, 1985; Phillips, 1968; Phillips, Phillips, Fixsen, & Wolf, 1971). More recently Sherman and colleagues (Sherman, Sheldon, Morris, Strouse, & Reese, 1984) had developed and evaluated reinforcement-based group homes in Kansas City communities. Saunders, Rast, and Saunders (1988) had applied reinforcement principles in their attempts to alter total institutional programs to meet the requirements of the Health Care Financing Administration.

Emergence of the Program Project

Several forces had led to the development of the first program project proposal. First, most of the investigators on the program project and the internal advisory group had a long-term interest in the problems of persons with severe and profound retardation. The investigators' casual and formal observations and the published data of many others indicated that a high proportion of such persons exhibit stereotypic, self-injurious, and aggressive behavior. In the course of studying other problems, such as communication, self-help, or social skills training, the investigators had frequently encountered these forms of aberrant behavior which can be severe enough to prevent any other habilitative programs. They either had to develop clinical programs for reducing such problems or develop research to study variables controlling them in order to proceed with other programs. Their cumulative experience with persons with retardation suggested that chronic aberrant behavior is prevalent among such people and that aberrant behavior interferes with training and rehabilitation efforts.

Second, approximately 6 years earlier, researchers at the Parsons Research Center had been funded by the Office of Special Education to study self-injury among school-age children. This project, headed by Robert Day, found that 40% of children with severe and multiple disabilities in the public school exhibited self-injurious behaviors. This project also conducted analogue evaluation (Iwata, Dorsey, Slifer, Bauman, & Richman, 1982) and then developed treatment programs (based on these analogues) that were conducted throughout the day in the classrooms (Day, Rea, Schussler, Larsen, & Johnson, 1988). Although the self-injurious behaviors of most of the children were reduced, Day and his colleagues were often disappointed by the lack of stability of these reductions. A second project was designed to delineate more carefully the social variables that affected the occurrence of self-injurious behavior and aggression. Its careful analogue analysis replicated findings by Iwata et al. (1982) that some aberrant behavior was controlled by (negative reinforcement) task avoidance and some by (positive reinforcement) the delivery of social attention, desired object, or food. However, for many self-injurious and aggressive persons, their aberrant behavior served either multiple functions or seemed somewhat unrelated to environmental conditions studied.

Two new and interesting findings resulted from these analogue studies: A small number of subjects exhibited aberrant behavior primarily when reinforcers were withdrawn (Larsen & Day, 1986) and subjects whose aberrant behavior took very mild, almost symbolic forms often performed aberrant behavior when reinforcement was presented.

Evaluations of institutions for persons with retardation by the Health Care Financing Administration found most institutional programs inadequate. Moreover, one of the most serious inadequacies was the failure to protect residents from harm. Observations showed that most residents' injuries occurred through self-injury and peer aggression. This was true nationwide and in Kansas as well. Urgent concern for protection from harm had led to the establishment of special units to manage self-injurious and aggressive behavior of the most difficult clients at PSHTC and KNI, and to the establishment of positions of directors of these units.

Although social environmental variables are important determinants of CAB, it is obvious that biological variables also play a role in determining aberrant behavior outcomes. Dr. Richard Tessel of the Department of Pharmacology and Toxicology in the School of Pharmacy was interested in studying the neurochemical actions of drugs and their effects on behavior. Rick had devoted much of his career to investigating the stimulus functions of specific drugs. Rick and his colleagues were the first to demonstrate that though fenfluramine had amphetamine-like actions, it was not addictive and that the discriminative properties of amphetamines were not mediated by dopamine. Moreover, he had published studies on neurochemical changes brought about by drug administration.

Tessel decided to turn his efforts toward conducting research aimed at developing a bio-social model of aberrant behavior development. He would not only make a major contribution to the understanding of aberrant behavior as a function of basic neurobehavioral pharmacological processes in his own project, but he also added greatly to the sophistication of the evaluation of the effects of neuroleptic and antipsychotic drugs proposed in other projects in the program project.

Thus, the history of the application of behavior analytic principles to the study of significant basic and applied problems, and recent developments in aberrant behavior research, as well as the linkage of behavior analytic and pharmacological researchers, allowed the investigators of this program project to make a broad-scale attempt to understand and treat chronic aberrant behavior in persons with developmental disabilities.

Significance of the Problem and Related Literature

Destructive behaviors, whether directed toward oneself or others, are always significant social problems. The rate of these behaviors among individuals with developmental disabilities is disproportionately high, and the behaviors are often dangerous. They may result in permanent physical deficits, blindness, and even death. These behaviors also have a high cost in terms of destroyed property and staff injuries. In addition, these behaviors significantly interfere with the attempts of treatment and educational personnel to facilitate development toward greater personal independence and the normal lifestyles associated with independence. In particular, such behaviors often preclude persons with developmental disabilities from attending a neighborhood school, living in a community group home, working on a job, or participating in normal leisure-time activities. Concurrently, such persons place enormous demands on the often meager resources of those responsible for their lives.

Unfortunately, even when resources are adequate, methods to eliminate these behaviors are not thoroughly reliable. The primary reason for these failures is an inadequate understanding of the determinants of these behaviors. Thus, many of the treatment approaches are simply attempts to override or mask the problems. A concentrated effort to clarify the determinants of these aberrant behaviors is needed.

Although the labels self-injurious, aggressive, and stereotypic suggest different intents, they do not always convey the cause or function of these behaviors. In some cases, the etiology or original cause of these behaviors may include organic factors; with other persons, the organic correlates are unknown or the behavior persists even when the presumably responsible physiological condition is removed.

A number of theories and models attempt to explain the causes of aberrant behaviors in people with retardation (Carr, 1977), yet these efforts have not resulted in an unitary explanation of CAB—nor is one likely. The severity of this problem is emphasized by the incidence of CAB among persons with severe or profound mental retardation. Schroeder, Bickel, and Richmond (1986) estimated that the total number of persons in the United States with severe or profound retardation is 250,000. This figure seems reasonable in light of the enumeration by White, Lakin, Hill, Wright, and Bruininks (1987), showing that of the approximately 107,000 persons residing in publicly operated facilities in fiscal year 1986, 82% of those in larger facilities and roughly 50% of those in smaller (less than 16 beds) had either severe or profound retardation.

In this subpopulation, estimates of the proportion of individuals who self-injure range from 14% (Schroeder, Schroeder, Smith, & Dalldorf, 1978) to more than 50% (Mulick, Dura, Rasnake, & Callahan, 1986; Rojahn, 1984). These estimates vary with the severity of self-injury defined by each survey. A recent survey in Kansas, conducted at the Parsons Research Center, revealed that 40% of the children in public schools classified as having severe and multiple disabilities exhibited SIB. Worse, Eyman and Call (1977) reported that 28% of persons with severe or profound retardation engage in aggressive behavior. Likewise, the incidence of stereotypic behavior in these individuals is also high. For example, previous estimates of the incidence of stereotypy in institutionalized persons ranged from 66% to 69% (Berkson & Davenport, 1962; Kaufman & Levitt, 1965). In addition, since then, estimates indicate an increase in the proportion of individuals with severe and profound retardation in these institutions. Thus, these estimates underpredict the percentage of those with stereotypy in those settings. Overall, a substantial proportion of persons with severe or profound mental retardation engage in one, two, or more forms of aberrant behavior.

The severity of this problem is increased for the majority of individuals with severe or profound retardation who must live and work together. Under such conditions, the incidence of aberrant behavior in the immediate social contexts of these individuals is much higher.

Many procedures have been used to control or eliminate severe stereotypic, self-injurious, and aggressive behavior. These include physical restraint and protective devices, superimposed contingencies involving reinforcement and punishment, a change in the motivational or setting conditions, alternate repertoire building, and psychoactive drugs, often in combination. Some of these procedures have been partially effective with some individuals, but no published or anecdotal accounts show that the incidence of chronic aberrant behavior in persons with severe or profound retardation has declined. Indeed, nearly all of the individuals observed in the large facilities mentioned above were being treated with specific behavior modification programs and many were also being medicated.

Routine time-based events, such as meals or activities with large response requirements, can produce very exaggerated and apparently nonfunctional behaviors that persist as long as the schedule of the events persists. These have been termed schedule-induced (or adjunctive) behaviors because the excessive rates and intensities are produced by the schedule of reinforcement for an unrelated activity (Falk, 1971). Behaviors such as aggression, polydipsia, excessive eating, pica, hyperactivity, and so forth have been observed in animals and humans (Falk, 1986) to be maintained not by their individual antecedents and consequences but by the pattern or schedule of significant events. There is little research available on the contribution of these molar relationships to the aberrant behavior of individuals with retardation.

A very likely possibility is that a person with retardation is not totally devoid of more complex and socially acceptable repertoires; and thus these repertoires are weak relative to the more primitive behaviors, and when deprivation states are high or aversive conditions intense or prolonged, this person reverts to the more primitive repertoires. A long history of research suggests that high deprivation or intense motivational conditions facilitate acquisition of simple tasks while interfering with more complex tasks (e.g., Lipsitt & LoLordo, 1963).

Other classes of variables can contribute to rates and intensity of aberrant behaviors in individuals already disposed to emit aberrant behaviors through the processes discussed above. Motivational or establishing conditions can affect the likelihood and intensity of aberrant responses. For example, reinforcer delay or denial would be more likely to result in aggression under deprivation than under satiation conditions (Talkington & Riley, 1971). It is also possible that escape or avoidance behaviors might depend on a variety of motivational or setting factors, including deprivation and existing emotional states arising from earlier aversive interactions. Certain episodes of self-injurious behavior seem to occur when temper tantrums and aggressive behaviors occur.

So the stage was set, and, after one revision, the first Aberrant Behavior Program Project at KU was funded in 1991. There were four interconnected projects.

Project I (Genetic and Prenatal Factors and Susceptibility to the Development of Aberrant Behavior among Rodents) by Rick Tessel studied the effect of isolation rearing, environmental stress, and unpredictable reductions in reward magnitude and frequency on susceptibility to aberrant-like behavior in a rat model of SIB using a neurotoxin, 6-hydroxydopamine, in Okamoto spontaneous hypertensive rats, and in rats with prenatally produced microcephaly. The project was aimed especially toward determining if these genetic and prenatal conditions result in aberrant-like behavior in the absence of shaping by reinforcement contingencies, whether reinforcement contingencies alone result in aberrant behavior, or whether persistent aberrant behavior results from the interaction of both biological conditions and reinforcement contingencies. Finally, the project investigated the effects of administration and withdrawal of various antipsychotic and antiepileptic drugs on aberrant behavior and fixed ratio discrimination of hypertensive and microcephalic rats. Neurochemical analyses also were made on the brains of animals in the various treatment conditions.

Project II (An Experimental Analysis of the Effects of Neuroleptic and Antiseizure Drugs on the Behavior of Persons with Mental Retardation) by Jim Rast proposed to use a comprehensive evaluation system to concurrently measure the effects of commonly used psychoactive drugs, alone and in combination, on aberrant behaviors, seizures, cognition, functional daily living skills, and general behavior (e.g., activity level, approach behavior, social responsiveness, and stereotypes) of individuals with developmental disabilities while monitoring the physiological side effects of the medications. The project would also attempt to determine whether different drugs affect aberrant behavior rates differentially according to their current controlling conditions. This project was withdrawn after the newly funded program project award was cut by 31%. It was withdrawn in order to save the other three projects.

Project III (The Effect of Factors Involved in Daily Routines on the Aberrant and Productive Behavior of Persons with Severe Mental Retardation) by Dick Saunders and Joe Spradlin investigated the occurrence of aberrant behavior in three common types of routines (linear, cyclical, branching) in group and individual settings. They analyzed how elements of the routine, such as type of instructions given, frequency of social reinforcement, pacing, or delays, affect the occurrence and type of aberrant behavior.

Project IV (Tolerance Training for Severely Self-Injurious and Aggressive Persons) by Don Baer attempted to first determine the antecedent stimuli that result in self-injurious and aggressive outbursts among a small group of extremely assaultive adults. Observation led the investigators to hypothesize that many of these outbursts were preceded by two classes of events, taunts from other clients and reinforcer denial or delay. The project proposed to develop tolerance for such antecedent events through systematic resensitization and reinforcement procedures.

The Second Program Project

Although considerable progress was made during the next 5 years, especially by Dick Saunders and Joe Spradlin on their research on routines and aberrant behavior and by Rick Tessel on his animal models on aberrant behavior, Don Baer's project was not going well. In doing extensive observations of the antecedents of aggressive behavior of their clients at KNI, and then doing conditional probability analyses of all of the antecedents, they found an endless string of antecedents and did not find a way to prioritize or group them in an empirically derived algorithm by the time of the renewal. So their project did not have much to show when they had to request more funds.

In addition, Joe Spradlin had just retired and Steve Schroeder took over as principal investigator. This fact led to more apparent uncertainty for the site visitors. The result was that the program project renewal was not funded, and resubmission was required. Don's project was dropped and Steve added instead a project on a double-blind crossover study of risperidone on aberrant behavior of children and adults with mental retardation and developmental disabilities (MRDD). Dean Williams also put in a section on behavioral evaluation of the behavioral selectivity of the drug effects of risperidone. These two projects dovetailed more theoretically with Rick's animal work, so that the whole program project was more conceptually cohesive. This program project was refunded, but Rick Tessel's animal modeling project was not funded. However, by this time he had other funding for his research, so we all proceeded with our planned work for the next 5 years.

Project I: Analysis of the Variables Affecting Response Allocation Between Aberrant and Productive Behavior

The investigator was Dick Saunders and the co-investigators were Muriel Saunders and Dennis Tucker. Project I was based on the hypothesis that marked changes can be made in the rate and frequency of aberrant behavior by establishing high rate performances of alternative behaviors. In the previous 5 years Dick Saunders and colleagues had shown that they could facilitate the development of nonaberrant performances by 1) selecting responses to reinforce those that were already in the individual's repertoire, 2) increasing the fluency of those responses with environmental manipulations, and 3) increasing discrimination of the relationship between those responses and the scheduled reinforcers. They referred to the high rate performances developed with these methods as indications of increased competence. The experiments described derived in general from these observations and conclusions from the preceding 5 years:

1. Reinforcement for behaviors alternative to aberrant behaviors can be a highly effective intervention.

2. Behavior cannot be reinforced, however, if not emitted and cannot be emitted if not in the repertoire.
3. Careful analysis of the existing repertoire and cognitive abilities of persons with severe or profound retardation leads to the identification of performable responses appropriate to serve as the cornerstone for the development of a socially relevant repertoire free of aberrant behavior.
4. Reinforcement of these performable responses under stimulus conditions (e.g., setting, adaptive devices, materials, reinforcement schedule) that leads to functional contingencies produces direct and generalized expansion of time allocated to responding with behaviors alternative to aberrant behavior.

Project II: Controlled Clinical Trials of Atypical Neuroleptics and Chronic Aberrant Behavior

The investigator was Steve Schroeder and the co-investigators were Jessica Hellings, Stephen Fowler, R. Matthew Reese, and Dean Williams. Project II had three complementary goals: 1) to conduct a double-blind crossover study of the effects of risperidone, clozapine, and olanzapine on CAB; 2) to generate a subject pool with a large enough taxonomy of CAB, in order to be able to study the interactions between behavioral and pharmacological treatments and various forms of CAB, especially aggression, stereotyped behavior, and SIB; and 3) to relate serotonin and dopamine hypotheses for CAB in humans to those studied in the Rick Tessel's animal models.

Risperidone, clozapine, and olanzapine are all considered "atypical" neuroleptics because they are less prone to produce negative motor symptoms of tardive dyskinesia, Parkinsonian tremors, or akathisia. Clozapine, in fact, is often used as a treatment for tardive dyskinesia among people with schizophrenia. However, it has other undesirable side effects. Although, at the time, there was only one double-blind study on risperidone for aberrant behavior in MRDD populations (Vanden Borre et al., 1993), it had come to be used widely among people with MRDD.

Interestingly, while clozapine at low doses tends to block primarily D1 dopamine receptors, it is psychoactive at 15 different receptor sites. Clozapine's affinity for 5HT2 serotonin receptors is greater than for D1 dopamine receptors. Action at multiple receptor sites appears to be a feature of atypical neuroleptics. Risperidone is primarily a D2 dopamine blocker and 5HT2 serotonin antagonist at low dose. Thus clozapine may work better with SIB, a primarily D1 dopamine dysfunction (Breese, 2002), whereas risperidone may work better with stereotyped behavior which is thought to be primarily a D2 dopamine dysfunction (Lewis et al., 1996). Lewis' in-depth study of a population of over 250 adults with severe or profound mental retardation and their repetitive movement disorders was very instructive as to how fruitful such a large *N* study can be. This project proposed a similar strategy with a larger age range (6–65 years) and a broader range of mental retardation (mild to profound), in order to extend the work on the taxonomy of aberrant behaviors among people with mental retardation.

Project III: Behavioral Selectivity of Atypical Neuroleptic Drugs: Effects on Cognitive and Social Behaviors

The investigator was Dean Williams and the co-investigators were Steve Schroeder, Jessica Hellings, Rema Menon, and Richard Shores. Project III was designed to address directly the issue of specificity of the effects of drugs commonly used to treat CAB among persons with retardation. Dean Williams and colleagues planned to explore the effects of psychotropic medications in the CAB population on aberrant behavior, basic performance, learning, memory, motivation, and social interaction. The effects on CAB, mood, daily activities, and side effects as measured by the treatment team were also monitored, but the main measures of interest for this project were the measures related to learning and memory. Three adult populations were sampled: 1) adults with mild to moderate mental retardation living at PSHTC where the program project is headquartered (CAB at Parsons usually consisted of aggressive behavior); 2) adults with mild to moderate mental retardation living in small intermediate care facilities in northeastern Kansas whose CAB is mostly SIB or aggression; and 3) a psychiatry outpatient population at the University of Kansas Medical Center in Kansas City which specialized in the psychopharmacology of people with mental retardation and mental illness or autism. This community clinic served a large urban area in which over 100 adults with developmental disabilities receiving psychotropic medication were evaluated and followed regularly at any given time. Clients in this sample had a wide variety of mental illnesses as well as developmental disabilities. The drug groups of interest were the same groups as those used in Projects II and IV (i.e., dopamine and serotonin modulators, blockers). The cognitive tasks proposed for study were also comparable with those used in the project on animal models of CAB (i.e., matching-to-sample and repeated acquisition of behavioral sequences).

The central theme of the program project remained gaining sufficient control over CAB to eliminate it. However, we wanted to be sure that, as we eliminated CAB, we did not also eliminate or reduce the capacity to learn new appropriate behaviors. In that sense, this project, which studied the effects of drug treatments for CAB on cognitive processes, was highly related to the central theme.

Major Findings of the CAB Program Project

The Severe Aberrant Behavior Program Project was not renewed in 2001 after Steve Schroeder retired. Rick Tessel also retired in 2002 and died of congestive heart failure following a bout of pneumonia in 2004. Nevertheless, much was learned and contributed by this team of investigators over the decade of its funding. They published over 100 peer-reviewed articles, 21 chapters, and a book on CAB, and there are still papers being published on the follow-up data collected since then. Some of the key findings are listed below.

Dick and Muriel Saunders (Analysis of Variables Affecting Response Allocation Between Aberrant and Productive Behaviors) developed a reliable real-time observation system and used it in the study of stereotypic, compulsive, and sometimes self-injurious behavior among people with severe or profound mental retardation. They developed computer software for viewing the data collected in a variety of ways and in a fraction of the time previously required. The data collected in multiple sessions per day can be combined easily and accurately into a single statistic for all of the sessions in a day. Conversely, individual sessions can be divided into discrete, consecutive intervals of a specified length (bins), and the local rates of behaviors presented for each interval. This latter capability permits visual inspection of the temporal relation between CAB, other subject behaviors, and environmental events within sessions. For certain analyses, rates and durations of multiple behaviors can be collapsed into a single statistic for an interval, session, or day representing the rate or duration of an hypothesized class of behaviors.

Dick and Muriel studied individuals with no apparent social basis for their aberrant behavior. These repetitive behaviors were maintained in the absence of contingent attention from others and in the absence of tangible reward. When the behaviors occurred in the context of demand situations, such as at work or in vocational training, removal of the demand had no effect. Some researchers have suggested that these behaviors are somehow automatically reinforced, perhaps by their proprioceptive effects. Others have suggested that the behaviors are default repertoires that emerge whenever other responses are insufficiently controlled by antecedent and consequent stimuli. Dick and Muriel studied typical schedules of reinforcement, such as variable interval (VI), fixed ratio (FR), and differential reinforcement of other behavior (DRO) for their treatment potential. They found that the schedules had measurable, but clinically insignificant effects on adaptive alternatives to the aberrant behavior.

The Saunders did find, however, that certain environmental modifications dramatically altered the effects of some schedules. FR schedules in particular can lead to nearly complete elimination of stereotypy and other repetitive behaviors when these modifications are introduced. A summarizing explanation would be that when the size of the ratio is made visually discriminable, the ratio schedule begins to produce its classic effects—rapid response runs and brief pauses following reinforcement. *Long-term exposure to the schedules results in work or vocational training periods that are largely free of the aberrant behavior.* The Saunders have further found that not all work responses or adaptive alternatives respond in this way. Successful intervention occurs when responses are selected for reinforcement that have the potential for increased rate. That is, the best responses are those for which the following adage would be applicable: "Practice makes perfect." Requiring responses or response chains that remain effortful or prone to error despite repeated practice does not result in achieving the desired treatment effect.

Steve Schroeder's project (Controlled Clinical Trials of Atypical Neuroleptics) began as a large-N double-blind crossover study to examine effects of different psychopharmacological agents (i.e., risperidone, clozapine, or olanzapine) and different taxonomic subtypes of CAB, especially stereotyped behavior, self-injurious behavior, aggression, as well as the main risk factors for CAB (e.g., level of mental retardation, age, gender, DSM-IV diagnosis, seizure disorders, residential placement, chronicity, presence of communication disorder, and age of onset). Previous research with risperidone in individuals with mental retardation and behavior problems has consisted primarily of case reports and had several limitations, including lack of double-blind conditions, no placebo condition, and concurrent medications with the risperidone.

Of the 52 participants eventually enrolled in the study to date, 58% showed a positive response to risperidone, based on clinical and caregiver ratings, in a dose–response fashion with few adverse side effects. However, several individuals dropped out prior to completing a dose condition because of personal reasons; of the remaining individuals who received at least one study dose, 73% showed a positive response to risperidone. The main side effects were sedation at the high dose and weight gain. This caused some early dropouts in the acute phase of the study, but attrition was decreased when the high dose was lowered from 0.06 mg/kg to 0.5 mg/kg. The positive responses to risperidone resulted in the limited testing of clozapine and olanzapine in adult participants.

One aspect of the research involved compiling consumer satisfaction information regarding the usefulness of the trial as well as staff responsiveness to caregiver concerns. Overall, the staff and the study have been rated favorably. In addition, naive observers rated brief videotapes of study participants both on medication and placebo. For four out of five study participants, raters were able to accurately determine when they were on medication and that the medication resulted in positive behavioral effects with limited side effects. Now completed, this study is the most comprehensive evaluation of risperidone in the treatment of CAB with severely developmentally disabled individuals to date.

A supplement to this project, directed by Jennifer Zarcone, enhanced the drug study by looking at the behavioral antecedents and consequences for destructive behavior and their interactions in response to risperidone by using functional analysis of their aberrant behavior. In all, 19 individuals participated in this portion of the study. Zarcone and colleagues found that functional analysis observations conducted throughout the course of the medication trial can determine the situations and settings in which the medication is likely to have the greatest impact. Specifically, they found that risperidone was more effective for those individuals whose CAB appeared to be maintained at least in part by negative reinforcement in the form of escape from tasks. In other words, the medication seemed to decrease the aversiveness of the negative reinforcer (e.g., tasks) in some manner. In addition, they found evidence that, for those individuals for whom the medication was not completely effective, results from the functional analysis observations may allow continued problem areas to be more easily identified and treated medically or behaviorally.

The Tessel project provided two very exciting types of data in the development of animal models for the study of aberrant and retarded behavior. These investigators used three animal models to study the development of retardation and aberrant behavior as a function of specific genetic and early developmental biological antecedents. They had selected the spontaneous hypertensive rats (SHR) as a model of genetic antecedents that may be related to subsequent aberrant behavior. Some have considered the SHR as a model for attention-deficit/hyperactivity disorders. Tessel selected this group as a group likely to exhibit aggressive behavior when subjected to such environmental stressors as shock or food deprivation. Their second animal model consisted of Sprague-Dawley rats exposed in utero to the antimitotic drug methylazoxymethanol (MAM), which results in experimentally produced microcephaly. These animals show *little motor disability* but should show cognitive deficiencies. If organisms with more limited competence are likely to show aberrant responses, then we might expect these subjects to show not only cognitive deficits, but also some form of aberrant behavior. The third animal model consisted of Sprague-Dawley rats lesioned neonatally by intercisternal injection of the catecholaminergic neuronal toxin, 6-hydroxydopamine (6-HD). Since isolate rearing is a condition that has been associated with high levels of aberrant behavior, one half of the subjects of each of the four groups (normal Sprague-Dawley controls, SHR, MAM, and 6-HD) were reared in isolation, while the remaining half was reared in group conditions.

The first set of interesting data was obtained when subjects of the eight groups were observed under a variety of conditions. Under conditions in which they were administered periodic unavoidable shock, members of the SHR group initially demonstrated aggressive responses by biting the bars of the chamber; however, after one session SHR animals became lethargic. MAM animals under these same conditions became hyperactive and engaged in stereotypic rearing behavior. No self-injurious behavior was observed in any group during shock sessions. However, when 6-HD animals who had experienced shock were exposed to apomorphine, self-injurious biting did occur. Periodic food delivery to food-deprived animals induced nonrearing stereotypies among SHR animals and rearing and hyperactivity among both SHR and MAM animals. Together these data suggest that there are *specific aberrant behavior patterns* associated with the different models. Now the question was raised: "Would drug or other treatments serve to reduce the aberrant behavior associated with the various models?"

The second set of fascinating data derives from observations related to fixed ratio discrimination training (Tessel, Loupe, & Schroeder, 2002; Tessel, Schroeder, Stodgell, & Loupe, 1995). Initially subjects were taught to discriminate between FR-1 and FR-16 schedules. This procedure involved having the subject respond to a center lever and then, when that lever was retracted and the side levers presented, the subject responded to the left lever if the center lever had been on one ratio and to the right lever if the center lever had been on the other ratio. When the discrimination started with the easy FR-1 versus FR-16 discrimination and then gradually progressed to FR-8 versus FR-16, all groups learned the discriminations and learning curves were essentially identical. However, when the discrimination was reversed, MAM rats reversed more slowly than the subjects of the other three groups. Moreover, when the fixed ratio discrimination started with the FR-8 versus FR-16 discrimination, MAM and SHR rats learned the discrimination at a significantly slower rate.

Analysis of brain structures and chemicals, however, yielded the most exciting findings. The 6-HD animals who had been given fixed ratio training showed a *reversal of cerebral and striatal catecholamine depletion*. Similarly, MAM animals that had been given FR discrimination training showed a *partial reversal of hippocampal hypoplasia* (*reversal of MAM-induced hippocampal weight and protein concentration reduction*). These observations are the first to suggest the possibility that susceptibility to CAB and the presence of cognitive deficits may not only be amenable to prevention, they may also be amenable to reversal. Although changes in behavior must be associated with changes in the brain, no one has pre-viously shown such specific and massive changes related to operant training. Moreover, the fact that changes were in the direction of nor-mality for animals with specific lesions was totally unexpected. These changes raise a number of fascinating questions. First, are the changes related to a specific kind of training involving progressive increase in problem difficulty or would training on a simple repetitive task result in the brain changes? Second, are such changes restricted to rats or do they occur in other animals including humans? Are these changes in brain structure and chemistry accompanied by more generalized changes in behavior? For example, do MAM animals who have been through fixed ratio discrimination training engage in less stereotyped rearing or do 6-HD animals no longer engage in self-biting when administered apomorphine and electric shock? Is it possible that such training will have a more generalized effect?

Many of the investigators in the CAB Program Project have gone on to pursue their individual interests, many of which are related to their early work on this project. Perhaps a fitting end to this chapter on the Bureau of Child Research/Life Span Institute work on CAB was an NICHD conference on SIB hosted in Bethesda in 1999 and published in 2002 in an edited volume entitled, *Self-Injurious Behavior: Gene–Brain–Behavior Relationships* (Schroeder, Oster-Granite, & Thompson, 2002). This conference convened most of the prominent geneticists, neurobiologists, and behaviorists responsible for the research over the past 35 years on the biological and behavioral bases of SIB and its treat-ment. It showed an impressive array of progress that has been made, and it still remains the benchmark in the field.

References

Baer, D. M., Peterson, R. F., & Sherman, J. A. (1967). The development of imitation by reinforcing behavioral similarity to a model. *Journal of the Experimental Analysis of Behavior, 10,* 405–416.

Baer, D. M., Wolf, M. M., & Risley, T. R. (1968). Some current dimensions of applied behavior analysis. *Journal of Applied Behavior Analysis, 1,* 91–97.

Bailey, J. S., Wolf, M. M., & Phillips, E. L. (1970). Home-based reinforcement and the mod-ification of predelinquents' classroom behavior. *Journal of Applied Behavior Analysis, 3,* 223–233.

Barton, E. S., Guess, D., Garcia, E., & Baer, D. M. (1970). Improvements of retardates' meal-time behaviors by timeout procedures using multiple baseline techniques. *Journal of Applied Behavior Analysis, 3,* 77–84.

Berkson, G., & Davenport, R. K., Jr. (1962). Stereotyped movements of mental defectives: I. Initial Survey. *American Journal of Mental Deficiency, 66,* 849–852.

Braukmann, C. J., Fixsen, D. L., Kirigin, K. A., Phillips, E. A., Phillips. E. L., & Wolf, M. M. (1975). Achievement Place: The training and certification of teaching-parents. In W. S. Wood (Ed.), *Issues in evaluating behavior modification* (pp. 131–152). Champaign, IL: Research Press.

Braukmann, C. J., Kirigin Ramp, K., & Wolf, M. M. (1985). *Follow-up of group home youth into young adulthood.* Washington, DC: Center for Studies of Antisocial and Violent Behavior, National Institute of Mental Health.

Breese, G. R. (2002). Age-dependent reduction of brain dopamine: Relationship to self-injurious behavior. In S. R. Schroeder, M. L. Oster-Granite, & T. Thompson (Eds.), *Self-injurious behavior: gene brain-behavior relationship* (pp. 279–288). Washington, DC: APA Books.

Carr, E. G. (1977). The motivation of self-injurious behavior: A review of some hypotheses. *Psychological Bulletin, 84,* 800–816.

Cotter, V. W., & Spradlin, J. E. (1971). A nonverbal technique for studying music preference. *Journal of Experimental Child Psychology, 11,* 357–365.

Cotter, V., & Toombs, S. (1966). A procedure to determine music preference of mental retardates. *Journal of Music Therapy, 3,* 57–64.

Cress, P. J., Spellman, C. R., DeBriere, T. J., Sizemore, A. C, Northam, J. K., & Johnson, J. L. (1981). Vision screening for persons with severe handicaps. *Journal of the Association for the Severely Handicapped, 6*(3), 41–50.

Day, R. M., Rea, J. A., Schussler, N. G., Larsen, S. E., & Johnson, W. L. (1988). Functionally based approach to the treatment of self-injurious behavior. *Behavior Modification, 12,* 565–589.

Dixon, L. S., Spradlin, J. E., Girardeau, F. L., & Etzel, B. (1974). Facilitating the acquisition of an "in front" spatial discrimination. *ACTA Symbolica, 5,* 1–22.

Dixon, M., & Spradlin, J. E. (1976). Establishing stimulus equivalences among retarded adolescents. *Journal of Experimental Child Psychology, 21,* 144–164.

Eyman, R. K., & Call, T. (1977). Maladaptive behavior and community placement of mentally retarded persons. *American Journal of Mental Deficiency, 82,* 137–144.

Falk, J. (1971). The nature and determinants of adjunctive behavior. *Physiology and Behavior, 6,* 577–588.

Falk, J. (1986). The formation and function of ritual behavior. In T. Thompson & M. D. Zeiler (Eds.), *Analysis and integration of behavioral units* (pp. 335–355). Hillsdale, NJ: Erlbaum.

Fulton, R. T., & Spradlin, J. E. (1971). Operant audiometry with severely retarded children. *Audiology, 10,* 203–211.

Fulton, R. T., & Spradlin, J. E. (1972). Effects of practice on SISI scores with normal hearing subjects. *Journal of Speech and Hearing Research, 15,* 217–224.

Girardeau, F. L., & Spradlin, J. E. (1964). Token rewards in a cottage program. *Mental Retardation, 2,* 345–352.

Guess, D., & Baer, D. M. (1973). Teaching productive noun suffixes to severely retarded children. *American Journal of Mental Deficiency, 77,* 498–505.

Guess, D., Sailor, W., & Baer, D. M. (1978). Children with limited language. In R. L. Schiefelbusch (Ed.), *Language intervention strategies* (pp. 101–143). Baltimore, MD: University Park Press.

Guess, D., Sailor, W., Rutherford, G., & Baer, D. M. (1968). An experimental analysis of linguistic development: The productive use of the plural morpheme. *Journal of Applied Behavior Analysis, 1,* 297–306.

Halle, J. W., Marshall, A. M., & Spradlin, J. E. (1979). Time delay: A K- technique to increase language use and facilitate generalization in retarded children. *Journal of Applied Behavior Analysis, 12,* 95–103.

Hollis, J. H. (1967). Development of perceptual motor skills in a profoundly retarded child: Part I. Prosthesis. *American Journal of Mental Deficiency, 72,* 941–952.

Hollis, J. H., & Meyers, C. E. (1982). *Life-threatening behavior: Analysis and intervention.* Washington, DC: American Association on Mental Deficiency.

Iwata, B. A., Dorsey, M. F., Slifer, J. K., Bauman, K. E., & Richman, G. S. (1982). Toward a functional analysis of self-injury. *Analysis and Intervention in Developmental Disabilities, 2,* 3–20.

Kaufman, M. E., & Levitt, H. (1965). A study of three stereotyped behaviors in institutionalized mental defectives. *American Journal on Mental Deficiency, 69,* 467–473.

Larsen, S., & Day, R. M. (1986). The effects of reinforcer removal on chronically aberrant behavior. Unpublished manuscript, University of Kansas, Parsons Research Center, Parsons, KS.

Lent, J. R., LeBlanc, J., & Spradlin, J. E. (1970). Designing a rehabilitative culture for mentally retarded adolescent girls. In R. Ulrich, T. Stachnik, & J. Mabry (Eds.), *Control of human behavior* (Vol. IV, pp. 121–135). New York: Scott, Foresman.

Lewis, M. H., Bodfish, J. W., Powell, S. B., Wiest, K., Darling, M., & Golden, R. N. (1996). Plasma HVA in adults with mental retardation and stereotyped behavior: Biochemical evidence for a dopamine deficiency model. *American Journal on Mental Retardation, 100,* 413–417.

Lipsitt, L. P., & LoLordo, V. M. (1963). Interactive effects and stimulus generalization on children's oddity learning. *Journal of Experimental Psychology, 66,* 210–214.

Lloyd, L. L., Spradlin, J. E., & Reid, M. J. (1968). An operant audiometric procedure for difficult-to-test patients. *Journal of Speech and Hearing Disorders, 33,* 236–245.

McLean, J. E. (1970). Establishing stimulus control of phoneme articulation by operant techniques. In F. L. Girardeau & J. E. Spradlin (Eds.), *A functional analysis approach to speech and language* (ASHA Monograph No. 14, pp. 24–48). Washington, DC: American Speech and Hearing Association.

Mulick, J. A., Dura, J. R., Rasnake, K., & Callahan, C. (1986, August). *Prevalence of SIB in institutionalized nonambulatory profoundly retarded people.* Poster presented at the American Psychological Association Annual Convention, Washington, DC.

Newsom, C, Favell, J. E., & Rincover, A. (1983). The side effects of punishment. In S. Axelrod (Ed.), *The effects of punishment on human behavior* (pp. 285–316). New York: Academic Press.

Phillips, E. L. (1968). Achievement Place: Token reinforcement procedures in a homestyle rehabilitation setting for "pre-delinquent" boys. *Journal of Applied Behavior Analysis, 1,* 213–223.

Phillips, E. L., Phillips, E. A., Fixsen, D. L., & Wolf, M. M. (1971). Achievement Place: The modification of the behaviors of pre-delinquent boys within a token economy. *Journal of Applied Behavior Analysis, 4,* 45–59.

Risley, T. R., & Hart, B. (1968). Developing correspondence between the nonverbal and verbal behavior of preschool children. *Journal of Applied Behavior Analysis, 1,* 267–281.

Rogers-Warren, A., & Baer, D. M. (1976). Correspondence between saying and doing: Teaching children to share and praise. *Journal of Applied Behavior Analysis, 9,* 335–354.

Rojahn, J. (1984). Self-injurious behavior in institutionalized, severely/profoundly retarded adults: Prevalence data and staff agreement. *Journal of Behavioral Assessment, 8*(1), 13–27.

Saunders, R. R., Rast, J., & Saunders, M. D. (1988). *A handbook for scenario-based active treatment.* Lawrence: University of Kansas.

Saunders, R. R., Saunders, K., Kirby, K., & Spradlin, J. E. (1988). The merger and development of equivalence classes by unreinforced conditional selection of comparison stimuli. *Journal of the Experimental Analysis of Behavior, 50,* 145–162.

Saunders, R. R., Wachter, J., & Spradlin, J. E. (1988). Establishing auditory stimulus control over an eight-member equivalence class via conditional discrimination procedures. *Journal of the Experimental Analysis of Behavior, 49,* 95–115.

Schroeder, S. R., Bickel, W. K., & Richmond, D. (1986). Primary and secondary prevention of self-injurious behaviors: A life-long problem. In K. D. Gadow (Ed.), *Advances in learning and behavioral disabilities* (Vol. 5, pp. 63–85). Greenwich, Ct: JAI Press.

Schroeder, S. R., Oster-Granite, M. L., & Thompson, T. T. (Eds.) (2002). *Self- injurious behavior: Gene–brain–behavior relationships.* Washington, DC: APA Books.

Schroeder, S. R., Schroeder, C. S., Smith, B., & Dalldorf, J. (1978). Prevalence of self-injurious behavior in a large state facility for the retarded: A three-year follow-up study. *Journal of Autism and Childhood Schizophrenia, 8,* 261–269.

Sherman, J. A., Sheldon, J. B., Morris, K., Strouse, M., & Reese, R. M. (1984). A community-based residential program for mentally retarded adults: An adaptation of the teaching-family model. In S. C. Paine, T. Bellamy, & B. Wilconx (Eds.), *Human services that work: From innovation to standard practice* (pp. 167–179). Baltimore, MD: Paul H. Brookes Publishing Co.

Spradlin, J. E. (1962). Effects of reinforcement schedules on extinction in severely retarded children. *American Journal of Mental Deficiency, 66,* 634–640.

Spradlin, J. E., Cotter, V. W., & Baxley, N. R. (1973). Establishing a conditional discrimination with direct training: A study of transfer with retarded adolescents. *American Journal of Mental Deficiency, 77,* 556–566.

Spradlin, J. E., & Dixon, M. (1976). Establishing conditional discrimination without direct training: Stimulus classes and labels. *American Journal of Mental Deficiency, 80,* 555–561.

Spradlin, J. E., Fixsen, D. L., & Girardeau, F. L. (1969). Reinstatement of an operant response by the delivery of reinforcement during extinction. *Journal of Experimental Child Psychology, 7,* 96–100.

Spradlin, J. E., Girardeau, F. L., & Corte, E. (1965). Fixed ratio and fixed interval behavior of severely and profoundly retarded subjects. *Journal of Experimental Child Psychology, 2,* 304–353.

Spradlin, J. E., Girardeau, F. L., & Horn, G. L. (1966). Stimulus properties of reinforcement during extinction of a free operant response. *Journal of Experimental Child Psychology, 4,* 369–379.

Spradlin, J. E., Lloyd, L. L., Horn, G. L., & Reid, M. (1968). Establishing tone control and evaluating the hearing of severely retarded children. In G. A. Jervis (Ed.), *Expanding concepts in mental retardation: A symposium from the Joseph Kennedy, Jr., Foundation* (pp. 170–180). Springfield, IL: Charles C Thomas.

Spradlin, J. E., Locke, B. J., & Fulton, R. T. (1969). Conditioning and audiological assessment. In R. T. Fulton & L. L. Lloyd (Eds.), *Audiometry for the retarded with implications for the difficult-to-test* (pp. 125–163). Baltimore, MD: Williams & Wilkins.

Spradlin, J. E., & Saunders, R. R. (1986). The development of stimulus classes using match-to-sample procedures: Sample classification vs. comparison classification. *Analysis and Intervention in Developmental Disabilities, 6,* 41–58.

Stokes, T. F., & Baer, D. M. (1977). An implicit technology of generalization. *Journal of Applied Behavior Analysis, 10,* 349–367.

Stremel-Campbell, K., & Campbell, C. R. (1982). Programming "loose training" as a strategy to facilitate language generalization. *Journal of Applied Behavior Analysis, 15,* 295–301.

Striefel, S., Bryan, K. S., & Aikins, D. A. (1974). Transfer of stimulus control from motor to verbal stimuli. *Journal of Applied Behavior Analysis, 7,* 123–135.

Striefel, S., & Wetherby, B. (1973). Instruction-following behavior of a retarded child and its controlling stimuli. *Journal of Applied Behavior Analysis, 6,* 663–670.

Striefel, S., Wetherby, B., & Karlan, G. (1976). Establishing generative verb-noun instruction-following skills in retarded children. *Journal of Experimental Child Psychology, 22,* 247–260.

Talkington, L. W., & Riley, J. (1971). Reduction diets and aggression in institutionalized mentally retarded. *American Journal of Mental Deficiency, 76,* 370–372.

Tessel, R. E., Schroeder, S. R., Stodgell, C. J., & Loupe, P. S. (1995). Rodent models of mental retardation: Self-injury, aberrant behavior and stress. *Mental Retardation and Developmental Disabilities Research Reviews, 1,* 99–103.

Tessel, R. E., Loupe, P. S., & Schroeder, S. R. (2002). Replacement therapy for the treatment of Lesch-Nyhan Syndrome. In S. R. Schroeder, M. L. Oster-Granite, & T. Thompson (Eds.), *Self-injurious behavior: Gene–brain–behavior relationships* (pp. 299–308). Washington, DC: APA Books.

Vanden Borre, R., Vermote, R., Buttiëns, M., Thiry, P., Dierick, G., Guetjens, J., et al., (1993). Risperidone as add-on therapy in behavioural disturbances in mental retardation: A double-blind placebo controlled cross-over study. *Acta Psychiatrica Scandinavica, 87,* 167–171.

Wetherby, B., Karlan, G., & Spradlin, J. (1983). Development of derived stimulus relations through training in arbitrary-matching sequences. *Journal of Experimental Analysis of Behavior, 40,* 69–78.

White, C. C, Lakin, K. C, Hill, B. K., Wright, E. A., & Bruininks, R. H. (1987). *Persons with mental retardation in state-operated residential facilities: Year ending June 30, 1986 with longitudinal trends from 1950 to 1986* (Report No. 24). Minneapolis: University of Minnesota, Department of Educational Psychology.

19

The Beach Center on Disability

H. RUTHERFORD TURNBULL III

On the one hand, my wife Ann and I are accidental co-founders of the Beach Center—accidental because we never sought to come to the University of Kansas (KU), Dick Schiefelbusch having sought us out and recruited us from University of North Carolina–Chapel Hill; because we never had an original plan to co-found and co-direct a research center; and because the fact that our son Jay has several disabilities and thus requires us to perform professional and family roles simultaneously is itself an accident of nature, there being no known explanation for his disabilities. On the other hand, we are quite deliberate co-founders, having formed a professional partnership with each other beginning in the late 1970s and then having competed for and won the federal competition that, in 1988, resulted in the funding that transformed us into the co-directors of a new research entity.

The launch of the Beach Center required not just the ideas we ourselves brought to the competition, but also the ideas and support that Jean Ann Summers, Paul Diedrich, Mary Beth Johnson, and Opal Folks added while, during weekends and evenings, we were writing the grant application from our sabbatical-home in Bethesda, Maryland. Their participation was deliberate and essential; without them, there would have been no initial grant.

Naming the Center and Honoring the Beach Family

Having secured the grant, we were obliged to re-name the center. We could not tolerate the federal name, the Rehabilitation Research and Training

Center on Family Support. We needed a family-friendly name. In addition, we needed to name our new center for a Kansas family who had distinguished itself in the field of disabilities and whose steadfast pursuit of excellence and unquestioned integrity represented all of the very best of Kansans and the University of Kansas.

Only one family fit those two criteria, and so, with Dick's blessing (for he knew them well and for a long time), we sought permission from Marianna and Ross Beach to name the center after them. They consented, and their consent radically changed our lives and our fledgling center. In naming ourselves the Beach Center on Disability, we sought to honor them. They and their entire family in turn have honored us and the Life Span Institute (LSI), Dick Schiefelbusch, and KU by their overwhelmingly generous gifts to the Kansas University Endowment Association for the center's benefit.

The naming and the gifts were never conditioned on each other. We named the center for Marianna and Ross because they unconditionally deserved that honor, and they later concluded that we merited their support.

One of the benefits of becoming involved with Marianna and Ross Beach is that we have become friends of their grandson, Ross Darby Edwards, and his mother and father, Terry and R. A. Edwards (Terry is one of the three Beach daughters). We often see Ross on campus or in town, and we delight in his life. And, of course, it is so good to be able to say that Terry and R. A. are friends.

Staying Put

If it is true of Paris, so it is of us: *Plus ça change, plus c'est la même chose.* The more she changes, the more she is the same. That is true of our physical site. When the Dole Center opened in 1990, many of our colleagues rushed to stake their claims there. We did not do so, believing it was better for the Beach Center if we were to continue to occupy the third floor of the Stewart Wing of Haworth Hall in order to create a collaborative culture. After all, people and methods make a university great, not libraries and laboratories.

So we stayed put. In return, we earned a gradual expansion of our space in Haworth; we now occupy the entire third floor. We cannot boast of beauty in our site. We can only embody competence, commitment, and character that lead to methods and wisdom that in turn make a difference for others.

Changing by Creating the Curve

Predictably, the center has changed. Evidence of the change comes from simply looking at the verbs that describe our past and present research on families. Instead of researching how policies and programs can support and then empower families, we now look to whether the outcomes of policy and practice enhance families' quality of life. The change of verbs is important: We continue to elevate families' status with respect to research and its outcomes.

In large part because we are the parents of a man with disabilities, we have spurred the Beach Center to ask the "so what" question: Now that our research has shown results, what difference can we make with that new knowledge? Simply studying over and over again what one has already studied or what others have done before you is not adequate or satisfying.

Reiteration is inadequate because it does not impel growth. And it is not satisfying because we and many of our colleagues like to be "curve makers." We have sought to create the swell under the surface of the ocean that causes the waves to curve and rush to the shores of philosophy, policy, practice, procedure, personnel, and funding. Psychic compensation is derived from riding the curve of a wave, but the satisfaction is greater when one creates the curve that makes the wave.

Changing by Expanding Our Scope of Work

Instead of working exclusively on family issues, we now have a much broader and deeper portfolio. Late in the 1990s, we recruited Michael Wehmeyer and, through his leadership, acquired an international leadership role in self-determination, assistive technology, and universal design of curriculum. And early in the 21st century, we recruited Wayne Sailor and, through his leadership, acquired an international leadership role in positive behavior support, standards-based school reform, and urban education.

Instead of corralling our talented research staff in only one area of work, we encouraged them to follow their interests. We now follow Jean Ann Summers as she explores how practitioners and their agencies advance or impede families' quality of life; Denise Poston as she researches family–professional partnerships; Matt Stowe as he investigates the legal, ethical, and social implications of the Human Genome Project; Sandra Padmanabhan and David Stowe as they push the frontiers of web-based research, training, and dissemination–utilization; and Mary-Margaret Simpson and Ray Pence as they make our products accessible to a wide audience.

Changing by Going Global

Rather than limiting ourselves to research that addresses conditions only in the United States, we now act globally. Our new scope began in 1989–1990, when Marianna and Ross made their first gift to the Beach Center. Marianna had been the president's appointed delegate to, and then president of the governing body of, the Inter-American Children's Institute, a specialized agency of the Organization of American States. (She also was a longtime member of the President's Committee on Mental Retardation.)

In her role as our nation's representative to the institute, she became a close friend of Maria Eloísa Garcia Etchegoyen de Lorenzo of Montevideo, Uruguay. Even then, Eloísa was an international star in disability advocacy and a longtime member of the institute's staff. She simply continued to shine more brightly the longer she lived.

Because of the gift from Marianna and Ross, we are now able to sponsor the Eloísa de Lorenzo Prize to honor excellence in research, teaching, service, and advocacy by individuals or entities in the institute's member nations and to sponsor international symposia on topics of emerging interest to families and others.

One of those topics relates to the intersection of policy and family quality of life. Because of our cutting-edge research, researchers, policy leaders, families, and practitioners throughout the world now look to the Beach Center for leadership on that topic. Predictably, students and faculty from other countries want to affiliate and collaborate with us around that issue, and we welcome them. Significantly, our web site reflects our globalization: We offer materials in English, Spanish, Korean, Chinese, and Japanese (*www.beachcenter.org*).

Benefiting from Enlightened Leadership and Reliable Allies

Of course, creativity and energy are not cabined only in the fecund minds and bodies of researchers. They reside, as well, in our colleagues within LSI who have embraced and advanced our vision. As LSI's directors, Dick Schiefelbusch, Steve Schroeder, and Steve Warren had one common, highly valuable trait: They stayed out of our way and cleared the way for us when we needed them to do so. As LSI's fiscal officers, Ed Zamarripa and Paul Diedrich brought their own creativity to the business of writing and administering grants.

Within the Beach Center itself, Opal Folks and then her daughter Lois Weldon have been our staunchest reliable allies. There have been other stellar employees, but Opal and Lois have seniority, individually and collectively.

Jim Martin, Dale Seuferling, and Clark Cropp, the senior officers of the Kansas University Endowment Association during the 1980s and thereafter, are rock-solid confreres, and Jim Roberts, now the director of the Kansas University Center for Research, always finds ways to bust the barriers that seem to impede us from time to time.

To surround ourselves with talent, enlarge the scope of our work, and justifiably believe that we are making a sustainable and significant difference for families is intrinsically rewarding.

That reward simply multiplies when Marianna and Ross Beach continue to participate in our work, when the late Betsy Santelli and her cousin James MacDonald Fowler and his parents endow our research and service to families, and when Julie and Scott Borchardt and their family create their own endowment so that we can support our graduate students. Those multipliers are accidents; we have never sought to do anything except be the best at our work and to create a culture within the Beach Center where the diligent pursuit of excellence, the daily honoring of people with disabilities and their families, and collaboration and trust prevail.

Documenting Our Work by the Fiscal Criterion

The Beach Center began in 1988, 8 years after we joined the faculty in special education and the Bureau of Child Research (now the LSI). Before that year (July 1981 through June 1988), Rud and Ann Turnbull had been responsible for earning $1,455,745 in federal, state, and private-entity grants. Since July 1988, Beach Center researchers have been responsible for earning $27,408,167 in federal, state, and private-entity grants. The ratio of federal to state dollars, represented in all of those grants between July 1988 and now, is, on average, 10 (federal or other) to 1 (KU).

That seems to be a decent leverage of Kansans' tax dollars: Invest $1, earn $10, each year. The principal investigators and senior research staff responsible for that level of peer-competed external support include those in the family-and-policy area (ourselves, Jean Ann Summers, Denise Poston, Matt Stowe); those in the self-determination area (Mike Wehmeyer and Susan Palmer); those in the school reform/PBS area (Wayne Sailor), and those in the area of the Human Genome Project (Matt Stowe and Rud Turnbull).

Documenting Our Work by the Publication Criterion

The Beach Center consists of prodigious researchers and scholars. They did some of their work before coming to the Beach Center but a great deal since then. One way to document the Beach Center's standing as a research entity is to take all of the published scholarship by all of the individuals named above (under "Documenting Our Work by the Fiscal Criterion") since they came to the Beach Center as a single, aggregated criterion of scholarship, count only once the publications co-authored by more than one of them, and then sum the scholarly publications.

The result is staggering. Rud and Ann Turnbull, Mike Wehmeyer, and Wayne Sailor alone have published a total of:

70 books—38 since they joined the Beach Center;
286 articles—153 since joining the Beach Center;
172 chapters—103 since joining the Beach Center; and
102 monographs, technical reports, and curricula—59 since joining the
    Beach Center.

(Co-authorships are counted only once. The publications of other staff are not counted; they often co-author with one of the four principal investigators.)

Documenting Our Work by the Educator Criterion

The Beach Center also consists of superb educators. "To educate" comes from a Latin word meaning "to lead forth," hence, to pull out of a person (a student) all that is in him or her, to bring to the light that which is innate and inchoate but not yet born and refined.

Again counting only from 1988 and including only those individuals listed above, the Beach Center's educators have served as chairpersons or members of the doctoral committees of more than 100 doctoral students who have graduated from the University of Kansas. Among these graduates are students from all across the United States in special education, human development, social welfare, and American studies. In addition, we have had doctoral students from China (People's Republic), Taiwan, India (by way of Great Britain), Korea, Japan, Israel, and Spain. In addition to teaching students in those doctoral programs, the Beach Center staff have offered full courses (not cameo appearances) in the Department of Special Education, other departments in the School of Education, and the Law School.

Documenting Our Work by the Service–Leadership Criterion

Service and leadership go hand in hand with each other. When we serve, we often also lead. Evidence of our service and leadership abounds.

Consider some of our work in the leadership category:

- Two presidents of the American Association on Mental Retardation;
- Two officers (vice president/president, and treasurer—both served as directors), of The Association for Persons with Severe Handicaps;
- One officer (secretary and director) of The Arc of the United States;
- Two directors of the University Center for Excellence in Developmental Disabilities;
- One chairman, Board of Trustees, Judge David L. Bazelon Center for Mental Health Law; and
- One chairman, American Bar Association Commission on Mental and Physical Disability Law.

Recognize some of our research awards:

- Distinguished early career award, Council for Exceptional Children;
- National Research Award, The Arc of the United States;
- Meritorious Performance and Professional Promise Award, San Francisco State University School of Education; and
- Faculty Achievement Award, University of Kansas.

Consider some of our teaching and mentoring awards:

- Gene A. Budig Teaching Professor, KU School of Education;
- Graduate Student Mentoring Award, KU School of Education;
- Co-recipients, The Arc of the USA Educator Award;
- Outstanding Woman Teacher, University of Kansas;
- Louise E. Byrd Graduate Educator Award, University of Kansas;
- Rotary International Teacher of the Handicapped Award;
- AAMR Education Award; and
- TASH Norris Haring Research Award.

Take into account that we serve(d) as editor (in chief, associate editor, or as reviewer) of 19 scholarly journals and as a reviewer or consultant for five major publishing houses.

Finally, acknowledge some of the miscellaneous awards:

- Two recipients, Century Award in Mental Retardation, 1999 (consortium of seven professional and family associations for changing the course of history in mental retardation during the 20th century);
- Two outstanding special educators, 20th century (peer-selected); and
- Two recipients, Elizabeth M. Boggs Award, Camphill Association of North America.

Adding Adjuncts

Our staff and student-trainee population consists of not only people from the United States and the countries we named, but also researchers who have or have had adjunct appointments with us.

They come to us from American institutions of higher education: Bob Schalock, former president of the American Association on Mental

Retardation and an internationally esteemed researcher in individual quality of life, from Hastings College, Nebraska; and Mian Wang, originally from China, formerly our doctoral student, and now at Rowan College, New Jersey.

They come, as well, from across the world: Canada (Ivan Brown and Roy Brown), Australia (Trevor Parmenter and the bi-national Roy Brown), Spain (Miguel Verdugo), and the People's Republic of China (Fei Zan and the already mentioned Mian Wang).

Practicing What We Preach and Teach

Fiscal, scholarly, educator, and colleague attractiveness are valid criteria for assessing whether the Beach Center has been a "curve maker." We could satisfy those criteria at high levels, however, and still not demonstrate our fidelity to people with disabilities and their families. So, another way of showing that we are faithful to our mission is to say that, since 1988, nearly one third of all Beach Center employees, at all levels and in all roles, have been people with disabilities or close family members (parents, sisters, uncles/aunts, cousins) of people with disabilities. We dare not research and teach without also practicing what we preach.

Impaling Values on a Phrase (or Two)

Exactly what do we preach and practice? There are two ways to answer that question:

1. By cutting to the jugular of our mission statement: to make a significant and sustainable difference in the lives of people with disabilities and their families, in Kansas, the United States, and the world, through excellence in research, training, and service; and

2. By reciting the five phrases that describe our aspirations for people with disabilities and their families:

   - *Great Expectations*—Raising our expectations for ourselves, people with disabilities, and their families, and thereby changing what "others" expect of us and them;

   - *Choices*—Making it possible for people with disabilities and their families to have the same choices in life that everyone else takes for granted;

- *Relationships*—Assuring that family and friendships grow because the greatest social security is in the arms of family and friends;
- *Strengths*—Building on the strengths that everyone has and not seeing people with disabilities and their families as poor, pitiful people;
- *Positive Contributions*—Affirming that people with disabilities and their families make positive contributions to society and making it possible for them to make those contributions; and
- *Full Citizenship*—Assuring that philosophy, policy, personnel, practice, procedures, and pennies (the six "P" approaches to an enviable life) favor people with disabilities and their families.

Telling the Stories of Real Lives

In part because "we are family" and in part because we adhere to our mission statement and the six values, we remain close to people with disabilities and their families. There is no ivory tower for us, nor do we want one.

Whether in our publications or our web site, we try to remain true to the narratives we hear from the families and individuals with whom we do our work. We tell about ourselves, because our lives—that is, the lives of many of us—are intimately connected to the lives of our family members with disabilities. We also tell about the people and families with whom we come into contact and about how professionals and practitioners daily serve those with disabilities and their families.

Some of the greatest teaching is by parable or allegory. We aspire to use those great teaching techniques to tell the stories of real people. Unless we are faithful to their narratives, we cannot be faithful to anyone's.

Recounting Our Psychological Journeys

The psychological journey may be the only one truly worth telling. Certainly the great novelists and dramatists say so, and so it is that our psychological journeys inform the Beach Center's founding, its present, and its future.

Some of us were transformed by the civil rights movements of the 1960s. Others by working in schools or state institutions that were horrifically insufficient to serve students or residents. Others by their experi-

ences as parents or brothers/sisters of people with disabilities. Others by
the compelling evidence that research can change people's lives. Others
by intellectual fascination with the constructs (and misconstructs) related
to disability. Whatever the origins of our journey, we have come to this
common land, this Beach Center, committed to making a significant and
sustainable difference in the world of disability, to adding value to our
communities, country, and world by serving others.

Being Partners and Trusting Each Other

If a visitor to the University of Kansas were to seek a research entity where
partnership prevails, that person would find it at the Beach Center. We
pioneered (in 1989) a new approach to research about families. We called
it "participatory action research" and we have practiced it ever since. It's
really quite simple: We ask families and individuals with disabilities to be
our partners in every step of the research enterprise, from shaping the
research questions to conducting the research, understanding our data,
and disseminating and assuring utilization of our research results. We have
benefited greatly by this work, because families and individuals with disabilities have a wisdom that too easily can escape researchers. We are quite
deliberate in trying to capture that wisdom and learn from it.

We also collaborate with each other. We work and play hard, often,
and collectively. And, of course, we struggle together, never against each
other but always in alliance with each other, to meet the challenges of
research, teaching, and making a significant and sustainable difference
for people with disabilities and their families. Candid, sometimes difficult, communications occur here; they have to and they retain, withal, a
civility and cordiality that enable the candor.

The consequence of our family partnerships and collegial collaborations is that families and individuals with disabilities have learned to
trust us, and we trust each other. Dissemblance has no place among us;
trust does. That is an inexpressibly valuable aspect of our lives at the
Beach Center.

Including Our Own Families

If you were to walk the corridors of the Beach Center, you would hear people talking face to face or on the telephone and the normal noise (and

silence) of people deep in thought, as is right and proper for researchers and their administrative support staff. But you would also hear the noises that babies and young children make. Like the others here, babies and children belong. So do our brothers and sisters and our parents and the other adults in our lives. Our families belong in our professional lives. Families are foundational to who we are and what we investigate; they are whom we seek to benefit. Of course, they belong here and are welcome here. They and the "issues" they bring into our lives are part of the ebb and flow of all human interactions; they are not distractions from but are instead central to our lives and our work, which is but a part of our lives.

We try to foster a mutual appreciation that we are whole persons with child, sibling, aging parent issues. Being whole is a lot more important than meeting our professional obligations every minute of every workday. Without wholeness and harmony, we most assuredly would belie our mission and be less capable in fulfilling it.

Adopting a Work Ethic

A collective culture does not simply happen. Support, money, productive people, personal histories, partnerships, and trust are necessary but not sufficient. Labor must occur.

Taped onto Rud's office door is a statement from the Latin poet/scholar Hesiod:

> Before the Gates of Excellence,
> The High Gods Have Placed Sweat.

And on a plaque in our suite is a saying from Ann's father:

> We have no conception of what our best effort is. So we must continually strive to do better today than we were able to do yesterday.

We work hard—period. We must remind ourselves of the "OPI" lesson that we teach our children: Organization and Perspiration precede Inspiration.

Making a Difference: Pointillistic Portraits

One way to know whether we are making a difference is to adduce data about grants, scholarship, teaching, and awards (none of which we have mentioned here). These are macrodata; they paint a big picture of outputs and outcomes.

Perhaps, however, an equally apt picture can be painted in a more pointillistic way. Do individuals and families seek us out? Do they "cold call"? Do they telephone, e-mail, write, drop by, stop us at conferences, and post their questions and stories on our web page? Yes, and perhaps the fact that we receive, hear, heed, and respond to them is solid evidence that we are making a difference. To know that we have affected just one life is, after all, to know that we will affect many, for that one life is connected to others, and thus our "difference making" multiplies.

Daring

Ann's father often told her that she should pray to be different because it's easy to be like everyone else. And Rud's family motto teaches that fortune favors the brave: Fortuna audaci favet. And so we dare to be different and brave. Put it another way: we never let our own ignorance or dullness stand in the way. When we lack knowledge, we seek it out or recruit people who bring the knowledge we need. When we lack courage, we look at the lives of our families and friends who are affected by disability, and we stiffen our resolve. When we begin to lose the thrill of making the force that makes the curve that shapes the wave, we try to recapture it by doing something we have not done before.

Life at the Beach Center should be exciting. If the time ever comes when "the thrill is gone," we'd better close up. To date, we're still having fun. IQ is important. But the JQ—the joy quotient—is just as important.

Looking Ahead

History can be a prelude to the future. It can tell us what we want to be, or not be; and how to achieve our goals.

What do we want to be? We want to be what we are now, only more so. We want to

Attract and retain international leaders,
Recruit superb researchers and doctoral students,
Deepen the culture that we have created, and
Continue to make a significant and sustainable difference for families
    and individuals affected by disability.

What do we need? Were we in a courtroom, the following dialogue would occur:

The reader: "Objection, your Honor, on the ground that the question is not relevant."
The judge: "Sustained."

And, turning to the lawyer who posed the objectionable question, His Honor would say:

"Mr. Turnbull, you are telling what happened, not planning your next activities. Proceed to your closing argument."

Concluding

This is not a history, though it may seem to be that. It is only an attempt to give you some sense of what we are all about here at the Beach Center. If you have liked what you read, let us know or come to see us. Otherwise, may you have good sailing on your journey and land safely on some other beach.

20

The Research and Training Center on Independent Living

JAMES F. BUDDE

The Research and Training Center on Independent Living (RTCIL) has a 26-year history of productive research, comprehensive training, and innovative dissemination of knowledge. It began with the quest to provide a home for a 21-year-old woman with quadriplegia. At that time, a planning group formed, including Roger Williams, Gary Condra, Cal Broten, Judy Bachelder, Franklin Shontz, and myself, unaware of an independent living (IL) model as we know it today. We struggled and failed to come up with a solution to our quest. Then Dick Royce, a graduate student working with us, discovered that the Department of Education under the Rehabilitation Services Administration had established three demonstration projects for independent living centers (ILCs) in Houston, Boston, and Berkeley.

I decided to visit the ILC in Berkeley and, to my excitement, found it was an effective storefront operation primarily run by individuals with severe disabilities. Their model was one that I believed would make a major impact on the world—and it has. This model contained three interrelated components. First, the services were what I later termed "undependency-creating" services. The services were all designed to help individuals become independent rather than dependent. For example, individuals were enabled to obtain their own home through accommodations, supports, and entitled benefits rather than being placed in a group home.

Second, the environment was viewed as the first obstruction to independence. At the time, the individual with the disability was rated

411

by what the person could and could not do rather than the restriction of the environment. For example, an individual might be rated as not being eligible for educational benefits because they could not attend classes in a wheelchair. The ILC service would be one of advocating for a ramp or elevator that would make educational access possible.

The third, and what I believe to be the most important, component, was consumer control. It was based on the concept that individuals with disabilities were to be treated as consumers of services. In other words, they could select services and participate in the process. Consumer control is also based on the concept that individuals with disabilities controlled their own lives. Early research reviews illustrated that when individuals cannot control their lives they become resentful, devalue what others force them to participate in, and even give up control after constantly being forced to make decisions that they do not value. The cornerstone and success of our country is individual freedom and independence; individuals with disabilities have the same rights and are encouraged and sometimes forced to control their own destiny.

Back in Lawrence, I reported my experience to the enthused planning group. We then created the model for what we decided to call Independence, Incorporated, which was launched with concession stand profits and Kansas Rehabilitation Services funding. That same year, in 1979, a Request for Proposal for a Rehabilitation Research and Training Center (RRTC) on IL became available through the National Institute on Handicapped Research, which later became the National Institute on Disability and Rehabilitation Research (NIDRR). Howard Moses, who had been recently appointed to the new, small independent living department of Kansas Rehabilitation Services and one of the nicest men whom I have ever met, and I decided to take our growing IL knowledge and University Affiliated Program (UAP) track record working with grassroots organizations and community innovation, to apply for the RRTC grant. To our favor, 10 additional points were to be awarded to any applicant from federal Region VII, including Kansas, because it was the only federal region that did not have a RRTC.

The grant challenged us because we had been using a UAP model that was less concerned with research and more concerned with innovation and training. Fortunately, the emerging IL field, too, placed a high value on innovation and training. To determine needs, we listened to the problems that individuals with disabilities had with services and the environment. This policy of involving the intended recipients of our research efforts and including them on our advisory boards would later be a NIDRR-mandated policy termed "Participatory Action Research," a mainstay at our center before it was even a center and integral to our long-term success.

As we wrote the RRTC application focusing on independent living foundations and services as well as self-help, we recruited researchers and staff and matched their interests with needs. We then worked with this staff nucleus, including Neil Salkind, Ann Turnbull, and Gary Clark to develop individual research and training projects overseen by Salkind as research director, Clark and Moses as training coordinators, and myself as center director. As we recognized the needs of the growing disability population, we developed the guiding statement: *Through research and training, improving services, enhancing the community environment, and facilitating consumer control, persons with disabilities are able to live independently.* Our target audiences were: 1) individuals with disabilities; 2) families and other social support groups of disabled individuals; 3) independent living service providers; 4) policy makers in rehabilitation and independent living; 5) rehabilitation and other professionals, and professional trainees in the university community; and 6) the general public, both locally and nationally.

When the peer reviews were completed, we scored highest when the 10 extra points were added, topping even the University of Nebraska and University of Missouri, both stunned that Kansas placed higher than their established rehabilitation centers. They and another entity contacted their Congressional delegations to challenge the decision, prompting site visits at each location to gain additional information. After our site visit, Kansas, of course, was awarded the grant, and the first Rehabilitation Research and Training Center on Independent Living was established within the Bureau of Child Research. And, through the advice and assistance of Edward Meyen, we requested that the Board of Regents grant the new RTCIL center status, which meant that the RTCIL would be a long-term entity that would conduct IL research at the University of Kansas.

Early Challenges and System Refinement

We initiated the grant with considerable enthusiasm under the watchful eye of Emily Cromar, our project officer, but our varied approaches conflicted. Richard Schiefelbusch became aware of the initial organizational problem and offered his usual helpful hand by suggesting that Todd Risley evaluate our progress. Risley identified the issues immediately and said we needed a more systematic approach to develop a needs-based research and development system. Risley, in his effective, analytic, problem-solving mode, joined us as our second research director, and made other valued recommendations.

For example, Risley required us to fine tune consumer needs and to develop intervention products tested through our research and then disseminated rapidly to improve services. This was a novel concept in 1980 because much of university research was based on researcher interest and resulted in journal articles or conference presentations. Today, our needs-based research, development, and dissemination model, involving a dynamic interplay between researchers and potential adopters, has become commonplace within most research projects and centers. One early use of this agenda-setting and organizing tool that involves consumers in shaping research questions and the survey instrument for later problem analysis and intervention was with our common concerns report method (CCRM), which summarized issues identified by 12,834 disabled consumers from 10 states in the late 1980s and identified consumer-generated solutions to each issue. We continue to use the CCRM and present results at public forums called "town hall" meetings to plan change in communities.

Another concept we pioneered and put into practice was the junior colleague model in which talented graduate assistants enrolled in departments such as counseling psychology, design, educational psychology, human development and family life, public administration, special education, social psychology, social welfare, and women's studies were selected to work on a center research team, beginning with routine data collection tasks and progressing to supervisory roles. At the highest level, graduate assistants also designed and submitted a research project to the management team for funding through the RTCIL grant. This "two-fer" proved successful because the graduate assistant carried out the RTCIL mission to a greater degree and the center provided funding and opportunity to manage and conduct research. Still used today at the RTCIL, this model has resulted in a number of graduate students becoming RTCIL staff after graduation who develop their own lines of IL research. Glen White, for example, the first scholarship recipient of the Independent Living Leadership Training Program, pursued a doctoral degree at the Department of Human Development and Family Life through the center and became our training director, then research director, and now directs the center.

Much of the RTCIL management model was patterned after Schiefelbusch and his management style of making the most of an individual's talents, interests, and opportunities to perform research and acquire research funds. The beauty of the model is that it enables researchers to be entrepreneurs within a major research university. Had it not been for this model, I doubt there would have ever been a RTCIL.

In keeping with the Life Span Institute model, we used regular and informal meetings to plan, increase productivity, and assist staff. New staff attended weekly meetings, or "counseling sessions" as Schiefelbusch might say, where information was shared and problem solving conducted. While we were not aware of what would be called "total quality management" much later, we were doing it from the start with staff communicating openly across lines of authority to achieve objectives efficiently and functionally while constantly refining our overall systems.

Today, our management team and a research and training team facilitate the center's work. The management team, composed of the center director, research director, training director, financial officer, and associate director, meet regularly to plan, monitor progress, and oversee expenditures. The management team interacts on a regular basis with the larger research and training team, made up of project directors and staff who manage individual timelines and budgets, but also have the responsibility to improve overall systems.

Additional quality control comes from outside advisors. Initially external, input came from the RTCIL Regional Advisory Council, Region VII Rehabilitation Services Administration (RSA) office, Kansas IL center directors, site reviews, and national peer review team that were used to ensure needed and quality research, aid in the management of the center, and provide a strong measure of accountability. The

Regional Advisory Council and independent living center directors describe consumer needs, review research and training activities, recommend projects, and provide guidance for keeping programs relevant to independent living needs. The council also serves to disseminate information about center accomplishments. The Region VII RSA office assists with these functions and also works to coordinate center activities with rehabilitation agencies, advises the center on appointments and future directions, and shares current information from other research programs. Site teams and the national peer review team provide a close look at the center's organization, operation, and projects, and help us improve both the center and its projects.

From the start, we have actively disseminated our research products with the goal of knowledge utilization. We initially used familiar methods (e.g., mail, in-service training, conference calls) as well as University of Kansas courses that began incorporating our research starting in 1982 and continue to be taught today, such as ABS Independent Living and People with Disability. For product promotion, we sent periodic announcements, promotional brochures, press releases, and catalogs to particular target audiences. We also presented research findings and issue discussions of specific interest and importance to that field beginning in the spring of 1981 through our quarterly *Independent Times* (later the *Independent Living Forum*) newsletter.

This dissemination system has provided the means to disseminate well over a million products and even more through information technology such as the Internet via our on-line catalog and Research Information for Independent Living database. Our research also continues to be published in journals and presented at national professional conferences.

Although we have provided technical assistance in numerous ways, such as the train-the-trainer model, one of our most noteworthy methods was the National Conference on Independent Living, initially organized by Gary Clark to further bring the state-of-the-art practices together in 1982. Through the years, national figures such as George H. Bush and Bella Abzug as well as IL leaders including Ed Roberts, Irvin Zola, and Marca Bristo were among the many presenters. Mike Jones, as the RRTC training director in 1983, oversaw future conferences based in Washington, DC during the 1980s and worked diligently to provide accessible conferences. The National Council on Independent Living took over the leadership of this conference that served as a rallying point for passage of the Americans with Disability Act.

Through the Years

1980–1985

While experiencing initial growing pains, at the end of the 2nd year, five research projects had been completed, work was in progress on six other research projects, and eight new projects were being designed. Our initial concentration included research projects examining development of independence in adults with disabilities, the influence of family on IL, survival skills for women with disabilities, involvement of people with disabilities in ILC operation, development of state IL policies, peer counseling programs, survey of technology in IL, and support groups.

Among our first projects was the development of efficient and effective methods for evaluating independent living center programs and services. These "Standards for Independent Living Centers," a set of minimum compliance indicators, were used by the Rehabilitation Services Administration and are still in use today. Providing research-based materials for independent living centers has been a continual practice for the RTCIL. Some of our many projects for this target audience include an ILC orientation manual; resource manual to help ILCs establish a funding base of local, nongovernmental support; a directory describing peer counseling services; and survey of ILCs to identify problems in serving underserved populations. We have also maintained an ILC directory, developed an assessment of community economic impact fostered by ILCs, and provided centers with extensive technical assistance.

Another stand-out project from the early years resulted from the study of media portrayal of people with disabilities. The end product, *Guidelines for Reporting and Writing About People with Disabilities,* is in its sixth edition and has been adopted by over 40 national disability organizations as well as the American Association for Advancement of Science, National Rehabilitation Association, *Journal of the Association for Persons with Severe Handicaps, Rehabilitation Counseling Bulletin, Associated Press Stylebook,* and *American Psychological Association Publications Manual.*

1985–1990

A new core RRTC funding grant concentrated research in monitoring the state of IL, facilitating consumer self-help, and improving IL services. Because of the RTCIL location, the state of Kansas was often a research beneficiary. For example, Concerns Report data resulted in the purchase of a transportation van and computer training program in Douglas County, accessible housing renovation in Shawnee County, a support group for people with disabilities in their families in Harvey and Linn Counties, and a utility loan program for residents with disabilities in Wyandotte and Johnson County, and Cass, Clay, Jackson, and Platte Counties in Missouri.

RTCIL researchers also collaborated with the Kansas Advisory Committee for the Employment of the Handicapped (KACEH) in preparing a statewide survey of the concerns of over 1,400 disabled citizens in Kansas to help set an agenda for executive and legislative activity for state agencies and advocacy groups serving persons with disabilities. KACEH also used RTCIL data to develop a state law on public building accessibility and mandate that public meetings of executive agencies be held in accessible places.

In 1988, four new research projects were added to investigate the impact of improved disability housing options, increase utilization of accessible housing by people with disabilities, build mentor relationships, and create and maintain an effective consumer volunteer program in ILCs. Seven new training projects and two new materials development projects also were added and completed, including the personal attendant care management training model, which increased the capacity of consumers to manage attendants, thus reducing management problems and the chances of institutionalization. Another training goal met was the identification of applied strategies that deterred unlawful parking in handicapped-designated parking spaces.

By the end of the decade, we were offering more than 150 products in our catalog and had filled more than 245,000 requests for materials. More than 2,000 people received our quarterly newsletter highlighting RTCIL research, and we averaged about 40 training events a year. In 1989 alone, RTCIL staff logged over 1,100 hours of technical assistance contacts provided to over 4,050 individuals and organizations.

We also moved from our offices in Haworth Hall to the new Dole Human Development Center building next door. It was through the efforts of Glen White that the Dole Center installed access ramps for people with disabilities. He had discovered that the plans for the newly constructed Dole Center did not include curb cuts, a violation of The Americans with Disabilities Act that requires wheelchair accessibility for public buildings, and ensured their provision.

1990–1995

We made a major effort in 1990 to write the RRTC proposal for the next 5 years. It was one of the best, if the not the best, ever written at the RTCIL. However, the best grants don't always win. We contemplated and rejected a challenge in which we might have won the battle but not the war in the long run. With the loss of major funding, we had to cut back on everything, including the hardest: letting valued staff go.

Our strategy was to maintain a core staff of individuals who could rebuild funding and maintain a minimum level of research and service. With the survival of the RTCIL at stake, Mark Mathews, Fabricio Balcazar, Glen White, and myself all wrote grants that were funded for more than what would have resulted from a new core RRTC grant. The three grants included exemplary IL practices in rural areas (Mathews), consumer recruitment of mentors (Balcazar and White), and consumer control (Budde).

Also during the early 1990s, Schiefelbusch was recalled from retirement to direct the Lawrence Campus Gerontology Center. We talked with him about the potential of IL in the gerontology field; then, fortuitously, Paul Kennedy, the innovative director of the Topeka Veteran's Administration (VA) hospital, contacted us about conducting research at the hospital. The RTCIL and Schiefelbusch accepted his offer to both work half-time at his hospital and soon found the VA was based on a traditional medical model managed with a somewhat military management model.

With Kennedy, we wrote and collaborated on a number of grants such as the Gerontology Research Education Center (GREC), which involved the Leavenworth, Kansas City, and Topeka hospitals, and a study of policies and procedures that facilitate discharge placement in less costly and more IL alternatives. In addition, we conducted a consumer conference where veterans were enabled to exchange information with staff and voice concerns—just as we did in IL; however, this met with limited success. Our greatest successes came in the form of planting IL philosophies and practices within services. We also met a number of consultants such as Rue Cromwell and graduate students who would play key roles in our next NIDRR RRTC grant.

During the last few months at the VA, we decided to respond to the request for proposal (RFP) on a RRTC for underserved populations and IL. One of our first efforts was to define the underserved population, which we determined were three key populations who had brain injury, psychiatric disability, or mental retardation (now called "intellectual disability"). Mathews took responsibility for the head injury core, Cromwell for the psychiatric disability area, and I for the intellectual disability area. With the help of Pam Willits and her staff, we edited, refined, produced, and forwarded the grant to NIDRR. Our efforts were rewarded: The application was successful and was funded to begin in October 1993.

The new Research and Training Center on Independent Living for Underserved Populations was designed to systematically address the many issues that would enable individuals from underserved populations to have opportunities to live independently. To achieve the mission and meet the NIDRR priorities for the underserved populations, six research and eight training projects were expedited by consumer-empowered teams that included consumer–consultants, advocate leaders, and IL experts in addition to researchers, trainers, and media personnel. Most products were developed around the concept that IL services do not need to be changed but rather augmented with accommodations for consumers from the underserved populations. Research projects included an IL needs assessment for underserved populations, assistive technology skills training for consumers with psychiatric disabilities, service accommodation for consumers with cognitive and intellectual disabilities, and facilitation of effective board skills for underserved IL populations.

1995–2000

In 1998, as we continued our research concentration on underserved disability populations, we began our Research Information for Independent

Living project (RIIL). With the Independent Living Research Utilization (ILRU) Program of The Institute for Rehabilitation and Research (TIRR), we worked to improve access and use of research information by people with disabilities and other nonresearcher stakeholders involved in the independent living, disability rights, and rehabilitation fields. Approaches used by RIIL include Webcasts, listservs, a review guide, and the interactive Internet database (*http://www.getriil.org*) that contains 2,000 research summaries on key IL topics.

2000–2005

Starting in January of 2001, with NIDRR funding, we built on previous research and expanded to include a new Rehabilitation Research and Training Center on Full Participation in Independent Living with a 5-year, $2.5 million NIDRR grant. Our initial research focused on learning how to get people with disabilities to participate fully in society, determining at what level they do participate, and identifying groups that may be underserved. The four core areas of research for the center have been increasing knowledge about disability; community participation and wellness; cultural independent living accommodations, and personal and systems advocacy with results readily available on our web site. Glen White, principal investigator for the new center, led a research team of co-investigators that included Michael Fox, David Gray, Daryl Mellard, Katherine Froehlich Grobe, Tom Seekins, Fabricio Balcazar, and myself. White also assumed a new leadership in 2002 when be became director of the RTCIL as I began a partial retirement and assumed the title of founder and past director.

Our research was directed toward 1) greater community participation (e.g., a qualitative interview study regarding barriers to full participation in IL); 2) the changing universe of disability (e.g., a population-based analysis to identify and to better understand emerging populations of persons with disabilities, such as those with chronic fatigue syndrome and violence-induced neurological impairments); 3) personal and systems advocacy (e.g., evaluation of cost-effective advocacy methods, and evaluation of a tribal disability concerns report method for community disability planning and building tribal disability action agendas); and 4) community participation and wellness (e.g., identification of exemplary ways to use peer networks and communication channels to enhance and maintain health and wellness for people with disabilities).

One full participation project, Self-Advocacy Training for Students with Disabilities, was completed by Yen Vo, a resident of Vietnam, who received a Ford Foundation International Fellowship in 2001 and came to the university to obtain her master's degree. Vo, at the RTCIL, researched a design for postsecondary students to lobby effectively for better accommodations at the University of Kansas, Emporia State University, and Washburn University. Her work has been made into a manual and also is being made into an on-line class.

Another exciting research project funded by a $615,000, 3-year grant from the Centers for Disease Control and Prevention through the Association of Teachers of Preventive Medicine in Washington, D.C. began in 2002. The research team, including Catherine "Cat" Rooney, project coordinator of our "Nobody Left Behind" project, investigated 30 randomly selected United States counties, cities, parishes, and boroughs where a natural or man-made disaster occurred between 1999 and 2004 to determine whether disaster plans and emergency response systems met the needs of people with mobility impairments.

Early results of the study were presented at the first Conference on Emergency Preparedness for People with Disabilities, supported by the United States Department of Homeland Security with the National Organization on Disability on September 23 in Arlington, Virginia. Through our Web survey, too, we have heard of the many public buildings with inaccessible escape routes, the lack of accessible transportation after a disaster event, and other problems. Because there is virtually no empirical data on the safe and efficient evacuation of persons with disabilities in disaster planning, we hope this study will lead to a national model that can prevent death and injury for this population in future disaster situations.

Looking Back While Looking Ahead

The RTCIL was conceived as a center without walls that would do what was necessary to enhance the IL field and the lives of individuals with disabilities. In this synergistic environment, consumers, researchers, trainers, and policy makers have worked to produce much more than they could have as individuals or groups. One of our greatest resources has been our department affiliations and talented staff.

It should also be noted that our support systems have had the mission to support research, training, and dissemination so that the center goals were achieved effectively and efficiently. Leadership in these systems was also key. Pam Willits is but one example. She has not only provided exemplary grants management, but created an effective, functional system to produce grants in a timely manner for over 20 years. Pam and I have often reflected that we are like a couple of old farmers working together to get the job done right the first time: You need a strong work ethic, you need to work with others, and you need to be just a tad bit stubborn about doing it right. Everyone is a link in the chain and is as important as any other on the RTCIL team.

Some former RTCIL staff have launched research in other fields at the University of Kansas, such as Steve Fawcett, founder and director of the nationally recognized Work Group on Health Promotion and Community Development; Jennifer Lattimore, research assistant professor; Jean Ann Summers, associate research professor; Ann Turnbull, co-director of the Beach Center on Families and Disability; and Mark Mathews, professor of applied behavioral science and associate director of the Gerontology Center. Other valued colleagues include:

Yolanda Suarez-Balcazar, associate professor, Department of Occupational Therapy, College of Applied Health Sciences, University of Illinois at Chicago;

Fabricio Balcazar, associate professor in the Department of Disability and Human Development at the College of Associated Health Professions and an associate professor in the Department of Psychology at the University of Illinois at Chicago;

Michael Jones, vice president for research and technology at the Shepherd Center in Atlanta, GA, and co-director of the Rehabilitation Engineering Research Center on Mobile Wireless Technologies Design;

Barbara Bradford Knowlen, founder of Barriers Breakers, which provides benefits counseling, assistance, training, in Oriskany Falls, New York, and author of the *How To Kick Ass and Win* manual;

Howard Moses, who served in key IL leadership positions within the Rehabilitation Services Administration and NIDRR;

Ray Petty, a disability consultant who has been involved in disability rights through research, the Kansas Commission on Disability Concerns, executive director of two ILCs; the Kansas Department of Health and Environment; and Kansas' Special Education Advisory Committee;

Todd Risley, professor of psychology at University of Alaska and author of more than 100 professional articles and book chapters and five books and monographs;

Tom Seekins, director of the Rural Institute on Disabilities (http://www. umt.edu) at the University of Montana since 1993; and

Gary Ulicny, president and chief executive office of Shepherd Center.

In 1980 when we first implemented the RTCIL, there really wasn't any IL knowledge base. The progress of the RTCIL over the past 25 years has contributed greatly to the IL knowledge base and is due to all of the fine people who have worked so hard at all levels of the RTCIL. Our grants have totaled over $16,945,000 and we have disseminated close to 2 million intervention products. We are proud to have contributed to the success of the more than 300 ILC in the United States and countless international organizations and also to have furthered IL for the millions of people with disabilities. Although I knew intuitively in 1979 that the ILC model would make a major impact in the world, I had no idea of the tremendous impact that it would make in both the disability and other fields as well.

We look ahead to an even brighter tomorrow, when individuals with disabilities will fully participate and contribute to their communities. We welcome new and exciting challenges that will allow us to use innovative ideas and quality research to develop and test interventions and new knowledge that will be disseminated broadly through new modes of information technology. We also look forward to new colleagues who will dedicate themselves to this important work.

Acknowledgments

This chapter is dedicated to the leaders, consumers, colleagues, and fallen heroes who have contributed unselfishly to the independent living knowledge base and to the formation and support of the RTCIL.

21

The Child Language Doctoral Program

MABEL L. RICE AND RICHARD L. SCHIEFELBUSCH

Research and research training activities within the Bureau of Child Research (BCR) have always included students at various stages of their training. The student's research skills were enhanced by research training grants, as well as by numerous seminars and colloquia, offered by the BCR in collaboration with their colleagues in the academic departments. For the most part, these arrangements went smoothly. However, certain graduate students who had come to the University of Kansas (KU) explicitly to earn graduate degrees in speech-language-hearing seemed concerned that content areas alluded to in the books and articles published at KU, for a national and international audience, did not match the content offerings of the academic department. Apparently, at that time, research protocols were more "interdisciplinary" than were the departmental curricular offerings. The only convenient way to adjust this reality for the student's purposes was to convene a special committee from several departments to design a special program for each innovative student—hardly a practical solution!

Since there were already several students wanting an interdisciplinary program of study and apparently there would be more in the future, it seemed desirable to develop an interdisciplinary curriculum. Students and faculty created informal discussion committees that eventually led to plans for a Child Language Doctoral Program. These events began as early as 1978 and continued until the new program was completed. The 1981–1983 group of language researchers who designed the Child Language Doctoral Program were from the Departments of Speech-Language-Hearing, Psychology, Linguistics, Human Development, and Special Education, and the Bureau of Child Research. As a theoretical and empirical base was established, the developers also sought out related disciplines of cognitive psychology, anthropology, and sociology. Child language at that time, of course, was a growing and productive area of research and scholarship that addressed questions regarding the nature of child language and how it is acquired. All of the disciplines contributed to both the basic and applied literature of child language. Models of the normal sequence of language acquisition were used as referents for determining the presence of language disorders.

The most active staff contributors were Frances Ingeman, linguistics; Susan Kemper, psychology; Mabel Rice, speech-language-hearing; John Wright, human development; and Richard Schiefelbusch, Bureau of Child Research. In addition, the proponents of the Child Language Doctoral Program were advised and encouraged in substantial ways by Frances Horowitz, vice chancellor for research, graduate studies, and human services. The student point of view was ably presented by Etti Dromi, now head of the Speech-Language-Hearing Program at the University of Tel Aviv; Amy Finch-Williams, now at Ft. Hays State University; Mike Cosby, now at Michigan State University; Mary Ann Romski, now at Georgia State University; Ann Kaiser, now at Vanderbilt University; and Steve Warren, now the director of the Life Span Institute.

The faculty used a range of theoretical approaches in the study of language and language disorders. Students and faculty of child language alike had available to them a rich variety of tools and databases. They drew upon well-established research facilities and field sites in pursuing their own research. Seminars in child language research, a proseminar in child language, workshops on special issues in language acquisition and intervention, and research practica were regularly held by KU faculty members and visiting experts. The principal investigators of the research projects were affiliated with the program in research training and language implementation.

The final version of the proposal for A Child Language Program was submitted to the Graduate School on October 7, 1981. The proposal was for the program to be housed in the College of Liberal Arts and Sciences, affiliated with four academic departments: human development and family life, linguistics, psychology, and speech-language-hearing. The approval process involved endorsement by each of the affiliated departments and various other committees. The interdisciplinary committee undertook the lengthy procedures involved in gaining the necessary approvals within the KU system and other settings where child language research was taking place. In this hierarchy of events, the Kansas Board of Regents gave the final approval. Perhaps the most complicated part of this approval effort, however, was the relationships within the relevant academic committees of the university. During the time of committee discourse, we sent a copy of our Child Language Program to a select group of academic and scientific leaders so as to secure their opinion and possible advice. The most helpful reply came from Roger Brown of Harvard University; however, it was not sent to us, but to Frances Horowitz, in the Graduate School:

Dear Frances,

There is no doubt in my mind that the proposed program in Child Language makes good sense both intellectually and vocationally and no doubt either that the University of Kansas has a faculty extraordinarily well qualified to carry out such a program. Indeed, seeing all the distinguished names listed together is quite overwhelming, and it would be so to prospective students and their advisers—which is part of the point.

Like many of the external scholars who wrote in favor of the program, I asked myself: "Why not here (Harvard)? Either today or in the past." Why should Melissa Bowerman, now at Kansas and one of the leading researchers in the world in child language, have to take a degree that reads "Social Psychology"? I think I know why it has not and does not happen here. The scholars interested in child language are, as with you, dispersed across several departments and even schools. Two problems do follow from this fact here but perhaps—probably—do not, at Kansas. If a program in child language were proposed to the relevant departments here, each would become greatly concerned that the graduates of such a program not be permitted to bypass any of the more difficult (especially if also distasteful) departmental requirements. The graduates must be fully credible psychologists, linguists, speech pathologists, etc. all at once. Impossible. Thirty years ago, Social Relations and Linguistics experimented with such a program here and the requirements were almost endless. Only two people took that degree: Jean Berko Gleason and Eric Lenneberg. Evidently the survivors had great adaptive powers, but few applied and fewer survived. The Kansas Departments seem to have risen above this kind of professional territoriality and the Program is both possible and well conceived.

The other problem that Departments can create is a little more subtle. A program of the kind described probably cannot succeed unless some minimal number of faculty members thinks of it as their primary affiliation. The affirmative pull of Departments is difficult to beat; they control resources and appointments. Simple physical propinquity and disciplinary socialization are also factors. What I take to be an extremely auspicious sign in this connection for Kansas is the quality of the proposal submitted. The proposal makes its case like a good lawyer's brief. There are letters from external scholars, evidence of employment prospects, student questionnaire results, titles of relevant dissertations, etc. This is a level of preparation unprecedented in my experience. Somebody—several or many bodies—has or have done a great deal of work. If I were in your position, I could not say no to so much impetus.

Roger Brown

The formidable group of faculty that Brown alluded to gave the proposal serious scrutiny. The plan was to use course offerings already available in the cooperating departmental graduate catalogues, to be supplemented by the development of new symposia by interested faculty. Our plan involved no new funding from university resources. A total of 27 faculty members indicated an interest in volunteering their efforts in the new interdisciplinary program. Approval was secured within the allocated time frame. The Board of Regents soon concurred. It is interesting to recall that the same week that the Regent's approval was transmitted to us we received notification that three federally funded Graduate Training Grants also had been approved. Furthermore, these grant approvals permitted us to undertake the timely task of seeking additional enrollees in the new doctoral program the following year! Mabel Rice soon became the director of the Child

Language Doctoral Program and Susan Kemper became the faculty representative to the Graduate School. The program promptly moved into fast forward. The practice of involving students in planning committee meetings continued. The cross-disciplinary Child Language Proseminar was added to the curriculum (co-taught by Susan Kemper, Clifton Pye, and Mabel Rice), cross-listed across the four sponsoring academic departments. It has been continuously offered in the more than 20 years since then.

Early on students were included in a second venture, a plan for a national conference project to be called The Teachability of Language. The actual conference was held in 1986. This conceptual, interdisciplinary model included the analysis of variables that influence the learning of language and that concurrently determine how it can be facilitated.

The Teachability of Language Model has three basic premises: The *language variability* thesis holds that the study of language development and language disorders must address significant sources of variation in language. These include accounting for variation within and across languages in terms of semantic variability, syntactic variability, and pragmatic variability. This variability within-English is mirrored across languages.

The second thesis is that of *learner variability*, which holds that the study of language development and language disorders must address significant sources of variation in language learners. These include accounting for both atypical patterns and typical patterns of development. Atypical language development in this context refers to a host of biological and psychological risk factors, which may influence the nature of language development. Such risk factors include prematurity, developmental delay, and specific-language development. Additional psychological variables that affect language development include variations across cognitive/developmental stages and the variations reflecting individual differences in cognitive processes and structures.

The third thesis of the teachability model is that of *environmental variability*, which suggests that the study of language development and language disorders must account for the effects of significant variations in the context of language development. While some contexts may promote language development for some children, other contexts may impede language development and foster language disorders. Conversely, variations in the environmental context of language may be designed to provide enrichments and interventions to remediate language disorders.

Brown's praiseful statements were useful and gratifying but they did not shield us from major changes that soon appeared in the collaborating disciplines and subdisciplines. These changes called for new integrative research in the fields of genetics and the environment. In 1993, Mabel Rice, director of the Child Language Doctoral Program, developed a language conference that included representatives from several relevant areas in the field of language acquisition and language disability. The conference resulted in a book in 1996, *Toward a Genetics of Language*, which was a call to arms for scientists from the following academic areas: genetics, behavioral genetics, linguistics, language acquisition, language impairment, and brain imaging. She explained that the purpose of the conference was to report and share across the disciplines so as to combine the information and to develop strategies for future interdisciplinary designs.

In the context of emerging work on genetics, the conceptual framework of language teachability was adjusted to include the biogenetic as well as behavioral dimensions of language intervention. In Rice's book she writes:

> There is an important distinction between the minimal conditions necessary for the activation of language for most children and the maximal conditions necessary for the support of language for children with limited language aptitude. Children with Specific Language Impairment (SLI) need environmental enhancements at the earliest possible ages. The implication from this work is that other children may have other genetically induced problems that require special developmental and environmental designers. (p. xvii)

Six years later, in 2002, a second conference was held under the auspices of the Merrill Advanced Studies Center entitled, "The Relationship of Genes, Environments, and Developmental Language Disorders: Research for the Twenty-First Century." The invited participants received the following message along with the invitation:

In the last ten years, we have experienced significant advances in our understanding of language disorders of children. Both inherited and environmental factors now complete the picture of human development and disability. Research programs that focus on a specific clinical area, such as Williams Syndrome, autism, or Specific Language Impairment, however, often have limited scientific knowledge. This conference is designed to bridge the gaps and build a unified theoretical framework on language and developmental disabilities across clinical populations. By bringing together experts in genetics, neuroscience, and behavioral development, we expect to find answers about: characteristics that the disorders share; the unique aspects of each disorder; and the reasons for shared characteristics among disorders. The ultimate purpose of this inquiry is to create more effective treatments for persons with disabilities.

Papers from the conference were subsequently published (Rice & Warren, 2004).

At this point in the discussion about the Child Language Doctoral Program it should be apparent that the interdisciplinary strategies that are used today do more than combine and share; they also create and evaluate. Evidence already exists that the Child Language Doctoral Program displays the arrangements for career-long distinguished work for students and the current and future staff alike. Currently the program offers students a wide choice of tools, facilities, and field sites including the Child Language Acquisition Studies Lab, which has the largest known archive of transcribed spontaneous samples from preschool children diagnosed as receptive/expressive specific language impaired. Research sites and practica are provided by the Life Span Institute, the Language Acquisition Preschool, and the clinical and research facilities of the Speech-Language-Hearing Clinic. This includes the following labs: Neurodevelopmental Disorders Lab (Steven Warren), Early Language Lab (Nancy Brady), Language and Reading Disabilities Lab (Hugh Catts), Word and Sound Learning Lab (Holly Storkel), and The Spoken Language Lab (Michael Vitevitch). The Child Language Program has been continuously funded by highly competitive National Institutes of Health training grants for more than 20 years. A total of 33 predoctoral and 27 postdoctoral trainees have been supported. Graduates of the program include colleagues in academic and research positions around the world, including administrators at the levels of dean and provost. The graduates maintain active communication networks via electronic communication networks dedicated to the group. In multiple ways, the dialogues started in planning for the Child Language Doctoral Program and in the ongoing implementation of the program are proving to be productive and long-lasting.

References

Rice, M. L. (Ed.). (1996). *Toward a genetics of language.* Mahwah, NJ: Erlbaum.

Rice, M. L., & Warren, S. F. (Eds.). (2004). *Developmental language disorders: From phenotypes to etiologies.* Mahwah, NJ: Erlbaum.

22

The Merrill Advanced Studies Center

MABEL L. RICE AND RICHARD L. SCHIEFELBUSCH

The Merrill Advanced Studies Center (MASC) was created in 1990 by a generous gift from Virginia and Fred Merrill of Leawood, Kansas. The center supports dynamic programs designed to stimulate advances in research across the human life span. In contemporary scientific pursuits, the development of successful collaborative research projects builds on a widespread community of scientific endeavor that extends beyond local resources. The MASC provides the mechanism to bring together scientists with similar interests, in both electronic and face-to-face conferences. These forums allow for scientific dialogues that lead to important new discoveries and opportunities for collaborative inquiry. These occasions serve to bring to the attention of local (University of Kansas, KU) scientists important new developments happening elsewhere, and to highlight notable KU-sponsored projects to visiting scholars.

Under the sponsorship of the MASC, KU experts can target a topic to be examined in cross-disciplinary contexts. By bringing local scholars together with noted national and international experts, common themes and collaborative approaches to research can be explored. Such occasions can lead to the development of collaborative proposals, joint publications, and a framework for continued interactions.

The MASC emerged during a period of major changes in the Kansas Center. The Bureau of Child Research had recently been renamed the Schiefelbusch Institute for Life Span Studies, and at roughly the same time Dick Schiefelbusch retired and Stephen R. Schroeder became the director of the institute. A third major event was the occupancy of the Dole Center for Human Development, located in a large new building adjacent to the Stewart Wing of Haworth Hall. The MASC was eventually provided space on the third floor of the Dole Building. When the MASC was first announced in late 1989, Dick Schiefelbusch was acting director of the Life Span Institute, the Gerontology Center, which was moving into the Dole Building, and the Merrill Center. Steve Schroeder, at the time, was preparing to move from Ohio State University to Kansas but was not expected to arrive in Kansas until early fall 1990. Also, all of the aspects of major changes were in the air, in the hallways, and in the protocols of the several research programs and academic departments soon to be located in the Dole Building. Literally, 21 years of tightly compacted arrangements were being expanded and reconfigured!

Steve Schroeder, director of the Life Span Institute, formed the initial "long-range" planning committee for the MASC in the fall of 1990. A report of the committee's work was made available on February 5, 1991. The committee (Frances Horowitz, Kathleen McCluskey-Fawcett, Dick Schiefelbusch, and Bob Senecal) were the recipients of the following information: "Enclosed is a draft brochure for our proposed Merrill Advanced Studies Center of the Schiefelbusch Institute for Life Span Studies. I would like to invite you to be part of a second planning committee, to set an agenda for 1991 and get this Center rolling in earnest." The brochure included the what, when, where, and why of the center. The brochure also included the mission statement, the professional profile, the program development objectives, and the initial thrust statement. In addition, the brochure included the initial plans for the Esther Katz Rosen Conference on Giftedness. Thus the center was officially launched.

The Initial Thrust

The second meeting of the Long-Term Planning Committee of the MASC was on February 19, 1991. The minutes of this meeting included the following information:

> The Inaugural Event for the Merrill Advanced Studies Center is set for Tuesday, March 5, 1991. Elizabeth Dole will be the keynote speaker. The Merrills will fly her in their private plane. The exact time, titles, and details of her visit are yet to be worked out, but her

visit will likely entail: (a) Time with Chancellor Budig; (b) time with the Merrills, and perhaps others; (c) an invited luncheon at the Alumni Center; (d) a dedication and keynote address in a large auditorium; and (e) tour of the Dole Human Development Center. Frances will call Elizabeth to get title and timelines.

The Merrill Advanced Studies Center brochure draft was approved with minor alterations and should be distributed at the luncheon and dedication on March 5, 1991. Plans for the next two Advanced Study topics will be: *Life Span: The New Initiative* for 1992 and *Communications and Language* for 1993.

On September 1993, Steve Schroeder sent a letter to the Merrills:

It has been several months now since the last Esther Katz Rosen Conference on Giftedness in February which the Merrill Advanced Studies Center cosponsors with the American Psychological Association. This conference series has received national attention and has been so successful that the American Psychological Foundation has renewed its grant support for another three years. So these February conferences will continue. I have more good news. Mabel Rice has agreed to become the director of the Merrill Advanced Studies Center. Mabel is currently the director of the Child Language Doctoral Program and Professor of Speech, Language, and Hearing at KU. Mabel is an international leading researcher in Speech and Language, Science and Disorders. She is the ideal person to direct the Merrill Advanced Studies Center. I would also like to make a public announcement of Mabel's appointment at a Merrill Center conference that Mabel has organized for November 11 and 12, 1993 on the Genetics of Language. This will be an outstanding conference, which will convene the main researchers in the United States on this topic. We would like to hold a dinner on the evening of November 11 or 12 with you and your family as our guests, at which we would announce Mabel as the new director of the Merrill Advanced Studies Center. We would like to recognize this event as the kick-off of the second phase in our long-term plan for developing the Merrill Advanced Studies Center.

Prior to Mabel Rice's appointment, there had been committee discussions and, before that, recommendations from Dick Schiefelbusch to

Steve Schroeder, that were discussed at length. In a period of less than 4 years, we had discussed many options—Schiefelbusch's options in 1989 and 1990 and Schroeder's in 1991 and 1992. Rice's options emerged in 1995. This brief chronology of events should be used to acknowledge the earnestness and the enthusiasm of our efforts. However, we should also acknowledge that the products of our committee meetings and our frequent discussions placed the work of the center largely in the future tense. Mabel Rice in a director's report to the Merrill Board introduced a new phase in October 12, 1995.

Under the heading of a *Director's Report,* Mabel Rice explained, "The purpose of this document is to summarize progress to date on the mission-related activities, and to project a plan for future developments. In effect, this constitutes architecture for building the future."

Organization of the Planning: An Overview

The building of the MASC can be thought of as four phases. In Phase 1: First Conferences, the early foundations have been laid. The MASC has sponsored three top-quality conferences that have been held or scheduled for the immediate future. In Phase 2: Conference Support System, a management plan for the sponsorship of conferences will be implemented in which there is an annual call for conference proposals, and a conference staff in place for coordination of the conference logistics. Central to this phase will be the development of an Internet dissemination system for reporting on the conference, the participants, outcomes, and future directions, to provide worldwide recognition of the work of the MASC.

In Phase 3: Visiting Conference Organizer, the system implemented in Phase 2 will be enhanced by one or more visiting scholars whose visit to the KU campus will be focused on the preparation and presentation of a conference. The visiting scholar will serve as a catalyst for discussions, planning sessions, new scientific insights, and integration of the work of local scholars with that of the visitors. In Phase 4: Conference Center, the existing operational structures will be enhanced by the development of a conference center building, to serve as a physical home for the support staff and visiting scholars, and as a suitable setting for study and reflection, small and large group discussions, and a moderate-sized conference setting.

Throughout these four phases, the commitment will be to the highest quality of scientific inquiry and discourse, the synthesis of emerging scientific findings with high relevance for understanding and remediating developmental disorders, the identification of important clinical issues worthy of targeted scientific investigation, the formulation of social policies of import for advocacy and intervention, and the development of the highest quality of scientific products in the way of printed materials and electronic dissemination on the information highway. In a real way, the outcomes are headed toward science with social relevancy.

Report on Conferences: 1995

For four years, the MASC co-sponsored the Katz–Rosen Symposium on Giftedness, with funds leveraged from the American Psychology Foundation. Next year (1996) is the final year unless other grant funds are found. The symposium proceedings will be published by the American Psychology Foundation as a two-volume set in 1996.

The first fully sponsored conference, Toward a Genetics of Language, was held in the fall of 1993, organized by Mabel Rice. This was an important scientific occasion in which international experts in genetics and language were brought together for the purpose of sharing new information and identifying new lines of inquiry. The group of participants also included local faculty scholars and students interested in language acquisition and impairments. The conference led to new professional collaborations, and the development of an edited volume, to be published by Lawrence Erlbaum Press in February 1996.

A third conference is scheduled for May 1996. This is the Third International Conference on Communication, Aging and Health. The conference organizer, Mary Lee Hummert, is a member of the Gerontology Center and a prominent scholar in the area. The work of Susan Kemper is also featured. The plan is for an edited volume of key papers from the conference.

Report of Conferences: 1997

Two Conferences were discussed at the MASC Board meeting on March 31, 1997. One was a Conference proposed by Sue Kemper—

Resolving the Communication Predicament of Aging to be held in Sedona, Arizona. This conference would involve some of the same people who participated in the 1996 Merrill-supported conference on Communication, Aging and Health, and would, in many ways, be a continuation of that conference.

It was announced, also, that the Merrill Center would be sponsoring a conference on "Planning for the Research Mission of Public Universities in the 21st Century," to be held at the Barn, a bed and breakfast retreat center, in Valley Falls on June 11–12, 1997. Board Members then moved to the Computer Applications Conference Room for a guided tour of the MASC website.

At the MASC Board meeting on September 18, Mabel Rice gave an overview of the conference—Planning for the Research Mission of Public Universities in the 21st Century. Participants appreciated this event's small, regional nature. The remoteness of the Barn seemed to make it easier for everyone to focus on the issues at hand. The overwhelming feeling of the attendees was that this should become an annual event.

The attendees at the three-day meeting at the Barn were drawn from four research universities in the region, Kansas, Missouri, Nebraska and Oklahoma. The intent was to bring together administrators and researcher-scientists for the purpose of informal discussions that would lead to the identification of pressing issues, different perspectives, and plans for the enhancement of research productivity. The following observations evolved from the papers and the discussions:

> "This is a time of intense pressure on the research mission of higher education. The pressure comes from multiple sources. First, in a time of reduced fiscal resources, there is a need for externally generated funding in order to support an on-going research enterprise. At the same time, these resources are more scarce, more competitive, and under heavy competition from prestigious research centers/ academic units. This situation in turn creates university-wide pressures on academic administrators and researchers. At the same time, the traditional academic departments follow the more conventional disciplinary boundaries. If research growth is to be achieved at the boundaries of the disciplines, it brings a world view often at odds with departmental priorities."

Four panel discussions were held during the conference. Chancellor, Researcher, Dean, and Vice-Chancellor/Provost panels focused on four defining issues:

- The challenge to encourage colleagues invested in traditional, conservative disciplinary boundaries to engage in more flexible, cross-disciplinary configurations of research enterprise.
- The need for externally generated funding in order to support an on-going research enterprise.
- The demands on researchers to be available for training graduate students in the laboratory and instructing undergraduate students on a more didactic level.
- The need to educate the public and non-participating regular faculty as to the highly technical, substantive and financial realities of today's externally funded research programs.

Special Note: Chancellor Hemmenway and Provost Shulenburger attended the panel meetings. This conference retreat resulted in the first of eight annual White Paper publications on topics of interest to the administrative and scientific domains of regional universities.

Director's Report for 1998

The MASC sponsored two Conferences in 1998. On March 15–18, 1998, a conference entitled "Constraints on Language: Grammar, Memory, and Aging," was held in Sedona, Arizona. This was an academic scientific conference with leading scholars in the topical area who convened to present formal talks and engage in informal discussions of research developments in the area of language change with aging. Klewer Academic Publishers published the conference proceedings in 1999. The conference organizers, Susan Kemper and Reinhold Kliegl of the University of Potsdam, edited it.

Our other conference was the second in what is shaping up as a series of regional conferences dedicated to developing the research potential for the public universities in Kansas, Nebraska, Missouri, Oklahoma, and Iowa. "Mobilizing the Research Opportunities in the Next Century" was held on July 15–17, 1998, at the Barn in Valley Falls, Kansas. This conference consisted of informal presentations by academic administrators, including the chancellors and provosts from Kansas and Nebraska, and academic deans from Kansas, Nebraska and Missouri, along with leading researchers and scholars. This year we invited an outside speaker, Mike Crow, of Columbia University. The conference proceedings will appear in a White Paper to be distributed by the end of 1998 in a hard copy version and an electronic version posted on the World Wide Web.

Director's Report for 1999

Building Cross-University Alliances That Enhance Research

On July 26–28, 1999 the MASC of the University of Kansas will host a regional Conference at the Barn in Valley Falls, Kansas. This informal Retreat will bring together university administrators and researchers for the purpose of discussing ways to enhance research productivity through cross-university alliances. The third annual event will build on discussions from past years. This year, top administrators from Iowa State University and Kansas State University will also attend. The keynote speaker is Luis Proenza, president of the University of Akron and former Vice Chancellor for Research at Purdue. He will discuss his experiences as a research administrator building cross-university linkages in the Big Ten.

Conferences

Self-Injurious Behavior, Mental Retardation and Autism

December 6–7, 1999—(Planned by Steve Schroeder)
The 1999 Merrill Conference in Rockville, Maryland brought together 25 of the leading scholars on self-injurious behavior. Researchers discussed the genetic, neurological and behavioral causes and treatments for self-injurious behavior, a problem that affects 5–17% of persons with mental retardation and autism. The ultimate goal of the 1999 Merrill Conference was to produce multidisciplinary models for more effective treatment. The conference was co-sponsored by the National Institute of Child Health and Human Development of the NIH. The resulting book was edited by Stephen Schroeder, Mary Lou Oster-Granite and Travis

Thompson. It was published by the American Psychological Association.

Director's Report for 2000

Principles for Emerging Systems of Scholarly Publishing (Tempe, Arizona, March 2–4)

The Association of American Universities, The Association of Research Libraries and the Merrill Advanced Studies Center sponsored the meeting. The meeting was held to facilitate discussion among the various academic stakeholders in the scholarly publishing process and to build consensus on a set of principles that could guide the transformation of the scholarly publishing system. Nine principles were developed and subsequently used to form plans for collaboration among relevant National Committees and Boards.

Fourth Annual Summer Conference on "Making Research a Part of the Public Agenda"

On June 7–9, 2000 The Merrill Center at the University of Kansas hosted a regional Conference at the Barn in Valley Falls, Kansas. The informal retreat brought together university administrators, researchers, and policy leaders for the purpose of making university research part of the public agenda. This fourth annual event was built on the experience of past years. The event had grown in scope to include 5 universities in the region: the University of Nebraska, the University of Missouri, Iowa State University, Kansas State University and the University of Kansas and KU Med.

Fifth Annual Summer Conference (2001): "Evaluating Research Productivity"

This Conference, held June 13–15, 2001, focused on the keynote speaker, Joan Lordon, Associate Provost for Research and Dean of the Graduate School University of Alabama at Birmingham. For our group, she provided a valuable overview of key elements to consider when selecting measures for evaluating performance, with a focus on the very important National Research Council (NRC) study. With this starting point, our conference participants elaborated and expanded on issues of research evaluation from the perspective of research administrators, faculty researchers, provosts, and the Executive director of the Kansas Board of Regents.

Biomedical Research Initiatives in Kansas City, Sept. 17–29, 2001

A meeting of the Kansas City Coalition for Excellence in Life Sciences (KC-CELS): Tempe Mission Palms Hotel. Sponsored by the Merrill Advanced Studies Center and the Kansas City Area Life Sciences Institute.

The conference created five work groups: Marketing, Scientists Talking and Working Together, Key Enabling Technologies, Workforce Development and Graduate Education Issues, Interface of Top Level and Individual Investigator Participation. Significant planning and development conferences and events have followed from this conference. The current expectations are for linkages between scientists in the greater Kansas City area and economic interests in Missouri and Kansas will result in a major corridor for research in the life sciences.

The Sixth Annual Summer Conference (2002): "Science at a Time of National Emergency"

The keynote speech was presented by Martin Apple, President of the Council of Scientific Society Presidents: "Science at a Time of National Emergency." He said, "*Universities must restore their role as bold big picture innovators. Our Universities must confidently collaborate with all other key institutions including government. Universities need to develop a 21st century social contract with society, industry, and virtual education.*"

Twenty-six participants identified a number of ways that scientists can come to the aid of the country, while also noting the difficulties and expense of increased security at the universities. We found a number of complementary strengths between institutions in the area of food safety and crisis management that will be the basis of collaboration in the next few years. We benefited from an unusually strong group of faculty participants as well as key administrators from the KU Medical Center, Kansas State University, Iowa State University, The University of Nebraska Medical Center, and the University of Nebraska at Lincoln.

Director's Report for 2002

Summary of Activities in 2002

Steven Warren and Mabel Rice directed the first of two conferences on "The Relationship of Genes, Environments, and Developmental Language Disorders" on May 2–4, 2002 in Tempe, Arizona. Seventeen scientists from across the country presented their research and discussed a unified framework on language that may prove useful for several clinical populations, including children with Down syndrome, Williams syndrome, Fragile X, specific language impairment and autism. This work spans the fields of linguistics, special education, psychology, neuroscience, medicine and genetics. Judith Cooper and Peggy McCardle from NIH participated and have agreed to co-sponsor the follow-up conference in May 2003.

Director's Report for 2003

Summary of Activities in 2003—Three Conferences

A. Regional Policy Retreat

2003 marked the seventh annual retreat in our series the Research Mission of Public Universities. The topic was: "The Recruiting and Training of Future Scientists: How Policy Shapes The Mission of Graduate Education." Twenty-three administrators and senior faculty came as teams from universities in the Midwest to discuss this topic. Two keynote speakers provided views from the top leadership levels in the United States and Canada.

B. Scholarly Conferences

Hugh Catts, KU Professor of Speech-Language-Hearing, directed a conference on "The Connections between Language and Reading Disabilities: Current Findings and Future Directions." A book on this topic is underway. Reid Lyon, an adviser to the Bush Administration on child development and education policies, participated in the conference and is writing the foreword to the book. He is a branch NIH chief in the National Institute of Child Health and Human Development.

Steven Warren and Mabel Rice directed the second conference of a two-part series on "The Relationship of Genes, Environments, and Developmental Language Disorders." This conference took place September 11–13 in Tempe, Arizona and involved the same group of scholars first assembled on May 2–4, 2002. From this second conference, several of the scholars are writing articles for a special issue of the journal *Applied Linguistics;* it will be devoted to a special topic "Language Impairment in Children: Current Status and Future Needs" and will be published next winter.

Project Activities for 2004

Modeling Developmental Processes in Ecological Context

(a conference sponsored by the Merrill Advanced Studies Center, the National Science Foundation and the Society of Multivariate Experimental Psychology, Tempe Mission Palms Hotel, Tempe, Arizona, March 4–6, 2004)

Riding the Momentum of Research: Leadership Challenges in Public Research Universities

Keynote Address: Mary Sue Coleman, President of the University of Michigan

(a Merrill Policy Retreat at the Barn, Valley Falls, Kansas, July 21–23, 2004)

Chapter Summary

The content of this chapter is drawn from the period 1989–2004. The authors are led to believe that during this time a maintaining program has evolved that will continue to grow in size and importance in future years. It is apparent that the procedures inherent in "advanced study" are timely, feasible, and productive for a number of purposes, such as planning new activities and programs; forming new collaborative relationships; designing significant policy and scientific interactions in crucial areas; and disseminating significant information to a relevant audience worldwide. The impact of leading-edge discussions by carefully chosen leaders from significant topical areas add dimensional meaning to the term "Centers of Excellence," which, of course, research universities are assumed to be. A further challenge is drawn from the observation that participants in advanced study activities also gain added competences for their role in the pursuit of excellence. Perhaps, it is not too much to expect that we may induce other research centers to aspire to similar goals (if they haven't already). An aphorism for the MASC: Future achievements always begin in the present.

23

The History of the Work Group for Community Health and Development

STEPHEN B. FAWCETT

T he mission of the University of Kansas (KU) Work Group is to promote community health and development through collaborative research, teaching, and public service. This is a story of a program begun at KU in 1975 that made use of diverse ideas and resources to invent new areas of research and development. It is a 30-year odyssey of a systematic program of research that has made use of many sources of influence and has in turn developed new areas of research by taking a fresh look at some old problems. In 2004, the KU Work Group was designated as a World Health Organization Collaborating Centre for Community Health and Development.

Early History (1975–1990)

Like the path of Odysseus, that of the KU Work Group has led to a variety of sources of knowledge and experience (but only a few life-threatening situations). If we were to do an archeological "dig" into the layers of influence on this work, it would yield a picture something like this:

- *Behavior Analysis*—The principles and methods of behavior analysis are prominent in this work. This subdiscipline gives us an edge in learning about and contributing to socially important goals.
- *Community Psychology*—By the late 1970s, we embraced the influence of community psychology. This subfield places a premium on

collaboration, the process by which we share resources and responsibilities with those with whom we learn and act.

- *Public Policy*—While a part of KU's Institute of Public Affairs and
  Community Development from the 1970s to the 1980s, we had opportunities to learn about public policy. We drew especially on ideas about
  agenda setting in public policy.
- *Independent Living*—During the 1980s, at the request of Dick
  Schiefelbusch, Todd Risley, and Jim Budde, we began working with
  our colleagues at KU's Research and Training Center for Independent
  Living. This helped us see how a university group's research and action
  agenda can be guided by the concerns of clients who are partners in
  the journey.
- *Public Health*—Beginning in 1990, with the support of the Kansas
  Health Foundation and their many mentors, we became very active in
  the work of public health. We embraced this field's commitment to
  social justice and to environmental change as a strategy for improving
  population-level outcomes.
- *E-Learning*—Since the mid-1990s, especially with work on the
  Community Tool Box (*http://ctb.ku.edu/*), we have been exploring the
  potential of Internet-based learning and *translation of knowledge to
  practice*. We are pursuing ways to use new communications technologies to support research, teaching, and public service.

Our common journey as a Work Group has traversed these (and
other) knowledge domains and experiences. As we make a home for ourselves in this work, our task is to welcome the contributions of each
domain, and to consider how their separate threads make up the fabric of
our work life.

During the past 30 years, our work has been in four primary areas of
activity:

1. *Instructional Technology*—From the mid-1970s to the 1980s, we did
   quite a bit of research on behavioral instruction. Using the medium
   of the Internet, we remain engaged in using behavioral instruction
   methods to build skills and capacities related to community health
   and development.

2. *Intervention Research*—Throughout our history, we have conducted intervention research studies for a variety of community problems and goals. We have examined the effects of modifiable features of the environment on behavior and related outcomes.

3. *Agenda Setting and Policy Research*—Particularly during the 1970s and 1980s, we worked with a methodology for agenda setting known as the concerns report method. We explored how empirical and qualitative information about community concerns could be used to help set the agenda for research and action.

4. *Comprehensive Community Initiatives*—Beginning in the 1990s and ongoing, we have focused on two core questions about comprehensive initiatives for community health and development: What factors affect their functioning in bringing about environmental change? Under what conditions is environmental change associated with improvements in community-level outcomes?

There is a wonderful saying attributed to the Dakota tribe: "We will be known forever by the tracks we leave." This composite picture represents *tracks* left by the activity of KU Work Group members over the past 30 years. It reflects the core story line: *Increasing diversity in response to unfolding opportunities to learn and contribute.*

But, where do these tracks lead? Is there an evolutionary path to be discerned? In his book, *Full House*, paleontologist Stephen Jay Gould suggests that the story line for evolution is *not* a "ladder of progress"—things moving slowly but surely upward toward some particular form of excellence. A better analogy for evolution, he suggests, is a "bush of diversity." The Work Group's "bush of diversity" really began bearing fruit in the 1990s when it seriously became involved in the field of public health.

Recent History (1990–2002)

In the early 1990s the Kansas Health Foundation (formerly the Wesley Foundation) in Wichita, a major Kansas foundation, decided to retool and refocus its philanthropic efforts toward health promotion. It convened a series of expert consultants from across the United States to set its agenda. The Work Group seized this golden opportunity to put into practice all it had learned in the past 15 years about community development and its measurement systems for studying the process of community change and improvement. It was deeply involved in framing the issues for the Kansas Health Foundation and then doing research to better understand and improve community efforts to create conditions under which health occurs.

Framing the Task of Building Healthy Communities

Globally and locally, people work together to better understand and improve the health and development of those in their communities. For example, consistent with objectives of the World Health Organization, regional and local projects take action to reduce the incidence and prevalence of alcohol and drug abuse, HIV/AIDS, and chronic diseases such as diabetes (Lee, 2003). Similarly, aligned with the United Nations' Millennium Development goals, local development work attempts to reduce violence, assure adequate income and shelter, and improve education for all (Annan, 2000).

The common aim of such efforts is to create conditions in which health and development can occur (Institute of Medicine, 2003; World Bank, 2001; World Health Organization, 1986). In this collaborative work, people who share a common place, such as a city or barrio, or interest, such as in promoting child health or reducing poverty, plan and take action together. People and organizations from different parts of the community work together to create environments that support widespread behavior change, such as caring engagements or health-promoting behaviors, and improvement in population-level outcomes such as levels of childhood immunization or educational achievement (Fawcett, Francisco, Hyra, et al., 2000).

The essence of the behavior–community paradigm is that problems and goals of individuals, communities, and societies are represented in the behavior of people and the environmental conditions they experience (Baer, Wolf, & Risley, 1968, 1987; Fawcett, 1991; Fawcett, Mathews, & Fletcher, 1980). Similarly, when public health experts McGinnis and Foege (1993) cited the "real, real causes" of death in the United States, they focused on key health-related behaviors, such as tobacco use and diet, and the environmental conditions, such as governmental policies, that affect them. By viewing societal problems as "mere behavior," we avoid the trap of seeing them as "intractable" or objects for description but not intervention. Analyses yield potentially modifiable features of the environment and broader conditions that may affect relevant behaviors of key actors in communities.

We—and our colleagues—have been learning about how communities affect conditions related to health and development. First, we describe briefly the *context for learning* including our research and training program at the University of Kansas, the related disciplines that have influenced our work, and some principles and values that guide community research and action. Second, we present a conceptual *framework* or theory of action for community efforts to create conditions that promote health and development. Third, we describe *how we are learning*—outlining the participatory research methods, and key measures, used to examine the functioning of collaborative partnerships for community health and development. Fourth, we describe *what we are learning*—including seven factors affecting the rate of community change and the conditions under which environmental change may contribute to improvement in population-level outcomes. Finally, we describe how we are using Internet-based capabilities to aid in translation of knowledge to practice.

Context for Learning and Contributing to This Work

Our attempts to learn and contribute to community efforts to promote health and development are grounded in the supportive context of our research group, influences from several related disciplines, and guiding principles and values. Our new World Health Organization Collaborating Center for Community Health and Development at KU has two primary objectives: 1) to expand the evidence base for community efforts to create conditions for health and development, and 2) to build capacity for this work including through dissemination of promising methods using Internet-based technologies.

We are supported by our home academic unit, the Department of Human Development, with its emphasis on applied behavioral science; and the broader research unit of which we are a part, the Schiefelbusch Institute for Life Span Studies, with its commitment to translating knowledge to practice. Throughout its nearly 30-year history, our KU Work

Group has attempted to integrate the core university functions of research, teaching, and public service in all its activities. As such, our discernment criteria for selecting among possible projects include: 1) opportunities to learn and contribute through research; 2) potential for impact on important outcomes; 3) client commitment to building capacity, discovery, and co-learning; 4) long-term relationships and commitment to this work; 5) potential links and synergies among projects; and 6) opportunities to collaborate with outstanding national and global partners.

Some Disciplinary Influences on Our Work

Our KU Work Group's efforts have been informed by several disciplines and traditions for research and practice. First, the field of applied behavior analysis focuses attention on socially important behaviors and outcomes, such as childhood immunizations or violence, of people in their actual communities (Baer et al., 1968, 1987; Fawcett, 1991). The field's analytic criterion promotes use of appropriate experimental designs and research methods to help identify evidence-based practices that produce effects of social significance. Its technological criterion encourages dissemination of these innovations to those who can create environments that support valued behaviors and outcomes.

Second, the field of community psychology (Jason et al., 2004; Rappaport, 1977; Tolan, Keys, Chertok, & Jason, 1990) offers an ecological perspective—the idea that multiple and interrelated factors, such as social support and access to resources, affect multiple and interrelated outcomes, such as school success or substance abuse. It highlights the process of collaboration (Himmelman, 1992): sharing risks, resources, and responsibilities for the work among all those in a position to learn and contribute, including community people most affected, researchers and technical advisors, and those grant makers who fund and support the work. It places a value on empowerment: the process by which people gain control over conditions and outcomes that matter to them (Fawcett, Paine-Andrews, et al., 1995).

Third, the field of public health draws attention to "what we as a society do collectively to assure conditions in which people can be healthy" (Institute of Medicine, 1988, p. 1). Globally and locally, the vision of "healthy people in healthy communities" (DHHS, 2000; World Health

Organization, 1986) is made concrete in specific health objectives, such as reducing rates of HIV/AIDS and the associated risk behavior of unprotected sexual activity, and related environmental strategies, such as making condoms more readily available and social consequences for their use more reinforcing. With its emphasis on population-level outcomes, such as prevalence of diabetes in a particular group or place, public health emphasizes engagement of people from multiple sectors, such as education and nongovernmental organizations, in changing community conditions that can affect widespread behavior change, such as physical activity and diet, and related health outcomes for all (Institute of Medicine, 2003).

Some Principles, Assumptions, and Values Guiding the Work

Grounded in the above-noted traditions, Table 1 outlines some principles, assumptions, and values that guide the work of understanding and improving community health and development (adapted from Fawcett, Francisco, Hyra, et al., 2000). For example, Value 1 reflects the public health goal of improving population-level outcomes. Value 2 directs attention to the behaviors and environmental conditions related to health and development goals. Value 4 acknowledges the importance of broader determinants of health and development (Tarlov & St. Peter, 2000), especially social connectedness (Berkman & Syme, 1979; Kawachi, Kennedy, Lochner, & Prothrow-Stith, 1997), income inequality (Wilkinson, 1996), and efficacy or ability to influence one's environment (Marmot, Bosma, Hemingway, Brunner, & Stansfield, 1997). Values 3 and 5 highlight the collaborative processes and ecological perspective of community psychology. We use the term *value* as Skinner (1972) used it: to refer to a statement of what is important, of what practices, if adhered to, might produce positive reinforcement from important audiences, such as those engaged in this work of understanding and improving community health and development (Fawcett, 1991).

A Framework for Community Efforts to Promote Change and Improvement

In this section, we outline a conceptual framework for community efforts to create change and improvement related to health and development,

Table 1. *Some Principles, Assumptions, and Values Guiding the Work of Understanding and Improving Community Health and Development*

- Improvement in community health and development involves the population as a whole, not merely individuals at risk for specific physical, mental, or social conditions.
- Community health and development requires changes in both the behaviors of large numbers of individuals and the environment and broader conditions that affect health and development.
- A healthy community is a local product with priority issues and strategies best determined by people most affected by the concern.
- Achieving health and development for all requires attention to key social determinants—in particular; income disparities, social connectedness, and efficacy or the ability to influence one's environment.
- Because health and development outcomes are caused by multiple and interrelated factors, single interventions are likely to be insufficient.
- The conditions that affect a particular health or development outcome are often interconnected with those affecting other concerns.
- Because the behaviors that affect health and development occur among a variety of people in an array of contexts, community improvement requires engagement of diverse groups bringing about change in multiple sectors of the community.
- Community health and development involves interdependent relationships among multiple parties in which none can function fully without collaboration with others.
- Collaborative partnerships, support organizations, and grant makers work together as catalysts for change; they convene, broker relationships, and leverage resources for those doing the work of community change and improvement.
- The aim of support organizations is to build capacity to address what matters to people over time and across concerns.

which has been adapted from Fawcett, Francisco, Hyra, et al. (2000) and grounded in the logic of health promotion (CDC, 2002; Green & Kreuter, 1991). This model was used by the Institute of Medicine to characterize collaborative public health action by communities in its report on the future of public health in the 21st century (Institute of Medicine, 2003). Figure 1 presents this five-component framework: 1) assessment and collaborative planning, 2) targeted action and intervention, 3) community and systems change, 4) widespread behavior change, and 5) improvement in population-level outcomes.

The model's components are interactive. For instance, assessment of community issues and concerns, such as levels of violence or safety, and developing plans to address them should inform targeted actions and

Figure 1. *A framework for community efforts to promote change and improvement in population-level health and development.*

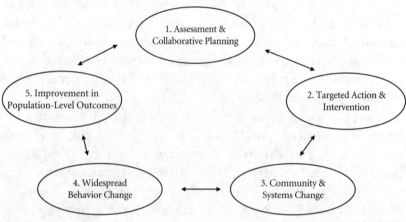

interventions. Similarly, information about the unfolding of new programs and policies (community change), and associated changes in rates of behavior and population-level outcome, may prompt adjustments in action plans and interventions. The framework's components are also iterative, or part of a repeating cycle. For example, when the process yields improvement in targeted population-level outcomes, such as rates of childhood immunizations or adolescent pregnancy, this may be followed by a renewed cycle of collaborative planning and intervention for other issues, such as early childhood development, that matter to local communities. Community capacity may be reflected in the demonstrated ability of generations of people working together to effect change and improvement over time, and across issues (Fawcett, Paine-Andrews, et al., 1995; Goodman et al., 1998).

Assessment and Collaborative Planning

Community members and outside experts work together to gather and use quantitative data (Green & Kreuter, 1991; Institute of Medicine, 1997) and information on community concerns (Fawcett, Seekins, Whang, Muiu, & Suarez de Balcazar, 1982; Paine, Francisco, & Fawcett, 1994) to target issues of importance, such as improved educational outcomes or caring engagements with children, that will be the focus of change efforts. In a multisectoral approach, representatives from different sectors of the community—such as schools, government, business, and faith communities—engage in the ongoing process of collaborative planning. The process should be inclusive, engaging those most affected by the issue, such as marginalized groups that traditionally lack power, as well as those in a position to effect needed changes, such as elected officials and community leaders.

The products of strategic planning include shared: 1) vision—the dream or what success would look like (e.g., "healthy children," "safe streets," "caring neighbors"); 2) mission—statement of what the group is going to do and why; 3) objectives—how much of what (e.g., increase/decrease in behavior or population-level outcome) will result by when; 4) strategies—how the effort will reach its objectives (e.g., providing information and enhancing skills, modifying access and opportunities, enhancing services and support, changing the consequences, modifying policies and broader systems); and 5) action plans—specific community changes to be sought and interventions to be implemented, including who will do what by when to bring them about (Community Tool Box, 2003).

Targeted Action and Intervention

Efforts often include targeted actions, such as personal contacts or group advocacy efforts, to bring about community and systems changes identified in action plans such as a new or modified program (e.g., after-school program for youth), policy (e.g., extended hours for access to service), or practice (e.g., more humane treatment of clients). They may also include implementation of evidence-based practices and interventions (e.g., Task Force on Community Preventive Services, 2000).

Community and Systems Change

Community and systems changes refer to new or modified programs, policies, and practices facilitated by the effort and related to its mission (Francisco, Paine, & Fawcett, 1993). For example, a community effort to reduce obesity and risk for diabetes might include public information programs displaying modeling and social reinforcement from peers for engagement in physical activity, policies that assure availability of healthy school lunches, and prompts for healthy practices, such as symbols for low-fat choices on restaurant menus and signs promoting use of stairs in public buildings. Community changes reflect the product of actions, an intermediate outcome between the process of collaborative planning and action and more distant changes in behaviors of group members and population-level outcomes (Fawcett, Francisco, Hyra, et al., 2000).

Widespread Behavior Change

The aim of targeted action and intervention—and resulting changes in communities and systems—is behavior change and improved health and development outcomes for the people in the defined community. For example, a citywide effort to reduce adolescent pregnancy would have behavioral objectives related to increased abstinence among unmarried teens and, for those who chose to be sexually active, increased use of appropriate contraceptives. Widespread change in targeted behaviors is more likely when community conditions address the array of relevant personal factors, such as knowledge and skill, and environmental factors, such as peer support and enhanced opportunities to respond. To effect behavior changes in the group, the specific components of a community intervention, such as the types of information or consequences, should reflect an analysis of the context and the environmental conditions that are associated with the behavioral problem or goal.

Improvement in Population-Level Outcomes

Improvement in population-level outcomes is the ultimate goal of community efforts to create conditions that promote health and development. Such efforts may aim to reduce adverse outcomes, such as the prevalence of alcohol abuse or exposure to environmental toxins, or promote positive health and development, such as increased rates of educational success or frequency of caring engagements with children. Often, a population-level outcome is the product of widespread change in multiple behaviors of those who share a place or group. For example, reduced prevalence of diabetes requires changes in engagement in physical activity and healthy diets in all children and adults, including those with multiple risk markers for diabetes such as impaired glucose toler- ance or a family history of diabetes.

How Are We Learning?: Using the Methodology of Community-Based Participatory Research to Document and Analyze the Contribution

This conceptual framework focuses our attention on: 1) processes (assess- ment and collaborative planning), 2) engagements (targeted action and intervention), 3) intermediate outcomes (community and systems changes), and 4) more distant outcomes (widespread behavior change and population-level outcomes). Since 1990, our research team has focused on two core questions: 1) What factors affect the rate of community and sys- tems change (intermediate outcome)? and 2) Under what conditions are community changes associated with improvements (in population-level outcomes)? In this section, we describe how we are learning—the methodology of community-based participatory research—and the use of a common measurement system, multiple case studies, and interrupted time series designs to examine the two core questions.

Methodology of Community-Based Participatory Research

Our methodology for studying the functioning of community efforts to promote health and development is grounded in the traditions of behav- ioral measurement (Johnson & Pennypacker, 1980), participatory research (Green et al., 1995; Whyte, 1991), ethnography and action anthropology (e.g., Stull & Schensul, 1987), and empowerment evaluation (e.g., Fawcett et al., 1996; Fetterman, Kaftarian, & Wandersman, 1996). A form of community-based participatory research (Fawcett, Schultz, Carson, Renault, & Francisco, 2003; Minkler & Wallerstein, 2003), it builds on other efforts to evaluate comprehensive community initiatives (e.g., Connell, Kubish, Schorr, & Weiss, 1995; Fawcett et al., 2001).

Figure 2 outlines our six-part framework for community-based par- ticipatory research (Fawcett, Boothroyd, et al., 2003). First, we support local community efforts in naming and framing the problem or goal ("What issues are we trying to address?"). For example, an initiative to

Figure 2. *A framework for community-based participatory research.*

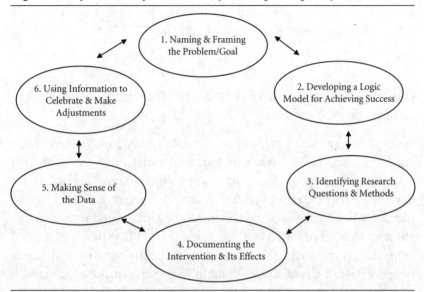

reduce adolescent pregnancy would focus on key behaviors—abstinence and use of contraceptives—and the environmental conditions that would reduce risk and enhance protection. Second, we aid in developing a logic model or framework for achieving success ("How will we get from here to there?") (See Figure 1 for a generic example of inputs, outputs, and an intended continuum of outcomes.) Third, we collaborate with members of the local effort in identifying research questions and appropriate methods ("What do we want to know and how will we know it?"). For instance, key stakeholders, such as community leaders and grant makers, might be interested in whether the effort results in environmental change and whether this yields improvements in population-level outcomes.

Fourth, we assist in documenting the intervention and its effects ("What are we doing? Is it making a difference?"). For example, we use Internet-based systems to provide on-line reports of accomplishments and graphs of the rate of community/systems change over time (Fawcett, Schultz, et al., 2003). Fifth, outside researchers and group members work together to make sense of the data ("What are we seeing? What does it mean?"). For instance, this may involve examining time series data for a population-level outcome, such as estimated pregnancy rates for young women aged 15–19 years, and comparing rates over time for both experimental and comparison communities. Finally, we support using the information to celebrate and make adjustments ("What do we do now, and how?").

Context and Collaborative Partners in Studying Community Change Efforts

Since 1990, our research group and collaborating partners have been studying the process, intermediate outcomes, and more distant population-level outcomes of community efforts to promote health and development (Fawcett et al., 2001; Russos & Fawcett, 2000). Typically, our KU Work Group provided integrated technical support and evaluation services as part of a broader collaboration that involved funded community or state initiatives, such as to reduce substance abuse or improve nutrition, and outside grant makers such as private foundations or government agencies.

Throughout, we used the same measurement system to document the product of community actions, community and systems change—new or modified programs, policies, and practices related to the mission (Francisco et al., 1993). To help assure the quality of the data, we provided training for documentation of the onset of discrete instances of community/systems change—for example, a new program for occupational safety, a modified policy extending health insurance coverage to low-income children, or a new practice to provide needed child immunizations during regular health care visits. Training included use of response definitions and scoring instructions, examples and nonexamples, opportunities to practice and receive feedback, and a mastery criterion of high levels of interobserver agreement before completion. Independent scoring of community/systems change and feedback on levels of interobserver agreement are used to help assess and assure consistency in the measurement system over time and across applications and contexts.

Consistent with the methodology of community-based participatory research (e.g., Minkler & Wallerstein, 2003), we supported community involvement in documenting the onset of discrete instances of community and systems change (i.e., new programs, policies, and practices) facilitated by the local efforts. Ongoing feedback on the rate of community change was presented in the form of graphs of the cumulative number of changes (aggregated monthly) over the course of the effort. Sense making by community members and researchers focused on: 1) examining discontinuities in rates of change and associated factors (e.g., marked increases in change following action planning; marked decreases following loss of leadership) and 2) analyzing the contribution (i.e., pie charts showing the distribution of community changes by goal [e.g., substance abuse, jobs], duration [e.g., one-time event, ongoing], strategy [e.g., providing information, modifying policies], and other aspects).

We focused the measurement system on the intermediate outcome of community/systems change. This is particularly strategic because population-level outcomes are often too distant—perhaps taking 5–10 years or more to improve—to be useful in making necessary corrections in project efforts. Documentation and feedback—in the form of graphs of the rate and distribution of community change—permitted ongoing learning, adjustments, and accountability.

Since 1990, we have used this common measurement system—and, as available, appropriate indicators of population-level outcomes—to support and evaluate over 30 collaborative partnerships (e.g., Fawcett et al., 2001). These community efforts have worked on a variety of issues/outcomes (e.g., adolescent pregnancy, substance abuse, nutrition, physical activity, childhood immunization, neighborhood development) in a diverse array of contexts (e.g., urban, rural, tribal communities). Taken together, this naturally unfolding social experiment might be considered a multiple case study design (Yin, 1988).

Core Research Questions and Related Method Systems

Our overarching research program has focused on two core questions: 1) What factors affect the rate of community and systems change? and 2) Under what conditions are community changes associated with improvements in population-level outcomes? To address the first question, we have used a natural social experiment involving different collaborative efforts that began and ended at different times and in different communities since 1990. For instance, the first initiative we studied, a community effort to reduce adolescent substance abuse in a midwestern city, began in 1990 and concluded several years later (Fawcett et al., 1997);

other efforts began and ended in subsequent years. This might be considered a naturally occurring multiple or interrupted time series design with the rate of community change as the dependent variable (Cook & Campbell, 1979; Johnson & Pennypacker, 1980).

Consistent with a natural science approach, investigators examined each case study for discontinuities—marked increases or decreases—in rates of community change. We also used qualitative methods, such as semi-structured interviews and reviews of archival records, to identify critical events or candidate factors associated with observed discontinuities (e.g., changes in leadership, completion of action planning, and announced contingencies for higher rates of change). To facilitate visual inspection for each case study, we overlaid the critical events on time series graphs of the cumulative rates of community change. To identify candidate factors, such as action planning, we looked for associated marked acceleration or deceleration in rates of change—systematic replication of these possible effects—in multiple case studies.

To address the second question, whenever possible, we used multiple time series designs to examine trends in population-level indicators (e.g., rates of adolescent pregnancy or childhood immunization) that may be associated with the unfolding of the independent variable (community change) over time. Consistent with the natural science approach, we looked for discontinuities in rates of population-level indicators and systematically analyzed the contribution of community changes to examine a possible dose–response relationship. For instance, in an adolescent substance abuse prevention initiative, we noted decreases in rates of single-nighttime vehicle crashes (a population-level indicator) in an experimental community compared with another similar community; the reductions in rates corresponded with the unfolding of over 200 community changes in the active community (Fawcett et al., 1997).

Our working hypothesis is that improvement in population-level outcomes (the intended "response") is more likely when community changes (the "dose") are of sufficient 1) amount by goal (e.g., targeted to one or a few goals, not distributed among many), 2) intensity of behavior change strategy (e.g., not merely weak behavior change approaches such as providing information, but also stronger variables such as modifying access and changing the consequences), 3) duration (e.g., not merely one-time events, but including ongoing events such as policy changes), and 4) penetration to reach intended targets (e.g., including all those at risk as well as those with multiple risk markers) through appropriate sectors (e.g., schools, business, government agencies) in specific places (e.g., areas with a high incidence of the problem). To make salient this analysis of contribution of community changes to more distant outcomes, we provide Internet-based feedback to community efforts in the form of pie charts displaying the distribution of community/systems changes for each dimension of contribution (e.g., by goal, by behavior change strategy, by neighborhood) (Fawcett, Schultz, et al., 2003; Paine-Andrews et al., 2002).

What Are We Learning?: Some Factors and Conditions

Affecting Community Change and Improvement

Based on these multiple case studies, and the work of other colleagues, we can summarize preliminary learning on two core questions: 1) factors affecting rates of community (systems) change and 2) conditions under which these environmental changes may "tip" or bring about improvements in population-level outcomes (Gladwell, 2000).

Some Factors Affecting Community and Systems Change

Reviewed elsewhere (Fawcett, Francisco, Paine-Andrews, & Schultz, 2000; Russos & Fawcett, 2000), we have identified seven factors associated with increases (or decreases) in rates of community (and systems) change:

1. *Clear vision and mission*—We have noted five- to sixfold higher rates of community change when community, initiatives have agreed on a clear vision and targeted mission (Francisco, Fawcett, Wolff, & Foster, unpublished data). In our observations, more targeted community efforts, such as those addressing substance abuse or nutrition, are associated with higher rates of change than diffuse efforts such as those addressing "healthy communities."
2. *Action planning*—Identifying specific community and systems changes to be sought in each relevant sector, such as an expanded after-school program or a new child care policy in business—and who would do what to bring them about—has been consistently followed by increases

in rates of community change (e.g., Fawcett et al., 1997; Lewis et al., 1999; Paine-Andrews, Harris, Fawcett, Richter, & Lewis, 1997). Action planning may be the single most important modifiable factor in accelerating change; leadership is very important, but not particularly modifiable.

3. *Leadership*—In the first community effort we studied, there was a marked decrease in the rate of community change following loss of leadership (Fawcett et al., 1997), a pattern that we have seen repeated fairly consistently when leaders have left community efforts. In some cases, a change in leadership, such as to those with strong commitment and social ties, had a facilitative effect (Lewis et al., 1999). Although challenging to assure, continuous leadership, including that distributed among multiple group members, may be a critical protective factor for continued high rates of change (e.g., Kegler, Steckler, McLeroy, & Malek, 1998; Paine-Andrews et al., 1997).

4. *Responsible community organizers*—Hiring community organizers with responsibility for assuring implementation of action plans has consistently led to increased rates of community change (e.g., Fawcett et al., 1997; Lewis et al., 1999; Paine-Andrews, Fawcett et al., 1996, 1997, 1999). When community workers are paid, there is often better accountability for the work of community change than when efforts rely solely on volunteers.

5. *Documentation and feedback on intermediate outcomes*—To provide a functional measure of intermediate outcome, we supported ongoing documentation of the unfolding of community change over time, and feedback, in the form of time series graphs of cumulative rates of change that are annotated to show factors (e.g., change in leadership) associated with discontinuities (Francisco et al., 1993). Since documentation and feedback are integral to the measurement system, we cannot tease out their separate effects on rates of community change. Functionally, such information may permit ongoing learning, adjustments, and accountability in the effort.

6. *Technical assistance*—To support community efforts, outside intermediary organizations, such as our KU Work Group, use training and technical consultation to build local capacity for key tasks, such as community assessment, strategic planning, and leadership development. Although not examined separately, such technical support may

prompt and provide modeling for appropriate activities, occasion reinforcement for these practices, and make them easier through Internet-
based supports (Fawcett, Schultz, et al., 2003).

7. *Making outcome matter*—Although we might expect intrinsic rewards
for progress, tangible contingencies of reinforcement for productivity,
such as increased resources for high rates of change and improvement, are rare. Following introduction of announced contingencies
of reinforcement (i.e., grant renewal based on evidence of progress by
a grant maker), we saw marked increases in rates of community
change (Fawcett et al., 1997). Other contingencies—including bonus
grants for particularly high rates of change and outcome dividends
for improvement in population-level outcomes (e.g., decreased rates
of adolescent pregnancy)—merit further examination (Fawcett,
Francisco, Paine-Andrews, et al., 2000).

Conditions Under Which Environmental Change May Be Related to Improvement in Population-Level Outcomes

Ultimately, community efforts must address the question: Whether (and
under what conditions) community/systems changes—those scores of
new programs, policies, and practices resulting from targeted action and
intervention—actually yield improvements in population-level outcomes
(Fawcett, Francisco, Hyra, et al., 2000; Institute of Medicine, 2003). In
complex adaptive systems (Eoyang, 1997), where multiple and interrelated
factors affect multiple and interrelated outcomes, attribution of cause and
effect can be difficult to impossible. Appropriate to such complex environments, the "proof" game may switch to the "plausibility" game (Baer,
1985; Fawcett, 1991); we adjust the analytic work from "attribution" to
"analysis of contribution" (Fawcett, Boothroyd, et al., 2003; Milstein &
Wetherall, 2001).

In an analysis of contribution, we examine how the "dose" of environmental change might contribute to the "response" of improvement in
population-level outcome. To analyze the contribution of community
health and development efforts, we use a working hypothesis of the conditions under which environmental (community/systems) change might
"tip," or bring about marked improvements in, outcomes for the population (Gladwell, 2000). Based on our research and that of colleagues, we

expect improvements in population-level outcomes to be more likely when community/systems changes are of sufficient:

- Amount by goal—when the environmental changes are many and focused on a few targeted categorical outcomes (e.g., substance abuse, nutrition, education);
- Intensity of behavior change strategy—when the community/systems changes resulting from the targeted action/intervention go beyond weak behavior change approaches, such as providing information, to use more potent strategies, such as modifying barriers and opportunities (e.g., reducing the time and effort for the desired behavior) and changing the consequences (e.g., price of tobacco products);
- Duration—when community changes include more ongoing events (e.g., policy changes) than one-time events (e.g., one-shot "health fairs"); and
- Penetration/exposure:
  - To reach targets—when community/systems changes are directed in a universal approach toward all those at risk or who could benefit (e.g., all adults in a place), and, in a targeted approach, toward those with multiple risk markers (e.g., for depression—family history, unemployment, social isolation, and other factors that increase risk for depression);
  - Through appropriate sectors or channels of influence—when community changes, such as new programs or policies, occur in community sectors through which targets can be reached (e.g., health organizations, faith communities, business, government, community/non-governmental organizations); and
  - In local places—when community changes are concentrated in places (e.g., cities, neighborhoods) where there is high incidence or prevalence of the concern.

For instance, we used this working hypothesis to analyze the contribution of community change to improvement in population-level rates of adolescent pregnancy in an urban community (Paine-Andrews et al., 2002). A reduced rate of adolescent pregnancy (the intended "response") was noted in the neighborhood in which a large number of community changes (the estimated "dose") were facilitated, but not in the contiguous neighborhood in which few environmental changes were made. Because other correlated events and associated conditions may account for differences, these findings are merely suggestive of how an analysis of contribution can contribute to our understanding of the functioning of community-level change efforts. Further research, perhaps using multiple case studies or interrupted time series designs, may help clarify how we can use this metric of community/systems change—a measure of the independent variable—to better understand the functioning of community efforts to improve population-level outcomes.

Using Internet-Based Capabilities in Translating Knowledge to Practice

How do we translate emerging knowledge—what we are learning about community-based efforts—into supports for best practice? Those working on community efforts to improve health and development often find it difficult to gain access to the knowledge and support they need, when they need it, at an affordable cost. Internet technology can help communities become more capable of understanding and effecting community-determined improvements by providing training and support for critical skills, processes, and practices (Fawcett, Francisco, Schultz, et al., 2000; Schultz, Fawcett, Francisco, & Berkowitz, 2003).

Core Competencies in the Work

Based on our experience and that of colleagues, we identified 16 core competencies for the shared work of promoting community health and development. Adapted from Fawcett, Schultz, et al. (2003), Figure 3 and the description that follows describe these abilities in relation to a framework for creating conditions for community health and development (see Figure 1).

CORE COMPETENCIES FOR ASSESSMENT AND COLLABORATIVE PLANNING. Six core competencies contribute to the work of assessment and collaborative planning. First, creating and maintaining coalitions is a common strategy for engaging individuals and organizations from a variety of sectors of the community, such as government or business, in common purpose. Second, assessing community needs and resources grounds the work in what is locally important and available. Third, working with community partners in analyzing problems and goals

Figure 3. *Translating knowledge to practice in promoting community health and development* (Community Tool Box, http://ctb.ku.edu/).

Assessment and Collaborative Planning	Targeted Action and Intervention	Community and Systems Change	Widespread Behavior Change and Improvement in Population-Level Outcomes	Sustaining the Effort
16 CORE COMPETENCIES SUPPORTED BY THE COMMUNITY TOOL BOX & CUSTOMIZED WORKSTATIONS				
What kind of community work do you want to do today?				
1. Create and maintain coalitions and partnerships				
2. Assess community needs and resources				
3. Analyze problems and goals				
4. Develop a framework or model of change				
5. Develop a strategic or action plan				
6. Build leadership	7. Develop an intervention			
	8. Increase participation and membership			
	9. Enhance cultural competence	10. Advocate for change		

11. Influence policy development
12. Evaluate the initiative
13. Implement a social marketing effort
14. Write a grant application for funding
15. Improve organizational management and development
16. Sustain the work or initiative

CAPABILITIES OF CUSTOMIZED ON-LINE WORKSTATIONS
What kinds of support do I need?

Building Capacity
- Help planning the work
- Solve a common problem
- Quick tips and tools for how to do the work
- See a story or example
- Learn a specific skill

Co-Learning and Adjustments
- Link to other online resources
- Connect with others about this work
- Ask a question of an advisor
- Knowledge base from collective experience
- See how this work fits together

Documentation, Evaluation, and Analysis of Contribution
- Document community and systems change
- Enter or see community-level indicators
- Display trends and discontinuities
- Analyze the contribution
- Sense making and adjustments
- Capture success stories
- On-line and print reporting

CTB TRAINING CURRICULUM—16 Modules, one for each core competency—AND GRADUATE CERTIFICATION

helps pinpoint the personal/group factors and environmental factors that may affect the current problem and future prospects for goal attainment. Fourth, developing a framework or model of change—including inputs, outputs, and a continuum of outcomes—helps define how the community intends to go from a problematic situation to sustained improvements in population-level outcomes. Fifth, developing strategic and action plans sets the blueprint for getting from a community's vision and mission to improvements in population-level outcomes. Sixth, building leadership helps people to develop and sustain relationships and transform conditions necessary for community improvement.

CORE COMPETENCIES FOR TARGETED ACTION AND INTERVENTION. Three additional core competencies apply to taking action. Seventh, developing an intervention involves selecting and using intervention components and elements based on an analysis of contributing factors and available resources. Eighth, increasing participation and membership promotes voice and influence from those with deep experience, such as youth or ethnic minorities, but limited prior engagement in the effort. Ninth, enhancing cultural competence helps build cross-cultural relationships and create more inclusive and respectful organizations and communities.

CORE COMPETENCIES FOR COMMUNITY AND SYSTEMS CHANGE. Several additional core abilities are associated with bringing about community and systems change. Tenth, advocating for change involves overcoming resistance and barriers to bring about new programs and policies related to the effort. Eleventh, influencing policy development requires being able to affect the policy agenda and the array of policy options presented to decision makers for consideration. Twelfth, evaluating the initiative includes being able to document the unfolding of community and systems changes over time and its potential impact on more distant population-level indicators of success.

CORE COMPETENCIES FOR WIDESPREAD BEHAVIOR CHANGE AND IMPROVEMENT IN POPULATION-LEVEL OUTCOMES. Thirteenth, implementing a social marketing effort involves using promotional techniques to effect widespread behavior change related to socially important goals. Other previously noted abilities, such as building leadership and evaluating the initiative, also have relevance to this aspect of the work.

CORE COMPETENCIES FOR SUSTAINING THE EFFORT. Several of the 16 core competencies are particularly important to this final aspect. Fourteenth, writing a grant application for funding can help gain access to financial and other resources needed for the work. Fifteenth, improving organizational management and development can create and enhance the needed institutional supports. Sixteenth, developing a plan for sustaining the work or initiative, such as how to share positions between agencies, helps ensure that human and financial resources are available long enough to make a difference.

Building Capacity Through the Community Tool Box and Customized Workstations

We have developed Internet-based resources and a training curriculum to support translation of knowledge—about factors affecting community efforts—into practice, such as enhanced skills in planning and other core competencies.

COMMUNITY TOOL BOX. In 1994, we began development of the Community Tool Box (CTB; *http://ctb.ku.edu/*), a comprehensive and widely used Internet-based resource for building capacity, or enhancing core competencies, among those involved in community efforts (Fawcett, Francisco, Schultz, et al., 2000). The mission of the CTB is to promote community health and development by connecting people, ideas, and resources. The CTB has over 6,000 pages of how-to information relevant to the 16 core competencies just discussed (e.g., assessing community resources and needs, facilitating meetings, evaluating programs). In a related effort, the KU Work Group has developed an Internet-based system for documenting and evaluating community initiatives, analyzing the contribution, and making ongoing adjustments.

CUSTOMIZED WORKSTATIONS. Based on these CTB capabilities and consistent with user needs and interests, we can now develop customized "workstations" for particular national, state, and community efforts (e.g., a multisite effort to improve child development outcomes or reduce chronic diseases). Each unique Workstation has several attributes (Fawcett, Schultz, et al., 2003). First, the resources are integrated in a one-stop workstation of multiple supports for the work. Second, its content is comprehensive, addressing all 16 core competencies (e.g., assessment, planning, evaluation). Third, the information is easily available on demand, providing a just-in-time response with the tools and links to resources a few clicks away. Fourth, the supports are useful, providing help in building capacity for doing this work, evaluation and sense making, and learning and making adjustments. Fifth, the resources are appropriate for diverse users and contexts, including for different types of: 1) users (e.g., community members, those providing technical support), 2) issues, and 3) contexts (e.g., urban, rural, indigenous communities). Sixth, it promotes equity by assuring equal access to guidance for all those having access to the Internet. Finally, carrying out the recommended activity results in a tangible product with benefits to the community initiative or organization (e.g., a strategic plan, an evaluation plan, a plan for sustaining the effort).

As outlined in Figure 3, a customized workstation offers capabilities to aid in three critical facets: 1) building capacity for the work, 2) promoting co-learning and adjustments, and 3) documenting, evaluating, and analyzing the contribution.

1. *Building capacity*—By offering multiple forms of support, a workstation makes it easier to enhance skills among those doing the work. First, each customized workstation provides help planning the work by connecting to tools that help develop useful products (e.g., a strategic pan, an evaluation plan, a plan for sustaining the effort). Second, the workstation provides help in solving commonly occurring problems through its *Troubleshooting Guide*, which presents: a) common problems and dilemmas in doing this work, b) questions to help clarify the issue, and c) links to appropriate sections in the CTB to provide support. Third, each workstation offers access to a growing database of quick tips and tools for how to do the work. Fourth, it features illustrative stories and examples of success doing this work. Fifth, the workstation provides access to relevant how-to sections for learning a specific skill. Finally, access to a training curriculum is available to those who pay for this service. The CTB training curriculum includes different modules and experiential activities for each core competency.
2. *Co-learning and adjustments*—A workstation promotes adjustments in community work through a variety of methods. First, it helps in

linking to other on-line resources for best practices in a particular area (e.g., promoting physical activity or school success). Second, it aids in connecting with others to learn about this work, such as the community of people experienced in planning or evaluation, and makes adjustments based on exchanges through an on-line forum or chat room. Third, as an optional feature, those in particular community efforts can gain expert guidance by asking a question of an advisor (e.g., a national expert on advocacy or social marketing approaches). Fourth, the on-line system can offer an evolving knowledge base from collective experience based on the emerging wisdom across generations of people in distributed communities of research and action. Finally, the workstation can outline a framework or pathway, such as illustrated by Figure 1, showing how this work fits together in a holistic way with links to appropriate practical information (e.g., for collaborative planning, for taking action).

3. *Documentation, evaluation, and analysis of the initiative's contribution—* Each customized workstation can also provide an Internet-based version of a widely field-tested measurement system for evaluating community efforts (e.g., Fawcett, Sterling, et al., 1995; Francisco et al., 1993). First, it supports the on-line documentation of community and systems change and other important events (e.g., services provided, resources generated). This includes the capacity to provide narrative information about accomplishments and code the events. Second, the system supports entering or seeing community-level indicators (e.g., rates of childhood immunizations or educational achievement). Third, it can display trends and discontinuities in coded events, such as community/systems change, allowing for a real-time review of trends and for an exploration of critical events (e.g., grant funding, change in leadership) that may be associated with increases or decreases in the pace of change. Fourth, the on-line system permits an analysis of contribution of how the initiative is aiding population-level improvement. On-line pie charts can show the amount and distribution of community and systems changes by key aspects of contribution (e.g., by goal, by place). Similarly, on-line time series graphs can display the relationship between levels of community and systems change, such as facilitated by an adolescent pregnancy prevention effort, and improvements in community-level indicators (e.g., estimated

pregnancy rate). Fifth, it supports sense making and adjustments. For example, users can go from a graph that shows a decrease in the rate of change associated with opposition to the effort to on-line guidance for how to respond to opposition (i.e., in the *Troubleshooting Guide* for solving common problems). Sixth, the system also captures success stories about accomplishments the initiative is particularly proud of, why it mattered, and its meaning for the people involved in the effort. Finally, the on-line documentation system supports on-line and print reporting about the initiative on demand, such as on-line grant reporting, for all those doing and supporting the work.

CTB CURRICULUM AND GRADUATE CERTIFICATION. We have also developed a 16-module curriculum that prepares learners in core competencies for this work (e.g., analyzing problems, strategic planning, designing interventions, evaluating efforts). Each module includes a *Participant's Guide* (e.g., key learnings, practical steps, experiential activities), a *Facilitator's Guide* and PowerPoint presentation, and a competence assessment or guided opportunity to put together a plan related to the particular skill (e.g., develop a strategic plan, develop an evaluation plan). Selected readings from the Community Tool Box serve as the textbook. To enhance benefits for those doing the work, we are also developing a formal course and practicum program that will result in a Certificate in Community Health and Development awarded by the Graduate School of the University of Kansas.

Taken together, these Internet-based tools, curriculum, and graduate certification opportunities offer integrated and comprehensive supports for translating knowledge about community efforts into widespread practice.

Conclusion

This report offered an overview of what we and our colleagues have been learning about how communities affect conditions related to health and development. We outlined a conceptual framework for efforts to create conditions that promote health and development. We noted how we are learning: using methods of community-based participatory research to examine the process, intermediate outcomes (community/systems change), and more distant (population-level) outcomes of community efforts to promote health and development. We described what we are learning, including seven factors affecting the rate of community change, and the conditions under which environmental change may contribute to improvement in population-level outcomes. Finally, we noted how we are using Internet-based capabilities to aid in translation of knowledge to practice.

In behavioral science, as in other sciences, we must decide what to measure, how to measure it, and what to do with what we see (Marr, 2004). To discover new things about community efforts to promote health and development, we focused the lantern on the intermediate outcome of community change. By studying patterns of community change (as a dependent variable) with different problems and contexts, we saw candidate factors, such as action planning, that appear to enhance change efforts. By analyzing the contribution of community change (as an independent variable) to population-level outcomes, we may be able to examine dose–response relationships associated with community improvement. Quantification of functional units, such as community change, and their visual representation in graphic feedback, convey "discoveries" or things that we did not know about how things work (Risley, 2004). Further systematic examination of community efforts—of what works and under what conditions—should enhance the science and practice of community change and improvement.

Consider a thought: how we might apply what we are learning to set conditions for success of a comprehensive effort to improve population-level outcomes. In an idealized social contract, key partners—state and community partnerships, support and evaluation organizations, and grant makers—might each commit to implementing the seven factors through a negotiated memorandum of agreement (Fawcett, Francisco, Paine-Andrews, et al., 2000). For instance, a comprehensive intervention to prevent violence or promote child well-being might include several components (and elements): 1) providing information and enhancing skills (e.g., training and certification in core competencies such as strategic planning and intervention); 2) modifying access, barriers, and opportunities (e.g., using Internet-based systems to make documentation of environmental change, and related adjustments in practice, easier and more rewarding); 3) changing the consequences (e.g., implementing bonus grants to enhance positive reinforcement for change and improvement); 4) enhancing support and services (e.g., providing responsive technical support for key tasks such action planning and implementing promising interventions); and 5) modifying policies and broader systems (e.g., assuring long-term financial support for community efforts sufficient to achieve population-level outcomes). Taken together, these components would change the conditions—the contingencies of reinforcement—operating on efforts to effect conditions that produce health and development (Biglan, 1995; Glenn, 1988; Russos, Fawcett, Francisco, Berkley, & Lopez, 1997).

Despite significant challenges, our emerging knowledge and capabilities permit unprecedented support for the work of community health and development. To realize the promise, we must discover new forms of working together—ways of "docking" our interlocking assets—across research teams and funding initiatives. Such broad collaborative efforts—across people, time, and contexts—can extend our capacity to understand and improve this work. Thus, locally and globally, we can create conditions that foster health and development for all those who share this world.

Epilogue

These last 30 years have been an amazing ride—from behavioral measurement and instruction to the world's largest Internet-based resource for promoting community health and development, the Community Tool Box. We continue to work locally, and now work globally through the World Health Organization Collaborating Centre for Community Health and Development.

Recall the saying attributed to the Dakota tribe: "We will be known forever by the tracks we leave." But, where do these tracks lead? We can hardly wait to find out!

Acknowledgments

We are grateful to our many colleagues who made this work possible. These include generations of KU Work Group colleagues and students who helped guide projects from which we learned. They include senior staff colleagues over the years, including: Jerry Schultz, Vince Francisco,

Adrienne Paine-Andrews, Jacquie Fisher, Rod Bremby, Renee Boothroyd, Valorie Carson, Rachel Oliverius, Bev Graham, Yolanda Suarez, Fabricio Balcazar, and Tom Seekins. They also include generations of wonderful students, both graduate and undergraduate. We also appreciate the patient teaching of colleagues in the many different efforts described here, and in the broader Community Tool Box team, including Bill Berkowitz and Tom Wolff. Finally, we thank the grant makers whose generous support enabled us to learn and contribute, including the Kansas Health Foundation, the Robert Wood Johnson Foundation, the John D. and Catherine T. McArthur Foundation, the Kansas Office of Social and Rehabilitative Services, the Ewing Marion Kauffman Foundation, and the U.S. Centers for Disease Control and Prevention. Special thanks to Dick Schiefelbusch who made room at the table for one more group trying to make a difference. We may be reached at: KU Work Group for Community Health and Development, 4082 Dole Center, 1000 Sunnyside Avenue, University of Kansas, Lawrence, Kansas 66045. For more information, go to the KU Work Group web site: http://www. communityhealth.ku.edu.

References

Annan, K. A. (2000). *"We the peoples": The role of the United Nations in the 21st century* (Millennium Report of the Secretary-General of the United Nations). New York: United Nations. Available on-line at http://www.un.org/millennium/.

Baer, D. M. (1985). Comment on Denkowski and Denkowski: Community-based residential treatment of the mentally retarded adolescent offender. *Journal of Community Psychology, 13,* 306–307.

Baer, D. M., Wolf, M. M., & Risley, T. R. (1968). Some current dimensions of applied behavior analysis. *Journal of Applied Behavior Analysis, 1,* 306–307.

Baer, D. M., Wolf, M. M., & Risley, T. R. (1987). Some still-current dimensions of applied behavior analysis. *Journal of Applied Behavior Analysis, 20,* 313–327.

Berkman, L. F., & Syme, S. L. (1979). Social networks, host resistance and mortality: A nine-year follow-up study of Alameda County residents. *American Journal of Epidemiology, 109,* 186–204.

Biglan, A. (1995). *Changing cultural practices: A contextual framework for intervention research.* Reno, NV: Context Press.

CDC (U.S. Centers for Disease Control and Prevention). (2002). *Syndemics overview: What procedures are available for planning and evaluating initiatives to prevent syndemics?* The National Center for Chronic Disease Prevention and Health Promotion Syndemics Prevention Network. Available on-line at http://www.cdc.goc/syndemics.

Community Tool Box. (2003). *Developing an action plan* (Chap. 8, Sec. 5). Available on-line at http://ctb.ku.edu/tools/en/tools_toc.htm.

Connell, J. P., Kubish, A. C., Schorr, L. B., & Weiss, C. H. (1995). *New approaches to evaluating community initiatives: Concepts, methods, and contexts.* Washington, DC: The Aspen Institute.

Cook, T. D., & Campbell, T. D. (1979). *Quasi-experimentation: Design and analysis issues for field settings.* Chicago: Rand McNally.

DHHS (Department of Health and Human Services). 2000. *Healthy People 2010.* Available on-line at http://www.health.gov/healthypeople/document.htm.

Eoyang, G. H. (1997). *Coping with chaos: Seven simple tools.* Cheyenne, WY: Lagumo Corp.

Fawcett, S. B. (1991). Some values guiding community research and action. *Journal of Applied Behavior Analysis, 24,* 621–636.

Fawcett, S. B., Boothroyd, R. I., Schultz, J. A., Francisco, V. T., Carson, V. L., & Bremby, R. (2003). Building capacity for participatory evaluation within community initiatives. *Journal of Prevention and Intervention in the Community, 26*(2), 21–36.

Fawcett, S. B., Francisco, V. T., Hyra, D., Paine-Andrews, A., Schultz, J. A., Russos, S., et al. (2000). Building healthy communities. In A. Tarlov & R. St. Peter (Eds.), *The society and population health reader: A state and community perspective.* (pp. 75–93). New York: The New Press.

Fawcett, S. B., Francisco, V. T., Paine-Andrews, A., and Schultz, J. (2000). A model memorandum of collaboration: A proposal. *Public Health Reports, 115,* 174–179.

Fawcett, S. B., Francisco, V. T., Schultz, J., Berkowitz, B., Wolff, T. J., & Nagy, G. (2000). The Community Tool Box: A Web-based resource for building healthier communities. *Public Health Reports, 115,* 274–278.

Fawcett, S. B., Lewis, R. K., Paine-Andrews, A., Francisco, V. T., Richter, K. P., Williams, E. L., et al. (1997). Evaluating community coalitions for the prevention of substance abuse: The case of Project Freedom. *Health Education and Behavior, 24*(6), 812–828.

Fawcett, S. B., Mathews, R. M., & Fletcher, R. K. (1980). Some promising dimensions for behavioral community technology. *Journal of Applied Behavior Analysis, 13,* 508–518.

Fawcett, S. B., Paine-Andrews, A., Francisco, V. T., Schultz, J. A., Richter, K. P., Lewis, R. L., et al. (1996). Empowering community health initiatives through evaluation. In D. M. Fetterman, S. J. Kaftarian, & A. Wandersman (Eds.), *Empowerment evaluation: Knowledge and tools for self-assessment and accountability* (pp. 161–187). Thousand Oaks, CA: Sage.

Fawcett, S. B., Paine-Andrews, A., Francisco, V. T., Schultz, J. A., Richter, K. P., et al. (2001). Evaluating community initiatives for health and development. In I. Rootman, M. Goodstadt, B. Hyndman, D. McQueen, L. Potvin, J. Springett, & E. Ziglio (Eds.), *Evaluation in health promotion: Principles and perspectives* (pp. 241–270). Copenhagen, Denmark: World Health Organization–Europe.

Fawcett, S. B., Paine-Andrews, A., Francisco, V. T., Schultz, J. A., Richter, K. P., Lewis, R. L., et al. (1995). Using empowerment theory in collaborative partnerships for community health and development. *American Journal of Community Psychology, 23,* 677–697.

Fawcett, S. B., Schultz, J. A., Carson, V. L., Renault, V. A., & Francisco, V. T. (2003). Using Internet-based tools to build capacity for community-based participatory research and other efforts to promote community health and development. In M. Minkler & N. Wallerstein (Eds.), *Community-based participatory research for health* (pp. 155–178). San Francisco: Jossey-Bass.

Fawcett, S. B., Seekins, T., Whang, P. L., Muiu, C., & Suarez de Balcazar, Y. (1982). The Concerns Report Method: Involving consumers in setting local improvement agendas. *Social Policy, 13*(4), 36–41.

Fawcett, S. B., Sterling, T. D., Paine-Andrews, A., Harris, K. J., Francisco, V. T., Richter, K. P., et al. (1995). *Evaluating community efforts to prevent cardiovascular diseases.* Atlanta, GA: Centers for Disease Control and Prevention, National Center for Chronic Disease Prevention and Health Promotion.

Fetterman, D. M., Kaftarian, S. J., & Wandersman, A. (Eds.). (1996). *Empowerment evaluation: Knowledge and tools for self-assessment and accountability.* Thousand Oaks, CA: Sage.

Francisco, V. T., Paine, A., & Fawcett, S. B. (1993). A methodology for monitoring and evaluating community health coalitions. *Health Education Research: Theory and Practice, 8,* 403–416.

Gladwell, M. (2000). *The tipping point: How little things can make a big difference.* Boston: Little, Brown, and Co.

Glenn, S. S. (1988). Contingencies and metacontingencies: Toward a synthesis of behavior analysis and cultural materialism. *The Behavior Analyst, 11,* 161–179.

Goodman, R. M., Speers, M. A., McLeroy, K., Fawcett, S. B., Kegler, M., Parker, E. A., et al. (1998). Identifying and defining the dimensions of community capacity to provide a basis for measurement. *Health Education and Behavior, 25,* 258–278.

Green, L. W., George, M. A., Daniel, M., Frankish, C. J., Herbert, C. P., Bowie, W. R., et al. (1995). *Study of participatory research in health promotion: Review and recommendations for the development of participatory research in health promotion in Canada.* Vancouver, British Columbia: Royal Society of Canada.

Green, L. W., & Kreuter, M. W. (1991). *Health promotion planning: An educational and environmental approach.* Toronto: Mansfield.

Himmelman, A. T. (1992). *Communities working collaboratively for a change.* Minneapolis, MN: University of Minnesota, Humphrey Institute for Public Affairs.

Institute of Medicine. (1988). *The future of public health.* Washington, DC: National Academies Press.

Institute of Medicine. (1997). *Improving health in the community: A role for performance monitoring.* Washington, DC: National Academies Press.

Institute of Medicine. (2003). Community. In *The future of the public's health in the 21st century* (pp. 178–211). Washington, DC: National Academies Press.

Jason, L., Keys, C., Suarez-Balcazar, Y., Taylor, R. R., Davis, M., Durlak, J., et al. (2004). *Participatory community research: Theories and methods in action.* Washington, DC: American Psychological Association.

Johnson, J. M., & Pennypacker, H. S. (1980). *Strategies and tactics of human behavioral research.* Hillsdale, NJ: Erlbaum.

Kawachi, I., Kennedy, B. P., Lochner, K., & Prothrow-Stith, D. (1997). Social capital, income inequality, and mortality. *American Journal of Public Health, 87,* 1491–1498.

Kegler, M. C., Steckler, A., McLeroy, K., & Malek, S. H. (1998). Factors that contribute to effective community health promotion coalitions: a study of 10 project ASSIST coalitions in North Carolina. *Health Education and Behavior, 25,* 338–353.

Lee J. (2003). Global health improvement and WHO: Shaping the future. *The Lancet, 362* (20/27), 2083–2088.

Lewis, R. K., Paine-Andrews, A., Fisher, J. L., Custard, C., Fleming-Randle, M., & Fawcett, S. B. (1999). Reducing the risk for adolescent pregnancy: Evaluation of a school/community partnership in a military community. *Family and Community Health, 22*(2), 16–30.

Marmot, M., Bosma, H., Hemingway, H., Brunner, E. J., & Stansfield, S. A. (1997). Contribution of job control and other risk factors to social variations in coronary heart disease incidence. *Lancet, 350,* 235–239.

Marr, J. (2004). Paper presented at the VIII Biannual Symposium on the Science of Behavior. Guadalajara, Mexico.

McGinnis, J. M., & Foege, W. H. (1993). Actual causes of death in the United States. *Journal of the American Medical Association, 270*(18), 2207–2212.

Milstein, R. L., & Wetherall, S. F. (2001). Framework for program evaluation in public health. *Mortality and Morbidity Weekly Review, 48,* 1–40.

Minkler, M., & Wallerstein, N. (Eds.). (2003). *Community-based participatory research for health.* San Francisco: Jossey-Bass.

Paine, A., Francisco, V. T., & Fawcett, S. B. (1994). Assessing community health concerns and implementing a microgrants program for self-help initiatives. *American Journal of Public Health, 84*(4), 316–318.

Paine-Andrews, A., Fawcett, S. B., Richter, K. P., Berkley, J., Williams, E. L., & Lopez, C. (1996). Community coalitions to prevent adolescent substance abuse: The case of the "Project Freedom" replication initiative. *Journal of Prevention and Intervention in the Community, 14,* 81–99.

Paine-Andrews, A., Fisher, J. L., Berkley-Patton, J., Fawcett, S. B., Williams, E. L., Lewis, R. K., et al. (2002). Analyzing the contribution of community change to population health outcomes in an adolescent pregnancy prevention initiative. *Health Education and Behavior, 29*(2), 183–193.

Paine-Andrews, A., Harris, K. J., Fawcett, S. B., Richter, K. P., & Lewis, R. K. (1997). Evaluating a statewide partnership for reducing risks for chronic diseases. *Journal of Community Health, 22,* 343–359.

Paine-Andrews, A., Harris, K. J., Fisher, J. L., Lewis, R. K., Williams, E. L., et al. (1999). Effects of a replication of a school/community model for preventing adolescent pregnancy in three Kansas communities. *Family Planning Perspectives, 31,* 182–189.

Rappaport, J. (1977). *Community psychology: Values, research and action.* New York: Holt, Rinehart, and Winston.

Risley, T. (2004). Paper presented at the VIII Biannual Symposium on the Science of Behavior. Guadalajara, Mexico.

Russos, S., & Fawcett, S. B. (2000). A review of collaborative partnerships as a strategy for improving community health. *Annual Review of Public Health, 21,* 369–402.

Russos, S., Fawcett, S. B., Francisco, V. T., Berkley, J. Y., & Lopez, C. M. (1997). A behavioral analysis of collaborative partnerships for community health. In P. A. Lamal (Ed.), *Cultural contingencies: Behavioral analytic perspectives on cultural practices* (pp. 87–106). Westport, CT: Praeger.

Schultz, J. A., Fawcett, S. B., Francisco, V. T., & Berkowitz, B. (2003). Using information systems to build capacity: The public health improvement tool box. In P. Carroll, W. A. Yasnoff, M. E. Ward, R. Rubin, & L. Ripp (Eds.), *Public health infomatics and information systems: A contributed work.* (pp. 644–646). Gaithersburg, MD: Aspen.

Skinner, B. F. (1972). *Beyond freedom and dignity.* New York: Knopf.

Stull, D. D., & Schensul, J. J. (1987). *Collaborative research for social change.* Boulder, CO: Westview Press.

Tarlov, A. R., & St. Peter, R. F. (2000). *The society and population health reader: A state and community perspective.* New York: The New Press.

Task Force on Community Preventive Services. (2000). *The guide to community preventive services.* Available on-line at www.thecommunityguide.org/home_f.html.

Tolan, P., Keys, C., Chernok, C., & Jason, L. (1990). *Researching community psychology: Integrating theories and methodologies.* Washington, DC: American Psychological Association.

Whyte, W. F. (Ed.). (1991). *Participatory action research.* Newbury Park, CA: Sage.

Wilkinson, R. G. (1996). *Unhealthy societies: The afflictions of inequality.* London: Routledge.

World Bank (2001). *World development report 2000/2001: Attacking poverty.* New York: Oxford University Press.

World Health Organization. (1986). The Ottawa Charter for Health Promotion. *Health Promotion, 1,* iii–v.

Yin, R. K. (1988). *Case study research: Design and methods.* Newbury Park, CA: Sage.

24

The Center for Multicultural Leadership

STEPHEN R. SCHROEDER AND JACOB U. GORDON

Instituted by the Board of Regents in 1986 as the Institute for Black Leadership Development and Research, it was renamed the Center for Multicultural Leadership (CML) and assigned to the Life Span Institute (LSI) in 1991 by Frances Horowitz, the vice chancellor for research, graduate studies, and public service. Its director was Jacob Gordon, an associate professor of African and African American studies at the University of Kansas (KU). Gordon was a well-known energetic activist on campus.

Upon coming to LSI, Jake Gordon began working on a number of projects related to multicultural leadership: 1) an annual Black Leadership Symposium; 2) an annual African-American Achievement Awards Banquet; 3) the *Journal of African-American Male Studies;* 4) Black family studies, with conferences and workshops; 5) alcohol and drug abuse studies in minority populations; 6) National Council of African-American Men; 7) establishment of the Kansas Multicultural Association for Substance Abuse; 8) a summer institute to prepare minorities for graduate studies; 9) African-American Youth Leadership Academy, to prepare high school students for college, with training sites in Wichita, Topeka, and Kansas City; 10) scholarship awards for gifted African American students; and 11) collaborative studies on multicultural issues with the Beach Center, African Studies, School of Social Welfare, the Gerontology Center, the Research and Training Center on Independent Living, and the Kansas University Affiliated Program. These efforts were totally funded through foundation grants from the Village Foundation, the Schumann Foundation, the Kellogg Foundation, and others. Many monographs and conference proceedings by Jake (over 20) came from this work.

All of Jake's projects were aimed at dispelling the myths, misconceptions, and stereotypes about minorities, especially Black males, that permeate United States society. He was determined to do something about that. In a sense, he was our conscience in academia.

One of Jake's projects that was particularly innovative was his Kellogg Foundation grant on the African American Male Leadership Academy (AAMLA). In this program, he identified talented African American men and boys and exposed them to leadership activities, partnerships with community organizations, businesses, and in summer institutes where they were trained in leadership skills. The great thing about these programs was that trainees were able to make contacts with prospective future employers. Here are some examples of the things they did in these summer institutes:

- *Kansas City, Kansas*—The Kansas City, Kansas summer institute trainees volunteered their services to Habitat for Humanity. The students were involved in initiating a local chapter of Students Together Rising Against Packing Pieces (STRAPP), an organization that promotes nonviolence among teenagers.
- *Kansas City, Missouri*—The program expanded to the Kansas City, Missouri School District. In cooperation with Project Neighborhood, Inc. and the Sprint Corporation, students would spend a day at Sprint and attended career seminars in the Sprint Corporation offices.
- *Topeka*—In the Topeka summer institute, students attended monthly career and leadership development seminars. The guest speakers were prominent African American male professionals in the Topeka community. They are also prepared for summer internships through resume and interview training. Several of the participants worked as interns with some of Topeka's local businesses during Christmas vacation.
- *Wichita*—During African American History Month, some of the students at the Wichita site prepared 2-minute speeches on Outstanding African American Heroes of the Past that were aired on a local

radio station throughout the month. They were also well known for their drill team. They competed annually at Langston University's Homecoming.

Some Staggering Statistics

Programs such as the AAMLA are important to all of us for the following reasons:

- *Population*—In 1990 the total United States population was 248,709,873. The total African American population was 29,930,524 (12%). Of this number, 14,170,151 were males (United States Census, 1990).
- *Health*—Black male life expectancy in 1991 was 64.6 years. White male life expectancy in 1991 was 72.9 years. The death rate for Black males with HIV in 1991 was 52.9%. The death rate for White males with HIV in 1991 was 16.7% (National Center for Health Statistics, 1994). Black males were more likely to be born to unwed teenage mothers who themselves have limited education and even more limited life choices (Gibbs, 1988).
- *Homicide*—The homicide rate in 1991 for African American males was 72.5 per 100,000, nearly 8 times higher than for White males (FBI, 1993).
- *Poverty*—The rate of poverty for all African Americans is 29.5% compared with 9.8% for Whites (United States Census, 1992). Nearly half (42.7%) of Black youth under 18 live in families below the poverty line (Curtis, 1996).
- *Family Life*—Of the 7,055,063 Black families, 3,045,283, or 43%, are headed by Black females; 26.3% of all Black families live in poverty, compared with 7.0% of White families (United States Census, 1992).
- *Incarceration*—Almost one in three (33%) Black males between the ages of 20 and 29 are under the control of the criminal justice system—in prison, jail, on probation, or on parole. This compares with one in 16 White males and one in 10 Hispanic males (Maurer, 1990). The number of African American males in prison and jail exceeded the number of African American males enrolled in higher education (Maurer, 1990). Black men in the United States were imprisoned at a

rate four times that of Black men in South Africa: 3,109 per 100,000 compared with 729 per 100,000 (Morton & Snell, 1992). Forty-four percent of all prisoners in the United States were Black; Black men made up 40% of the condemned on death row (Sentencing Project, 1990).

- *Education*—More than 20% of the Black male adolescents in the 12- to 17-year age groups were unable to read at the fourth-grade level (Brown, 1979).
- *Stereotypes*—The Black male has been more negatively portrayed in the media and the literature than any other group in American history (Drake & Cayton, 1945; Gibbs, 1988).
- *Jobs*—Unemployment among Black youth was 34%—twice the rate of 17.4% among all teenagers (Gibbs, 1988).

By most demographic indices, morality, health, crime, homicide, life expectancy, income, education, unemployment, and marital status, African American men have the smallest chance to achieve the American dream. In fact, of the four comparison groups (Black males, Black females, White males, White females), social indicators show that Black males experience the highest rates of health and social problems, including heart disease, hypertension, diabetes, homicide, suicide, unemployment, delinquency and crime, school dropout, imprisonment, and unwed teenage parenthood (Gordon & Majors, 1994). As Gibbs (1988) put it, "Black males have been miseducated by the educational system, mishandled by the criminal justice system, mislabeled by the mental health system, and misread by the social welfare system." In fact, she argued that Black males have become rejects of the American affluent society and misfits in their own communities.

Conclusion

The Center for Multicultural Leadership was discontinued in 2003 by Jake in preparation for his retirement in 2004. He was often a loner in championing his causes. He was not afraid of controversy, but his work was always positive and constructive. His contribution to the LSI and KU was substantial.

25

The History of the International Program of the Life Span Institute

STEPHEN R. SCHROEDER

The Bureau of Child Research (BRC) and the Life Span Institute (LSI) have a long and distinguished history of extending their programs to developing countries, especially in Latin America. The early history of these exploits is recounted by Dick Schiefelbusch in chapters 7 and 8 and by Bob Hoyt in chapter 10.

These programs were quite extensive in several countries in Central and South America. They had to be adapted to the political cultures in the various countries of interest. Unfortunately, many of these programs ended when the BCR's representatives were no longer involved, or with the ouster of some president or dictator who was sponsoring the interaction. Those programs that lasted and flourished all worked with the infrastructure of the culture and the country and developed native talent into the decision-making bodies who carried on the program no matter who was in power and who was representing the BCR or LSI at the time.

By 1990, there were three programs remaining, upon which members of the LSI concentrated their efforts: 1) the Inter-American Children's Institute, an Organization of American States (OAS)-sponsored program based in Montevideo, Uruguay; 2) the Alegria School based in Asuncion, Paraguay; and 3) the Centro Ann Sullivan del Peru based in Lima, Peru. Each of these is discussed in this chapter. There were also many other trips during this period to Latin America by BCR and LSI scientists for conferences and so forth that were not part of these programmatic efforts.

The Inter-American Children's Institute

In 1979 Dick Schiefelbusch was invited to visit a school run by Eloísa de Lorenzo, a very charismatic teacher and advocate for children with mental retardation and developmental disabilities in Uruguay and the rest of Latin America. Her connection with the Instituto Interamericano del Nino (IIN), an OAS-sponsored affiliate based in Montevideo, Uruguay, facilitated a relationship of the BRC with IIN. Ross Copeland of the BRC had been appointed to the IIN Director's Council by President Nixon in the early 1970s, which gave him entrée into many other countries in Central and South America. Both he and Bob Hoyt traveled extensively disseminating BCR programs and fostering exchange of visiting scientists. At the time, the BCR had produced over 50 training films on many aspects of disabilities, many of them in Spanish, and these were very useful for dissemination purposes.

In about 1980, another important development occurred. With the intercession of Senator Bob Dole, Marianna Beach was appointed the next U.S. representative to the director's Council of the IIN. The Beaches are one of the supernumerary families for which Kansas is famous—influential families with a strong social commitment who have had a substantial impact on their generation.

Marianna Beach represented the United States at the IIN in an exemplary fashion for more than a decade. In 1989, she and her husband Ross also endowed the Beach Center on Disability, headed by Ann and Rud Turnbull of LSI, to extend and continue research on children with disabilities and their families within Uruguay and Paraguay. Over the years, the Beach Center has flourished and has expanded greatly. It has now broadened its mandate to cover all aspects of disabilities. A fuller treatment of the Beach Center can be found in chapter 19.

A major contribution by the Beaches through the Beach Center was to fund a $5,000 biennial award for advocacy and service to people with disabilities in Latin American countries. Co-sponsored by the IIN, the competition was open to individuals and organizations in the Americas who have demonstrated an unusually high degree of excellence in the provision of services in some country of the Americas, especially Latin America and the Caribbean.

This is an important award because it recognizes values-based services to people with disabilities. The services must reflect a belief and practice of the following principles: 1) persons with disabilities and their families have the potential for development and can make positive contributions to society; 2) the potential for such self-fulfillment is possible in each person with a disability, but it is dependent upon the support of individuals and institutions in the community; and 3) persons with disability have the same rights as other citizens in all aspects of life. The judges were a distinguished panel of people in the disability field in many countries of Latin America.

Although these values seem self-evident to us today, they were not necessarily the values in delivering services to people with disabilities for many Latin American countries at the time. As a matter of fact, the IIN had been spending most of its time trying to find, count, and care for homeless children and children of war, rather than to care for its people with disabilities. Their approach to people with disabilities was very paternalistic and custodial. In some countries (e.g., Chile), this is still true today, a relic of the Pinochet regime.

Eloísa de Lorenzo was the role model in pioneering the rights of children with disabilities in Latin America. Starting as a teacher in rural Uruguay in the 1940s, she later completed graduate work in the United States in the education of children with special needs. She became famous all through Latin America for developing programs for children. In 1966 the IIN appointed her to develop programs on their behalf for children with disabilities in education and rehabilitation. She extended collaborations of the IIN with PAHO, WHO, the UN, UNESCO, UNICEF, and many other international organizations to promote the rights of people with disabilities in Latin America.

So the Eloísa de Lorenzo Award was a lasting contribution that still continues today, even though Marianna Beach retired as the U.S. representative to IIN in 1991 and the Beach Center reduced its activities in Latin America in the late 1990s, focusing more on Hispanic and other minority populations in the United States, such as La Raza, a national organization for Hispanic families.

The Alegria School

In 1979 the Bureau of Child Research sent John Throne as its IIN representative to begin work in Asuncion, Paraguay at the Alegria School. John was an interesting personage who had come to the BCR from the

Kennedy Foundation, where he had been the executive director during some of the landmark legislation on mental retardation and disabilities during the Kennedy administration. As he liked to say, he was the "throne behind the power." He was a radical behaviorist, even for the University of Kansas, which was the hotbed of behavior analysis at the time. He was fearless in championing the application of behavior analysis to the causes of people with mental retardation. At one time, he even developed a correspondence with B. F. Skinner about some of his ideas.

When the opportunity to operationalize some of his ideas in Latin America came about, John seized it. So began a 15-year state-of-the-art model school integration program (i.e., the Alegria School) in Asuncion, Paraguay. This was an integrated private elementary school far ahead of its time, in which 50% of the students had mental retardation and 50% were typically developing children. The instruction was highly individualized, using functional assessments of the child's strengths and weaknesses and teaching the behaviors directly, using behavioral objectives, step-by-step programming, time-to-criterion performance measures, prompts, backward chaining, and instructional fading techniques. Brighter students helped tutor slower students. After acquisition, there was an overlearning phase, to routinize what was learned, then another evaluation by the teacher to make sure the instructional steps were appropriate for each child's performance. The program was very successful in teaching academic skills and allowing each child to succeed as much as possible at his or her own rate.

How was such an avant garde program possible in a developing country? Like many cutting-edge programs in Latin America, it was a nongovernmental organization (NGO) sponsored by influential parents who served on the board of directors and whose children were students in the Alegria School.

The Paraguayan government was not involved at first. However, when the Alegria School became so successful and its students fared better than those in the public school system, the government began to take notice. In 1984 a special committee was activated to facilitate advances in these fields in service, training, and research. Under the auspices of the minister of education and culture, the committee consisted of key figures in the public and private sectors, including the minister himself, the director of the National Institute for the Rehabilitation of Exceptional Persons, the director of the Department of Special Education, the president of the National Association of Parents of Exceptional Children, the president of the Paraguay–Kansas chapter of the Partners of the Americas, and John, representing the Bureau of Child Research. They identified 11 projects which needed technical assistance, from early identification and intervention to parent training programs. The mechanism was to be a partnership between the IIN, the Bureau of Child Research, and the Ministry of Education and Culture of Paraguay.

This was a truly national plan for special education for all of Paraguay. But the problems were lack of funding and the lack of support from the government of Paraguay. At the time, the president was a dictator named General Alfredo Stroessner, who had been running Paraguay for 35 years like a feudal state. Indeed, Paraguay was viewed in South America as "an island surrounded by land." Democracy and the rights of people with disabilities were not in favor with his government.

However, the forces of democracy were stirring in the late 1980s and protests in the streets were common. Eventually, Stroessner was unseated in 1989 by one of his own generals in a coup, General Andres Rodriguez. To everyone's surprise, Rodriguez freed the press, pushed for economic reform, and promised democracy. For the disability community, this meant an opportunity to write a Bill of Rights into their new Constitution. This was done. At the same time, John sent his lead teacher at Alegria School, Claudia Pacheco, to the University of Kansas (KU) to take her graduate degree in special education. This she did, and the program seemed to be off and running.

Then tragedy struck: both John Throne and Eloísa de Lorenzo contracted cancer. Two of the key figures in Paraguay special education would soon be out of the picture. John continued to go to Paraguay until his death in 1993. The Alegria School continues, but the national program for special education based on the Alegria model never materialized. The Life Span Institute did not have the resources to fund another person to follow up on John's program. The truth is that he was the right person at the right time, a maverick who was an independent thinker, who had the courage of his convictions, which he put into practice.

John had a way of getting your attention by trying to shock or irritate you. He was constantly making up new words, taking ideas and standing them on their heads, shaking them up, and looking for a new way to view things. I give just one example: the last paper he gave at a conference in Quito, Ecuador just before his death, called "Interpendence." Interpendence was John's alternative to interdependence, which is said to be a cultural difference between the dynamics of Latino families and United States families in their attitude toward children and siblings with disabilities. Latino families are thought to foster dependence of children with disabilities within the nuclear family, whereas United States families are said to foster independence. John's Hegelian synthesis of interpendence occurs even if all the family stays together in later life, but if each member still has the ability to make independent life decisions and be a valued member of the family. We refer to this circumstance currently as consumer empowerment.

In Latin America, the nuclear family is the most important unit of resources for a person with disabilities. In the United States, the government is expected to share this responsibility more. As a model, John pointed to the Family Resource Project developed by Todd Risley, another research scientist of the BCR and the LSI. Todd had developed this project to help provide wrap-around services to people with disabilities living in remote areas of the state of Alaska, where the circle of friends may involve all of the members of a village. John recommended that this model of a wrap-around community resource network be adapted for Latin American families who have more limited financial resources, to foster "interpendence." Until his death, John was always thinking of a better way to serve the people with disabilities and their families in Latin America.

Centro Ann Sullivan del Peru

A third very successful program sponsored by the LSI in Latin America is the Centro Ann Sullivan del Peru (CASP) in Lima, Peru. The name Ann Sullivan was chosen in recognition of the famous teacher of Helen Keller. In the late 1970s, Liliana Mayo was a newly graduated clinical psychologist from San Marcos University in Lima, Peru. Her area of expertise and responsibility was behavior modification programs. San Marcos University was also home to the Shining Path, the terrorist maoist organization that later became violent and caused havoc in Peru for almost two decades. Being a radical behaviorist, Liliana and her friends were considered "radicals." To punish her, the then-chairperson of psychology changed Liliana's internship from a clinical program to one working with people with disabilities. In those days in Peru no one wanted to work with this population.

Liliana fell in love with the population. She was especially fascinated by children with autism. She moved into the field of special education and devoted herself to working full time with people with autism—a group who fascinated her. Since there were no educational facilities for children with severe autism or severe behavior problems in Peru, she enlisted the help of three colleagues and started a program for eight pupils in the garage of her parents' house.

Although Liliana had read many of the works of Bijou, Sidman, and Skinner, she felt she "was in over her head" and needed some help to know how to develop her center. Her parents sold some property to fund a trip for her to visit programs in Mexico and California for people with autism. In 1980, while in Los Angeles attending an American Psychological Association conference, she was looking for professionals willing to assist and consult with her in her endeavor. There she met Judy LeBlanc, who at the time was the co-chair of the Department of Human Development and Family Life (now the Department of Applied Behavioral Sciences) at KU.

Liliana found out that Judy was to be consulting and giving a series of workshops at the Central University of Venezuela in Caracas, Venezuela the following year. She thus persuaded Judy to extend her trip to visit the CASP program in Lima. When Judy arrived, there were already 50 children attending classes at CASP and the classrooms had spread throughout the first floor of the house. Judy, like many professionals after her, was impressed with how much the staff already knew of behavior analysis and was transported by their dedication, enthusiasm, and industriousness. They were determined to make a difference and to do whatever was necessary to succeed. So began a long partnership between Judy and Liliana in developing a state-of-the-art program for children with severe disabilities and autism and severe behavior problems.

Once again we might ask how such a successful NGO program happened in a developing country with little help from the government and often with a severe shortage of funding due to crises in the Peruvian economy. The key ingredients seem to be: 1) a strong commitment by the nuclear family, friends, and professionals to educating and caring for their children with disabilities; 2) effective utilization of expert consultation and technical assistance from experienced consultants who do not "take over" the program, but problem solve with teachers and parents; and 3) mutual respect between professionals and families regardless of differences in culture, family values and preferences, or political orientations.

Judy LeBlanc was especially gifted as a consultant. A master teacher herself, she began teaching the staff and working directly with them as they worked with the students and their families. She also had years of administrative experience and knew how to guide them toward making sound decisions regarding their future directions. She never made decisions for the CASP staff, but instead encouraged them to problem solve, with guidance and prompting as only she could do. After first visiting CASP in 1981 and again in 1983, she took a 1-year sabbatical in 1986–1987 in Peru to begin developing the curriculum. Since 1986, she has returned to Peru each year for a period of 4 to 6 months each year to teach and consult with the staff. In 1985–1986 Liliana completed her MA degree in the Department of Human Development and completed her PhD in 1996, attending only one semester (5 months) a year and returning to Peru to direct CASP the remainder of the year. Judy was her advisor and together they were developing the programs at CASP and teaching the staff. The net result was a group of master teachers who could attack any problems that arose at CASP, and who could effectively evaluate their own progress. The staff, in turn, became teachers of other professionals and parents throughout the provinces of Peru. The approach resulted in a multiplicative effect of the program. Because so many wanted to learn how to establish similar programs in other regions in Peru, veteran parents and friends became teachers, mentors, and evaluators of other new parents of children with disabilities. Veteran students became coaches of newer students.

There are 14 consultants who have taught the staff over the years: From KU, they are Judy LeBlanc, Barbara Thompson, Eva Horn, Steve Warren, Wayne Sailor, Matt Reese, Jessica Hellings, Carolyn Schroeder, Glen White, Georgina Peacock, and Steve Schroeder; from the University of Georgia, David Gast; from Tampa, Florida, Mary Aangeenbrug; and from the University of Dublin, Christy Lynch.

In 1990, CASP was in a financial crisis. The Peruvian economy was in shambles with 1,000% inflation. Alberto Fujimori had just been elected president of Peru and had instated economic hardship measures, devaluing the currency and essentially canceling all debts. This led to ruining Peru's credit and investment status internationally and cutting the purchasing power of all people in Peru. CASP now did not have enough income to pay its bills and was facing closure. Liliana and Judy contacted Heinz Heiner, a Dutch psychologist they met at the Association for Behavior Analysis Convention the previous year and asked for suggestions to help them pay the staff and start the program again the next year. Heinz, a board member of Stichting Kinderpostzegels Fonds in Holland, suggested to the other board members that they help CASP and it was immediately decided to send CASP sufficient funds to allow them to begin the new year.

At this point the LSI began to sponsor CASP as an international affiliate program. Judy LeBlanc also became the LSI director of international programs and was funded part time to continue her work with CASP. In 1997 she took early retirement from the university in order to devote herself full time to the work at CASP, a great part of which was fund raising. Fortunately she and Liliana found several philanthropists and foundations to help support the program. Chief among them were the Christian Foundation for Children and Aging, based in Kansas City; Stichting Kinderpostzegels and Lilian Fonds in the Netherlands; the Rotary Club of Sudbury, Ontario, Canada, as well as Rotary International; and the Mary Spader family, an entrepreneurial farm family from Oldham, South Dakota. Project money from these sources has allowed CASP to annually wave tuition for about 60% of the families because they have insufficient income to pay.

A third fortuitous event was that Annie Sullivan Enterprises, Inc., a U.S.-based, private, nonprofit corporation headed by Carolyn and Steve Schroeder, began to sponsor the CASP program. This gave CASP a U.S.-approved base to receive and administer donations and project funds, to assure that the money could not suddenly be devalued by another government coup in Peru. Also foreign foundations could be assured of proper fiscal accountability for their donations. Steve and Carolyn's son, Matthew, who is in international business, went to CASP over a 2-year period to help organize their administrative structure and to develop business and accounting plans to make the organization more stable. Annie Sullivan Enterprises, Inc. subsequently gave scholarships for key teachers at CASP, such as Yemi Oyama, to complete graduate training and also helped professionals from other countries to come to Peru to learn how to develop a similar program in their country.

Good fiscal accountability encouraged more giving. In 2000, Lilian Fonds of Holland nominated CASP for an award of $1 million from the Nationale Postcode Loterij de Holanda (a Dutch lottery for charitable purposes) to complete a new building, which had been started with a donation of nearly $250,000 from the Spader family. Thus the first totally accessible, state-of-the-art facility was completed to support CASP's state-of-the-art program that was now rapidly growing.

Current Status

Today CASP is a model international research, demonstration, and training center where about 450 people with disabilities and their families are educated annually. Nine similar programs in different parts of the world (three in Spain, two in Argentina, two in Brazil, one in Bolivia, and one in Chile) actively follow the functional/natural curriculum model developed at CASP. There are three or four other professionals and parents who are in contact with CASP and are learning in hopes of starting such programs in their home country. CASP has a program that requires annual reports from these associated programs in exchange for continuing consultation and, when possible, visitation by CASP staff members.

CASP has four areas of operation: education, inclusion, parent and professional training, and administration. The education and inclusion areas are concerned with education of students enrolled in CASP and their families. The parent and professional training area is involved in the education of parents both within CASP and from other areas of the country and the world. The administration area is concerned with the overall operation of the CASP programs, the directions of CASP growth, the image of CASP, and the financial and administrative concerns of CASP.

At CASP, students have individualized life plans and educational programs that are designed to make them independent, productive, and happy now and when they become adults. For students who are nonverbal, CASP uses the PECS (Picture Exchange Communication System). PECS was created by Andy Bondy and Lori Frost to teach students to initiate communication and to respond spontaneously. CASP also has a read–write program and a mathematics program developed by Mary Aangeenbrug and Judy LeBlanc. The educational program of CASP is based on the functional/natural curriculum created by Judy LeBlanc with the CASP staff. It prepares students for success in the integration of life, while becoming independent, productive, and happy. The curriculum emphasizes teaching functional abilities that are immediately useful today and in the future.

Education

CASP has an Early Intervention Program to teach parents how to teach their infants and to aid in their development; a Preschool Program that focuses on socialization, self-care, language, and preacademics; a School Program that includes academics, independent functioning, socialization, and work skills; and a Prevocational Program that places emphasis on teaching students to do real contracted work in the classroom, as well as in commercial establishments of the community, such as minimarkets, carpentry shops, bakeries, restaurants, car repair shops, superstores, banks, and so forth. In this kind of teaching, students can apply their knowledge of academics, communication, and courtesy in the real world. All programs emphasize teaching students to be independent and focus on their integration into their homes, schools, and communities.

Inclusion

The inclusion area includes a Supported Employment Program, a School Inclusion Program, and an Open School Program, which is similar to a clinical parent training program. Supported employment in the CASP program is real work with a competitive salary in real work places. Supported employment programs teach people with different abilities to use their special abilities in specific jobs. The CASP Supported Employment Program assumes that the only way to learn a real job is to do the job in the work place.

Currently the Supported Employment Program at CASP has over 60 adults with severe autism, Down syndrome, cerebral palsy, or other limitations working in high-quality companies. The coaches who teach the students in the work places are CASP family members or volunteer university students. Several CASP students who are working in these jobs support their families with their salaries because their parents cannot find work at a time of economic difficulties in Peru. Despite the high rate of unemployment in Peru, CASP students can compete with others for jobs because they are hired on the basis of the quality of their work and not for charity. Some workers have been in their jobs for more than 9 years, producing quality precise work exceeding company expectations, even though they cannot talk, read, or write.

CASP began inclusion programs in the regular schools of Peru in 1979. Currently there are 50 students included in schools throughout Lima and the Provinces. The integration team is comprised of the parents, the teachers of the regular school, the integration specialist from CASP, and the other students in the classroom.

The Open School Program began in 1993 as an alternative for families who live far from CASP in Lima and for those for whom CASP has no immediate vacancy. It now has over 150 students and families. There is a weekend program for those parents who cannot take time off from their jobs to participate in the program. In this program, advances that the students make are primarily due to the efforts of the parents to be good teachers of their children.

Professional and Parent Training

Families of students in programs in the education and inclusion areas are also educated in a School of Families Program in which they must be enrolled as long as their child with limitations is enrolled in CASP. When Liliana created CASP, she created this School of Families which is perhaps the first of its kind in the world and certainly the largest with its 450 families who are enrolled. When a child is admitted to CASP, the parents must agree to learn how to teach their child. They are then graded on their participation in the education of their child. If they do not participate, they will receive low grades. If after a year or two their participation does not improve, it will be suggested to them that they find another placement for their child, because the success of the CASP program depends on ensuring that what is taught in the classroom is taught and practiced in the home and community so generalization can occur. The objective is to continually educate parents, helping them to be the best parents possible for their children. The best scholastic programs in the world are useless if children are not given the opportunity to practice their recently acquired skills in their homes, communities, and work. CASP annually offers 132 hours of training to each family, in large groups, small groups, individually in the classrooms, and in the homes. From the time brothers and sisters are 4 years old, they are included in the family training.

The CASP parent and professional training area is also responsible for training over 14,000 parents and professionals in workshops all over Peru. The educational programs use many examples and demonstrations as well as opportunities to role-play real-life situations for attendees. Many other professionals and family members also come to the center to receive more hands-on training.

The parent and professional training area is also responsible for the Long Distance Education Program, created in 1997. This program is for teaching professionals and parents in the provinces of Peru and is again based on the multiplicative education approach. People who will be facilitators come from each of the sites to spend a couple of weeks at CASP learning the current topic to be taught in their province. The topics are based on the educational videos produced at CASP to teach others how to do what is done there. Currently there are eight videos and there are about 15 more planned for developing in the future. The facilitators then return to their provinces and teach the currently enrolled group by showing and discussing the video with the aid of the manuals created at CASP. Each of 7 to 10 sessions per unit includes a part of the current video and this is shown at the beginning of the session, after which an hour is spent with a CASP consultant discussing issues and answering questions. This is a way that CASP can more rapidly extend knowledge to many people who are interested in working with people with disabilities. There are currently 14 sites involved in this program, thanks to funding provided by Integra, Inc. of Peru, who is providing the necessary funding to simultaneously teach in 14 areas of Peru. Each of the sites is assigned one staff member from CASP for their permanent consultant and that consultant makes one trip to the site for direct consultation during each unit that is studied.

The next projects for the parent and professional training area will be a Long Distance Education Program involving interactive video conferencing from KU Medical Center to CASP in Peru; and a web-based certification program that will be based on the same educational videos used in the Long Distance Education Program.

Awards

CASP and Liliana Mayo have received many local and Peruvian national awards as well as the three-country regional South American INICTEL award for innovative uses of technology in education; the Queen Sofia of Spain award for outstanding education and rehabilitation programs; the Association for Behavior Analysis International Dissemination Award; and the University of Kansas Distinguished Service Award. Liliana Mayo is also a senior social entrepreneur member of ASHOKA International.

26

The History of the University of Kansas at Parsons Providing Access to Information and Technology

CHARLES R. SPELLMAN, PAMELA J. CRESS, AND SARA H. SACK

The University of Kansas at Parsons has a long history of research, demonstration, and service that has greatly impacted individuals with disabilities having greater access to information and technology. The first section briefly describes some of programs that were designed to provide increased access to information. The second and third sections focus on activities that resulted in increased access to technology.

Access to Information

Access to information involved improving the way students with disabilities were served by schools, by providing individuals with disabilities the skills needed to work, by identifying and correcting vision problems of infant, toddlers, and school-aged students with disabilities, and by developing programs to teach students to manage an individual health fitness program. Project MESH (Model Education for Severely Handicapped) focused on developing strategies that would allow students with severe disabilities to have access to information that is generally available through public schools. The grant for this project was awarded as a result of collaboration among most of the researchers associated with the University of Kansas' Bureau of Child Research in Parsons, Kansas in the early 1970s. The purpose of this project was to demonstrate that students with severe disabilities could successfully be served in community-based, rural, public schools. This was the first "Zero Reject" school in Kansas. Thirty years of additional research and demonstration evolved from this initial project that began the process of applying evidence-based instruction in nonlaboratory settings.

A subsequent grant allowed researchers to replicate the Project MESH model in three rural school districts in Kansas (Programming Regional Intervention for Difficult to Educate [PRIDE]). Concurrent with this grant, a state-funded project was established to replicate the vocational training component from Project MESH in community-based programs serving adults with disabilities (Adult Service Provider In-service [ASPIN]). This project was designed to teach individuals with disabilities critical work skills. Another grant was funded to demonstrate that students with severe disabilities could work in "high-tech jobs" in competitive employment settings (Innovative Vocational Education in Technological Areas for Severely Handicapped Youth). This was one of the first demonstrations that individuals with severe cognitive disabilities could be successful in real jobs in Kansas.

During the 1st year of Project MESH, it was discovered that most of our students could not perform on vision screening procedures that were available and that Kansas law required public schools to provide regular vision screening to all students. During the 2nd year of this project, staff began pilot research that led to the development and marketing of the Parsons Visual Acuity Test, the first commercially available tool for testing students who were unable to perform on standard vision screening tests. Two field-initiated research projects validated these procedures for individuals with severe disabilities and preschool children who were unable to perform on standard vision screening procedures (Research and Development of Subjective Visual Acuity Procedures of Severely Handicapped Persons; Research and Development of Subjective Visual Acuity Procedures for Handicapped Preschool Children). This was followed by a series of federal grants including:

- National In-Service Training Project for Vision Screeners of the Difficult-to-Test;
- Statewide Program for Early Identification of Deaf–Blind Children;
- Five-Year National Communication Skills Center for Young Children with Deaf–Blindness;

- Early Behavioral Identification and Referral to Developmental Services (Early BIRDS);
- Personnel Preparation Project to Provide Vision Screening and Evaluation Services to Children from Birth to Three Years; and
- Knowledge Dissemination for Vision Screeners.

In 2000 the work in visual acuity research and training was completed with the development of an interactive CD-ROM for training others to screen the vision of infants, toddlers, and school-aged students.

Another major activity that was initiated during Project MESH was the development of a picture reading curriculum for students who were unable to read traditional textbooks. At that time there were no textbooks for students with moderate and severe cognitive disabilities. Project staff developed a crude, but useful, series of books that were used to teach a wide variety of tasks. Students and staff found these "homemade books" to be very useful. Data suggest that they were not only useful in teaching the task and as a reference source once the task had been learned, but also that these students were "learning how to learn." Another series of research grants was generated related to the picture reading curriculum originally developed by Project MESH. These federal research grants included a transition curriculum for students with moderate and severe disabilities (A Picture Symbol Transitional Curriculum for Moderately and Severely Handicapped Adolescents) and a literacy research grant (Picture Reading to Promote Literacy of Students with Moderate and Severe Disabilities) that developed an innovative way to use a small number of verbs to represent the "universe" of verbs needed to complete almost any task.

In 2003 a small business grant (Picture Reader: Behavioral Technology for Teaching Task Sequencing Skills) was funded to develop web-based software that would allow individuals with disabilities to learn new tasks in which the learner could receive the level of instruction needed to complete a task through computerized instruction (e-books for individuals with disabilities). The e-books use words or pictures to represent nouns and 23 symbols that represent the universe of verbs or prepositions needed to complete any task. For example, the verb "bake" is not used. Rather "bake" is where you put the pan, for how long, and at what temperature. This would be represented by: "pan in oven, turn dial to 350 degrees or a color-coded mark on the dial, turn to 45 minutes or color-coded mark on dial." Again, pictures represent nouns and verbs and prepositions are represented by symbols. If pictures represent objects to the individual and if he or she knows the actions associated with the 23 verbs, the learner can complete any manual task.

For example, the step in a cooking program "pan in oven" is represented by a picture of a pan, the symbol for "in," and a picture of an oven. This three-word sentence, "pan in oven," also has the written word (available in English and several other languages) below the pictures and symbols. If the learners do not know how to put "cake in oven," they can view a short movie clip of this step. Finally, individuals can practice the step or demonstrate that they understand the step by "clicking and dragging" a picture of a pan into the oven. Some problems of generalization can be reduced because the program allows one to change any of the pictures in the e-books to be the same stove or pan the individual will be using. This is accomplished by using a digital camera to take pictures and downloading them to the program. A prototype was recently completed and the Phase 2 grant was awarded; the project began in August 2005. Because of the universal design features, this also has implications for use with non-English-speaking individuals and other non-disabled populations.

In 1988 two grants were awarded to develop methods for teaching health fitness to individuals with disabilities and to train others to replicate these efforts (Preparation of Personnel to Deliver Health Fitness Programs to Students with Moderate and Severe Handicaps; Health Fitness Transition Program for Students with Severe Handicaps). These programs developed techniques for teaching students with moderate and severe disabilities to monitor their health fitness activities as a part of their school program. This program was a collaboration with the SEK Special Education Cooperative serving multi-school districts in southeastern Kansas. The curriculum was marketed nationally through a joint effort of the University of Kansas and a commercial publisher.

The experiences from Project MESH were useful in the development of the first public school programs in Kansas that served special education students in their neighborhood schools and in the regular classroom. A series of grants from 1985 through 1993 provided training and technical assistance to public schools in southeast Kansas (Supported Integration Project; Full Inclusion Project). These projects were a collaboration between the State Department of Education, the Parsons Public Schools, the Greenbush Educational Service Center, and the Kansas University Center on Developmental Disabilities at Parsons, Kansas. The Inclusion Project was replicated in the SEK Special Education Cooperative. As a result of this demonstration, the State Department of Education began supporting and advocating for inclusion classrooms on a statewide basis.

Access to Technology

Advances in technology have resulted in the development of many tools that can help people with disabilities and health conditions that affect a person's vision, hearing, memory, walking, balance, or other abilities. These new tools are called "assistive technology" and can help a person live, learn, work, and play more independently and more easily. Assistive technology includes items such as: powered mobility, adapted employment-related equipment, voice-activated remote controls, computer software programs that can read text on the screen out loud, software programs that reduce the number of keystrokes needed to type on a computer, magnification systems to enlarge print and visual input, and communication devices, to name but a few. There are more than 40,000 commercially available items and thousands of individually produced solutions to increasing independence and productivity.

The Rehabilitation Act of 1988 (the Tech Act) provided support for the development of a statewide assistive technology network to link services and supports and to identify barriers to assistive technology. In 1992, the University of Kansas at Parsons was able to convene over 600 consumers and nearly 70 representatives from agencies and organizations supporting persons with disabilities to respond to the Tech Act mandate requiring education and rehabilitation programs to be consumer directed. The grant was submitted this time through the Parsons University Affiliated Program.

In 1993 a multiyear technology grant, the Assistive Technology for Kansans (ATK) project, had a major impact on the quality and quantity of assistive technology devices and services for Kansans. The goal of this project was to increase access to assistive technology devices and services. More specifically, the project initiatives included:

- Monitor and respond to laws, regulations, policies, and practices that influence Kansans' access to, provision of, or funding for assistive technology devices and services;
- Expand the definition of assistive technology in regulatory language within the systems of the state;
- Establish private, public, and corporate support designed to increase the availability of funds;
- Establish policies, procedures, regulations, and activities designed to facilitate timely access to, provision of, and funding for assistive technology devices and services;
- Increase access to comprehensive assistive technology evaluations designed to assist individuals with disabilities to identify and obtain appropriate devices and services;
- Establish/maintain a competency-based training program and a public awareness effort designed to provide a mechanism for staying current with continued advancements related to the field of assistive technology;
- Assist and encourage consumer involvement, including underrepresented groups, in legislative and advocacy activities related to assistive technology;
- Coordinate activities between state agencies and organizations in order to facilitate access to, provision of, and funding for assistive technology devices and services; and
- Identify project components that need to be continued once federal funds are no longer available to the project and design strategies for continuing needed functions with federal and nonfederal support.

The Kansas project is unique in that individuals with disabilities were actively involved in planning and implementation of the project activities. For example, individuals with disabilities selected the five organizations that would be the project's regional assistive technology access sites and they selected the project coordinator.

This collaboration with individuals with disabilities has served the project well. For example, Kansas Rehabilitation Services (KRS) requested that the legislature approve $75,000 of state money that could be used to match federal dollars. Individuals with disabilities rallied around this request and began calling their legislators. They overwhelmed the phone system in Topeka and demonstrated that Kansans supported the match dollars for ATK services. This resulted in $375,000 per year (including the federal matching funds) that is used to provide core support for the five regional assistive technology access sites!

KRS and ATK work together to ensure that vocational rehabilitation customers have access to the assistive technology devices and services they need to achieve their goals for employment and independence. This award of $75,000 per assistive technology access site underwrites information, evaluation, training, and technical assistance services for the KRS counselor/customer/employer team. Assistive technology specialists work with the customers, counselors, Cerebral Palsy Mobile Shop staff, and other service providers in situations where customized technology solutions are needed. Specific outcomes of this project are: 1) more people employed, 2) increased employee productivity, 3) increased customer and employee job satisfaction, and 4) increased consideration given to assistive technology as a solution to independence and employment-related issues.

Early on, ATK recognized that a major barrier that prevents people from accessing the assistive technology they need is the lack of knowledgeable service providers in the state. Staff became involved with a federally funded program at the University of New Mexico that develops and delivers distance education coursework focusing on assistive technology. Through funds contributed by several state agencies, over 250 Kansans completed one or more distance education courses to increase their knowledge of assistive technology devices and services.

The collaboration between ATK and the staff at the University of New Mexico was expanded through a jointly written grant (Distance Education in Assistive Technology for Speech/Language Pathologists, Occupational Therapists, and Early Intervention and Preschool Personnel Project) that funded the development and delivery of additional distance education courses. The new courses targeted the assistive technology information needs of preservice students in the fields of early childhood education, speech language pathology, and occupational and physical therapy. These courses are currently offered throughout the

United States and abroad through a number of universities and professional development programs.

ATK receives case management funds from Kansas Medical Policy (Medicaid). Kansans with medical cards are eligible to receive assistive technology services from their regional assistive technology access sites. Each of the five assistive technology access sites is reimbursed for these services thanks to the addition of assistive technology case management as a covered service in the state Medicaid plan. Funds were allocated by the Kansas legislature, and Kansas Medical Policy and ATK laid out the parameters of the services.

Assistive technology specialists and information and referral managers at the assistive technology access sites are reimbursed for providing a range of services to Medicaid customers. The services include: evaluation; loan and lease of equipment; training on specific devices for consumers, families, and others; maintenance and upgrading of equipment; monitoring appropriateness of existing technology solutions; reassessment of assistive technology needs; coordination with other needed services; resource and funding development; assisting with eligibility determination; assisting in determining dual eligibility; advocacy support related to promoting self-sufficiency and self-empowerment; and consultation to support groups, consumers, medical professionals, government agencies, schools, and employers.

Kansas Infant-Toddler Services was the first state agency to develop collaborative activities with ATK. The initial intent of the contract was to encourage local infant/toddler teams to consider the assistive technology needs of the children and families they serve and to develop relationships between local providers and the regional assistive technology access sites. These activities resulted in increased attention to access issues for infants and toddlers in addition to introducing a new resource that was particularly important for rural networks.

The scope of the contract has remained somewhat constant, but there has been a change in how the services have been used over time. The primary activities of the contract are comprehensive assistive technology assessment, regional and state training, and loan of equipment.

Local infant/toddler teams are encouraged to participate in the comprehensive assessments conducted by evaluation teams. These experiences, in conjunction with participation in annual training activities, appear to have influenced the capacity of the state to respond to children's and families' needs. Local infant/toddler teams report that they are comfortable independently conducting the simpler assessments. The loan of equipment has saved thousands of dollars for both public funding agencies and families. Infants/toddler teams are allowed to borrow equipment to determine if it meets their needs.

The Kansas AgrAbility program is a partnership between Kansas State University, the University of Kansas, and Southeast Kansas Independent Living. The many collaborating partners include County Extension educators, Centers for Independent Living, Rural Independent Living, Easter Seals, Vocational Rehabilitation, and the Kansas Livestock Association.

The program has identified four levels of service for farmers with disabilities, their families, and farm workers with disabilities. The identified barrier of limited rural rehabilitation necessitates a strong focus on public awareness. The project coordinator collects and develops materials, and along with the agricultural (ag) specialists and ag assistive technology specialists, disseminates to the collaborating partners. This grass roots network assists in identification and referral of consumers. Training and public awareness activities reach 1,000 Kansans annually.

Access to the Kansas AgrAbility program is streamlined through use of a toll-free phone line located at the five regional assistive technology access sites. These sites provide information and referral services. When more intensive services are needed, the assistive technology access site staff connects the caller with the ag assistive technology specialist serving his or her region. This level of service includes assessment, customized accommodation, and assistive technology solutions. The ag specialists, ag assistive technology specialists, and the local team conduct an on-site evaluation. Some requests require assistance from specialists in areas such as low-incidence specialized farm operations, some forms of fabrication, and complex mobility/safety issues.

The program offers a peer-to-peer counseling network and is guided by a state consumer advisory group. Training session evaluations and measures of consumer satisfaction with services and appropriateness of recommended accommodations are routinely collected.

A grant from the National Institute on Disability and Rehabilitation Research (Reusing Durable Medical Equipment Acquired Through

Public Funds: Developing a Cost-Neutral Consumer Driven Program) and a contract with Kansas Medical Policy (Kansas Equipment Exchange) has allowed the ATK project, durable medical equipment providers, and consumers to develop an equipment reuse program. The program tracks certain types of equipment purchased by Medicaid, and conducts follow-up with the recipients to assure that they are getting the maximum benefit from the equipment. If a device is not being used, the contact person offers to arrange training and technical assistance. In situations where the individual no longer needs the device, it is picked up, reconditioned, and donated to another individual who needs it.

Kansas Equipment Exchange is designed to move equipment quickly that is not being used and that is still in good shape (or could be returned to good shape) to Kansans who need equipment. The five regional assistive technology access sites affiliated with the ATK project work with organizations in their region to operate regional reuse teams that can pick up, clean up, conduct minor maintenance and repair, and deliver equipment. If more substantial maintenance is required, certified durable medial equipment vendors will conduct the repair.

In 2001, ATK became a collaborating partner with the Great Plains Disability and Business Technical Assistance Center. The purpose of this subcontract is to increase access to information technology for persons with disabilities. Project staff played a major role in enacting a state requirement that all Kansas state agency web sites meet accessibility standards. Current efforts focus on helping public schools, universities, and colleges develop and implement plans to make information technology in educational settings accessible to students with disabilities.

Assistive Technology Program Expansion

ATK recognized that funding was a primary barrier to access of assistive technology devices and services for persons with disabilities. A consumer-run organization, Kansas Assistive Technology Cooperative (KATCO), was developed to operate an alternative financial loan program. The requirement of a state match was met through the support of state general fund dollars, and Kansas received one of the first six federal awards in 2000 to operate a financial loan program. Loan applications are reviewed by persons with disabilities. The success of this program demonstrated the need for additional funds for a broad range of assistive technology, including adapted vehicles and home modifications. ATK wrote the successful 2003 Alternative Finance Program application that brought $9.8 million to continue these efforts. In 2004, KATCO made over 120 loans for slightly over $2 million.

In 2003, ATK wrote a successful Telework application for KATCO. The state received nearly $1.1 million to provide low-interest loans to persons with disabilities and their employers when engaged in distance employment. Both the Telework and Alternative Finance Program applications required a financial match. The disability community located the financial match by working with state government to emphasize the need for increased employment and independence efforts for persons with disabilities.

The ATK program has been in operation for 13 years and, although activities have changed over time, much of the structure that consumers set in motion is still in place 13 years later. Chuck Spellman and Sara Sack direct the efforts and work with Advisory Council to select project staff, subcontractors, and develop strategies to address identified barriers. The program operates five regional assistive technology access sites, an interagency equipment loan program, and for 6 years conducted an annual conference with over 800 attendees, 100 vendors of assistive technology, and 60 instructional sessions. The project has a strong legislative and policy component that has resulted in assistive technology being included in Medicaid waiver programs, communication technology being purchased for adults through Medicaid, the implementation of a lemon law under the auspices of the attorney general, and many other funding supports for home modifications and technology purchases. The program has established strong collaborative relationships with Vocational Rehabilitation, Mental Health and Developmental Disability, Infant–Toddler Services, Kansas Medicaid, Department on Aging, the Statewide Independent Living Council, and others.

The Assistive Technology Program receives only a small award from the federal government (approximately $320,000), but, through leveraged funds, has a staff of about 24 technology specialists across the state. This collaborative funding of activities has evolved over the years and is a direct result of the trust built among partners and their active participation in program activities. ATK was successful in getting state general

Table 1. *Accomplishments of the Assistive Technology for Kansans Project*

ATK Accomplishments	Oct. 2002– Sept. 2003	Oct. 2003– Sept. 2004
Assistive technology services provided	19,000	20,100
Assistive technology goals created	2,986	2,976
Persons received hands-on training	2,000	4,200
Objectives for obtaining employment	5,900	6,100
Objectives for maintaining or improving employment	1,600	1,800
Services provided to farmers, agricultural workers, family members	700	1,300
Device/equipment loans	900	1,200
Consumers requested assistive technology site staff at critical planning meetings	600	700

fund dollars that were federally matched by Rehabilitation Services to support the program. This allocation was made immediately following the legislators receiving over 600 calls and faxes within a 24-hour period from consumers advocating for the program. Additional state general funds were set aside by the legislators and leveraged by Kansas Medicaid in 1998 to provide further support of the work of the assitive technology access sites. As Table 1 illustrates, this collective effort has resulted in the development of a program that serves many Kansans in identifying and acquiring technology to increase independence, employment, education, and community living. Table 1 provides an example of how this project has increased access to assistive technology devices and services in Kansas. The University of Kansas at Parsons has had a significant impact on the access to information and technology of Kansans with disabilities for more than 35 years.

27

The Legacy of the Bureau of Child Research and the Life Span Institute

RICHARD L. SCHIEFELBUSCH AND STEPHEN R. SCHROEDER

The Bureau of Child Research (BCR) had an official beginning in 1921 when the founder, Dr. Florence Sherbon, succeeded in getting a bill passed in the legislature authorizing the BCR. During the following years, she created a program of child care and child research, even though she was hampered by funding problems brought on by "the Great Depression" and World War II. Those were the years at the University of Kansas (KU) when everyone was expected "to cut back."

At that time, building a research program was truly a difficult undertaking. We must understand that, although Sherbon was both a registered nurse and a physician, she was given little support for her efforts. Also, women in the 1920s were seldom allowed to have the mantle of leadership in American universities. In this, and other essential respects, Sherbon was a pioneer. (See the account of how child research came to Kansas in chapter 1.)

So, in spite of the obstacles, what was the legacy left by this pioneer woman? This question is best answered in two ways: 1) in the short term and 2) in the long term. In the short term, Sherbon was able to develop two courses at KU in child care, for which she wrote two published books, one for each course. She created seven preschools, one for each grade school in Lawrence. She undertook to do research on the histories of women graduates of KU. She initiated demonstrations of effective infant care. She developed a program of women's physical education that included dance therapy. But, best of all, she spoke to groups, at the university and in the community, in order to awaken interest in child care and child health.

Now for the long term—in 1942, 2 years before her death, but while she was still an active staff member of the Department of Home Economics, the Kansas Council for Children and Youth was created. The council members represented 52 agencies and service centers across the state. What a remarkable change in the status of children in the social ecology of the state of Kansas! At that time, also, there were social workers and trained preschool teachers and child psychologists. KU had both a demonstration preschool and a child psychology clinic. It should be noted that it is difficult to put together the full range of information about Kansas' evolving interest in early childhood, at that time. But, when Dick and Ruth Schiefelbusch arrived in Lawrence in 1945 with their 25-month-old son, Larry, there was a remarkably good, university-sponsored, preschool located west of the university's football stadium. The preschool included skilled teachers, student trainees, and parent volunteers. When asked, "Where did this come from?" Professor Edna Hill, the director of the Preschool Program and chairman of the Department of Home Economics said, "It was built by Dr. Florence Sherbon." Hill noted that she never tired of talking about Sherbon. Subsequently, as Hill's time was drawn away from the preschool and focused on the transitions from the Department of Home Economics to the Department of Human Development and Family Life, Sherbon's legacy largely disappeared from published accounts, until Professor Viola Anderson published *Fifty Year History of the Department of Home Economics*. Thus, it is now possible for members of the BCR to include her lasting contributions, which include the statute, with our own historical summaries and label them as the legacy of the Bureau of Child Research.

However, there is one more preliminary explanation that should be made about this historical perspective. The Bureau of Child Research has not been expunged! It is still an active statute and it is still a division of the Life Span Institute (LSI). So, at the right time and the right place, some future leader or leaders may bring it forth again and they may say, "We need a greater emphasis on child care and child health. So, we should reexamine the 1921 statute." (The State Attorney General's

Office has agreed that it is still valid and available for our use.) They may even examine our legacy statement. The following foci are taken from Sherbon's work and used in framing our legacy statement for 1955 up to the present day, which includes the combined periods of BCR (1955–1989) and LSI (1990–2006). The following issues will be used as a bridge between the past and the present, but the main bridge would then need to be between the present and the future.

These issues are based on Sherbon's wording in the statute:

1. Precedents and strategies for *collaborations*—"organized for the scientific study of child life through cooperative efforts of all groups in the state which are equipped and willing to contribute to such study";
2. Designing *interdisciplinary* arrangements and activities;
3. *Disability* project activities;
4. *Combining research, teaching, and service* resources on behalf of children and families; and
5. Demonstrating *leadership* functions.

These five items could have been taken from Sherbon's legislative statutes that she wrote in 1921 and/or from her published materials in the following years. However, although she wanted to engage in these activities, she could not have implemented most of them fully because she did not have resources to do so. During the second period, however, we have found resources to undertake extensive work in each of her legacy priorities. So, now in retrospect, we can describe a legacy for the BCR/LSI (1921–2006).

First, we will pursue the legacy transfer idea from the 1921–1944 period to the 1955–2006 era. In order to pursue this exercise conveniently and flexibly, we will need five code/phrases: 1) collaborations; 2) interdisciplinary; 3) disability; 4) combining research, training, and service; and 5) leadership.

Collaborations

The collaboration history of the BCR began with a combined research effort between the University of Kansas and the Parsons State Hospital and Training Center. It soon became necessary to add the Board of

Social Welfare in Topeka to the collaboration activities. Then, in turn, came the chancellor of the University of Kansas, the vice chancellor of KU Medical Center, the project officers of the National Institute of Child Health and Human Development, many citizens of the Juniper Gardens district of Kansas City, Kansas, and finally, a number of emergent scientists from George Peabody College of Vanderbilt University and from the University of Washington in Seattle, Washington, who joined the program at Kansas as research associates. It is not incidental that as research activities grew and programs enlarged, the collaborations also enlarged and multiplied. It is a fact, of course, that the BCR, now LSI, has engaged in a steadily growing number of other collaborations. So, it is likely that future growth experiences will evoke still more collaboration as needed. Count on it! The next major collaboration is already under way, among university/community research laboratories and (for profit) private corporations. The most recent collaboration program, known as the Life Sciences, has been created by multidimensional collaborations that include several research laboratories in the greater Kansas City area and the Kansas state legislature. The details of this emergent collaboration are in the hands of planning committees.

Interdisciplinary

Universities relate to students primarily through academic departments. Each department has faculty members who teach and supervise students, representing their discipline with its fields of organized information (knowledge). For the most part, each discipline also organizes the research tactics that are taught to students within that discipline, by using minor fields, correlate areas, and the use of seminars in selected areas. In this manner, departments have been able to adjust to the encroachment of interdisciplinary curricular practices, until recently. Now the pressures for an interdisciplinary curriculum, training tactics, and larger research programs have combined to force the use of an interdisciplinary system of scientific planning and implementation. Then too, some prominent research areas are more likely to require an interdisciplinary team than are other areas.

The first research project of the Bureau of Child Research brought together an interdisciplinary research team. We proposed to teach new language and communication to children with mental retardation at Parsons State Hospital and Training School. The four researchers who were brought together on this project became our first interdisciplinary team. That occurred in 1958. This event set in motion other projects for research training, programmatic research, and community outreach research. Also, finally, it led to an interdisciplinary Child Language Graduate Program. This series of interdisciplinary research activities and interdisciplinary planning were probably unique in the field of language and communication research, at that time. Additional interdisciplinary programs soon followed in other fields of research at other locations of the BCR's research program.

During the years 1965–1972, 14 disciplinary departments located at KU and KU Medical Center combined their efforts in creating the Center for Research in Mental Retardation and Human Development and the Kansas University Affiliated Program. This was done under a combined leadership system headed by the Bureau of Child Research.

More recently, university representatives from four states (Nebraska, Iowa, Missouri, and Kansas) met under the auspices of the Merrill Advanced Studies Center, a component of the Institute for Life Span Studies, to discuss future research developments in our four-state region. In a concluding discussion at the 2-day meeting, a prominent issue was considered: Interdisciplinary combinations are not only increasing but there may need to be further discussions leading to a substantial addition of them across the board. This was followed by a recommendation extended by Provost David Shulenburger of KU that the assembled university representatives form committees to explore the priorities, strengths, and possibilities for framing interuniversity plans for future research development.

Disability

Disability has been a prominent focus for the BCR since it was included in the statute in 1921—studies of the "diagnosis, treatment, and prevention of delinquency, defectiveness, and dependency. . . ." Included in the BCR/LSI cluster of centers and projects are: 1) the Kansas Mental Retardation and Developmental Disabilities Research

Center, (MRDDRC) dedicated to the scientific investigation of the causes, prevention, and treatment of intellectual and developmental disabilities; Kansas University Center on Developmental Disabilities (KUCDD), including virtually all of the institute's direct service, technical assistance, and postdoctoral, pre-, and in-service training; the Life Span Institute at Parsons; the Juniper Gardens Children's Project; the Beach Center on Disability; the Research and Training Center on Independent Living; the Gerontology Center; the Center for Biobehavioral Neurosciences in Communication Disorders; the Work Group for Community Health and Development; the Center for Physical Activity and Weight Management; and other newly developed projects, including Preventing Child Neglect in High-Risk Mothers, the Fragile-X Syndrome (a national project), Twins and Singletons with Specific Language Impairment, and Language Building for Deaf–Blind Children. The last cluster of projects is explained further in chapter 28.

Combining Research, Training, and Service: The Compounding System

In the Epilogue in chapter 8, we explained how the concept of research compounding emerged in our review of the combined research and service chapters. This legacy subsection provides an opportunity to extend the concept. We should first look at the ecology of an entrepreneurial research center that includes research–training–service objectives. We have informally labeled the system as a research–information–dissemination–utilization–response (RIDUR) system.

These functions naturally emerge in an entrepreneurial research system that acknowledges the importance of research planning and evaluation. Interestingly, the compounding features occur without formal time allotments. They occur naturally as a function of the interaction of features within the "ecology." In short, they occur because people learn from each other; because the system invites give and take; because there are emergencies in which people need each other and seek each other's help; and, finally, because a group of interactive participants are brighter and more competent and more productive than is a single operator.

Leadership

(The following brief document is taken from a memo that Dick Schiefelbusch sent to Ann Kaiser and Joe Spradlin on July 28, 1982 regarding the final report of the Future Planning Committee.)

During the early years, the Bureau was stimulated by a group of hard working collaborators. Your report gives me too much credit and does not give adequate acknowledgment to a number of colleagues who both tutored and supported me. For instance, I think the existence of this development team during the first ten years ('58–'68) of the Bureau's growth cycle was the dramatic feature of that time frame. I realize that the issue at hand is the change of directors so you need to set the stage for that event but I think the cooperating team, especially Spradlin, Girardeau, Copeland, Hollis, Fulton, McLean, Lent, Horowitz, Rosenfeld, McReynolds, and after '65, Baer, Risley, Wolf, Hall, Sherman, etc. should be given primary credit, nevertheless. My role was only one among many.

The Bureau is a big functional system of contingencies, inconsistencies, imperfections, and incentives. The director is not above the system but, rather, is part of it. Thus, his or her behavior must 1) reduce (not escalate) problems, 2) create excitement, 3) help to select important projects, 4) help to meet deadlines, 5) evoke cooperation, and 6) give credit to others. Most of this must be done across campuses and settings. Ninety-nine percent of all administrative initiatives and reactions should be positive in nature.

The director should build relationships, form covenants, and share risks with staff and collaborators. We all strive to be totally honest but sometimes are unable to fulfill all of our intentions. Nevertheless, the director must build trust. Essentially trust evolves from successes, crises, strife, difficulties, and the give and take of unstructured, untidy transactions. Essentially good administrative relationships are earned.

I am convinced that good human transactions are essential to good administration. Our challenge for the future is clearly defined by the way we support each other. If we can persuade someone to take this complex role (it will be far more complex for the new director than for the old one) we can add greatly to his or her success by the positive support we provide.

Conclusion

Perhaps, our greatest legacy is our 50-year research program in which we weathered several generations of peer reviewers, sometimes called gatekeepers. The peer review system has provided us with about 90% of our operating budget. As our reviewed efforts increased in number and as our successes became better known, our aspirations grew and so did the scope of our work. We have crossed the half-century marker and we are still growing, as chapter 28 will describe. So, we have now engaged in a group writing effort called a History, which is, in part, an exercise in retrospection. We have tried to describe how we think we have impacted our fields of effort and have provided support and new opportunities for our clients. In our scientific and service domains this is called accountability. But the strongest realization that emerges is best explained in the language of eager, young behavioral scientists. "We set out to shape them and eventually came to realize that they have shaped us."

28

The Future of the Schiefelbusch Institute for Life Span Studies

STEVEN F. WARREN

In August of 2001 I became the director of the Life Span Institute (LSI). This is a humbling role to assume for at least three reasons. First, the individuals who preceded me in this role did so much and were so obviously successful. Second, the mission of the LSI—to discover or invent solutions to the problems of human and community development, disabilities, and aging—is as ambitious as it is noble. Third, as has always been the case and should always be for a research institute, we must live by our wits. We are not like the English department. No one guarantees our future. Instead, our future depends entirely on the extent to which we can achieve our ambitious mission.

Most of this book has been about the past. Thus, it is fitting that this final chapter be directed at the future. Where are we going? Are we positioned to continue our rich legacy of making a difference? What are some of the enduring challenges and opportunities that lie ahead? What values and principles will ensure our future success? Before I attempt to answer these questions, I will provide a "2006 snapshot" of the LSI. This is relevant since where we are today will have a lot to do with where we go tomorrow.

A Snapshot of LSI in 2006

By most measures the Life Span Institute continues to be a highly successful organization. We are both the oldest and largest research program at the University of Kansas (KU). For the 2004–2005 fiscal year, more than 140 investigators associated with more than 20 academic departments were involved in more than 110 externally funded research projects totaling nearly $22 million in grants and contracts. This is the largest amount of external funding we have ever had and was our 9th straight year of overall growth. Indeed, by this metric we are twice as large as in 1996 and more than $6 million larger than we were in 2001. For each dollar we received from the university, we generated approximately $6.50 in external support (in 1990 the ratio was just 3:1). Forty-two percent of our funding came from the National Institutes of Health and another 35% from the United States Department of Education. Approximately 15% of all graduate research assistants at KU were funded by LSI projects. An estimated 49,000 Kansas citizens benefited from the institute's technical assistance, training, and direct services. Too many individual LSI investigators were honored for their contributions to list here. As impressive as these indicators are, they tell little of the impact of the institute. Fortunately, when we look for such indicators, they abound even if they are not easily captured in numbers. Here are just a few examples.

- A diagnostic test for children with specific language impairment;
- The Actifer—a high-tech device that determines the ability of preterm babies to suck and then quickly trains them to do this critical skill if necessary;
- The Actometer—a device for measuring fine motor movements in rodents that is paving the wave for new research on the effects of various drugs on the nervous system as well as the effects of neurodegenerative diseases;
- New and effective approaches for enhancing the physical fitness of children and preventing childhood and adult obesity;
- The translation and large-scale application of schoolwide approaches to support positive behavior by all students;
- The development of increasingly effective early communication intervention approaches;
- The development of cognitive and behavioral measures that reveal early evidence of neurodegenerative disorders such as Alzheimer's years before such disorders are normally detected;

- The discovery that two fatty acids found in breast milk are necessary for optimal cognitive development in infants—leading to major infant formula companies to begin including these substances in infant formula;
- The novel use of the Internet to quickly gather data on key indicators of child development, graph these data, and immediately provide recommendations for intervention to clinicians and teachers throughout North America;
- The development and worldwide dissemination of the Community Tool Box—an Internet-based resource with more than 6,000 pages of critical information to help communities anywhere in the world develop effective programs to deal with HIV/AIDS, nutrition, water quality, crime, and a whole host of challenges; and
- The widespread dissemination of assistive technologies to citizens throughout Kansas to enhance communication, work, independence, and quality of life of individuals with virtually any type of serious physical or intellectual disability.

The problem with starting a list like this is that I could go on and on. In so many areas, LSI investigators are developing solutions to problems of human and community development, disability, and aging. Our span is "womb to tomb," thus the appropriateness of our name. Indeed, our mission is so expansive that we have found it useful to organize ourselves into centers. These centers reflect areas of emphasis and their structure is fluid and flexible. Thus many investigators claim membership in more than one center, which we in fact strongly encourage. The idea is not to create "silos," but instead use the notion of centers as an intellectual tool that helps us to focus our efforts and resources. None of these centers are permanent. Each will exist only as long as it continues to be a useful mechanism for achieving our mission. Indeed, several LSI-affiliated centers have disappeared over the years. This should not be viewed as a bad thing. Instead, it is simply a sign of a dynamic environment that is always moving ahead, unencumbered by a structure that loses its function but still stands nonetheless.

For the record, a brief description of our 12 current centers follows.

Kansas Mental Retardation and Developmental Disabilities Research Center

The Kansas Mental Retardation and Developmental Disabilities Research Center (MRDDRC) is our oldest (40 years of continued funding) and largest center. It is an "all university" entity shared principally between KU–Lawrence and KU Medical Center (KUMC) with a significant presence at the Juniper Gardens Children's Project. It is one of 14 national centers dedicated to the scientific investigation of the causes, prevention, and treatment of intellectual and developmental disabilities supported by the National Institute of Child Health and Human Development (NICHD). Research is conducted in labs, clinics, and the community by 60 investigators from the biological and behavioral sciences who seek solutions to the challenges of intellectual and developmental disabilities. Research projects are organized around four themes: 1) language, communication disorders, and cognition in mental retardation; 2) risk, intervention, and prevention in mental retardation; 3) the neurobiology of mental retardation; and 4) the cellular and molecular biology of early development. Steven F. Warren is the director and Peter Smith is the co-director.

Kansas University Center on Developmental Disabilities

More than 30 years ago, as the institute's research on developmental disabilities took root, efforts began to translate this research into practice through what is now known as the Kansas University Center on Developmental Disabilities (KUCDD). A significant portion of the institute's direct service, technical assistance, and postdoctoral, pre- and in-service training are associated with KUCDD. These include clinics at KUMC to diagnose and treat children with disabilities, a Parsons-based statewide project that provides assistive technology to people with disabilities, and training child care providers and social workers how to support individuals with disabilities. KUCDD research has state, national, and international impact in areas such as self-determination, positive behavior supports, inclusive educational practices, early childhood education, community and workplace supports, and family systems and supports. The following individuals run the center: Michael L. Wehmeyer, director; Glen W. White, associate director; Wendy Parent, Lawrence assistant director; David P. Lindeman, Parsons director; Chet

D. Johnson, KUMC director; and R. Matthew Reese, KUMC assistant director.

The Life Span Institute at Parsons

For more than 40 years, the University of Kansas has maintained research, service, and training programs housed on the campus of the Parsons State Hospital, including a major component of the Kansas University Center on Developmental Disabilities. This institute, located in rural southeast Kansas, currently has research addressing early literacy and reading, maladaptive/challenging behavior, and program evaluation strategies. Additionally, this program has provided significant service and training across the state of Kansas, addressing the assistive technology needs of Kansans, early intervention and early childhood, and training for community organizations and agencies serving persons with developmental disabilities. David P. Lindeman is the director.

Juniper Gardens Children's Project

The Juniper Gardens Children's Project (JGCP) began in 1964 when citizens from the northeast Kansas City, Kansas neighborhood joined with faculty from KU to devise solutions to specific problems in educational achievement and parenting in that low-income community. The JGCP has grown over the years from a small, community-based research initiative housed in the basement of a liquor store to a unique internationally recognized research center that includes multiple community sites, projects, and investigators. The JGCP is particularly recognized for its contributions to the development of effective approaches for accelerating learning and reducing classroom conduct problems in both special and general education. In 1996, the JGCP was given the Research Award of the International Council for Exceptional Children in recognition of its outstanding research contributions. Charles R. Greenwood is the director.

Beach Center on Disability

The Beach Center on Disability has a steadfast commitment to making a difference in the quality of life for persons with disabilities and their families. It is committed to listening to the priorities of families, service providers, policy makers, and researchers, and incorporating those priorities into the center's research agenda, related training, technical assistance, dissemination, and utilization activities. Primary areas of Beach Center research include the effects of public policy on the quality of life and community integration of families; the ethical, legal, and social implications of the Human Genome Project; disability policy generally; family professional partnerships; access to the general curriculum; self-determination; assistive technology for individuals with cognitive disabilities; and positive behavioral supports in schools, homes, and communities. The Beach Center was named for Ross and Marianna Beach in 1988 in honor of their significant roles in advocating for families affected by disabilities. The following persons serve the Beach Center: H. Rutherford Turnbull III, co-director; Ann P. Turnbull, co-director; Michael L. Wehmeyer, associate director; and Wayne Sailor, co-associate director.

Research and Training Center on Independent Living

Since 1980, the Research and Training Center on Independent Living (RTCIL) has worked to improve the lives of people with disabilities using systematic research and training initiatives to help them increase their health and independence to take control of their lives. The RTCIL uses a participatory action research approach to address research questions and outcomes, actively recruiting the involvement of consumers who are affected by the problems being investigated. The Independent Living Core activities address advocacy, services, and interventions; the Health Promotion Core promotes health practices that reduce the risk of health problems; and the Disability Policy Core is concerned with policy issues that impede or facilitate independent living. The RTCIL continues to strengthen international connections with colleagues in Vietnam, Korea, and Peru. Glen W. White is the director.

Gerontology Center

The Gerontology Center's affiliation with the Bureau of Child Research in 1990 paved the way for an extended research agenda of the newly formed Life Span Institute. Center researchers are interested in all areas of aging, but are distinguished by seminal research in communication and aging, long-term health care and housing alternatives, and decision making in later life. The center coordinates an interdisciplinary graduate certificate program in gerontology for students enrolled in any master's or doctoral program at the university as well as a multidisciplinary graduate program that offers both masters and doctoral degrees in gerontology. Center staff members also work with a wide variety of public and private agencies in developing programs for older persons and their families and assisting agencies and organizations with evaluations of programs and public policies. David J. Ekerdt is the director.

The Center for Biobehavioral Neurosciences in Communication Disorders

The Center for Biobehavioral Neurosciences in Communication Disorders (BNCD) became the Life Span Institute's newest affiliated research center in 2002 when the National Institute on Deafness and Other Communication Disorders awarded a core grant to establish the center. The BNCD is a natural outgrowth of the Life Span Institute's long-standing focus on communication and language development and intervention. The BNCD's research spans a wide range of issues relevant to the causes and treatment of communication disorders from infancy to old age, including studies on infant attention, the genetics of language impairments, language intervention, the decline of working memory in old age as reflected in speech, and more precise measures of hearing loss to aid cochlear implant design. Mabel L. Rice is the director.

Child Language Doctoral Program

The Child Language Doctoral Program was established in 1983 as the first specialized degree program in the emerging field of child language acquisition. The program focuses on the interdisciplinary academic preparation and research training of child language specialists. The internationally recognized faculty brings diverse approaches to the study of how children communicate and speak. The program offers students a wide choice of research tools, facilities, and field sites, including the

Child Language Acquisition Studies Lab that has the largest known archive of transcribed spontaneous samples from preschool children diagnosed as receptive/expressive specific language impaired. Research sites and practica are provided by the Life Span Institute, the Language Acquisition Preschool, and the clinical and research facilities of the Speech–Language–Hearing Clinic. Mabel L. Rice is the director.

Merrill Advanced Studies Center

The Merrill Advanced Studies Center, founded in 1990 with an endowment from Virginia Urban Merrill and Fred Merrill, is a catalyst for scholarship on disabilities and policies that shape university research. Merrill conferences and publications establish new directions and build collaborative projects in both science and policy. World-class experts often meet as a group for the first time at Merrill conferences and go on to develop national projects that answer key questions in science. The center publishes books on topics relevant to developmental disabilities and makes policy papers available on-line and in print. The Merrill web site at *merrill.ku.edu* has fact sheets and discussions on science and policy for the general public. Mabel L. Rice is the director.

Work Group for Community Health and Development

The mission of the Work Group for Community Health and Development is to promote community health and development through collaborative research, teaching, and public service. Formed in 1976, the Work Group has focused on measurement and analysis of the process of community/system change, and on building capacity for efforts to create conditions that improve community-level outcomes. Its current work is in three domains: community/public health (e.g., substance abuse, adolescent pregnancy), child/youth health and development, and community development. Many years of the group's work has been distilled into an Internet site, the Community Tool Box at *ctb.ku.edu*. This site provides comprehensive technical assistance, consultation, and distance learning to connect people, ideas, and resources for promoting community health and development. In 2004, the Work Group was designated as a World Health Organization Collaborating Centre for Community Health and Development at KU. Stephen B. Fawcett is the director.

Center for Physical Activity and Weight Management

The Center for Physical Activity and Weight Management joined the institute in 2001 and supports research, training, and clinics for weight loss and weight maintenance. The center is interested in the metabolic syndrome—abnormal values for blood lipids, glucose, insulin, and blood pressure that accompany overweight and obesity. The center also has a major effort aimed at preventing overweight and obesity in children by increasing physical activity and reducing high-fat, energy-dense foods in elementary schools. The center's Energy Balance Laboratory features a whole-room indirect calorimeter that measures energy expenditure precisely under a variety of experimental conditions. Joseph E. Donnelly is the director.

Centro Ann Sullivan del Peru

In addition to these 12 centers, the LSI has a long-term collaborating relationship with the Centro Ann Sullivan del Peru (CASP). CASP was founded in Lima in 1980 by Liliana Mayo. In 1981, Judy LeBlanc, a KU faculty member and longtime LSI investigator, began a long-term collaboration with Mayo and the two of them have created an extraordinary program for children and adults with disabilities. CASP has been recognized around the globe as a model for developing countries. CASP staff have translated many approaches and techniques developed by LSI investigators so that they are appropriate for use in developing countries. CASP increasingly serves as an international training center and has established satellite centers in several other Latin American countries to date. Many LSI investigators have contributed to the success of this effort over the years.

LSI Services

The LSI provides over 100 specific services to enhance the success and impact of these centers and the more than 80 associated investigators. These services range from the essential but mundane (i.e., bookkeeping, budget management, inventory) to the services that literally make the science more effective and generative. A good example of this would be the array of services provided by the Research, Design, and Analysis Unit. Like the work of the centers, the nature of services we provide to investigators continues to evolve and change. We assist this evolutionary process by regularly conducting rigorous evaluations of our services and of investigator need.

Three Characteristics That Position Us for the Future

LSI is old enough to have a number of enduring "characteristics." Some of these may be of nothing more than cosmetic interest. But several of these characteristics look suspiciously like contributors to our long viability and success. Three of these are worth special note: flexibility, adaptability, and persistence.

There are a number of ways the LSI demonstrates its flexibility. One example is our use of wide-array investigator appointments—ranging from full-time regular tenure-track to many investigators with 100% appointments in the institute and virtually everything in between. This wide range of appointments reflects the university's willingness to allow us a substantial degree of flexibility. We also exhibit flexibility in how we use funds to support our mission. For example, we provide partial salary support to a number of experienced full-time investigators so that the pressure on them is not unreasonable in terms of how much of their salary they must continuously generate from grants. We also back up investigators with salary when they encounter funding problems to the extent we can. This degree of flexibility allows us to maintain a certain stability essential to long-term success.

It is a paradox, perhaps, that to be stable we have to evolve and change. This highlights a second enduring characteristic—adaptability. If a research center stands still, it will quickly die. We are about the creation of useful knowledge. If we don't generate important new knowledge, we won't be around for long. For this reason, we are largely a flat organization and essentially function as a federation of interests—not a top-down hierarchy. Specific centers can be added or discontinued from this federation, thus allowing the overall organization to thrive even as specific pieces struggle or even die. To operate this way, one must give lots of flexibility and autonomy to individual center directors and investigators. Consequently, the LSI central office does not micromanage. Furthermore, all of our directors are active scientists and leaders in their fields as well. None of us are full-time administrators. For example, even though I direct the Life Span Institute and our largest single center (the Mental Retardation Research Center), I maintain a lively program of research just like all other LSI investigators. This is important for my credibility both locally and nationally. It also means that I am impacted by the same forces and policies that all our investigators face. Thus, when I say to our center directors and investigators that we are all in this together, that is exactly what I mean. This flat, minimally intrusive model is capable of rapidly adapting to even very specific changes in the environment.

Evolve or die is a fact of life for a research center. Research centers should die when they are no longer meeting their mission and no longer on the cutting edge of knowledge generation. Research centers should be seen as an intellectual tool—a way of organizing talent and resources to solve important problems. Right now the rapidly changing nature of science is a significant challenge for us. It has had a huge impact on behavioral science and this is central to us. We cannot just keep doing what we have been doing. There are changing federal research priorities—as there should be. We are stretching the infrastructure and our talent to meet these. In practice, this is a little bit akin to the idea of rebuilding an airplane while you fly it. This is what we must do in a large mature program to keep it moving forward. There is no time to simply stop and retool— you have to make changes on the fly. In applying this metaphor to the LSI, a federation of research centers, it becomes easy to see how the LSI can keep flying while individual research centers come and go over the years.

This brings us to the third enduring characteristic—persistence. Why do individuals persist in the face of failure? Why do they keep attempting to move forward when funding is drying up, or their research efforts struggling? I cannot claim to truly answer this. But it is clear that belief in the importance of your work in the long term has something to do with this. But perhaps as important is actual experience in some failing, only to eventually turn things around and succeed. Because LSI has been in business for more than half a century, we have lots of experience surviving rough times and eventually thriving. This experience resides in many of our senior investigators, who in turn model this for our more junior investigators. This importance of persistence is likely to be tested over the next few years. We seem to be entering another period in which external funding may be hard to come by after a decade of rapid growth. This period will again test many of our investigators. However, the past teaches us that we can survive and move forward as long as we are flexible and adapt. And that is how these three enduring characteristics create their magic—by working together to ensure we evolve and more forward even when the going gets tough.

The Future

Here on the edge of the future, this country and the rest of the world are encountering all sorts of challenging problems. There are 54 million Americans with a disability, including 1 in 12 children. A completely preventable, mostly behavioral problem, obesity, has become a major health epidemic. We aging baby boomers are already creating a host of major economic, social, and health problems. The education system in the United States is being challenged to finally create a scientific basis for its practices. New medical practices are saving more and more very low birth weight, very premature babies, but these survivors face a host of developmental challenges. The vast majority of adults with developmental disabilities are unemployed or seriously underemployed. Two thirds of fourth graders are reading below grade level. Autism as a diagnosis is exploding onto families, schools, and more. This list could obviously go on and on. But you get the picture. Despite the enormous gains and accomplishments of the past 100 years, we still have plenty of work to do. And attacking these and other problems is of course our enduring work. We are armed with an enormous amount of experience and an equally enormous amount of evidence that we can make a meaningful difference. Consequently, although these problems concern us deeply, we know that given the opportunity and a reasonable amount of resources, we can make headway on a whole range of human challenges.

That said, the way we work now and in the future has changed a good deal since the Bureau of Child Research was restarted in the 1950s. It is common knowledge among life scientists that the easy problems have all been solved. The day of the lone-wolf scientist isolating herself in the lab and chipping away at some basic question from the perspective of her relatively narrow discipline is all but over. Although it is built solidly on the backs of thousands of lone-wolf types who toiled away for decades on basic research, further progress in solving the major problems of human development, disability, and aging will require an unprecedented degree of cross-disciplinary collaboration. This fact is made all the more daunting by the realization that however noble such collaborations may appear to outsiders, to those trying to collaborate it often feels like an unnatural act between two or more nonconsenting adults. Will future progress be held hostage to ancient human emotions like jealousy, vanity, and a caveman-like protection of turf? In the end, I believe these natural human tendencies will be circumvented by a more powerful human desire to cooperate to ensure mutual survival and success. Still, the road ahead will be rough.

Beyond the challenge of collaboration lies a seemingly paradoxical challenge just beginning to confront life scientists. It is evident that biological organisms are inherently tuned to their environment. Genetic factors alone typically account for only a fraction of variance in human behavior. To account for the remaining variance, that is, to fully understand development and behavior, scientists must increasingly move toward analyses of functional interactions between biology, environment, behavior, and culture. This is surely a surmountable challenge, but it will require the integration and creation of new analytical models growing out of many disciplines. In many respects, this is the greatest intellectual challenge that faces the science of human development and functioning over the long term.

Concluding Thoughts

The Life Span Institute and its earlier manifestation, the Bureau of Child Research, have created a remarkable legacy of impact on a wide range of problems associated with human and community development, disability, and aging. Our history positions us well to continue this noble legacy far into the future. Infused with a potent combination of prairie pragmatism and empiricism, we will surely continue to make a difference through an unwavering commitment to high-impact, hard-nosed empirical science combined with innovative research to practice efforts. As we move ahead into the future, we readily admit to being unbridled optimists—the kind who occasionally look to the sky on a Midwest summer evening and recall that famous Helen Keller quote: "No pessimist ever discovered the secrets of the stars or sailed to an uncharted land or opened a new heaven to the human spirit."

Name Index

Page numbers in *italics* indicate references to published research. Page numbers followed by a *t* indicate tables.

Subject Index

Page numbers followed by an *f* or *t* indicate figures and tables.